HISTORY
OF THE
AMERICAN AUTO

BY THE AUTO EDITORS OF CONSUMER GUIDE®

Publications International, Ltd.

Manufactured in China.

8 7 6 5 4 3 2 1

ISBN: 0-7853-9874-0

Library of Congress Card Catalog Number: 2004106036

ACKNOWLEDGMENTS

PHOTOGRAPHERS

Scott Baxter; Ken Beebe; Les Bidrawn; Joe Bohovic; Terry Boyce; Scott Brant; Michael Brown; Chan Bush; Thomas Cannell; Joseph Caro; Jim Frenak; Diane Garnett; Bob Garris; Gene's Studio; Tom Glatch; Ed Goldberger; David Gooley; Sam Griffith; Mike Hastie; Bob Havorka; Jerry Heasley; Alan Hewko; Bill Hill; Scott Hutchinson; Bert Johnson; Bud Juneau; Bill Kanz; Laurel H. Kenney; Milton Kieft; Kugler Studio; Randy Lorentzen; Dan Lyons; Vince Manocchi; Bill McCall; Tom McGann; Mark McMahon; Doug Mitchel; Mike Mueller; Jerry Naunheim; Bob Nicholson; Morton Oppenheimer; David Patryas; Jay Peck; William Schintz; Gary Smith; Robert Sorgatz; Richard Spiegelman; Dan Stockum; Gerald Sutphin; Rich Szczepanski; Tom Storm; David Talbot; David Temple; Bob Tenney; Marvin Terrell; Thomas Photo; Jim Thompson; Kris Trexler; Rob Van Schaik; W.C. Waymack; Joseph Wherry; Willoughby Photographic; Hub Wilson; Nicky Wright; Vince Wright; Zoom Photographic.

We would like to thank the following for providing us with many of the images used in this book:

DaimlerChrysler Corporation; Ford Motor Company; General Motors Corporation; Wieck Media Services.

CHAPTER 1

American Automotive Manufacturers Association; Bill Bailey; National Automotive Museum; Oldsmobile Division Public Relations; Oldsmobile History Center.

CHAPTER 2

American Automotive Manufacturers Association; American Motors Corporation; Auburn-Cord-Duesenberg Museum; Bob and Lori Babcock; Bill Bailey; Gene Baldwin; Cadillac Motor Car Division; Chevrolet Public Relations; Crawford Collection; Ford Motor Company; GM Photographic; Richard M. Langworth; Panhandle Plains Historical Museum; "Pinky" Randall; Carl M. Riggins; William and Joseph Schoenbeck; Carroll Studebaker; Joseph H. Wherry.

CHAPTER 3

American Automotive Manufacturers Association; H. Fred Bausch; Richard Bayer; Briggs Cunningham Museum; Chrysler Historical Center; Ron Dehler; Dennis Fink; Ford Motor Company; Stanley C. Fuller; Gilmore Car Museum; GM Photographic; Frank Gonsalvez; Dan and Carol Hansen; Ken Havekost; Owen Hoyt; Jonnie Keller; Richard M. Langworth; Wayne Loomis; W.M. Lyon Collection; National Automobile Museum; Darrell A. Rader; "Pinky" Randall; Carl M. Riggins; Bob and Karyn Sitter; Stan Sokol; William F. Stever; Earl Timko; Ernest V. Toth; Ruth M. Toth.

CHAPTER 4

Daniel Allen; American Automotive Manufacturers Association; Armand A. Anneread, Jr.; Norm Anselment; Robert Atwell; Dr. Barbara Atwood; Les Aubol; Auburn-Cord-Duesenberg Museum; Robert Babcock; Michael Bancroft; Ed Barwick; Richard Bayer; Ronald Benach; Spencer L. Bing; James H. Bowersox; Ron Bransky; Bob Briggs; Howard A. Bring; Brooks Stevens Museum; Donald A. Burkholder; California Custom Coach; James L. Carlson; Mrs. Benjamin R. Caskey; J.F. Cassan; Bob Clarke; Edward and Arlene Cobb; Debbie Colaniro; Joe Consalvo; Briggs Cunningham; Ralph Davis; Harry A. DeMenge; Dick Dennis; Larry Desenville; Donald E. Desing; Gerald Dewey; Harold Dinger; Harvey Doering; Alex and Beverly Dow; Michael Doyle; Donald D. Duffy; Dr. James Dunkel; Ken and Stephanie Dunshire; Bill Dyke; Jerry Emery; Alfred Ferrara; Fred C. Fischer; Jim Flicek; Joseph B. Folladori; Fraser Dante, Ltd; Francis Frisch; Gilmore Car Museum; Wayne R. Graefen; L.D. Grandey; Lee Greer; Elwood Griest; Peter Guido, Jr.; Ed Gunther; Tom Hall; Jeff Harbaugh; John F. Hare; Jacques Harguindeguy; Dick and Nancy Harvey; Dr. Frank Hayward; Earl Heintz; Harold Hofferber; Dave Holls; Bill and Berta Honey; Tim Hrudka; Ray Hunter; Julius Ironhat; Terry Johnson; Robert Joynt; John Kaelin; George D. Kanaan; Craig Karr; Bruce B. Kennedy; John Kepich; Vernon A. King, Jr.; Larry Klein; James Kozbelt; Everett A. Kroeze; Darvin and Becca Kuehl; Phil Kuhn; Ron and Debbie Ladley; Peter Lampert; William Lauer; Michael P. Laureno, Jr.; Warren and Sylvia Lauridsen; Basil Lewis; Donald D. Lyons; Maurice W. Ludwig; W.M. Lyon Collection; John Madison; James P. Manak; James Martin; Mr. and Mrs. Paul Mather; Gerard and Lorraine May; Robert L. McAfee; Bill McCall; Jim McGrew; Frank McLiesh; Ray Menefee; Paul Miller; S. Ray Miller; S. Ray Miller, Jr.; Chuck Mitchell; Armin F. Mittermaier; Erville W. Murphy;

Marshall R. Nelson; Ralph Neubauer; Clay Nichols; Jack Passey, Jr.; N. Gene Perkins; John Poochigian; Ester Price Candies Corp.; Terry Radey; Ted and Jo Raines; Glen and Vera Reints; Theodore J. Risch; Philomena Ronco-Kohan; Fran Roxas; Eugene Roy; Jess Rupp; Ronald N. Schneider; Ed and Judy Schoenthaler; Sam H. Scoles; Walter G. Serviss; Ed Siegfried; Harv Sjaarda; Thomas B. Smiley; Peter A. Spear; Samuel Spedale; Thomas P. Spenny; Carroll Studebaker; David Studebaker; Mick Thrasher; Eric M. Thurstone; Ed and Eleanor Todd; Ernest J. Toth, Jr.; Bill Trnka; Gene Troyer; Billy F. Wilson; Larry Wilson; William L. Wilson; Harry Wynn; William Young; Marvin E. Yount, Jr.; Robert Zaitlin; P. Alvin Zamba.

CHAPTER 5

American Automotive Manufacturers Association; Thomas Barratt III; Norman and Joyce Booth; Terry Davies; Dominoes Farms; Roger A. James; Bill Lauer; James R. Lauzon; Dr. R Leia; Dr. Gerald M. Levitt; Charlie Montano; Robert Reeves; Raymond J. Reiser, Sr.; Al Wilkiewicz; Harry Wynn.

CHAPTER 6

Joe Abela; Al Adams; Jim and Mary Ashworth; Jack Bart; Neil S. Black; Gordon Blixt; Robert Bradley; Elmer F. Brawn; Robert N. Carlson; Tom L. Carver; Chrysler Historical Center; Joseph Clameitt; Dr. Steven Colsen; Donald W. Curtis; Rayond E. Dade; Vincent Daul; Gary L. Faulk; Bev Ferreira; Fraser Dante, Ltd.; Terri Gardner; GM Photographic; Ed Gunther; Ken Havekost; Harvey Hedgecock; Sharon Hielefeldt; Chris and Pete Jakubowski; Blaine Jenkins; Bud Juneau; Robert Kash; Bill Knudson and John White; Peter M. Krakowski; William H. Lauer; Jerry and Adell Laurin; Dr. Roger Leir; Thomas F. Lerch; David Marshall; Robert L. McAfee; Ralph G. McQuoid; Robert M. Messinger; Mike Moore; Michael Morris; Rod Morris; Melvin Mull; Harry Nicks; Louise and Inez Nosse; Oldsmobile History Center; John Otto; Donald Passardi; Dick Pyle; Steve Roberts; William C. Rohley; Arthur Sabin; Roy A. Schneider; H. Robert and Kathryn Stamp; Suburban Motors; Ronald Szymanowski; Chip Turtzo; Burt Van Flue; Jerry Windle.

CHAPTER 7

Jim Bauldauf; Donald and Phyllis Bueter; Tony Capua; Myron Davis; Harry A. DeMenge; David Doyle; Glenn Eisenhamer; Ford Motor Company; GM Photographic; Sonny and Mari Glassbrenner; Bill Hill; David Hill; Thomas A. Hoffman; Bud Juneau; Press and Janet Kale; Russell A. Liechty; Verl D. Mowery; Tenny Natkin; Charles Newton; Oldsmobile Historic Center; Rader's Relics; Myron Reichardt; Bill Reinhardt; Arthur J. Sabin; John Segedy; Donald Sharp; Raymond Silva, Jr.; John Spring; Danny L. Steine; Sam Turner; Bob Ward; Anthony and Boise Wells.

CHAPTER 8

William D. Albright; Edward George Allen; Nancy L. Beauregard; George A. Buchinger; Bill Burgun; Earl J. Carpenter; Steve Carey; Bob and Brad Chandler; Dick Choler; Chrysler Historical Collection; Phil and Louella Cruz; James E. Dinehart; James L. Dowdy; Ford Motor Company; Bob Frumkin; GM Photographic; Anthony J. Gullata; Dix Helland; Melvin R. Hull; Victor Jacobellis; George S. Jewell; John Keck; John and Minnie Keys; Gary J. Kistinger; Larry K. Landis; Paul A. Leinbohm; Bud Manning; Richard Matson; Steve Megyesi; Loren E. Miller; George W. Mills; Ken Netwig; Greg Pagano; Donald W. Peters; Peters Motor Cars; John Pollack; Lewis E. Retzer; Robert Rocchio; Homer Jay Sanders; John Sanders; Robert G. Seals; Charles O. Sharpe; Henry Smith; Bonnie and Dennis Statz; Jerry Tranberger; Charles and Charlotte Watons.

CHAPTER 9

Bob Aaron; Robert and Diane Adams; Mervin M. Afflerbach; Albie Albershardt; William D. Albright; Jeff Alexander and Scott Holldraw; Andrew Alphonso; William Amos; Eldon Anson; Len Antrim; Mark Apel; Lynn Augustine; Robert Babcock; John Baker, Sr.; Barry and Barbara Bales; Kathy Barber; Paul Batista; Bob Baumgardner; Chuck Beed; Charles R. Bell; Raymond and Marilyn Bendy; Michael L. Berzenye; Patrick R. Billey; Neil S. Black; Norman Bloggs; Bill Bodnarchuck; Pete Bogard; Ernest Bollerud; Clayton E. Bone; Peter Bose; James Bottger; Richard and Marilyn Bourgie; Bob Brannon; Dr. Douglas Bruinsma; Joseph R. Bua; David Burkholder; Vern Burkitt; Dr. Art Burrichter; Paul A. Buscemi; Richard Carpenter; Dwight W. Cervin; Chicago Car Exchange; Dick Choler; Gordon Christl; Classic Car Center; Jim Clark; Roger Clements; Kathy Crasweller; Bill Curran; Arthur and Suzanne Dalby; Gail and John Dalmolin; Richard Daly; T. Davidson and H. Rothman; Charles Davis; Myron Davis; Harry DeMenge; Deer Park Car Museum; Ray and Nancy Deitke; Tom Devers; Jim

DiGregorio; Orville Dopps; Harry E. Downing; Jeff Dranson; Stanley and Phyliss Dumes; Dale and Marilyn Dutoi; Sherry Echols; William B. Edwards; Galen and Fay Erb; Stan Farnham; David L. Ferguson; Al Ferreira; Bob Flack; Jeff Franklin and Scott Hallaran; Tom Franks; Fraser Dante, Ltd.; Kurt Fredericks; Theodore Freeman; John M. Galandak; Michael Gallagher; F. James Garbe; Bob Gautschy; Ray Geschke; Harold Gibson; G.R. Good; Roger and Connie Graeber; Art Gravatt; Tim Graves; Jim D. Gregoria; Greg Gustafson; Tim and Sharon Hacker; Robert P. Hallada; Jim Hardy; Sam Harpster; Jay Harrigan; Billy and Dorothy Harris; Ralph M. Hartsock; Dennis J. Hauke; Bob Heffman; Henry T. Heinz; Dr. Ernie Hendry; Paul Hern; Carl Herren; Carl Herrin; Charles Hibert; Bill Hill; Roger Hill; David D. Horn; Mac Horst; Tom Howard; Virgil Hudkins; Dennis L. Huff; Melvin R. Hull; Elmer and Shirley Hungate; Fred and Diane Ives; Mary Jaeger; Blaine Jenkins; Roger and Betty Jerie; Gary Johns; Dennis and Kathy Johnson; Aaron Kahlenberg; Sherwood Kahlenberg; Thomas L. Karkeiwicz; William Kipp; Edwin C. Kirstatier; Gerry Klein; Bud Knudsen and John White; Don R. Kreider; John Krempasky; Andrew Krizman; David and Anne Kurtz; Edward S. Kuziel; William H. Lauer; David Lawrence; Donald R. Lawson; Dr. William H. Lenharth; Kenneth G. Lindsey; William R. Lindsey; George Lucie; Andrew and Bonita MacFarland; Joe Malta; Mike Matheson; Gene Mauburger; Michael D. McCloskey; Gordon McGregor; Virgil and Dorothy Meyer; Gary Mills; Dennis B. Miracky; Bob Montgomery; Bob Moore; Jack E. Moore; Guy Morice; Jim Mueller; M. Randall Mytar; Richard Nassar; Paul F. Northam; Tim Null; Ray Ostrander; Paul Oxley; Robert W. Paige; Alan C. Parker; John E. Parker; John Petras; Robb Petty; Richard and Janice Plastino; A. La Rue Plotts, Jr.; Michael Polsinelli; Joel Prescott; Richard Presson; Priceless Classic Motorcars; Norman W. Prien; Leonard Quinlin; Larry and Annis Ray; Jerry Retka; Gary Richards; Glendon and Betty Rierstead; John and Judy Riordan; Gary Robinson; Bob Rose; Otto T. Rosenbusch; Dick and Judy Rosynek; Glyn-Jan Rowley; Jess Ruffalo; Dan and Kate Santoro; Jim Scarpitti; Al Schaeffer; Peter and Jane Schlacter; Lester Schnepen; Bill Schwelitz; John Scopelite; Robert N. Seiple; Bob and Ronnie Sue Shapiro; Don Simpkin; Karl W. Smith; Walter J. Smith; Don and Bonnie Snipes; Ray Somers; Allan Spethman; Frank and Gene Sitarz; Tom Stackhouse; David L. Stanilla; Dennis M. Statz; Dan Streik; John Struthers; Studebaker National Museum; David L. Studer; Duane and Steven Stupienski; Neil W. Sugg; Robert G. Swanstrom; Frank Talarico; Kris Trexler; William E. True; Kenneth and Wayne Turner; Dean Ullman; Bill Ulrich; Roy Umberger; Charles F. Vandervelde; Eugene Vaughn; James and Susan Verhasseldt; Don L. Waite; Christine and Robert Waldock; Bob and Wendi Walker; Marvin Wallace; Glen Warrick; Edward E. Wassmann; Bob Weber; Herbert Wehling; Michael Wehling; Ron Welch; Jeff and Aleta Wells; H.H. Wheeler, Jr.; John White; Lee Willett; Brian H. Williams; Dale Williamson; Bill Wilt; John Wood; Frank E. Wrenick; Charles and Vernocia Wurm; Richard Zieger.

CHAPTER 10

Arnie Addison; Carolyn and Mark Badarno; Barry and Barbara Bales; Joseph Barrera; Wayne F. Beran; Rod and Claudia Bjerke; Ken Boorsma; Dave Brown; Bob Burroughs; Patt and J.T. Buxman; Richard Carpenter; Kenneth J. Caswell; Chrysler Photographic; Mike Congelose; Virgil K. Cooper; Mike Cowles; Thomas Crockatt; Claude E. Daniel, Jr.; Jim Davidson; Myron Davis; Dell's Auto Museum; Robert Dowd; Jack Driesenga; Roger Eberenz; Mike Elward; Greg Englin; Phil Fair; Clifford R. Fales; Robert and Gene Fattore; John T. Finster; Bob French; Paul Garlick; John Gaylord; GM Photographic; Ben Gipson; Gary A. Girt; Stephen Gottfried; Jack Gratzianna; Wanda Habenicht; Robert Hallada; Rex Harris; Ken Havekost; Chuck Henderson; David Hooten; Andy Hotton; Bill Jackson; Vic Jacobellis; Blaine Jenkins; Charles E. Jenkins; Michael and Patricia Kelso; Ron Kendall; Robbie Kincaid; Goerge Kling; William Korbel; Bob and Phyllis Leach; Melvin Lewis; Harold Lee Lockhart; Terry Lucas; Guy Mabee; Donald Maich; Darryl McNabb; Ed Meurer; S. Ray Miller, Sr.; Amos Minter; Frank J. Monhart; Bob Montgomery; Dean J. Moroni; Jim Mueller; Bob Newman; Jack L. Nichols; Jim Noel; Barry Norma; Ed Oberhaus; Oldsmobile History Center; Anthony Patane; Bob Patrick; Rear Admiral Thomas J. Patterson; Joseph A. Pessetti; Roger and Kathy Porep; Les Raye; Vivian Riley; Richard M. Rusnak; Tom Schay; Charles Schnetlage; Sam H. Scoles; Mike Shafsnitz; M.J. Shelton; Ray Shinn; Ray Sklarin; Mike Spaziano; Frank Spittle; Larry Stumpf; Rusty Symmes; Gary Thobe; Keith Thompson; Steve Thompson; Robert Thornton; Marion and Lindy VanWormer; Harold VonBrocken; John Wacha; Alois Peter Warren II; Joyce and Jim Wickel; James Carter Wright; Lou Zanon.

CHAPTER 11

Sam and Char Adams; Chuck Aiello; Norman Andrews; Jim Ashworth; Doug and Judy Badgley; Trever Badgley; Howard L. Baker; Jeffrey Baker; Delores Banuls; Ray Banuls; John Baritel; Ben Barlage; Larry Barnett; Dave Bartholomew; Alan N. Basile; Carl J. Beck; Beechy Family; Larry Bell; Tom Bigelow; John Breda; Rodney Brumbaugh; Jerry and Carol Buczkowski; Joe Burke; Richard L. Burki; Bill Bush; Ken Carmack; Richard Carpenter; Ed Catricala; Vince Cesena; Mary Lee Cipriano; Charles and Marie Cobb; Dave Cobble II; Mick Cohen; James E. Collins; John Cook; Ed Coughlin; Gordon Cowan; Dr. Mike Cruz; Allen Cummins; Nick D'Amico; Sandy D'Amico; Dan and Linda Davis; David Dawes and Bob Painter; Harry DeMenge; Rocky D'Orio; Patrick and Barbara Dugan; Keith Duncan; Donald F. and Chris Dunn; Jay Dykes; Joseph J. Eberle; Neil Ehresman; Glenn Eisenhamer; Ray and Gil Elias; Rob Embleton; James and Mary Engle; Eugene Fattore, Jr.; Mark E. Figliozzi; David Fink; Christina Finster; John T. Finster; Bob H. Firth; John Fobair; Frank Frandsen; Al Fraser; Charles P. Geissler; Tony and Suzanne George; Michael S. Gray; David Griebling; Mike Guffey; Earl F. Hansen; James Harris; Ralph M. Hartsock; Tom Hasse; Michael E. Hatch; Jon F. Havens; Grady Hentz; Ray Herman; Steve Hinshaw; Jeff and Trish Holmes; Steven Jenear; William Jenn; Aaron Kahlenberg; Jack Karleskind; Lawrence Keck; Dago and Cindy Keetch; Don and Karen Kerridge; Michele King; Robert and Ann Klein; Frank Kleptz; Barry L. Klinkel; Scott R. Koeshall; Darrell Kombrink; William W. Kramer; Mark Kuykendall; Jim Labertew; Leroy Lasiter; William G. Lajeunesse; Harold Lehman; James Lojeski; Dan and Joyce Lyons; George Lyons; Richard and Madeline Martindale; Ralph M. Mathiot; Steve Maysonet; Donald C. McCallum; Bryan McGilvray; Paul McGuire; Michael Mennela; Horace and Susan Mennella; Greg and Rhonda Meredyk; Bruce Meyer; Larry and Karen Miller; Rick Mitchell; Manny Montgomery; Bud Moore; David R. Mullett; Allan S. Murray; M. Randall Mytar; Yoshio and Eric Nakayama; Ken Nelson; Rich Neubauer; Burt and Lynda Neuner; Ed Oberhaus; Alfred L. Olson; Jay F. Painter; Samuel Pampenella, Jr.; Patricia and Rexford Parker; Dan Parrilli; Lawrence Pavla; Lee M. and Jeanette Pawilratz; Andrew Peterson; Paul D. Pierce; Sam Pierce; Joseph Pieroni; Charles Plylar; Thomas and Carol Podemski; Edwin Putz; Ed Raden; David Ramaly; Ramshead Auto Collection; John and Shirlee Rasin; Les Raye; T.M. Raymond; Jim Regnier; Jim Reilly; Bruce Rhoades; Roman Robaszewski; David L. Robb; Dennis D. Rosenberry; Jim and Chriss Ross; Sam and Wanda Roth; Darryl A. Salisbury; Walter Schenk; Allen Scherer; Rick Schick; Tom Schlitter; Howard Schoen; Lou Schultz, Jr.; Hans Schumacher; Owen Schumacher; Steven Schuman; Robert and Mary Lu Secondi; Brad Shull; Larry Simek; Russ Smith; David Snodgrass; Frank Spittle; Vince and Helen Springer; Tom and Katherine Stanley; Charles E. Stinson; Tom and Nancy Stump; Scott Swaydrak; Steve Sydell; Michael Tesauro, Jr.; Gary R. Thalman; Brian and Elvira Torres; David A. Ulrich; Dennis A. Urban; Charles A. Vance; Volo Auto Museum; Ron Voyles; Ron Walker; Bob Weggenmann; Odus West; William E. Wetherhost; Sherman Williams; Stephen M. Witmer; Patrick Wnek; Ron Wold; Bill Woodman; David Yordi; Andrew and Phyllis Young; Dr. Richard Zeiger; C.L. Zinn.

CHAPTER 12

Kirk Alexander; Mark Alter; Fernando Alvare; Orville L. Baer; Sam Bardic; Charles D. Barnette; James H. Carson; Gordon and Dorothy Clemmer; Ann C. Coffin; Rick Cybul; Leonidas Demopoulos; J. Glenn Dowd; Tony and Betty Fabiano; G. Benjamin Graves; Alan L. Gray; Gary M. Gurnushian; Gregg Gyurina; David L. Hardgrove; Bud Juneau; Charles M. Kerr; Kevin Kloubek; William Korbel; Tony and Larry Lawler; Bob Masi; Ken McDowell; Keith W. Meiswinkel; Ralph Milner; Delores Ann Mitchell; Dick Nelson; Ed Oberhaus; John Phillips; Thomas and Carol Podemski; Dennis W. Riley; Patricia A. Schelli; Doug Schliesser; Paul Swenson; Frank Trummer; Rosanne Winney; Peter Zannis; Larry Zidek.

CHAPTER 13

Grazina and Lloyd Biciunas; Corvette Mike; Bill Daubney; Robert and Bonnie Griffith; Dennis Helferich; Dan and Joyce Lyons; James Marino; Edward E. Ortiz; Bill and Sherri Souther.

CHAPTER 15

DuPont Automotive.

CONTENTS

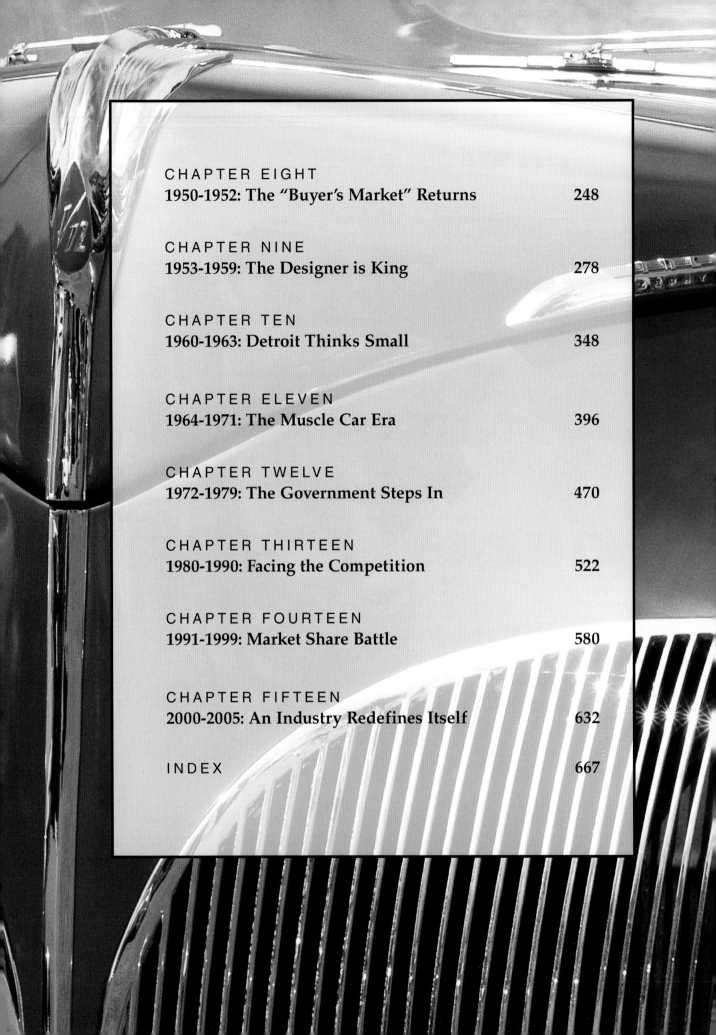

AN AMERICAN ODYSSEY

Welcome to a great story well told. The American automotive saga is rich in color and variety, and if there's a better way to convey its pace, scope, and excitement than with more than 4000 photos and captions, we haven't seen it. Think of *History of the American Auto* as a "family album" of the American automobile: a scrapbook of the major and minor, the good and ghastly, the memorable and forgettable.

Actually, it's a tale that spans more than 100 years, so this album does, too. But the automobile is the quintessential twentieth century device, and its story is the story of the American Century. Indeed, our chronicle is divided according to historical periods, with highlights of significant events and trends included in the introduction to each chapter. As for the automotive subject matter itself, we have striven to portray as many representative models as possible. If we have omitted things you think should have been included, we can only plead that there's never enough room for everything—except maybe in the Smithsonian Institution.

We've designed this book to inform and entertain readers of every age in every land, and there's a good reason why it should. Just as America is like no other country and Americans like no other people, American automobiles have a unique character.

Although born in Europe, the automobile really "grew up" in America, becoming an expression of the nation's values and technology, as well as an engine of economic and social change. In fact, nowhere else has the automobile been a more pivotal player on a national stage. We were quick to adopt the "horseless carriage" as our own. We paved landscapes so we could drive the machines everywhere (to the ultimate decline of our railroads). We perfected interchangeable parts so we could build cars consistently, then made Detroit the Motor City by devising the mass-production assembly line to turn automobiles out so efficiently that everybody could afford one—the very essence of democracy.

Americans made cars bigger and heavier than Europeans did, if only for comfort and durability in a large nation full of wide open spaces. The cars were also made to be as fast and powerful as possible. And why not, when gasoline was so much cheaper and more plentiful here? Historically, inexpensive gas not only hastened America's acceptance of the internal combustion engine over steam and electricity, it made Detroit the home of horsepower—all the better for covering, say, 500 miles in a day. The typical European road trip doesn't cover half that distance.

One thing you may glean from these pages is the way American automobile design still reflects the can-do flamboyance of Americans. This holds true not only for appearance, which Americans tend to alter more often and capriciously than Europeans, but also for technical features; which have often been something less than advertised. Yet if Detroit was once ridiculed for gaudy gimmicks and faddish "planned obsolescence," it was only because Americans most always believed that "new" really was "better." Besides, how else to encourage people to buy from an industry that came to account directly or indirectly for one of every three American jobs?

Not that the American car industry hasn't done its share to advance the state of automotive art. The modern high-compression engine, safety-rim wheel, power steering and brakes, automatic transmission, air conditioning, and the airbag were all invented here. These innovations deserve due credit, if only to balance more dubious Detroit achievements, such as tailfins and wraparound windshields. Then again, "styling" was invented here, too.

To browse though this book is to be struck by how far the automobile has come in only a hundred years—from the crude, costly, slow, and smoking rattletrap at the turn of one century to the clean, quiet, safe, and sophisticated conveyance at the turn of another. It's been a remarkable ride. And it's only just begun.

The Editors of Consumer Guide®

CHAPTER ONE

1893-1902

IN THE BEGINNING

Though first in countless technical developments, America came late to the automobile. By the time the Duryea brothers of Mass-achusetts took their horseless carriage for a spin in 1893, such European motorcars as Benz and Panhard et Levassor had been marketed for several years.

Clearly, American inventors had the engineering skills to have created an automobile earlier. Many were aware of European develop-ments. Nevertheless, the American auto industry lagged at the start-ing gate.

Roads presented one major obstacle. America was a vast land of muddy ruts—where any pathway existed at all. Besides that, poten-tial backers feared the financial risk, so countless automakers would fail due to lack of sufficient capital.

Three power sources vied for attention: steam, electricity, and gasoline. Steam locomotives had helped tame the American West. Couldn't a steam-powered conveyance also run on roads? Oliver Evans had proposed such a wagon in 1801. Sylvester Roper had built a steam carriage in 1863. Finally, by 1897, the Stanley twins were producing steam-powered automobiles. Though powerful, steamers demanded skilled maintenance. Stanleys lingered through the mid Twenties, but their heyday was over long before then.

Electric motors powered carriages by the early Nineties. Despite their short range, electrics were genteel: clean, silent, perfect for ladies. At the turn of the century, electrics grabbed an impressive 38 percent of the market, but their share soon plummeted. More than a century later, the long-expected battery "breakthrough" still remains elusive.

No single inventor earns credit for the internal-combustion engine, first patented in 1826. Etienne Lenoir patented a two-cycle motor in France in 1860. George Brayton's American-built gasoline engine ran at the 1876 Centennial in Philadelphia. Inspired by Bray-ton's two-cycle motor, George Selden applied for a patent on a "road engine." Years later, Selden's patent would cause American automakers grave consternation.

In 1885, Karl Benz and Gottlieb Daimler, of Germany, indepen-dently created the world's first vehicles with internal-combustion engines, operating on the four-cycle principle devised by Nicholas Otto. Charles and Frank Duryea read about the Benz in the *Scientific American* and—on September 21, 1893—drove their motorized phaeton. Was theirs really the first in America? No one knows for sure. Charles Lambert, for instance, claimed to have produced one in 1891.

If any one event paved the way for gasoline power it was Chicago's *Times-Herald Race*, held in November 1895. The grueling contest, run in the snow, was won by a two-cylinder Duryea.

By 1895, *The Horseless Age* magazine estimated that 300 Amer-icans had attempted to build a motorized carriage. Like Daimler and Benz, nearly all worked alone, unaware of others' efforts.

In March 1896, Charles King drove his car in Detroit. Three months later came Henry Ford's Quadricycle. Before the year was out, Ransom Olds and Alexander Winton had cars ready for pro-duction. By 1897, the auto industry was rolling full steam—or gaso-line—ahead.

An impartial observer might have pronounced the gasoline engine's prospects limited. The operator had to start it with a crank, tinkering with various controls. It shook and clattered, smoked and stank. Shifting gears was no picnic. Farmers were angered, horses frightened. Genteel, it was not. Soon, though, the trend narrowed to the water-cooled, four-cycle gasoline engine.

Many of the visions of our pioneer automakers faltered quickly. Others carried on for several years. A handful, like the Curved-Dash Runabout named for Ransom Olds, and the soon-to-arrive Buick and Ford, persisted into modern times.

Pre-1893

• Credit for the first self-propelled land vehicle goes to the 1770 French Cugnot, a steam-powered artillery tractor

• By 1865, Sylvester Roper mounts a steam engine on a carriage to create a self-propelled runabout

• Even earlier, in 1862, Jean Joseph Etienne Lenoir experiments with a gasoline-powered road vehicle in Europe

• Oldsmobile founder Ransom Eli Olds begins experiments with three-wheeled steam vehicles as early as 1886

• An improved Olds steamer of 1891 earns national attention and a mention in *Scientific American* magazine

• Lucius D. Copeland builds a steam-powered bicycle in the early 1880s, steam tricycles are produced later in the decade

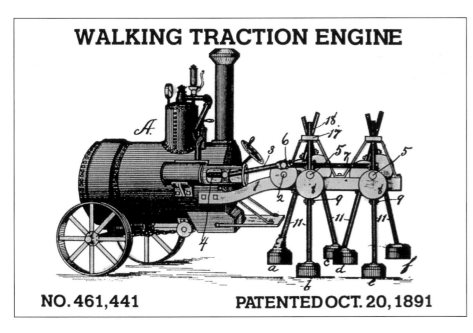

WALKING TRACTION ENGINE

NO. 461,441   PATENTED OCT. 20, 1891

◄ Wheeled motorcars already dotted Europe, but this 1891 patent was basically for a six-legged mechanical horse.

▼ The popularity of bicycles in the 1880s led various inventors to envision mechanization. Lucius D. Copeland attached a small boiler to his Star bicycle's front frame tube, and a small steam engine below the saddle.

▲ Henry Ford began work on a motorized bicycle in 1893 in a brick shed behind his Detroit home. Completed in 1896, his Quadricycle used belt and chain drive and a two-cylinder, water-cooled engine. This replica of Ford's workshop may be viewed at Greenfield Village in Dearborn, Michigan.

- Early French automotive tinkerer DeLamarre De Bouteville receives a patent for the carburetor in 1884

- Two German motor vehicles make news in 1886: Benz three-wheeler and Daimler side-wheeler cycle

- Benz obtains a German patent for a gasoline-powered "Motorwagon" in January 1886

- Karl Benz and Gottlieb Daimler earn credit as developers of the first workable gasoline-powered vehicles

- European automobiles are in regular production by the 1890s, makes include Delahaye and Panhard & Lavassor

- After several attempts, William Morrison drives his first "truly successful" electric vehicle in Chicago in 1888

- Early vehicles that claim title to the first American car include Lambert and Nadig, both built in 1891

- The three-wheeled, surrey-topped Lambert gets a price tag of $550, about $11,000 in current dollars, but fails to sell

- The Nadig carriage uses a one-cylinder gasoline engine drive—but is never patented by creator Henry Nadig

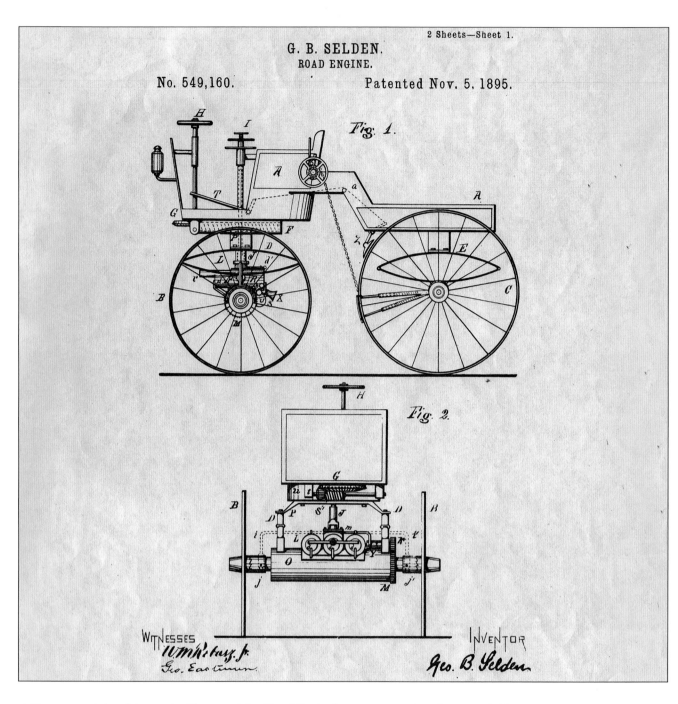

G. B. SELDEN.
ROAD ENGINE.

No. 549,160.

Patented Nov. 5, 1895.

Fig. 1.

Fig. 2.

WITNESSES
W. M. Witney, Jr.
Geo. Eastman.

INVENTOR
Geo. B. Selden

▲ Few grasped the ultimate significance of the "Road Engine" patent granted to George B. Selden on November 5, 1895. Later, Selden would demand royalties from infant automakers, claiming that his patent covered their efforts.

1893-94

• The Duryea brothers run the "Buggyaut" on September 21, 1893, in Springfield, Massachusetts; it's considered the first successful gas-engine vehicle built in the U.S.

• An early Duryea magazine advertisement explains to readers that the new vehicle "actually operated under its own power"

• Elmer and Edgar Apperson and Jonathan Maxwell build the single-cylinder Haynes; conceived by Elwood Haynes, it is first tested in autumn 1893

• Henry Ford builds and bench tests his first engine in 1893. Ford's first automobile won't arrive for another three years

▲ Elwood P. Haynes tends the tiller of his first motorcar, which he drove in Kokomo, Indiana, in 1894. Haynes bought a single-cylinder, two-stroke Sintz engine, then asked the Apperson brothers to build a vehicle around it.

▲ Charles Duryea sits at the tiller of one of the machines built with brother J. Frank. The Duryeas are considered by most authorities to have built the first American gasoline-powered car.

▲ Years later, many Americans would incorrectly believe that Henry Ford invented the automobile. Ford was an engineer at the Edison Illuminating Company when he started work on his first vehicle.

▲ Henry Ford's Quadricycle drew scant attention when he drove it around Detroit on June 4, 1896, at 2:00 A.M. Its two-cylinder engine produced roughly four horsepower, good for 20 mph.

• The U.S. Office of Road Inquiry is established in 1893, a result of the "good roads" movement spearheaded by cycling fans

• The first brick-surfaced road is laid in 1893, on Wooster Pike in Cuyahoga County, Ohio. Construction cost: $16,000 per mile.

• A son, Edsel, is born to Henry and Clara Ford on November 6, 1893. Edsel would be the couple's only son

• The Duryea brothers file papers to incorporate the Duryea Motor Wagon Company in 1893

▶ Charles Brady King grasps the tiller of his first automobile, in 1896. Beside him is assistant Oliver E. Barthel, who was later associated with Henry Ford.

▼ Ransom E. Olds (*left*) formed the Olds Motor Vehicle Company in 1897. His passenger in the one-cylinder '97 model, M.F. Bates, claimed to have built the first internal combustion engine in Michigan.

1895

• U.S. Patent Office grants a patent on a motorcar to George B. Selden

• A Duryea wins the *Times-Herald Race* in Chicago, at an average 7.5 mph

• Hiram Percy Maxim opens a motor-carriage department for Pope Mfg. Company, a Connecticut bicycle maker

• The first four-wheeled Riker Electric is built, but no vehicles are sold until 1897

• Two automotive trade journals debut: *The Horseless Age* and *The Motocycle*

• The American Motor League, the first U.S. automotive association for enthusiasts, is formed in Chicago

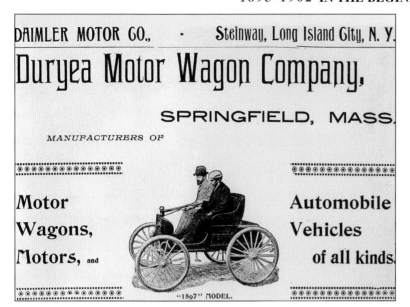

▲ Dr. Carlos G. Booth, of Youngstown, Ohio, may have been the first American physician to use a motorcar in his practice. Dr. Booth assembled his own vehicle.

▲ After building 13 vehicles in 1896, the Duryea brothers were definitely in business as the Duryea Motor Wagon Company. Note the early use of the term "automobile" in this ad for their 1897 model.

▼ Henry Ford built his second Quadricycle in 1898–99, with a far more finished appearance than the 1896 model. Note the tiller handgrip.

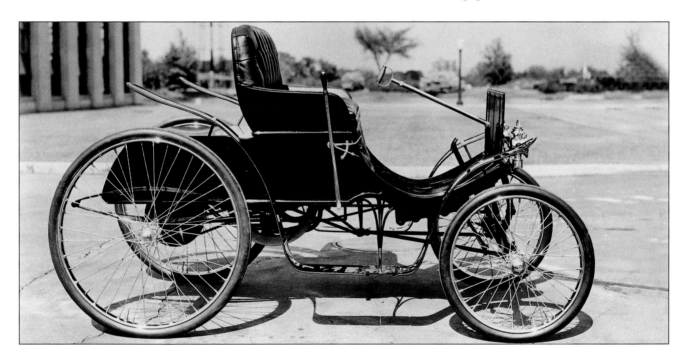

1896

- *The Horseless Age* claims more than 300 people or firms have built motorcars

- Charles B. King drives his water-cooled, four-cylinder, four-cycle vehicle in Detroit

- Track races are held for the first time on September 7 at Narragansett Park, Rhode Island; a Riker Electric is the winner.

◄ Cadwallader W. Kelsey had built a four-wheeled vehicle in 1897, at age 17. He then teamed with college friend Sheldon Tilney on this three-wheeled, single-cylinder "Autotri."

► Alexander Winton turned from bicycle production to an experimental auto in 1896, then formed Winton Motor Carriage Company. A total of 22 were sold in 1898.

▲ Built by the Detroit Automobile Company in 1899, this delivery van was the first Ford-related truck intended for sale. Henry Ford had left his job at Edison and was named superintendent at Detroit Automobile, but serious production never happened. The company collapsed late in 1900.

- Alexander Winton builds an experimental two-seat, single-cylinder motor carriage

- The American Electric Vehicle Company offers its first wares

- Ransom E. Olds drives a one-cylinder, six-horsepower, gasoline-engined motorcar

- Duryea builds third through sixteenth car—the first design used for multiple autos

- Frank Stearns constructs his first auto, at age 17, in his father's machine shop

- Henry Ford drives his two-cylinder Quadricycle in Detroit on June 4

- Pope Manufacturing Company builds its first electric motor carriage

- Originally a French term, American publications first use the word *automobile*

▲ Francis E. and Freelan O. Stanley, owners of a photographic equipment company, attempted in 1884 to build a steam car based on the Field steamer. They failed, but would later produce the fabled Stanley Steamer.

◄ Kelsey & Tilney's 1899 experimental three-wheeler ultimately went to the U.S. National Museum. Kelsey's father forbade him to put it into production, but a decade later he developed a Motorette, aimed to rival Ford's new Model T.

1897

• The Oldsmobile Motor Vehicle Company is formed in Lansing; it is Michigan's first registered automobile manufacturer

• Studebaker Brothers, a carriage-building firm since 1852, begins building motor-vehicle prototypes

• Pope Manufacturing holds first American auto press conference to introduce its Mark III Electric Phaeton

• The first Stanley Steamer is assembled by identical twins Francis E. and Freelan O. Stanley

• Bicycle manufacturer Thomas B. Jeffery builds his first auto; it will eventually evolve into the Rambler

• Winton automobiles enter regular production, following the formation of the Winton Motor Carriage Company

▲ The first White Steamcar, a Stanhope model, appeared in 1900. Former sewing-machine maker Thomas White adopted the newly invented semiflash boiler for his motorcars.

▲ In 1900, the first electric ambulance rolled through New York City to St. Vincent's Hospital. A year earlier, Akron, Ohio, police had acquired an electric patrol wagon.

"OLDSMOBILES"

ELECTRIC
AND
GASOLINE.

PRICE,
$600.00
AND
UPWARD.

Write
for Catalogue.

VARD LOOMIS
Dixie Hwy. at M 87
SBURG, MICHIGAN
Phone Can be 5-5601
Operated by
the
Inexperienced.

OLDS MOTOR WORKS, 1299 Jefferson Ave., DETROIT, MICH.

◀ Ransom Olds had planned both electric and gasoline vehicles for 1901, but when a fire gutted the Detroit plant in March, only a gasoline-engined runabout was saved.

1898

• Joining the ranks of automobile manufacturers this year are General Electric and Waverly Electric

• Auto builder F. B. Stearns & Company is founded; but serious production is delayed until 1901

• Nation's first franchise auto dealer, H. O. Keller, sells first commercially available Winton in Reading, Pennsylvania

• In Detroit, William E. Metzger establishes the country's first independent auto dealership

• One of the first used-car dealerships opens in New York as The Empire State Motor Wagon Company

• Horse-drawn taxis are joined by electrics on American streets, appearing first in New York City

▲ In 1900, New York's Madison Square Garden hosted the National American Automobile Show. Forty manufacturers displayed more than 300 vehicles.

▲ Photographed near his Kenosha, Wisconsin, shop, Thomas B. Jeffery's experimental vehicle—forerunner to the Rambler—had been complete three years prior.

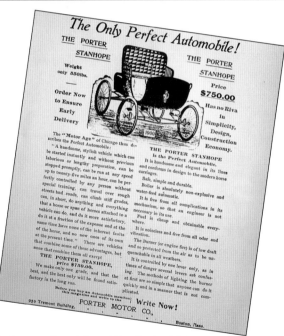

▲ Modesty wasn't a virtue at the Porter Motor Company, yet its steam-powered "perfect automobile" lasted only from 1900 to 1901. The light runabout featured aluminum body panels.

1899

• Olds Motor Works, Ransom's second company, is established and moves from Lansing to Detroit

• James Ward Packard constructs his first automobile and runs it on November 6 in Warren, Ohio

• Henry Ford goes to work for the Detroit Automobile Company as engineer

• The Bridgeport, Connecticut-based Locomobile Company builds its first steam car.

• Mrs. John Howell Phillips of Chicago becomes the first woman to obtain a driver's license

• A Winton franchise becomes New York City's first automobile franchise

▲ Introduced in 1899 as the American, the renamed Gasmobile appeared at the New York Auto Show in 1900—but left the auto scene in 1902, after about 140 examples had been produced.

▲ The Mobile Company of America acquired production rights from the Stanley brothers for the 1900 Mobile steamer.

▲ Back in 1900, a filling "station" had to come to the motorist, carrying barrels of fuel. Not until 1901 was the first gasoline storage tank installed, in New York.

- A. L. Dyke establishes the first American auto-parts business, in St. Louis

- The U.S. Army takes delivery of its first electric vehicle

- The U.S. Post Office experiments with electric delivery vehicles

- Boston restricts automobiles in parks to avoid spooking horses

- Merchants in New York and Boston add electric vehicles to their delivery fleets

- New York's American Motor Company advertises "competent mechanics"

- The first issue of *Motor Age* magazine hits the newsstands

- The Automobile Club of America is formed, regional branches are added in 1900

- Freelan Stanley drives a Stanley Steamer, built by him and brother Francis E., to the top of New Hampshire's Mount Washington

- Alexander Winton drives his own automobile from Cleveland to New York City in just under 48 hours

- Engine emissions gain attention by the turn of the century, including the concept of a catalytic converter

▲ By 1901, seven Locomobile models were being built, including this Locosurrey. A period ad promised "no noise, jar, or odor." By 1904, 5000 Locomobiles had been built.

▲ The Waverly Electric was a product of the American Bicycle Company, of Indianapolis, Indiana. In 1900, this 1050-pound Model 22 Road Wagon carried a $925 price.

▲ Production of Model A Rambler runabouts began in 1901. A steering wheel (left-hand drive) and front engine were planned, but cars introduced for 1902 had a right-hand tiller and one-cylinder engine located under the seat.

New Makes 1899

- Baker Electric
- Baldwin Steam
- Chicago Electric
- Dyke
- Grout
- Gurley
- Holyoke
- Kensington
- Kidder
- Leach Steamer
- Locomobile
- Media
- Oakman-Hertel
- Orient
- Packard
- St. Louis
- Strathmore
- Victor Steam
- Woods Electric

1900

- Just under 4200 automobiles are produced in America this year, by approximately 40 different manufacturers

- Some 48,000 fans attend the first National American Automobile Show in November in New York City

- The first automobile show included seven steam-powered models and 11 parts and accessory manufacturers

- Prices for the approximately 300 models on display at the first automobile show ranged from $280 to $4000

- The Mobile Company of America builds a 200-foot ramp for use in demonstrating the hill-climbing ability of steam vehicles

- By the end of the year, America's streets and rural roads will be dotted with an estimated 14,000 automobiles

▲ Henry Ford's third car, sporting fancy fenders and a steering wheel (no tiller), was built by the Detroit Automobile Company while he was superintendent there in 1901.

▲ Soon after Ford's third car was built, the Detroit Automobile Company folded.

▲▼ Drivers (and passengers) had to bundle up, but early automobiles could brave the toughest blizzards, as this circa-1901 Olds runabout demonstrates. Even so, flat tires and mechanical problems were inevitable on most trips.

• The Auburn and Peerless makes arrive, along with the Knox three-wheel runabout and the first White Steamcar

• After three years of development, Walter C. Baker introduces his car, the Baker Electric

• Latest Packard model features a steering wheel, in place of the popular tiller

• Several makes move gasoline engines to a new location, under a "hood" creating space in back for a "trunk"

• An automobile advertisement appears in *The Saturday Evening Post* for the first time

• Average new car has top speed of eight mph and goes 35 miles on a gallon of gas

• The price of the average new car in America is now $1168, approximately half the cost of a single-family home

• William McKinley is the first U.S. President to ride in an automobile

• R.E. Dietz Company introduces a kerosene auto lamp that casts a beam 200 feet

▲ In this demonstration, three 1901 Oldsmobiles ride a seesawlike contraption to prove their agility. The Curved-Dash Olds used a horizontal single-cylinder, 4.5-bhp engine.

▲ John Maxwell pilots a 1901 Oldsmobile up a harsh hill. Rough roads served as "proving grounds" in the early years. Mass production of gasoline-engined cars began in 1901—425 "Curved-Dash" Model R runabouts were built.

• Leach Motor Carriage adds an antitheft device to some models, a removable steering lever

• Alexander Winton is the first American to participate in foreign auto competition, The Gordon Bennett Race, in France

• Of the approximately 8000 automobiles in use, 40 percent are steam, 38 percent electric, and 22 percent gasoline powered

• Ransom E. Olds is credited with constructing the first U.S. factory purpose-built for the manufacture of automobiles

• New York City is the first American municipality to employ a motorized vehicle in its ambulance fleet

• As America's population swells to 76 million, approximately one in 20,000 people owns an automobile

▲ Henry Ford sits in his first racing car, powered by a 26-bhp, two-cylinder engine. On October 10, 1901, it averaged 43.5 mph over a 10-mile course at Grosse Pointe, Michigan, beating a Winton.

1899-1900 Production Figures	
1. Columbia (1900)	1500
2. Locomobile (1900)	750
3. Winton (1899)	100
4. Packard (1900)	49
5. Stanley (1899)	30
6. Stearns (1899)	20
7. Knox (1900)	15
8. Oldsmobile (1899-1900)	11
Some figures are estimated or calendar year	

1901

• In several areas of the country, license plates are required for the first time

• Approximately 7000 automobiles are built in the U.S. this year

• Some 88 exhibitors display products at the second National American Automobile Show, held again at Madison Square Garden

• First Packard ad urging readers to "Ask The Man Who Owns One" appears

• The short-lived Henry Ford Company is organized by investors

• The Electric Vehicle Company, holder of the Selden patent, threatens legal action for infringement by unlicensed manufacturers

▶ Henry Ford experimented with this two-cylinder runabout in 1901–02. By early '02, his short stay with the Henry Ford Company was over. Barney Oldfield set an American speed record in the Ford "999" racer in October: 5 miles in 5 minutes, 28 seconds.

▲ Racing dominated Henry Ford's mind at the time, but he nonetheless constructed a third Quadricycle in 1901. After Ford left the Detroit Automobile Company, a version of this car would become the first Cadillac.

New Makes 1900

- Akron
- American De Dion
- Auburn
- Automobile Fore-Carriage
- Boston
- Buffalo
- Canda
- Clark Steam
- Collins Electric
- Crest
- Crowdus
- Eclipse Steamer
- Friedman
- Gasmobile
- Hasbrouck
- Hewitt-Lindstrom
- Holley
- Imperial
- International
- Keene Steamobile
- Keystone
- Klock
- Knox
- Lane Steam
- Marlboro
- Milwaukee
- Peerless
- People's
- Remington
- Robinson
- Searchmont
- Skene Steam
- Springfield Steam
- Strong & Rogers Electric
- Triumph
- White Steamer

- Ransom E. Olds builds 425 Curved-Dash models, making them the first "mass-produced" engined auto in the world

- Oldsmobile begins using parts and subassemblies produced under contract by other companies

- "Spindletop" gusher comes in near Beaumont, Texas, sinking the price of crude oil below five cents per barrel

- Roy Dikeman Chapin drives an Oldsmobile from Detroit to New York City in 7½ days, averaging 14 mph

- The Automobile Club of America launches a roadside-information-sign program between New York City and Boston

- New York State begins licensing automobiles, and generates $1000 in revenue the first year

- The George N. Pierce Company of Buffalo introduces its first car, the Pierce Motorette

- The first White automobile, a steamer, is produced by a division of the White Sewing Machine Company

- Henry Ford defeats Alexander Winton in a head-to-head track race in Grosse Pointe, Michigan, on October 10

▲ A "hedgehog" engine, nicknamed for the appearance of its air-cooled cylinder, powered this 1901 Knox. The three-wheeled Knoxmobiles soon were joined by four-wheeled runabouts. In this one, passengers sat up front.

▲ Production of the 1901 Locomobile Steamer was limited to four cars per day, implying that the car was built with precision. An early Locomobile might hit 40 mph, but couldn't travel far—usually only 20 miles—before it needed more water.

▼ Like many start-up ventures, the Niagara Car, built at Niagara Falls, quickly failed: begun in 1901, gone a year later. The little runabouts had a four-bhp gas engine.

◄ In 1901, company president George N. Pierce posed in a Pierce Motorette, whose one-cylinder engine developed 2¾ horsepower. About 150 were built through 1902.

1902

- American automobile production rises by 1000 this year, to 9000

- First Studebakers hit the road, originals are electrics

- The Detroit Automobile Company becomes Cadillac Automobile Company

- Wisconsin-based Rambler is founded, produces 1500 vehicles

- The Ohio Automobile Company changes its name to the Packard Motor Car Company

- A Locomobile is the first U.S. front-engine, water-cooled, four-cylinder automobile

- Northern becomes the first car to wear running boards

- Packard patents the "H" layout for floor-mounted shifters

◀ Nattily dressed occupants of this "double-seated" 1901 Locomobile enjoyed the benefits—and failings—of steam power. Early Locomobiles used tiller steering and chain drive; frames were welded together.

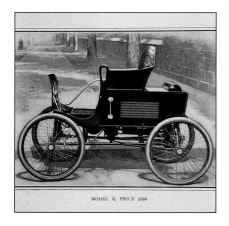

▲ Ads for the 1901 Reading Steam Carriage optimistically promised that it "runs indefinitely without attention." This Model B sold for $750 with a four-cylinder engine, two more than most of its steamer competition.

New Makes 1901

• Ajax Electric	• Crestmobile	• Hudson Steamer	• Rogers & Hanford
• Autocar	• Darling	• Lewis	• Steamobile
• Automotor	• Desberon	• Long Distance	• Stearns
• Brecht	• Empire Steamer	• Moncreif Steam	• Storck Steam
• Buckeye	• Essex	• Murdaugh	• Taunton Steam
• Buffalo Electric	• Fanning	• National Electric	• Thompson
• Buffum	• Foster	• Norton	• Toledo
• Century	• Geneva Steam	• Pawtucket Steam	• Walls
• Conrad	• Halsey Steam	• Prescott Steam	• Warwick
• Cotta Steam	• Hoffman	• Reading Steamer	

• Autocar's Louis S. Clarke designs the porcelain spark plug insulator and patents the double reduction gear for the rear axles

• While attending Cornell University, Clarence W. Spicer builds the first driveshaft U-joint

• T. H. Shevlin is fined $10 in Minneapolis for traveling in excess of 10 mph more than the posted speed limit

• Motor Mart opens in New York City, the multifranchise dealership sells new and used cars

• Henry Ford's "999" racer sets a speed record, covering five miles in five minutes, 28 seconds

• A Pierce Motorette is victorious at the Automobile Club of America's first endurance run

▲ The 1901 Toledo Steam Carriage, whose engine used 3×4-inch piston valves, came from the American Bicycle Company. This Model A was priced at $900.

▲ This single-cylinder Winton Surrey started at $1200. In 1901, a Winton drove 810 miles to the New York show in just under 38 hours. Sales reached 700 units this year.

▲ Displayed at the first National American Automobile Show in New York, this 1901 Winton was driven there from Cleveland—the longest known drive at the time.

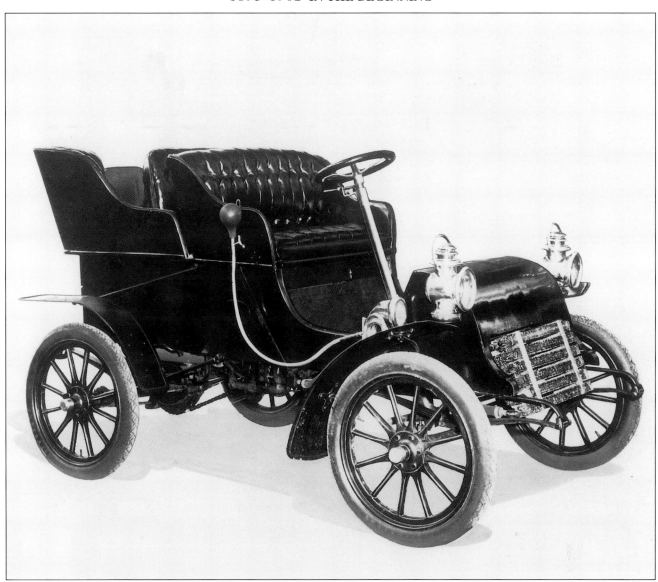

▲ The Detroit Automobile Company reorganized as the Cadillac Automobile Company in autumn 1902. The guiding light for the venture was Henry M. Leland, widely known for precision machining. The first Cadillacs, all with 10-bhp, one-cylinder engines, were built late in '02. Almost 2300 orders for the new Cadillac were placed at the New York Auto Show in January '03.

▲ Shown here with an experimental automobile of his own design, W. K. Ackerman later joined Cadillac's engineering department.

▲ Hyped as the "first shaft driven car," an '02 Autocar went from Philadelphia to New York in a record 6 hours, 10 minutes. The car cost $800.

1901 Model-Year Production Figures

1. Locomobile	1500
2. Winton	700
3. Oldsmobile	425
4. White	193
5. Autocar	140
6. Knox	100
7. Packard	81
8. Stanley	80

Some figures are estimated or calendar year

▲ Edgar and Elmer Apperson enjoy a spin in the first Apperson car, built in 1902. Their venture followed a split from Haynes in 1901. A Sintz-built two-cylinder, 16-bhp gas engine powered the Model A.

▲ Even after Edgar and Elmer Apperson departed for their own auto venture, the Haynes-Apperson name lingered for a couple of years. Here, the brothers are pictured in a two-passenger 1902 Haynes-Apperson.

▲ Locomobiles hailed from Bridgeport, Connecticut. The $1600 1902 Model A Touring held four people above a 73-inch wheelbase. Its steam engine had a 42-gallon water tank and a 16-inch boiler/burner.

▲ Begoggled and single-mindedly intent on victory, Dan Wurgis wields the tiller of the '02 racing Olds Pirate. Note how he leans over as he rounds the turn, as if driving a motorcycle. The one-cylinder Pirate, whose twin "rockets" are fuel tanks, ran in the first race at Daytona Beach, Florida, in April 1902 against Winton's four-cylinder Bullet 1. The Olds, renamed Flyer in 1903, set a lightweight one-mile record over the sand: 54 mph.

New Makes 1901

- Apperson
- Baldner
- Blomstrom
- Brasier
- Bristol
- Centaur
- Cloughley
- Covert
- Davenport Steam
- Decker
- Flint Steam
- Franklin
- Fredonia
- Gaethmobile
- General
- Graham
- Holsman
- Ideal
- Kunz
- Model
- Motorette
- Murray
- Northern
- Pomeroy
- Rambler
- Reber
- Rockaway
- Sandusky
- Santos-Dumont
- Tourist
- Union
- Upton
- Walter
- Wildman
- Yale

▶ With the exception of Henry Ford's Model T later in the decade, few automobiles earned the popularity of the Curved-Dash Oldsmobile. In fact, the 1901 fire at the factory proved providential, letting Olds focus on a single model. This 1902 Runabout carried a single-cylinder, 95.4-cubic-inch engine with a 4½×6-inch bore and stroke. The motor, turning at a leisurely 500 rpm, was said to emit "one chug per telegraph pole."

◀ Dos-a-Dos (2+2) seating was a $25 option on the 1902 Rambler Model C Runabout, which retailed for a modest $750.

▲ Everyone on this family outing looks grim, despite the virtues of their 1902 Rambler Dos-a-Dos. Wheelbase measured a compact 72 inches; wheel size 28×2½ inches.

▲ By 1902, Studebaker was building a wagonlike Electric Runabout. Ads boasted it "can be run any day in the year by any member of the family."

▲ "It starts from the seat," boasted the catalog for the 1902 Stevens-Duryea. J. Frank Duryea joined forces with the J. Stevens Arms & Tool Company to manufacture this five-bhp flat-twin runabout for $1200.

1902 Model-Year Production Figures	
1. Locomobile	2750
2. Oldsmobile	2500
3. Rambler	1500
4. White	385
5. Knox	250
6. Packard	179
7. Stanley	170
8. Union	60
Some figures are estimated or calendar year	

▲ Dr. George B. Crissman and his bride-to-be guide their 1902 Rambler Model C Runabout through a public park in Fort Collins, Colorado. The 1902 model was the first production Rambler; its one-piston engine developed four bhp.

CHAPTER TWO

1903-1919

UP AND RUNNING

Not much time passed before the trickle of pioneering automobiles turned into a steady flow. Buyers had countless cars to choose from—though most were too costly for the middle class. In addition to the companies that prospered and grew into giants, hundreds more turned out a handful of vehicles, then disappeared.

Because most early cars were assembled, not built from scratch, entry into manufacturing wasn't terribly difficult. Automakers typically bought components on credit, and then sold finished automobiles for cash.

In 1903, seven years after driving his first Quadricycle, Henry Ford founded the Ford Motor Company. By 1906, Ford ranked first in sales. Henry Leland focused on precision craftsmanship with the first Cadillac, also in 1903. The adoption of interchangeable parts was a giant leap forward from the practice of hand-fitting every piece.

The Electric Vehicle Company, having acquired George Selden's "road engine" patent, claimed that it covered nearly all motorcars. Most manufacturers fell in line, paying royalties to the Association of Licensed Automobile Manufacturers. Henry Ford was one of the few who resisted.

Detroit quickly grew into an automotive power, but cars were built all over the nation. Studebaker turned to gasoline cars in 1904, when Ransom E. Olds launched Reo (or Reo). William C. Durant gained control of Buick, then founded General Motors. In 1908 came Hupmobile; then Hudson, Chevrolet, and the Dodge Brothers. Higher up the scale, sportsmen might have preferred a Stutz Bearcat or Mercer Raceabout.

Taking an early day spin wasn't exactly a picnic. Gearboxes were balky; steering required muscle. Drivers faced hand throttles, spark levers, drip oilers—each unit demanding attention. Carbide and kerosene lamps gave little illumination.

Farmers might threaten—or even aim a gun at fast-moving machines. Motorists needed special apparel, and one had to expect a succession of flat tires, if not more serious troubles. Owners (or their chauffeurs) were expected to do their own repairs.

By 1908, nearly 400,000 vehicles were registered. Charles Duryea (no longer an industry force) estimated that 515 companies had entered production—but more than half had failed. Then, Ford announced the car that would alter America: the Model T, destined to live for two decades and sell more than 15 million copies. Adoption of the moving assembly line in 1913 helped make Ford's "flivver" easily affordable, the first "car for the masses."

Innovations were many, but the gasoline engine had elbowed aside electrics and steamers, and cars took a standardized form. Still, plenty of inventors thought they had a better idea, such as the Charter Water-Gasoline car of 1903. A decade later came a short-lived fad of fragile "cyclecars." Air-cooled engines had their proponents. Highwheelers came and went. Friction drive and electric transmissions were tried. Among the strangest: the eight-wheeled Octoauto.

Few technological advances would change the automobile's future as much as the electric self starter, installed in 1912 Cadillacs. Elimination of the dangerous hand crank meant more Americans, particularly women, could drive.

In the Teens, the "Sunday drive" took hold. Vacationers were turning to autocamping. Automobiles carried comedians to their destinies in silent films, and played a major role as America finally entered the Great War. After the Armistice, American women won the right to vote, and were ready for their own flirtation with the automobile.

1903

- A total of 11,235 automobiles are built in the United States this year

- New features include mechanical valves (Olds and Rambler), compensating carburetors, square "bonnets," honeycomb radiators

- Enclosed cars are displayed at the New York auto show for the first time, are described by some as "glass front"

- New features on display include T-head engines and shock absorbers

- Ford Motor Company is incorporated with $28,000 capital. The company earns enough money to pay a dividend in the same year

- Henry Ford is the company's vice president and chief engineer, with 25.5-percent interest; John S. Gray is president

▲ Chief engineer Walter Marr (*at wheel*) and Thomas Buick—son of David Dunbar Buick, the company's founder—drive the first Buick built in Flint, Michigan. The Model B had a two-cylinder, 21-bhp engine.

► William Crapo Durant, co-owner of the Durant-Dort Carriage Company, took over Buick on November 1, 1904.

▲ Ford Motor Company began life in 1903 in this modest factory on Mack Avenue in Detroit, with John Gray serving as president. Ford paid $75 a month rent for the building, which initially had a single floor. A second story soon was added.

- Initial Ford stockholders include John and Horace Dodge, Albert Strelow, Alex Y. Malcomson, and James Couzens

- The Dodge Brothers agree to supply completed chassis to the new Ford company, for $250 each

- The first Ford Model A runabout is sold in July; its L-head engine has twin opposed cylinders displacing 100.5 cubic inches

- The Ford Motor Company pays its first dividend in November, a staggering 10 percent of share value

- The Association of Licensed Automobile Manufacturers (ALAM) is established, includes nine automakers

- Until 1911, nearly all manufacturers of gasoline automobiles pay Seldon patent royalties through the ALAM

- Rejected membership, Ford is sued by Selden. Selden claims to have patented the automobile, in its current form, in 1877

- The first Cadillac appears at the National Automobile show. The single-cylinder Caddy is sold on site

- Two Oldsmobiles, "Old Scout" and "Old Steady," run in a 4000-mile transcontinental race. "Old Scout" won.

▲ Three daring travelers had to squeeze to fit into a 1903 Ford Model A "turtleback" runabout. One ad promised that a Ford was "so simple that a boy of 15 can run it."

▲ Ford's first production auto, the $850 1903 Model A, had a two-cylinder, 100.5-cid engine under the seat, yielding eight horsepower. A removable tonneau was a $100 option.

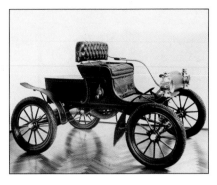

▲ Oldsmobile production rose to 4000 units in calendar-year 1903. The popular Curved-Dash Runabout continued with a tiller and a seatside crank for the 4¼-horsepower engine.

▲ Two Oldsmobile runabouts, "Old Scout" and "Old Steady," line up in New York City for the start of the first transcontinental auto race in the spring of 1905. Destination: Portland, Oregon. Old Scout won, arriving after 44 days, to help open the Lewis & Clark Centennial Exposition.

• Some 88 new companies are added to the ranks of autobuilders, Buick and Overland are among them

• The four-cylinder Packard Model K debuts, joins the firm's original single-piston model in the lineup

• Peerless adopts an easier-to-produce pressed-steel frame, other manufacturers quickly follow suit

• Power steering, operated by a seperate electric motor, is installed in a Columbia Electric Motor Truck

• C. Harold Wills signs on with the Ford Motor Company as chief engineer and factory manager

• Packard moves operations to Detroit, occupying the world's first factory made of reinforced concrete

• White Steamers perform flawlessly during 650-mile reliability trials conducted in Britain and Ireland

• Bicycle racer Berner Eli "Barney" Oldfield hooks up with Ford, pilots Henry's "999" racer

• The Jackson Automobile Company issues both a gasoline-powered runabout, and a larger Jaxon steamer

◄ The first car to travel a mile in less than a minute (42 seconds) was the 1903 Oldsmobile "Pirate," at Daytona Beach. Torpedolike tanks suggest the Olds "Rocket" of the Fifties. Early race drivers were dangerously exposed—note the driver's shoe at the axle.

▲ Detail refinements for the 1903 Packard Model F runabout included a sloped hood, longer 88-inch wheelbase, and lower $2000 price tag.

▲ Mom and Pop occupy the center seat of a one-cylinder 1903 Rambler; the kids are tucked in up front. Wheelbase: a compact 78 inches.

▲ Barely a dozen single-cylinder, Overland runabouts were built in 1903. Steering was still by tiller. They cost just $595.

New Makes 1903

- Austin
- Bates
- Berg
- Blackhawk
- Buckmobile
- Cadillac
- Cameron
- Cincinnati
- Clarkmobile
- Columbus Electric
- Commercial
- Country Club
- Eldredge
- Ford
- Glide
- Greeley
- Hall
- Hammer-Sommer
- Howard
- Iroquois
- Jackson
- Jaxson Steam
- Jones-Corbin
- Lyman & Burnham
- Mackle-Thompson
- Marble-Swift
- Marr
- Matheson
- Mercury
- Mitchell
- Mohawk
- Monarch
- Moyea
- Niagara
- Overland
- Parkin
- Phelps
- Pope-Robinson
- Pope-Toledo
- Premier
- Randall
- Rapid
- Regas
- Rotary
- Russell
- Shelby
- Smith
- Springer
- Star
- Thomas
- Tincher
- Warner
- Waterloo
- Welch Tourist
- Zentmobile

1903 Model-Year Production Figures

1.	Oldsmobile	4000
2.	Cadillac	2497
3.	Ford	1708
4.	Pope-Hartford	1500
5.	Rambler	1350
6.	Winton	850
7.	White	502
8.	Knox	500

Some figures are estimated or calendar year

▲ Riding an 87-inch wheelbase and sporting curved fenders, the 1904 Buick Model B touring car used a right-hand steering wheel. A 159-cid, two-cylinder engine gave 22 bhp. Price was $950, but only 37 were built.

▲ Henry Ford dreamed of a cheap car, but this 1904 four-cylinder Model B touring went for a hefty $2000.

▲ Henry Ford topped 91 mph when he piloted the 1904 Arrow "999" racer (left) on icy Lake St. Clair in January of that year.

◄ Cadillac's Model B succeeded the Model A in 1904, with a one-cylinder "Little Hercules" Leland & Faulconer engine. Advertised at 8¼ horse-power, the motor displaced 98 cubic inches and used a new pressure-fed oiler.

▲ The roots of the Orient make can be traced to 1893, and Orient bicycles. Car production began in 1902. The 1904 Orient Buckboard rode on a wooden platform without springs, and could reach 30 mph with its one-cylinder engine.

▲ Early day designers are busy at their boards in Oldsmobile's main drawing room, at the Seager Engine Works. The Curved-Dash's engine got a larger bore in 1904, for a seven-horsepower rating, plus a new Holley carb. R.E. Olds departed from the firm he founded to form the Reo Motor Car Company.

New Makes 1904

- Acme
- American Napier
- Beverly
- Black Diamond
- Brew-Hatcher
- Buick
- Cantono Electric
- Chadwick
- Christie

- Compound
- Courier
- Dawson
- De Motte
- Detroit
- Dolson
- Duquesne
- Four Wheel Drive
- Frayer-Miller

- Gibbs Electric
- Hill
- Logan
- Luverne
- Mahoning
- Marion
- Marmon
- Michigan
- Moline

- Ormond Steam
- Pierce-Racine
- Pope-Hartford
- Pope-Tribune
- Pope-Waverly Electric
- Pungs-Finch
- Reliance
- Queen
- Standard

- Stoddard
- Stoddard-Dayton
- Studebaker
- Sturtevant
- Synnestvedt Electric
- Walworth
- Wayne
- Wolverine

1904

- Total industry output excedes 22,000, double that of 1903

- The fourth National Automobile Show is the largest yet, of the 185 exhibitors, 87 are vehicle manufacturers

- Many of the new makes feature removable "demountable" wheel rims that allow for easy service

- Autocar is among the makes to offer automatic lubrication for the first time

- The first Buicks are sold, feature an under-floor engine and valve-in-head two-cylinder engine

- Sturtevant offers America's first automatic transmission, using a centrifugal clutch it features one high and one low gear

▲ A total of 2342 Rambler motorcars left the T. B. Jeffery plant in 1904, all equipped with steering wheels instead of tillers.

▶ Visible to the right of the Jeffery plant is this steep-grade test bridge. A tree-lined oval test track is also visible (*above*).

- A huge factory fire delays Cadillac production, forcing the company to return dealer deposits on 1500 automobiles

- Ransom E. Olds sells his interest in Olds Motor Works, then organizes Reo Motor Car Company

- Leland & Faulconer Manufacturing merges with Cadillac Automobile Company to become Cadillac Motor Car Company

- At least 240 businesses are established in America between 1904 and 1908 for the sole purpose of manufacturing automobiles

- The United States surpasses France in automobile assembly, remains the world's largest producer until the mid-1980s

- Some Maxwells and a few experimental Marmons are built and sold, but volume sales for both brands begin in 1905

- Though Ford announces air cooling for upcoming Model A, the company's first-ever four-cylinder engine arrives water-cooled

- The last single-cylinder Packard until 1911 is produced; four-bangers become the company's bread and butter

- Pope-Hartford becomes the first auto builder to include headlamps as standard equipment

◀ Buick output rose to 750 cars in 1905. Billed as "The Car of Quality," the $1200 Model C touring car differed little from the Model B, but wore a new Royal Blue body and used a footbrake. Wheelbase was again 87 inches.

◀ Engine and wheelbase of Ford's Model C grew in 1905, to 113.4 cid and 78 inches. In addition to the tonneau (*shown*) and runabout, a Model E panel delivery debuted. Windshield, headlights, and top cost extra.

1904 Model-Year Production Figures

1. Oldsmobile	5508
2. Cadillac	2457
3. Rambler	2342
4. Ford	1695
5. White	710
6. Stanley	550
7. Franklin	400
8. Packard	250

Some figures are estimated or calendar year

• The Prest-O-Lite Company is founded, stated goal is to develop safe-to-use acetylene headlamp

• Henry Ford pilots his Arrow racer to a record 91.37 mph; but William Vanderbilt reaches 92.31 in a Mercedes a week later

• Frenchman Louis E. Rigolly is the first driver to exceed 100 mph, reaching 103.56 in a Gabron-Brille

• Ford displays cars at seven auto shows, including the Louisiana Purchase Exposition in St. Louis

• Buick is reorganized and Charles Nash is brought on board. Nash will later become president of General Motors.

• Maxwell Motor Car Company is founded by former Oldsmobile associate Jonathan Dixon Maxwell

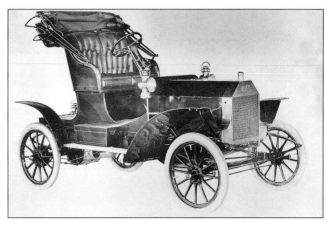

▲ Elegant it was, but the 1905 Ford Model B touring car, carrying a 283.6-cid, 24-bhp four-cylinder engine, was heavy—and, at $2000, cost too much to attract many buyers.

▲ A 77-cid, two-cylinder engine went into the curious looking 1905 Overland Model 17 runabout ($750). Also available: a $1500 four-cylinder Model 18 with side-entrance tonneau.

▶ Sporting gents in 1905 could have quite a time tooling around the countryside in a $750 one-cylinder Oldsmobile Touring Runabout. This one is driven by Howard Coffin, who later co-founded Hudson. Gus Edwards and Vincent Bryan wrote the famous tune, "In My Merry Oldsmobile," but R. E. Olds himself had turned to the Reo automobile.

1905

- Combined production reaches 24,250, plus an additional 750 trucks

- Rear-entry tonneaus are giving way to longer bodies with side doors

- Larger gasoline cars are the trend at the Fifth National Automobile Show. Exhibits include 177 gasoline-powered cars, 31 electrics, and just four steamers

- Show emphasis now on comfort, rather than just speed

- Several displayed makes feature "cape," or folding, tops

- Innovations on display include Goodyear universal rims, ignition locks, power tire pumps, Gabriel exhaust horns, and Weed tire chains

◀ Road signs were still rare when the occupants of this 1905 Rambler Type One Surrey, with two-cylinder, 18-bhp engine, needed directions on a rural byway. This was the final year for one-cylinder Ramblers, as total output hit 3807 units.

▼ The first automobile with an automatic transmission was the $5000, six-cylinder 1905 Sturtevant. High- and low-speed clutches worked by centrifugal force, based on engine rpm.

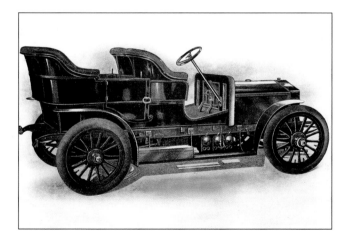

New Makes 1905

• A.B.C.	• Eagle Air Cooled	• Morse Steam
• Adams-Farwell	• Forest City	• Oxford
• American Mercedes	• Fritchle Electric	• Parsons Electric
• Ardsley	• Gale	• Pullman
• Ariel	• Gas-Au-Lec	• Rauch & Lang
• Aurora	• Halladay	• Rainier
• Banker	• Hammer	• Reeves
• Berkshire	• Johnson	• Reo
• Boss	• La Petite	• Speedway
• Breese & Lawrence	• Leader	• Victor
• Cartercar	• Lozier	• Walker
• Corbin	• Maxwell	• Watrous
• Crawford	• Monarch	
• Culver	• Moon	

• First year production begins for the Cartercar, Lozier, Moon, and Reo

• The last Adams is produced, features a rotary three-cylinder gas engine

• New Ariel features an engine that is air cooled in winter, water-cooled in summer

• American Mercedes produces an exact replica of its German-built motorcar

• The first four-cylinder Cadillac debuts, features a three-speed transmission

• Oldsmobile adds a side-entrance touring model, features a two-cylinder engine

• Like many makers, Overland abandons one-cylinders engines for twos and fours

• The Society of Automotive Engineers is founded

• A White Steamer leads President Theodore Roosevelt's inaugural parade

• Ramblers are now two or four cylinder, single-cylinder models are dropped

• A nod to affordability, the first automobiles are sold on the installment plan

• The American Motor Car Manufacturers Association is chartered

◄ Shoppers took kindly to Ford's dashing $500 "boat-tail" Model N run-about, introduced in 1906—predecessor of the legendary Model T. A front-mounted, four-cylinder engine developed 15 bhp, good for 45 mph.

▲ Henry Ford sits at the wheel of a Model K, powered by a 405-cid, 40-bhp, six-cylinder engine. Priced at $2500 (soon $2800), the big roadster with "mother-in-law" seat was guaranteed to hit 60 mph—for anyone foolhardy enough to try.

1906

- Vehicle production climbs to 33,200 passenger cars, and approximately 800 trucks

- By this time, an estimated 42,000 cars have been built in accordance with the Seldon patent

- The National Automobile Show features a move to more durable materials such as high-carbon steel and chrome-nickel alloy

- The show features boasts of lighter construction, including Marmon with its cast-aluminum body

- Six-cylinder engines become more common; new models come from Ford, Franklin, Pierce-Arrow, and National

- Ford introduces the forerunner to the Model T; the low-priced, 45-mph Model N

1905 Model-Year Production Figures	
1. Oldsmobile	6500
2. Cadillac	3942
3. Rambler	3807
4. Ford	1599
5. White	1098
6. Stanley	1016
7. Franklin	864
8. Packard	823
Some figures are estimated or calendar year	

▲ William C. "Billy" Durant (*second from left, in car*) was originally hired by Buick to help promote the brand. In 1904 he became Buick's president and began work assembling the components that would eventually become General Motors. This 1906 Model F touring car boasted 33 bhp and right-hand drive.

• Ford's huge, six-cylinder Model K costs $2500 and is guaranteed to reach 60 mph; production ends in 1908

• Production of the Kissel Kar begins in Hartford, Wisconsin; cars reach showrooms in 1907

• All Buick models now come with a storage battery as standard equipment

• Buick's 30-bhp Model D is launched as an early 1907; with a $2000 price tag it costs nearly twice as much as other Buick models

• Cadillac joins the ranks of manufacturers dropping single-cylinder engines from their lineups

• Front bumpers are offered as optional equipment on several makes

• The $2250 four-cylinder Model S joins the Oldsmobile line and is billed as "the best thing on wheels"

• Henry Ford buys out partner Alexander Malcomson, takes over as company president following the death of John S. Gray

• Some Packards sport the marque's new T-head engine, it produces 24-bhp

▲ From 1906 to 1909 the St. Louis Car Company built the French Mors under license, calling it the American Mors. This 1907 American Mors limousine sold for $4500.

▲ Four-cylinder engines were available in Ramblers for the first time in 1906, in 226- and 432-cid sizes (25 and 35/40 bhp). Seen here is a two-cylinder Type II Surrey. Rambler prices ranged from $800 to $3000.

▲ The 1906 model year brought this Packard roadster, and the first of the marque's T-head engines, which incorporated magneto jump-spark ignition. The T-head, a four, displaced 350 inches and made 24 bhp.

◄ No roof was included in the $800 base price of a one-cylinder 1907 Cadillac Model K runabout. An extra $40 bought a rubber top; $70, a leather top; $100, a Victoria top.

▼ Buick output rose to 4641 units in 1907—second only to Ford—as four-cylinder models joined the line, including this Model H touring car. The T-head produced 30 bhp.

◄ Four-cylinder Cadillacs, with L-head engines rated at 20 horsepower, were far more posh than the one-cylinder models. This 1907 Model G touring car sold for $2000, $2120 with "Cape Cart Top"; 1030 Model Gs were produced in four models for 1907. Cadillac was already well known for precision manufacture, as well as easy maintenance.

1906 Model-Year Production Figures

1.	Ford	8729
2.	Cadillac	3559
3.	Rambler	2765
4.	Reo	2458
5.	Maxwell	2161
6.	Oldsmobile	1600
7.	White	1534
8.	Buick	1400

Some figures are estimated or calendar year

◀ A $750 Model R Ford (*shown*) and less-equipped S joined the cheaper N in 1907. Each had a 15-bhp four.

▶ Sales of Ford's Model K roadster never took off. Near the end of its 1906-08 run, prices plunged $1000.

▲ Driving was no picnic in the early days of motoring. Here, a 1907 Packard roadster bogs down in goo.

◀ The 1907 Rambler Model 24 and 25 had four-cylinder engines, but two-cylinder cars were also available. Wheelbase on this Model 24 was 108 inches.

New Makes 1907

- Albany
- Anderson
- Atlas
- Aurora
- Bailey Electric
- Barnes
- Bay State
- Belden
- Brush
- Bugmobile
- C-F
- Chase
- Colt
- Conover
- Continental
- Corbitt
- Cosmopolitan
- Craig-Toledo
- Crescent
- Cunningham
- C.V.I.
- Detroit Electric
- Diamond T
- Duer
- Durocar
- Earl
- Euclid
- Eureka
- Everybody's
- Falcon
- Fee-American
- Four Traction
- Gearless
- Gifford-Pettitt

- Great Smith
- Griswold
- Harper
- Hatfield
- Hay-Berg
- Haydock
- Ideal
- International
- Jenkins
- Kermath
- Kiblinger
- Kingston
- Klink
- Lauth-Juergens
- Lorraine
- Marvel
- Maryland
- Miller
- Monarch
- Oakland
- Pennsylvania
- Perfection
- Ranger
- Regal
- Selden
- Senator
- Simplex
- Simplicity
- Speedwell
- Staver
- Stilson
- Trebert
- Triumph
- Wolfe

1907

- Auto-industry production reaches 43,000 cars and 1000 trucks, despite a deep economic recession

- Total U.S. vehicle registration passes the 140,000-unit mark

- Selective-gear transmissions—similar to modern H-pattern shifters—are a trend at the seventh National Automobile Show

- Other auto-show trends include stronger brakes and better paint

- Reversing a trend, six-cylinder models out-number single-piston vehicles at the New York show

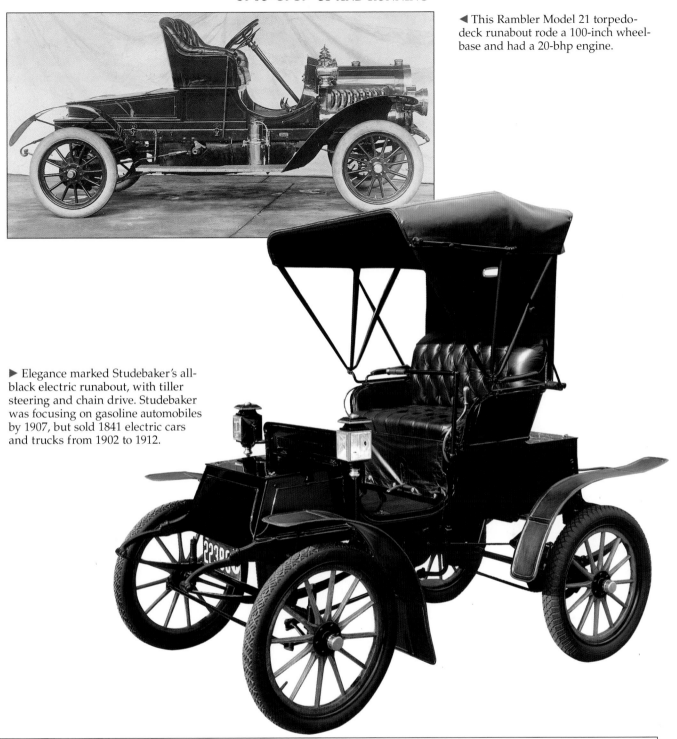

◄ This Rambler Model 21 torpedo-deck runabout rode a 100-inch wheelbase and had a 20-bhp engine.

► Elegance marked Studebaker's all-black electric runabout, with tiller steering and chain drive. Studebaker was focusing on gasoline automobiles by 1907, but sold 1841 electric cars and trucks from 1902 to 1912.

- The Oakland Motor Car Company is established by buggy maker Edward M. Murphy, with designs by Alanson Brush

- The final right-hand drive Fords, Models R, S, and N, are produced

- The last Curved-Dash Olds is produced, replaced by the four-cylinder Model M

- Hewitt claims its $4500 touring car is the first American car with V-8 power. Buffum also offers a V-8 this year

- Glencoe, Illinois, becomes the first town to use "humps" to control automobile speed

- Reducing weight and cost, Olds begins nickel-plating trim that had been brass

- The Association of Licensed Automobile Manufacturers issues a standardized formula for calculating horsepower

- The first official White House car, a White Steamer, is order by William Howard Taft

- Despite a weak economy, Ford and Packard post $1-million-plus profits

▲ William Durant incorporated General Motors on September 16, 1908, in New Jersey.

◀ The Apperson Jack Rabbit made its debut in 1908. Top speed was 75 mph.

▲ A 255-cid, 30-bhp T-head four again powered the 2000-pound 1908 Buick Model D touring car. Price: $1750.

▲ Buick's popular new car for 1908 was the $900 Model 10 runabout; 4002 were produced. It had a 22.5-bhp four.

▲ Three oil lamps and a bulb horn were included in the $850 price of this Cadillac Model S runabout.

▲ A Buick Model 10 runabout could have a two-passenger rear seat. Price included acetylene headlights.

▲ Cadillac's Model G Limo started at $3000. A "speaking tube" facilitated communication with the driver.

1907 Model-Year Production Figures	
1. Ford	14,887
2. Buick	4641
3. Reo	3967
4. Maxwell	3785
5. Rambler	3201
6. Cadillac	2884
7. Franklin	1509
8. Packard	1403

Some figures are estimated or calendar year

▶ J. Frank Duryea (*near right*) and Charles Duryea earned credit for producing the first true working automobile in America in 1893, but the brothers went their own ways before the turn of the century. J. Frank helped issue the Stevens-Duryea, while Charles produced vehicles under the Duryea nameplate as late as 1917.

New Makes 1908

- Allen-Lingston
- Bendix
- Benner
- Bertolet
- Black
- Browniekar
- Chalmers-Detroit
- Chicago Motor Buggy
- Chief
- Clark-Hatfield
- Clymer
- Crown
- Davis
- Deal
- DeSchaum
- De Tamble
- Duplex
- Economy
- E-M-F
- Fairbanks-Morse
- Famous
- Fuller
- Garford
- Hobbie
- Imperial
- Jeannin
- Lincoln
- Marathon
- Midland
- Mier
- Owen-Thomas
- Palmer-Singer
- Paterson
- Pittsburgh
- Rider-Lewis
- St. Joe
- Stafford
- Sears
- Sharp Arrow
- Sultan
- Viking
- Waldron
- Webb Jay

◀ This 1908 Ford Model S roadster sold for $700 as a two-seater, or $750 with tonneau. Curb weight was about 1400 pounds. Even with a top, weather was a problem.

◀ Oakland began in 1908 with two-cylinder power, but sold only 300 cars, so a new 40-horsepower, four-cylinder Model 40 seen here was introduced in time for 1909.

1908

- Annual industry production rises to 63,500 cars and 1500 trucks

- Longer wheelbases and better ride quality are the buzz at the eighth National Automobile Show, again in New York City

- Left-hand-side steering is becoming the norm at this year's show

- Ford's C. Harold Wills develops high-strength vanadium steel

- The General Motors Company is incorporated in New Jersey by Buick's William Crapo Durant.

- General Motors includes Buick, Olds, and truck-builder Rapid Motor

◀ This 1908 Oldsmobile four-cylinder Series M carries a limousine body. A six-cylinder series was introduced this year.

▲ This Model M tourer was one of 1145 cars built by Oldsmobile in 1908.

▶ In 1908, Overlands used a 173-cid, 20/22-bhp four-cylinder engine and 96-inch wheelbase.

▼ Overland came back a bit in 1908, with 465 cars built. Crude bodywork belied the car's mechanical qualities.

- Studebaker enters into an agreement with the Everitt-Metzger-Flanders company to sell Studebaker-EMF cars under license

- Ford launches the Model T on October 1; New York's Grand Central Station hosts a formal debut on December 31

- Charles Knight quiets gas engines with sleeve-valve invention; it will slowly replace less-reliable poppet valve

- The Fisher Body Company is formed by Fred and Charles Fisher. The new firm will eventually become part of General Motors

- A 60-bhp Thomas Flyer claims victory in the New York-to-Paris race, traveling 13,341 miles in 88 days

- Cadillac is awarded the Dewar Trophy for its use of interchangeable parts; it is the first American maker to claim the prize

- Oldsmobile adds its first six-cylinder engine to the line, a 505-cid Series Z touring car priced at $4500

- Frequent clutch failure is addressed as makers begin sealing against dust and road grime

- Ex-bicycle manufacturer John North Willys becomes president of the Willys-Overland Company

▲ Buick's Model 16 Tourabout, which sold for $1750, featured "modern" rounded fenders and a 318-cid four.

▲ The 1909 American Simplex Toy Tonneau seven-passenger touring car had a two-stroke "valve-less" engine rated at 50 bhp. This car features a body by Holbrook.

▼ Bob Burman raced a stripped Buick against a plane at Daytona Beach in 1909.

1908 Model-Year Production Figures	
1. Ford	10,202
2. Buick	8820
3. Studebaker	8132
4. Maxwell	4455
5. Reo	4105
6. Rambler	3597
7. Cadillac	2377
8. Franklin	1895
Some figures are estimated or calendar year	

▲ The Ocean-to-Ocean race ran from New York City to Seattle, but the eventual 1909 winners took an unplanned break as their Model T succumbs to one of Kansas' many unpaved rural roads. The durable "T" was eventually disqualified for using a modified engine, but not before Ford was able to capitalize on its success in the press.

New Makes 1909

• Abbott-Detroit	• Croxton-Keeton	• Firestone-Columbus	• Kauffman	• Paige-Detroit	• Salter
• Alco	• Cutting	• G.J.G.	• Kearns	• Petrel	• Sellers
• Babcock	• Detroit-Dearborn	• Herreshoff	• Keystone	• Pickard	• Spoerer
• Black Crow	• Emancipator	• Hudson	• Lexington	• Pilot	• Sterling
• Broc Electric	• Empire	• Hupmobile	• McCue	• Planche	• Toledo
• Coates-Goshen	• Enger	• Illinois	• McIntire	• Pratt-Elkhart	• Velie
• Cole	• Everitt	• Inter-State	• Metz	• Ricketts	• Washington
• Correja	• F.A.L.	• Jonz	• Ohio	• Roebling	• Westcott

1909

• Total industry output: 123,900 cars—including 17,771 Fords—and 3255 trucks

• By year's end, more than 290 makes are built in America, in 24 states: 45 from Michigan, 44 from Indiana, and 39 from Ohio

• The ninth National Automobile Show focuses on customer satisfaction, not merely on taking orders from dealers

• Some 71 percent of gas-engined cars displayed are four cylinder, 27-percent are sixes

• Some steering wheels feature a corrugated underside to help prevent hand slippage when conditions are damp

• A U.S. District Court holds that the Selden patent is valid, and that the Ford Motor Company has infringed upon it

▲ Two Fords entered the 1909 Ocean-to-Ocean race. Number 1, driven by Frank Kulick, got lost along the way.

▲ The St. Louis-built Moon lasted from 1905 to 1929. Here, the 1909 Model D: 32.2-bhp four; 121-inch chassis; $3850.

▲ A peek inside the Oakland Motor Company factory, in 1909, reveals a few of the 4500 vehicles produced that year. On January 20, General Motors purchased a half interest in Oakland. The Oakland name would be changed to Pontiac in 1932.

▲ This $2750 Model DR, one of Olds's four-cylinder models, helped boost total 1909 output to 6557 units.

▲ This Overland Model 34 four-passenger roadster offered the company's first six-cylinder engine.

- Cadillac, Oakland, and other automakers enter the expanding General Motors fold

- The new Hupmobile places the transmission and multiple-disc clutch integral with the engine

- The Hudson Motor Car Company is formed, with the first cars produced in July as 1910s

- Construction of the Indianapolis Motor Speedway in completed

- Ford's Model T adopts the increasingly popular three-pedal arrangement, production lags far behind demand

- Buick's four-cylinder Model 7 is huge, with 5 × 5-inch bore and stroke for 392.6 cid; only 85 are sold for 1909-10

- Race driver Louis Chevrolet begins building his own six-cylinder car

- The first rural section of concrete pavement, a one-mile stretch, opens on Woodward Avenue, near Detroit

- Mrs. John R. Ramsey is the first woman to drive across America, in a Maxwell touring car

▲ Not even a roof protected the driver of the '09 Overland Model 31 taxicab. This four-cylinder model sold for $1400.

▲ President William Howard Taft (*rear*) leaves the Georgia home of Major Cummings in 1909 in a Rambler touring.

▲ This 1909 Model 34 touring car employed Overland's new six—which would last only one year. John North Willys renamed the company Willys-Overland in 1909.

◀ The 1910 American Simplex touring car had a 117-inch wheelbase.

▶ Apperson Jack Rabbits raced frequently. This is a 50-bhp 1910 model.

▲ Buick built 11,000 Model 10s in 1910.

▲ A publicity stunt pitted a 1910 Brush against a horse.

◀ Buick had its 622-cid "Bugs" ready when the Indianapolis Speedway opened in 1910. Bob Burman drove a time-trial record 105.87 mph.

1909 Model-Year Production Figures

1. Ford	17,771
2. Buick	14,606
3. Maxwell	9460
4. Studebaker/EMF	7960
5. Cadillac	7868
6. Reo	6592
7. Oldsmobile	6575
8. Willys-Overland	4907

Some figures are estimated or calendar year

1910

- Industry production tops 181,000 cars and 6000 trucks

- Ford produces 32,000 vehicles, good for almost 18 percent of the market

- Featured at the National Automobile Show are "torpedo" bodies, basically open cars with sporty-looking lowered coachwork

- Buick offers its first closed body, Model 41 Limousine; only 40 are built this year

- James J. Storrow is named president of General Motors

- Ford begins production at its new Highland Park plant, the largest such facility under one roof

▲ The Everitt was a 1910 outgrowth of EMF (Everitt-Metzger-Flanders). This is the Model 30 touring car.

▲ A Ford Model T runs in the 1910 Munsey Tour. Ford's market share neared 18 percent, with 32,053 cars built.

◄ Oldsmobile boasted that its huge 1910-12 Limited set a "new standard of luxury." Limiteds rode a 130-inch chassis powered by a 505-cid six.

New Makes 1910

• American Fiat	• Continental	• Great Western	• Mercer	• Republic
• Ames	• Courier	• Henry	• Morse	• Sebring
• Amplex	• Demot	• Kenmore	• Norwalk	• Spaulding
• Anchor	• Dispatch	• Kimball	• Ohio	• Warren
• Anhut	• Everitt	• Kline Kar	• Otto	• White
• Bergdoll	• Flanders	• K-R-I-T	• Owen	• Wilcox
• Borland	• FWD	• Lion	• Parry	
• Burg	• Great Eagle	• McFarlan	• Plymouth	

• Ford markets a $700 chassis for use under other automakers' coachwork

• A four-cylinder Reo earns a perfect score in The Gordon Bennet Race

• For 1910 only, every Ford model sports all-wood bodies

• Ford begins using front-hinged doors on its coupe models

• The Reeves Company experiments with six- and eight-wheeled automobiles, neither vehicle saw production

• Ford's Model T now boasts a speedometer as standard equipment

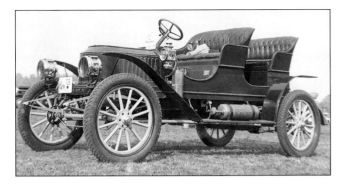

▲ Best known (if not the most sophisticated) of the steam cars, Stanley offered four 1910 models. This one cost $1150.

MODEL FORTY

MODEL 40 is a fast, powerful Roadster, capable of sixty miles an hour, but so mechanically perfect that it will throttle down to a walking pace and run at any speed with the smoothness of an electric motor. This model offers everything desirable for the man who knows and wants a good car. The chassis is similar to that in Model 42, except that it is equipped with the Overland Planetary Transmission; the big, strong engine is the same, and the options in seating arrangements give a purchaser ample space for two, three or four passengers, as he may desire.

SPECIFICATIONS

Wheel Base 112 inches.
Tread 56 or 60 inches.
Seating Capacity Two, three or four.
Motor 4-cylinder, cast singly, 4¼ x 4½ inches.
Horse Power Forty.
Transmission Planetary, two speeds forward, one reverse.
Clutch Multiple Disc.
Ignition Magneto and battery.
Carburetor Schebler, float feed.

Brakes Internal and external on rear hubs.
Springs 2 x 38 inches, semi-elliptic and 2x44 inches, three-quarter elliptic, front and rear respectively.
Steering Gear Worm and segment adjustable.
Front Axle Drop-forged I-section.
Rear Axle Semi-floating.
Wheels Artillery.

Tires 34x3½ inches.
Frame Pressed steel.
Equipment Two Gas Lamps, Three Oil Lamps, Generator, Horn, Tools, Pump and Repair Kit.
Trimming Black leather.
Finish Dark Blue, with Gold Striping.
Price $1250, including Single Rumble Seat. Double Bucket Seat in lieu of regular equipment, $35 extra.

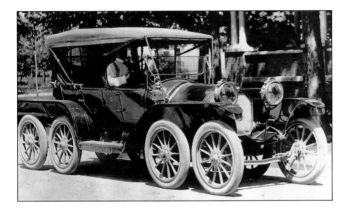

▲ Eight wheels on the huge 1910 Reeves Octoauto promised a smoother ride and longer tire life. The firm also created a six-wheel Sextoauto. Ultimately, neither went on sale.

▲ A 35-bhp, four-cylinder Overland Model 40 roadster, with a two-speed planetary gearbox, could do 60 mph.

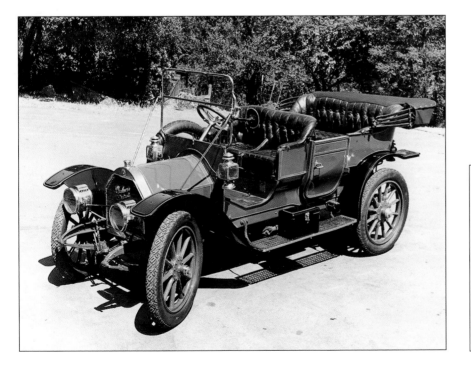

1910 Model-Year Production Figures	
1. Ford	32,053
2. Buick	30,525
3. Willys-Overland	15,598
4. Studebaker/EMF	15,020
5. Cadillac	10,039
6. Maxwell	10,000
Brush	10,000
7. Reo	6588
Some figures are estimated or calendar year	

▲ A 226-cid four powered the 1910 Chalmers-Detroit. Renamed Chalmers for 1911, it remained popular through the teens.

▲ Hill climbing was still a popular means of evaluating a car's potential in 1911-12. Here, a $900 Buick Model 34 roadster with a 165-cid four scampers up a steep slope.

▲ The American was most commonly known as American Underslung—named for a frame that hung below the axles.

▲ Model 39 was Buick's designation for the touring-car version of the 38, priced identically at $1850; 905 found buyers.

1911

• Industry production totals: 199,319 cars and 10,681 trucks

• Nearly every automaker at the 11th National Automobile Show in New York exhibits a four-door model

• A truck show, held in conjunction with the National Automobile Show, features 286 exhibitors

• Several self-starting mechanisms emerge, including the Amplex compressed-air starter

• Chevrolet Motor Company is organized in November 1911; production quickly gets underway with a handful of models

• Little, a low-priced companion to Chevrolet, is announced on October 30, but doesn't go into production until 1912

◄ The wheelbase of Cadillac's "Thirty" grew to 116 inches in 1911. This closed three-seater cost $2250.

► The first open-air Cadillac with a front door was the "Thirty" Fore-Door touring. Asking price: $1800.

▲ A prototype of the Chevrolet Classic Six was finished early in 1911. The first Chevrolet, a large car, used a cone clutch and three-speed gearbox on the rear axle. Its 299-cid, six-cylinder T-head engine gave up to 40 bhp.

• Studebaker acquires full control of the Everitt-Metzger-Flanders Company

• Stutz goes on sale after an 11th-place finish at the Indianapolis 500; production versions virtually duplicate the racer

• Mercer's Model 35 Raceabout becomes one of the first true sports cars

• Hudson's "fluid-cushioned" clutch rotates in a blend of oil and kerosene

• The U.S. Court of Appeals reverses the U.S. District Court Selden Patent decision, holding it "valid but not infringed" by Ford and others; payment of royalties stops

• Studebaker becomes a corporation, drops steam cars from its lineup

• Buick sets a speed record, traveling over 20 miles in just over 13 minutes

• Ford's Model T gets a new body and a price cut to as low as $680. Sales double and market share reaches 35 percent

• William S. Knudsen joins Ford—later leaves to head Chevrolet

▲ Ford touring cars adopted steel-over-wood framing in 1911, instead of wood-only construction. Metal running boards wore the famous "Ford" script.

- Automobile-manufacturer securities are listed on the New York Stock Exchange for the first time

- The Detroit area becomes home to the nation's first painted highway center lines

- The Diamond T Motor Car Company abandons its automobile models to concentrate on trucks

- General Motors Truck Company is formed by combining recently acquired automakers Rapid and Reliance

- Ray Harroun wins the first 500-mile Indianapolis Speedway Race in a six-cylinder Marmon Wasp

- A combination starter-motor/generator is developed by Cadillac, freeing drivers from hand-cranking their cars

▲ A dusty duo in a Ford Model T navigate the 1911 Glidden Tour. Extra spare tires were vital to make the distance.

New Makes 1911

• Alpena	• Havers	• Roader
• ArBenz	• Hupp-Yeats	• Rogers
• Atterbury	• King	• S.G.V.
• Carhartt	• Lenox	• Standard
• Case	• Mighty Michigan	• Stutz
• Chevrolet	• Motorette	• Stuyvesant
• Colby	• Nyberg	• Virginian
• Crow-Elkhart	• Penn	• W.F.S.
• Dalton	• Rayfield	
• Gaylord	• R.C.H.	

▲ In 1911, Ramblers came in a choice of three wheelbases: in this case, 112 inches for the 34-horsepower Model 63 coupe.

▲ The biggest 1912 Buick was the Model 43 touring, on a 116-inch wheelbase with a 318-cid four-cylinder engine and sliding-gear transmission. Buick stood fourth in sales.

▲ The first car to use an electric starter was the 1912 Cadillac, winning the make a second Dewar Trophy in 1913. A new slogan boasted: "Standard of the World."

◄ A combination starter motor/generator was installed on 1912 Cadillacs, freeing drivers from cranking the engine. A 1983 Cadillac cranking motor is also shown.

1911 Model-Year Production Figures

1. Ford	69,762
2. Studebaker/EMF	26,827
3. Willys-Overland	18,745
4. Maxwell	16,000
5. Buick	13,389
6. Cadillac	10,071
7. Hudson	6486
8. Chalmers	6250

Some figures are estimated or calendar year

▲ The 1912 Cadillac had a steel body; closed cars wore aluminum skin.

1912

• No longer a fledgling industry, automakers crank out 356,000 cars and an additional 22,000 trucks

• The new Automobile Board of Trade takes over sanctioning of the New York Show

• Crankless starters are the rage at the 12th auto show. Units use a variety of power sources including electricity and acetylene

• Cadillac adopts an integrated starter/generator/ignition system developed by Charles F. Kettering

• A total of 3000 Chevrolets are built, including the popular six-cylinder touring car which cost $2150

• Ford slashes Model T prices another $80, prices for the "car for the masses" now start at just $590

▲ Louis Chevrolet (*far right*) poses with a 1912 Chevrolet touring car. Initial examples used a compressed-air starter.

▲ Henry Ford sits at the wheel of a Model T "Fore-Door" Touring. Despite the name, the driver's "door" didn't open.

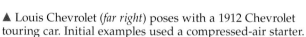

◄ The 20-bhp Little was built from 1912 to 1913, when the Durant-launched make merged with Chevrolet.

• Ford production rises to almost 75,000 vehicles, but market share skids to 22 percent as competition increases

• Edward Gowen Budd creates the first all-steel car body. The Dodge Brothers are among the first to use Budd bodies.

• The Boyce MotoMeter is introduced to monitor engine temperature, radiator-cap and dash-mounted units are offered

• A short-lived cyclecar craze begins; the low-cost, often fragile vehicles draw some buyers, much scorn

• Charles W. Nash is named president of General Motors; Walter P. Chrysler goes to work as Buick's plant manager

• Packard introduces its first-ever six-cylinder series, featuring a massive 525-cid engine

• Chicago introduces an ordinance restricting automobile horn usage within city limits

• Hudson's Mile-A-Minute Roadster is guaranteed to do—predictably—60 miles per hour

• White separation lines are painted on the streets of Los Angeles-area Redlands, California

▲ In 1911-12, Oldsmobile produced this brash, low-slung Autocrat Speedster, a $3500 two-seat roadster with twin-barrel gas tanks. Underhood lurked a 471-cid, T-head four.

▲ The enclosed $2000 45-bhp Overland 61-C coupe featured Bosch duplex ignition, gas lamps, and electric pillar-mounted lamps.

▲ Ransom E. Olds called the 1912 Reo the Fifth his "Farewell Car," the culmination of his efforts. A top and extras added $100 to the $1055 price tag, a self-starter $25.

▲ Even the model names of the 1912 Rambler lineup—Gotham, Country Club, Valkyrie—suggested regal traveling. Four-cylinder engines with 38 or 50 bhp displaced 286 and 432 cid, respectively.

64

1912 Model-Year Production Figures	
1. Ford	78,440
2. Willys-Overland	28,572
3. Studebaker/EMF	28,032
4. Buick	19,812
5. Cadillac	12,708
6. Hupmobile	7640
7. Reo	6342
8. Oakland	5838
Some figures are estimated or calendar year	

▲ Production of the tall, stubby, stately Studebaker Electric coupe would end by 1912, but some drivers—especially city women—still liked their silence and tiller steering.

New Makes 1912

- Argo Electric
- Atlas-Knight
- Car-Nation
- Chevrolet
- Chicago
- Church-Field

- Crane
- Detroiter
- Dodo
- Edwards-Knight
- Great Southern
- Grinnell

- Henderson
- Little
- Marquette
- Modoc
- Omaha
- Pathfinder

- Perfex
- Pratt
- Stoddard-Dayton Knight
- Touraine

▲ Buick's rakish $950 24 roadster found 2850 buyers in 1912. Buick sales rose from 19,812 in 1912 to 26,660 in 1913, a nearly 35 percent improvement.

▲ Charles F. Kettering at the wheel of a 1913 Buick, testing the self-starter that had debuted on the 1912 Cadillac.

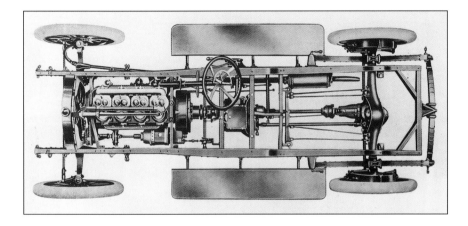

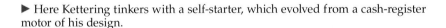

▲ All 1913 Buicks used four-cylinder engines and a three-speed gearbox with cone clutch. Brakes worked on two wheels. Electric lighting was available.

▶ Here Kettering tinkers with a self-starter, which evolved from a cash-register motor of his design.

1913

- Total Industry output spurts to 461,500 cars and 23,500 trucks

- The 13th National Automobile Show is split: Madison Square Garden for high-end makes, Grand Central Palace for modestly priced cars

- Many of this year's cars display sloping fronts and hoods, with smoother body lines and longer curves

- Chandler automobiles arrive on the scene, assembly takes place in Cleveland

- Mass production of the Ford Model T begins, using an overhead drop to lower completed bodies onto waiting frames

- Annual Ford output more than doubles to 168,220 cars; production reaches 1000 per day

▲ This $1975 Torpedo touring was one of seven Cadillac body styles offered for 1913. All controls were now inside.

▲ In mid 1913, Chevrolet launched the Series H, with a 171-cid, 24-bhp four. This "Baby Grand" touring cost $875.

▲ "Royal Mail" was Chevrolet's $750 104-inch-wheelbase Series H roadster. It came with top and windshield.

▲ The $2500 Chevrolet Classic Six sported a European flair. Only the windshield mount changed for 1913.

▶ Closed bodies in various states of completion are being readied for installation on Chicago Electrics at the Seaman Body Company in 1913. Note how much wood was used. Scores of U.S. manufacturers still turned out vehicles, but the total was beginning to decline. Electrics were fading fast, but the short-lived "cyclecar" craze was gaining momentum.

• New on the market are the Imp and Twombly cyclecars, continuing a short-lived trend that began a year earlier

• The Bendix electric-starter drive appears, accelerates the demise of crank starting

• A new six-cylinder engine and a bigger four cylinder are found under Hudson hoods; the four departs after this year

• Pierce-Arrows sport "frog-eye" headlamps set on the mudguards, a design that endures until the marque's demise in 1938

• Automobiles are increasingly being financed by installment loans

• Dealers fear the impact of used cars on new-car sales; the National Association of Automobile Manufacturers investigate

• The Automobile Board of Trade and National Association of Automobile Manufacturers combine to form the National Automobile Chamber of Commerce, which recommends a standard, industrywide 90-day new-vehicle warranty

• Gulf Oil Company is the first gasoline retailer to offer free road maps

▲ A winter roundup of Fords en route to a New York dealership pauses for a photo. Brass had nearly disappeared from Fords by 1913, as bodies received another revamping. Soon, as mass production really took hold, far more Fords would be built each day.

▲ At $800, the most costly Ford of 1913 was the seven-passenger Model T Town Car. A runabout cost only $525. Ford output more than doubled to 168,220.

New Makes 1913

• Chandler	• Lyons-Knight
• Coey	• Monarch
• De Soto	• Partin-Palmer
• Grant	• Read
• Holly	• Tribune
• Howard	• Vulcan
• Imp	• Wahl

◄ Delco electric starting/lighting was available on 1913 Oldsmobiles, including this Model 53 touring car, on a long 135-inch wheelbase. Its 380-cid six-cylinder engine made 50 horsepower. Olds hoped it would sell better than the now-extinct Limited. Four-cylinder Defenders also were offered.

◄ Overlands came in two series for 1913: Model 69, on a 110-inch wheelbase; and Model 71, at 114 inches. A touring roadster, like this one, and coupe bodies were sold. Overlands were well built, but sporting folks had other choices, such as a Mercer Raceabout or Stutz Bearcat.

1913 Model-Year Production Figures

1. Ford	168,220
2. Willys-Overland	37,422
3. Studebaker	31,994
4. Buick	26,666
5. Cadillac	17,284
6. Maxwell	17,000
7. Hupmobile	12,543
8. Reo	7647

Some figures are estimated or calendar year

▲ Only one car from the Pope empire remained in 1913: the Pope-Hartford, seen here as a $2250 Model 31 touring.

▲ Steam engines had powered Whites since 1900, but the firm sold only four- and six-cylinder gasoline autos by 1912. Here, a 1913 touring car.

▲ Buick's first overhead-valve six, rated at 48 bhp, went into this $1985 1914 B-55, riding on a 130-inch wheelbase.

▲ The first of Buick's closed coupes was the 1914 Model B-38, with a 35-bhp four, and a 112-inch wheelbase.

◄ Four-cylinder Buick engines came in two displacements for 1914: 165 and 221 cubic inches. The latter, like the new six, had a five-inch stroke. With 13,446 units built, the best-selling Buick for '14 was the $1050 B-25 touring car.

▼ General Motors would never have enjoyed its success without the talents of such luminaries as Henry Leland (*second from right*), who would leave Cadillac and six years later launch Lincoln; and electrical wizard Charles Kettering (*far right*), who later founded GM Research Laboratories.

New Makes 1914

- Benham
- Briscoe
- Dile
- Doble Steamer
- Dodge
- F.R.P.
- Hercules
- Jeffery
- Jones
- Lewis
- Milburn
- Moline-Knight
- Monroe
- Saxon
- Singer
- Sphinx
- Vixen
- Willys-Knight

1914

- The "Great War"—World War I—begins in Europe; the Dow Jones stock average falls 24.4 percent on December 12

- Uncertain times fail to slow auto builders, as industry output rises again, to 548,139 autos and 24,900 trucks

- Construction of the Lincoln Highway—the first transcontinental road, stretching from New York to San Francisco—begins

- The National Automobile Chamber of Commerce sponsors the 14th National Automobile Show

- Cyclecars for one or two passengers, introduced in 1912-13, are the fad of the season, including the $295 Argo

- Five show exhibits help cyclecars rise from the status of "toy" to relative popularity, though the trend will soon evaporate

◄ Innovations on the 1914 Cadillac included a new Timken two-speed rear axle, plus a hinged steering wheel and driver's cushion to ease entry/exit. All Cadillacs, like this $1975 roadster, had a 365.8-cid four-cylinder engine and rode a 120-inch wheelbase.

CHEVROLET "BABY GRAND"
climbing State Capitol Steps
at Des Moines, Iowa,

Steps are full City Block long and 45° grade, 18 miles per hour—no stop—loaded with passengers.

The "CHEVROLET" is a great car.

◄ A fully loaded Chevrolet "Baby Grand" climbs the State Capitol steps at Des Moines, Iowa. This feat, up a 45-degree grade, was achieved at 18 mph. The touring car sold for $875.

◄ Louis Chevrolet was well-known as a racing driver before his name went on a production auto. Here, he wields the wheel of a Buick at Atlanta.

► A 1914 Chevrolet "Royal Mail" flat-deck roadster could be ordered in plum color or basic gray. Price: $750.

- Dodge cars, produced by brothers Horace and John Dodge, debut late in the year

- Notable new nameplates include Briscoe (with a single "cyclops-eye" headlight), Doble Steamer, and Willys-Knight

- Rambler cars, still made by the Thomas B. Jeffery Company (though founder Thomas B. had died in 1910), are renamed Jeffery

- Cadillac introduces a "high-speed" V-8 in September 1914 for the '15 model year

- Henry Ford announces an eight-hour day with a $5 minimum daily wage for certain workers; 15,000 qualify. The new Ford Sociological Department's duty is to see that workers use the wage "properly"

- Ford output soars to more than 308,000 vehicles, a new calendar-year record

- Ford intends for the new $5 wage to slow worker turnover and to keep the Industrial Workers of the World (union) out

- Not yet concerned with fashion, the Model T is made available "in any color, as long as it's black"

▶ Outside builders produced the wooden bodies for Ford's Depot Hack back in 1914. Ford wouldn't get around to producing its own station wagons until years later. Riders got plenty of fresh air in the Depot Hack, or the vehicle could carry cargo. A bare Model T chassis, of which Ford sold tens of thousands over the years, weighed in at about 960 pounds.

▲ John and Horace Dodge launched their first car in 1914.

▲ By 1914, black was the Ford Model T's only color.

▲ Women eagerly took to Ford Model Ts, including the driver of this new "turtledeck" runabout.

▲ The Rambler was gone, but Thomas Jeffery's son Charles replaced it with Jeffery, maker of cars and trucks.

- Buick's first six-cylinder car, the Model B-55, appears with 331 cubic inches and 48 horsepower

- Cadillac's final four-cylinder model has a Timken two-speed rear axle with an electro-magnetic shifting mechanism

- Chevrolet drops its six-cylinder car to focus on four-cylinder models

- Ford offers a $40-$60 rebate to Model T buyers—if 300,000 are sold in a one-year period. The refund actually comes to $50

- The first street sign appears on Detriot streets; meanwhile, a city ordinance prohibits curbside gasoline pumps

- A new 288.6-cid, six-cylinder engine is available in Hudsons

- A Chevrolet promotion pitted a "Baby Grand" against the Iowa State Capitol steps; the car won, at 18 mph

- Besting the Model T by one, Chevrolet's "Royal Mail" roadster can be ordered in plum as well as black

- Electrical systems add $125 to Chevrolets, almost 20 percent over base price on some

▲ This rakish two-seater—with a 348-cid, 48-bhp six-cylinder engine—was one of 10,417 Jefferys built in 1914.

▲ Vehicles don't get much more impenetrable looking than this 1914 armored car, which betrays little of its Jeffery basis.

▲ One of the higher-quality cyclecars was this 1914 Scripps-Booth Rocket, which featured belt drive, tandem seating, and some weather protection.

◄ An air-cooled, 70-cubic-inch Spacke vee-twin engine drove the Scripps-Booth Rocket to a 45-mph top speed.

1914 Model-Year Production Figures

1. Ford	308.162
2. Willys-Overland	48,461
3. Studebaker	35,374
4. Buick	32,889
5. Maxwell	18,000
6. Reo	13,516
7. Jeffery	10,417
8. Hupmobile	10,318

Some figures are estimated or calendar year

▲ Belts drove the machinery in this General Motors plant. By 1914, Ford had turned to full mass production at his Highland Park, Michigan, plant, building on systems that had been used at Oldsmobile years earlier.

▲ This was no ordinary 1915 Buick, but ranks as one of the earliest special-bodied "dream cars" created to flaunt fresh ideas. A total of 43,946 conventional Buicks were built.

▲ One of Buick's popular 1915 cars was this $1235 Model C-37 touring, with a 37-bhp four. Like other midpriced cars, Buicks were owned by relatively affluent families.

1915

• Materials shortages are felt as a result of World War I, even though the U.S. is not yet an active participant

• Industry volume leaps again, now 895,930 cars and 74,000 trucks

• Images of the usefulness of trucks in the European war improves the image and sales of trucks in America

• Eight-cylinder engines, all V-8s, are featured at the National Automobile Show in Cadillac, King, Briggs-Detroiter, and Remington

• More than a half-million Ford cars and trucks are built this year

• The Ford Model T is restyled with curved rear fenders and electric headlights; a Coupelet and Center-Door Sedan are added

▲ All Cadillacs, designated Model 51 in 1915, boasted a brand-new L-head V-8 engine. The touring cars came in both five- and seven-passenger versions.

▲This $2800 1915 Cadillac center-door "Sedan for Five Passengers" boasted a three-piece "rain vision" windshield.

▲ Cadillac's V-8 wasn't the first ever, but was the first to reach volume production in the U.S. It developed 70 bhp.

- Cadillac's new mill is the first successful V-8 built in America. Initially developing 70 horsepower, it lasts into 1927

- Packard announces a V-12, appropriately called "Twin Six," in May, as a 1916 model

- The first standard-size Scripps-Booth cars appear. The company had formerly built the Rocket cyclecar

- Dodges go on sale, with a 35-bhp four and cone clutch—it's the first mass-produced car with an all-steel body (by Budd)

- The Gadabout cyclecar roadster features a wicker body on a wood frame

- Packard, Winton, Kissel, and Kline offer a "sociable" body with an aisle between the front seats, so passengers can move freely between front and rear

- All Oldsmobiles are filled with a standard top and windshield, still extra-cost items on most cars

- General Motors declares its first dividend, a healthy $50 per share

- All but a few makes have moved to easy-to-serve, removable, "demountable" rims

► Louis Chevrolet (*behind wheel*), could barely fit behind the wheel of this unibodied Cornelian, but nonetheless raced it at Indy.

▲ The $750 Chevrolet "Royal Mail" cut a dashing figure in 1915, with shapely fenders and a rear-of-seat gas tank.

▲ A special Seaman formal body graced this 1915 Jeffery. Eight models were priced from $1450 to $2900.

▲ The $975 Ford center-door sedan, which soon swapped aluminum bodies for steel, came with electric lamps.

1915 Model-Year Production Figures	
1. Ford	501,462
2. Willys-Overland	91,904
3. Dodge	45,000
4. Maxwell	44,000
5. Buick	43,946
6. Studebaker	41,243
7. Cadillac	20,404
8. Saxon	19,000
Some figures are estimated or calendar year	

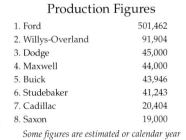

◄ The 1915 Olds Model 42, offered as a touring car (*shown*) or roadster for $1285, had a 194.2-cid, 30-bhp four.

◄ Buick's first sedan, the 1916 center-door Model D-47, boasted a new 45-bhp ohv six. At $1800, 881 were sold.

▼ The 1916 Cole touring had a 39.2-bhp eight-cylinder engine built by GM's Northway division.

▲ Buick output hit 124,834 in 1916. The Model 55, with its 331-cid ohv six, was in its last year.

1916

- Industry output nearly doubles to 1,525,578 cars and 92,130 trucks

- Petroleum prices rise during the year, prompting increased public interest in fuel-economy testing

- Falling prices and more power are trends at the 16th National Automobile Show, with most cars priced below $1250

- Five automakers display V-12 models at the show: Packard, Enger, Haynes, National, and Pathfinder

- Some 18 carmakers now offer V-8 engines: Abbott, Apperson, Briscoe, Cadillac, Cole, Daniels, Hollier, Jackson, King, Monarch, Oakland, Oldsmobile, Peerless, Pilot, Ross, Scripps-Booth, Standard, and Stearns-Knight

▲ Cadillac dubbed its 1916 touring a "Seven-Passenger Car." Total Cadillac output for 1916: 13,002 units.

▲ Chevrolet launched the 490 roadster and touring (*shown*) as '16 models, both priced at $490; 70,701 were built.

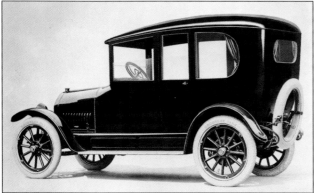

◄ Many companies issued elegant, top-of-the-line limousines; shown here, the 1916 Jeffery.

▶ Save for the Chesterfield Six model, Jefferys were four-cylinder cars, such as this Special Touring model.

- Design trends include slanted windshields and dual-cowl bodies, as well as wider availability of wire wheels

- Packard's Twin Six, the first American V-12, is the first engine to make use of aluminum pistons

- The Cadillac Motor Car Company becomes a division of General Motors

- Hudson's Super Six is the first American car with a balanced, counterweighted crankshaft to help quell engine vibration

- Ford slashes Model T prices again: The entry-level Runabout dips to $345, touring cars to $440

- A lower-cost four-cylinder Chevrolet 490 lists at, predictably, $490

- Packard abandons its six-cylinder engine (temporarily) after 1916, producing only the Twin Six until 1921

- Charles W. Nash leaves General Motors to take over the Thomas B. Jeffery Company, which will become Nash Motors Company

- William C. Durant succeeds Charles Nash as president of General Motors

◄ Ford cut 1916 Model T prices to combat Chevy's new 490. This $590 Coupelet found 3532 buyers.

New Makes 1916

- Anderson
- Bell
- Birch
- Bour-Davis
- Brewster-Knight
- Bush
- Columbia
- Daniels
- Dixie Flyer
- Drummond
- Economy
- Elcar
- Elgin
- Fergus
- H.A.L.
- Hatfield
- Homer-Laughlin
- Jordan
- Kent
- Laurel
- Liberty
- Maibohm
- Marion-Handley
- Moore
- Murray
- New Era
- Riddle
- Roamer
- Stephens
- Sun
- Waco
- Yale

▲ Sleeve-valve engines powered all 1916 Willys-Knight automobiles. Unique wraparound glass added elegance to this $1500 coupe.

- Oaklands available with four- or six-cylinder engine, or a new V-8

- Oldsmobile launches a V-8 engine: 246.7-cid and 40 horsepower

- The Federal Road Aid Act, approved by President Wilson, paves the way for an interstate highway system

- Alvan Macauley is named president of Packard Motor Car Company

- Henry Ford is sued by the Dodge Brothers over dividend payments

- Cross-licensing agreements, which allow for sharing the benefits of patents, take effect throughout the auto industry

- Total Buick sales nearly triple, to almost 125,000 cars

- The United Motors Corporation is established, Alfred P. Sloan is president

- The Model T's "brass era" comes to a close, with the final use of the metal on radiators and hubcaps

▲ For $1040, the '17 Buick D-44 roadster provided a 224-cid, 45-bhp six-cylinder engine.

▲ After extensive tests in 1917, the Cadillac V-8 was chosen as a "standard model" for service in WWI.

▲ Though not overly impressive to look at, Chevrolet's V-8 was advanced inside—yet it was gone by 1919.

1916 Model-Year Production Figures

1. Ford	734,811
2. Willys-Overland	140,111
3. Buick	124,834
4. Dodge	71,400
5. Chevrolet	70,701
6. Maxwell	69,000
7. Studebaker	65,536
8. Saxon	27,800

Some figures are estimated or calendar year

▲ Chevrolet's new 1917 Series D—$1385 for touring car or roadster—boasted a 288-cid ohv V-8 and lush interior. Note the tiny round portholes in the top.

1917

- American automakers offer their full cooperation as the U.S. enters World War I on April 6

- American auto manufacturers help in the development and production of Liberty aircraft engines

- A total of 1,745,792 cars and 128,157 trucks are produced, a 15 percent increase over 1916

- The first true Ford truck is built, and 39,000 go to the allied forces by the end of the war

- Ford's Model T gets a facelift, but sales fall slightly to 622,351 units; market share slides marginally as well to 36 percent

- The first Nash appears; initially just a rebadged Jeffery, the redesigned "true Nash" arrives for 1918

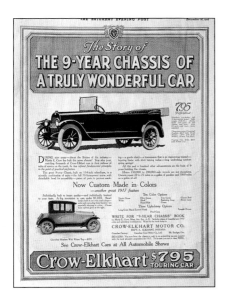

▲ Peak production year for the mid-priced Crow-Elkhart was 1917: 3800 units, touring car or roadster.

▲ The Wisconsin-built "All-Year" Kissel had a detachable top. A V-12 "Double-Six" joined the sixes in 1917.

▲ Continental six-cylinder engines powered the midpriced 1917 Liberty, built from 1916–23 in Detroit.

New Makes 1917

- Amco
- American-Piedmont
- Ben Hur
- Comet
- Commonwealth
- Cruiser
- Disbrow
- Eagle-Macomber
- Rotary
- Fageol
- Geronimo
- Ghent
- Hackett
- Harroun
- Napoleon
- Nash
- Nelson
- Olympian
- Pan-American
- Pennsy
- Phianna
- Sayers
- Seneca
- States
- Tulsa
- Woods

▲ A V-8 had been offered, but the 1917 Mitchell ran with a six. A power tire pump came standard.

▲ The driver of a 1917 Premier changed gears via pushbuttons, which actuated a magnetic gearshift.

- Notable new nameplates include Geronimo, Harroun, and the short-lived $12,000 Fageol luxury car

- The National Automobile Dealers Association is established, originally a congressional lobbying group

- Henry M. Leland, former head of the Cadillac Motor Car Company, forms the Lincoln Motor Company

- Chevrolet introduces a long-stroke, overhead-valve V-8 in its $1550 Series D cars, the engine disappears in 1919

- The Essex Motor Car Company is formed by Hudson to produce and sell lighter, less-expensive automobiles

- Ford division Fordson produces its first farm tractor in October

- Premier automobiles offer buyers the convenience of pushbutton gear changes, made possible by a magnetic shifter

- Continental Motor Manufacturing supplies power for smaller makes, including Liberty autos and Ahrens-Fox fire engines

- Wisconsin-based Kissel advertised an "All-Year" car, it came standard with a detachable hardtop

▼ Oldsmobile listed sixes and V-8s in 1917, the latter a 58-bhp unit. This Light Eight Touring car cost $1185.

◄ Since 1913, Pierce-Arrows had come with fender-mounted "frog-eye" headlights, but this 1917 limousine has the optional drum headlamps.

▼ The V-8 powering this 1917 Willys-Knight 88-8 cape-topped Victoria was rated at 65 bhp. A sedan, limo, and town car were sold at $2800-$2900.

1917 Model-Year Production Figures

1. Ford	622,351
2. Willys-Overland	130,988
3. Buick	115,267
4. Chevrolet	111,877
5. Dodge	90,000
6. Maxwell	75,000
7. Studebaker	39,686
8. Oakland	33,171

Some figures are estimated or calendar year

▲ Cars and trucks shared billing in this 1917 Reo ad, touting the make as "The Gold Standard of Values." The four-cylinder models began at $875.

1918

- Industry output sinks to 943,436 cars and 227,250 trucks, partly due to steel shortages and production for the military

- Americans endure "gasless Sundays" to conserve fuel, while automobiles are excise-taxed as luxury items

- War efforts prompt manufacturers to offer carburetors designed to run on low-grade fuels or kerosene

- Women enter factories as men go off to war; carmakers build tanks, plane engines, antiaircraft guns, and military vehicles

- Ford's civilian volume drops to 436,000 vehicles, as the war restricts volume and sends car prices skyrocketing

- The show does go on, as the 18th National Automobile Show is held as usual, despite the war

▲ A uniquely bodied $4250 Town Landaulet joined the Cadillac line in 1918, featuring tilting headlights.

▲ General John J. Pershing steps out of a specially built Cadillac sedan. More than 2000 served in World War I.

▲ Still called the 490, Chevrolet's cheapest model jumped to $685 for 1918. Closed cars now had rear-mounted gas tanks.

• Borrowing from military designs, several makes offer models equipped with steel wheels

• Nash becomes the world's biggest truck producer, the result of an Army contract for 11,494 four-wheel-drive "Quads"

• An all-new Nash arrives with an overhead-valve six-cylinder engine and three-speed gearbox

• The Chicago-built Deering Magnetic features an electric transmission, licensed from the makers of the Owen Magnetic.

• Chevrolet becomes a member of the growing General Motors group

• White abandons passenger-car production, focuses all its efforts on trucks

• California gets the first section of highway built under the Federal Road Aid Act

• Malcolm Loughead develops four-wheel hydraulic brakes; they will soon see use under the "Lockheed" name

• An armistice is signed on November 11, 1918, but car prices fail to drop as quickly as anticipated

▲ A 212.3-cid four drove the Dodge Bros. Model 30 roadster, which was priced at $985. Leather upholstery came standard, as did a speedometer. As the fifth-ranked automaker, Dodge produced some 62,000 cars in 1918.

▲ As the U.S. entered World War I, the government ordered car production slowed. Regardless, Ford continued sending products to auto shows around the country.

▶ Chevrolets get a final inspection at the assembly plant in Flint, Michigan.

New Makes 1918

• Cleveland
• DuPont
• Briggs & Stratton

▲ The police had special requirements for their "screenside" Ford Model T trucks.

▲ After offering two four-cylinder series and a six in 1918, Overland sold only a light four the following year. Prices rose sharply industrywide following the Great War.

▲ For business or fun: the 1918 Overland 90 roadster, whose 179-cid Light Four was rated at 32 bhp. Price: $780.

▲ With side pillars removed, Overland's Model 85 Big Four Touring Sedan foretold the hardtop craze of the '50s.

1918 Model-Year Production Figures	
1. Ford	435,898
2. Willys-Overland	88,753
3. Chevrolet	88,717
4. Buick	77,691
5. Dodge	62,000
6. Maxwell	34,000
7. Oakland	27,757
8. Oldsmobile	19,169
Some figures are estimated or calendar year	

85

▲ Buick's priciest was the $2585 H-50. Buick was second in sales to Chevrolet in the General Motors family.

▲ Big Cadillacs were billed as the "Standard Seven-Passenger Car of the United States Army."

▲ Chevrolet's $1110 FB touring car of 1919 rode a 110-inch chassis and wore flowing "reverse-curve" front fenders.

▲ Mechanics had easy access to Chevrolets in 1919. They also were as likely to fix a part as replace it. Note the foundry, for making "adjustments" in component fit.

1919

- Coal shortages worry industry leaders, who doubt they can meet the surprisingly strong postwar demand for automobiles

- Dealers demand product, but cars are in short supply—partly due to strikes, partly because of materials shortages

- A total of 1,651,625 passenger cars are built, nearly double the 1918 figure, plus 224,731 trucks

- Ford produces 820,445 cars, including the three-millionth Model T; market share nears 50 percent

- The Essex, the only new car at the National Automobile Show, immediately makes the low-cost closed sedan popular

- The Hudson-built Essex employs a four-cylinder engine with rocker-actuated intake valves and 55 bhp.

▲ Essex debuted in 1919 with an F-head four that produced an impressive 55 horses. Seen here is the two-door roadster, which sold for $1595.

◄ An electric starter finally became standard on Ford's Model T, but only on closed cars like this center-door sedan. The added equipment helped explain a price hike from $645 to $875 for this model in 1919. Demountable rims were also standard on closed models; later, open cars gained both.

- General Motors Acceptance Corporation is formed; automobile financing continues to gain popularity

- After 67 years, Studebaker drops carriage-building to focus solely on motor vehicles

- Auto-repair shops experiment with a flat-rate pricing system, an idea that gradually gains acceptance

- General Motors buys a majority interest in the Fisher Body Company; Nash acquires interest in the Seaman Body Company

- The first three-color stoplight is installed, in Detroit

- After payments of $75 million, the Ford family becomes sole owner of Ford Motor Company, with Edsel named president

- NADA sponsors the National Motor Vehicle Theft Act to curtail movement of stolen vehicles across state lines

- Oregon, opening a floodgate, enacts the first state gasoline tax

- A Duesenberg racing car with two straight-eight engines sets a landspeed record at Daytona Beach, reaching 158 mph

▲ An Entz electric gearbox, shifted via hand lever, was the foremost feature of the big, expensive Owen Magnetic, "Car of a Thousand Speeds." The firm failed in 1920.

▼ Hudson's rugged Super Six boasted an even tougher chassis for 1919.

▲ This 1919 Oldsmobile four-door sedan was the one-millionth car manufactured by General Motors. Both a Pacemaker V-8 and Series Six were marketed at $1395-$1895.

▲ After leaving GM, Charles Nash bought out Jeffery in 1916 and launched Nash. This $1395 1919 Model 681 was one of four six-cylinder touring models offered.

1919 Model-Year Production Figures	
1. Ford	820,445
2. Chevrolet	129,118
3. Buick	119,310
4. Dodge	106,000
5. Willys-Overland	80,853
6. Oakland	52,124
7. Maxwell	50,000
8. Oldsmobile	39,042

Some figures are estimated or calendar year

▲ Hyped as the "Most Beautiful Car in America," the six-cylinder Paige was known for clean, graceful styling.

CHAPTER THREE

1920-1929

ANYTHING GOES

Novelist F. Scott Fitzgerald called it "the greatest, gaudiest spree in history." Newspaperman-philosopher H.L. Mencken coined the term "boobus Americanus" to describe provincial adherents of the booming consumer society.

Either way, this was the "Jazz Age"—a decade of silliness and sophistication; of evangelists and literary giants; of fads from marathon dances to flagpole sitting. Bobbed-haired "flappers" cavorted to the aptly named shimmy. Prohibition was the law, speakeasies the rule. Broadcast radio was born by 1920, "talking" movies a few years later.

Despite the boisterousness, conformism was the "American Way." Except for the 1920–21 depression, prosperity seemed permanent. Canny politicians promised such goodies as a "car in every garage." Salesmanship ruled the business world, bolstered by small-town boosterism. Money gained unprecedented importance.

An automotive culture was emerging, as the car shifted from frivolous plaything to virtual necessity. Roadside stands, tourist camps, and gasoline stations spread throughout the land. Affluent families began their migration to suburban subdivisions, linked by automobile to downtown businesses. Young blades did their courting in cars. Chain stores were displacing independent retailers.

Ford remained king of the automotive pack, but the faithful flivver wouldn't long remain the vehicle of choice—not for those who could hustle the bucks to select from the fast-unfurling array of consumer goods. By late 1927, something fresh from Ford awaited: the perky Model A.

Alfred P. Sloan ushered in an era of efficiency at General Motors. GM also cleverly pioneered "planned obsolescence," introducing new models designed to make customers dissatisfied with the cars they'd recently loved so much.

Those fortunate enough to possess wealth often elected to flaunt it. What better way than a flamboyant automobile? Duesenberg, Lincoln, Marmon, Cadillac, Pierce-Arrow, Packard Twin Six—for the well-heeled, a cornucopia of choices awaited. And with such expert coachbuilders as Derham and LeBaron to create the bodywork, the fine machinery wore a cloak to match its inner magnificence.

For less-affluent folk, middecade saw the founding of Chrysler Corporation, then its addition of Dodge, DeSoto, and Plymouth.

Automotive technology was moving forward. Closed bodies were displacing the open roadster and touring car, using less wood and more steel. Hydraulic brakes began to replace mechanical units, stopping four wheels instead of two. Introduction of synchromesh soon would make gear clashing a distant memory. Driving was becoming easier and safer.

Ned Jordan's essay, "Somewhere West of Laramie," changed the face of automotive advertising, but not everyone was able to join the automotive whirl just yet. Even when the Model T bottomed at $260 in 1925, the average worker earned just $1434 per year. As many as three-fourths of new cars were bought on installments, however, as automakers urged customers to "pay as you ride."

One Indiana resident told researchers Robert and Helen Lynd that the dominant force changing America amounted to "just four letters: A-U-T-O." Others were more direct, insisting they'd "rather do without clothes," or even food, "than give up the car."

All the ballyhoo came crashing down in October 1929, as Wall Street responded to the speculation and overproduction of the Twenties. A slimmed-down America was coming, but the automobile had already cut too deep a path to retreat.

1920

- The "Roaring Twenties" begin with Prohibition in force and American women now eligible to vote

- America now has 191 miles of highway at least partially funded by federal programs

- Production for the year totals 1,905,560 passenger cars (a quarter million more than 1919) and 321,789 trucks

- Despite the industry gain, Ford output drops by half, but still leads Chevrolet, Buick, and Oakland

- The Duesenberg Model A is introduced late in 1920—the first American production car with all-wheel hydraulic brakes

- The Kurtz Automatic, made in Cleveland, uses a preselector gearshift, with shift levers at the steering wheel

▲ Critics acclaimed the arrival of the revised Type 59 Cadillac for 1920, like this $4750 four-door sedan.

▲ As it had in the Teens, the new Cadillac featured a 315-cid V-8 and tilt steering. This is the $3590 roadster.

▲ Except for new reverse-curve front fenders, the Chevrolet 490 and costlier FB changed little for 1920.

▲ Ray Lampkin sits at the wheel of a stripped Essex, which won a series of southern races in 1920. The Essex four, built by Hudson, debuted in 1919.

◄ Henry Ford—now one of the wealthiest men in the world—poses here in his modest office.

- The first Gardner is built in St. Louis, power comes from a four-cylinder Lycoming engine

- LaFayette, a V-8 luxury make, goes into production late in the year; prices start at $5025

- Flat windshields are slowly giving way to slanted glass, as wire wheels gain favor over wood

- Essex ranks as the first low-priced closed car, courtesy of a sedan model added late in 1919

- William C. Durant loses control of General Motors for the second and final time; Pierre S. DuPont becomes president

- Walter P. Chrysler takes charge at Willys-Overland via a two-year contract and a $1-million-per-year salary

- Auto pioneers John and Horace Dodge die within nine months of each other; pneumonia claims the brothers

- Heaters are becoming standard equipment, usually built in the car floor to make use of exhaust-gas heat

- General Motors Research Corporation is created, includes recently acquired Dayton Engineering Laboratories Company (Delco)

▲ At $3400, a 1920 Hudson sedan was fairly costly. The Super Six—with 76 bhp, 289 cid—came in three series.

- Ace
- Adelphia
- Alsace
- Beggs
- Bradley
- Cyclomobile
- Duesenberg
- Economy-Vogue
- Ferris
- Gardner
- Gearless Steam
- Globe
- H.C.S.
- Huffman
- Innes
- Kelsey
- Kenworthy
- Kessler
- Kurtz Automatic
- LaFayette
- LaMarne
- Leach-Builtwell
- Lorraine
- Manexall
- Marshall
- Moller
- Parenti
- Premocar
- R&V Knight
- Ranger
- Severin
- Shaw
- Simms
- Skelton
- Southern Six
- Stanwood
- Texan
- Wasp

▲ The Indiana-built Lexington survived from 1909 to 1927. This "Convertible Sedan" was among 6000 six-cylinder cars built in 1920. A pair of Lexingtons ran first and second at Pikes Peak this year.

▲ Dubbed the "Sensible Six," Oakland carried a 44-horse, 177-cid engine. Optional sun visors were common accessories in 1920.

▲ Though exposed, the chauffeur got some shelter in this 1920 Packard Twin Six limousine with a 424-cid V-12. Wheelbase could be either 128 or 136 inches.

▲ The 1920 Oldsmobile Sixth Series came with a 44-bhp, 177-cid, ohv six; the Thorobred series boasted more power, from a 58-bhp V-8.

- Ford Model T prices are cut drastically, but average $150 reduction fails to impact sagging sales

- Bulging Ford inventories force a protracted Christmas-holiday factory shutdown that extends until February 1921

- Ford market share dips to 22 percent, as exaggerated rumors of the company's financial woes circulate

- As the country adjusts to a new, more mobile culture, roadside stands and gas stations begin to dot the landscape

- Lexington billed its Minute Man Six as a "Convertible Sedan," featuring a roof that opened "instantly" when weather permitted

- A prize fight is America's first public radio broadcast; radio-equipped cars come later in the decade

1920 Model-Year Production Figures

1. Ford		806,040
2. Chevrolet		146,243
3. Dodge		141,000
4. Buick		115,176
5. Willys-Overland		105,025
6. Studebaker		48,831
7. Hudson/Essex		45,937
8. Chandler		45,000

Some figures are estimated or calendar year

▲ The first Checkers were based on the short-lived Commonwealth. They were built in a plant near Chicago.

▲ Chevrolet production dropped to 130,885 in 1921. A firm of engineers advised GM to drop the make.

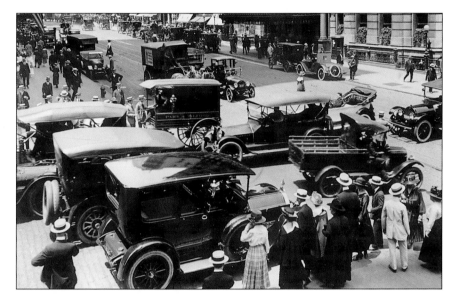

▲ Traffic congestion was a growing problem, as this 1921 scene on New York City's Fifth Avenue reveals. Some 4500 vehicles used the Avenue every hour.

◀ Essex was a lower-priced, four-cylinder mate to Hudson. This 1921 Essex roadster sold for $1595.

New Makes 1921

• Adria	• Henney
• Ambassador	• Lincoln
• Automatic	• McGill
• Birmingham	• Merit
• Bowman	• Murray-Mac Six
• Carroll Six	• Northway
• Checker Cab	• Peters
• Colonial	• Raleigh
• Commodore	• Rees
• Curtis	• Rodgers
• Drake	• Rolls-Royce
• Driggs	• Romer
• Durant	• Sheridan
• Fox	• Spencer
• Fremont	• Sperling
• Friend	• Washington
• Handley-Knight	• Wills St. Claire
• Hanover	• Winther
• Heine-Velox	• Wizard

1921

• Automobile sales sag severely as does rest of the U.S. economy, the result of a brief, but brutal, depression

• Total passenger-car production dips to 1,468,067; truck output sinks by nearly half, to 148,052

• New price cuts help stimulate Ford Model T sales, as does an eventual upturn in the U.S. economy

• Ford production more than doubles to a record-setting 1,275,618 units; market share triples to 61.5 percent

• Chevrolet output runs a distant second to Ford, followed by Buick, Dodge, and Studebaker in order

• Lincoln's first car, the Model L, is introduced, powered by an 81-bhp, 358-cid V-8.

▲ Cars didn't have to be costly to wear custom-built bodywork. Bodies for Ford's Depot Hack came from outside suppliers. A Model T chassis alone cost $360.

▲ Angular styling helped distinguish the new 1921 Essex Cabriolet, which rode a 108.5-inch wheelbase, from the competition. Its 179-cid F-head four developed 55 horses.

▲ Ford's Center Door Sedan dropped sharply in price, from $975 in 1920 to $795—then lower yet. Rear quarter panels were now an integral part of the bodysides, not split in two.

- Durant Motors is organized by William C. Durant following his retirement from General Motors; the first Durant car debuts

- The new Wills St. Claire boasts an advanced overhead-cam engine featuring aluminum and molybdenum components

- Checker Cab goes into production again; an earlier version was built by Commonwealth Motors in 1920

- Glass wind wings, long popular in California to reduce wind buffeting, gain popularity in the East

- Hydraulic brakes are installed on several makes, gradually replace mechanical systems

- Nickel-plating appears on some radiators and headlamps, wide use of chrome is still a few years away

- Cadillac carburetors gain thermostatic control, drivers relieved of all fuel-related adjustments except choke

- William S. Knudsen leaves Ford for Chevrolet, had engaged in policy battles with Henry Ford

- Warren G. Harding is the first American President to ride to inauguration in an automobile, a Packard Twin Six

▲ A padded roof and side windows made this 1921 Nash seven-seat touring car, with a 249-cid six, appear impenetrable. Nash added several four-cylinder models during the year.

◄ One of the best-known—and most coveted—sporty autos was the Stutz Bearcat, still sporting right-hand drive in 1921. An enormous 361-cid four provided plenty of thrust.

▲ A slightly smaller 234-cid V-8 went into the $1825 Model 47 Oldsmobile in 1921. Also new: a four-cylinder Olds.

▲ Walter P. Chrysler had taken charge of the Willys empire for a time, but John North Willys regained control. Here, a $2195 Model 20 sleeve-valve Willys-Knight touring car.

- The three-towered, $19 million General Motors Building opens on Grand Avenue in downtown Detroit

- The nation's first drive-in restaurant, The Pig Stand, opens in Dallas, Texas. The Pig Stand Special cost 25 cents.

- Increased traffic spurs the Detroit police to synchronize traffic lights; pedestrians get raised-platform safety zones

- General Motors researcher Thomas Midgley, Jr., discovers that Tetraethyl "lead" is an effective antiknock gasoline additive

- Walter P. Chrysler temporarily wrangles control of the Willys Automobile Company from founder John North Willys

- Despite Henry Ford's resistance to offering credit to buyers, 73 percent of Fords are purchased on installment plans

▶ Closed coupes, like this $1475 Buick Model 22-4-136 kept a tall profile. Some 2225 were sold. Four-cylinder Buicks rode a 109-inch wheelbase, sixes were 118 or 124 inch.

▲ Buick's overhead-valve, 242-cid six-cylinder engine with multidisc clutch powered the $1495 22-6-44 roadster. New sport roadster and touring models had wire wheels.

▲ At $2435, this Buick Model 22-6-47 six-cylinder sedan had many rivals in the midprice closed-car field, including Auburn, Case, Chalmers, Elcar, and Reo.

▶ Open touring cars, such as this $1735 Buick 22-6-49, continued to sell well, but their days were numbered as buyers gradually turned to the all-weather versatility of closed sedans and coupes.

1921 Model-Year Production Figures	
1. Ford	1,275,618
2. Chevrolet	130,885
3. Buick	82,930
4. Dodge	81,000
5. Studebaker	65,023
6. Willys-Overland	48,016
7. Hudson/Essex	27,143
8. Nash	20,850
Some figures are estimated or calendar year	

▲ A year after this 1922 taxi was built by the Checker Cab Manufacturing Company in Illinois, assembly was moved to a production facility in Kalamazoo, Michigan.

◀ Price cuts—down to $510 for the 490 roadster—helped bolster Chevrolet sales for 1922. Dodge outsold Chevy this year, knocking the Bow Tie brand to third place overall.

1922

- Passenger-car output rises sharply to 2,274,185 units, while truck production increases to 269,991

- Model T Ford output nears 1.2 million, accounts for more than half of all cars sold in America

- Far behind with 152,653 automobiles produced is Dodge; followed closely by Chevrolet and Buick

- Roadster-coupes—roadster bodies with fixed tops—are popular exhibits at the National Automobile Show

- Rickenbacker, a new make built in Detroit, is named for race driver and World War I flying ace Edward "Eddie" Rickenbacker

- The budget-priced Star is launched by Durant, ready to rival Ford's Model T; 100,000 are produced in less than a year

▲ Wooden station wagon-type bodies generally came from outside suppliers. This 1922 Dodge had bodywork from the J. T. Cantrell & Company of Huntington, New York.

► This Essex Cabriolet looked sharp in 1922, but the big news was the new coach—with a low profile and equally low $1245 price tag, it hastened the demise of open cars.

▲ As before, a 55-bhp, F-head four powered the '22 Essex touring car.

- New Dagmar serves as a sporty companion to the Crawford; both are built in Hagerstown, Maryland

- With a midpriced six, the new Jewett brand is introduced as a subsidiary of the Paige-Detroit Motor Car Company

- A one-piece windshield is installed on the short-lived Earl touring car, which is basically a reworked Briscoe

- Low-pressure "balloon" tires introduced by Firestone, provide more comfortable ride, higher speeds

- Rickenbacker is the first make to use nonoiled "dry" air-cleaner elements to protect engines from dirt

- Nash reduces felt vibration by introducing rubber engine mounts, already in use on several lower-volume makes

- Replacing the dipstick, more convenient fuel gauges appear on the instrument panel of several makes

- Ford Model T prices are lowered again; the entry-level touring car can now be had for as little as $298

- Ford buys the Lincoln Motor Company out of receivership for $8 million, Edsel Ford takes the helm of the struggling make

▲ Three six-cylinder and V-12 Haynes series vied for sales in 1922. Shown is a $1785 Model 55 touring, with 50-bhp six. Haynes would survive into 1925.

▲ Introduced a year earlier by Henry Leland, Lincoln became a division of Ford in 1922. Under the hood was a 357.8-cid V-8 rated at 90 horsepower.

▲ Two Henrys, Ford and Leland, stand behind their sons as Ford purchases the ailing Lincoln Motor Company.

- The struggling Locomobile Company is placed in receivership, is later purchased by Locomobile

- Charles M. Schwab takes the helm at Stutz; two years after founder Harry Stutz had left the firm

- William S. Knudsen becomes vice president in charge of operations at Chevrolet

- Henry Ford publishes *My Life and Work*, it runs 296 pages and is eventually translated into 14 languages

- About 73 percent of cars are now bought on time, but Henry Ford still disapproves of installment payments

- George Selden dies; he claimed to have developed the first automobile, but lost his patent suit to Henry Ford

- An electrically synchronized traffic-signal system is installed in Houston, Texas; becomes model for nation

- Car insurance policies, previously based on purchase price, are revised to reflect actual vehicle values

- Country Club Plaza in Kansas City, Missouri, becomes the nation's first suburban shopping center

▲ Beneath the hood of this $1045 Nash Model 41 sat a four-cylinder engine, but Nash also produced sixes in 1922.

▲ Three-seat Oldsmobile coupes, with a four or V-8, had this angled windshield. Olds output for '22: 21,499.

▼ New in 1921, the Wills St. Claire made use of expensive molybdenum. Perfectionism demanded by founder Harold Wills led to its demise in '27.

◄ Willys-Knight sales rose in the early '20s. Willys claimed its sleeve-valve four-cylinder "improves with use.... Carbon only makes it better."

New Makes 1922

• American Steamer	• D.A.C.	• Goodspeed	• Metropolitan	• Stratton-Bliss
• Bay State	• Dagmar	• Gray	• Richelieu	• Tarkington
• Commander	• Earl	• Gregory	• Rickenbacker	• Trask
• Corinthian	• Falcon	• Jewett	• St. Louis	• Waltham
• Crane-Simplex	• Frontenac	• McCurdy	• Star	• Wharton

▲ A big car with an old name: The 1923 Apperson shown here was priced at $2620. Power was V-8.

▲ Six-cylinder Buicks rode a 118- or 124-inch wheelbase. This $2195 Model 23-6-50 sedan saw 10,279 copies built.

▲ Cole, previously known as the Aero Eight, built just 1522 cars for 1923. This $2685 touring car had a V-8.

1922 Model-Year Production Figures	
1. Ford	1,147,028
2. Dodge	152,653
3. Chevrolet	138,932
4. Buick	123,152
5. Studebaker	105,005
6. Willys-Overland	95,410
7. Durant (all makes)	55,300
8. Maxwell/Chalmers	44,811
Some figures are estimated or calendar year	

▼ In addition to this low-cost four-cylinder model, Buick added a six-cylinder roadster this year. More than 201,000 Buicks were built in calendar-year 1923.

1923

• Industry production soars upward again, totaling 3,624,717 passenger cars and 409,295 trucks

• More than two million Fords are built this year, including more than 1.8 million cars—half the industry total

• Chevrolet output increases to 323,182 cars—comfortably more than third-place Buick's 201,572

• Fixed-top phaetons and closed five-seat cars are popular at the 23rd National Automobile Show

• Dodge is first make to offer an all-steel closed body, developed by Edward G. Budd

• Durant's short-lived Eagle is introduced. Meant to slot between the maker's Durant and Star cars, it disappears after 1924

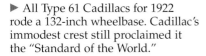
▲ DeLuxe Chevrolets, introduced during 1923, came with disc wheels, bumpers, step plates, and a number of other fancy extras.

▶ All Type 61 Cadillacs for 1922 rode a 132-inch wheelbase. Cadillac's immodest crest still proclaimed it the "Standard of the World."

• Durant also launches the Flint brand; it's priced between the builder's Durant and Locomobile makes

• The first factory-produced station wagon is introduced by Star, Durant's lowest-priced car line

• The Doble Steamer is back after a brief absence, it features a new burner for shorter warm-up times

• Maker Jordan expands the realm of auto advertising with its legendary "Somewhere West of Laramie . . ." campaign

• Four-wheel brakes, power wipers, and foot-controlled dimmer switches are standard on several makes

• The first car radios available for factory installation are built by the Springfield Body Corporation

• Ethyl (leaded) gas, developed by General Motors Research Corporation, goes on sale; Standard Oil distributes the fuel

• Floor-type heaters slowly lose favor due to safety concerns, makers worry about exhaust gas in the cabin

• Buick produces its one-millionth car while Ford closes in on its nine-millionth car; Dort reaches 100,000 produced

▲ The 1923 Essex coach carried the last of the company's four-cylinder engines: a 179-cid, 55-bhp unit. At $1145, a coach cost just $100 more than a touring car.

▲ The 1923 Dorris was a big, powerful car, with a 132-inch wheelbase and 377-cid six. The Dorris brand survived from 1906 to 1926, chalking up about 3100 cars and 900 trucks.

▲ Restyling gave Ford's 1923 Model T a lower profile with sloped windshield. The new look was an instant hit with buyers, who snapped up nearly two million copies.

• Nash introduces a vacuum-powered windshield-wiper motor; Buick and Cadillac follow suit soon after

• The Model T Ford is restyled, finally gets front-hinged doors; "Fordor" and "Tudor" sedans debut

• Ford announces a weekly purchase plan; The customer gets the car only after the full amount is paid, in $5 installments

• Ford advertising resumes after a six-year lapse; ads focus on quality and price—as low as $295 for the touring car

• Chevrolet, selling mostly sixes, abandons its larger four-cylinder engine, but keeps the smaller version through 1928

• Alfred P. Sloan, Jr., is named president of General Motors, Roy D. Chapin retires as president of Hudson

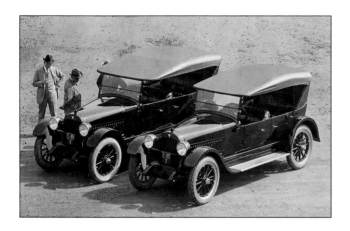

▲ Differences between Hudson's 1923 seven-passenger Phaeton (*left*) and Speedster aren't evident at a glance. Both Super Six models rode a 125.5-inch wheelbase.

▲ Charles Nash launched the luxurious LaFayette, shown here in 1923 touring sedan form. This 4200-pound Model 134 with its 348-cid V-8 engine cost a whopping $5500.

▲ Edsel and Eleanor Ford enjoy their Lincoln. Model L wheelbase grew to 136 inches in 1923. Sales rose, too.

▲ The 1923 Moon Sport Touring Model 6-58 was priced at $1985 and rode on a 128-inch chassis.

▶ When "Cannon Ball" Baker drove this Olds coast-to-coast in 12½ days, all gears but high had been removed.

New Makes 1923

- Barley
- Cardway
- Courier
- Deemster
- Delling
- Detroit
- Eagle
- Flint
- Harris Six
- Leon Rubay
- MacDonald
- Princeton
- Rollin
- Sekine
- Sterling-Knight

▲ Wartime ace Captain Eddie Rickenbacker, with the car that bore his name and featured a dual-flywheel engine.

▲ Challenging Ford, William Durant built 100,000 Stars—like this $443 1923 touring car—during the first year.

◀ This square-rigged 1923 Nash Model 694 seven-passenger sedan listed at $2190. It rode a 127-inch chassis, and, like most cars of the day, placed the rear passengers atop the axle.

▲ Willys-Knight was one of several makes popular with taxi services. Other manufacturers had tried the Knight's sleeve-valve engine design, but none lasted as long as Willys.

▲ Hydraulic brakes and a high-compression six marked the new 1924 Chrysler.

▲ Bigger and roomier, this '24 Buick Model 50 six saw 9561 copies built.

1923 Model-Year Production Figures

1. Ford	1,831,128
2. Chevrolet	323,182
3. Buick	201,572
4. Willys-Overland	196,038
5. Durant (all makes)	172,000
6. Dodge	151,000
7. Studebaker	146,238
8. Hudson/Essex	88,914

Some figures are estimated or calendar year

▲ New for 1924 was Chevrolet's Coach—a bargain at $695. Some DeLuxe models had disc wheels and bumpers. Ads promoted "economical transportation."

▲ Essex adopted a longer, lower profile for '24, though not quite as radical as this prototype. A new 130-cid L-head six replaced the make's dated 180-cid F-head four.

▲ The little Essex six was quickly bored and stroked to 144.5 cid and an estimated 40 horses. Note the "suicide" (rear-hinged) door on this $975 coach.

◄ An integral rear deck replaced the removable "turtleback" on Ford's new five-window coupe. Demountable rims were standard. Closed cars had "rotary regulator" window roll-up cranks.

New Makes 1924

- Balboa
- Chrysler
- Kleiber
- Luxor
- S&S
- Schuler
- Traveler

1924

- Steam is a no show; for the first time, all cars at the National Automobile Show are powered by gasoline

- Maxwell-Chalmers Corp. introduces the Chrysler, with four-wheel hydraulic brakes and a high-compression engine

- The six-cylinder Chrysler 70 draws crowds at the show; features instruments grouped behind an oval glass panel

- Passenger-car output dips moderately to 3,185,881 units; truck production climbs slightly to 416,659

- Ford Model T production slips to 1.75 million, but Ford maintains its 50-percent market share

- Dodge ousts Buick from third place in output; Chevrolet volume drops sharply, but still retains second spot

▲ Franklin "Desert Camels" relax at Scotty's Furnace Creek Ranch in Death Valley, California, in May 1924. Treks through the blazing California-Nevada desert tested the stamina of the air-cooled engine—and passengers.

▲ The last LaFayette was built in '24, shown here in dapper two-seat, $5000 roadster form. Total 1921–24 output: 2267. Nash clung to the name, and would use it again in the '30s.

▲ Only six-cylinder engines went into 1924 Oldsmobiles, all 42-bhp and 169-cid units. This $1075 30-B Series coupe attracted 8839 customers. Note the chains mounted on the rear tires.

◄ Two Nash lines were available in '24: a six-cylinder 690 and four-cylinder 40 series (last year for fours). Landau bars, as on this Brougham, decorated many cars of the day.

- Oakland cars are now sprayed with quick-drying Duco lacquer, the new paint helps reduce assembly time

- Packard offers the first mass-produced straight eight, a 358-cid engine producing a claimed 160 bhp

- Other straight-eight engines are introduced by Hupmobile, Auburn, Duesenberg, Jordan, Rickenbacker, and others

- The last four-cylinder Buicks are produced; the make will sell only sixes until the Depression

- Oakland drops its overhead-valve six, replacing it with a new L-head of roughly the same dimensions

- Balloon (low-pressure) tires and four-wheel brakes are standard on a number of makes

- Twin-filament headlight bulbs and baked-enamel paint become common on lower-priced cars

- Ford builds its 10-millionth automobile, enters the aftermarket with factory-built accessories

- Ford prices drop to $265 for the Runabout, $295 for the Touring. The average employed American earns $1293 annually

▲ New "enclosed" touring cars, with a permanent top and sliding side windows, joined the 1925 Buick line. This $1475 Master Six was one of 160,411 Buicks built for the year.

▶ The Aluminum Corporation of America (later ALCOA) joined with Pierce-Arrow in 1925 to produce 10 experimental aluminum cars powered by a 75-horsepower six.

▲ In 1925, the $735 Chevrolet closed coach, with wooden wheels and balloon tires, was a popular family car.

1924 Model-Year Production Figures

1. Ford	1,720,795
2. Chevrolet	264,868
3. Dodge	193,861
4. Willys-Overland	163,000
5. Buick	169,411
6. Hudson/Essex	133,950
7. Durant (all makes)	111,000
8. Studebaker	105,387

Some figures are estimated or calendar year

• Nash Motors purchases LaFayette Motors Corp., then drops it after only 2267 cars have been built in three and a half years

• Chandler adopts a "traffic transmission" with constant-mesh gearing, a forerunner of the forthcoming synchromesh

• General Motors completes its new proving ground at Milford, Michigan, names William Knudsen president of Chevrolet

• Ethyl Corporation is formed by GM and Standard Oil of New Jersey. Ethyl (leaded) "antiknock" gasoline goes on sale

• The Winton Company drops out of automobile production, concentrates on diesel engines

• After just two years, the 300,000th Ford is sold on the company's weekly credit plan

Two Millionth Chevrolet

The Chevrolet Motor Company is the first manufacturer of selective gear shift automobiles to produce 2,000,000 cars. The coach shown above is the two millionth car made Sept. 8. Standing at left is C. E. Dawson, assistant general sales manager; right, W. S. Knudsen, president.

◄ Chevrolet's two-millionth car happened to be a closed coach, assembled on the line above. Assistant general sales manager C. E. Dawson (*left*) poses proudly with Chevrolet president William S. Knudsen.

New Makes 1925

- Ajax
- Barbarino
- Bauer
- Diana
- Julian
- Majestic
- Mayfair

1925

- Passenger-car production climbs to 3,735,171; truck volume reaches 530,659 units

- Ford automobile production declines to 1,669,847, but truck output climbs to a record 268,411

- The industry reaches a milestone in 1925: The 25-millionth American motor vehicle is produced

- Continuing a trend, closed automobiles outsell open-air alternatives for the first time this year

- Safety and comfort draw customers: Most automobiles now boast four-wheel brakes and standard bumpers

- Companion makes appear: the $865–$995 Ajax is introduced by Nash, the $2000 Diana by Moon, but neither will last long

▲ Workers are busy with the new Chevrolet engine for 1925. Series K looked similar to the prior F, but was better mechanically. The engine had a new block, heavier crankshaft, drop-forged rods with bigger bearings, and an enclosed flywheel.

▼ Ford dealers grew worried as Chevrolet and other rivals gained strength. Even with a weekly payment plan available to bolster sales, many had trouble meeting sales quotas. A mid-1925 facelift didn't help as much as expected.

▲ As elsewhere, closed bodies gained favor at Ford. For example, this $580 Tudor sedan attracted 195,001 buyers.

▼ Even though the '25 Ford Fordor sold for $660—about twice the price of a touring car—81,050 were sold.

- Lighter steering is featured on several car models with balloon tires, including the new Diana, which aims at female drivers

- Straight-eight engines are among the hot new trends at the 25th National Automobile Show, again in New York City

- Other notable trends include rumble seats, one-piece windshields, mohair upholstery, and crank-type window lifts

- The last Stanley Steamers are smaller and cheaper, with hydraulic brakes; the well-known make fades away after 1925

- Quick-drying synthetic pyroxylin paints permit wide color choices—and can be sprayed and baked

- A Fisher ventilating windshield for GM cars retracts vertically, forming a watertight seal when closed and ventilation when opened

- The nation's first chain of car-rental agencies is established, features Hertz "Drivurself" automobiles

- Available aftermarket accessories include stop signals, mirrors, ashtrays, cigar lighters, locking radiator caps, trunk racks

- The "improved Ford" gets a major facelift during the summer, its second update ever, and the first since 1917

▲ Angular styling didn't diminish the appeal of the Nash Special Six, which replaced the make's four-cylinder line. This Model 133 two-door sedan, with its 207-cid engine, cost $1225.

▲ Landau bars had no function, but they looked good on a 1925 Hudson Special.

▲ Model 48, Locomobile's biggest 1925 car, had a 142-inch chassis, 525-cid six, and $7400 price tag for the Sportif.

- Model T prices reach all-time lows: $260 for the Runabout, $290 for the Touring car

- Lawrence P. Fisher is named president of the Cadillac Motor Car Division

- The Pennsylvania-based Fleetwood custom-body firm is acquired by GM

- General Motors purchases the Yellow Truck and Coach Manufacturing Company

- Maxwell-Chalmers Corporation is reorganized as Chrysler Corporation

- Motor buses are now in use by over 150 electric railway systems across the country

- The Lincoln Highway is completed—the world's first transcontinental highway

- A trade paper, *Automobile Daily News*, is established and commences publication

- Uniform markings for federally funded highways are adopted—even numbers for east/west roads, odd for north/south

- Ralph Mulford drives a Chandler 1000 miles in a record-setting 689 minutes, an 87-mph average

- Miller front-wheel-drive racing cars appear at the Indianapolis 500 race, foretelling a front-drive production model of 1929

▲ Oakland was the first car to sport new Duco paint with its "True Blue" model. A larger 185-cubic-inch six powered this $1905 roadster in 1925.

▼ Willys-Knight added a six-cylinder model to the line, with 60 horses and 236 cid. Shown here is the $1750 Model 66 roadster for 1925.

▲ Conventional poppet-valve engines powered the Willys-Overland, which was priced considerably lower than Willys-Knight models. This $850 Overland Model 91 Standard sedan featured a 154-cid four-cylinder engine on a 100-inch wheelbase. The Model 93 sixes rode a longer 113-inch chassis.

▲ Buick's six was boosted to 75 bhp for 1926. This $1795 Master Six four-passenger coupe sold 10,028 copies.

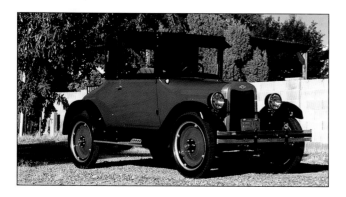

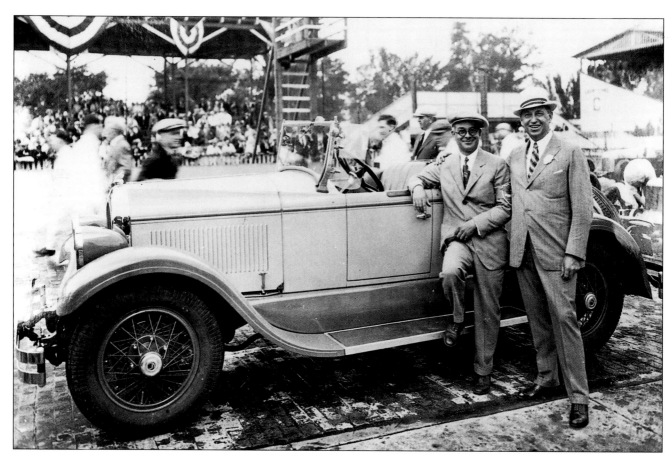

▲ Chevy's $510 roadster—with ample rear storage—was one of Ford's most serious sales challengers.

◀ Accessories—such as bumpers and step plates added pizzazz to the '26 Chevrolet Superior two-passenger coupe.

▲ Walter P. Chrysler (*right*) and C. Walrich pose with the new, distinctively styled, $2885 Chrysler Imperial E-80 roadster, which paced the Indianapolis 500 in 1926.

▲ New Hudson-built steel bodies and a nickel-plated radiator highlighted the '26 Essex, here the $735 coach. Output this year totaled 157,247 units.

▶ This stunt illustrated the Essex's rugged construction, particularly the piano-hinge doors adopted late in '26.

▲ Edsel Ford sits at the wheel of the 15-millionth Ford, built in May 1926.

▶ Closed Fords now sported a nickel-plated radiator shell. This $660 Fordor ($545 later) posted 102,732 sales.

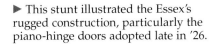

1925 Model-Year Production Figures

1. Ford	1,669,847
2. Chevrolet	306,479
3. Hudson/Essex	269,474
4. Willys-Overland	215,000
5. Dodge	201,000
6. Buick	192,100
7. Studebaker	133,104
8. Chrysler/Maxwell	132,343

Some figures are estimated or calendar year

▲ A Brougham with Biddle & Smart body joined Hudson's line in mid 1925.

▲ The durable Hudson made sense in taxi service. The 76-bhp Super Six was potent for the day. Price: $1650.

▲ Oldsmobile produced 53,015 cars in 1926, among them 3296 copies of the landau coupe. Price: $990.

◀ Two new Hupmobiles arrived in '26: A-1 Six on a 114-inch wheelbase and E-2 Eight on a 125-inch chassis.

1926

• U.S. vehicle output remains relatively stable at 3,692,317 passenger cars and 608,617 trucks

• Chevrolet edges closer to Ford in the production battle, but is still far behind with 547,724 cars compared to Ford's 1,426,612

• Narrower windshield pillars improve visibility of several models displayed at the 26th National Automobile Show

• Rubber engine mounts hold Pontiac's six-cylinder L-head mill in place

• The new Pontiac, first seen at the National Automobile Show, is a low-priced companion make to the Oakland

• Both Oakland and Pontiac models are produced through 1931, with different bodies and engines

▲ In addition to the cars issued under its own name, Nash offered the lower-priced Ajax (*right*) for one year only. It was replaced by the Nash Light Six by 1927, with the same 40-bhp, 170-cid L-head engine. "True" Nashes used overhead-valve sixes.

▲ The first Pontiacs rolled off the line in 1926, lower-priced mates to the long-established Oakland. This Pontiac is enduring a test run inside the plant, its front tires blocked. Pontiacs featured a 40-bhp, 187-cid L-head six and rode a 110-inch wheelbase.

- The Willys-built Whippet debuts in the fall as the smallest American automobile; it has a 134-cid, four-cylinder engine

- The Maxwell nameplate disappears; the four-cylinder car is renamed Chrysler 58 and marketed next to the six-cylinder Model 70

- Chrysler's new distinctively styled, higher-priced Imperial carries a more powerful six-cylinder motor and bullet-shaped headlamps

- Stutz adopts an overhead-cam "Vertical Eight" engine with silent chain drive and an advertised 92 horsepower

- Cadillac introduces shatter-resistant safety glass; Stutz and Rickenbacker offer "shock-proof" windshield glass

- GM opens the first styling studio, the impressively titled Art & Colour Section, directed Harley J. Earl

- Packard develops quiet-running hypoid gears for the rear axle, first produced for the 1927 model years

- Glass "eyes" at the rear of many headlight housings allow the driver to confirm the lights are on

- Chandler offers a one-shot lubrication system, a setup that soon will appear on many higher-priced cars

▲ All '26 Willys-Knights had a six: 178 or 236 cid, 53 or 60 horses. This is a $2295 Great Six. In the Twenties, Willys usually sold more than 50,000 Knights a year.

▲ Buick's engines for 1927 were hyped as "vibrationless beyond belief." Here, the $1275 coupe; 7178 were built.

◄ The Willys-Knight Model 70, shown here in roadster guise, was new to the make for 1926. Price: $1525.

- More rubber for Chrysler: engine mounts, spring shackles, and seat parts now made of the shock-absorbing material

- An electric starter finally becomes standard on open Model T Fords

- E. G. "Cannon Ball" Baker drives a loaded General Motors truck cross-country in 5 days, 17½ hours

- The *Encyclopedia Britannica* contains a Henry Ford article on "mass production" (formerly referred to as "Fordism")

- Ford workers work week reduced to five days, from six

- Model T Fords come in a choice of colors for the first time since 1913, though fenders stubbornly remain black

▲ Opera windows and landau bars adorned Buick's Model 51 Brougham, a $1925 sedan that sold 13,862 copies.

▲ The top-selling '27 Chevrolet was the $695 coach: 239,566 units. Closed cars were still growing in popularity.

▲ All seven Fisher brothers attended groundbreaking ceremonies for the Fisher Building in Detroit, in August 1927. Each of the brothers except Howard (*second from right*) was in the automobile business. GM had bought all the remaining stock in the Fisher Body Company in 1926, but the Fisher name remained on GM cars for years afterward.

New Makes 1926

- Cavalier
- Hertz
- Pontiac
- Saf-T-Cab (taxi)
- Whippet

119

► The last of an era: the '27 Ford Model T. More than 15 million had been built. The Model A was next.

▲ Most 1927s, like this Hudson, had centrally mounted gauges. An F-head engine replaced the L-head Super Six.

▲ In the late Twenties, "boattail" rear ends transformed the look of otherwise ordinary roadsters. Here, a 1927 Essex Speedabout, with six-cylinder power. Price: $700.

1926 Model-Year Production Figures

1. Ford	1,426,612
2. Chevrolet	547,724
3. Buick	266,753
4. Dodge	265,000
5. Hudson/Essex	227,508
6. Willys-Overland/Whippet	182,000
7. Chrysler	135,520
8. Pontiac/Oakland	133,604

Some figures are estimated or calendar year

▲ Legendary stylist Harley Earl earned credit for the new 1927 LaSalle, which had a 75-bhp, 303-cid L-head V-8. GM slotted it between Buick and Cadillac.

▲ Prince William of Sweden (*at wheel*) visited the Nash plant in Kenosha, Wisconsin, in 1927. Scandinavian workers presented him with this newly available Nash Ambassador Six (Model 267) four-door Brougham sedan.

▲ Capacity of the $1475 Nash Advanced Six roadster for '27 was four, but two had to squeeze into the rumble seat. Wheelbase measured 127 inches; power came from a 69-bhp, 278-cid six. Special and Light Six Nashes were smaller.

1927

• General Motors president Alfred Sloan leads the industry toward the annual model change, heralding what will become known as "planned obsolescence," whereby motorists will be encouraged to grow dissatisfied with their cars—and eager to obtain the very latest model

• Passenger-car volume skids to 2,936,533; trucks dip to 464,793 units

• Chevrolet out produces Ford by an enormous margin, but only because the Model T era finally draws to a close

• A small-car trend is evident at the 27th National Automobile Show

• The Studebaker-built, $995 Erskine—"The Little Aristocrat"—debuts with a 146-cid Continental six; it lasts only into 1930

▲ Idle at the moment, this array of cutters at the Hudson axle plant produced ring gears. A single-disc, oil-filled clutch replaced the multidisc unit in 1927.

▲ Dramatic restyling lowered Hudson bodies, led by bullet-shaped headlamps and a taller radiator. A new 289-cid F-head six made 92 bhp. Total 1927 sales: 66,034.

▲ Long known for massive cars, the Marmon company added a Little Marmon 8 in 1927—but it lasted only one season. Shown is a Locke-bodied four-passenger Victoria.

- The Little Marmon and Little Custom Playboy join the Marmon and Jordan lineups, but buyers resist pricey compacts

- LaSalle is created as a companion brand to Cadillac: lower in price ($2496 and up), but comparable in quality

- LaSalle helps establish Harley Earl's Art & Colour Section, giving it a status separate from GM's engineering department

- Reo launches the Flying Cloud series—the first car to use Lockheed's newly developed internal-expanding hydraulic brakes

- The $1195 Wolverine is introduced by Reo as a more affordable companion to the Flying Cloud

- Hudson's trusty six-cylinder engine, an L-head, adopts overhead intake valves, creating the new F-head

- Packard and the Little Marmon employ compact hypoid rear axles, which permit a lower body profile

- Carl Breer begins to study auto-related aerodynamics, which will lead to Chrysler's Airflow design and monocoque construction

- Most cars now have four-wheel brakes, air cleaners, oil and gas filters, crankcase vents, mirrors, and automatic windshield wipers

▲ For 1927, Oldsmobile bored its little six to 185 cubic inches, upping output to 47 bhp. Deluxe equipment for this $975 30-E roadster included front/rear bumpers; 2342 were sold.

▲ Crossing the continent with minimal fuel was no problem for the little 1927 Willys-built Whippet four. A Whippet six set a 24-hour endurance record at Indianapolis.

NEVER in the history of fine motor cars have body and chassis lines been so perfectly blended as in the Safety Stutz, with its much lower center of gravity, its greater stability and safety, and its improved roadability and performance.

The Improved New

SAFETY STUTZ

▲ Ads promoted the roadability of the '27 Stutz. Lush, low Weymann Flexible Bodies enhanced its appeal. Thin wires in the safety glass could actually be seen. Black Hawk Speedsters earned 1927 AAA stock-car honors.

◄ A notable feature of the $1635 '27 Velie 60 Royal Sedan was its front door, slanted to match the windshield. Built in Illinois, Velie lasted for two decades: 1909–29.

New Makes 1927

- Brooks
- Calvert
- Erskine
- Falcon-Knight
- LaSalle
- Wolverine

- The Paige-Detroit Motor Car Company is now Graham-Paige Motor Corporation

- Studebaker celebrates its 75th Anniversary; it built carriages before making cars

- GM stockholders receive nearly $135 million in dividends; Chrysler stockholders divvy up a $10 million bounty

- Sharing success, employees now own $20 million in Nash stock

- The final Model T Fords are built, ending an impressive 19-year run

- An all-new Model A Ford is announced on May 25, 1927, but is not unveiled until December as a 1928 model

- Ford built 1,548,478 Model Ts, a record finally beaten by the Volkswagen Beetle

- Hudson develops a single-disc, cork-insert clutch, and keeps that design into the 1950s

- Packard builds a 500-acre proving ground in Utica, Michigan; it includes a 2.5-mile high-speed oval track

▲ New Lovejoy hydraulic shock absorbers and a double-drop frame altered the ride and stance of this $1765 Buick Country Club coupe.

▲ At $1765, buyers couldn't resist this '28 Chevrolet Imperial Landau sedan. This was the first Chevy styled by Harley Earl's Art & Colour Section.

◄ Gear clashing was a common sound until Cadillac launched the synchromesh transmission in 1928, as on the Fisher-bodied Imperial sedan.

▲ Even though Chevrolet was selling nose to nose with Ford's new Model A, salesmen weren't always busy with customers. Engine output rose substantially for 1928 from 26 to 35 bhp.

▲ The five-millionth Chevrolet was a coach—Chevy's top '28 seller by far.

▲ Top GM men pose with Delco-Remy manager C. F. Wilson (*center, front*) in 1928. Flanking Wilson are GM president Alfred Sloan and vice president W. S. Knudsen.

▲ Although Essex was considered a fairly small car, this woman looks tiny at the wheel of the $750 '28 Phaeton.

▲ Maurice Lichtenstein of Chicago won this Essex Speedabout in a "College Humor" art contest.

125

▲ Customers clamored to see the new Model A Ford, like this $480 roadster.

◄ The $550 Tudor shows the Model A's sweeping hoodline and crowned fenders—like a scaled-down Lincoln.

1927 Model-Year Production Figures

1. Chevrolet	1,001820
2. Ford	367,213
3. Hudson/Essex	276,414
4. Buick	255,160
5. Pontiac/Oakland	188,168
6. Willys-Overland/Whippet	188,000
7. Chrysler	182,195
8. Dodge	180,000

Some figures are estimated or calendar year

1928

- The new Model A Ford has a conventional three-speed gearbox, 40-bhp L-head four, four-wheel brakes, and shatterproof glass

- An estimated 10 million people flock to see the Model A within 36 hours of its unveiling

- Horsepower and compression-ratio increases are the news at the 28th National Automobile Show

- Passenger-car output rebounds to 3,775,417; truck production climbs to 583,342 units

- Car prices continue falling, while eight-cylinder engines grow in popularity

- Chevy wins again: 1,193,212 cars to Ford's 607,592. But its lead will be short-lived as Ford Model A production increases

▲ Aircraft developer Eddie Stinson poses with his favorite plane and a brand-new $735 Essex Coach. Celebrity endorsements became popular during the Twenties.

▲ Spare tires moved to front fenders during the Twenties, giving this 1928 LaSalle convertible coupe a dashing air. Model-year LaSalle production came to 14,806 units.

▲ The top-line 1928 Nash, as before, was the Advanced Six, on a 121- or 127-inch chassis with a 70-bhp, 279-cid six. This $1775 rumble-seat coupe sports paint-matching wheels.

◄ A taller radiator distinguished this 1928 Nash two-door sedan. Nash production was up sharply to 138,137 units for the calendar year—and wouldn't be topped until 1949.

• Chrysler Corporation launches the Plymouth brand in July, DeSoto in August, both as 1929 models

• Plymouth is the only Chrysler brand with four-cylinder engines

• Chrysler Corporation takes over Dodge Brothers on July 30, with K. T. Keller at the helm

• Dodge offers a pair of sixes to replace the former four: 208 cid in Standard and Victory models, 224 cid in the Senior model

• Chrysler Corporation turns out 360,398 cars, up from 137,668 in 1928

• Graham-Paige automobiles emerge, with four-, six-, or eight-cylinder engines; most have a four-speed transmission

• Chandler adopts a Westinghouse-built vacuum brake system that cuts pedal pressure by two-thirds

• Cadillac uses safety glass for side and rear windows as well as windshield

• Cadillac introduces synchromesh transmission—no more need for double-clutching to change gears

▲ Folding down the windshield enhanced the sporty flavor of the patriotically named Oakland All-American Six Sports Roadster. At $1075, it boasted a bigger 211-cid six.

▲ Partially obscured in this picture, extra passengers are relegated to the jump seat. This Oldsmobile Sport Coupe had a 197-cid, 55-bhp six and a base price of $1145.

▲ European styling touches flavored the extravagant 1928 Stutz "BB" line, including the Versailles and Biarritz models. Copious racing success earned the brand's lighter Blackhawk model the title of "America's fastest production car."

- Hudson is first with a hard-rubber, steel-core steering wheel, containing finger scallops around the rim

- LaSalle has a 303-cid V-8; big-brother Cadillac turns to a 341-cid version

- Lincoln's V-8 grows to 385 cubic inches, but delivers the same 90 horsepower as its smaller predecessor

- The new President boasts Studebaker's first eight-cylinder engine, the 313-cid mill boasts an even 100 horsepower

- A number of makes offer factory-installed radios for the first time

- Martin minicar prototypes appear, aiming to be the smallest practical car on the market; production never begins

- Combined Ford Motor Company assets swell to nearly a $1 billion; Model A development costs run $250 million

- Studebaker takes over control of Buffalo-based Pierce-Arrow

- Milestones: James Ward Packard dies, Buick celebrates 25th anniversary, coast-to-coast bus service is first offered

▲ Bulging side panels on the restyled 1929 Buick made it appear "pregnant" to harsher critics. This $1525 Sport Sedan featured twin electric wipers.

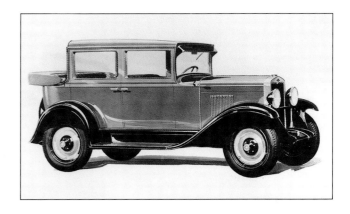

▶ The rarest '29 Chevrolet (300 built) was the $725 Landau Imperial sedan, with convertible fold-down rear quarter.

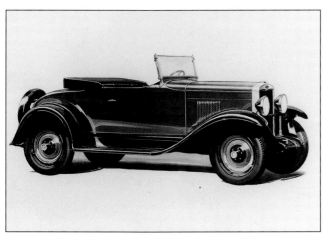

▲ Under the hood of the '29 Chevrolet lurked a new 46-bhp "Stovebolt Six." The $525 roadster sold 27,988 copies.

▲ For 1929, Chrysler debuted a major styling change, led by the 75 series: 75 horsepower, 75 mph. This is the $1550 road-ster, of which 6414 were built.

▲ Chrysler launched a new marque for 1929: DeSoto. This sharp Roadster Espanol sold for $845. DeSoto's first-year output topped 80,000.

▼ DeSotos undergo inspection at the Highland Park, Michigan, plant.

▲ Introduced on August 4, 1928, DeSoto offered seven models on a 109.75-inch wheelbase. All models, including this $845 Phaeton, had hydraulic brakes.

▲ Double-daters enjoy an $895 Essex convertible, named Challenger for '29. Its 160-cid six produced 55 bhp.

◄ A "Rumble Roof" gave the impression of shelter to rear occupants in a '29 Essex coupe. A graceful exit wasn't easy.

▲ Leather (or leatherette) went on the back and top of Ford's Briggs-bodied Fordor "leatherback" sedan. Far more complex than the primitive Model T, the Model A cost more, $625 in this case—but buyers appreciated the extra refinement.

1928 Model-Year Production Figures

1. Chevrolet	1,193,212
2. Ford	607,592
3. Willys-Overland/Whippet	315,000
4. Hudson/Essex	282,203
5. Pontiac/Oakland	244,584
6. Buick	221,758
7. Chrysler	160,670
8. Nash	138,137

Some figures are estimated or calendar year

New Makes 1929

- Blackhawk
- Cord
- Fargo
- Marquette
- Roosevelt
- Ruxton
- Viking
- Windsor

1929

- Automobile sales start the year strong, but "The Roaring Twenties" grind to a halt on "Black Thursday"

- The "Great Depression" begins with the stock market crash of October 29, and grips the nation until the outbreak of WWII

- Automobile production rises on the strength of early year sales, to 4,445,178 units; truck output climbs to 881,909

- The millionth Ford Model A is built, followed by the two-millionth only a few months later

- Ford's market share doubles to 32 percent, sufficient to reclaim the annual sales title from surging Chevrolet

- Chevrolet counters Ford's Model A dreadnought with a new overhead-valve six good for 46 horsepower

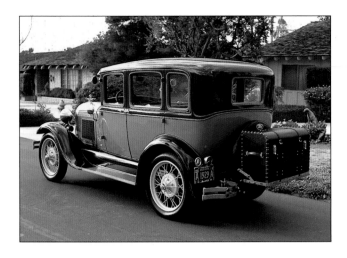

▲ Small rear side windows identified the Murray-bodied Ford Town Sedan; other Fordors had blank quarters.

▲ Over-the-shoulder visibility was better in the five-window Model A coupe than in some of its Ford mates.

▲ Henry Ford's son Edsel created the formal-looking Town Car, with an open chauffeur's compartment. At $1400, it cost more than twice as much as any other Ford Model A.

◄ Bright colors could be had on Model As. This $670 Model A cabriolet was Ford's first true convertible since the Model T Coupelet. External trunks were a popular add-on.

• Oldsmobile introduces an upmarket companion brand, the $1595 Viking V-8; it survives only two model years

• Buick introduces the $1000 Marquette at midyear; it's an early 1930 model with an L-head six-cylinder engine

• Duesenberg announces the Model J, with a 265-bhp, dual-overhead-cam, straight-eight engine; it's huge, fast, and expensive

• A Duesenberg Model J reaches 116 mph in tests at the Indianapolis Speedway

• Even nonmotor enthusiast Americans soon come to appreciate the Duesenberg-inspired accolade "its a Duesy"

• The new luxurious Cord L-29 features front-wheel drive; so does the recently introduced, equally luxurious, Ruxton

• Ruxton's developers have trouble finding a production facility; eventually farm out production to Moon Motor Car Company

• Ruxton, one of few cars without running boards, is soon known for its narrow Wood-Lite-supplied headlights (actually an option)

• The Marmon-built Roosevelt and Stutz-built Blackhawk appear; both less powerful and expensive than their big brothers

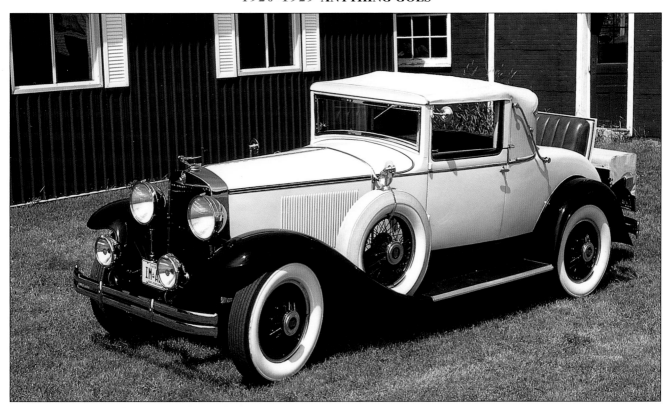

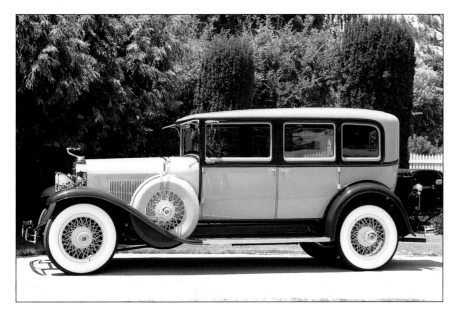

▲ A 322-cid, L-head straight-eight engine powered this '29 Model 827 rumble-seat cabriolet, but Graham-Paige also offered six-cylinder cars. The marque had bowed a year earlier.

◄ Even in sedan form, the 1929 LaSalle had graceful lines. The Series 328 line borrowed its synchromesh transmission and safety glass from upmarket big-brother Cadillac.

- DeSoto is officially on the market with a 174.9-cid, L-head six that cranks out 55 bhp

- More than 80,000 DeSotos are sold—a first-year record for a new make

- The Franklin "le Pirate" models have concealed running boards under the doors

- Dual taillights begin to appear, but some makes keep single lights well into the '30s

- Chrysler incorporates downdraft carburetors for improved fuel distribution

- Auburn exhibits an aluminum Cabin Speedster with an aircraft-inspired interior

- The Fargo line of commercial sedans and wagons is introduced by Chrysler

- The Kleiber Motor Company experiments with diesel truck engines

- Aerocar introduces a "house trailer"; auto-camping has become a popular pastime

- Nearly 90 percent of all cars sold are closed models, up from 10 percent in 1919

- Nash develops its first straight-eight engine, it produces 100 horsepower

- Automotive pioneer David Dunbar Buick passes away on March 6

▲ Magnificent is the word for a 1929 Lincoln dual-cowl phaeton.

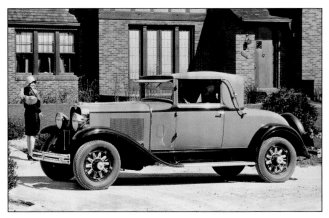

▲ The Nash Standard Six kept single ignition for its L-head engine, standard on the $935 phaeton shown here.

▲ Oldsmobile introduced a costlier companion make for 1929: the Viking V-8. This is the $1595 convertible.

▶ This drawing shows the nearly identical 1930 Viking convertible with the top down. Its 259-cid V-8 produced 80 horsepower.

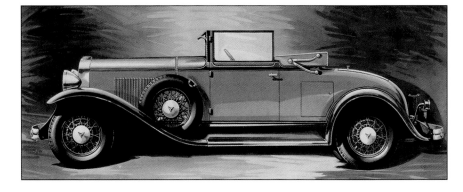

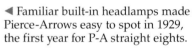

▲ The biggest of the 1929 Packards: the 645 DeLuxe Eight, in extravagant dual-cowl phaeton form.

◄ Familiar built-in headlamps made Pierce-Arrows easy to spot in 1929, the first year for P-A straight eights.

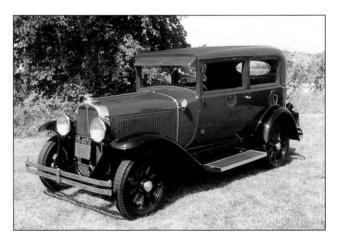

▲ Ready for inspection, Marmon's newly introduced lower-cost, straight-eight Roosevelt. Prices started at $995.

▲ Early '29s had horizontal hood louvers, but complaints of overheating led Pontiac to switch to vertical openings.

▲ This dashing 1929 Stutz Series M roadster wears a LeBaron-designed body. The 322-cid, overhead-cam straight eight worked through a four-speed gearbox.

▲ Note the unusual cut-down door on this 1929 Stutz M dual-cowl phaeton. Known for sport and luxury, Stutz offered an appetizing selection of bodies.

◄ Launched in '29, the sleek Ruxton had a straight eight with a twist: front-wheel drive. This made possible the low overall height.

1929 Model-Year Production Figures	
1. Ford	1,507,132
2. Chevrolet	1,328.605
3. Hudson/Essex	300,392
4. Willys-Overland/Whippet	242,000
5. Pontiac/Oakland	211,054
6. Buick	196,104
7. Dodge	124,557
8. Nash	116,622
Some figures are estimated or calendar year	

▼ The low-roofed, fabric body by Weymann on this '29 Stutz Monte Carlo hints at chopped hot rods of later vintage.

CHAPTER FOUR

1930-1941

SURVIVAL OF THE FITTEST

"Brother, can you spare a dime?" Those words became a veritable anthem of the Great Depression, as millions of workers hit the street.

Americans were confused, downhearted, and downtrodden. After three rough years, voters ousted President Hoover in favor of Franklin Delano Roosevelt's "New Deal." Industrial output sank to half the 1929 level, and one-fourth of the workforce was jobless. Soup lines fed the hungry.

Even as the Civilian Conservation Corps (CCC) and Works Progress Administration (WPA) provided government-sponsored jobs, the Great Depression lingered on. In 1937, FDR still saw "one third of the nation ill-housed, ill-clad, ill-nourished."

Movies and radio tried to boost morale. "Art deco" design added brightness to daily life. Such utopian concepts as "technocracy" and Huey Long's "share our wealth" campaign drew legions of followers.

The Dust Bowl of middecade added more misery, sending thousands of "Okies" on the road. Labor strife culminated in a bitter sit-down strike at GM's Fisher Body plant in 1936–37. Then a heated battle between Ford-employed thugs and strikers erupted a few months later.

Hard times made the used car king, and an astounding number of families somehow did manage to keep a motor running. The Depression notwithstanding, car ownership was still a big part of the "American Dream." Cowboy-philosopher Will Rogers noted that America was the first country "to go to the poor house in an automobile."

Both style and technology made great strides. Ford issued the first V-8 engine in a low-cost car. Plymouth became a major player. Cadillac and Marmon launched magnificent V-16 models. Cars became lower, streamlined (like the latest locomotives), and easier to handle. Graham introduced a supercharger. Auburn submitted its sumptuous Speedsters, while Cord debuted its timeless "coffin-nosed" 810/812.

Gearshifts became synchronized. Seats broadened to hold three. Built-in trunks were adopted. Independent front suspensions helped smooth the bumps. Even Henry Ford finally gave in to hydraulic brakes. By 1940, sealed-beam headlights led the way, gear-shifts rode the steering column, and running boards were rapidly becoming extinct.

Not every innovation lasted long. Freewheeling faded after a few years—in part because some states made such "coasting" illegal. Startix units enjoyed a brief fling. Overdrive boosted the economy of 1934 Chrysler Airflows and spread to other makes, but never quite captured the imagination.

As for automatic shifting, Reo's "Self Shifter" of 1933–34 drew modest attention. GM's Safety Automatic Transmission made a smaller splash. When Oldsmobile introduced Hydra-Matic for 1940, the public was interested, but widespread adoption wouldn't come until after the war.

The number of significant makes slimmed from about 60 in 1929 to 18 in 1941. A brief stab at minicars started with the American Austin and its Bantam successor; later came the Crosley.

Paved roads more than doubled in a decade, as the automobile culture grew. Drive-ins lured moviegoers. Tourist courts dotted the landscape.

At the New York World's Fair of 1939, GM's Futurama predicted the world of the Sixties, including 100-mph superhighways. The modern age was imminent, but Americans had to face another world war before enjoying all its fruits.

1930

- As the Great Depression grips the nation, industry volume skids to 2,910,187 passenger cars and 599,991 trucks

- Ford continues to top Chevrolet in total output—1,140,710 cars to 640,980—but Chevy's "Stovebolt Six" is gaining popularity

- A sign of things to come, many General Motors cars sport rakish tilted windshields

- Looking upmarket, Oakland abandons its six-cylinder engine, turns to a much-anticipated but unreliable V-8

- Studebaker pioneers "freewheeling," a drivetrain system that allows clutchless shifts after leaving first gear

- Cadillac ups the power ante, offering V-12 and V-16 engines, plus power brakes

◄ The American Austin—based on its British counterpart—was built in Pennsylvania. The S465 coupe seated two and rode a short 75-inch wheelbase.

► Americans weren't ready for mini-cars when Austin arrived. Annual output reached 8558, then skidded. This roadster weighed in at 1100 pounds.

◄ A beltline molding and lower stance minimized Buick's "pregnant" look, as on this 1930 Series 40 phaeton. Its 258-cid six developed 81 bhp. Priced at $1310, only 1100 were sold.

▲ Chevrolet offered one 1930 series: AD Universal. Shown is the $615 Sport Coupe; 45,311 were sold. The rear window lowered for ventilation or communication with people in the rumble seat. The 194-cid six had 50 bhp.

▲ Launched in 1929 as a '30 model, Buick's Marquette lasted only one season despite a production run of 35,007 units. Smaller than a Buick, it had a 67.5-bhp L-head six.

▲ To trounce such rivals as Packard and Peerless, Cadillac launched a V-16 for 1930. The 452-cid engine made 165 horsepower—second only to Duesenberg. Some 33 V-16 variants were listed, starting at a pricey $5350.

- A front-drive Gardner is announced (to join existing rear-drive lineup), but new model never advances beyond protype stage

- Cadillac, Chrysler, Dodge, LaSalle, Marmon, and Roosevelt cars are available prewired for radio installation

- A new-look Model A Ford debuts in January with higher hood-to-body lines, smaller balloon tires

- Chrysler's new "Steelweld" bodies all but abandon wood components

- Hupmobile claims to be the first American-built car with an oil cooler

- Franklins sport new styling and a reworked supercharged engine

- The "Great Eight" Hudsons are introduced as company's sixes depart

- Cadillac engines have automatic hydraulic tappet-clearance adjustment to reduce maintenance and noise

- The American Austin Car Company is formed to build a variant of the British Austin Seven in the U.S.

- The National Automobile Chamber of Commerce plans to scrap 360,000 obsolete vehicles to combat the "used car problem"

▲ Launched in 1929 by E. L. Cord, the Classic Cord L-29 featured a 125-bhp, 299-cid straight eight driving the front wheels. Long and low, it rode a stately 137.5-inch chassis. This 1930 dual-cowl phaeton wears custom coachwork by Murphy.

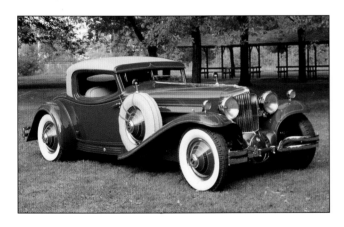

▲ Celebrities loved the L-29 Cord. An appetizing array of custom bodies included this coupe by Sakhnoffsky, sporting unique roof and window treatments.

▲ An L-head eight drove this $985 Model CF roadster, but DeSotos also offered more economical six-cylinder engines: first 175 cubic inches, later enlarged to 190 cid.

- Graham-Paige uses rubber-cushioned springs and drops the "Paige" suffix from car badges

- Chrysler's new "CJ" is the "lowest-priced six ever to bear the Chrysler name"

- DeSoto's K-Series starts the season, but is replaced in May by the CK Finer Six

- A Speedster is DuPont's most notable model; it features cut-down doors, narrow headlights, and a $5000+ price tag

- Willys adds a new straight-eight engine; Whippet disappears early in 1931

- Essex and Hudson launch "Sun Sedan," a two-door convertible sedan body style

▲ Coachbuilder Murphy supplied the body for this 1930 Duesenberg Model J
Torpedo Berline. Bare chassis began at $5000, bodywork could double that price.

◄ Company founder William Crapo
Durant was forced to sell his stake in
the Durant Motor Company when his
loans were called in by debtors left
cash strapped by the stock market col-
lapse of 1929. This Model 407 roadster
was largely unchanged for 1930.

1930 Model-Year Production Figures	
1. Ford	1,140,710
2. Chevrolet	640,980
3. Buick	181,743
4. Studebaker	123,216
5. Hudson/Essex	113,898
6. Plymouth	108,350
7. Dodge	90,755
8. Chrysler	77,881
Some figures are estimated or calendar year	

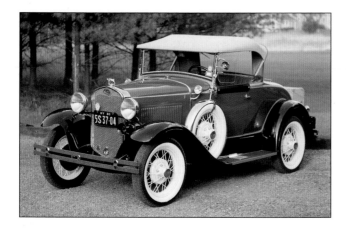

▲ Ford's Model A earned a bit of touch-up work in 1930. Fenders were lower and wider, the hood taller, wheels smaller. DeLuxe roadsters sported cowl lights and twin taillights.

▲ Eight-cylinder Hupmobiles, like this $1695 1930 Model C coupe, were built in Detroit, sixes in Cleveland. Riding a 121-inch wheelbase, the C boasted 267 cid, 100 bhp.

▲ Longer and costlier, 1930 LaSalles rode a 134-inch wheelbase; 14,986 were produced. Six Fleetwood bodies were offered, plus Fisher coachwork, as on the $2590 Model 340 soft-top shown.

▶ A Twin-Ignition Six powered this $1365 rumble-seat roadster, but Nash also added a Twin-Ignition Eight for 1930. Eights rode a longer wheelbase and had a dashboard starter button.

1931

- As the economy stalls, output plummets to 2,038,183 cars and 434,176 trucks

- Automakers, in coping with the deepening Depression, are unsure whether to risk creating new models or to cut prices on existing ones

- Chevrolet squeaks past Ford's model-year production, but both sink to nearly 620,000 units; Buick remains a distant third

- Plymouth makes a move, up from seventh to fourth place in production race

- A milestone is reached, the 50-millionth American motor vehicle is built

- A National Automobile Chamber of Commerce recommendation suggests grouping all new-model introductions in November or December, to stimulate fall/winter buying

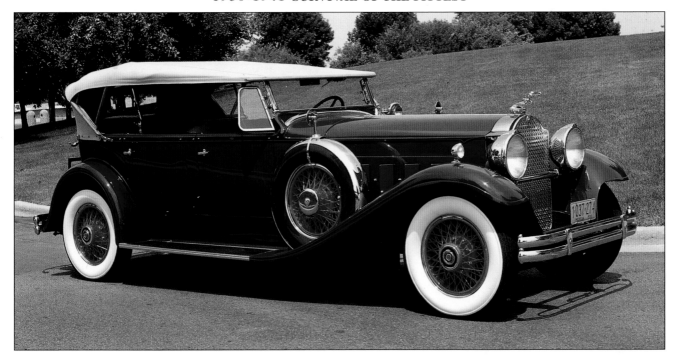

▲ Packard offered the Sport Phaeton in Standard, Custom, or DeLuxe Eight form for 1930. All models had straight-eight engines: 320 or 385 cid. A tiny number of racy Speedster Eights were built on a shortened Sport Phaeton chassis.

▲ Coachwork by Weymann, featuring a chopped roofline, made the $4495 1930 Monte Carlo one of the most celebrated Stutz custom sedans.

▲ With side curtains snapped in place, this $895 Oakland roadster was reasonably well-bundled-up for winter in 1930. The 85-horsepower, 250-cid V-8, with a 180-degree crankshaft, tended to vibrate badly at higher speeds.

- Chrysler launches its first eight-cylinder engines; they're L-head straight units

- Marmon launches a new Sixteen with styling by Walter Dorwin Teague

- Oakland appears for the last time but companion make Pontiac continues

- Startix is available on several makes—it recranks the engine in the event of a stall

- A freewheeling clutch is offered on Auburn, Chrysler, DeSoto, DeVaux, Dodge, Essex, Graham, Hudson, Hupmobile, Lincoln, Marmon, Peerless, Pierce-Arrow, Plymouth, Studebaker, and Willys

- Oldsmobile offers a "Synchro-Mesh" transmission for smoother, clash-free shifting—it will eventually become standard on most makes

- Restyled Auburns grow stylistically similar to Cord and Duesenberg

- A Buick-powered racer qualifies for the Indianapolis 500 Memorial Day Race

- Packard and several other makes offer dashboard shock-absorber adjustment

- The last Model A Ford is built in November to be replaced by the first low-priced V-8

▲ Cadillac offered a catalog of 30 different Fleetwood-supplied bodies for its 1931 V-16, priced from $5350 to $15,000. Note the wire wheels and extra-cost wind wings on this rumble-seat roadster.

▲ Chryslers for '31 featured "Floating Power" (rubber engine mounts) and freewheeling. In addition to six-cylinder models, Chrysler offered new straight eights in four sizes.

▲ At $575, a 1931 Chevrolet DeLuxe Sport Coupe with optional rumble seat cost only $30 more than a business coupe. Wheelbase stretched 109 inches.

- Chrysler's "Floating Power" engine mounts debut, initially on Plymouth, which claims its four has the smoothness of a six

- The National Automobile Chamber of Commerce recommends a 90-day/4000-mile warranty for new cars

- Graham adds a low-cost "Prosperity Six" to its line, but the economy has few buyers feeling prosperous enough to purchase one

- Lincoln is one of the few automakers to raise prices, defying a trend; the Model K rides a longer wheelbase than the old model

- Stutz experiments with a supercharged engine, but turns instead to a 32-valve twincam head for its DV32 model

- Two new straight-eight engines join the Reo list—the bigger one goes into the impressive streamlined Royale

- Twin-Ignition Nash Eights adopt Bijur automatic chassis-lubrication systems

- Carryover Plymouths are replaced midyear by an all-new PA-Series

- Willys-Knight continues in production, but Willys now pushes conventional engines

- A retractable hardtop convertible is patented by B. B. Ellerbeck

◀ Traction could be troublesome when driving an L-29 Cord, shown here in $2495 cabriolet form. Front-wheel drive was unproven, thus difficult to sell.

▶ The Durant line shrank to two body styles for '31, priced from $675 to $775, with a four or six. After just 7270 sales in '31, the firm folded early in '32.

▶ Ford added a Town Sedan in 1931, featuring a slanted windshield and cowl lamps. Priced at $630, it found a place in the hearts of 65,447 buyers.

▼ Despite the romantic aura of boattail bodies, Hudson's Greater Eight sport roadster—with an 87-bhp—was built for only six months.

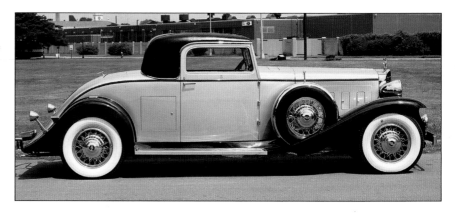

▲ Lincoln launched the massive Model K for '31, among them this $4600 dual-cowl Sport Phaeton on a 145-inch chassis. A 385-cid V-12 produced 120 bhp.

▲ After five years of research, Marmon debuted the Sixteen. Guaranteed to do 100 mph, this coupe cost $5220. About 390 Sixteens were built between 1931 and 1933.

▲ Boattail speedsters were the rage in 1931, exemplified by this dapper Packard. Engines provided either 100- or 120-bhp.

1931 Model-Year Production Figures	
1. Chevrolet	619,554
2. Ford	615,455
3. Buick	138,965
4. Studebaker	96,173
5. Pontiac	84,708
6. Plymouth	75,510
7. Willys	65,800
8. Chrysler	65,500
Some figures are estimated or calendar year	

▲ Amos Northup designed the streamlined 1931 Reo Royale.
Straight-eight Royales wore Murray bodies on a 131- or 135-inch
wheelbase. Pictured here is the handsome $2745 Victoria coupe.

◄ New versions
of Reo's mid-
price Flying
Cloud, the 6-25
six and 8-30
eight, borrowed
elements of
Royale styling
but stuck to flat
radiators. An
80-bhp version
of the six drove
this $1705 Model
20 Sport Sedan.

1932

• As the Depression deepens, vehicle
production drops to the lowest level since
1918: 1,186,185 cars and 245,284 trucks

• An astounding 12 million American
would-be workers are unemployed

• Franklin D. Roosevelt is elected President

• Olds and Packard get automatic chokes

• Ford's eagerly awaited 221-cid, 65-bhp
flathead V-8 arrives; production of an
upgraded four-cylinder model continues

• Chevrolet ends the model year in the
number-one spot; despite building only
313,404 cars, well ahead of Ford's 210,824

• Plymouth reaches number three for the
first time, ahead of Buick and Pontiac

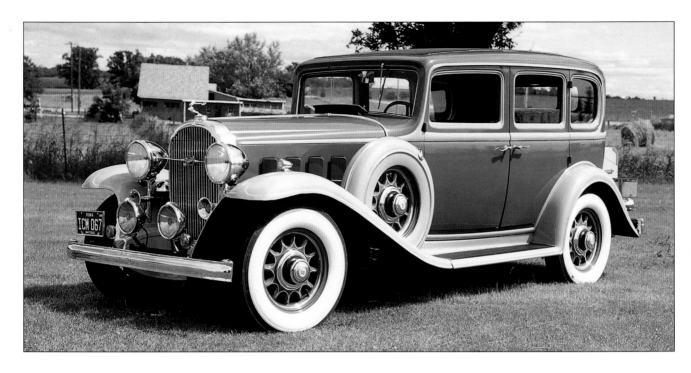

▲ All Buicks had straight-eight engines in 1932, including this Series 60 sedan. "Wizzard Control" and "Silent Second SynchroMesh" were new features.

▲ Cadillac's 353-cid V-8 was boosted to 115 bhp for 1932, as bodies grew more rounded. Eights sold far better than Twelves; V-16s were very rare.

▲ Many consider the 1932 Confederate models, including the Sport Coupe, one of the sharpest Chevys of all time. This DeLuxe with sidemount tires cost $505.

◄ Long rear-quarter windows gave this '32 Chevrolet Confederate DeLuxe coupe a roomy look. This body saw 7656 units built. A synchromesh transmission was new.

- Pierce-Arrow drops Eights, launches two new V-12 engines boasting quieter hydraulically operated valve lifters

- Studebaker introduces the low-priced companion Rockne ($585–$695); Hudson launches the Essex Terraplane ($425–$610)

- Chrysler focuses on silent running, advertises quieter fans, air intakes, and exhaust systems

- Lower-effort vacuum-actuated clutches appear on Buick, Cadillac, Chrysler, DeSoto, Dodge, and LaSalle models

- Interior-mounted sun visors gain popularity, will gradually replace bulky-looking outside units

- Auburn introduces a V-12 series, it features a "Dual-Ratio" Columbia rear axle that shows up later on other models

- Unemployed workers hold a "hunger march" at Ford's Rouge assembly plant after layoffs; four are killed in rioting

- Buick's "Wizard Control" combines an automatic clutch with freewheeling; other makes offer similar setups

- Cadillac adopts softer, more-rounded styling, boosts V-8 output to 115-horsepower, a gain of 20

▲ DeSoto launched an "All New Six" SC series in 1932, here the Custom roadster with a 75-bhp, 211.5-cid engine. A 77-bhp straight eight was also sold, but dropped after '32.

▲ The $545 DeLuxe V-8 phaeton had cowl lights and pinstripes; a Standard phaeton cost $50 less. Production of both versions totaled only 2705 units.

▲ A Ford Sport Coupe (*shown*) had a rumble seat; regular three-window coupes didn't. Four-cylinder cars cost $50 less than their V-8 cousins.

▲ Graham offered a variety of six- and eight-cylinder models in 1932, including this $1225 Special Eight coupe—plus a new Blue Streak Eight.

- The last L-29 Cords are offered—the Indiana-based marque will disappear temporarily, returning in 1936

- Three Essex series are listed: Standard, Pacemaker, and Terraplane; the latter is destined to help save the Hudson brand

- A supercharged, air-cooled V-12 with 150-horsepower is available in Franklins, initially in the new Airman series

- Hupmobile Eights are styled by Raymond Loewy; the dramatic shape doesn't translate directly into impressive sales

- The new Twin Six Packard boasts a 160-bhp V-12, while the Light Eight gives Packard a lower-priced model

- Ab Jenkins drives a Pierce-Arrow V-12 prototype 2710 miles in 24 hours at the Bonneville Salt Flats in Utah

- Plymouth offers its last four-cylinders; the lineup is bolstered by a convertible sedan and seven-passenger sedan

- Pontiac sales sag; William S. "Big Bill" Knudsen is named general manager

- Nash introduces the Ambassador Eight, it rides atop a 142-inch wheelbase

- Lincoln adds a V-12 "KB" Series

▲ A $1195 Hudson Special Coupe, part of the '32 Greater Eight Standard line, cost $100 more than a regular coupe, and sported deluxe exterior fittings. Bored to 254 cid, Hudson's straight eight now cranked out 101 horses.

▲ "Cannon Ball" Baker, well-known for transcontinental runs, drove this 1932 Hudson Standard sedan in record time between Ohio cities. With several models capable of speeds over 90 mph, Hudson frequently staged stunts of this type.

▲▼ Designer Raymond Loewy drew Hupmobile's 1932 F-222 (*above*) and I-226 Eight (*below*), featuring vee'd grilles, and sloping windshields.

▲ One of seven 1932 models, this 130-inch-wheelbase LaSalle convertible coupe sold for $2545. All 3386 '32 LaSalles built used a 353-cid V-8.

▲ Packard lowered its bodies in 1932 and launched a Twin Six (V-12). This $1940 Series 900 Coupe-Roadster was part of the new Light Eight line.

▲ "Syncro-Safety Shift," transmission with a dash-mounted lever, was new on the '32 Nash. This is a $1785 Advanced Eight Victoria coupe.

▲ Created as a showpiece by designer Philip Wright, the Pierce Silver Arrow claimed to be "in 1933 the car of 1940." Five were built; one paced the Indy 500.

1932 Model-Year Production Figures	
1. Chevrolet	313,404
2. Ford	210,824
3. Plymouth	186,106
4. Hudson/Essex	57,550
5. Buick	56,790
6. Pontiac	45,340
7. Nash	30,834
8. Willys	27,800
Some figures are estimated or calendar year	

◀ This Pierce-Arrow Eight coupe, on a 137-inch wheelbase with a 125-bhp, 366-cid engine, cost $2985 in 1932. Biggest news was the availability of a V-12.

▲ Nash offered a rumble-seat coupe in each of its many model lines for 1932, except for the long-wheelbase Ambassador Eight. Ads touted the Second Series' "slip-stream body" and "beavertail" sloped back panel.

▲ Jazzy striping and a low windshield must have made this 1932 Plymouth PB "Collegiate Special" Sport Roadster a hot number on campus. Rated at 65-bhp, the L-head was Plymouth's last four until the Seventies.

▲ A new 135-inch platform carried this '32 Studebaker President Eight convertible roadster, in $1750 basic or $1855 "State" trim. Its 337-cid engine made 122 bhp. Stude also offered Dictator and Commander Eights.

▲ Stutz revived the old Bearcat name for a new line, topped by this stubby $5895 Super Bearcat on a special 116-inch wheelbase—guaranteed to reach 100 mph.

1933

- Chevrolet tops Ford in production by a sizable margin; Plymouth ranks a solid third; Dodge moves up to fourth, passing Pontiac and Buick

- Continental debuts as the only major new make; descended from DeVaux, it survives for about a year in the weak economy

- Aerodynamic styling and streamlining are the hot new design trends at the 33rd National Automobile Show

- In May, Reo introduces its "Self Shifter," a semiautomatic transmission that's controlled by a T-handle mounted under the dash

- New technical innovations for 1933 include valve-seat inserts, independent front suspensions, and "reflex" glass taillights

- Studebaker falls into receivership and slips to 14th place in production, company chairman Albert R. Erskine resigns

▲ The sparkling lines of a 1933 Auburn Salon Twelve Dual-Ratio Phaeton Sedan failed to translate into strong sales, as only 7939 Auburns were built this year.

▲ American Austin prices were cut in 1933, down to $275 for the business coupe and $315 for a roadster. Just 4726 were built, and fewer yet in '34.

▲ Fresh styling by Harley Earl gave this 1933 Cadillac V-16 Victoria skirted fenders and a unique vee'd grille, on a long 149-inch wheelbase. Note the elegant four-bar bumper.

▲ Kinship with the legendary Auburn-Cord-Duesenberg empire seems bizarre, but E. L. Cord bought Checker Taxi in 1933. A 98-bhp Lycoming straight eight powered the '33 cabs.

▲ Chevrolet's two-seat roadster was gone in 1933, and its rumble-seat mate fading, as buyers turned to cabriolets. Two Chevy series were sold: a Mercury and upmarket Eagle (*shown*).

▲ GM's 1933 models featured "No-Draft Ventilation" (pivoting wind wings), developed by Fisher Body.

◄ This 1916 Chevrolet was driven to Chicago's Century of Progress, where the 1933 Chevy coach was built in a plant at the fair's GM building.

• GM president Alfred Sloan combines Chevy and Pontiac manufacturing to cut costs, then merges Buick, Olds, and Pontiac sales divisions, so dealers must sell all three

• Power-assisted brakes are offered on various makes, most are vacuum

• General Motors's Fisher division offers "No-Draft Ventilation," with pivoting front ventwings to control airflow

• Competition forces Ford to finally succumb to annual model changes

• Cadillac limits the sale of V-16 models to 400 per year—but sells only 125

• The nation's first drive-in theater opens in Camden, New Jersey

• Roy Chapin returns as president of Hudson after a stint in the Hoover Administration

• Willys-Overland, reorganized after bankruptcy, pins its future on the small 100-inch-wheelbase Model 77; production is initially under court supervision

• C.L. McCuen named president of Olds; Harlow H. Curtice is president of Buick

• The National Automobile Dealers Association (NADA) publishes its first *Official Used Car Guide*

153

▲ The cheapest DeSoto for 1933 was the $665 business coupe. Prices were cut as production hit an all-time low: 24,896 units. The straight eight was gone, but the 218-cid six made 82 horsepower—five more than the previous year's eight.

▼ A vee'd grille was new to LaSalle for '33, as was GM's No-Draft Ventilation. This Series 345C RS coupe, complete with rumble seat, sold for $2245.

▲ Gracefully restyled, the '33 Ford got a more potent 75-bhp V-8 and rode a longer 112-inch wheelbase. The $510 DeLuxe roadster had a rumble seat.

▲ Graham's Blue Streak was renamed Custom Eight for 1933, topping the line at $1095. Ads called Graham "The Most Imitated Car on the Road."

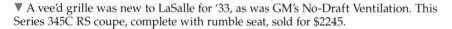

- Stutz, enduring its worst year yet, loses an estimated half-million dollars

- Newly streamlined Cadillacs sport skirted fenders, narrowly vee'd radiators

- The rakishly futuristic Pierce-Arrow Silver Arrow appears, but only five are built

- Hudson's Pacemaker series get new Super Six engines borrowed from the Terraplane

- In its last year, Essex lineup pared to only Terraplane models; all are available with an optional straight-eight engine that sets more than 100 stock-car records

- Low-slung Fords adopt "suicide" (rear-hinged) doors; the V-8 is boosted to 75 horsepower

- Plymouth switches from a four- to a six-cylinder engine, sales zoom

▲ Dietrich supplied bodies for Packard V-12s, including the $6070 Victoria. Standard and Super Eights were also sold. Total '33 Packard output: 4803.

▼ A 175-bhp, 462-cid V-12 went into this '33 Pierce-Arrow convertible sedan. Other models had a 160-bhp V-12 or 135-bhp eight. Total output this year came to only 2298 cars.

▲ Only three Dietrich-bodied Packard Sport Phaetons were built in 1933, on a 147-inch wheelbase, for auto shows. The rear windshield/windows folded.

1933 Model-Year Production Figures	
1. Chevrolet	486,261
2. Ford	334,969
3. Plymouth	298,557
4. Dodge	106,103
5. Pontiac	90,198
6. Buick	46,924
7. Studebaker/Rockne	43,024
8. Hudson/Essex	40,982
Some figures are estimated or calendar year	

▲ Reo trimmed its '33 line, which saw only 4112 sales. The Flying Cloud Eight was dropped, so this S-2 convertible got a 268-cid six. To raise cash, Reo sold bodies to Franklin.

▲ Stutz offered its straight-eight engine with 161 bhp in the DV32 (*shown*) and 133 bhp in the smaller SV16. Production dwindled to fewer than 50 cars for 1932-33.

◄ Hudson's Essex Terraplane debuted in mid 1932 on a new 106-inch wheelbase, with a 70-bhp, 193-cid six. An eight joined in '33. Capable of 80 mph and 25 mpg, Terraplanes earned a deserved "Hill-Buster" nickname.

▲ Willys hyped the 25-30 mpg economy of the 77, plus its 70-mph top speed. The all-steel bodies weighed around 2100 pounds. The lightweight coupes became popular with racers.

1934

- Industry labor disputes are on the rise, increase in frequency, intensity

- Industry production rises dramatically, to 2,270,566 cars and 599,397 trucks

- Chevrolet again tops Ford's calendar-year volume, this time by close to 10 percent

- Graham debuts the Supercharged Custom Eight, the first moderately priced blown engine

- Chrysler launches the daring Airflow, but excellence in engineering fails to tempt customers, who fail to appreciate the car's startling avant-garde design

- LaFayette debuts as the "junior" series from Nash; prices start at a modest $585

- The Brewster nameplate returns after nearly a decade; unique bodies go mainly on Ford V-8 and Buick chassis from 1934 to 1936

▲ Cadillac's 1934 restyling featured pontoon fenders, a slanted grille, and torpedo headlamps. Shown here is a $3045 355-D Eight convertible sedan.

▲ Like other GM makes, Buick adopted "Knee-Action" suspension geometry in '34. A 100-bhp, 278-cid straight eight powered this $1495 Series 60 convertible; 263 were sold.

▲ Chrysler failed to predict public response to the shape of its radical new Airflow. This $1345 CU sedan was the most popular '34 Airflow, accounting for just over 7000 sales.

▶ GM's "Knee-Action" front suspension went into Chevrolet's Master series, but not Standard versions. Only 1974 Sport Roadsters were built in '34.

- The "Hupp Aerodynamic" features a three-piece windshield; Archie Andrews captures control of Hupmobile

- Although the restyled Pierce-Arrow line includes a less-radical Silver Arrow, the company is forced to file for bankruptcy

- Many General Motors cars now available with new "Knee-Action" (independent) front suspension systems

- Terraplane officially becomes a separate make, rising from the ashes of the fallen Essex brand, only sixes are offered

- The last of Nash's big 322-cid straight eights go into Ambassador models this year; all Nash engines have Twin-Ignition

- Ford V-8s earn high praise from "folk hero" outlaws John Dillinger and Clyde Barrow

- Several makes now have integrated radio controls built into the instrument panel

- Cadillac introduces a battery-preserving controlled-current generator

- American Austin builds the last of its small, British-designed cars

- Auburn displays new "Aero-Streamlined" styling; six-cylinder power returns

▲ Dodge lost straight-eight engines for 1934, and never produced an Airflow. This $765 DeLuxe convertible, of which 1239 were built, carried Dodge's new 87-bhp, 218-cid L-head six.

▶ Baseball great Babe Ruth (*left*), division manager Byron C. Foy, and Walter P. Chrysler (*right*) attended a bash to introduce the DeSoto Airflow. Whereas Chrysler also offered an ordinary model, DeSoto sold only the Airflow.

▲ A 95-bhp straight eight drove this '34 Model 67, but the big news at Graham was a Supercharged Custom Eight, blasting out 135 bhp—the first blower on a midprice car.

▶ Wooden station wagons started looking a little dated by 1934. Ford (*shown*) now built its own wagon bodies, but other automakers still turned to outside suppliers.

◀ "Suicide" doors gave this $615 '34 Ford DeLuxe Fordor a jaunty stance. This model saw 102,268 sales.

1934 Model-Year Production Figures

1. Ford	563,921
2. Chevrolet	551,191
3. Plymouth	321,171
4. Dodge	95,011
5. Hudson/Terraplane	85,835
6. Oldsmobile	79,814
7. Pontiac	78,859
8. Buick	71,009

Some figures are estimated or calendar year

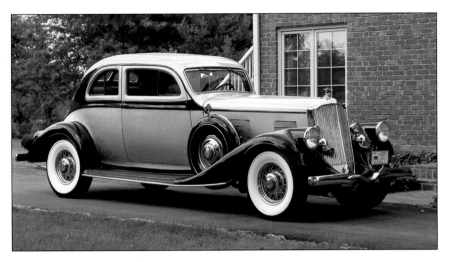

▲ This Plymouth $660 PE DeLuxe sedan sports a Gabriel "form-fit" trunk. It found 108,407 buyers.

▲ For 1934, Pierce-Arrow borrowed the name of its stunning Silver Arrow show car for a less radical fastback coupe, sold as a DeLuxe Eight or Salon Twelve. Bankruptcy brought production to a halt in August.

▶ Rumble seats were fading fast, but some models like this Pontiac still offered them. The 1934 Sport Coupe sold for $725 and featured GM's much-touted new Knee-Action independent front suspension, plus a boost to 84 horsepower.

▶ Produced by Hudson, the Terraplane lost its "Essex" prefix for 1934, and was listed as a separate make. Most examples didn't look quite as curious as this custom-bodied tourer from Australia. Straight eights were gone, but a new 212-cid six boasted 80/85 bhp. Terraplane output: 51,084.

1935

- Showing new vitality, industry output jumps to 3,387,806 cars and 732,005 trucks

- Chevrolet produces 820,253 cars during the model year, easily besting Ford's 48,215

- The Automobile Manufacturers Association skips a season, sponsors the 36th National Automobile show in November; meanwhile, the 35th show is sponsored by the Automobile Merchants Association of New York

- A conventionally styled "Airstream" series joins Chrysler's (and DeSoto's) slow-selling Airflow

- Fords appear at the 1935 National Automobile Show—for the first time in 25 years

- Lower-priced "affordable" cars are the primary trend at this year's Automobile Show; models with fewer features or less power are announced by Chrysler, DeSoto, Graham, Hudson, Hupmobile, Packard, Pontiac, and Reo

▲ Seeking a cheaper heir to the Duesenberg, Gordon Buehrig and August Duesenberg wound up creating a revived Auburn Speedster for 1935—one of the most striking Thirties machines, complete with a supercharged straight eight. At $2245, the new Auburn cost roughly half as much as an average Lincoln.

▲ Buick called its open Series 60 four door a Convertible Phaeton in 1935. It sold for $1675, and its 278-cid eight made 100 bhp. Longer, pricier Series 90 cars boasted a 335-cid 116-bhp eight.

• General Motors cars begin the switch to Fisher all-steel "Turret-Top" roofs, eliminating the customary fabric inserts

• Sedan bodies, particularly "trunkback" versions, grow in popularity; open cars slip slowly into obscurity

• Chevrolet introduces the Suburban Carryall, the first all-steel station wagon, on its panel-delivery light-truck chassis

• Nash offers a new "sealed-in" engine with the manifold cast inside the block

• The failed American Austin firm is taken over by Roy S. Evans, who later will introduce the American Bantam

• Pierce-Arrow is reorganized and resumes auto operations, but fewer than 1000 cars are built by the new organization

• Walter P. Chrysler turns the presidency over to K.T. Keller; F. M. Zeder is the new Chrysler vice chairman

• The stunning Auburn Speedster, destined to spawn replicas decades later, has the 150-bhp Super-Charged engine

• "Second Series" Graham sedans veer from the prior Blue Streak styling; like many, the company is suffering financially

▲ Chevy's upscale Master roadster was gone, and this $465 Standard Sports Roadster saw only 1176 sales in '35. Closed Master DeLuxe models adopted an all-steel "Turret Top."

▲ At a dealership, a '35 Dodge DU four-door sedan would have sold for $760 ($735 as a trunkless fastback). The new Airstream sported a waterfall grille and skirted fenders.

◄ Dodge named its 1935 line the "New Value Six," again with the 218-cid L-head as sole engine. Coupes came with or without a rumble seat, and 22,299 of both types were produced.

► Engine designer Harry Miller teamed with Preston Tucker to enter a set of Miller-Fords in the 1935 Indy 500—the first front-drive Indy cars with all-independent suspension.

◄ Ford greeted 1935 with a new longer, wider, sleeker look, plus front-hinged front doors. This was the final year for wire wheels and outside horns. Woody wagon bodies were built in Ford's Iron Mountain, Michigan, plant. The wagon listed at $670, the DeLuxe five-window coupe for $560.

- A $925 convertible coupe is added to Buick's low-priced Series 40 lineup

- Chevrolets wear sleek new bodies with rakish vee'd windshields

- Dodge's "New Value Six," displaying the "Airstream" look, enjoys a sales surge

- Duesenberg offers the Rollston-bodied, 153.5-inch-wheelbase JN; only 10 are built

- Fords get an all-new look and front-hinged front doors; the convertible sedan is revived

- Six-cylinder engines return to Pontiac after running only straight eights for two years

- Reo loses its eight, fields only six-cylinder models: Flying Cloud and Royale

- Paul G. Hoffman appointed new president of Studebaker

- Hudson expands lineup with six-cylinder models, but still loses market share

- A new 105-bhp, 248-cid straight eight is available in some LaSalle models

- Nashes sport "Aeroform Design" and new hydraulic brakes

- Packard launches its lower-priced One Twenty line, which starts at $980

◄ Built for the Maharajah of Indore, India, this right-drive '35 Duesenberg SJ Speedster-Roadster wore a body by J. Gurney Nutting of England.

▼ Graham's 1935 Special Six, including coupes and a convertible as well as this Touring Sedan, had an 85-bhp engine. Overall sales increased to 15,965.

• A more streamlined Plymouth features new "Chair-Height" seats and carryover 82-horsepower "economy" six

• Studebaker Dictators are available with conventional or Planar independent front suspension—this unwisely named series hangs on through the end of 1937

• Looking for loose change, Oklahoma City installs the first parking meters

• Driver Harry Mack pilots a Ford Model 48 convertible sedan to pace the 1935 Indianapolis 500

• The experimental Stout Scarab—a rear-engined conceptual forerunner of the modern minivan—debuts; it draws much attention, but only five buyers

• Ford repositions passenger seating, markets result as "Center-Poise Ride"

◀ Studebaker fielded three series in 1935: Dictator Six, Commander Eight (*shown*), and President Eight—on 114-, 120-, and 124-inch wheelbases.

▼ Not all sidemounted spares integrated this naturally. Restyled for '35, Plymouth prices now started at $510.

▶ Only a $475 basic coupe (*shown*) and sedan made up the '35 Willys Model 77 line, hyped as "The New Era Car." Note the recessed spare tire.

1935 Model-Year Production Figures	
1. Ford	820,253
2. Chevrolet	548,215
3. Plymouth	350,884
4. Pontiac	178,770
5. Dodge	158,999
6. Oldsmobile	126,768
7. Hudson / Terraplane	101,080
8. Buick	53,249
Some figures are estimated or calendar year	

▲ Tucking a big 320-cid eight into a light Special body, Buick created the spritely Century—perhaps the first "factory hot rod." Note the covered spare on this $1090 Touring Sedan.

◄ Auburn Eights, including this Supercharged cabriolet, got an 852 label for 1936, but changed little. Sixes were called Model 654. Only 1848 cars were built in Auburn's final year.

▲ Only 52 huge Series 90 Cadillacs were built in 1936—and just six Fleetwood V-16 convertible sedans. All except Sixteens had hydraulic brakes.

▲ The most popular Standard '36 Chevy was the $605 Town Sedan, which sold 220,884 units. It had new hydraulic brakes and a steel roof.

▲ Even Checker taxis had "suicide" doors in 1936. Morris Markin regained control of the Checker firm following three years of E. L. Cord ownership.

1936

• Industry output totals 3,669,528 cars and 784,587 trucks for the best year since 1929

• Ford tops Chevrolet in model-year output with a gracefully facelifted line, but lags in calendar-year production 975,238 to 791,812

• Plymouth breaks the half-million production mark for the first time, while Oldsmobile rises to fifth place, just behind Dodge

• The $1275 Lincoln-Zephyr, with a Ford V-8 derived V-12, is the make's first midpriced car

• The front-drive "coffin-nose" Cord 810 debuts three years after the last L-29. Many consider it one of the most beautiful designs of all time

• After building 3206 cars in 1936, Reo abandons the car business to concentrate exclusively on trucks

▲ With a "coffin" nose and crank-up headlights, this dazzling new 1936 Cord 810 could never be mistaken for any lesser auto. A fingertip preselector activated its four-speed gearbox.

  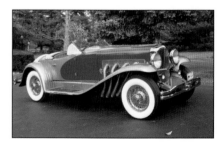

▲ The final DeSoto Airflows came in 1936 as a sedan or this $1095 coupe, which saw only 250 built. Chrysler's version lasted a year longer.

▲ Dodge dubbed its '36s "Beauty Winner," an apt title for this $795 rag-top coupe; 1525 were sold. A convertible sedan was revived at $995.

▲ Apex of the Duesenberg legend was the supercharged, short-wheelbase SSJ Speedster. Only two were built—one each for Clark Gable and Gary Cooper.

- The American Bantam minicar tries to take up where the American Austin left off; prices start at a miser-appealing $295

- Graham abandons eight-cylinder engines, introduces the first supercharged six; bodies are shared with Reo's Flying Cloud

- E. L. Cord returns from England to face government inquiries into his financial dealings; plans for a '37 Auburn fade

- Cord 810s have disappearing headlights, Lycoming V-8, and "Electric Hand" shifting (with a supercharger optional in 1937)

- Many new models have repositioned the handbrake to the driver's left, allowing for a roomier front seat

- Advancing the causes of style and convenience, many cars now have sloping side windows and built-in defrosters

- Buick models now have names as well as numbers and a streamlined steel-roof design courtesy of Harley Earl's Art & Colour group

- The Century mixes Buick's lighter-weight body with the Roadmaster's big engine, creating a "banker's hot rod"

- A less-expensive Series Sixty is added to the Cadillac line; all except the V-16 are fitted with hydraulic brakes

▲ A facelift made the '36 model a prime choice of Ford fans. This $560 DeLuxe roadster sold only 3862 copies; the cabriolets were far more popular.

▲ Add-on skirts added flash to a '36 Ford DeLuxe Touring Sedan. With trunk, a Tudor cost $590. Horns were hidden; steel wheels replaced wires.

▲ Hupmobile trimmed its line for '36 to the 618-G Six (*shown*) and 621-N Eight, rated at 101 and 120 bhp. Hupp then closed down for 18 months.

▲ Fresh "art deco" styling with a tall grille gave 1936 Hudsons a slick look. DeLuxe and Custom Eights (*shown*) were available, plus a Custom Six. Terraplanes sold far better.

◀ Produced by GM Truck and Coach and borrowing Chevrolet components, the General Taxi was similar—though not identical—to the regular 1936 General Motors products.

• The U.S. Dept. of Commerce finds that 54 percent of American families own cars

• Nash Motor Company merges with Kelvinator Corporation to form Nash-Kelvinator Corporation, with George W. Mason as president and Charles W. Nash as chairman

• Willys-Overland Motors is reorganized and moves out of receivership in February; 30,826 Model 77 cars are built

• Nash displays a car with twin travel beds

• The final ill-fated DeSoto Airflow is built; Chrysler's version will last one more season

• Winding down, Stutz offers its last automobiles, including a Bearcat speedster

• The entire Chevrolet car line now benefits from hydraulic brakes, but loses roadster and phaeton variants

• Hupmobile shuts down its assembly plant; it remains closed for 18 months

• The Packard One Twenty's engine is stroked to 282 cid and a convertible sedan is added to the line—production output doubles to 55,042 units

• The "Beauty Winner" Dodge line includes a revived convertible sedan and long-wheelbase sedans/limos

▲ Packard assaulted the upper mid-priced market with the One Twenty in 1935. Aimed at folks who couldn't previously afford a Packard, it was powered by 120-bhp eight for 1936. A '36 convertible like this paced Indy.

▲ Lincoln added the lower-priced, unibody Zephyr for '36, styled by John Tjaarda. This $1320 four door had a 110-bhp, 267-cid V-12; 13,180 were built.

▲ Packard still built high-end models, such as this massive Super Eight dual-cowl phaeton with hang-on trunk, but the cheaper One Twenty stole the sales show.

- Hudsons feature all-new, all-steel bodies

- A single 105-bhp eight powers all LaSalles

- Nash debuts lower-cost, six-cylinder "400" models; prices start at $675

- "Hill Holder" clutch is introduced by Studebaker; with the pedal depressed, the car will not roll backward on a hill

- Studebaker drops the Commander

- Reo drops Self Shifter, offers overdrive

- Redesigned Pierce-Arrow is billed as the "World's Safest Car," but sales still slip

- A supercharged Graham wins the Gilmore-Yosemite Economy Sweepstakes, recording a miserly 26.66 mpg

▲ Pierce-Arrow prices started at $3115 in 1936. Eight-cylinder models rose to 150 bhp. With overdrive, this $3795 Model 1602 Club Berline Twelve might nudge 100 mph.

▲ Even if ad claims of "America's Finest Six" were true, Reo neared extinction, building only trucks after 3206 cars for 1936. The final Flying Clouds came basic or DeLuxe.

◄ No other 1936 automobile could be mistaken for the radical Stout Scarab, created by William B. Stout. Only Buckminster Fuller's earlier Dymaxion came close. Stout's teardrop-shaped future machine, sporting flush glass, was rear-wheel drive, using an 85-bhp rear-mounted Ford V-8. Stout planned production of 100 cars, starting at $5000, but fewer than 10 were built.

▲ Only the Dictator Six and President Eight (*shown*) made Studebaker's 1936 lineup. Most Studes had "Planar" independent front suspension.

▲ Still frisky with its 88-bhp engine, the $640 '36 Terraplane DeLuxe Six coupe rode a longer 115-inch wheelbase and wore a narrow grille.

1936 Model-Year Production Figures	
1. Ford	930,778
2. Chevrolet	918,278
3. Plymouth	520,025
4. Dodge	263,647
5. Oldsmobile	200,546
6. Pontiac	176,270
7. Buick	168,596
8. Hudson/Terraplane	123,266
Some figures are estimated or calendar year	

169

▲ Buick offered a convertible phaeton in its 1937 Special and Century series, as well as a more costly $1856 Roadmaster (*shown*), which had debuted a year earlier.

▲ Rearward visibility wasn't a strong point of the '37 Cord 812 Custom Beverly sedan, but who cared with a body this luscious to gaze upon? Note the bustleback trunk.

▲ Styled by a crew under Gordon Buehrig, the 810/812 Cord was one of the top industrial designs, yet only 2320 were produced in 1936-37. Shown is the 1937 Beverly sedan.

1937

- Industry production volume totals 3,915,889 cars and 893,085 trucks

- Ford beats Chevrolet in model-year output, 942,005 cars to 815,375, but trails for the calendar year

- Cadillac builds its final V-12 and ohv V-16, but a new L-head V-16 will appear for '38; the 346-cid V-8 is by far Cadillac's most popular engine

- Chrysler products move to all-steel roofs and all-around standard safety glass

- Oldsmobile introduces the Automatic Safety Transmission, a "semiautomatic" system that still requires clutching to engage first gear

- Pierce-Arrow sales plunge and production is halted; the company files for bankruptcy protection in December, having built a small number of 1938 models

◄ Specials earned a bigger straight eight, while the upper-level 320-cid engine gained 10 horsepower, to 130. Buick promoted a new steering-wheel horn ring and front/rear antiroll bars.

▲ Both the Hudson Custom Six and this smaller Terraplane (still a separate make) used a 212-cid six in 1937. As always, Terraplane sold a lot better.

◄ A $611 standard Ford Tudor could be formidable on police duty with the 85-bhp V-8, but economy-minded folks in '37 could choose the milder V8/60.

◄ After three years with an Olds straight eight, LaSalle turned to a 125-bhp, 322-cid V-8 in 1937, borrowed from the prior year's Cadillac Series 60. Wheelbase grew to 124 inches, while output rose to a record 32,000 units. Prices began at $1155, but this Model 5067 convertible coupe went for $1350, with a rumble seat optional.

- With 77,000 cars produced, Nash enjoys its best year of the decade

- Willys, offering slightly enlarged cars with a full restyle and a bulging nose, increases production to 63,467 units

- Chrysler shows off a safety-padded adjustable seat that moves up-and-down as well as forward and aft

- Unionized Autoworkers win their first major labor contracts

- Striking union leaders are beaten by Ford thugs at the infamous "Battle of the Overpass" on May 26

- Hudsons break 40 official performance records; one of them was for 24 hours, covering 2104.22 miles at 87.67 mph

- In Cord's final season, supercharging and long-wheelbase sedans are available

- LaFayette, mounted on the chassis of the prior 400 series, becomes Nash's lowest-priced offering

- Buick builds great-looking models and enlarges the Special's engine to 248 cid, good for 100 horsepower

▲ Not many cars in 1937—or any other year—had a rear deck as long and shapely as the new $1295 Lincoln Zephyr three-passenger coupe, accentuated by rear fender skirts.

▲ Upright formal models with open-air driver's compartments—like this Brunn-bodied Pierce-Arrow Metropolitan V-12 Town Car—looked dated by 1937.

▲ Packard output doubled in 1937, topping 122,000 for the year. This two/four-passenger convertible listed for $1060. The smaller One Ten was Packard's best-selling model.

▶ Safety glass was standard on all Chrysler products in 1937, including the restyled Plymouth P4 DeLuxe. This coupe, which cost $650, attracted 67,144 new-car buyers.

- Chrysler spends $22 million on assembly plant improvements

- Buick claims its steering-wheel horn ring is a "first" in the auto industry

- Chevrolet's six-cylinder engine is redesigned; Master and Master DeLuxe series are offered

- Streamlined Fords get steel roofs, choice of 60- or 85-horsepower V-8 engines

- A three-passenger coupe and Town Limousine join the Lincoln-Zephyr line

- Big Lincolns sport integrated headlamps and a vee'd windshield; the V-12 engine gets quieter hydraulic lifters

- A Ford V-8-powered racer wins the prestigious Monte Carlo Rally

- Plymouth's crank-open windshield makes its last appearance; production hits 566,128

- All Packards now have independent front suspension; a lower-cost six-cylinder model is added to lineup

▲ Only in 1937-38 did Pontiac offer a convertible sedan. Shown here is the $1235 DeLuxe Eight, which was costly for the day. The DeLuxe Six was less pricey: $1197.

▼ Fully restyled for '37, Willys kept the old 48-bhp engine and 100-inch wheelbase. The bulged front end hinted at the forthcoming "Sharknose" Graham. Standard and DeLuxe models cost $499–$589. Willys output reached 63,467.

▲ At $595, the DeLuxe business coupe was Terraplane's lowest-cost 1937 model—shown here with the awkward-looking slide-in cargo box.

1937 Model-Year Production Figures

1. Ford	942,005
2. Chevrolet	815,375
3. Plymouth	566,128
4. Dodge	295,047
5. Pontiac	236,189
6. Buick	220,346
7. Oldsmobile	200,886
8. Packard	122,593

Some figures are estimated or calendar year

▲ Buick's major 1938 news was a new all-coil suspension and more powerful 248- and 320-cid engines.

▼ Optional fender skirts and spotlights added a purposeful look to a 1938 DeSoto S5 coupe. Price: $820.

▲▼ Series 60 Cadillacs, like this $1730 four-door sedan, kept their former shape for '38, adding a column gearshift. Meanwhile, the Series 90 (*below*) switched to a smaller 431-cid V-16, now an L-head, but still rated at the same 185 horsepower.

1938

- After a modest middecade recovery, a sharp recession sinks the still-fragile economy

- Auto-industry output plunges 40 percent, to 2,000,985 cars and 488,100 trucks—one of the industry's worst slumps ever

- Chevrolet is again number one, as Ford production tumbles by more than half. With only occasional exceptions, Chevrolet is destined to hang onto the lead well into the Eighties

- Hupmobile is back in business, with six- and eight-cylinder models, but only 2001 are built

- Nash develops Weather-Eye, a "conditioned air" heating/ventilation system that heats and filters air before it reaches the cabin

- After four years as a separate make, Terraplane officially becomes a Hudson model; a new low-cost Hudson "112" undercuts Terraplane prices

▲ Graham referred to the look of its new cars as the "Spirit of Motion." This is the line-topping Supercharger Custom.

▲ Hupmobile's return to action for 1938 brought two sedan series: 822-E Six (*shown*), and the less-popular Eight.

▲ Wheelbase grew to 125 inches as part of Lincoln Zephyr's '38 restyle. Note the wind wings on this coupe.

◀ Terraplane became part of the Hudson line in '38. Four-door sedans listed from $864 to $915.

- William L. Mitchell, protégé of Harley Earl, designs Cadillac's elegant new Sixty Special sedan with concealed running boards

- Several automakers offer steering-column-mounted gearshift levers

- Several automakers, catching up with Buick, turn to coil-spring rear suspensions

- Graham introduces radically shaped "Spirit of Motion" styling, featuring a "sharknose" front-end design

- Ford spends $40 million on plant expansion and renovation

- Dodge produces its last convertible sedans—only 132 find buyers

- Buicks gain modified "Dynaflash" engines with up to 141 bhp; the division ranks as GM's second-best-seller from 1938–47

- GM builds the first experimental "dream car," the Y-Job, on a '37 Buick chassis

- Chrysler introduces the midline $1378 New Yorker Special Touring Sedan

▲ Packard's One Twenty was simply called the "Eight" for 1938; this handsome convertible coupe sold for $1365.

▶ Packard offered a convertible Victoria in both the Super Eight and Twelve series (*shown*) for 1938.

▲ Only a handful of Pierce-Arrows went on sale in 1938, including this massive V-12 limousine. Liquidation quickly followed bankruptcy in December 1937. Pierce was best known for its fender-mounted headlights, initiated in the Teens.

- Ford adopts two-tier styling: DeLuxe models are restyled, Standards keep the '37 DeLuxe body; slantback models are gone

- An early sunroof: LaSalle adds a four-door sedan with a sliding steel top

- Oldsmobile offers sidemounted spares for the last time; Automatic Safety Transmission is available on all models

- Plymouth's station wagon rides the passenger-car chassis; bodies come from the U.S. Body and Forging Company

- Packard calls the One Twenty the "Eight" this year and stretches the wheelbase

- Studebakers are restyled by Raymond Loewy, the first of many such projects for the famed industrial designer

▲ The 1938 Plymouth coupe didn't win many styling kudos, but America's Number Three automaker went on to produce 45,451 examples of this body style, priced from $645 to $770. A hardy 82-bhp L-head six promised reliable service.

▲ The '38 Willys lineup included new two-door sedans, plus coupes (here a $574 DeLuxe) and four-door sedans. Output fell from 63,476 units to 26,691.

▲ A three-inch-shorter 122-inch wheelbase marked this $1130 '38 Studebaker State President three-passenger coupe, a rare model adorned here with a sidemounted spare. A 250-cid straight eight made 110 horsepower.

1938 Model-Year Production Figures

1. Chevrolet		465,158
2. Ford		410,263
3. Plymouth		285,704
4. Buick		168,689
5. Dodge		114,529
6. Oldsmobile		99,951
7. Pontiac		97,139
8. Packard		55,718
Some figures are estimated or calendar year		

► Buick received a mild but pleasant facelift for 1939, with optional hidden running boards. A rumble seat was no longer offered for this $1077 Special convertible.

▲ Cadillac Sixteens strutted front-end styling wholly unique from eight-cylinder models.

◄ Fender-mounted headlights led Chrysler's 1939 redesign. This New Yorker sedan listed at $1298.

▲ This top-line Master DeLuxe Town Sedan with trunk was Chevrolet's best-seller in 1939: 220,181 units.

◄ Radio/refrigerator tycoon Powel Crosley, Jr., developed a minicar bearing his name. The 1939 Crosley had an 80-inch wheelbase and an air-cooled two-cylinder engine. Early convertible coupes and sedans were sold in hardware stores.

1939

- The New York World's Fair opens; thousands marvel at technology to come, including television and futuristic highways

- Chevrolet leads Ford in sales by nearly 100,000 units; Plymouth runs a close third

- The Bantam-size two-cylinder Crosley debuts, created by Powel Crosley, Jr.

- The midpriced Mercury is introduced; though mechanically similar to Ford, it boasts a longer wheelbase and bigger V-8 engine

- Studebaker spends $3.5 million in tooling for the new low-cost, lightweight Champion series

- Most cars (except Fords) now have a column-mounted shift lever

▲ Ford finally switched to hydraulic brakes for 1939. This $742 Tudor was a hot seller, finding 144,333 buyers.

▲ The Hayes company built bodies for this rakish limited-edition, thin-pillared Dodge Town Coupe, well-equipped for $1055. Only 363 were produced.

▶ Since 1937, Ford offered two V-8s: "Thrifty Sixty" with 60 or 85 bhp. Only three 1939 Series models were available with the small V-8: coupe, Tudor, and Fordor.

THE NEW 1939 *"Thrifty Sixty"* FORD V-8

▼ A "Combination" coupe (*shown*) and two-door sedan—both $940 ($1070 Supercharged)—joined the "Sharknose" Graham line for 1939. But sales continued to languish: just 5392 units.

▲ Fully reworked, the 1939 LaSalles looked modern—and sales rose 50 percent to 21,127 units.

- Packard builds its last V-12 models

- New Chrysler models: Windsor, New Yorker, Saratoga

- Lincoln-Zephyr is one of several models to discard running boards

- At long last, Ford adopts hydraulic brakes, as do Mercury and the Lincoln-Zephyr

- The 75-millionth American vehicle is built

- Chevrolet introduces an easier-to-use vacuum-operated gearshift

- Chrysler brands are restyled by Ray Dietrich—headlamps move into the fenders

- Chrysler introduces a fluid-coupling powertrain, Fluid Drive, for Imperial

- Dodge is redesigned for 25th anniversary

- Pontiac adopts "Duflex" rear springs, featuring smaller auxiliary leaf springs

- Ford's convertible sedan is in its final year; the phaeton is already gone

- Under-seat heaters and pushbutton radios appear in several models this year

▲ This Lincoln-Zephyr convertible coupe was new for '39; 640 were sold at $1747 apiece. Zephyrs adopted hydraulic brakes, while the big Model Ks stuck with mechanical binders. Gearshift levers remained on the floor for one last year. Zephyrs could have any of six bodies: coupe-sedan, three-passenger coupe, four-door sedan, Town Limousine, convertible coupe—even a convertible sedan. Vestigial running boards were now covered by skirts. Total Lincoln output for the '39 model year rose slightly to 21,134 units.

▲ Overshadowed by the less-costly Zephyr, the '39 Lincoln lineup still included a long list of massive Model Ks. This LeBaron convertible sedan is one of only nine built.

▲ Mercury's 95-horsepower V-8 was slightly larger than Ford's 85-horse unit. Prices started at $916.

▲ The Mercury brand debuted in 1939, filling the position between the Ford DeLuxe series and Lincoln-Zephyr. Lushly curved, it rode a 116-inch chassis (Ford, 112; Zephyr, 125) and had a 95-horsepower V-8 engine.

▶ Both the big Nash and the less-expensive LaFayette were treated to a total restyling for 1939, featuring flush headlamps and a prowlike hood. LaFayettes like this one sold in the $770-$950 range.

- Chrysler develops the "Superfinish" method of finishing parts with no scratches deeper than one-millionth of an inch

- DeSotos come in DeLuxe and Custom series; open cars are gone, and a planned sliding sunroof never makes production

- A two-door sedan and "Combination Club Coupe" are added to Graham's "Sharknose" series, but sales remain sluggish

- Terraplane leaves the Hudson lineup, but 101-bhp Pacemaker and Country Club sixes debut, as do "Big Boy" sedans

- Packard designs and builds marine engines for U.S. Navy PT boats; White is selected to build Army scout cars

- Poland is invaded by Germany on September 1, the implications for the auto industry are still unclear

▲ Ray Dietrich penned the neat 1939 Plymouth restyle, which featured rectangular headlights. This $775 Touring Sedan has the new column shift.

▲ Clean styling, miserly mileage, and sprightly performance marked the new 1939 Studebaker Champion, here a $720 DeLuxe coupe.

▲ Light-truck buyers could enjoy the benefits of Studebaker passenger-car styling for 1939 by choosing the dual-purpose Coupe-Express.

▲ Pontiacs wore wider "pontoon" fenders in 1939, sharing some body panels with Chevrolet. This is the $1046 DeLuxe Eight ragtop.

1939 Model-Year Production Figures

1. Chevrolet	577,278
2. Ford	487,031
3. Plymouth	423,850
4. Buick	208,259
5. Dodge	186,474
6. Pontiac	144,340
7. Oldsmobile	137,249
8. Studebaker	85,834

Some figures are estimated or calendar year

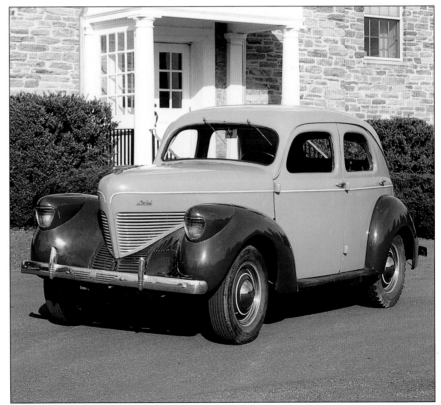

▲ Willys kept its Model 38 for '39, but added a revived Overland, coupe or sedan (*shown*). Overlands had a 62-bhp four and hydraulic brakes.

181

▲ Buicks came in six series for 1940. Special, Super, Century, Road Master, Limited 80, and top-of-the-line Limited 90. Only 550 copies of this $1343 Century convertible were built. This was the last year for the sidemounted spare tire.

▲ Modern profiles on longer wheel-bases marked the 1940 Chrysler line, like this $960 six-cylinder Royal coupe.

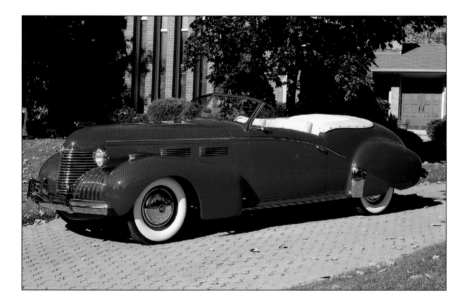

▲ No ordinary 1940 Cadillac, this dazzling convertible wears a custom body, with neatly dipped-down doors by Bohman & Schwartz. Built on a Series Sixty-Two chassis with the stock 135-bhp, 346-cid V-8, this car even sports bucket seats.

▲ Running boards were a $10 option on the Dodge DeLuxe sedan; 84,976 were built. Starting price: $905.

1940

- A war buildup is underway in the U.S.; automakers' European branches convert production to military output

- General Motors president William S. Knudsen is tapped by FDR to direct production for national defense

- Industry production totals 3,692,328 cars and 777,026 trucks

- Chevrolet builds nearly 765,000 cars in the model year, topping archrival Ford by more than 220,000 units

- The Lincoln Continental debuts with the Zephyr's V-12 engine; it's regarded as one of the most striking designs of all time

- The last of the huge K-Series Lincolns are built; model-year production is only 133

▲ The racy-looking DeLuxe convertible coupe, priced at $849, was Ford's only open car in 1940. This was the final year for the smaller of Ford's two V-8 engine offerings.

▲ Taking one last stab at the market, Graham issued the $1250 Cord-based Hollywood (*shown*). Only 1597 were built for 1940–41. Output ceased in late 1940.

◄ LaSalle was in its final year when this 1940 Series 52 Special sedan was assembled. Featuring Harley Earl's "torpedo" look, it became the top-selling model: 10,250 units.

◄ "Bob" Gregorie had designed a custom Lincoln-Zephyr convertible for Edsel Ford in 1939, "continental style" with a rear spare. A year later, it was produced as the Continental. Sold as a $2783 coupe or $2916 soft top, Continental featured mechanical elements from the far-cheaper Zephyr.

• The Graham Hollywood and Hupp Skylark share a Cord-based body, but are rear-drive; Grahams are supercharged

• LaSalle's final cars come in two series, one featuring GM's new "Torpedo" design

• Cadillac's huge V-16 engine makes its last appearance, but only 61 are sold

• Nearly all makes, including resistant Ford, have a column gearshift and enclosed running boards

• Nash produces the last LaFayettes, low-cost series dropped after 1940

• Sealed-beam headlights become the industry standard this year

• Hydra-Matic Drive—the first truly clutchless automatic transmission—is introduced by Oldsmobile

• Chrysler develops Safety-Rim wheels that keep the tire on the rim after a blowout

• Most car models now have a standard heater and windshield defroster

► This 1940 Mercury convertible coupe listed for $1079. More than 86,000 Mercs were sold for '40.

▲ Mercury's $987 "Coupe-Sedan" was chosen by 16,819 buyers in 1940. A 95-horsepower V-8 was standard.

▲ Packard V-12s were gone by 1940, replaced by straight eights. This One Twenty model cost $1166.

▲ Glamour in Packard's 1940 lineup came from custom-built Darrins, styled by Howard "Dutch" Darrin. This is the $4593 Super Eight One Eighty Victoria.

- A demonstration of what will become the "Jeep" is held by Colonel Arthur W.S. Herrington; it's to be built by Willys

- Walter P. Chrysler dies in August

- A larger 50-cid, 22-bhp engine goes into the little American Bantam

- The final Buick Century convertible sedans are built; the Super series debuts

- Cadillac's Series Seventy-Two lasts just one season, but the new Series Sixty-Two will become the top seller

- Chevrolet's new "Royal Clipper" styling imparts a fresh look; three series are offered, as is Chevy's first true convertible coupe

- Crosley cuts prices to as low as $199; a convertible, woody wagon, and "covered wagon" are added to the lineup

- Four striking custom-built Darrin models, led by a low-slung Convertible Victoria, capture the attention of Packard fanciers

- Hudson adopts coil springs up front

- Mercury lists a $1212 convertible sedan, it is discontinued by year's end

- Oldsmobile offers its first convertible sedan; only 50 are built

▲ Replacing Oldsmobile's Series 80 for 1940 was the new top-of-the-line Series 90, featuring a 110-horsepower straight eight. More than 33,000 of the $1131 sedans were sold.

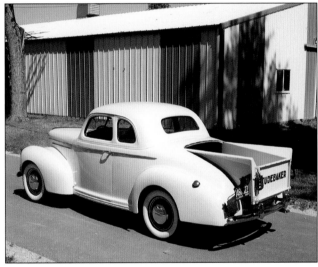

▲ Oldsmobile's Series 90 models, like this $1069 Custom Cruiser club coupe, were notable for their smoother tails and rear rooflines. Hydra-Matic quickly gained converts.

▲ Studebaker offered a Coupe-Delivery in 1940, with a short pickup bed stuffed into the trunk. Except for styling touch-ups, Champion, Commander, and President changed little.

Makes That Expired 1930-41

American Austin	Duesenberg	Kissel	Roosevelt
American Bantam	Du Pont	LaFayette	Ruxton
Auburn	Durant	LaSalle	Sterns-Knight
Blackhawk	Elcar	Marmon	Stutz
Brewster	Erskine	Marquette	Terraplane
Continental	Essex	Oakland	Whippet
Cord	Franklin	Peerless	Viking
Cunningham	Gardner	Pierce-Arrow	Willys-Knight
Detroit	Graham	Reo	Windsor
De Vaux	Hupmobile	Roamer	
Doble	Jordan	Rockne	

1940 Model-Year Production Figures

1.	Chevrolet	764,616
2.	Ford	541,896
3.	Plymouth	430,208
4.	Buick	278,784
5.	Dodge	225,595
6.	Pontiac	217,001
7.	Oldsmobile	192,692
8.	Studebaker	107,185

Some figures are estimated or calendar year

▲ Now available on Buick Fireball eights was "Compound Carburetion," or dual carburetors. This two-tone Century coupe started at $1241.

▲ Convertible phaetons still existed in Buick's 1941 Super and Roadmaster series. At $1555 and $1775, sales reached only 508 and 326 units, respectively.

▲ Cars don't get much prettier than this '41 Cadillac Series Sixty-Two convertible sedan, benefiting from a major styling update. Only 400 of these $1965 ragtops were produced. A new Series Sixty-One replaced the departed LaSalle.

◄ Chevrolet added a top-of-the-line Special DeLuxe series for 1940, then restyled the line handsomely for '41 on a longer 116-inch wheelbase. This $949 Special DeLuxe "cabriolet," of which 15,296 were sold, sports many extras.

1941

- The massive war buildup helps expedite the end of the Great Depression

- Pearl Harbor is bombed on December 7; Congress declares war a day later

- Following a violent wildcat strike, Henry Ford concedes to a union vote and the first closed shop in the automobile industry

- Total industry production comes to 3,744,300 cars and 1,094,261 trucks

- Just over a million Chevrolets are built in the '41 model year, far ahead of Ford's 691,455

- Packard becomes the first make to offer air conditioning, but priced at $1080 it's a *prohibitively* expensive proposition

◄ Only 2045 Chevrolet Special DeLuxe station wagons were built in 1941—a price topper at $995. Lots of extras could be ordered, from vacuum shift to turn signals to bumper guards.

▼ Blanked rear quarters marked the $1760 Chrysler Crown Imperial Town Sedan, of which 984 were sold. "Vacamatic" semiautomatic changed gears with little use of the clutch.

▲ This '41 DeSoto Custom convertible struts a load of extras to compliment its "toothy" new grille. Priced at $1240, it found just over 2000 buyers. DeSoto ranked tenth in the sales race this year.

▲ Like other '41 Dodge Customs, this $995 club coupe (18,024 built) had extra trim and Airfoam cushions. Long-wheelbase sedans and limos remained, but only 654 were ordered.

▲ Running boards were shrinking, but still there, on the 1941 Ford Super DeLuxe convertible, which came with a power-operated top. Price was $946 with a V-8, $931 with the more economical 90-horsepower L-head six.

• Nash's new "600," which replaces the LaFayette, features unitized construction; Nash sales expand to 84,007 units

• Buick offers "Compound Carburetion" for the Fireball eight—a second carb kicks in when the gas pedal is pressed to the floor

• Hydra-Matic becomes available for $110 in Cadillacs; 30 percent of buyers choose it

• Chrysler offers a semiautomatic transmission that delivers a low-to-high shift when the driver lets up on the gas

• Willys-Overland names all its cars Americar, begins deliveries of "jeeps" to the U.S. Army

• Hudson earns nearly $4 million, but mostly from defense contracts

• Buick builds its last Super and Roadmaster convertible sedans, 834 of them find buyers this year

• Fastback sedans join the Buick line; the two Limited lines meld into a single high-line 90-Series Limited

• Cadillac's revived, lower-priced Series Sixty-One takes the place of LaSalle

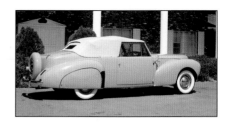

▲ Graham halted production of the Cord-based Custom Hollywood sedan in September 1940, but a fair number of remaining cars were sold as '41s.

▲ Like the similar Graham Hollywood, the handful of Hupmobile Skylarks sold in 1941 were leftovers from '40. All had the 101-bhp "Hornet Six."

▲ Pushbutton door handles gave the 1941 Lincoln Continentals a high-tech touch. Only 400 of the $2865 cabriolets (*shown*) were produced this year.

◄ Nash turned to unit construction in 1941 for the new, smaller "600" series, but not for the big Ambassador, here a fastback sedan. The Ambassador six delivered 105 bhp; the eight, 115 bhp.

▼ Inboard headlamps made Oldsmobiles easy to spot in '41. This $1089 Model 68 "Special 8" convertible coupe rode a new 119-inch wheelbase, with a 110-bhp, 257-cid straight eight.

- All redesigned Chevrolets now have an independent front suspension; a formal-look Fleetline sedan appears at midyear

- Chrysler's new Town and Country is the make's first station wagon

- Crosley modifications include the addition of driveshaft U-joints and a new engine smaller than the 1939–40 version

- DeSotos boast first prominent grille "teeth"; 10th-place sales ranking is the make's best showing ever

- Ford replaces the V-8/60 with an inline L-head six developing 90 horsepower

- Convertible sedans are still available in the Hudson line, and there's now a station wagon and a "Big Boy" car/pickup

- Packard's Clipper four-door sedan debuts at midyear, predicting postwar styling; an "Electromatic" clutch is newly available

- Oldsmobile adds fastback sedans, and reaches sixth place in industry rankings

- A new lower-priced Cadillac Series Sixty-One replaces the departed LaSalle on showroom floors

▲ The top-priced Packard series for 1941 was the One Eighty, including this $4695 Custom Super Eight All-Weather Cabriolet by Rollson.

▲ All Studebakers, like this President Skyway sedan, gained a handsome Raymond Loewy restyling for '41. Presidents cost between $1140 and $1260.

▲ Willys called its slightly enlarged 1941 models "Americar." In Speedway, DeLuxe, and Plainsman trim, each had a 63-bhp, 134-cid four.

▲ Unlike most '41s, Plymouth clung to running boards. This $1007 Special DeLuxe convertible showed off the facelift; 10,545 were sold.

▲ Most convertibles were still without rear side windows in 1941. Pontiac's handsome $1048 DeLuxe Torpedo Eight was no exception to the rule.

▲ Studebaker bored the Champion six to 167 cid, getting 80 bhp for '41. Note the two-toning on this $860 Champion DeLux-Tone Cruising Sedan.

1941 Model-Year Production Figures	
1. Chevrolet	1,008,976
2. Ford	691,455
3. Plymouth	522,080
4. Buick	374,196
5. Pontiac	330,061
6. Oldsmobile	270.040
7. Dodge	215,575
8. Chrysler	161,704
Some figures are estimated or calendar year	

189

CHAPTER FIVE

1942-1945

DETROIT GOES TO WAR

The winds of war aimed toward America as the '42 models debuted in the autumn of 1941. Across the Atlantic, combat had been raging for two full years, and Hitler controlled nearly all of Western Europe. Despite its biggest peacetime military buildup ever, the U.S. had steered clear of the conflict—while shipping war materiel to beleaguered Britain. Isolationist sentiment was strong, and the initiation of the military draft in 1940 had drawn considerable criticism. People were wary, if not quite worried, so the news of the Japanese bombing of Pearl Harbor, on December 7, 1941, came as a profound shock.

President Roosevelt placed the nation on an immediate wartime footing, and Detroit quickly followed. By early February 1942, production of civilian automobiles screeched to a halt. In fact, those few cars built after the first of the year, billed as "blackout" models, lacked their customary brightwork. Quite a few '42s were impounded by the government, earmarked for use by officials. Car registrations fell by about 1.6 million in 1942, as departing GIs put their cars up on blocks for the duration.

Packard had obtained a contract to produce aircraft engines in 1940, so conversion to war work came easily. Ford dedicated its huge government-financed Willow Run plant to the production of B-24 Liberator bombers. Dodge's new Chicago factory, also paid for by the government, built B-29 engines. Chrysler issued Sherman tanks and antiaircraft guns.

All told, automakers turned out $29 billion worth of armaments and related products for the war effort—everything from trucks and planes to lifeboats and sandbags. General Motors became the biggest producer. Second was Curtiss-Wright, followed by Ford. "Cost-plus" contracts provided the incentive to get the work done—and earn big profits.

Best known of the wartime products was the four-wheel-drive Jeep initially designed by American Bantam. Bantam produced fewer than 3000, but Willys and Ford were responsible for some 650,000.

On the "home front," gasoline rationing began in the Northeast during 1942, spreading nationwide in December of that year. Accompanied by a 35-mph national speed limit, rationing's major purpose was to conserve rubber. A motorist with the basic "A" sticker was entitled to four gallons of gas per week (later, three). "B" stickers went to priority workers, "C" to doctors and officials—or people with "connections."

Not every citizen cooperated eagerly. A black market in fraudulent and stolen ration coupons grew rampant as the war dragged into 1944–45. Used-car dealers were supposed to stick to government pricing limits, but more than a few vehicles sold for more than they'd cost when new.

Young men went off to war, but their bobby-soxer girlfriends—and exempted fellows—jitterbugged and jalopied in search of a good time. Jobs were easy to find, wages high—in stark contrast to the recently departed Depression. Women were applauded for their "Rosie the Riveter" roles, though their efforts would quickly be forgotten when returning veterans reclaimed those factory jobs.

By V-J Day in 1945, some $49 billion in War Bonds had been bought. Urban dwellers planted Victory Gardens to grow vegetables, and participated in scrap drives. Air-raid wardens enforced blackouts and scanned American skies for enemy planes—none of which were ever spotted.

The end of hostilities found many Americans with stuffed wallets from wartime work, and hungry for the civilian goods—especially cars—of which they'd been deprived. Postwar would be a new world.

1942

- As America enters the war early in the 1942 model year, customers worry that production will be halted rather than simply curtailed

- Under government mandate, automakers quickly convert from civilian to full wartime production, turning out shells, aircraft engines, antiaircraft guns, Jeeps, and more

- "Blackout" '42 automobiles—those produced after January 1—get government-ordered painted parts instead of chrome trim; most cars look lower, longer, more massive

- Fleetline Chevrolets include a Torpedo two-door Aerosedan and a four-door Sportmaster sedan

◀ Preparation for war had helped bring an end to the Great Depression and sparked car sales, but American two-lane highways would feel less carefree when the government placed strict limits on pleasure driving.

▲ Stylists drew from GM's "Y-Job" show car when reworking '42 Buicks. Sweeping full-length "Airfoil" fenders graced most models, including this Roadmaster convertible.

▲ Cadillac got a fresh new look for 1942 with big bullet-shaped fenders, plus a fastback roofline for Series Sixty-One (shown) and Sixty-Two sedanets.

◀ Two-tone paint looked fine on a 1942 Chevrolet Fleetline Aerosedan. This body style had been popular in other GM divisions in 1941, and sold well in the short '42 season. Chevrolet claimed the title "America's Most Popular Car." The new Fleetline subseries included a "torpedo-style" Aerosedan and conventional Sport-master four door.

- Chrysler's "alligator-style" hood opens from the front; running boards are hidden beneath flared door bottoms

- After a hefty price increase, Crosley prices start at $413; the versatile "covered wagon" model is dropped

- While Dodge strokes its engine to 230 cid, the cars are subject to a heavy facelift, getting a broader grille

- Ford gets a "big-car" look thanks to a revised grille and big-shoulder fenders

- Hudson cars can be ordered with Drive-Master semiautomatic shift

- Nash produces its final straight-eight engines; only sixes will return after the war

- Officially, Oldsmobile is now a division of GM—the Olds Motor Works name is history

- Turbo-matic Drive, a semiautomatic gearbox, is optional on Studebaker Commander and President models

- Civilian car production comes to an end on February 9; civilian-truck output ceases on March 3

- A national 40-mph speed limit is imposed to conserve fuel and rubber; later, it's reduced to 35 mph

▲ Introduced a year earlier, Chrysler's steel-roofed 1942 Town & Country was unlike any other "woody" wagon— and was the first such model offered by the company. A sloping rear roof and "clamshell" doors gave the original Chrysler Town & Country a unique spot in wagon history.

▲ DeSoto convertible coupes came in DeLuxe and Custom trim in 1942. A plush Custom Town Sedan, dubbed Fifth Avenue, featured leather and Bedford cloth upholstery trim. Only DeSoto presented a dramatically different face for 1942, in the form of hidden "airfoil" headlights, billed as "out of sight except at night." A larger six made 115 bhp.

◄ The final prewar Chrysler rolls off the assembly line on January 29, 1942, less than two months after Pearl Harbor. After facelifting its line-up for 1942, with grillework that reached around front fenders, Chrysler joined industry colleagues in the war effort. Cars built in January had painted metal trim, per government edict.

- Strict rationing of remaining new automobiles begins on March 2

- Gas rationing is ordered effective December 1, 1942

- Pontiac is the first automaker to win the Navy's "E" (Efficiency) Award; Chrysler earns the first Army-Navy "E" distinction

- Graham-Paige builds amphibious tanks

- By midyear, output of war materiel by auto manufacturers exceeds the normal peacetime production rate

- The Automotive Council for War Production reports $4.665 billion in arms production for the year

▲ Just 1185 Dodge Custom convertibles were built in the brief model year, with a larger (230-cid) 105-bhp six.

▲ A new frame gave 1942 Fords a lower stance. Both the V-8 and the six made 90 bhp. Shown: a DeLuxe Fordor.

▲ Mahogany paneling graced Ford's 1942 Super DeLuxe station wagon, while maple or birch went on DeLuxe versions.

▲ Could this 1942 Hudson Commodore Eight sedan be aspiring to official duty with that red spotlight?

1942 Model-Year Production Figures

1. Chevrolet	254,885
2. Ford	160,432
3. Plymouth	152,427
4. Buick	92,573
5. Pontiac	83,555
6. Dodge	68,522
7. Oldsmobile	67,783
8. Studebaker	50,678

Some figures are estimated or calendar year

◀ That final '42 Hudson had better last, because there would be no more civilian autos for more than three years. Hudson turned out 40,661 cars for the year.

1943

• In January, the Office of Price Administration (OPA) bans nonessential driving in 17 eastern states; 25 million gasoline ration books are issued to motorists nationwide

• As the war rages on, Income-tax withholding is introduced to help finance the effort

• With 1.25 million workers going strong, annual war production from 1000 automobile plants is twice the rate of the top prewar (peacetime) year

• The Automotive Council for War Production reports 1038 auto plants cooperating voluntarily in the war effort; this year, the combined value of materiel produced totals $13 billion

• Cadillac's wartime output includes tanks, aircraft engines, munitions

• Crosley develops an overhead-cam "CoBra" engine for the U.S. Navy; its block is made of brazed copper and sheet steel

◀ The Lincoln Continental's V-12 engine earned a 1942 enlargement to 305 inches, for 10 extra horsepower. Only 200 club coupes were produced, with a $3000 price tag. Facelifting of the 1942 Lincoln Continental roughly foretold its postwar look. Fenders were taller and longer, with headlamps flanked by dual parking lights.

▶ Still sitting in the shadow of the classic Continental, Lincoln's Zephyr earned a similar restyling for the abbreviated 1942 season. Note the pushbutton-operated doors on this $2150 convertible, like those on the Continental. A three-passenger coupe, club coupe, and four-door sedan also made the 1942 lineup. The last prewar Lincoln left the factory on February 10, 1942, after a run of just 6547 cars.

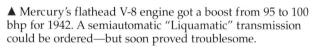

▲ Mercury's flathead V-8 engine got a boost from 95 to 100 bhp for 1942. A semiautomatic "Liquamatic" transmission could be ordered—but soon proved troublesome.

▲ A spotlight wasn't standard fare on a 1942 Mercury convertible coupe. Like other makes, "blackout" Mercurys produced after December 1941 had painted, not chromed, trim.

- Chrysler's contributions include antiaircraft guns, Wright Cyclone aircraft engines, land-mine detectors, radar units, marine engines, tanks, harbor tugs

- Ford also turns out gliders and gun carriers—plus the vital bombers from Willow Run, led by the B-24 "Liberator"

- Henry Kaiser announces a plans for postwar automobile production

- Studebaker's varied contributions mainly include trucks and aircraft engines, plus "Weasel" personnel carriers

- Hudson produces Invader landing-craft engines and body sections for Curtiss Helldiver aircraft, Martin B-26 bombers, Boeing B-29 super bombers, and Bell Aircobra helicopters—plus a number of naval munitions, including the Oerlikon antiaircraft gun

- During the war years, Oldsmobile turns out some 350,000 precision aircraft-engine components, 175 million pounds of gun forgings, 140,000 machine guns, and vast quantities of ammunition

- Packard produces Rolls-Royce Merlin aircraft engines, PT boats, and power units

- Joseph Frazer leaves the Willys-Overland firm in 1943 to take over Graham-Paige

▲ A Nash Ambassador rode a a 121-inch wheelbase and could be powered by either a six- or eight-cylinder engine.

▲ Just 31,780 Nashes were made before the government-ordered closing. The last of the line were "blackout" models.

▶ Packard's own designers penned this upright '42 One Eighty limousine, far removed from the pending "Clipper" shape.

◀ Packard unveiled the trendsetting Clipper in mid 1941, positioned between the One Twenty and One Sixty. Both "Dutch" Darrin and Packard's stylists contributed to the modern design, which featured a slim grille and a flush-sided "envelope" body, wider than it was tall.

- With $20 million in defense contracts, Graham-Paige is finally profitable

- Edsel Ford dies on May 26; Henry Ford is again elected company president on June 1, 1943; he is 80 years old

- Henry Ford II is released from the U.S. Navy on July 26, and elected vice president of Ford Motor Company on December 15

- Another Ford in service is Edsel's brother Benson, serving as an Army lieutenant

- Typical wartime advertisements included images of the company's combat hardware and reminders to purchase war bonds

- Two thirds of all wartime heavy truck production comes from various General Motors assembly plants

▲ "Fuselage fenders" edged into doors on 1942 Oldsmobiles, including this Special Series Sixty "torpedo" styled club sedan. Series Sixty and Seventy could have a six or an eight; the Ninety was straight eight only.

◀ More than 152,000 Plymouths went to buyers in the brief 1942 building season, keeping the the company third in the annual sales race.

1944

- Franklin D. Roosevelt is elected to an unprecedented fourth term as President of the United States

- Even more U.S. auto plants are converted to war production by 1944, as most automotive items are rationed

- The War Production Board authorizes Detroit to build one million trucks for military and civilian use

- In November, the Board approves the manufacture of light civilian trucks for the first time since 1942

- More than 13 percent of Allied war materiel comes from comes from American automobile manufacturers

- The value of armaments produced by American auto builders exceeds $9 billion during 1944

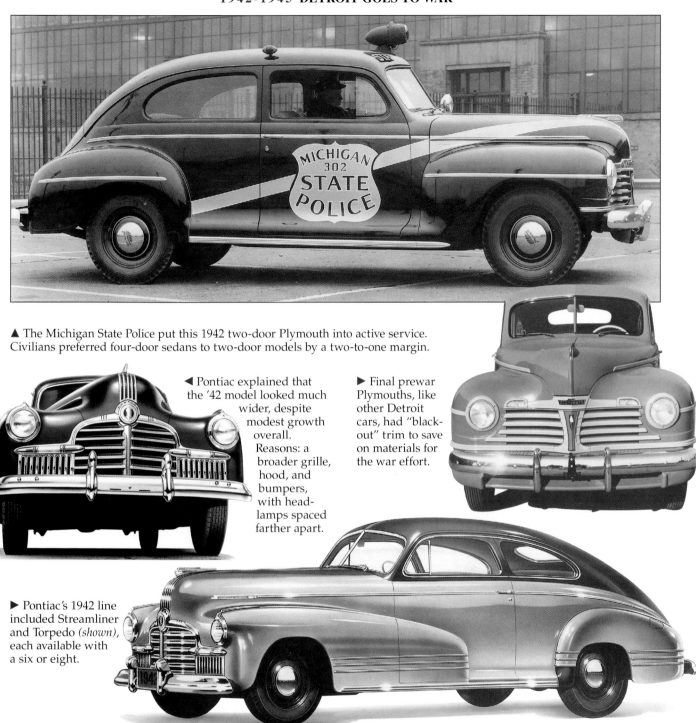

▲ The Michigan State Police put this 1942 two-door Plymouth into active service. Civilians preferred four-door sedans to two-door models by a two-to-one margin.

◄ Pontiac explained that the '42 model looked much wider, despite modest growth overall.
Reasons: a broader grille, hood, and bumpers, with head-lamps spaced farther apart.

► Final prewar Plymouths, like other Detroit cars, had "black-out" trim to save on materials for the war effort.

► Pontiac's 1942 line included Streamliner and Torpedo (*shown*), each available with a six or eight.

• Automakers build 57 percent of the tanks that go to U.S. and Allied forces

• The basic civilian gasoline ration is reduced to two gallons per week

• Per the Office of War Information, 4000 passenger cars are being scrapped daily

• Petroleum-based synthetic rubber is invented during the war years

• The G.I. Bill of Rights is signed in 1944 to provide benefits to veterans; millions of returning vets will attend college in the late Forties and eagerly buy new homes and automobiles in the Fifties

• The War Production Board commissions the Automobile Industry Advisory Committee to consider basic problems involved with the eventual resumption of civilian car and truck production

• Willys-Overland announces its plan to manufacture a civilian version of the Jeep after the war ends

• Joseph W. Frazer, now chairman of Graham-Paige, announces his intent to build cars after the war

• The Army taps the North American Dealer Association (NADA) for help in recruiting qualified mechanics for duty

▲ Wartime ads helped bolster morale, emphasizing the expertise of auto plants that now served the military.

▲ Rather than deal with gasoline rationing, or because car owners were serving overseas, thousands of motorists put their cars into storage for the war's duration.

◄ Conversion to all-out military production began right after war was declared. Eight million artillery shells came out of Chevrolet plants. Here, the St. Louis Shell Division.

1945

- FDR dies on April 12; Vice President Harry S Truman is sworn in as President

- Germany surrenders on V-E Day, May 8

- Restrictions on production of replacement automotive parts are lifted on May 22

- Ford closes the enormous Willow Run, Michigan, aircraft plant on June 23 after producing 8685 bombers

- The War Production Board announces a program for the transition back to civilian vehicle production, to resume on July 1

- Kaiser-Frazer Corporation is formed on July 26; automobile production will begin in a leased aircraft plant at Willow Run

- Atomic bombs are dropped over Hiroshima and Nagasaki on August 6 and 9; Japan surrenders on V-J Day, August 14, 1945

U.S. Automakers' Contributions to the War Effort

American Bantam
Fire pumper trailers
Jeeps
Jeep trailers (amphibious)

Chrysler Corporation
Aircraft engines
Airplane components/
  body sections
Ammunition of various types
Bofors antiaircraft guns
Chrysler-Bell air-raid sirens
Duraluminum forgings
  and castings
Explosive rockets
Fire pumper units
Fuselage sections for Martin
  B-26 Marauder bombers
General Grant M3 tanks
  (also M4/M26)
Gun barrels/shells
Landing-gear assemblies
Land-mine detectors
Magnesium and bronze parts
Marine engines
Medium-tank major
  assemblies
Personnel boats
Pontoons
Radar units
Refrigerating and
  heating equipment
Sea Mule marine/
  harbor tugs
Searchlight reflectors
Sherman tanks
Sperry Gyro-Compasses
Submarine nets
Tank engines
Trucks (Dodge)
Wright Cyclone aircraft
  engines (Dodge)

Crosley
CoBra four-cylinder engines

Ford Motor Company
Aircraft generators
All-terrain trucks
Amphibian Jeeps
Antiaircraft detectors
Armored personnel carriers

B-24 Liberator bombers
GAA four-valve, dohc V-8s for
  Sherman tanks
General Electric
  Turbosuperchargers
Gliders
GPW Jeeps
Gun carriers
Jettison gas tanks
M-4 Sherman tanks
M-10 tank destroyers
M-20 Utility Commando Cars
Magnesium castings
Moto Tugs
Pratt & Whitney R-2800
  radial engines
Rate-of-climb indicators
Tires
Trucks

General Motors
Aircraft-engine components
Aircraft engines
Airplanes
Ammunition (Olds)
Amphibious Ducks
Antiaircraft torpedoes
Artillery shells (Chevrolet)
B-26 bomber landing gear
Bofors automatic field guns
Cannons, 20-mm/37-mm
Car/truck parts (Chevrolet)
Crankshafts (Olds)
Forgings
GMC buses for the civilian
  market (Pontiac)
Grumann Avengers
Gun forgings (Olds)
Hellcat M-18 tank destroyers
High-explosive shells
Hydra-Matic for tanks
Machine guns (Olds)
Military cannons (Olds)
Munitions (Cadillac)
Oerlikon antiaircraft cannons
Pratt & Whitney aircraft
  engines (Buick)
Precision parts for aircraft
  engines
Staghound T-17 armored cars,
  4-wheel (Chevrolet)
T-19 armored cars, 6-wheel

Tanks/motor gun carriages:
  M-5/M-8/M-19/M-24
  (Cadillac)
Trucks (Chevrolet/GMC)
V-8s for tanks (Cadillac)

Graham-Paige
Amphibious tanks

Hudson
Ailerons for pursuit planes
Aluminum aircraft pistons
Ammunition boxes
Auxiliary fuel tanks
B-29 bomber parts
Body sections for aircraft
Bomb fuse adapters
Fire-control apparatus
Gun mounts
Invader landing-craft engines
Marine mine anchors
Oerlikon antiaircraft guns
Torpedo tubes

Nash
Pratt & Whitney aircraft
  engines

Packard
Marine engines
P-T boats
Rolls-Royce Merlin aircraft
  engines
Shells, 37–40-mm

Studebaker
Military trucks, mainly 6×6s
  and 6×4s
Pratt & Whitney R-2800
  radial aircraft engines
Weasel personnel carriers
Wright Cyclone R-1820
  radial aircraft engines

Willys
Jeeps

Note: This list is not comprehensive; rather, it is intended to provide a general idea of how involved the auto industry was in the war effort. Much work was subcontracted, even among the automakers themselves.

▲ Just weeks after Pearl Harbor, Chrysler president K. T. Keller *(left)* helped celebrate production of the company's 60,000th gun barrel.

▲ Ford produced components for the four-engine Boeing B-24 "Liberator." A new plant at Willow Run, Michigan, turned out 8685 bombers.

▲ Henry Ford *(left)* and wife Clara pose with grandson Henry Ford II, who was released from the U.S. Navy in 1943 to assist with war production.

• Gasoline rationing ends on August 15; restrictions on truck production are lifted five days later

• Health gradually failing, Henry Ford finally resigns; Henry II becomes company president on September 21, 1945, and soon hires a team of management "Whiz Kids" to revitalize the ailing company

• The Automotive Council for War Production is dissolved on October 15

• The new 1946 Fords are shown to the public on October 26, 1945

• A wave of strikes (authorized and "wildcat"), absenteeism, and general labor unrest mark the early postwar recovery period, beginning in late 1945

• Many materials, such as sheet steel, are scarce—and remain so for several years

• O.P.A. price ceilings try to curb inflation, but unwittingly help to curtail production and earnings in the early postwar period

• Crosley announces its plan to manufacture more small cars, but now with four-cylinder engines (instead of the prewar two-bangers)

▲ Millions of women entered the workforce during World War II, including this 1943 group that helped produce Hudson-built aluminum aircraft pistons.

▲ Independent automakers—Crosley, Hudson, Packard, Studebaker, Willys—turned to war work with gusto. Shown is Hudson's B-29 bomber production facility.

▲ Some top executives did more than contribute to the war effort from home. William S. Knudsen (*shown*) served as a lieutenant general.

▲ Developed by the GMC Truck & Coach Division, the amphibious "Duck" saw duty worldwide during World War II, carrying troops on land or water. All five GM passenger-car divisions also turned their facilities over to the war effort. Many M-24 light tanks used Cadillac V-8 engines and Hydra-Matic transmissions.

◀ General Motors produced 854,000 trucks for wartime use, including these near-ready light-duty models.

▶ Two-thirds of the heavy trucks employed during World War II came from GM plants.

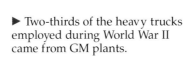

- The '46 models generally are lightly facelifted '42s, but this does nothing to dampen the pent-up demand for new cars

- In an effort to get production underway quickly, some makers at first offer only a limited selection of models and options

- Although most companies are producing by October, Chrysler Corporation and Studebaker don't get rolling until December

- Clayton Moore—who portrays *The Lone Ranger* on radio—buys the first '46 Pontiac

- As sales of conventional cars boom after the war, executives begin to doubt the market viability (or profitability) of small cars in the postwar marketplace

- On December 8 in Japan, Toyota is given government permission to resume vehicle production, but only trucks and buses

▲ GM built 206,000 engines for planes like this Lockheed P-38 "Lightning."

▲ The Fisher Body plant in Trenton, New Jersey, built Grumman Avengers for the Navy. Forty percent of GM's $12.25 billion in war material was aviation related.

▲ Chrysler president K. T. Keller *(right)* and General Dwight D. Eisenhower, commander of Allied Forces in Europe.

▲ The star on the door marks this 1942 Packard sedan as a military staff car.

▲ Henry Ford II drives the first civilian postwar Ford off the assembly line on July 3, 1945. Production resumed just after V-J (Victory in Japan) Day.

◀ Henry Ford *(left)* and grandson Henry Ford II sign the 5000th "Liberator" built by Ford. Henry II would soon be a Ford vice president.

201

CHAPTER SIX

1946-1948

THE POSTWAR "SELLER'S MARKET"

Even before World War II ended, automakers began promising cars for discharged troops. One Buick ad featured a '42 model accompanied by the headline, "So nice to come home to!"

Because automakers had trouble rebuilding their assembly lines after the war ended in August 1945, and because materials were in short supply, just over 83,000 cars were built that fall. Labor unrest didn't help, highlighted by a 119-day strike against General Motors in 1945-46. Production soared during 1946, even if the cars themselves differed little from the final '42 models.

Ford ushered in a new postwar regime, after Henry Ford II took over the helm from his illustrious grandfather. He soon brought in a team of "Whiz Kids" to help transform the company's antiquated management—and financial fortunes.

Automakers expected a massive "seller's market" to develop, and they were correct. After 15 years of economic hardship and wartime limits, shoppers were eager to buy just about anything Detroit could supply. In fact, many were willing to pay jacked-up prices for new cars in those heady postwar days, snapping them up as soon as they hit the dealerships—if not before. Bargaining? Not a chance.

At first, the Office of Price Administration limited prices to 1942 levels, but the scarcity of new cars created long waiting lists. Still, shoppers who wanted a car badly enough could usually find a way to obtain one. Dealers were known to accept—or solicit—bribes, and customers might have to accept high-priced (and unwanted) extras tacked onto the list price. A "gray market" sent new models onto used-car lots, priced hundreds of dollars higher than their official new-car price. Some buyers even turned around and resold their cars and pocketed the profit.

Studebaker was the first among the existing automakers to offer a totally restyled model. Though some derided Stude's "which-way-is-it-going?" shape, eager crowds marveled at the Starlight coupe with its wraparound back window. A year later, Hudson's dramatic "Step-down" design was ready, wearing a startlingly low roofline.

Willys left the passenger-car market, except for a civilian version of the Jeep and some offshoots, but Americans had two brand-new makes from which to choose: Kaiser and Frazer. Introduced before the '47 Studebaker, but in actual production slightly later, both sold well at first, as did the other independents.

Preston Tucker's sensational new Torpedo drew even more attention. Packed with ahead-of-its-time safety features and technological advances, the rear-engined "Car of Tomorrow" attracted eager crowds—until the Securities and Exchange Commission charged Tucker with fraud. Though exonerated by a jury, Tucker's dream was dead on arrival.

Visionaries proposed three-wheeled cars, flying cars, cars that turned into boats. Few progressed beyond the prototype stage (if that). None went past minimal production. Americans weren't quite ready for a minicar, either, as the eventual failure of the improved Crosley demonstrated.

No less acute than the automobile shortage was the housing shortage. Returning veterans often had to move into Quonset-hut developments, and some looked closely at the new prefabricated homes. Many vets returned to school, earning benefits under the G.I. Bill of Rights. Christian Dior penned the "New Look" for women's fashions. Television was entering a handful of American homes. What Americans appeared to want most, however, was a new car, and Detroit scurried to fulfill those aspirations.

1946

- Thanks to the wartime production halt, the average car on the road is now nine years old

- With pockets full of money from wartime work, car-starved Americans eagerly snap up the warmed-over '42s as they slowly begin to trickle off Detroit's assembly lines

- Price increases over 1942 are huge; Chevy's most-popular '46 model, the Stylemaster Sport Sedan, is up 43 percent—from $760 to $1205

- Car price and wage controls are lifted

- More than 28 million vehicles are registered, 2,155,924 of them having been built in the 1946 model year

- An early startup helps Ford leads in model-year production: 468,022 cars

- Chevrolet builds 398,028 cars; Plymouth and Dodge come in third and fourth

▲ Like other 1946 makes, Cadillac got only a mild facelift. This $2284 Series Sixty-Two sedanet had larger rear windows than its Sixty-One line mate.

▲ Cadillac's Sixty Special Touring Sedan returned for 1946, priced at $3095. All Cadillacs added a crest and "V" on the hood and deck.

• Despite impressive volume, Ford Motor Company posts an $8.1 million loss

• Chevrolet's reduced production total is partially attributed to strikes and shortages; GM's 1946 output is just 45 percent of '41

• A January steel strike closes assembly lines; in addition, the industry faces critical shortages of copper, brass, and lead

• An April coal strike causes layoffs in the auto industry; rail strikes also hurt

• The Ford Light Car Division is formed to develop an economy car with a five-cylinder engine, but the project is quickly axed

• Studebaker's '46 Skyway Champion has only a brief production run before the all-new '47 models are introduced

• William Stout develops a fiberglass prototype with a rear-mounted engine

• Kaiser-Frazer begins production late; the cars are sold as '47 models, and, along with Studebaker, are the only new postwar cars

• Crosley announces its intent to build a four-cylinder engine instead of the two-cylinder that powered prewar cars

▲ New names for Chevrolet: Master DeLuxe became Stylemaster, Special DeLuxe was now Fleetmaster. Fleetlines ranked top-of-the-line, led by the Aerosedan.

▲ Because the wood-trimmed Town & Country was Chrysler's glamour car, celebrities were engaged to hawk its virtues. Here, Marie "The Body" McDonald shows off a convertible.

◄ Comedian Bob Hope with a 1946 Chrysler Town & Country convertible.

- Detroit's Automotive Golden Jubilee celebrates the 50th anniversary of the auto industry in America

- Disabled veterans can get cars with special equipment developed by the Society of Automotive Engineers

- Chevrolet is one of first automakers to advertise on network television: Other makes will soon follow

- Some 82 million automotive tires are produced in 1946—an all-time high

- Tucker Corp. announces its plan to issue $20 million in common stock

- Dodge's former Chicago war plant, intended for lease to Tucker, is awarded instead to Lustron Corporation for building prefabricated homes

- Automakers announce plans for the construction and/or purchase of 25 factories needed to meet demand

- The Century series is gone from Buick's lineup, but its "gunsight" hood ornament is widely copied by accessory manufacturers

- Chevrolets face the postwar world with a new grille; Fleetlines sport triple chrome speedlines on all four fenders

▲ Two of these 1946 Chrysler "Continental" coupes were specially built. Both went to the same man, who liked the look of the Lincoln Continental. Priced at $17,000 apiece, the cars had squared-off, top-opening trunks with exposed spare tires, and padded leatherette tops. The coupes rode on a Saratoga chassis and carried 135-bhp eights. From B-posts forward, they looked all-Chrysler.

▲ Despite a longer look, Crosley's wheelbase again spanned 80 inches. The new four made 26.5 bhp—twice the prewar rating—but the "CoBra" copper-brazed engine block proved troublesome. Prices doubled, too.

▲ Crosley took a serious stab at styling with a sedan that measured 28 inches longer than prewar models. A station wagon joined in '47.

• Chrysler's Town & Country is now a wood-trimmed convertible and sedan; a new "harmonica" grille rides up front and front fenders blend smoothly into the bodysides

• An enlarged Crosley platform is introduced with a sedan first, later a convertible; a more-reliable cast-iron engine block soon displaces the much-touted but failure-prone copper-steel "CoBra" unit

• DeSoto fields a new long-wheelbase Suburban sedan with a fold-down rear seat; headlamps are again exposed

• Lincoln gains a two-layer cross-hatch grille and loses its Zephyr name

• Ford borrows Mercury's 239.4-cid V-8, adding 10 horsepower; a handsome wood-trimmed Sportsman convertible debuts

• Unlike most makes, Hudson keeps its '42 semiautomatic transmission option; a grille with a recessed center is the styling keynote

• Dodge receives a bold eggcrate grille

• Nash drops the Ambassador Eight to concentrate on six-cylinder engines: an L-head for the 600 series, and an overhead valve for the Ambassador

▲ Except for a new cross-hatch grille, the 1946 Dodge Custom convertible was similar to its prewar counterpart. Its 102-bhp six now started with a dashboard button.

▲ Headlights were no longer hidden on the postwar DeSotos. This 1946 Custom convertible went for $1761.

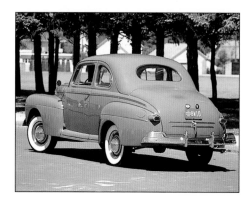

▲ Only one Ford was new for 1946: the $1982 wood-trimmed Super DeLuxe Sportsman.

◄ The 1946 Ford "coupe sedan" came only in top Super DeLuxe trim. Price: $1307 with a V-8.

1946 Model-Year Production Figures	
1. Ford	468,022
2. Chevrolet	398,028
3. Plymouth	264,660
4. Dodge	163,490
5. Buick	153,627
6. Pontiac	137,640
7. Oldsmobile	117,623
8. Nash	94,000
9. Hudson	91,039
10. Mercury	86,608
11. Chrysler	83,310
12. DeSoto	66,900
13. Packard	30,793
14. Cadillac	29,214
15. Studebaker	19,275
16. Lincoln	16,645
17. Crosley	4999

Some figures are estimated or calendar year

• Self-shift Hydra-Matic gains popularity in Oldsmobiles, which feature a new four-bar grille that tapers downward at ends

• Willys introduces an all-steel skin Station Wagon with Jeep-like styling

• Mercury trades its '42 three-passenger coupe for a '46 Sportsman woody convertible; only 205 will be built

• Kaiser-Frazer negotiates with Fiat to build a lightweight car, but nothing comes of it

• Bobbi Motor Car Corp. acquires an option for a factory to produce the "Bobbi-Kar"

• The Cushman Motor Scooter Company offers lightweight "shopping cars"

• Two three-wheeler, rear-engined cars debut—the 4½-bhp Comet and the 10-bhp Brogan—production is minuscule

• Californian Frank Kurtis also develops a three-wheeler; it evolves into the '47 Davis

• The buckboard-style King Midget, sold as a kit (later assembled), is advertised in *Popular Mechanics* and similar magazines

▲ In September 1945, workmen at the Detroit plant prepare the first batch of facelifted '46 Hudsons for shipment.

▶ This 1946 Hudson Super Six convertible Brougham could also come as a Commodore Eight, for $171 more.

▲ A boost to 82 bhp gave the 1946 Nash 600 a little extra oomph. Ambassador sixes also gained some horsepower.

▲ Looks like this 1946 Mercury sedan, sporting a modest postwar facelift, is nearing the end of the assembly line.

THE NEW
1946 PACKARD CLIPPER

▲ The 1946 Clipper still looked impressive. Eights came in 282- and 356-cid versions; Clipper was also available with a 105-bhp six.

▲ Nash pushed the roominess and economy of its "600," promising 25-30 mpg and

▲ Topping the Oldsmobile lineup was the 98 Custom Cruiser convertible. Its 257-cid straight-eight, which unleashed 110 horsepower, also went into the Dynamic Cruiser 78 series.

▲ Plymouths took DeLuxe or Special DeLuxe form for '46, with the same 95-bhp, 217.8-cid six as in 1942. Utility models were deleted from the line.

◄ "Silver Streak" styling for the 1946 Pontiac included a bell-shaped grille and triple fender trim strips. Looks differed little from '42.

▲ One of several roadsters planned for postwar America, the Bobbi-Kar rode an 80-inch wheelbase, with a 25-bhp four. Production of the two-seater never began.

▲ Except for a revised grille, Buick's '47 Roadmaster hadn't changed much. Postwar inflation kept pushing prices upward, sending the convertible to a heady $2651.

▲ The big Series Seventy-Five Cadillacs stuck with traditional styling. This seven-passenger sedan, weighing 4895 pounds and priced at $4686, appeared in *The Godfather*.

▲ Cadillac convertibles came only in Series Sixty-Two in 1947, priced at a princely $2902. Hydro-Lectric window lifts were standard—an uncommon extra for the day.

▲ Even Cadillac's Series Sixty-Two sedanet (also called a club coupe) was no lightweight at 4145 pounds.

▲ Only a prototype of the three-wheeled Californian was built, by former racer Frank Curtis. With a 58-bhp engine, it promised 100-mph top speed and 40 mpg.

▲ If Ford could offer a woody-look convertible, why not Chevy? This 1947 Fleetmaster wears a dress-up "Country Club" kit, offered by Engineering Enterprises for $148.50.

▲ Chevrolet's 1947 Fleetmaster station wagon was the most-expensive model ($1893) as well as the slowest seller (4912 built). Grilles changed slightly this year.

▲ General manager Nicholas Dreystadt (*left*), sales manager T.H. Keating, and manufacturing boss Hugh Dean pose with, and partially obscure, the 20-millionth Chevy.

◄ Idaho troopers didn't have to endure spartan patrol duty, while driving this Fleetline Aerosedan—the most-costly two-door Chevrolet sedan, and also the most popular.

1947

- Pent-up demand for autos continues to strain supply, it is still a seller's market

- Automobile prices reach an all-time high; inflation becomes a serious problem throughout the entire economy

- Automobile production reaches 3,555,792 units in calendar year 1947

- Chevrolet is again number one with 671,546 cars built; Ford is second with 429,674, followed by Plymouth and Buick

- Studebaker has already introduced its all-new postwar design, with a similar front and rear shape—critics joke that the Champion and Commander models look the same coming or going

▲ Only straight-eight engines went into the 1947 Chrysler Town & Country convertible. With 135 horsepower and Fluid Drive, Chrysler Eights weren't terribly quick at startup, but delivered smooth takeoffs and luxurious rides.

▲ Almost forgotten amid the flurry of attention given to convertibles was the similarly styled wood/steel Chrysler Town & Country sedan. Only a six-cylinder engine was installed.

▲ Body components for Chrysler's Town & Country were assembled in this rig, claimed to deliver fit and finish comparable to all-steel-body models.

- The most-striking Studebaker, the five-passenger "Starlight" coupe, boasts a huge four-piece wraparound rear window

- Two all-new makes, Kaiser and Frazer, have already gone on sale; Kaiser-Frazer purchased the assets of the prewar Graham-Paige Motor Corp.

- A total of 164,492 convertibles and 82,665 station wagons are built this year

- Kaiser-Frazer achieves the highest calendar-year production of any of the independent automakers: 139,249

- Most makes differ little from '46 except for trim and detail revisions; in fact, the '47s receive even fewer changes than did the '46s

- After declining in the Thirties, outside sun visors regain favor as an accessory

- The auto industry and millions of Americans mourn the death of Henry Ford on April 7, 1947, at the age of 83

- In January, the government agrees to let the Tucker Company lease the former Dodge war plant; the Tucker Torpedo is unveiled in Chicago, but only 51 will be built

- Packard offers hydraulic power seats and windows in some top-line models

◄ Fluid Drive eased clutch operation in the 1947 Dodge. A fluid coupling between the engine and three-speed transmission gave smooth startups, but gears had to be shifted manually.

▼ Early '47 Fords showed little change, but a midyear tweaking brought round parking lights.

- Ford's luxury division Lincoln celebrates its 25th anniversary

- Ford and the United Auto Workers reach a tentative labor agreement in June; foremen have been on strike

- Chrysler and GM also sign new autoworkers' union contracts

- The Taft-Hartley Labor Act is passed, brings a halt to strikes

- The Automobile Manufacturers Association approves a motion to standardize bumper heights

- A new synthetic rubber is developed by Phillips Petroleum Company

- All Chryslers now boast Goodyear low-pressure "Super Cushion" tires

- Crosley adds a station wagon to its two-door sedan and convertible lineup; production nearly triples to 19,344 units

- Fluid Drive semiautomatic transmission becomes standard on all Dodge models

▲ A long wheelbase helped give the Frazer Manhattan a smooth ride. Power came from a Continental L-head six, rated at 100 horsepower. The sedan's front seat was the widest in the industry. Overdrive was optional for the three-speed gearbox. Early examples had a tiny "Darrin-styled" logo on the trunklid and a "Graham-Paige" plate on the firewall.

▲ Top-of-the-line at Kaiser-Frazer was the 1947 Frazer Manhattan. Frazer produced only four-door sedans, priced at a hefty $2712 for the Manhattan, or $2295 for the less-posh "standard" model.

▼ Hudson retained its basic prewar look for one more season. The 3-millionth car (a Commodore Eight) was built in 1947. Hudson president A.E. Barit is shown here seated in the Commodore; other execs in Number One, a 1910 roadster.

- Ford announces lightly facelifted "Spring Models" for all three of its car lines in April; many consider these to be the "true" '47s

- Although the first few Frazers are built at the Graham-Paige plant in Detroit, production quickly shifts to Kaiser's sprawling Willow Run facility

- Kaiser and Frazer wear slab-sided sedan bodies styled mainly by Howard "Dutch" Darrin; Frazer is the more costly of the duo

- The Davis Motor Car Co. is organized to build a three-wheeled vehicle; the first car is built in October, but only 17 more will be assembled through 1949

- Ford's Lincoln-Mercury Division, established in October 1945, now has its own distinct dealer network

- The War Assets Administration accepts a bid from Playboy Motor Car Corp. for an abandoned Chevrolet plant; the three-seater convertible features a novel folding steel top

▲ Hudson Eight sedans came in two levels: $1862 Super and $1972 Commodore, both with a 128-bhp, 254-cid six-cylinder engine.

▲ Ray Russell designed the 1100-pound three-seat Gadabout on a short wheelbase, during the war. The prototype had a Duraluminum body on an MG chassis.

◀▲ Kaiser sold Special and Custom models its first year out. This well-equipped Custom came with a 100-bhp six, but a 112 horse could also be had. Only sedans were offered.

• Lincoln adopts pull-type door handles, replacing traditional pushbuttons

• Packard unveils a major restyling on the '48 convertible in March, to be followed in the fall by the rest of the '48 line

• Eight-cylinder Pontiacs outsell the sixes for the first time, a sign that customers are willing to spend money for upgrades

• Kaiser-Frazer acquires the rights to build the Scarab rear-engined car

• Although the fold-up Airscoot three-wheel car is developed, production never begins

• Bobbi-Kar changes its name to Keller Motors Corp. and moves from California to Alabama

▲ Postwar Lincoln Continentals got a fresh grille. Output for 1947 totaled 831 coupes and 738 convertibles.

► Non-Continental Lincolns swapped their pushbutton doors for pull-style handles. The Zephyr name no longer was used for the sedan, club coupe, or convertible. Lincoln's L-head V-12 shrunk to its 1941 size: 292 cid.

1947 Model-Year Production Figures	
1. Chevrolet	671,546
2. Ford	429,674
3. Plymouth	382,290
4. Buick	272,827
5. Dodge	243,160
6. Pontiac	230,600
7. Oldsmobile	193,895
8. Studebaker	161,496
9. Chrysler	119,260
10. Nash	101,000
11. Hudson	92,038
12. DeSoto	87,000
13. Mercury	85,383
14. Kaiser	70,474
15. Frazer	68,775
16. Cadillac	61,926
17. Packard	51,086
18. Lincoln	21,460
19. Crosley	19,344

Some figures are estimated or calendar year

▲ This Mercury wagon went for $2202. Lincoln-Mercury became an independent division of Ford in 1947.

▲ Nash turned to wood trim for its fastback 1947 Ambassador Sedan Suburban, which sold for $2227.

▲ Notchback versions of the 1947 Nash Ambassador four-door sedan (*shown*) went for $1464; "slip stream" fastbacks cost $44 less. Note the spotlight and sun visor—two popular add-ons. Two-toning highlighted the rooflines of many late-'40s models.

▲ Virtually identical to the 1946 models, this 1947 Packard Custom Super Clipper four-door sedan sold for $3449. Packard produced 51,086 cars this year, ranking 17th (down from 13th). Only serial numbers distinguish '46s from '47s.

◀ General Motors chairman Alfred P. Sloan. Jr. (*right*) congratulates Ransom E. Olds at a dinner to mark the auto pioneer's 80th birthday in 1947. Olds had left the company that bore his name years earlier to begin production of the Reo.

217

▲ Plymouths looked virtually identical from 1946 to early '49. The 1947 woody station wagon came in Special DeLuxe trim only, priced at $1765.

▲▼ A total of 5690 two-door (*above*) and four-door (*below*) sedans were produced in Packard's posh Custom Super Clipper series. Interiors featured broadcloth or leather upholstery. Packard offered no convertibles or station wagon models.

▲ Pontiacs wore a simplified grille for 1947, when a six-cylinder Torpedo convertible sold for $1811 ($1853 in DeLuxe trim). Eights added $43 to the price.

▲ Streamliner Pontiacs, including this 1947 Eight DeLuxe woody station wagon, rode a 122-inch wheelbase. Slightly less-expensive Torpedo models measured 119 inches.

◀ "Dramatic" barely describes the 1947 Studebaker, styled by Virgil Exner and Robert Bourke.

▲ Willys launched its all-steel Jeep wagon in 1946, with "Planadyne" semi-independent front suspension.

▲ Most daring of all the new '47 Studebakers was the Starlight coupe (*right*), with wraparound back window. All Studes featured self-adjusting brakes.

◀ The Beech Aircraft Company built this Beechcraft Plainsman sedan prototype. An air-cooled, four-cylinder Franklin engine drove an electric generator, powering separate electric motors located at each wheel.

▼ Dynaflow—the first passenger-car torque converter—joined Buick's option list in 1948, available for $244 on Roadmasters. This Estate Wagon weighed a whopping 4460 pounds and cost $3433. Only 350 were built.

◀ Buick offered a convertible in the Super and Roadmaster series for 1948, priced at $2518 or $2837. Sluggish, droning takeoffs prompted some critics to nickname the new automatic transmission "Dyna-slush."

1948

- Critical material shortages and labor unrest continue through the year; sheet steel remains in tight supply

- Wage disputes close many auto plants in the spring; suppliers are struck, too

- Calendar-year auto production rises to 3,910,213 cars despite all the problems

- With 696,449 built, Chevrolet is tops in model-year production; Ford is second with 430,198, followed by Plymouth and Dodge

- Chrysler Corp. ranks second in total car production, behind GM, ahead of Ford

- Independent automakers earn a 22 percent market share, versus 9.3 percent in 1941

▲ Leather upholstery and Hydro-Lectric windows were standard in the 1948 Cadillac Sixty-Two convertible. The masterful, aircraft-inspired redesign featured curvaceous roof and fender lines, plus a shapely hood.

▲ Modestly sized when they first appeared on the 1948 Cadillac, tailfins would soon grow enormous. This Series Sixty-One sedanet, at $2728, was Cadillac's cheapest model.

▲ Chevy was given Indianapolis 500 pace car honors in 1948. A standard-issue Fleetmaster Cabriolet cost $1750.

▲ Chevrolet's Fleetline Sportmaster looked a lot like pricier GM sedans in 1948. It cost $1492, with 64,217 built.

• After a short 1948 model year, Lincoln and Mercury introduce their all-new '49s in April, followed by Ford in June

• Chrysler Corp. continues to sell its '48 models into early 1949 (as "First Series" '49s), waiting until the modern postwar replacements are available for sale

• The all-new Cadillac introduces tailfins, inspired by the Lockheed P-38 fighter plane

• Hudson introduces a new, revolutionary "Step-down" series for '48: safe, stylish, and with a surprisingly low center of gravity

• Ford Motor Company is in financial chaos, but orders for the 1949 model pass two million by July, an all-time industry record; many of the orders will go unfilled

• The bulk of 1948 models differ little—if at all—from last year's offerings

• Buick introduces its Dynaflow torque-converter automatic transmission, which is available on Roadmasters

• Dodge announces the development of a protective oil coating for the cylinder walls of its newest engines to prevent scoring during the critical break-in period

• Pontiac offers optional Hydra-Matic; it is ordered in most 1948 eight-cylinder models

▲ M.E. Coyle, GM's executive vice president, contrasted a 1948 Chevrolet to a 1929 Buick to demonstrate to a congressional committee how cars had risen in value.

▲ Whatever wouldn't fit inside a leather-upholstered 1948 Chrysler Traveler four-door sedan could be loaded onto the wood/chrome roof rack. Travelers sold for $2163.

▲ The lowest-priced 1948 Chrysler New Yorker was the three-passenger business coupe. Only 701 of these strictly business, compact-cockpit coupes were ever produced.

◀ Deluxe versions of DeSoto's 1948 four-door cost $1825; better-equipped Customs started at $1892.

▲ "Tip-toe" shift cost $121 extra on DeSotos. Shown is a 1948 Custom convertible, priced at $2296.

- Borg-Warner announces that it intends to supply automatic transmissions to automakers—and it will do so before long

- Green is the year's most-popular color; black is considered to be a "Depression" hue and falls from popularity

- Tucker operations are halted in July so that the Securities and Exchange Commission can examine the firm's accounting records

- The U.S. auto industry builds its 100-millionth vehicle (cars and trucks)

- B.F. Goodrich develops the tubeless tire, which will soon dominate the industry

- Henry J. Kaiser plans to build an inexpensive car "at some future date"

- Cadillac Series Seventy-Five sedans carry on with an old prewar design

- Production of the rear-engine/front-drive Gregory is projected to begin in June, but only one car is actually built

- The Playboy convertible is ready for pilot production in April; an announced three cars per day will soon be constructed

- Keller enters minimal production, evolved from the earlier Bobbi-Kar; fewer than 20 will be produced through 1950

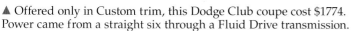

▲ Offered only in Custom trim, this Dodge Club coupe cost $1774. Power came from a straight six through a Fluid Drive transmission.

▲ Most Dodge offerings rolled into 1948 virtually unchanged. This spacious Custom sat seven. Price: $2179.

▲ San Diego scofflaws faced a tight fit in the back seat of this Ford coupe-sedan, supposedly able to carry six. Civilian versions started at $1330.

▲ Despite the growth of suburbia, the era of wood-bodied wagons was ending. This 1948 Super DeLuxe Ford seated eight, and 8912 were built.

▲ Kaiser-Frazer touted 35 improvements in style and mechanical details for 1948. In reality, this $2746 Frazer Manhattan didn't look much different from the '47, though its price rose moderately. Posh interiors helped the Manhattan attract customers, but a standard Frazer was a less-expensive alternative.

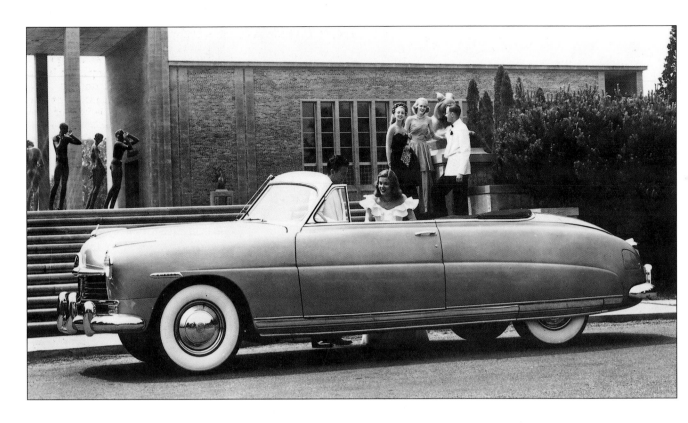

▲ Hudson had a radically new design in 1948: the stunning "Step-down," named for its dropped floorpan. Note the heavy upper-windshield molding on this Commodore Eight Brougham, a feature of 1948-54 Hudson ragtops.

◄ "Step-down" Hudson occupants rode within the unitized body's girders. Hudsons like this Commodore gained a reputation for great handling.

1948 Model-Year Production Figures	
1. Chevrolet	696,449
2. Ford	430,198
3. Plymouth	412,540
4. Dodge	243,340
5. Pontiac	235,419
6. Buick	213,599
7. Studebaker	184,993
8. Oldsmobile	172,852
9. Chrysler	130,110
10. Hudson	117,200
11. Nash	110,000
12. DeSoto	98,890
13. Packard	92,251
14. Kaiser	91,851
15. Cadillac	52,706
16. Mercury	50,268
17. Frazer	48,071
18. Crosley	26,239
19. Lincoln	7769

Some figures are estimated or calendar year

▶ Last examples of the classic Lincoln Continental came off the line in 1948. Henry Ford II drove a convertible to pace the Indianapolis 500 this year.

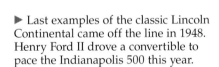

◄ The last American-built V-12 engines were delivered to customers in 1948, under the hood of the Continental and standard Lincolns.

◄ Like other automakers, Nash clung to the past in 1948, planning a major update for '49. Two-toning looked tidy on the Ambassador brougham.

► This 1948 Nash DeLuxe 600 business coupe came stripped for $1478. This example is loaded with optional add-ons, including a huge sun visor.

▲ An even thousand Ambassador Custom cabriolets went to buyers in 1948—the first convertible Nash model since the war.

► GM fastbacks, two- and four-door, continued to lure a fair share of buyers. This Olds Series 76 club sedan, at $1726, changed only in detail for '48.

▶ The 1948 Oldsmobile "Futuramic" 98, from Harley Earl's Art & Colour studio, was one of GM's first totally new postwar designs.

▼ Modern shaping—especially in the rear—gave the new Oldsmobile 98 a longer, lower look. More than 65,000 "Futuramic" 98s were built in '48.

▲ Even in four-door form, the fresh lines of Oldsmobile's Futuramic 98 are evident. This two-toned DeLuxe sedan was the top 1948 seller.

▼ Packard's 1948 redo evolved from a "Phantom" car built for vice president Ed Macauley. This $3250 Super Eight rode on a 120-inch wheelbase.

▲ Though its price leapt from $1289 in 1947 to $1529 in '48, the Plymouth Special Deluxe was unchanged.

▲ Roof, decklid, and inner panels remained from the prior Clipper, but Packard stylists packed on metal to give a modern "flow-through-fender" effect. This seven-passenger Custom Eight limo rode a 148-inch wheelbase.

▶ Custom Eight Packards like this one used a new 145-bhp 327-cid engine, while the standard eight was 288-inch unit. Convertibles came in Super and Custom trim.

▼ In DeLuxe trim, a 1948 Plymouth sedan cost $1441. Moving to Special DeLuxe meant nicer upholstery, a bright windshield frame, hoodside lettering, and an additional $88.

▶ Spotlights weren't part of the $1857 price of a 1948 Plymouth Special DeLuxe convertible, which had no rear side windows.

▼ Pontiacs sported "Silver Streak" nameplates for the first time in 1948. Here, a fastback Streamliner.

▲ Big Pontiac news for 1948 was Hydra-Matic, available for an extra $185. This DeLuxe Streamliner woody cost $2490.

▶ Americans clamoring for a "car of the future" thought they had one in the Tucker. Hailed as the "First Completely New Car" in half a century, the four-door fastback looked like nothing on the road in 1948. Styled by Alex Tremulis—on a 128-inch wheelbase—the sedan stood only 60 inches tall.

Tucker Sets a New Pattern of Safety

▲ Carrying a 94-bhp, 226-cid six, the Studebaker Commander Regal DeLuxe convertible cost $2431.

▲ Though exonerated, Tucker's dream of a radical—and safe—auto was dashed. Innovations had included fully independent suspension and a moving "Cyclops-eye" headlight.

▲ Preston Tucker (*left*) together with radio personality Art Baker (*holding microphone*), son Preston Jr., and public relations agent Charles Pearson. By the time 51 cars were built, Tucker was indicted on charges of securities fraud.

▼ Tuckers were roomy, powerful, and aerodynamic. The rear-mounted flat-six engine delivered 166 bhp and a walloping 372 pound-feet of torque.

◄ Driving the $1765 Jeepster was the same engine that had powered prewar Americars: a 134-cid four, rated at 63 bhp. First-year output topped 10,000.

► Details of the 1948 Willys station wagon were similar to the Jeepster. Early models were painted maroon, with a woodlike trim pattern.

CHAPTER SEVEN

1949

A NEW ERA BEGINS

Never had American automobiles changed more in a single year than in 1949. Of course, Cadillac, Hudson, Oldsmobile Ninety Eight, Packard, and Studebaker had been redesigned for 1947-48—which hindsight suggests was a bit ahead of necessity—and Kaiser-Frazer had been an astounding success since opening for business in mid 1946. Now everyone else made the much-anticipated "big switch" from warmed-over prewar products to all-new postwar styling, and many nameplates offered new or improved engines to go with it. The result was a record industry year (eclipsing 1929), as Americans eagerly gobbled up more than six million cars.

"New" was the biggest factor in this banner sales performance, hyped to the heavens in most every showroom. But new didn't mean the same thing to every automaker. Chrysler, for instance, stayed on the conservative path it had started down after the mid-Thirties Airflow disaster, issuing high and boxy new models that were long on practicality but short on pizzazz. Such cautiousness would cost Chrysler dearly—but not this year.

At the opposite end of the Big Three styling spectrum was General Motors, whose sleek new '49 Chevys, Pontiacs, Buicks, and junior Oldsmobiles continued the aircraft-inspired themes favored by corporate design chief Harley Earl. These cars confirmed GM as the industry's design leader, a role it would play for most of the next 40 years. A further jewel in GM's '49 styling crown was a new concept that would soon sweep the nation. This, of course, was the glamorous "hardtop convertible."

Between GM's stylishness and Chrysler's stuffiness stood Ford Motor Company, whose biggest attraction by far was the most-changed Ford in a generation. A trim and tasteful design, the all-new '49 Ford was an instant hit—a good thing, too, as Dearborn was still teetering on the brink of financial ruin. Had it not sold well, Ford might not have lived to celebrate its 50th birthday. But fortunately, the '49 Ford did sell.

"Bathtub" styling, a legacy of sporadic wartime design work at Ford and elsewhere, was fairly popular in '49. Its best expressions were a burly new Lincoln and Mercury, and Hudson's year-old "Step-down"; the worst was arguably Nash's advanced, but awkward, new Airflyte. Packard offered bathtubs for a second season in '49, though the later "pregnant elephant" sobriquet still seems more appropriate.

Other '49 developments were more predictive. Compression ratios began sneaking up in preparation for an industrywide "horsepower race," with GM looming as the odds-on favorite thanks to the introduction of America's first modern, short-stroke overhead-valve V-8s at Oldsmobile and Cadillac. What's more, Olds chief Jerrod Skinner had the foresight to drop his lively "Rocket" engine into a smaller, lighter platform to create the granddaddy of all "muscle cars," the speedy new Olds 88. Automatic transmissions were still a high-cost feature, but GM offered one in more models for '49—and where GM led in those days, others were bound to follow. The year also saw the death of structural-wood models and the birth of all-steel wagons at GM and Chrysler.

Upstart Kaiser-Frazer could financially manage only facelifts for 1949, and president Joe Frazer advised that wasn't nearly enough against so much new competition. But chairman Henry Kaiser refused to retrench, and ordered tooling up for 200,000 cars. He should have listened. With 1949 sales of only 100,000 cars, K-F began a long, sad, downward spiral.

1949

- Industry production hits a record high: 6,253,651 vehicles roll off of American assembly lines

- All Big Three automakers display modern postwar redesigns, at least on some models

- Ford's model-year production beats Chevrolet by more than 100,000, topping 1.1 million; Plymouth ranks third, Buick fourth

- Calendar-year production totals favor Chevy for the number-one spot, comfortably ahead of perennial rival Ford

- Inflation continues to drive new-car prices spiraling upward

- With so much new to see, regular auto shows finally return to the American scene, though many are smaller, local events

▲ Buick's Super Estate Wagon lost a lot of wood with the new '49 styling, though the timber remained structural. List price was $3178, and 1847 were produced for the model year.

▲ Buick—along with fellow GM makes Cadillac and Olds—pioneered the hardtop convertible with the '49 Roadmaster Riviera. At $3203, it cost $53 more than the soft top; 4343 were built.

- Chevrolet and Pontiac adopt curvaceous modern bodies like other GM makes, while Ford and Chrysler turn to boxier profiles

- Buick, Cadillac, and Oldsmobile offer the first true pillarless "hardtop convertible" coupes, blending the coziness of a closed car with the airiness of a ragtop

- Hardtop look gives GM a lead on this striking body style that will dominate auto design throughout the Fifties

- The emergence of all-steel station wagons from Chevrolet, Olds, Plymouth, and Pontiac sets a new trend for burgeoning suburbia; "woody" wagons will soon be extinct

- The first two Volkswagens arrive in America—few suspect the import invasion that's destined to follow in the Fifties

- Nash displays new "inverted bathtub" Airflyte styling; aerodynamics are excellent and sales are fairly impressive, but the shape draws scorn from critics

▲ The Series Sixty-Two Coupe de Ville "hardtop convertible" was Cadillac's new style leader for 1949.

▲ Cadillac's new postwar styling saw only minor changes for '49, when the Series Sixty-Two convertible sold for $3442.

▲ Fleetline fastbacks wore Chevy's 1949 restyling well. A DeLuxe four-door cost $1539. More than 130,323 were built.

- GM touts high-compression, overhead-valve V-8 engines; Cadillac's 331-cid version cranks out 160 horses, the 303-cid Olds Rocket boasts 135

- GM's new V-8s allow higher compression ratios with available gas; they're lighter in weight and "breathe" more easily, while shorter strokes cut friction and reduce wear

- Studebaker thwarts Ford's attempt to purchase exclusive rights to Borg-Warner's automatic transmission

- The Renault 4CV and other minisize European cars are available, especially in the Northeastern states; sales are slow

- A sleekly restyled Buick lineup includes the pillarless two-door Riviera hardtop

- Cadillac holds over its 1948 tailfins, but launches a radically new Coupe de Ville pillarless hardtop as a Series Sixty-Two model late in the model year

- Chevrolet adopts a modern streamlined body with a curved, two-piece windshield; the model lineup gets new names, but the overhead-valve six harks back to the Thirties

▲ Chevy replaced its woody wagon with a look-alike all-steel model in mid 1949, still a Styleline DeLuxe, listing at $2267. This is one of the 3342 "true" woodies built.

◀ A 1949 model from each of GM's car divisions poses on the banked high-speed oval at the firm's Milford, Michigan, proving grounds.

▲ Nonfastback '49 Chevys, like this $1508 DeLuxe Sport Coupe, were dubbed "Stylelines." Less-expensive Specials were also available.

- Buicks feature front-fender VentiPorts, commonly called "portholes," plus an aircraft-inspired appearance

- Chrysler starts the new season with carryover 1948 models; an all-new, boxy-but-modern Silver Anniversary series debuts at midyear

- Fleetline fastbacks and all-steel station wagons are part of the Chevrolet lineup for '49; vacuum shift is gone

- The similarly restyled "Second Series" DeSoto, Dodge, and Plymouth models also arrive in the spring—all powered by the old, reliable L-head sixes

- A restyled Crosley with integral front fenders sags sharply in sales, despite adding a sporty new Hotshot roadster

- The handsome, slab-sided Ford restyle earns credit for helping to save the company, evidence that the youthful team under Henry Ford II is now in charge

▲ A convertible was the only wood-bodied Town & Country in Chrysler's new '49 lineup. The price was a stiff $3970, so production only reached 1000 units.

▶ Chrysler dashboards, as on the ragtop T&C, still dazzled for 1949, and they were padded, too. The pistol grip to the left controls a spotlight.

▲ The eight-cylinder New Yorker topped Chrysler's standard line. The $2726 four-door was the series' best-seller.

▶ Windsor stood a step above Royal among six-cylinder Chryslers. Again, the four-door was the series' mainstay.

- Dodge offers a new single-seat, three-passenger Wayfarer roadster; it lacks roll-up windows—a throwback to the '30s

- Fords are quick and nimble with a 100-bhp L-head V-8; Mercurys are too, with 110 horses on tap; overdrive is optional for both

- Hot-rodders continue to clamor for aftermarket add-ons to hop-up the legendary Ford/Mercury flathead V-8 engines

- Chrysler and DeSoto use semiautomatic "Tip-Toe" Fluid Drive, so no gear shifting is needed when moving forward; GM cars all offer true automatic transmissions

- DeSoto offers an all-steel Carry-All "sedan-wagon" with a fold-down back seat, along with a "woody" wagon and nine-passenger Suburban sedan

- Coil-spring front and semielliptic-leaf rear suspension replaces Ford's antiquated front- and rear-transverse-leaf setup

- The Frazer lineup includes an odd-looking but unique four-door Manhattan convertible sedan, sales are dismal

- Kaisers and Frazers receive a facelift amid a serious corporate shake-up; sales of both makes falter perilously

▲ Crosley took a shot at sports-car fans with the new doorless $849 Hotshot, which surprised many people with its racing prowess. Only 752 '49s were built.

▲ The "Cubster" roadster was one of many short-lived kit-car ventures that sprang up after World War II.

▶ Like the new-for-'49 Chryslers, DeSoto was fresh but boxy. The $2156 Custom Club Coupe found 18,431 buyers.

▲ The four-cylinder, 30-mpg Del Mar from San Diego was a no-hope '49 newcomer. Fewer than 10 were built.

- Hudson returns with its modern "Step-down" body, as introduced in mid 1948, without significant change

- Recessed headlights mark the 1949 Lincolns, which wear heavy-looking, slab-sided bodies; an L-head V-8 is new

- The curved Mercury attracts hot-rodders and customizers; small Lincolns share the Merc bodyshell, and get attention, too

- A mildly customized 1949 Mercury club coupe will later be immortalized as the car that actor James Dean drives in the 1955 movie, *Rebel Without a Cause*

- The aerodynamic Nash Airflytes are packed with innovations, including a "Uniscope" gauge pod atop the steering column and traditional reclining front seatbacks that form a bed

- Packards are carryovers until midseason, when mildly facelifted 50th anniversary "Twenty-Third Series" models bow

- Plymouth offers a new all-steel station wagon to rival those issued at midseason by Chevrolet, Oldsmobile, and Pontiac

- Restyled Silver Streak Pontiacs wear notchback or fastback bodies, again carry six- or eight-cylinder L-head engines

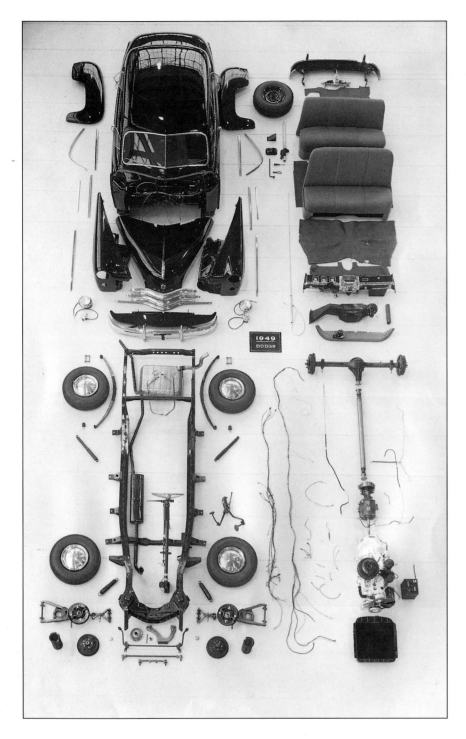

▲ Dodge's most affordable 1949 model was this trim, three-seat Wayfarer business coupe priced at $1611. Though inexpensive, just 9342 were sold.

◄ A '49 Dodge was "broken down" to show all its new components. Prices this year ranged from $1611 to $2865.

▲ Ford's wagon still used structural wood, but changed from a four-door Super DeLuxe to a two-door Custom.

- Crosley introduces Goodyear-Hawley four-wheel disc brakes at midyear; all-disc brakes also appear on the limited-production Chrysler Crown Imperial

- The ignition key operates the starter on Chrysler products; key-actuated starting will soon become nearly universal, but for now most cars still use a dashboard button

- The separate foot-operated starter pedal is gone from all General Motors cars, but some makes cling to the pedal starters for a few more years

- Earl "Madman" Muntz buys out the Kurtis operation and begins production of the Muntz Jet, one of the most-noticed sports-type cars of the early Fifties

- The $500, 475-pound Imp mini-convertible has a 7.5-bhp air-cooled engine and a no-door fiberglass body; it will be produced in minimal quantity as late as 1951

- The Davis Motor Car Co. is organized to build a three-wheeler; the first car is completed in October, but fewer than 20 will be built through 1949

▲ The new-look 1949s, like this upmarket $1511 Custom V-8 Club Coupe (150,254 built), were the most completely updated Fords in many years.

▲ Ford built 433,316 1949 Custom Tudor sedans. This $1590 V-8 model shows off its neat, all-new lines.

▶ President Henry Ford II drives the one-millionth '49 Ford built with brothers Benson and William Clay.

▶ A heavy-looking facelift marked the '49 Frazer, here the new Manhattan convertible sedan, which cost $3295—just $147 less than a Cadillac ragtop.

▲ Sedans remained Frazer's sales mainstay, but the up-market $2595 Manhattan attracted only 9950 buyers.

▲ Looking rather Studebaker-like, the small four-cylinder, rear-engine, front-drive Gregory saw only a prototype.

▲ Joe Frazer (*here circa 1945*) protested when Henry Kaiser tooled up for 200,000 1949 sales. Only 100,000 were sold.

▲ "Toylike" describes the aptly named Imp, a rear-engined prototype that would never see volume production.

▲ Hudson's bold "Step-down" design returned little-changed for '49; output rose to 159,100. This is the $3041 Commodore Eight Brougham convertible.

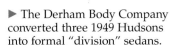

◀ A 1949 Hudson Super Six sedan sports rare two-toning and "cadet" windshield visor. Price: $2207.

▶ The Derham Body Company converted three 1949 Hudsons into formal "division" sedans.

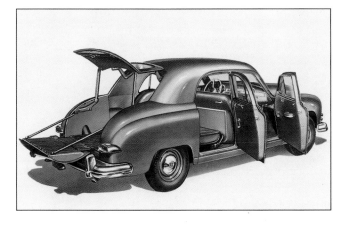

▲ Kaiser added the Special Traveler "hatchback" sedan for 1949, a wagon substitute conceived by chairman Henry Kaiser. About 22,000 were built at a price of $2088.

▲ For an extra $200, Kaiser offered the $2088 Traveler as this DeLuxe Vagabond. Output was only 4500 units through model-year 1950. The left-rear door didn't open.

1949 Model-Year Production Figures

1. Ford	1,118,308	8. Dodge	256,857	15. Cadillac	92,554
2. Chevrolet	1,010,013	9. Hudson	159,100	16. Kaiser	79,947
3. Plymouth	520,385	10. Nash	130,000	17. Lincoln	73,507
4. Buick	409,138	11. Studebaker	129,301	18. Frazer	21,223
5. Pontiac	304,819	12. Chrysler	124,218	19. Crosley	7431
6. Mercury	301,319	13. Packard	116,955		
7. Oldsmobile	288,310	14. DeSoto	95,051	*Some figures are estimated or calendar year*	

▶ Kaiser Virginians sported leather-look tops. They had a curb weight of 3541 pounds, meaning the standard 112-horse six had its work cut out for it.

▼ Like Frazer, Kaiser was able to field only a modest 1949 facelift against all-new Big Three models; here, the $2195 DeLuxe sedan.

◀ Famed race-car designer Frank Kurtis sold his sleek Kurtis Sport both as a kit and fully built. Only 35-36 were completed in 1948-49.

▲ Lincoln offered junior and senior ragtops for '49. This "Junior" standard model listed at $3116.

▲ Lincoln dropped the bulbous Sedan after '49 due to slow sales. Price: $3238.

▲ The elegant standard Sport Sedan was Lincoln's best-seller. Total Lincoln output was 73,507 units.

▲ Still with one nameless series but a bigger flathead V-8, Mercury offered this $2410 convertible for 1949.

▶ Mercury's '49 price leader was this $1979 coupe. It became a favorite with "Kustom Kar" fanatics in the '50s.

▲ Mercury's '49 wagon retained the wood-look dash trim used in previous years, but the dash itself was somewhat cleaner and better organized.

▲ Like Ford, Mercury switched from four-door to two-door wagons for '49. Base price for this eight-seater, of which 8044 were built, was $2716.

▲ A quartet of radically new 1949 Airflytes, of which 130,000 were sold, departs Nash's California plant.

▶ Ambassador was Nash's senior series in 1949. This Airflyte in top-line Custom trim listed at $2363, which put it in the medium-price field.

◀ Nash's new Airflyte dash with bullet-shaped "Uniscope" instrument pod was definitely futuristic for '49.

243

▲ The Oldsmobile Ninety Eight, here a $2594 DeLuxe four-door, retained its new-for-'48 "Futuramic" styling.

▲ Lansing's news for '49 was the modern "Rocket" V-8. In Series 88 models like this one, it made Olds a hot performer.

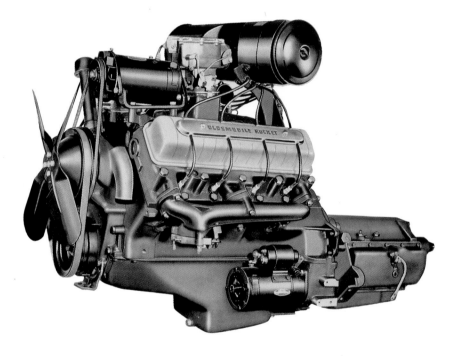

▲ Along with Buick and Cadillac, Olds debuted a hardtop for 1949, the luxurious Ninety Eight Holiday.

◀ Arriving at 304 cubic inches, Oldsmobile's "Rocket" pioneered the modern short-stroke, high-compression, overhead-valve V-8 that would sweep Detroit. Horsepower for '49 was a lively 135.

▲ Olds 88s quickly began setting stock-car racing records. Symbolizing this performance, an 88 soft top served as the Official Pace Car for the '49 Indy 500 Memorial Day Race.

▲ From Buffalo, New York, the four-cylinder Playboy boasted a manual-folding steel top for just $985, but tiny size and only two seats held total production to about 90 cars.

244

▲ Packard was restyled for 1948, so its '49s offered little new except the debut of Ultramatic Drive. This 50th anniversary '49 Eight DeLuxe was priced at $2383.

▲ This view of a '49 Super Eight Club Sedan shows why Packards of this period came to be called "pregnant elephants." No matter—the cars sold well.

▶ The 1949 Plymouth Special DeLuxe convertible found 15,240 buyers.

▼ Plymouth's four-door Special DeLuxe was a hot seller: 252,878 units.

▲ Plymouth also looked to the future with its all-steel Suburban wagon. It sold for $1840; 19,220 were sold.

▲ Despite the new all-steel Suburban, Plymouth offered woody wagons for '49. Here a Special DeLuxe four-door.

▲ Pontiac's "Silver Streak" hood trim was bolder than ever for '49. This DeLuxe Chieftain Eight listed at $1924.

▶ This full-page magazine ad presented but a sampling of Pontiac's broad 36-model lineup for 1949.

246

▲ Fastbacks fast faded from public favor after 1949, when Pontiac offered this rakish four-door Streamliner DeLuxe Eight for $1903.

▲ This oddity is the wood-bodied Pup, one of many here-today/gone-tomorrow autos that sprouted postwar.

▲ Another would-be hit was the Towne Shopper. Fuel was sipped at the claimed rate of 50 mpg.

▲ Studebaker's '49 ads talked value—and 129,301 buyers agreed. The Champion four-door was the firm's best-seller.

1950-1952

THE "BUYER'S MARKET" RETURNS

The American auto industry might have been expected to pause after its frantic product pace of 1948-49, and it did. Yet there was still plenty to keep buyers interested in 1950-52.

In fact, 1950 saw record calendar-year production of nearly 6.7 million cars, up more than 1.5 million from banner '49, though this wasn't entirely Detroit's doing. In June, President Truman committed U.S. troops to support the United Nations "holding action" against an incursion by Communist insurgents into South Korea. It looked like the start of a new world war, and Americans rushed to buy, fearing another drought of consumer goods á la World War II. That fear proved exaggerated, but the government did curb civilian production for a time and diverted strategic materiels to military production while awarding fat contracts to car companies. With that, the booming postwar seller's market was over.

Predictably, 1950 was a quiet model year. The all-new 1948-49 designs were still fresh, so changes were evolutionary, not revolutionary, though Studebaker's bizarre "bullet-nose" facelift was a notable exception. A more predictive one was Nash's new Rambler, which quickly became America's best-selling compact car based on a combination of sturdy, unitized construction and thrifty, reliable engines. The "hardtop convertible"—that '49 General Motors innovation—spread to encompass Chevrolet and Pontiac models, as well as belated entries from Hudson and most divisions at Chrysler Corporation, which had blown a chance to pioneer this fast-selling style back in '47.

Elsewhere on the '51 scene, the ungainly "pregnant elephants" gave way to the first fully fresh Packards since the elegant Clipper of a decade earlier. Designer John Reinhart called them "high pockets" because of a high beltline, but they were clean, modishly square, yet dignified. Alas, they were but a temporary help. Like Hudson, Packard would be stuck with a platform it could not afford to change very much, to the detriment of sales.

More stunning was a new second-generation Kaiser shaped by the redoubtable "Dutch" Darrin. Sleek, ground-hugging, and low-waisted, it offered superb visibility, a fine ride, a predictive safety-styled interior—and the same staid old Kaiser six. It really should have had a V-8, but most of the money for that had gone into a new 1951 compact. Egotistically named for the company chairman, the Henry J was sturdy but little more, and though it sold well at first, it didn't have the staying power of the Rambler.

While most automakers offered light touch-ups for 1952, Ford Motor Company overhauled its entire fleet. Like the newest Packards, these were square and slab-sided but neat—perhaps too neat for a public gone gaga for glitz. But they sold well enough to restore Dearborn to the number-two spot in industry volume, helped by true hardtops at Lincoln-Mercury—and continued bungling at Chrysler. Also, Lincoln gained a new ohv V-8 destined to sire a whole slew of such engines throughout the Ford family.

Nash also redesigned along similar lines, but its new Airflytes were arguably less pleasing despite aesthetic assistance from Italy's renowned Pinin Farina. After a decade's pause, Willys reentered the auto business with its compact Aero line, which included two- and four-door sedans and a neat Eagle hardtop.

Out on the fringes were more small-time sports cars, minicars, and even electrics; most were poorly planned, underfinanced ventures that were present one day and gone the next. The low-volume Nash-Healey roadster was an interesting exception. So was a Kurtis Sport puffed up from two to four seats to become the Muntz Jet, launched by California radio and used-car baron Earl "Madman" Muntz, also with visions of vast fortune. But the car game was fast becoming one for major-league players only, as events would soon prove.

1950

- Auto sales smash seemingly optimistic predictions and set an industry record at better than 6.3 million units

- Ford slips to second place with 1.2 million cars built; Chevrolet turns out nearly 290,000 more for the model year

- More than 40 million passenger cars now travel on American roads—40 percent more than a decade ago

- On June 25, President Truman orders U.S. troops to Korea in a "police action," which officials will call the Korean "conflict"

- The National Production Authority orders conservation of raw materiels; a "state of emergency" is proclaimed in December

- Defense work rises: Cadillac wins a contract to produce tanks; Ford inks an agreement to build Pratt and Whitney aircraft engines

▲ Like all 1950 Buicks, the Roadmaster Riviera hardtop wore more-shapely styling and higher prices. This new Deluxe-trim version listed for $2854.

▲ Buick grilles were "toothier" than ever for 1950, as on this $1909 Special "Jetback" four-door sedan. It enjoyed a production run of 58,700 units.

▲ Cadillac also adopted a bolder look for 1950. The Sixty Special sedan cost $3797 and attracted 13,755 customers.

▲ Cadillac's posh new Sixty Special sedan listed for $3797. Riding on a longer wheelbase for 1950, it attracted 13,755 buyers.

▲ Picking up where the 1939 Futurama left off was GM's 1950 Motorama, the first of many glitzy annual traveling auto shows. An Olds lurks behind the column.

- Fear of wartime shortages triggers a national car and truck buying frenzy

- Chrysler endures a 104-day worker walkout beginning January 25

- Briggs Cunningham's Cadillacs surprise many by coming in 10th and 11th at the Le Mans road race in France

- A coal strike early in the year leads to eventual steel shortages

- The Federal Reserve Board places stricter limits on automobile credit

- Chevrolet prices start at $1329, while a Crosley can be bought for just $872; average full-time workers earn $2992 yearly

- About 60 percent of American families own a car, whose average age is 7.8 years

- GM's fastback body styles are rapidly losing popularity in the marketplace

- The new Chevrolet Bel Air is a true pillarless coupe; hardtops are also offered by Pontiac, Chrysler, Dodge, and DeSoto

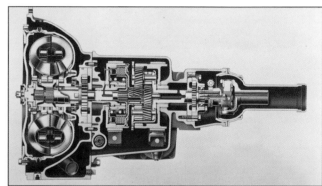

▲ A $1529 Styleline DeLuxe Sport Sedan rolls off the assembly line. This model was easily Chevy's best-seller in 1950.

▶ Chevy scored a first in the low-priced field with a fully automatic two-speed Powerglide transmission, a $159 option for DeLuxe models. Here the original 1949-50 design.

▲ Chrysler kept its boxy year-old styling, but simplified the grille for 1950. At $3232, the New Yorker convertible attracted only 899 buyers.

▲ GM beat Chrysler to hardtops, but Highland Park got one for 1950 and called it Newport. This is a $3133 New Yorker, of which 2800 were built.

▲ Imperial came down in price for 1950, to $3176 for a Deluxe Sedan like the one shown here. Almost 11,000 of the luxury Chryslers found a home.

- Chevrolet's DeLuxe models can now be ordered with a two-speed Powerglide automatic transmission, a $159 option

- Chrysler products receive a mild facelift of the three-box shape introduced in 1949

- Chrysler's Town and Country employs disc brakes, but just on the front axle

- Crosley introduces the Super Sports roadster, a Hot Shot with doors, and returns to drum brakes after a flirtation with discs

- Lacking a pillarless "hardtop convertible" body style, Ford offers a sporty two-tone Crestliner two-door sedan with a padded vinyl top and deluxe interior; Mercury's Monterey coupe has a similar theme

- The Wayfarer roadster continues in the Dodge lineup, with roll-down windows phased in late in the 1949 model run

- Kaiser-Frazer fields reserialed '49s until the completely restyled '51s arrive in the spring

- Lincolns may be ordered with Hydra-Matic transmissions, purchased from GM

▲ DeSoto was also new to hardtops in 1950. Its sole entry was this top-of-the-line Custom model called Sportsman.

▲ Dodge stood mostly pat for 1950, but a cleaner "face" was notable. This four-door sedan wears top-line Coronet trim.

◄ Ford was still a year away from hardtops in 1950, so it offered a jazzed-up Custom Tudor called Crestliner, with wild two-toning, padded roof, and deluxe interior.

◄ Diagonal grille bars and detail changes marked the 1950 Hudsons, here the top-line Commodore Eight Custom Brougham convertible. At $2893, only 425 were built.

• A surprisingly popular shorter Pacemaker series joins the Hudson lineup, accounting for half of model-year production

• Lincoln finishes ninth in the first grueling *Carrera Panamericana* (Mexican Road Race), which is won by an Oldsmobile 88

• In March, Nash launches the Rambler line on a 100-inch wheelbase—the first volume-built U.S. "compact" car

• The Rambler debuts as a unique convertible, followed in June by a two-door station wagon

• Hydra-Matic transmission is available on Nash Ambassador; the engine is started by lifting the gearshift lever

• Oldsmobile produces its final six-cylinder Series 76 models

• A Rocket 88 Oldsmobile shatters a class speed record at Daytona, averaging more than 100 mph

• Many Packards are available with Ultramatic—the only automatic developed by an independent maker

• The last-ever Plymouth wood-bodied station wagon rolls off the line; an automatic choke is new for all models

▲ Hudson reached down to the lower medium-priced field for 1950 with a five-model Pacemaker line that included this $1933 four-door.

▲ This nicely restored Hudson Commodore Six Club Coupe is well-accessorized. Base price was a moderate $2257 in 1950.

▲ Mercury's 1950 wagon sales sank from 8044 in 1949 to 1746 in 1950, despite a cut from $2716 to $2561.

- Oldsmobile models win 10 of 19 major stock-car races for the year

- Packard's "pregnant elephant" bathtub shape is in its final season

- Crosley announces the "Quicksilver" engine with 10.0:1 compression, running on gasoline plus water-alcohol injection

- Plymouth displays the Ghia-styled XX-500, the first of Chrysler's new "idea cars"

- Studebaker front ends display a "bullet nose," and sales soar to a record 320,884

- Willys Jeepsters get an F-head four-cylinder engine and a bigger six (also F-head) at midyear

- Akron-based Goodyear develops a puncture-sealing tubeless tire

- Late in the season, Studebaker introduces "Automatic Drive" automatic transmission

- Nash-Kelvinator exhibits the NXI two-seater on a Fiat chassis; it will evolve into the Metropolitan minicar of 1954

▲ Mercury settled for minor changes for 1950—and raised the price of its ragtop only $2 to $2412; 8341 were built.

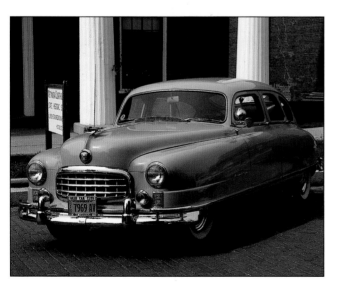

▲ Nash enjoyed higher volume for 1950—160,354 units. Among the Ambassadors was this $2064 Super sedan.

▲ Nash celebrated a production milestone in 1950 with its two-millionth car, an aerodynamic Airflyte sedan.

▲ Nash's Rambler bowed as a convertible in March 1950, followed by a two-door wagon in June. It would quickly prove to be America's most successful postwar compact.

▲ Rambler's other new model bowed on June 23. This is the 100-inch-wheelbase Custom two-door wagon; 1713 were sold.

1950 Model-Year Production Figures

1. Ford	1,498,590	8. Studebaker	320,884	15. Packard	42,627
2. Chevrolet	1,208,912	9. Mercury	293,658	16. Lincoln	28,190
3. Plymouth	610,954	10. Chrysler	179,299	17. Kaiser	15,228
4. Buick	588,439	11. Nash	171,782	18. Crosley	6792
5. Pontiac	446,429	12. DeSoto	136,203	19. Frazer	3700
6. Oldsmobile	408,060	13. Hudson	121,408		
7. Dodge	341,797	14. Cadillac	103,857	*Some figures are estimated or calendar year*	

▲ Oldsmodile's little-changed 88 convertible remained fast,
flashy, and highly desirable in 1950—and 9127 were sold.

◄ Oldsmobile
98s, such as this
$2641 Holiday
hardtop, looked
lower and
longer for 1950;
8263 were built.

► The 1950 Packards were identical to the "Second-Series" '49s—sales plunged from 116,955 to 42,640 for the year.

▼ Plymouth dechromed for 1950—and looked better for it. The convertible was sold only in Special DeLuxe trim.

▲ Aside from station wagons, the sporty $2190 Chieftain Eight DeLuxe convertible was the priciest Pontiac for 1950.

▲ Pontiac added four new Chieftain Catalina hardtops for 1950. This is the $2069 DeLuxe Eight version.

▶ Pontiac's 1950 wagons looked a little plain without Di-Noc wood-look trim. Price range: $2264 to $2411.

▲ Dwindling demand led Pontiac to drop four-door Streamliners (*Deluxe Eight shown*) after 1950.

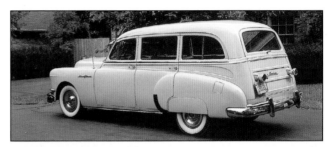

▲ Studebakers got a new "bullet-nose" grille for 1950. It's worn here by a $1644 Champion Regal DeLuxe two-door sedan, of which 21,976 were sold.

▲ An inch-longer wheelbase improved 1950 Studebaker profiles. This $2018 Commander Regal DeLuxe rode a 120-inch wheelbase and had 102 bhp.

▶ Willys's Jeepster phaeton sold well in debut 1948-49, but demand dropped sharply for 1950 despite a new grille and more-modern F-head engines. Jeepster vanished after '51.

▲ Buick again listed long-chassis Super and Roadmaster Riviera sedans for '51, here the $3044 Roadmaster; 48,758 were produced.

▲ At $3780, the '51 Roadmaster Estate Wagon remained the costliest Buick—and the rarest, as only 679 were sold.

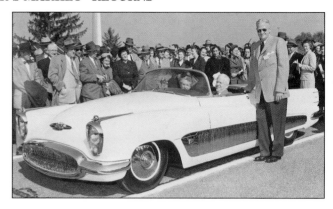

▲ Buick chief engineer Charles Chayne with the '51 XP-300 show car. Seated are GM president Charles Wilson and wife.

▲ Even with a hefty base price of $3987, the Series Sixty-Two ragtop attracted 6117 lucky buyers.

▶ Cadillac's $3843 Series Sixty-Two Coupe de Ville hardtop more than doubled its sales for model-year '51.

1951

- As the Korean War intensifies, production cutbacks are ordered by Washington, by way of the the National Production Authority

- Under siege, auto manufacturers face government-ordered ceiling caps and increasing labor costs

- A rail strike in February temporarily cuts off supplies of critical raw materiels

- More than three-fourths of all cars are considered "deluxe" models, as postwar prosperity and public optimism continue

- Hardtops gain in popularity as convertibles decline; 480,597 hardtops are built (nine percent of total), versus 140,205 ragtops

- Industry output of 5.3 million cars is second only to record 1950 tally

▲ Chrysler's new "Firepower" 180-bhp V-8 won Indy Official Pace Car honors for the New Yorker ragtop.

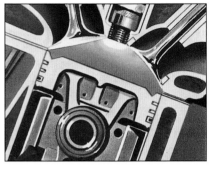

▲ This drawing appeared in 1951 Chrysler brochures to help explain the superior power and efficiency of the company's Hemi engines.

▲ The $2030 Chevy Styleline DeLuxe convertible wore a broader "smile" for '51, captivating 20,172 customers.

► Bolder grille aside, Chryslers were still dull and boxy for '51—but 25,000 New Yorker sedan buyers disagreed.

- Hardtop pillarless coupes join Ford, Plymouth, Hudson, and Packard lineups

- Chrysler introduces its 331-cid, 180-bhp "Hemi" Firepower V-8 engine in the Saratoga, New Yorker, and Imperial

- The "hemispherical-head" V-8 offers technical advantages, but is costlier to produce than conventional engines

- The Town and Country nameplate now applies only to Chrysler's all-steel wagon

- Bill Sterling places third in the *Carrera Panamericana* (Mexican Road Race) driving a Chrysler Saratoga

- Dodge continues the all-steel Sierra wagon introduced in 1950; the Wayfarer Sportabout roadster returns for its final season

- Hydraguide power steering, an industry first, becomes available on Chryslers

- Ford-O-Matic and Merc-O-Matic transmissions, built in cooperation with Warner Gear, are introduced

- Hudson ads promise "Miracle H-Power" from the H-145 engine, the most-powerful and largest six built in the U.S.

◄ Briggs Cunningham's Chrysler Hemi-powered C-2R, evolved from his C-1, competed in 1951 with no real success. Only three were built.

► Like all '51 DeSotos, the $2438 Custom four-door sedan wore a lower, wider, but still toothy grille. Total DeSotos built it reached approximately 106,000 units.

▼ A trio of '51 Ford Customs about to face the future: the $1949 convertible (*top left*), new $1925 Victoria hardtop coupe, and $1505 Tudor sedan (*on road*).

- Ford's Custom Victoria is the only low-priced hardtop with a V-8

- This is Frazer's final year; it sports a rather radical restyling front and rear

- Hudson's hot new Hornet—which debuts with a 145-bhp, 308-cid six—begins to earn a long list of stock-car racing victories

- The restyled "Anatomic" Kaiser, penned by Howard Darrin, debuts as a '51 model

- Kaiser promotes safety with a padded dash and pop-out windshield

- The Kaiser-built Henry J economy car debuts, lacking many common amenities, including a glovebox and trunklid

- Restyled "Rocket" Oldsmobiles win an impressive 20 of 41 stock-car starts

- The Super 88 series joins the Oldsmobile lineup; station wagons are dropped

- The new two-seat Nash-Healey sports car places bodywork penned by Donald Healey atop an existing Nash chassis

► Though late to respond to Chevy's pillarless Bel Air, Ford's new 1951 Custom Victoria Hardtop boasted 110,286 model-year sales.

▼ Ford's Crestliner returned for '51 at $1595 (a $116 price cut!). But after only 8073 were built it was dropped.

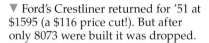

▲ Forget the ugly setting. This photo of Ford's $1465 DeLuxe Fordor was turned into brochure artwork.

▲ Another '51 brochure-art photo shows off the newly named Country Squire wagon; 29,017 were built.

- The first Muntz Jets are produced in Evanston, Illinois, courtesy of the colorful Earl "Madman" Muntz

- Nash Rambler adds a Country Club hardtop coupe to the lineup, but the wagon is far more popular

- The "bathtub" Nashes make their final appearance, adding prominent rear fenders for a "racing teardrop tail"

- The Pontiac Streamliners are dropped during the model year; fastback bodies are quickly going the way of the dinosaur

- Studebaker Commanders are finally available with V-8 power; a 232-inch, 120-horsepower unit at first

- A Comet two-seat roadster is offered in kit or assembled form; it reportedly can do 40 mph and gets 60 mpg

- The Paxton Phoenix, styled by Brooks Stevens, is to be offered with a steam engine, but never leaves the drawing board

- The factory soon offers "severe usage" parts for the Hudson Hornet to boost its already-swift performance for racing

- Top-line Hudsons get Hydra-Matic, making the Drive-Master/Super-Matic semiautomatic transmissions obsolete

▲ Part of the final Frazer Standard line was this novel Vagabond utility sedan.
Kaiser pioneered the hatchback body in 1950. About 3000 were sold at $2399 each.

▲ The Henry J was styled by an outside company, some
would argue poorly. Almost 82,000 were built for 1951.

▲ Like Ford and Plymouth, Hudson introduced hardtop
models for 1951; here, the $2869 Hornet Hollywood.

- Studebaker is the first to install durable synthetic Orlon convertible tops

- Packard gains a modern squared-off profile, adds a lower-priced 200 series

- Packard is awarded the title of "the most beautiful car of the year" by the Society of Motion Picture Art Directors

- Oriflow-brand shock absorbers improve Plymouth's ride and handling

- Pontiac production is the second-best ever, more than 370,159 units

- Chrysler's K-310 show car, designed in Detroit but built in Italy, demonstrates some of Virgil Exner's early ideas

► Besides the Hollywood, Hudson's debut Hornet line included this $3099 Brougham convertible.

▲ Low and sleek, the all-new '51 Kaiser was a styling sensation and a good handler. Here a $2296 Club Coupe.

▲ The 1951 Kaiser was the work of famed designer "Dutch" Darrin. The Deluxe four door was the most-popular model.

▲ Kaiser persisted with utility sedans in its new second-generation '51 line. All were called Traveler, and included this $2433 four-door DeLuxe.

1951 Model-Year Production Figures

1. Chevrolet	1,229,986	8. Oldsmobile	285,615	15. DeSoto	106,000
2. Ford	1,013,381	9. Studebaker	246,195	16. Packard	100,713
3. Plymouth	611,000	10. Nash	205,307	17. Henry J	81,942
4. Buick	404,657	11. Chrysler	163,613	18. Lincoln	32,574
5. Pontiac	370,159	12. Kaiser	139,452	18. Frazer	10,214
6. Mercury	310,387	13. Hudson	131,915	18. Crosley	6614
7. Dodge	290,000	14. Cadillac	110,340		

Some figures are estimated or calendar year

▲ Lincoln still lacked hardtops for '51, so the stand-in Cosmopolitan Capri coupe returned at $3350 with a wider "mouth" and reshuffled trim.

▲ Lido, which remained Lincoln's standard-series pseudo-hardtop for '51, measured 214.8 inches overall.

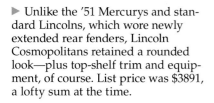

▶ Unlike the '51 Mercurys and standard Lincolns, which wore newly extended rear fenders, Lincoln Cosmopolitans retained a rounded look—plus top-shelf trim and equipment, of course. List price was $3891, a lofty sum at the time.

▲ Nash Airflytes like this '51 Ambassador Custom were once seen on TV's
Highway Patrol. Airflyte output totaled 153,398 units this year.

▲ The Nash-Healey roadster resulted from a chance meeting between Nash's
George Mason and British sports-car builder Donald Healey.

▲ Rambler remained its trim self into '51, but added a third model in June, a neat Custom-trim hardtop coupe dubbed Country Club that attracted 19,317 happy buyers.

▲ Semienclosed front wheels gave early Nash Ramblers, like the $1968 Custom Country Club hardtop, an overly large turning circle. This model weighed 2420 pounds.

▲ As if to remind everyone how much cars had changed since horseless carriage days, Olds issued this publicity photo of a new '51 Super 88 Holiday hardtop posed with the little Curved-Dash Oldsmobile of 1900-04. Olds dropped its six for '51, making the 88 the base series.

► Packard still relied heavily on medium-priced 200 Series two- and four-door sedans for '51, but also hopped on the hardtop bandwagon with the Mayfair, tagged at $3234.

▲ At $3662, the luxurious Patrician 400 sedan was the priciest of Packard's 1951 models. Just 9001 of the hefty 4115-pound sedans were produced.

▲ Cranbrook replaced Special DeLuxe as Plymouth's poshest for '51. Like other models, this $1826 four-door wore a new face but had no major changes.

▲ Total Pontiac production reached 370,159 units for the model year. Here a Chieftain Eight Super Catalina.

▲ Studebaker muted its "bullet-nose" for '51 by painting the chrome ring around it. Here a Champion two-door sedan.

◄ The '52 Golden Anniversary Cadillacs gained 30 horsepower (to 190) via a four-barrel Quadra-Jet carb. The posh $4323 Sixty Special sedan saw 16,110 examples built.

▼ Buick's '52 Special line again used Chevy/Pontiac tooling. Exclusive to the series was this $2115 "Tourback" two-door sedan; only 2206 were built.

1952

- The Korean conflict restrains auto production: the National Production Authority limits build to 4,342,000 cars

- Ford Motor Company is the only Big Three automaker to fully restyle its cars this year; Chrysler and GM field lightly facelifted '51s

- More than two million automatic transmissions are installed this year

- Chevrolet output drops to 818,142 cars, Ford builds only 671,733; Plymouth clings to its traditional number-three position

- Sears, Roebuck markets a new compact Allstate, essentially a Henry J with a different grille and tweaked styling

- Installation of V-8 engines exceeds one third of total production

► Despite a $100 bump, Chevy's
DeLuxes still handily outsold Specials
in 1952. This $1761 four-door sedan
topped the line with 319,736 sales.

▲ The '52 Chryslers were identical to
the '51s. Here, the $3969 New Yorker
Newport.

► Chrysler's 180-bhp Hemi V-8 gave
the best performance in its lighter '52
models, like this $3215 Saratoga.

▼ The Chrysler Special show car was
built by coachbuilder Ghia of Italy, but
designed by Highland Park's Virgil
Exner. It was one of several "idea
cars" used to jazz up Chrysler's image
during a period of dull production
styling.

- Power steering becomes available on
Buick Roadmasters as a $199 option

- Cadillacs now sport stylish dual-exhaust
outlet tips in the rear bumper

- Now with a four-barrel carburetor,
Cadillac's V-8 has the highest horsepower
rating in the industry: 190

- Crosley production ceases as the company
merges with General Tire and Rubber

- A 160-bhp Firedome "Hemi" V-8 becomes
available across the DeSoto line

- Three hemi-powered C-4R Cunninghams
compete at Le Mans; Briggs Cunningham
drives to a fourth-place finish

- All-steel Ford station wagons debut,
including a woody-look Country Squire

- Ford's all-new cars get new "Power-Pivot"
suspended brake and clutch pedals

- Ford introduces an overhead-valve,
six-cylinder engine; the long-lived
"old-tech" flat-head V-8 soldiers on

▲ Except for the hubcaps, the '52 Dodges were literally 1951 reruns. The Coronet four-door sedan, $2256 in 1952, was the best-seller in both years.

▲ Ford offered four-door wagons for '52, its first since 1948, but now with steel bodies. The Country Sedan in the midrange Customline series saw 11,927 sales, but the cheaper two-door Ranch Wagon did best: 32,566.

▲ Ford was all-new for 1952, thus more competitive against holdover Chevy and Plymouth—but Korean War-related conservation forced production cutbacks.

▶ Glamour leader of Ford's '52 line was the new Sunliner convertible, priced at $2027; 22,534 were built.

- The Henry J "Vagabond" wears a "continental" spare tire in the rear

- Hudson launches the 119-inch-wheelbase Wasp series and drops the Super Six; Hydra-Matic is now available in all models

- Marshall Teague wins 12 of 13 stock-car events at the wheel of a Hudson Hornet; Hudsons claim 27 NASCAR victories

- Mildly facelifted Kaiser sedans are launched late in the 1952 model year

- Lincoln adds ball-joint front suspension, a 317.5-cid overhead-valve V-8, and hardtops for the redesigned Cosmopolitan and Capri

- Lincolns claim all top five spots in the 1952 grueling 2000-mile *Carrera Panamericana* (Mexican Road Race)

- Power steering and a four-way power seat are newly introduced Lincoln options

- Studebaker joins the "hardtop" ranks with its Starliner coupe; the bullet-nose front end is replaced by a "clam-digger" grille

- Mercury's flathead V-8 gets a much needed boost to 125 horsepower via a higher 7.2:1 compression ratio

▲ Hudson's "Step-down" design, now in its fifth season, was starting to look dated when this Hornet Club Coupe was built.

▲ Hudson scored 27 NASCAR wins in 1952, but that didn't help sales of this Hornet sedan. Overall, output fell from 131,915 units in 1951 to 70,000 in 1952.

- Mercury dashboards now feature aircraft-inspired sliding levers

- Italian stylist Pinin Farina helps redesign the Nash line, replacing the "bathtub" look with a more-modern squared-off shape

- Nash-Healey is also restyled with help from designer Pinin Farina

- Nash-Healey scores a first in class, third overall at Le Mans

- A three-wheel electric shopping car, the Autoette, is built from 1952 to 1957; it's little more than a golf cart

- Packards now equipped with power brakes for the first time

- James Nance takes the helm at Packard, promising a new focus on luxury cars

- Skorpion two-passenger roadsters, made of fiberglass in Anaheim, California, from 1952 to 1954, come as a kit or assembled

- Dual-Range Hydra-Matic is installed in Pontiac, Oldsmobile, and Cadillac cars

◀ Kaiser got a heavier-looking face during model-year '52, but it did little for sales, which began a long downward spiral (only 32,131 this year). Here, a $2654 Manhattan sedan.

▼ Lincoln was all-new for '52. Cosmopolitan was now the baseline series, and came as a Sport hardtop coupe or this $3198 four-door sedan.

◀ The '52 Lincoln also boasted a modern overhead-valve V-8 and its first hardtops; here, the $3518 uplevel Capri. With 12,916 produced, it was the year's most-popular Lincoln.

- Overdrive transmission is available in Plymouths and DeSotos

- Studebaker celebrates its 100th anniversary, it built carriages long before producing automobiles

- Willys Aero sedans arrive sporting L-head or F-head six-cylinder engines

- Ford's Continental show car features phone, dictaphone, and automatic jacks

- The 1952-56 Woodill Wildfire sports car with a Glasspar fiberglass body is sold as a kit, although 15 will be sold fully assembled

- Experimental Packard Pan-American will evolve into the 1953 Caribbean

▲ New in 1951, the four-place '52 Muntz Jet was a literal extension of Frank Kurtis's 1949-50 Sport two-seater.

▲ Mercury shared in Ford Motor Company's linewide overhaul for '52. This $2370 convertible, one of three new Monterey models, had a production run of 5261 units.

▲ The Muntz Jet, priced at $4450, was arguably America's first "personal-luxury" car. Nearly 400 were built from 1951 to 1955.

▶ Wagons remained the costliest '52 Mercs, but were now four-doors with fake wood trim on all-steel bodies.

▲ Nash was all-new for '52, entering the hardtop race at last with this $2829 Ambassador Custom Country Club; 1228 were built. A shorter $2433 Statesman version saw 869 built.

▲ Like all '52 Nashes, this $2716 Ambassador Custom sedan wore the badge of Italy's Pinin Farina, but the actual styling work was by Nash's in-house chief designer, Ed Anderson.

▲ Oldsmobile's base series for '52 was tagged 88 DeLuxe and included this $2262 two-door sedan, plus a four-door. The more-potent Super 88s outsold the 88s six-to-one.

▶ Plymouth's first hardtop bowed for '51 as the $2114 Cranbrook Belvedere. This nearly identical '52 model added the distinctive "saddleback" two-tone treatment.

1952 Model-Year Production Figures

1. Chevrolet	818,142	8. Mercury	172,087	15. Packard	62,921
2. Ford	671,733	9. Studebaker	167,662	16. Kaiser	32,131
3. Plymouth	396,000	10. Nash	154,291	17. Willys	31,363
4. Buick	303,745	11. Cadillac	90,259	18. Henry J	30,585
5. Pontiac	271,373	12. DeSoto	88,000	19. Lincoln	27,271
6. Oldsmobile	213,490	13. Chrysler	87,470	20. Crosley	2075
7. Dodge	206,000	14. Hudson	70,000	*Some figures are estimated or calendar year*	

◀ Pontiac offered a sedan delivery in the early '50s, but sales were slim—only 984 units for '52. The famous "Silver Streak" trim is evident on this example.

▲ This 1952 Chieftain Eight DeLuxe droptop shows how little Pontiac Styling changed from the '49 redesign.

▲ The all-new Studebaker planned for the firm's 1952 centennial was delayed, so this Champion Starlight coupe and other models were changed only at the front.

▲ Willys returned to passenger cars for '52 with the Aero Willys. Among the three two-door models offered, was this $1989 Aero-Wing; 12,819 copies were sold.

▼ Willys claimed 24 cubic feet of trunk capacity for its '52 Aero—good even today. Note the rear-fender kick-up.

▲ A look inside the '52 Aero Willys shows uncommon roominess for a compact, and simple, functional trim.

CHAPTER NINE

1953-1959

THE DESIGNER IS KING

Americans were still seeking their promised postwar peace and prosperity when they a new President in 1952. With the Korean War dragging on, the specter of the atomic bomb hovering over the new "Cold War" with Communist powers, and increasingly thorny domestic challenges like inflation, McCarthyism, and civil rights, it was perhaps no great surprise when General Dwight David Eisenhower of D-Day fame swept into office on the Republican ticket ahead of "egghead" Democrat Adlai Stevenson. Ike went to Korea to help end the fighting, then returned home to usher in eight years of self-absorbed prosperity. In many ways, the Eisenhower years were a triumph of style over both substance and science. How else to explain a time when Cinerama made as much news as the first polio vaccine?

Detroit reflected the national bent for good times and free spending by spewing forth a dazzling array of cars. Each yearly crop was seemingly more colorful, complex, and contrived than the last—as well as longer, lower, wider, heavier, and more powerful.

Year-to-year changes were often far more dramatic than young people could now imagine. Between 1954 and '55, for example, Chevrolet, Dodge, Plymouth, and Pontiac were all transformed from relatively simple, low-suds family haulers to hot V-8 performers with acres of new "dream car" sheetmetal, miles of chrome, and gallons of multicolor paint.

Designers were the true kings of Detroit in 1953-59, and the public paid homage by buying cars like crazy, peaking with 1955's record seven-million-plus. Many of those buyers were newly better-off middle-class types still fast forsaking cities for suburbia, where the station wagon was the family's new vehicle of choice. Yet, hardtops kept increasing even faster in popularity, and if two-door models were good, why not four-doors? General Motors again led

the way, and by 1956 you could find hardtop sedans in most every showroom—and two cars in many driveways.

Alas, there were fewer makes to choose from by decade's end. One factor was the frantic 1953-54 Ford/GM price war that mortally wounded surviving independents. The second was the sharp 1958 recession that turned Americans away from frivolous flash toward more-sensible cars. Thus, Nash and Hudson consummated a desperate 1954 marriage to form American Motors, only to vanish in three years after AMC decided to focus on more salable Rambler compacts. Similarly, once-proud Packard hoped for better times with its 1954 takeover of struggling Studebaker, but was sacrificed for the corporate good in 1958. Even heady 1955 couldn't save postwar upstart Kaiser-Frazer, and Willys likewise abandoned the U.S. car market to concentrate on Jeeps.

No such retrenchment for Ford, which regained its position as the industry's number two in 1952, then set its sights on giant GM by ambitiously expanding from two divisions to five. Among the results were the elegant Continental Mark II and the spectacularly unsuccessful Edsel. Meanwhile, number-three Chrysler roared back with bold new Virgil Exner styling for '55, then seized industry design leadership with its befinned "Forward Look" '57s.

Throughout these years, Detroit waged a "horsepower race" to rival the U.S.-Soviet arms buildup. Sadly, handling and braking were anything but ideal (ditto fuel efficiency—gas was a quarter a gallon), yet a few automakers timidly tried selling safety features like seatbelts and padded dashboards.

But that's the way it was in an age when glitter, go, and gadgets were the principal keys to automotive success. The Fifties was the last decade in which America was truly innocent, and American cars, like the country itself, would never be the same again.

1953

- Auto-production controls are lifted in February, as Dwight D. Eisenhower takes over the presidency from Harry S. Truman

- The Korean War ends July 26, 1953

- The postwar "seller's market" is over; auto-makers are forced to focus on style as well as engineering

- A selling "blitz" begins as Ford mounts an all-out challenge on Chevrolet; factories literally force cars onto dealer lots

- Calendar-year cars built soars to 6,134,534

- Ford comes within 100,000 units of Chevrolet's 1.3 million, the closest the two rivals have been since 1949

▲ The 1953 Buick Roadmaster Skylark sold just 1690 copies at $5000 each.

▲ Save Skylark, the Roadmaster Estate Wagon was again the costliest Buick for 1953 with a $4031 price tag.

▲ The $3002 Super boasted vastly improved performance over predecessors with Buick's new ohv "Fireball" V-8.

▲ Though denied the ohv new V-8, the $2197 Special four-door remained Buick's most-popular car for 1953: 100,312 units.

- The Ford/Chevrolet blitz of 1953-54 helps kill off the independent automakers

- Automakers Ford and Buick celebrate a half century in the auto business

- GM's Motorama "dream car" show tours for six months, hosting 1.7 million visitors

- Chevrolets start at $1524; the average worker now earns $3581 annually

- The average American motorist now drives 10,000 miles annually

- Popping up everywhere, motels now outnumber hotels by a two-to-one margin

- American cars, such as Buick, begin to adopt 12-volt electrical systems

- Half of all new cars are built with automatic transmissions

- Hardtop production accounts for almost 15 percent of total production

- Restyled, still-boxy Chrysler products finally adopt one-piece windshields

- Full-size Chevrolets are restyled; a new 235.5-cid six delivers up to 115 bhp

- Chevrolet introduces the Corvette sports car with a 150-bhp six-cylinder engine

▲ Cadillac's Eldorado was one of three limited-edition GM ragtops for '53. A $7750 price held production to only 532.

▲ Small rear-fender scoops were part of Cadillac's optional air conditioning for '53, as shown here on a Sixty Special.

▲ Unlike Eldorado, Cadillac's '53 Series Sixty-Two ragtop had a full-height windshield and a flexible top boot.

▲▶ Despite smart new looks outside, the 1953 Chevrolets were largely 1949-52 carryovers under the skin.

- Buick offers a limited-production Skylark convertible with a lowered beltline, rounded wheel openings, and wire wheels

- Eldorado and Fiesta, limited-edition ragtops from Cadillac and Oldsmobile, boast "Panoramic" windshields

- All Buicks except the Special have V-8 engines; most also have improved Twin-Turbine Dynaflow transmission

- Because of an August fire at GM's Hydra-Matic plant, many Cadillacs and Oldsmobiles come with Dynaflow this year

- Briggs Cunningham drives a Chrysler-powered Cunningham C-5R to third place at Le Mans

- PowerFlite two-speed fully automatic transmission is installed in Chrysler models beginning in June

- A Red Ram "Hemi" V-8 engine delivering 140 horsepower is available in the all-new Dodge

- Dodge is one of the first production makes styled for Chrysler by Virgil Exner (formerly of Studebaker)

- A Dodge V-8 averages 23.4 mpg in the Mobilgas Economy Run, and also breaks 196 AAA stock-car records at Bonneville

◄ Chevy offered another ragtop in its midline Two-Ten series. Priced at $2093, it found only 5617 buyers.

▲ At $3513, the '53 Corvette offered modern lines but some oddly old-timey features like side curtains.

▲ Corvettes began coming off a small Flint assembly line in June 1953. Early fiberglass-body problems limited '53 model output to 315 units. Production moved to St. Louis for '54.

▲ Chevy's long-lived "Blue Flame Six" gave 1953 Corvettes 150 horsepower via triple carburetors and other tweaks.

• Ford's venerable—and dated—flathead V-8 engine is in its final season

• Twin H-Power for Hudson Hornets sports dual carburetors; the "7-X" race engine yields 210 horsepower

• Hudson's economy-priced compact Jet debuts, but sells below expectations

• Lincolns capture the first four spots in the *Carrera Panamericana*

• Kaiser's posh Dragon sedan flaunts gold-plated body trim, padded roof, and innovative interior detailing

• The Nash-Healey convertible is joined by a LeMans coupe

• Packard's line-topping Caribbean convertible outsells Cadillac's Eldorado

• A LeMans option for Ambassador adds dual carburetors and high-compression head, bringing the Nash to 140 bhp

• Plymouths gets Hy-Drive, combining manual shift with a torque converter

▲ Staid styling remained a Chrysler sales drawback for 1953. This New Yorker DeLuxe convertible sold for $3945.

▲ The '53 Chrysler Custom Imperial Town Limousine offered opulent seating for six at $4762. Just 243 were sold.

◄ DeSoto again offered long sedans for 1953. This $3529 FireDome with a 160-bhp V-8 found 200 buyers.

► The lone DeSoto convertible again came only in top-line FireDome form for '53. Just 1700 were sold at $3114.

► A hot new "Red Ram" V-8 gave '53 Dodge Coronets extra sizzle. The $2494 ragtop saw just 4100 sales.

- Studebakers enjoy a Euro-style redesign by Robert Bourke of the Raymond Loewy Studio

- Demand for the stunning Starlight and Starliner coupes tops sedans, to the surprise of Studebaker executives

- A Ford V-8 powers the short-lived Detroiter fiberglass-body convertible

- The Edwards American convertible enters limited production; about a half-dozen are built from 1953-55

- The Fibersport roadster, based on the Crosley Hot Shot, is sold either as a kit or fully assembled

- Fina Sport combines bodies from Vignale of Italy with Detroit V-8 power

- A fiberglass-bodied Buick Wildcat appears at the GM Motorama; the sporty Oldsmobile Starfire wears an aircraft-inspired oval grille

- Appropriately named, Studillac sports a large Cadillac V-8 into the light Studebaker coupe body; sales are slow

- Lincoln's show-stopping XL-500 concept car features an all-glass roof

▲ Ford marked its 50th birthday in '53 by making few changes to its all-new '52 models. This woody-look Country Squire wagon sold 11,001 copies at $2203.

▼ This '53 Crestline Sunliner did official pace car duty at that year's Indianapolis 500, honoring Ford's 50th anniversary.

▶ The Ford Crestline Victoria hardtop listed at $2055 for '53; 128,302 were sold. This one wears a dealer-installed "continental kit," a popular accessory.

▲ A facelifted Henry J bowed during 1952, so the '53s were little-changed.

▲ The original '48 Hudson "Stepdown" styling was aging by '53, and output fell to 66,143. This Hornet Club Coupe has optional "Twin-H Power."

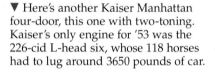

▲ Luxury $3924 Dragon was Kaiser's newest '53. Just 1277 were built.

▼ Here's another Kaiser Manhattan four-door, this one with two-toning. Kaiser's only engine for '53 was the 226-cid L-head six, whose 118 horses had to lug around 3650 pounds of car.

▲ Mercury offered its first two-series line for 1953. Here, the four-door sedan in uplevel Monterey trim.

▲ Lincolns like this '53 Capri were winning big in the brutal *Carrera Panamericana*.

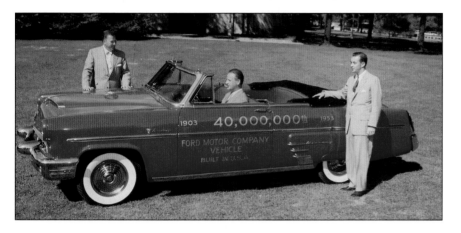

◄ This '53 Mercury Monterey played a part in Ford Motor Company's 50th anniversary hoopla. Posing (*from left to right*) are Ford brothers Henry II, Benson, and William Clay.

▲ A new face with "floating" grille helped spruce up the compact Rambler, giving it a look closer to bigger Nashes. Here a $2125 Custom Country Club with "continental kit."

▲ Only minor detail changes marked the year-old "Farina" Nashes for 1953. Rear fender skirts grace this Statesman Custom two-door sedan, which retailed for $2310.

1953 Model-Year Production Figures

1. Chevrolet	1,346,475	8. Mercury	305,863	15. Hudson	66,143
2. Ford	1,247,542	9. Chrysler	170,006	16. Willys	42,224
3. Plymouth	650,451	10. Studebaker	151,576	17. Lincoln	40,762
4. Buick	488,755	11. DeSoto	132,104	18. Kaiser	27,652
5. Pontiac	418,619	12. Nash	121,793	19. Henry J	16,672
6. Oldsmobile	334,462	13. Cadillac	109,651	20. Metropolitan	743
7. Dodge	320,008	14. Packard	90,252		

Some figures are estimated or calendar year

▲ A new long-chassis Nash-Healey Le Mans coupe bowed for 1953 at a staggering $6399. Styling was again the work of Italy's famed Ferrari designer, Pinin Farina.

▲ The Ninety Eight Fiesta completed GM's trio of flashy, limited-edition '53 convertibles. Olds sold only 458.

▲ Packard joined the fray, proffering its take on the pricey low-volume rag-top for 1953, the $5210 Caribbean.

▲ The 1953 Packard Patrician sedan came in this $3740 base model and as a $6531 Formal Sedan by Derham.

◄ Packard debuted Clipper in two new 1953 subseries as a first step to divorce itself from a "medium-priced" image. This DeLuxe club sedan sold for $2691, and 4678 were sold.

▼ Plymouth got a heavy restyle for 1953, but still looked short and stubby in profile. The $2064 Belvedere hardtop was again included in the top-line Cranbrook series.

▲ The Pontiac line sported a new look for 1953. This well-chromed Chieftain Eight Catalina hardtop sold for $2446.

▲ With sales sagging, the Pontiac Sedan Delivery was in its second-to-last year in 1953; 1324 were built.

◄ Studebaker's all-new '53 "Loewy coupes" were a strong indication of how automotive styling would evolve during the Fifties. Base price: $1868.

▲ "Loewy" Studebaker coupes came as a pillared Starlight and pillarless Starliner. This Starliner started at $2488.

▲ Loewy-based lines also appeared on Studebaker's new 1953 sedans like this $2316 Commander Land Cruiser.

▲ Willys was also celebrating 50 years in 1953. Aero models, like this $2157 Eagle hardtop, changed little.

▲ Willys's Aero-Ace two-door sold in 1953 for $1963, nearly as much as some less-expensive full-size cars.

287

▲ GM show-car styling arrived on the '54 Buicks. Here, the $2964 Super.

▲▶ Riding a 122-inch wheelbase, the Buick Skylark and Special wagon.

▲ Cadillacs like this 1954 Eldorado sported new wraparound windshields and a blockier shape.

▲ Relatively rare and very pricey, Cadillac built 2150 Eldorados for the car's sophomore year. Base price: $5738.

1954

- The horsepower race is underway: 15 makes announce higher engine ratings

- Ford's model-year production of 1,165,942 beats Chevrolet's by a slim 22,381 cars—a new ohv V-8 gets much of the credit

- Nash-Kelvinator and Hudson combine to form American Motors Corporation—George Romney is newly named chief

- Studebaker and Packard consolidate into the Studebaker-Packard Corporation

- Buick launches its hot Century, stuffing a Roadmaster V-8 engine into the lightweight two-door Special body

- Giving the home team its due, the Detroit Public Library unveils its automotive history collection; it's open to the public

▲ Though little-changed from its introduction, Chevy's Corvette saw 1954 output jump to 3640.

▲ Chevy's 1954 Bel Air hardtop was officially called Sport Coupe. At $2061, it garnered 66,378 sales.

◄ The Bel Air convertible remained the most glamorous standard Chevy for 1954. The base price was $2185.

▲ Still on an exclusive chassis, the 1954 Chrysler Custom Imperial sedan listed at $4260; 4324 were built.

▲ Extra chrome again marked the DeLuxe Chrysler New Yorkers for 1954. Here, the $3406 four-door sedan.

• Ford's "Y-Block" overhead-valve V-8 replaces the long-lived flat-head engine

• The wraparound windshield is a new design trend, led by General Motors makes Buick, Cadillac, and Oldsmobile

• The Buick Special runs with a new over-head-valve 264-cid V-8 engine

• Henry Kaiser buys the Willys-Overland firm, moves all production to Toledo, Ohio

• A revamped Buick Skylark is festooned with tacked-on fins, more chrome—lacks the elegant stylishness of 1953

• Cadillacs are longer, lower, wider, and the first make with standard power steering

• The Dodge Royal 500 convertible sports a "continental" spare tire and wire wheels

• DeSotos and Dodges are available with PowerFlite automatic transmission, but a three-speed manual is still standard

• Chrysler and DeSoto six-cylinder models appear for the last time

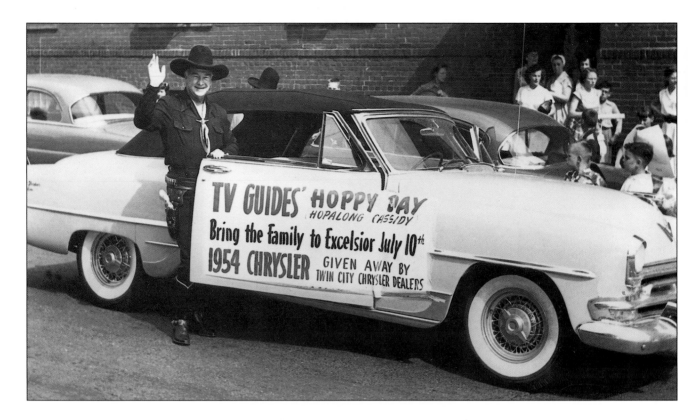

▲ Dodge wooed buyers in mid 1954 with two-toned "spring specials" like this Coronet Sport Coupe hardtop. Prices started at $2380.

▲ William Boyd of *Hopalong Cassidy* TV fame saddles up a '54 Chrysler New Yorker DeLuxe ragtop.

▲ A hot mid-1954 Royal 500 ragtop was inspired by the Indy 500 Dodge pace car. Just 701 were built.

- Dodges finish in five of the top six positions in the Medium Stock class at Mexico's *Carrera Panamericana*

- Ford is the first low-priced car with ball-joint front suspension geometry

- The Ford Crestline Skyliner and Mercury Monterey Sun Valley hardtop models debut with tinted Plexiglas roof panels

- Hudson's dramatic aluminum-bodied Italia, built by Carrozzeria Touring in Italy, sees minimal production of just 26 units

- Designer "Dutch" Darrin later buys 100 leftover Kaiser-Darrins, installs Cadillac V-8s

- The fiberglass Kaiser-Darrin sports car features horizontally sliding doors, landau top, and a Willys F-head engine

- Plymouths gain the PowerFlite automatic transmission option in March, making the Hy-Drive semiautomatic redundant

- Facelifted Kaiser Manhattan sedans boast a new supercharged engine

- DeSoto's Adventurer I show coupe rides a shortened wheelbase, sports outside exhausts—and comes close to production

◄ San Franciscan Sterling H. Edwards built but six cars in 1953-55, including this handsome one-off hardtop.

◄▲ Ford's new '54 Crestline Skyliner sported a green-tint Plexiglas front half-roof that brought the outside inside—and, according to critics, made people perspire on sunny days.

▲ With 293,375 built, the Customline Tudor remained a mainstream Ford for 1954. It cost $1744 with six, but the big news was a modern ohv V-8.

• Packard adopts tubeless tires during the year; other manufacturers will follow for '55

• An overdrive-equipped Studebaker Land Cruiser V-8 wins the Mobilgas Economy Run

• New Jomar blends a British TVR chassis with a lightweight aluminum body

• Chrysler road tests an experimental gas turbine engine in a Plymouth Belvedere

• A Dodge Firearrow roadster, initially a mock-up show car, is made road ready; the Firearrow coupe and convertible appear later, leading to the Dual-Ghia

• Experimental/show cars include a Corvette-based Nomad wagon, Buick Wildcat II, Packard Panther, GM turbine-powered Firebird, Plymouth Explorer, Ford FX-Atmos, and Mercury Monterey XM-800

► Hudson updated its "Step-down" for '54, but the effort was too late. Here, the Hornet convertible.

▼ Hudson's dumpy Jet compact bowed for '53 and promptly bombed. Here, a '54 Jet-Liner two-door.

▲ The radical 1954 Italia was eyed as the next new Hudson, but only 26 were built before funds ran out. All wore aluminum bodywork.

▲ Narrow sliding doors and a novel three-way soft top were featured on the '54 Kaiser-Darrin roadster.

◄ Styled by Dutch Darrin, the Kaiser-Darrin featured a fiberglass body. The $3668 ragtop was a slow seller; just 435 were built.

1954 Model-Year Production Figures

1. Ford	1,118,308	8. Dodge	256,857	15. Cadillac	92,554
2. Chevrolet	1,010,013	9. Hudson	159,100	16. Kaiser	79,947
3. Plymouth	520,385	10. Nash	130,000	17. Lincoln	73,507
4. Buick	409,138	11. Studebaker	129,301	18. Frazer	21,223
5. Pontiac	304,819	12. Chrysler	124,218	19. Crosley	7431
6. Mercury	301,319	13. Packard	116,955		
7. Oldsmobile	288,310	14. DeSoto	95,051	*Some figures are estimated or calendar year*	

▲ The aptly named King Midget bowed in 1946 and hung on until 1970. All came with a one-cylinder engine.

▲ Lincolns wore a bolder face for 1954. Price for this ragtop Capri was $4031, and 1951 were sold.

▲ Here's a replica of the Lincolns that ran 1-2 in the Stock Class of the final *Carrera Panamericana* of 1954.

▲ Lincoln priced its '54 Capri sedan at $3711.

▲ The '54 Mercury Custom two-door listed for $2194.

▲ Like Ford, Mercury got a new ohv V-8 for '54, with 256 cid and 161 horses, versus a 239 with 130.

▲ The singular Muntz Jet was near the end of its road in 1954.

293

▲ Mercury's $2582 Monterey Sun Valley was a cousin to Ford's popular '54 Skyliner, but sold only 9761 units.

▲ Looking like a big toy Nash, the two-seat Metropolitan coupe and ragtop were fair sellers in the mid Fifties.

▲ Metropolitan prices started at $1450. This convertible listed for $1469 not including the continental kit shown.

◄ This 1954 Nash Statesman Custom Country Club hardtop is a rarity (2726 were built). It sold new for $2423.

▲ A trendy wrapped windshield and blockier contours marked the 1954 Oldsmobiles. The Super 88 Holiday saw a healthy 42,155 sales.

◄ Olds added the Starfire name to its Ninety Eight convertible for '54. Base price was $3249. Just 6800 were built.

▼ Oldsmobile's Ninety Eight Holiday hardtop came in standard and DeLuxe versions for '54, priced at $2826 and $3042. The DeLuxe was more popular.

▲ Packard's handsome standard convertible listed for $3935 and saw total production of just 863 copies.

▲ Pacific replaced Mayfair as Packard's senior-line '54 hardtop. Sales were slow; only 1189 copies were produced.

◄ Caribbean came back for '54 as Packard's glamour leader, but the price went up to a staggering $6100.

► Belvedere became Plymouth's top-selling series for '54, and again listed a hardtop, up-priced to $2145.

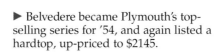

▲ The '54 Plymouths were the last of the staid and stubby generation introduced for '49. This ragtop Belvedere was one of only 6900 built.

▲ Pontiac moved upmarket for '54 with four new top-line Star Chief models on a longer wheelbase. Among them was this $2557 Custom Catalina hardtop.

▲ Like all '54 Pontiacs, the new $2630 Star Chief convertible wore a light redo of 1953's facelift, which included more-prominent rear fenders.

▲ Studebaker added wagons for '54 with two-door Conestoga models like this $2448 Commander DeLuxe.

▲ The 1954 Studebaker "Loewy" coupes showed few changes to their stunning year-old styling. This pillared Commander Regal Starlight sold for $2341.

▼ A "continental kit" graced the '54 Willys Aero Custom models like this Eagle hardtop, but the now-struggling firm could afford few other changes.

▲ Once Buick's best-seller, the next-to-the-top Super line again included this $2831 Riviera hardtop coupe.

▲ Buicks were occasionally chosen for police work, as was the relatively light Century two-door sedan shown here.

◄ Only 4243 Buick Century Estate Wagons were built for 1955. The hefty $3175 base price may have held down sales.

▼ Cadillac's own 1955 Series Sixty-Two convertible wore a tasteful facelift of its all-new '54 styling. List price: $4448.

1955

- The first McDonald's drive-in opens

- Detroit's big boom year: Automobile output leaps an amazing 44 percent

- American production totals 7,920,186 cars and 1,249,090 trucks—setting a new record

- Ford's output is the highest since 1923, yet one-quarter million below Chevy's 1,704,667

- Buick takes over third spot in sales, bumping Plymouth to fourth

- The average car retails for $2300, while the average worker earns $3851 yearly

- Led by Buick and Oldsmobile, the four-door hardtop ranks as the trend of the year

- The Corvette also adopts V-8 power

▲ The Series Sixty-Two four-door sedan remained Cadillac's best-selling model for banner 1955: 45,300 units.

▶ Distinctive "shark" fins graced Cadillac's '55 Eldorado, and would do so for several years. Price was up sharply to $6286, and so were sales.

▲ Every '55 Chevy was all-new, but none was more desirable than the $2305 Bel Air V-8 convertible.

▲ Chevy's first V-8 since 1917 bowed for 1955 with 265 cubic inches and 162 or 180 horsepower.

▲ Chevy's new '55 Bel Air Nomad pioneered the "hardtop" wagon, but attracted just 8386 buyers.

- V-8 engines are new to Chevy, Plymouth, Pontiac, Hudson, Nash, and Packard

- Seven out of 10 new cars have an automatic transmission; 80 percent are built with V-8 engines

- Car air conditioning is on the upswing: 184,027 installations in 1955 versus just 57,469 units installed in 1954

- Installment buying expands: The National Automobile Dealers Association (NADA) warns buyers of "crazy credit terms"

- Automatic-transmission shift levers poke from the dashboards of Chrysler products, which get new "Forward Look" styling inspired by designer Virgil Exner

- Three-tone color schemes appear on Chrysler brands, as on the DeSoto Coronado

- Dodge's La Femme hardtop features a pink/white exterior and interior, folding umbrella, and a fitted purse

- Ford's Thunderbird, a "personal car," bows—and sells 16,155 first-year copies versus Corvette's 674

▲ Chevy's '55 Chevy Bel Air Sport Coupe hardtop listed at $2067 with a six. This one, though, carries a V-8.

▲ Part of Chevy's Two-Ten line was the $1835 Delray, a standard $1775 two-door sedan with uptown interior trim.

▲ This '55 Chevy Bel Air Sport Coupe is the 50-millionth car built since General Motors's founding in 1908.

▲ Chevy's Corvette retained its original styling for '55, but was nearly dropped as sales sank to just 674.

◀ Chrysler Corporation spent $100 million to restyle its entire 1955 line, so Chrysler Division boasted its cars had the "$100 Million Dollar Look." This New Yorker DeLuxe Newport hardtop sold 5777 copies at $3652.

- The completely restyled Chevrolet offers a 265-cid V-8 engine—its first V-8 since 1917

- A Nomad wagon is Chevrolet's style leader; Safari is Pontiac's equivalent model

- Chrysler's Hemi-powered C-300 supercar dominates NASCAR racing

- Imperial is now listed as a separate make, no longer a Chrysler series

- The C-6R, Cunningham's final stab at racing, fails to finish at Le Mans

- The rakish Ford Crown Victoria gets an optional transparent half-roof

- Ramblers and Metropolitans now wear both Nash and Hudson badges

- The final few Kaiser Manhattans and Willys sedans are built

- Nashes feature a wraparound windshield and an available 320-cid Packard V-8

▲ Chrysler put an Imperial-look front on a New Yorker hardtop and added a new 300-bhp Hemi V-8 to create the first of its memorable high-performance 300s for 1955.

▲ Chrysler started offering more elaborately trimmed limited-edition "spring specials" like this 1955 Windsor four-door sedan to spark midseason interest.

▲ The Nassau was a lower-priced hardtop fielded to replace the club coupe in Chrysler's 1955 Windsor DeLuxe line. List price: $2703.

▲ DeSoto was handsomely restyled for '55, though a heavy, toothy grille remained. The new top-line Fireflites included a $2939 Sportsman hardtop; 26,637 were produced.

▶ Optional wire wheels added extra sportiness to this '55 DeSoto Fireflite convertible, which sold for $3151. Just 775 examples were built for the year.

- Tech-oriented Packard offers "Torsion-Level" ride, with motorized torsion bars instead of springs

- Studebaker's Speedster features wild two-tone paint, quilted-vinyl interior, and tooled dashboard

- Tubeless tires are now standard on almost all American cars

- The American Automobile Association halts sanctioning of auto races

- Michigan is the first state to require a driver's education course before issuing a license to applicants under 18

- The Glasspar Company develops the two-seat Ascot roadster for buyer assembly

- The tiny American Buckboard roadster prototype uses a two-cylinder motorcycle engine and fifth-wheel drive

- The Gaylord luxury two-seater, styled by Brooks Stevens, features a Spohn body and a Chrysler Hemi V-8; six are built

- The Tri-Car three-wheeler has a rear engine, plastic body, and few buyers

▲ DeSoto helped pioneer the triple-tone paint job. Here the mid-'55 Fireflite Coronado sedan.

▲ Dodge also offered a tri-color paint treatment. This Lancer hardtop listed for $2543; 30,499 were built.

 ► Also included among Dodge's top-line '55 Custom Royals was this Lancer convertible. Just 3302 were built.

► The $2944 Thunderbird promptly trounced the 'Vette in sales. Svelte good looks and a lift-off hardtop were two of the reasons. Buyers quickly ordered 16,155 examples.

◄ The '55 "standard" Fords were so heavily restyled they looked all-new. The $2095 Victoria hardtop sat in a new Fairlane series; 133,372 were sold.

▲ Wagons became a separate Ford series for '55, but with 106,284 sold, the four-door Country Sedan remained the most-popular model.

▲ Ford's new '55 Fairlane group also embraced the glamorous Sunliner convertible, which rose $60 to $2224 with a six. Buyers snapped up 49,966 copies.

▲ Hudson used Nash-based bodies for 1955. The $3145 Hornet V-8 Custom Hollywood topped the lineup.

▲ AMC restyled Ramblers for 1955. Here, the Custom Cross Country.

► "Hash" is often used to describe the 1955-57 Nash-based Hudsons, but the '55s at least looked good. Wasp models like this four-door shared Nash Statesman tooling, but ran with a 202-cubic-inch Hudson six.

1955 Model-Year Production Figures

1. Chevrolet	1,704,667	8. Dodge	276,936	15. Hudson	45,535
2. Ford	1,451,157	9. Chrysler	152,777	16. Lincoln	27,222
3. Buick	738,814	10. Cadillac	140,777	17. Imperial	11,432
4. Plymouth	705,455	11. Studebaker	116,333	18. Willys	6565
5. Oldsmobile	583,179	12. DeSoto	115,485	19. Metropolitan	6096
6. Pontiac	554,090	13. Nash	96,156	20. Kaiser	1291
7. Mercury	329,808	14. Packard	55,247		

Some figures are estimated or calendar year

▲ Chrysler made its luxury Imperial a separate make for '55. Designer Virgil Exner made it handsome. At $4483, this four-door sedan captured 7840 buyers.

▲ The '55 Imperial introduced distinctive "gunsight" tail-lamps that would become a make trademark.

▲ Kaiser abandoned the U.S. car market after 1955 and a brief run of little-changed '54 Manhattan sedans. Of the 1291 built for '55, only 270 were sold. However, Dutch Darrin's design would find new life in Argentina, where it was built through 1962 by a Kaiser subsidiary as the Carabela.

▲ Lincoln was one of Detroit's few '55s without a trendy wraparound windshield. This Capri hardtop sold new for $3910, and 11,462 were built.

▲ Mercury's "bubbletop" Sun Valley joined the Montclair line for 1955. Only 1787 were built. Price was $2712.

▲ All '55 Mercs shared a brighter look and a bigger new V-8. This Montclair convertible cost $2712; 10,668 were built.

▲ Nash got a wraparound windshield in a major '55 restyle. This Ambassador Country Club carried a $3095 price tag.

▲ This is the 1955 Nash Rambler Custom Country Club hardtop, base priced at $1995.

▲ A new oval grille announced the facelifted 1955 Oldsmobiles like this $2984 Super 88 convertible.

▲ The Olds Ninety Eight Starfire convertible again sported flashy side trim and two-toning for '55. Price: $3276.

▲ Stylist Dick Teague conjured a remarkable '55 facelift that made Packard's '51 bodyshell look almost new. The Caribbean ragtop again topped the line at $5932.

▲ Packard's senior 1955 hardtop was named "The Four Hundred," after the social elite of bygone days.

▲ The Belvedere convertible was the only '55 Plymouth with a standard V-8, an efficient new 260-cid "poly-head" design with 167 or 177 horses.

▲ Plymouth was dramatically new for '55 in both looks and performance. The $2217 Belvedere Sport Coupe hardtop attracted 33,433 buyers.

▲ Plymouth's top-line 1955 wagon was the $2425 Belvedere Suburban.

◄ Chrysler first experimented with gas-turbine power in a '54 Plymouth. A '55 Belvedere sedan was used to test an improved engine the following year.

▲ Silver Streak hood trim was about the only styling holdover on Pontiac's all-new '55s. This $2691 Star Chief convertible enticed 19,762 eager buyers.

▲ A modern new 287 V-8 was standard across a smaller, but more focused, '55 Pontiac line. Here is the Star Chief Custom Catalina hardtop, priced at $2499.

◄ Studebaker offered jazzy new two-tone colors on its 1955 models. This $2456 President State hardtop wears "lemon and lime."

▼ Another look at the Willys '55 Bermuda hardtop, which replaced the Aero-Eagle but was much like it except for styling details. Exactly 2215 of these were built with either the 161- or 226-cid six.

◄ Faltering Willys hoped for a sales miracle with a contrived facelift, but it didn't happen, so the firm quit building cars in the U.S. after only 6565 '55s. This newly named Bermuda hardtop listed at $1895 or $1997.

▲▶ Buick's Century (*above*) and Roadmaster (*right*) both received minor but effective facelifts for 1956.

◀ Cadillac was in the last year of a three-year design cycle for 1956. Here, the popular Coupe de Ville hardtop.

▲ Cadillac's Eldorado convertible now carried the Biarritz name to distinguish it from the Eldorado hardtop, a new two-door named Seville. Both were priced at a princely $6556.

▲ An instant hit, Cadillac's new $4753 Sedan de Ville was the division's first four-door hardtop and, with 41,732 sales, its most-popular 1956 model.

1956

- Industry output eases slightly to 6.3 million cars for the model year

- A 41,000-mile Interstate Highway Network is approved; the federal government will pay 90 percent of the construction costs

- The 156-mile Indiana Toll Road opens, joining the Ohio Turnpike for an uninterrupted Chicago-New York superhighway

- Ford builds 1.4 million cars, but is edged out by Chevrolet's 1.56 million

- Four-door Chevy and Ford hardtops debut; they're also sold by Plymouth, Dodge, DeSoto, Chrysler, Imperial, and Pontiac

- Pushbutton automatic transmission selectors are installed on Imperial, Chrysler, DeSoto, Dodge, Plymouth, and Packard

◀ Corvette wizard Zora Arkus-Duntov greets NASCAR officials after his record run up Pikes Peak.

▲ Chevy facelifted to good effect for 1956, as shown on this Bel Air Sport Coupe hardtop. Asking price: $2176.

▶ The restyled 1956 was right in tune with buyer tastes. This is the popular $2344 Bel Air convertible.

▼ Chevrolet joined the movement to four-door hardtops for 1956 with the pillarless Sport Sedans.

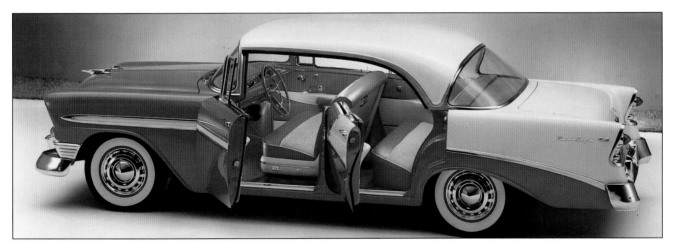

- Ford joins the Automobile Manufacturers Association; Henry II is elected president

- Ford goes public; stock in the automaker is sold for the first time since 1919

- A limited-edition Adventurer is DeSoto's response to the high-performance Chrysler 300-B, Dodge D-500, and Plymouth Fury

- Four-fifths of all 1956 cars have a V-8 engine; only eight makes offer a six

- A dozen makes offer leather interiors, most often as an extra-cost option

- Fords are offered with seatbelts, padded dash, and other safety features—but they fail to take hold with the buying public

- Highway Hi-Fi record players are optional in Chrysler Corp. cars

- Chrysler's 300-B engine is uprated to 355 bhp—one horsepower per cubic inch

- The $10,000 Continental Mark II coupe debuts, separate from the Lincoln line, with a 285-bhp V-8

▲ Chevrolet's Corvette was all-new and dramatically improved for 1956. A new lift-off hardtop option shown here helped boost model-year output to 3467.

▲ Corvette prices started at $3149 for 1956. That bought more amenities and more power: 210 horsepower standard and 225 with the optional "Power Pack."

◄ Built for General Motors designer Bill Mitchell in mid 1956, the experimental Corvette SR-2 racer saw action at Daytona, Sebring, and Road America.

▼ Detroit resident Ruben Allender began offering "Cadillacized" Chevrolets during 1956 under the name El Morocco. Of the 20 built for 1956, 18 were ragtops.

- Ford's Thunderbird adds a "continental" spare tire and "porthole" roof option

- AMC's new V-8 replaces Packard's V-8 in the Hudson Hornet and Nash Ambassador

- Packard's Clipper is now listed as a separate make, but sales go nowhere

- Packard Caribbean gets leather/fabric reversible cushions and 310 horsepower

- Packard offers electrically controlled door latches and a limited-slip differential

- Rambler's Cross Country is the first four-door hardtop station wagon

- Plymouth's experimental gas-turbine car is driven from New York to Los Angeles

- American Motors develops an air-cooled V-4 that weighs only 200 pounds

- Plymouth's Plainsman show wagon has its spare tire hidden inside the rear fender

- Firebird II, a gas-turbine vehicle, appears at the '56 GM Motorama

- Pontiac's wild Pontiac Club de Mer dream car stands only 38.4 inches tall

- Olds's Golden Rocket show coupe sports roof panels that rise when a door is opened

▲ Sheetmetal fins flew on Chrysler's facelifted 1956s, including this $3995 New Yorker St. Regis hardtop.

▲ Only 921 Chrysler New Yorker convertibles were built for 1956, making this restored survivor all the more interesting.

▲ The 1956 Chrysler 300-B beat the magic "1 hp per cu. in." ideal by milking 355 horses from 354 cubic inches.

▲ Chrysler's 1956 Windsors wore their own unique grille for the first—and last—time. This four-door sedan was the line's best-selling model with 53,119 orders.

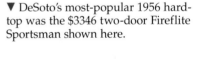

▼ DeSoto's most-popular 1956 hardtop was the $3346 two-door Fireflite Sportsman shown here.

◄ Topping DeSoto's nicely reworked line was the new Adventurer. It developed 320 horsepower from a 341-cid Hemi V-8. Price: $3728.

• Studebaker launches a quartet of sporty Hawk models, highlighted by the top-line Golden Hawk sporting Packard's big 352-cubic-inch V-8 powerplant

• A "quad" four-headlamp system is introduced by the Automobile Manufacturers Association; it will be available for 1958 models

• Dual-Ghia features a Dodge chassis and Italian coachwork; the international hybrid captures the attention and wallets of a number of Hollywood celebrities

• The El Morocco convertible and hardtop is based on the 1956-57 Chevrolet, but is intended to impart the look of a Cadillac Eldorado

▲ Like sister MoPar makes, Dodge sported prominent tailfins for 1956, as on this $2513 V-8 Royal sedan.

▲ Also decidedly well-finned, Dodge's 1956 V-8 Royal Lancer hardtop coupe. Asking price: $2583.

▲ Dodge and Chrysler makes offered a futuristic new feature for 1956: pushbutton controls for the two-speed PowerFlite automatic transmission.

▲ Fender skirts grace this 1956 Dodge La Femme two-tone lavender specialty model that came with a compact and umbrella for milady. Sales were slow.

▲ For 1956, Ford added a $1985 Victoria hardtop coupe as a low-cost alternative to the $2194 Fairlane.

◀ Like Chevy, Ford added a hardtop sedan for '56, a $2249 Town Victoria in the top-line Fairlane series, but model-year sales were modest at 32,111.

▼ Seen here are a solid-roof '56 Ford Crown Vic and that year's Thunderbird, which was modestly updated with a "continental" spare and hardtop "portholes."

◀ Atypical for a wagon, this '56 Ford Country Squire wagon wears fender skirts. 23,221 were built.

▶ Contrived "V-Line" styling and tri-tone paint made the '56 Hudsons look a lot busier than the '55s. This V-8 Hornet sedan is one of only 3490 built.

313

▲ Lincoln was dramatically restyled for 1956. A new uplevel Premiere series included this $4601 hardtop.

▲ Imperial grew longer and higher rear flanks for '56, but remained tastefully restrained. The mainstay four-door sedan listed at $4832 and found 6821 buyers.

▲ The $4747 Premiere convertible topped Lincoln's five-model 1956 lineup, but garnered only 2447 sales.

▲ A big new 368-cubic-inch V-8 with 285 horses powered all '56 Lincolns, like this $4601 Premiere sedan.

▶ Elegant lines, superb workmanship, and a startling $10,000 list price made Lincoln's reborn Continental, called the Mark II, unique among 1956 cars.

1956 Model-Year Production Figures					
1. Chevrolet	1,567,117	8. Dodge	240,686	15. Hudson	22,588
2. Ford	1,408,478	9. Cadillac	154,577	16. Clipper	18,482
3. Buick	572,024	10. Chrysler	128,322	17. Imperial	10,684
4. Plymouth	571,634	11. DeSoto	109,442	18. Packard	10,353
5. Oldsmobile	485,458	12. Nash	83,420	19. Metropolitan	9068
6. Pontiac	405,730	13. Studebaker	69,593	20. Continental	2550
7. Mercury	327,943	14. Lincoln	50,322		

Some figures are estimated or calendar year

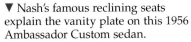

▲ Most 1956 Mercs wore jazzy Z-line moldings. Top-line Montclairs, like this $2765 hardtop, got more go from a standard new V-8 with 235 horses.

▲ The '56 Customs again included Mercury's cheapest wagons: six- and eight-passenger models at $2722 and $2819. A new V-8 gave them 210/225 horses.

◄ Mercury moved to hardtop sedans in a big way for 1956. This is the $2700 Monterey, which found 10,726 buyers.

▼ Nash's famous reclining seats explain the vanity plate on this 1956 Ambassador Custom sedan.

▲ Added tinsel did nothing for Nash sales in 1956. Ambassadors, like this Custom, found just 15,271 buyers.

▲ The last of Nash's tiny Series 54 Metropolitans were sold in 1956.

▲ At $3740, the 1956 Ninety Eight Starfire convertible was Oldsmobile's priciest offering. 8581 were built.

▲ Oldsmobile's Rocket V-8 packed 230 horses in 88 models, such as this $2599 Holiday hardtop coupe, which topped the line in 1956 sales at 74,739 units.

▲ Now at $5995, the Caribbean ragtop again led the Packard line for 1956, which would be the last "real" Detroit-built models. Only 276 were sold.

▲ Clipper became a separate make for 1956, but was still obviously a Packard. Here, the $3164 Custom Constellation hardtop coupe. Only 1466 found buyers.

▲ The Executive was Packard's new entry-level model for 1956. Base price: a less-than-entry-level $3500.

▲ Heating up Plymouth's performance image for 1956 was the new $2866 Fury hardtop with a 240-horse V-8 and special gold-tone side trim. Just 4485 were built.

◀ All Plymouths returned for 1956 with a modest facelift marked by higher fins and revised trim. Here, the Belvedere convertible, which was priced at $2478.

▲ The 1956 Pontiacs had a new, brighter face. The line's only convertible again appeared in the top-shelf Star Chief series, priced at $2857, and 13,510 were sold.

▲ Pontiac's Safari "hardtop" wagon returned for 1956 to score slightly improved sales of 4042 units. All models got a larger V-8 engine, with 192-285 bhp.

▲ Ramblers were redesigned for 1956. The $2494 Custom Cross Country was Detroit's first hardtop wagon.

▲ Studebaker pitched its 1956 Hawk line as "family sports cars." Here, the $3061 V-8 Golden Hawk.

▲ A step down from Studebaker's 1956 Sky Hawk was the still-handsome pillared Power Hawk, which carried a 259-cubic-inch V-8 and sold for $2101.

▲ Another look at Studebaker's pillarless $2477 Sky Hawk. Designer Raymond Loewy supervised its remarkably effective restyle.

▲ Studebaker's most-affordable '56 family sports car was this six-cylinder, 101-bhp Flight Hawk. Price: $1986.

▶ Despite fast-falling sales, noncoupe Studes were also fully restyled for '56. This lush, new long-wheelbase President Classic sedan sold for $2489.

▲ The '57 Buicks were longer and more rakish. A $4373 Riviera coupe highlighted the new Roadmaster 75 series.

▲ GM considered making pillarless wagons like the $3706 Buick Century Caballero long before its 1957 models bowed.

▲ A new, smaller ultraluxury Caddy made its debut for '57 as the Eldorado Brougham, a show-car-inspired hardtop shockingly priced at $13,074.

▲ Cadillac also rebodied for 1957, nicely blending boxy and rounded lines on the Eldorado Biarritz, whose price was up to a staggering $7286.

▶ Non-Eldorado '57 Caddys bore flat-top fins and blocky rear contours. Sales fell off—the $5256 Sedan de Ville dropped 43 percent to 23,808 units.

1957

- The 42nd National Automobile Show—the first since 1940—is held at New York's new Coliseum in late 1956 to display the '57s

- This year's National Auto Show is the first to be televised; Vice President Nixon speaks at the banquet, gaining national exposure

- The Automobile Manufacturers Association bans factory-sponsored racing, resolves to eliminate speed from auto advertising

- Ford, with all-new styling, outsells Chevrolet for the model year: 1.67 million cars to 1.5 million

- Plymouth retakes the number-three sales position, ranking ahead of GM makes Buick and Oldsmobile

- The five-mile-long Mackinac Bridge opens, finally linking Michigan's Upper and Lower Peninsula

▲ More than 165,000 customers found garage space for the "classic" $2399 Bel Air V-8 Sport Coupe.

▲ Disappointing sales were the death knell for the Bel Air Nomad. Just 6103 were produced for 1957.

▲ Compared with Ford's canted blades and Plymouth's rear fenders, Chevy's fins were quite modest.

► A rapid rarity, this 1957 Chevy One-Fifty two-door with fuel injection is identified by the rear-fender insignia and script.

- An average car sells for $2749; the average worker now earns $4230 yearly

- Nash and Hudson names are dropped after the 1957 model year; '58 models are to be part of the Rambler line

- Virgil Exner's second-generation "Forward Look" styling is featured on all Chrysler products

- Chrysler Corp. cars replace front coil springs with a torsion-bar suspension

- American cars begin the switch to quad headlamps, but they're ruled illegal (temporarily) in several states

- Pontiac celebrates its Golden Anniversary; Oldsmobile marks its 60th year of building automobiles

- Mechanical fuel injection is optional on certain Chevrolet and Pontiac models

- Buicks get an ambitious restyle; Cadillac's reworking is inspired by the earlier Eldorado Brougham and Park Avenue show cars

- Cadillac's $13,074 Eldorado Brougham features a brushed-aluminum roof, air suspension, and quad headlights

► Chevy crafted the lightweight Corvette Sebring Special to win the 12-hour Florida race in 1957. It was fast—but unfortunately failed to finish.

▲ Production Corvettes changed little on the surface, but available fuel injection boosted horsepower to 283.

▲ Ruben Allender's Chevy-based El Morocco looked even more Cadillac-like for '57, but only 16 were built, spread among three body styles.

▲ Chrysler's all-new 1957 300-C got its own front end and 375 or 390 horses. Here it leads a 1957 Speed Weeks parade at Daytona Beach.

- Corvette boasts a 283-cid V-8 that develops one horsepower per cubic inch with fuel injection

- Packards, now built in South Bend alongside similar Studebakers, are powered by a supercharged V-8

- A super-quick Rambler Rebel four-door hardtop arrives at midyear, powered by a 327-cubic-inch V-8

- Triple-turbine Turboglide automatic transmission is available on Chevrolets

- A D-500 package boosts Dodge's Hemi V-8 up to 340 horsepower

- Ford sports a sculptured restyle; Fairlanes are inspired by the Mystere show car

- Ford's unique Skyliner retractable hardtop debuts; so does the Ranchero car/pickup

- The "classic" Ford Thunderbird sports canted fins in its final two-seat season; a supercharged 312-cubic-inch V-8 thunders out 300/340 bhp

- Imperial displays curved side-window glass and almost outproduces Lincoln

- The gadget-packed Mercury Turnpike Cruiser features a retractable rear window and 49-position driver's seat

▲ All '57 Chryslers were stunningly restyled. Here, the New Yorker convertible, which listed for $4638.

▲ DeSoto's top-line Adventurer series added this $4272 convertible for 1957. Only 300 were built.

▲ Like Chryslers, the '57 DeSotos were dramatically restyled, though the "Tri-Tower" taillamps remained.

▲ Dodge's new 1957 look was billed as "Swept-Wing Styling." This Coronet Lancer hardtop coupe sold for $2580.

◄ The limited-edition Dual-Ghia evolved from the 1953-54 Dodge Firearrow show cars. It bowed in 1957 as this $7646 Dodge-powered ragtop. Only 104 were built through 1958.

- Station wagons return to the Olds lineup for the first time since 1950

- A J-2 Rocket triple-carb option gives Oldsmobiles 300 horsepower

- The Packard Clipper comes in station wagon form—Packard's first since 1950

- Pontiac's Bonneville ragtop gets fuel injection or Tri-Power (three carburetors)

- Studebaker offers budget-priced, minimal-trim Scotsman models

- The freshly finned Golden Hawk is boosted by a Paxton supercharger

- Most domestic cars now ride on 14-inch wheels, up from 13-inchers

- Several makes offer the luxury of optional six-way power seats

- Most luxury cars now come with electric door locks

- Several makes offer optional limited-slip differentials for better traction

- Jack Kerouac publishes *On the Road*, the "bible" of the forthcoming Beat Generation

- John Keats writes *The Insolent Chariots*, a brutal comic critique of the auto trade

▲ Model-year 1957 saw the first all-new Fords since 1952. A new Fairlane 500 series included this $2404 Victoria hardtop; 68,550 were built.

▶ The '57 Ford Sunliner was another new Fairlane 500 model offering V-8 options from 272 to 312 cubic inches and 190 to 245 horses. Price: $2505.

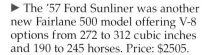

◀ Ford scored a Detroit first with the '57 Fairlane 500 Skyliner and its novel retracting metal hardtop. This multiexposure view shows how it worked.

▲ Reviving the car/pickup idea was Ford's '57 Ranchero, offered in Custom trim (*above*) and as a standard model.

▲ At about $2500, the Ford Country Sedan (186,889 built) seated six or eight folks.

▲ Thunderbird was handsomely restyled for '57, the last year for the original two-seater. Exactly 21,380 were built.

▶ Years of declining sales sealed Hudson's fate. Just 4180 final cars were sold in 1957. Here, the $3011 Hornet Custom.

▼ Hudson got only minor styling changes for '57. The "Continental" spare shown here was a factory option.

1957 Model-Year Production Figures

1. Ford	1,676,449	8. Mercury	286,163	15. Imperial	37,593
2. Chevrolet	1,505,910	9. Cadillac	146,841	16. Metropolitan	15,317
3. Plymouth	726,009	10. DeSoto	126,514	17. Nash	10,330
4. Buick	405,086	11. Chrysler	122,273	18. Packard	4809
5. Oldsmobile	384,041	12. Rambler	91,469	19. Hudson	4180
6. Pontiac	334,041	13. Studebaker	63,101	20. Continental	462
7. Dodge	287,608	14. Lincoln	41,123		

Some figures are estimated or calendar year

▲ Imperial was all-new for '57, and sales would prove the best in the make's history: 37,593 units. Seen here is the $5406 Crown Southampton hardtop sedan.

▲ The 1957 Imperial Crown Southampton was available with a faux trunklid spare, a dubious but expanding trend.

▲ The '57 Lincolns were little more than '56s with big canted fins and stacked quad headlights tacked on.

▲ The ultraluxury Continental Mark II returned for 1957 with 15 additional horsepower, 300 total, as the only significant change.

◄ Mercury added a Turnpike Cruiser ragtop to its line of 1957s. One of the 1265 built was this Indy 500 pace car.

▲ All '57 Mercurys looked like something from outer space, but none more than Turnpike Cruisers like this $3758 hardtop coupe. Only 7291 were sold.

▲ The $3849 Cruiser hardtop sedan had a drop-down rear window among many "space age" gimmicks.

▲ Nash, like partner Hudson, finally succumbed to insufficient sales and was put out to pasture after 1957. Among the last produced, this $2847 Custom Country Club hardtop.

▲ One of Nash's last styling tweaks was the move to quad headlights. A total of 10,330 1957 Nashes were built.

325

▲ Olds was all-new for 1957. This Starfire Ninety Eight Holiday cost $3937, and attracted 17,791 customers.

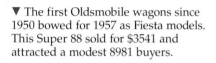

▼ The first Oldsmobile wagons since 1950 bowed for 1957 as Fiesta models. This Super 88 sold for $3541 and attracted a modest 8981 buyers.

▲ All '57 Olds Ninety Eights were Starfires, not just the convertible (shown with a nonfactory "continental kit"). This ragtop listed at $4217; 8278 were built.

▲ A Plymouth redesign for 1957 netted a bigger, bolder, and better-handling car. Here, the $2419 Belvedere Sport Sedan.

▲ The limited-edition Fury hardtop returned for 1957 with Plymouth's new styling, a 290-horse V-8, and a $2925 price.

▲ The 1957 Packards were little more than dressy Studebakers. Here, the $3212 Clipper Town Sedan.

▲ Packard's only other 1957 was the Country Sedan wagon. It cost $3384. Total Packards built for '57: 4809.

▲ Pontiac's original "hardtop" Safari wagon departed after the 1957 model year and a final run of 1292 units.

▲ Only a bit more salable than the two door, Pontiac's other 1957 Safari, a $3636 four-door; 1894 were built.

▶ A surprise from Rambler, the limited-edition '57 Rebel hardtop sedan with a 255-horse 327 V-8.

▲ These $1995 wagons were part of the new lower-cost Scotsman line from Studebaker. Sales were meager.

▲ Studebaker also offered new four-door wagons for 1957. This is the well-appointed $2666 President Broadmoor.

▲ Stude's other 1957 two-door sportster was the $3182 Golden Hawk.

▲ New for 1957 was this $2263 Studebaker Silver Hawk V-8.

327

▲ Buick vied with Olds as 1958's "glitter king." This $5125 Limited ragtop was one of only 839 built.

▲ Buick's shiny '58 Limiteds also included the Riviera. This coupe cost $5002; just 1026 were built.

◄ This ragtop Buick Century is a now quite a rarity—only 2588 were built.

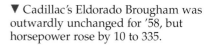

▼ Cadillac's Eldorado Brougham was outwardly unchanged for '58, but horsepower rose by 10 to 335.

1958

- America suffers its worst recession of the postwar era—car sales plummet almost 34 percent for the model year

- Only 987,945 Fords are built, compared to Chevrolet's 1.14 million; Plymouth retains its grip on third place in the sales race

- Oldsmobile captures fourth place, ahead of rapidly falling Buick

- The long-rumored midprice Edsel debuts with pushbutton transmission controls located in the steering wheel

- Studebaker-Packard announces a halt to Packard production to focus on the upcoming compact Lark

- Imported cars grab more than eight percent of total new-car sales

▲ The Eldorado Biarritz and its hardtop Seville cousin retained a rounded tail for 1958. Also priced at $7500, the ragtop garnered a lowly 815 sales.

▲ All-new styling dressed the 1958 Chevys (*bottom*) and the Corvette (*middle*). Providing a glimpse of the future, the experimental Biscayne (*top*) and Sebring SS (*far right*).

▲ Chevy reached upmarket with its new 1958 Bel Air Impala models. This ragtop stickered at $2734.

▲ Chevy's midrange series for '58 was the new Biscayne. This is the $2236 two-door sedan version.

- Unemployment reaches 5,437,000 Americans in June—the highest since 1941

- Chrysler products begin to abandon Hemi V-8s in favor of the cheaper-to-produce "wedge-head" power plants

- The Automobile Information Disclosure Act passes; window stickers must show make, model, and suggested retail price

- Nearly all domestic makes/models adopt the quad-headlamp setup

- Ford marks the 50th Anniversary of the Model T by reassembling a 1909 model at its New Jersey plant

- The chrome-laden "B-58" Buick ranks as one of most garish designs of the year; Flight-Pitch triple-turbine Dynaflow debuts

- General Motors celebrates the 50th Anniversary of its incorporation

- Buick dealers now sell the German-built Opel subcompact; Pontiac dealers distribute the the British-sourced Vauxhall

- The four-passenger Thunderbird debuts, pioneering the "personal-luxury" car; it easily outsells the former Ford two-seater

▲ Chrysler facelifted its year-old "Forward Look" for 1958. The New Yorker hardtop coupe listed at $4347.

▲ The third-generation Corvette arrived for 1958 with a quad-headlamp front, more chrome, and slightly increased weight. Horsepower rose to 290.

▲ DeSoto suffered more than most medium-priced makes in the 1958 recession, as output skidded to 49,445. Seen here is the top-line Adventurer hardtop coupe.

- Chevrolet adds two luxury Impala models and a big 348-cubic-inch V-8 option

- DeSoto production slips to under 50,000 units, the lowest since 1938; even fledgling Edsel sells more cars

- Adventurer is the most costly DeSoto ever—and the fastest

- A handful of Dodges go on sale with fuel-injected 361-cubic-inch engines

- Lincoln fields the largest unibody cars ever built; the Continental Mark III is now based on a Lincoln chassis

- Fords get a heavy-duty facelift and new, larger V-8 engines

- Lincoln's new 430-cubic-inch V-8 earns the title of America's largest car engine

- The last Packards go on sale; the Hawk is a weird luxury version of the Studebaker Golden Hawk, sporting outside "armrests"

- All GM makes offer troublesome air suspension; the option is soon abandoned

▲ Like sister Chrysler brands, the "Swept-Wing" Dodges were modestly facelifted for '58. This factory photo shows a sampling of the lineup.

▶ Dodge added this Regal Lancer hardtop coupe to the Custom Royal line at mid 1958 as a limited-edition paint-and-trim "spring special."

• General Motors's failure prompts other automakers to drop air-suspension plans

• Short-wheelbase Rambler Americans return along with a new long-wheelbase Rambler Ambassador series

• Remote-controlled mirrors are offered on Cadillac and Lincoln/Continental

• Cheap-to-replace paper air-cleaner elements are found on some new engines

• Some Chrysler Corporation cars sport double-compound windshields that extend deep into the roofline

• Automatic speed control is offered on Cadillac, Chrysler, and Imperial

• Studebaker President and Commander series add a hardtop body option

• GM shows the Firebird III concept with a joystick controller; it steers itself via a control wire planted on the road surface

• Plymouth's Cabaña hardtop show wagon lets the breeze in through a sliding sunroof

▲ Ford president Henry Ford II chauffeurs brothers Benson and William Clay in this publicity shot staged to launch the new 1958 Edsel. This top-line Citation ragtop cost $3801.

▼ Edsel's second 1958 ragtop was this Ford-based Pacer version, priced at $3028. Just 1876 were built.

▲ Edsel general manager Richard Kravke stands behind Ford design chief George Walker and Benson Ford.

▶ A popular 1958 Edsel Pacer was the $2805 hardtop coupe, which attracted 6139 buyers.

- Ford displays a model Glideair vehicle that travels on a thin cushion of air

- The independently produced Bocar XP-4 sports car goes into production with Chevrolet or Pontiac V-8 power

- A two-seater economy car, the Colt, uses a one-cylinder engine, finds few buyers

- The Corvette-powered Devin SS sports car is marketed in kit or fully assembled form

- The German-built Ford Taunus enters the U.S. market; the first few Toyotas—called Toyopets—and Datsuns arrive from Japan

- Studebaker-Packard halts Packard build to focus resources on the upcoming Lark

▲ The 1958 passenger Fords borrowed styling cues from the new T-Bird. Here, the Fairlane 500 Victoria coupe, priced at $2435; 80,439 were built.

▲ The $2397 two-door Ranch Wagon, Ford's least-expensive 1958 wagon, accounted for 34,578 deliveries.

▲ Ford's Thunderbird switched from two to four seats in a full 1958 redesign. The convertible was a late arrival at $3929, limiting output to 2134 units.

◄ This 1958 Ford Fairlane 500 Sunliner is outfitted with fender skirts and a "Continental kit." Priced at $2650, the model sold 35,029 copies.

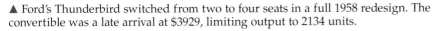

1958 Model-Year Production Figures

1. Chevrolet	1,142,460	8. Dodge	137,861	15. Lincoln	17,134
2. Ford	987,945	9. Mercury	133,271	16. Imperial	16,133
3. Plymouth	443.799	10. Cadillac	121,778	17. Metropolitan	13,128
4. Oldsmobile	294,374	11. Chrysler	63,681	18. Continental	12,550
5. Buick	342,892	12. Edsel	63,110	19. Packard	2622
6. Pontiac	217,303	13. DeSoto	49,445		
7. Rambler	162,182	14. Studebaker	44,759	*Some figures are estimated or calendar year*	

▲ A 1958 restyle preserved Imperial's good looks, as on this Crown Southampton coupe. Build was down to 1939 units.

▲ Pride of the Lincoln line for 1958 was this massive new Continental Mark III convertible, priced at a stiff $6283.

▲ The restyled 1958 Mercurys sported even more gingerbread, as on this $3536 Montclair with "cruiser skirts."

◄ A pair of Lincoln-Mercury executives try out a Mark III convertible in this 1958 factory press photo taken at Ford's Dearborn Proving Grounds.

▲ Mercury's Turnpike Cruiser line thinned to a pair of Montclair hardtops for 1958. Base price: $3498.

▼ For 1958, Olds again offered a convertible in all three of its series. This midrange Super 88 version cost $3529 and attracted 3799 customers.

▲ Fiesta wagons returned with the same excessive use of chrome as other 1958 Oldsmobile models.

▲ The first and only Packard Hawk was a Studebaker Hawk with a "fish-mouth" grille and a supercharged V-8.

▲ After a year off, Packard's hardtop coupe returned for 1958 as this thinly disguised Studebaker with chrome add-ons. Buyers didn't bite—only 675 were built.

▲ Rarest of 1958 Packards is this wagon—a mere 159 had been assembled when management abandoned Packard as no longer profitable.

▲ Quad headlights and a horizontal bar lower grille were among the trim changes marking the 1958 Plymouths. The Belvedere Sport Sedan hardtop stickered at $2528.

◄ Plymouth's midrange Savoy series again included a Sport Coupe two-door hardtop for 1958. Base price was $2329.

◄ Bonneville was Pontiac's top-line model for 1958. This $3481 hardtop coupe was new to the line. Fender script here identifies optional fuel injection with 310 horsepower.

▲ Dummy side scoops identified '58 Pontiac Star Chiefs like this Catalina hardtop coupe, which sold for $3122.

▲ Like Chevrolet, the '58 Pontiac would be a one-year-only design. This Star Chief Safari sold new for $3350.

▲ "Ambassador by Rambler" bowed for '58, replacing Nash and Hudson. Here a $3116 Custom Cross Country.

▲ Regular 1958 Ramblers were divided into V-8 Rebels and six-cylinder models. The latter included this $2327 Custom four-door sedan.

▲ This $2378 Studebaker Commander four-door sedan found fewer than 7000 willing buyers in 1958.

▶ Three bare-bones Scotsman models were Stude's best-sellers—20,872 units—though this $1795 two-door sedan chalked up just 5538 sales.

► The LeSabre four-door sedan took over from its Special predecessor the title of Buick's best-selling model: 51,379 were built in 1959.

▼ Invicta replaced the Century as Buick's midrange series for '59. Among its five models was this hardtop sedan priced at $3515.

▼ Buick's 1959 flagship was this $4192 Electra 225 convertible, one of three models in that new top-line group. Total production came to only 5493 units.

1959

- Model-year auto output expands by 31 percent to more than 5.5 million units

- Studebaker-Packard launches the compact Lark; the compact-car race begins in earnest

- Chevrolet and Ford race neck-and-neck in production, topping 1.4 million cars; Chevy barely edges ahead for the model year

- Plymouth finishes third, followed by Pontiac and then Oldsmobile

- All General Motors cars share a basic bodyshell, but wear vastly different styling

- Buick renames its entire model lineup, and makes a new 401-cubic-inch V-8 engine standard in high-end models

▲ Tailfins reached record heights with the 1959 Cadillacs. This is the $7401 Eldorado Seville hardtop coupe.

▲ Like Buick, Cadillac gained all-new styling and huge fins for 1959. Here, the $5455 Series Sixty-Two ragtop. Sales rose to 11,130.

▲ Cadillac's '59 hardtop sedans offered six-window styling, as on this $5080 Series Sixty-Two, or a flat-top four-window roofline for the same money.

▲ The '59 Cadillac Eldorado Brougham was a larger hardtop sedan built by Italy's Pinin Farina, but workmanship wasn't as good as on the 1957-58 original. Base price: $13,075.

▲ All 1959 Cadillacs used a newly stroked 390-cubic-inch V-8 with 325 horsepower (except Eldorados which got 345). Here, an Eldorado Biarritz ragtop. Base price: $7401.

- Imported cars reach record sales levels with a 62 percent increase over 1958

- The federal gasoline tax is raised from 3 to 4 cents per gallon

- The Automobile Manufacturers Association reports that a crankcase-ventilation device to reduce emissions will go on all cars sold in California, effective with the '61 models

- Cadillacs boast a new 390-cid V-8 and flaunt new more-massive tailfins

- Most Chryslers are now powered by a 383-inch "wedge" V-8; Hemis are gone

- Studebaker drops the Golden Hawk and introduces a nonsupercharged Silver Hawk; the new Lark comes with an L-head six-cylinder engine or an optional V-8

- Chrysler's 300-E gets 380 horsepower from a standard 413-cubic-inch V-8

- Swivel bucket seats are available to ease ingress/egress on some Chrysler products

- A caravan of 16 vehicles drives 4239 miles, from Detroit to Alaska's Susitan Valley, to establish homesteads in the country's vast new 49th state

▲ Chevy was "all new all over again" for '59, and wilder-looking than ever. The Impala Sport Coupe shown here was part of a new full top-line series.

▲ Like all '59 Chevrolets, the Impala convertible sported a new "batfin" tail. The $2967 ragtop was popular—65,800 were sold.

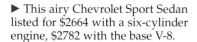

▶ This airy Chevrolet Sport Sedan listed for $2664 with a six-cylinder engine, $2782 with the base V-8.

▲ Chevy replied to Ford's Ranchero in 1959 with the El Camino, a two-door wagon with a pickup bed instead of a rear cargo bay. An abbreviated roofline mimicked that of the hardtop sedans.

- Chevrolet offers an optional fully synchronized four-speed manual gearbox; Corvette already has one

- This is the final year for the dated Dodge/Plymouth L-head six

- DeSotos receive a heavy facelift, but sales continue to be glum

- Curtiss-Wright Corporation and NSU Werke of West Germany test a "rotary" engine with few moving parts

- A Galaxie luxury series sporting a Thunderbird roofline joins the Ford line

- Ford Thunderbirds can be had with the enormous 430-cubic-inch Lincoln V-8

- Buick introduces a seat-lock mechanism to prevent the passenger's front seatback from moving forward suddenly

- Lincoln's Continental Mark IV line includes a limited-production Town Car and limousine

- Nash Metropolitan is spruced up with a trunklid and vent windows

▲ Chevy's Corvette output rose by roughly 500, to a healthier 9670 units. Curb weight was 2840 pounds.

▲ GM's design chief Bill Mitchell built this experimental Stingray. The same basic shape would appear on post-1962 showroom Corvettes.

▶ Chrysler Division chief engineer Bob Rodger fathered the original 300. Here he shows off the new 380-horse wedge-head engine of the '59 300-E.

- Pontiac introduces a split grille design and aggressive "Wide-Track" stance

- American Motors Corporation (the union of Nash and Hudson) posts a $60 million profit, builds a record 374,000 Ramblers

- The Checker Superba passenger car, an upgraded taxicab, goes on display in May

- Willys announces a deluxe Jeep Station Wagon known as the Maverick Special

- Chrysler offers an electronic control that changes the rearview mirror to nonglare when a headlamp beam hits its surface

- Oldsmobile introduces flanged brake drums for more-efficient cooling

- The Asardo, a fiberglass-bodied sport coupe carries an Alfa Romeo engine, shows promise but never sees production

- Experimental cars include the DeSoto Cella, which converts liquid fuel into electrical energy; Cadillac Cyclone, with a radar warning system; plus the Ford Levacar, which floats on a cushion of air

▲ A rather uninspired facelift marked 1959's "Lion-Hearted" Chryslers. Windsors like this $3289 hardtop coupe used a new 305-horse V-8.

▲ The 1959 Chryslers gained more than 6000 sales over the '58s, but the $4890 New Yorker convertible dropped from 666 to a mere 286.

▲ Chrysler's 1959 300-E kept the big trapezoid grille from 1957-58 and looked better for it. The $5319 hardtop weighed 4290 pounds.

▲ The '59 300-E ragtop listed at $5749, but garnered a mere 140 orders versus the hardtop's 550, a Letter-Series low.

▶ Optional swivel front seats were a new Chrysler gimmick for 1959, demonstrated here on a Dodge Royal hardtop.

◀ Like its Chrysler corporate kin, Dodge's '59 facelift was heavy but not that popular. This $3422 Custom Royal ragtop was one of only 974 built.

▲ Special badges signal the hot D-500 engine option on this $3201 Custom Royal Lancer hardtop coupe.

▲ DeSoto's Adventurer was still a hot seller for 1959, but overall make output cooled to 45,734 units.

▲ This '59 DeSoto Fireflite four-door sedan wears a simple monotone finish. The base price was $3763, and 4480 were produced for the model run.

1959 Model-Year Production Figures

1. Chevrolet	1,462,140	7. Buick	285,089	13. DeSoto	45,734
2. Ford	1,450,953	8. Dodge	156,385	14. Edsel	44,891
3. Plymouth	458,261	9. Mercury	150,000	15. Lincoln/Continental	26,906
4. Pontiac	383,320	10. Cadillac	142,272	16. Metropolitan	22,209
5. Oldsmobile	382,865	11. Studebaker	126,156	17. Imperial	17,269
6. Rambler	374,240	12. Chrysler	69,970		

Some figures are estimated or calendar year

► Reacting quickly to disappointing first-year sales, Edsel returned for 1959 with only Ford-based models, lower prices and more-conservative styling. The top-line Corsair convertible cost $3072 and found only 1343 buyers.

▲ A part of the 1959 Ford Fairlane 500 Galaxie family, the Skyliner managed 12,915 sales—too few to be continued.

► Pretty in pink or burgundy, Ford's '59 Thunderbird weighed 3903 pounds and attracted 10,261 buyers.

◄ The Ford Galaxie Club Sedan two-door attracted a healthy 52,848 buyers in 1959. Base price: $2528.

344

▲ The rarest of post-1954 Imperials are the special Ghia-built Crown Imperial limousines. This is one of only seven built to 1959 specs. Cost: $15,075.

▲ Mainstream Imperials got a toothier grille for 1959, plus a big new 413-cid, 350-bhp wedge-head V-8.

◄ Continental went from separate make to Lincoln series for 1959. The little-changed Mark IV Landau hardtop sedan attracted 6146 buyers.

▲ Mercury's 1959s were fairly tasteful despite newly added bulk. At $4206, this Park Lane convertible was the priciest model. Only 1257 were built.

▲ Olds continued offering three ragtops for 1959, with the Dynamic 88 the most affordable at $3286. Here is one of 8491 examples built during the model run.

▲ Oldsmobile four-door sedans were called Celebrity for 1959. The $3890 Ninety Eight found 23,106 buyers and ran with a new 315-bhp Rocket V-8.

▶ The restyled '59 Plymouths were basically 1957-58 underneath. Part of the Sport Fury line, this is the $3125 convertible. Almost 6000 were built.

▶ Sport Fury was Plymouth's performance offering for '59. The $2927 hardtop coupe enjoyed a production run of 17,867 units.

▲ Here's a Bonneville Sport Coupe hardtop. It went for $3257, and 27,769 buyers left Pontiac stores with one.

▲ Pontiac soared to fourth in industry sales with its all-new "Wide-Track" '59 models. This $3478 Bonneville convertible attracted 11,426 sun worshippers.

▲ American Motors president George Romney poses with his company's 1959 Rambler Ambassador Custom Country Club hardtop sedan outside AMC headquarters.

▲ A quiet year for AMC, only minimal styling changes marked the 1959 Ramblers. The $2327 six-cylinder Custom four-door sedan shown here found 35,242 buyers.

▲ For 1959, AMC added two-door wagons in Super (*shown*) and DeLuxe trim at around $2100—and sold 32,639 of them.

347

CHAPTER TEN

1960-1963

DETROIT
THINKS SMALL

Suddenly it was 1960, and the times began changing as never before. True, the Cold War was far from over, the specter of nuclear armageddon remained all too tangible, and the civil rights struggle had barely begun. Worse, a new Cuban dictator named Fidel Castro had brought the Communist threat to just 90 miles from U.S. shores. Yet America had reasons for optimism. The economy continued its slow but steady recovery from the doldrums of 1958, and the country's space program had finally—and literally—gotten off the ground.

As if to herald the momentous times ahead, Detroit's Big Three automakers offered their smallest cars in 30 years. American Motors's Rambler had pioneered compacts in the Fifties, and Studebaker belatedly chimed in by trimming the fat from its old platform to find sales salvation in the tidy '59 Lark. For 1960, Chevrolet added the rear-engine Corvair, Ford the utterly conventional Falcon, and Chrysler the rather oddly styled Valiant. Mercury came along at mid model year with a spiffier Falcon called Comet. Though Corvair was the most radical in engineering terms, all four of these compacts were new designs conceived to stem the growing tide of import sales. And to an extent, they did, reducing the foreigners' market share from just over 10 percent for calendar '59 to 7.6 percent in 1960.

But that only meant that most of the 6-7 million cars Americans bought each year from 1960-63 were full-size or "standard" models. Yet, even here there were changes aplenty. Though Falcon promptly ran away with the compact market, a mid-1960 Corvair offering called Monza accidentally unearthed a sizable demand for sporty cars with bucket seats, floorshift, and other "foreign" features. An instant—if modest—hit, Monza saved Corvair from an early grave and set the stage for a far greater success, though that would be another Ford, much to Chevy's chagrin. But the industry took immediate note of Monza's popularity, and by 1962 most every nameplate was offering bucket-seat interiors and snazzy appearance touches like vinyl roof coverings.

Meanwhile, Buick, Olds, and Pontiac stoked the compact craze with clean, trim new '61 models mirroring another period trend: the swift public rejection of Fifties styling excess. With certain bizarre exceptions from Chrysler Corporation, Detroit fast abandoned fins, needless chrome, and outsized proportions for more rational and tasteful designs.

Compacts may have been on Detroit's mind, but performance was still closest to its heart. Indeed, the Fifties "horsepower race" had not really abated—it had merely gone underground with the 1957 manufacturers' agreement to abandon racing and performance advertising. In 1961, however, the race came above ground when Chevrolet unleashed its "real fine" 409 big-block V-8, along with a sporty new big car, the Impala SS. Ford replied for '62 with a burly 406, and Chrysler kept pace with a husky 413 wedge-head. At the performance pinnacle in these years were two 1963 stunners, Studebaker's Avanti and the first all-new Corvette since 1953.

With all this, the U.S. car market was fragmenting into specialized size/price segments. Ford furthered the process for 1962 by successfully pioneering the "midsize" car with a new Fairlane. Intriguingly, Chrysler tried the same tactic that year with "resized" standard Plymouths and Dodges, but they bombed because they were too small and looked weird.

Finally, America lost another old friend as DeSoto departed after a token '61 model run. The same fate attended the once-ballyhooed Edsel, dropped in late 1959 after just three model years and far more controversy than Ford Motor Company had ever expected.

1960

- Industry production edges past the six million mark; 12 percent are two-door hardtops, 11 percent four-door hardtops

- Ford output slips slightly to 1,439,370 cars; Chevrolet's rises to 1,653,168, strengthening its stranglehold on the number-one spot

- Plymouth holds third place for the last time until the Seventies; Rambler is fourth, with the highest production ever from an independent

- Three new compacts debut early: Chevrolet Corvair, Ford Falcon, and Plymouth Valiant; Mercury's Comet arrives later in the year

- More than 9100 miles of the Interstate Highway System are completed, with 4700 more under construction

- Four-fifths of all American families own at least one automobile—that number is up almost a third since 1940

▲ American Motors gave 1960 Rambler Ambassadors a heavy facelift and a "Scena-Ramic" compound-curve windshield. This Custom hardtop sedan cost $2822.

▲ The '60 AMC Ambassador Custom Cross Country hardtop wagon carried a $3116 price tag—and garnered only 435 orders. A 250-horse V-8 was standard, 270 bhp optional.

▲ American remained AMC's smallest compact, and not greatly changed save for the addition of four-door sedans like this top-trim Custom. It found 2172 buyers.

▲ Buick's 1960 styling was a slightly muted version of '59. A $3145 convertible again headed the entry-level LeSabre line and saw slightly better sales of 13,588 units for '60.

◄ Like all 1960 Buicks, this $2915 hardtop coupe offered a 364-inch V-8 with 250 horsepower. Production reached 26,521.

- All Chrysler Corporation cars save Imperial adopt unibody construction; so do the new Chevrolet Corvair and Ford Falcon

- The last of the cheeky little Metropolitans are built in England at midyear

- Studebaker offers a $100 rebate on late-year models to clear dealer lots

- Checker's new passenger cars—Superba sedan and wagon—look similar to the ubiquitous work-a-day taxis

- Total output for the Superba Standard and slightly fancier Superba Special reaches about 1050 units (plus 5930 taxis)

- Buick introduces a separate rear heat control, is billed as an "industry first"

- Chevy's radically engineered Corvair sports an air-cooled, six-cylinder engine at the rear and a swing-axle rear suspension

- A new "Slant Six" engine replaces the L-head under Dodge and Plymouth hoods

- Ram-induction manifolding is available for Chrysler 300-F and Dodge/Plymouth V-8s

◀ Like Buick, Cadillac's styling was somewhat simplified for 1960, as seen on this Eldorado Biarritz convertible. At a stiff $7401, only 1285 were built.

▼ The Cadillac Eldorado Seville said goodbye after 1960, when sales amounted to only 1075 units.

▲ The standard-size 1960 Chevys weren't appreciably changed from the '59s, but available horses went up 20 to a maximum 335. Here, the $2769 Impala Sport Sedan hardtop.

▲ The Nomad name continued to grace Chevy's best top for 1960, but the car was very different from the 1955-57 original. The sticker read $2996 with the base V-8.

- Chrysler 300-F buyers can specify a French *Pont-a-Mousson* four-speed manual gearbox (this year only)—but only seven do

- Chrysler touts an "electro-luminescent" dashboard for some models; automatic swivel seats are newly optional

- Plymouth Valiant gets an alternator in place of the traditional generator; this device will soon be standard on all U.S. cars

- The final Edsels go on sale—production is halted in November 1959 after just 3008 cars are built for the abbreviated 1960 run

- A sliding metal sunroof (unseen on U.S. cars since prewar days) is offered on the Ford Thunderbird hardtop; 2536 are ordered

- T-Bird convertibles, borrowing 1957-59 Ford Skyliner technology, stow their tops neatly out of the way—in the trunk

- Led by the slippery semifastback Starliner, the new big Ford models are considerably longer, lower, wider than their predecessors

- A dragstrip-ready Pontiac delivering 348 horsepower is predictive of the performance cars to come during the '60s

- An overhead-valve six replaces the ancient L-head engine in the Rambler American at midyear

▲ Chevrolet built 65,800 Impala convertibles for 1960, priced at $2967 with the 283-inch V-8. Full-size Chevys kept their 119-inch wheelbase and weighed 3455-3960 pounds.

▲ A more conventional face appeared on all full-size 1960 Chevrolets, including the popular Impala Sport Coupe hard-top, which sold for $2599 with the standard 135-horse six.

▲ Corvair bowed with neat four-door sedans in two trim levels. This upper 700 model, which sold for $2103, saw output reach 139,208 units. Coupes were added at mid model year.

▲ A number of design tweaks—and up to 315 fuel-injected horses—made Chevy's 1960 Corvette the best yet. Sales finally broke the 10,000 mark.

▲ Less exterior chrome and fewer frills marked Chevy's low-rung $2038 Corvair 500 sedan, which found 47,673 buyers. The costlier 700 sedan outsold it by nearly three-to-one.

1960 Model-Year Production Figures

1. Chevrolet	1,653,168	8. Mercury	271,331	15. Imperial	17,719
2. Ford	1,439,370	9. Buick	253,807	16. Metropolitan	13,103[1]
3. Plymouth	483,969	10. Cadillac	142,184	17. Edsel	3008
4. Rambler	458,841	11. Studebaker	120,465	18. Checker	1050[2]
5. Pontiac	396,716	12. Chrysler	77,285		
6. Dodge	367,804	13. DeSoto	26,081		
7. Oldsmobile	347,142	14. Lincoln/Continental	24,820		

[1] *Calender-year sales*
[2] *Estimate, excludes taxicabs*

▲ Fins flew high on the all-new 1960 "Unibody" Chrysler lineup. The $4875 New Yorker convertible (*above*) snared only 556 buyers.

▲ The 1960 Chrysler 300-F hardtop cost $5411. Available horsepower: 375 or 400.

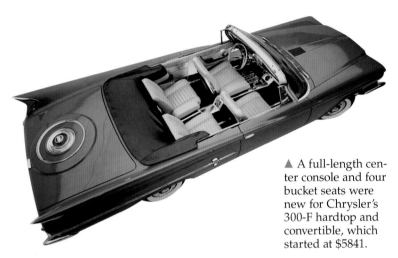

▲ A full-length center console and four bucket seats were new for Chrysler's 300-F hardtop and convertible, which started at $5841.

◄ This $3663 hardtop coupe was one of six models available in DeSoto's 1960 Adventurer lineup.

- Rambler station wagons feature an innovative side-hinged rear door

- Studebaker's Lark adds a four-door station wagon and convertible to the line; Hawks come only with V-8 power

- Oldsmobile models get an optional vacuum-operated decklid opener; many Chrysler models offer vacuum door locks

- Lee Iacocca takes the helm at Ford Division, is ready to focus on "excitement"

- GM announces an experimental "electric fence" that would warn a driver if the vehicle nears the pavement's edge

- Chevrolet displays the XP-700 Corvette show car; Plymouth exhibits its asymmetrically styled XNR sports car

▲ A new two-tier 1960 Dodge lineup included this $3506 hardtop wagon in the senior (larger) Polara series.

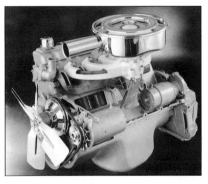

▲ A sampling of the 1960 Dodge line-up; the smaller Darts are on the right.

◄ Dodge and Plymouth boasted Chrysler's new "Slant Six," it will be a corporate mainstay for three decades.

◄ The Plymouth-based Dart doubled Dodge's 1960 sales: 367,804 versus 156,385 in '59. This car was built on April 7 in Hamtramck, Michigan.

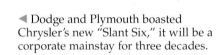

▲ Edsel was canned in November 1959 after a brief run of 1960 models, including 76 Ranger convertibles. Sticker price was an even $3000. Production for all three years: 110,847.

▲ This $2697 Ranger four-door sedan was the most-popular 1960 Edsel, yet only 1288 were produced.

▲ A no-nonsense type, Robert S. McNamara (left) served briefly as Ford Motor Company president in late 1960 when Henry Ford II (right) became the firm's chairman.

▶ A prototype for a two-door 1960 Edsel Villager wagon that wasn't offered; 275 four-doors were built.

▲ Simple in both look and concept, Ford's Falcon was by far the most popular of the Big Three's new 1960 compacts, with 435,676 sales. Price: in the $2000-$2300 range.

▲ This Galaxie Victoria hardtop sedan displays the linear styling common to all 1960 standard-size Fords. Sticker priced at $2675, this model attracted 39,215 buyers.

▲ An accessory hood ornament graces this restored 1960 Ford Galaxie Sunliner convertible, which sold 44,762 copies at a base price of $2860. Wheelbase measured 119 inches.

▲ Imperial was restyled for 1960, but arguably not for the better. This $5774 Crown convertible saw only 618 copies built. Top-line honors went to two new LeBaron models.

◄ A sliding metal sunroof was a new option for the Thunderbird hardtop in 1960, the last year for the original '58 "Squarebird" design. Sales hit a record 90,843.

▲ The last of Lincoln's square-rigged giants appeared for 1960 with only minor changes from '59. That year's Continentals were dubbed Mark V; 2044 were built.

▲ Lincoln's 430-inch V-8 was detuned from 350 to 315 bhp for 1960 in a faint nod to buyers' gas-mileage concerns. Now a Mark V, this Continental hardtop sedan again cost $6845.

▲ The big 1960 Mercurys offered a rounded-off version of '59 styling, plus engines that guzzled a bit less gas. The base-line Montereys sold the best. Here, a $3077 ragtop.

▶ At $2631, the Monterey two-door sedan remained the most afford-able "Big M," and 21,557 were sold. A 312-inch V-8 was again standard, but horses were down to 205.

▲ Once meant for Edsel, Comet bowed in mid 1960 to put Mercury into the new compact market. This four-door sedan was the most popular of the four models, with 47,416 sales.

▲ The '60 Comets were basically Ford's Falcons in Mercury trim, and likely sold well because of that fact. Wagons were offered as two- or four-doors, the latter priced at $2365.

▲ Oldsmobile traded 1959's "Linear Look" for cleaner "Balanced Design" on its 1960 models, shown here by a pair of Ninety Eight hardtops. Prices: $4086 and $4162.

▲ Again for 1960, Super 88s carried Oldsmobile's 394 V-8 with 315 horsepower, as did Ninety Eights. Here, the Super convertible, of which just 5830 were sold.

▲ The 1960 Plymouths had a new "Unibody" platform and styling that was nothing if not different. This top-line $2967 Fury convertible managed a meager 7080 sales.

◀ With up to 330 horses from its 383-inch V-8, the 1960 Plymouths made fast mounts for the law. The styling, though, made spotting by speeders easy.

▲ Just visible in this view of Plymouth's 1960 Fury hardtop sedan is an optional squared-off (and odd) steering wheel. This $2656 model attracted only 9036 customers.

▲ The Valiant arrived with a large Chrysler-style rhomboid grille, dual headlights, blade-type fenderlines, long-hood/short-deck profile—and surprisingly enough, no fins.

▼ Chrysler released this "teaser" shot in late 1959 to herald the arrival of its new Valiant compact, which it described as bearing "crisp lines and completely fresh silhouette."

◄ Valiant also offered four-door wagons for 1960 with seating for six or eight, in V100 and V200 trim. This V100 stickered at $2365.

▶ The successful 1959 "Wide Track" Pontiacs gained a slightly different look for 1960. Here, the Bonneville convertible, which enticed 17,062 buyers. It listed at $3476.

◄ Fresh from saving Studebaker in '59, the '60 Lark line got new four-door wagons; 18,797 were sold. This is the $2591 "VI" in top Regal trim.

▲ Now just plain Hawk and looking quite dated, the 1960 edition of Studebaker's "family sports car" sold for $2360, or $2495 with V-8.

▶ Though little-changed, Studebaker's compact Lark had another good year in 1960, with sales only a bit short of 1959. Here, the workaday $2040 "VI" (six-cylinder) DeLuxe four-door sedan.

◀ Lark was alone among 1960 compacts in offering a convertible. Sold only in top-line Regal trim, it listed for $2621 with the standard six, $2756 with a V-8.

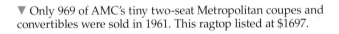

▲ AMC's Ambassador Custom Cross Country four-door wagon offered only pillared styling for '61, and its base price went up $85 to $3111. Only 784 were produced.

◄ A mild facelift marked American Motors's midsize 1961 Ramblers, now called Classic. This Custom sedan sold for $2413 or $2512 (six or V-8); 28,568 were sold.

▼ Only 969 of AMC's tiny two-seat Metropolitan coupes and convertibles were sold in 1961. This ragtop listed at $1697.

▼ New outer sheetmetal made AMC's '61 Rambler Americans blockier looking and a tad shorter. Here, the $2165 midrange Super two-door wagon.

1961

- Due to a brief recession early in the year, industry output slips to 5.4 million cars

- The National Automobile Show, held at Detroit's new Cobo Hall in October 1960, attracts 1.4 million visitors

- President Eisenhower speaks at a banquet during the show, and the U.S. Post Office issues a commemorative "Wheels of Freedom" stamp

- Four upmarket compacts debut: Buick Special, Dodge Lancer, Olds F-85, and Pontiac Tempest

- Ford output edges past Chevrolet as both makes top 1.3 million cars; Plymouth drops to fourth, behind Rambler

- Checker's Superba Special becomes the Marathon; total Superba and Marathon sales equal an estimated 860 units

▲ A pair of pillared coupes bolstered Buick's Special sedans and wagons in mid '61. This uplevel $2621 bucket-seat model resurrected the Skylark badge; 12,683 were sold.

▲ Buick's big 1961s were a bit lighter than before and much cleaner looking. This LeSabre convertible attracted 11,951 satisfied shoppers at a $3382 base sticker price.

◄ Stylingwise, the full-size '61 Buicks were light-years removed from the excesses of 1958-59. As on all full-size GM cars that year, new arc-shaped A-pillars replaced the "dogleg" knee-bangers of old. Buick's top-line '61 four-door sedan was this Electra model with "six-window" roof styling and a $3825 base price—all of which appealed to 13,818 customers.

▼ Buick revived its familiar Special name for new 1961 compacts with crisp lines, small all-aluminum V-8, and standard or Deluxe trim.

- General Motors faces sporadic strikes, limiting production

- New-car warranties are extended to at least 12 months/12,000 miles

- AMC offers a U.S. Savings Bond to buyers as a conditional rebate

- The "Special" nameplate is revived on the smallest Buick in 50 years: a compact with an aluminum V-8, plus a sporty Skylark Sport Coupe that debuts in May

- Chevrolet's tauter, fin-free look shows the influence of GM design chief Bill Mitchell

- A Super Sport option is offered on Chevy Impalas—it's available with a 409-inch V-8

- Chevrolet Corvair Monza can be ordered with a four-speed manual gearbox

- Corvettes display a new flowing "ducktail" rear seen earlier on the XP-700 show car

▲ Save for tiny front-fender script, the $6477 '61 Cadillac Eldorado Biarritz looked the same as this $5455 Series Sixty-Two convertible.

▲ Likewise, this $4892 '61 Cadillac Sixty-Two hardtop looked much like the uplevel $5252 De Ville.

▲ Chevrolet sparked an industrywide move toward sporty big cars with its new '61 SS (Super Sport) package for Impala hardtop coupes and ragtops. It cost just $53.80.

▲ Shown here, the popular Impala Sport Sedan hardtop. It sold for $2662 with a six, $2704 with the base 283-inch V-8. A potent 350-horse 348-inch V-8 was the top power option.

◄ The influence of GM design chief Bill Mitchell is seen in the 1961 Corvette's new "ducktail," lifted directly from his 1959-60 Stingray racer. Chevy sports-car sales reached 10,939 units; base price was $3934.

- Chrysler issues its last Windsors, while launching a cheaper Newport series

- DeSoto makes a final short appearance; production halts in November 1960 after only 3034 '60 models are built

- Dodge fields a new Valiant-based Lancer compact, output of 74,776 units is considered a modest success

- A new, thumping 413-cid V-8 is available in Dodges and Plymouths

- The third-generation Thunderbird has a new optional "Swing-Away" steering wheel allowing easier driver ingress

- The massively finned Imperial displays freestanding headlights in an attempt to revive the "Classic" look of the Thirties

- Ford offers a new option: its first four-speed manual transmission

- Lincoln launches a downsized Continental, including the first U.S. convertible sedan since the 1951 Frazer Manhattan

- Continentals come with an unprecedented 2-year/24,000-mile warranty; several other makes will soon follow suit

▲ Corvair added nifty Lakewood wagons for 1961 in base 500 and, as shown here, spiffier 700 form. The latter was preferred four-to-one.

◄ Detail changes improved the '61 edition of Chevy's rear-engine Corvair compact. This 700 coupe sold for $1985; 24,786 were built.

► Chevy's sporty Corvair Monza coupe got this $2201 sedan companion for '61. It managed only 33,745 sales.

▼ Who says it was Chrysler that invented the minivan? Chevy's new Corvair Greenbrier "Sports Wagon" offered much the same thing back in 1961. The new '61 Corvair-based Greenbrier "Sports wagon" was the spiritual predecessor of the modern minivan.

◄ Chevy hoped to win back more of its Corvair investment with new 1961 utility models, including the novel "Rampside" pickup.

- Oldsmobile's new "personal-luxury" Starfire convertible rides a Super 88 chassis; 7600 are built

- The Pontiac Tempest offers GM's first postwar four-cylinder engine, plus a unique flexible "rope" driveshaft and rear transaxle

- A rebodied Rambler American line gets a pert little convertible; 12,918 are sold

- AMC offers an aluminum-silicon alloy engine for the Rambler Classic—a first for an American automaker

- Studebaker updates the Champion-based L-head six to overhead valves for the Lark; horsepower increases from 90 to 112

- Studebaker Lark can be ordered with a "Skytop" sliding fabric roof

- Fords are prelubed with 30,000-mile grease fittings; Cadillacs boast lifetime maintenance-free chassis lubrication

- Experimental vehicles for 1961 include Chrysler's Turboflite, the Dodge Flite Wing, and the gyroscope-controlled Ford Gyron

- The handbuilt Fitch GT rides a modified Corvair chassis; it is short-lived

▶ Sales improved only slightly for the '61 Chryslers, mainly due to the Newport models. This New Yorker hardtop sedan snared 5862 buyers.

◀ Here, the 1961 "Letter-Series" Chrysler 300-G. The hardtop coupe cost $5411, and saw sales of only 1280 units.

▲ The front of the last DeSotos looked a tad overwrought. The car itself was basically a retrimmed Chrysler Windsor.

▲ Chrysler's ragtop New Yorker was a slow seller for 1961, just 576 were built.

1961 Model-Year Production Figures

1. Ford	1,338,790	7. Mercury	317,351	13. Lincoln	25,164
2. Chevrolet	1,318,014	8. Buick	276,754	14. Imperial	12,258
3. Rambler	377,902	9. Dodge	269,367	15. DeSoto	3034
4. Plymouth	356,257	10. Cadillac	138,379	16. Metropolitan	969[1]
5. Pontiac	340,635	11. Chrysler	96,454	17. Checker	860[2]
6. Oldsmobile	317,548	12. Studebaker	59,713		

[1] Calender-year sales
[2] Estimate, excludes taxicabs

◄ Dart remained Dodge's mainstay seller for '61, when a heavy facelift made it look more like senior models. Seen here is the top-line Phoenix hardtop coupe.

▼ Senior '61 Dodges slimmed to a single line of Dart-look-alike Polaras with a standard 265-horsepower 361-inch V-8. This ragtop sold for $3252.

▼ Mid-'61 Dodge Darts added an extra taillamp inboard of each tapered fin, among other "spring special" trim changes. Total '61 Dart production: 183,561. Dodge's senior-series Polaras managed only 14,032 units.

▲ Dart wagons in 1961 consisted of Seneca and Pioneer models, the latter with room for six or nine. Wagon prices ranged from $2695 to $3011.

▲ Although base priced at $2849, this '61 Galaxie Sunliner carries several accessories, including fender skirts, "continental kit," special hubcaps, and factory hood ornament. Ford built 44,614 Sunliners this year, slightly less than its 44,762 total for 1960.

▲ The Fairlane was the volume low-priced big-Ford series for '61; here, the $2317 four-door sedan. Production neared 100,000 units.

▲ Lincoln lost many pounds, inches, and models with 1961's all-new Continental. This revived convertible sedan, of which only 2857 were built, retailed for a lofty $6713. Wheelbase was now 123 inches, down by eight.

◄ Mercury's compact Comet came back for '61 with modest changes, but a new bucket-seat S-22 coupe was the big news. Here, the standard two-door, which listed at an even $2000.

▲ Big Mercurys were smaller for 1961. Montereys topped the line. This $3128 ragtop was the choice of 7053 buyers.

▲ The top-line '61 woody-look $3191 Mercury Colony Park saw 7887 copies built. A 175-bhp 292-inch V-8 was standard.

▲ Oldsmobile helped start the swing to sporty big cars with the new mid-1961 Starfire, a specially trimmed Super 88 convertible priced at $4647. Just 7600 found buyers.

▲ Unlike sister GM divisions, Oldsmobile's full-size '61s looked busier than the 1960 models. This $4159 Ninety Eight Sport Sedan hardtop boasted a 325-bhp "Skyrocket" V-8.

▲ The 1961 Olds Ninety Eight line also embraced this more formal "six-window" Holiday hardtop sedan at $4021. Weighing in at 4269 pounds, it found 13,331 buyers.

▲ The smallest Olds in decades, the new F-85 (*right*) was a compact companion to the full-size Super 88 Holiday (*left*), and looked much like it up front. The four-door here sold with the coupe and four-door wagons in the $2300-$2900 range. F-85 output totaled 76,394 for '61.

▲ Olds continued with Dynamic and Super 88 wagons for 1961. This eight-seat Super 88 sold for $3773, but only 2170 were sold.

▲ Sportiest of Oldsmobile's new F-85s was this Deluxe-trim, bucket-seat pillared coupe called Cutlass. At $2621, it attracted 9935 sales in 1961.

▼ Full-size Plymouths went from finned to finless for '61. Here, the Fury hardtop coupe; 16,141 buyers drove one home.

▲ Plymouth's 1961 full-size sales fell sharply. The $2967 Fury V-8 convertible appealed to just 6948 customers.

▲ The Sport Suburban remained Plymouth's top-line wagon for '61. The nine-passenger model cost $3134.

▲ The '61 Valiant line added this spiffy $2137 V200 hardtop coupe, which pleased exactly 18,586 new-car shoppers. The Plymouth's rear-quarter windows were stationary.

▲ Valiants changed little for 1961, but again sold well—143,078 units—though they couldn't entirely offset Plymouth's big-car losses. This V200 wagon listed at $2423.

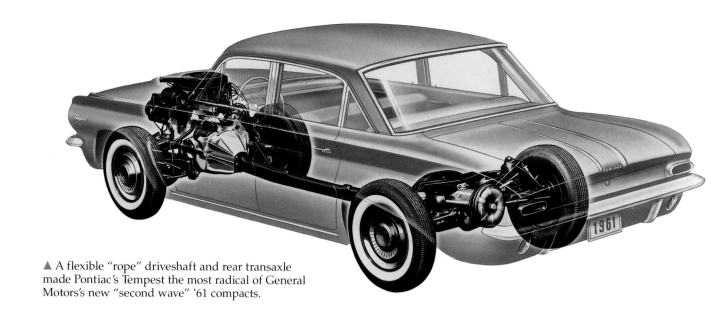

▲ A flexible "rope" driveshaft and rear transaxle made Pontiac's Tempest the most radical of General Motors's new "second wave" '61 compacts.

▲ Tempest bowed with four-door sedans and wagons, adding coupes at midyear. All offered base or Custom trim.

▲ Tempest's first "face" evoked thoughts of '59 Pontiacs and was related to full-size '61 styling. Total build: 100,783 units.

▲ Returning from 1960, the '61 Ventura was an upmarket Catalina two-door Sport Coupe costing $2971 (*shown*), or four-door Vista hardtop.

▶ The 1961 Bonneville Sport Coupe revived 1959's split-theme grille. All "Bonnies" rode a 123-inch chassis.

▲ Another Regal ragtop, also an "VIII" (V-8), shows off the dual headlamps worn by upper-trim '61 Larks. This model topped the line at $2689, $135 more than the standard six.

▲ Studebaker's Lark compacts were lightly facelifted for '61, and sales slipped. Here, the top-line Regal convertible; 1981 were produced. This Lark weighed 3315 pounds.

▲ AMC's first Rambler American convertible returned for '62 with a new look. At $2369, it enticed 13,497 frugal sun lovers.

▲ AMC demoted the '62 Ambassador to the smaller 108-inch Classic chassis, and cut prices a bit in the process. The new $2605 top-line 400 sedan saw production of 15,120 copies.

▲ Sales of AMC's mini Metropolitan reached 412 for '62, though assembly had actually ceased in mid 1960.

▲ Buick broadened the appeal of its compact Special for 1962 with convertibles in Deluxe and, shown here, bucket-seat Skylark trim. At $3012, it attracted 8913 buyers. The $2879 Deluxe sold 8332 copies.

1962

- Chevrolet output passes the two million mark, but Ford builds fewer than 1.5 million cars; industry volume hits 6.7 million

- New '62 offerings include the Chevy II, Ford Fairlane, Mercury Meteor, Pontiac Grand Prix, Studebaker Gran Turismo Hawk

- Pontiac reaches number three in total production and holds that spot through 1970; Plymouth skids to eighth place

- Bucket-seat installations triple to 14.3 percent of American production, as the sporty "personal-car" trend expands

- Big-engine power grows again: Chevrolet's 409-cid V-8 delivers up to 409 bhp; Ford's 406-inch unit reaches 405 horsepower

- Studebaker drops the Packard name from the corporate title and acquires Paxton Products, a manufacturer of superchargers

◀ Buick joined the sporty big-car crowd for '62 with the Invicta-based Wildcat hardtop coupe. A vinyl roof and buckets-and-console interior were included for $3927, as was a 325-bhp 401-cid V-8. Sales totaled exactly 2000.

▼ Like Buick, Cadillac took on a slightly huskier, more-blunted look for 1962. As in '61, all models carried the division's 390-inch V-8 with 325 horses. This $5588 Series Sixty-Two convertible was one of 16,800 examples built.

▲ Cadillac offered six different hardtop sedans for '62. The "six-window" Series Sixty-Two model, with a $5213 price tag, attracted 16,730 buyers.

▲ Though still much like the standard Series Sixty-Two ragtop, the '62 Eldorado Biarritz cost $1022 more: $6610. Production totaled 1450, same as the '61 model run.

- Close to one-third of all American-made cars sold are "pillarless" body styles

- Ford withdraws support of the 1957 AMA resolution against promoting power/speed

- A Plymouth Fury hits 190.073 mph at the Bonneville Salt Flats—the highest speed ever for a stock-body production car

- Dual braking systems are standard in American Motors and Cadillac models

- Buick debuts Skylark and Special Deluxe ragtops, and an optional four-speed gearbox

- American Motors debuts factory-installed seatbelts for both front and rear seats; all cars have anchors for belt installation

- The bucket-seat Wildcat attracts 2000 customers and boosts the Buick image

- Cadillac now offers optional front-fender cornering lights

- Chevrolet's 283 V-8 expands to 327 cid, but the 283 remains through '67; Super Sport is now an Impala subseries

◄ Chevy II bowed for 1962 as a more conventional, more salable, compact to supplement the Corvair. This is the $2465 Nova 400 convertible, which managed 23,741 sales.

► At the other end of the '62 Chevy II spectrum were base-trim 100 sedans and wagons. This two-door sold for $2003 with a four-cylinder engine, $2063 with a six. No V-8s were offered.

▼ It looks stock, but this '62 Chevy Bel Air "bubbletop" Sport Coupe sports a very rare aluminum front end, part of a package offered for serious drag racers.

- The Chevy II compact, Chevrolet's orthodox response to Ford's Falcon, employs single-leaf rear springs

- Midyear brings a Corvair Monza ragtop, plus a turbocharged, 150-bhp Spyder

- Corvettes run with new 327-cid engines rated up to 360 bhp with fuel injection

- Dodge and Plymouth "standard" cars shrink to near-compact size, and sales suffer; the full-size Custom 880 arrives at midyear to boost Dodge sales

- The Ford Fairlane and similar Mercury Meteor pioneer the "intermediate-size" field; small V-8s are available

- Full-size, bucket-seat Fords—the 500/XL Victoria hardtop and Sunliner ragtop—arrive as part of the "Lively Ones" promotion

- The Thunderbird Sports Roadster arrives with a fiberglass tonneau over the rear seat

- Mercury issues the full-size S-55 hardtop and ragtop with bucket seats

▶ The "duck-tail" Corvette returned for '62 with even tidier looks (no two-toning), plus enlarged V-8s with up to 360 horses. Base price was also up—to $4038—but so were sales, to a record 14,531 units.

▲ Unlike the Bel Air, Chevy's 1962 Impala hardtop coupe (*SS shown*) wore a new, more "formal" roofline.

▲ Chevy's Corvair Monza line added this wagon for '62, but only 2362 were called for by buyers. Base price was $2569.

◀ Shown here is the Chrysler New Yorker hardtop sedan, which listed at $4263 and found 6646 buyers.

- The last AMC Metropolitans, 412 of them, are finally sold

- A handsome hardtop coupe joins the Oldsmobile Starfire convertible

- The Pontiac Grand Prix hardtop, based on the Catalina, makes its debut

- "E-Stick" manual shift with automatic clutch is new on the Rambler American

- A Rambler American wins the Mobil Economy Run, averaging 31.11 mpg

- Shelby-American begins production of the AC Cobra roadster

- The Apollo sports car features an Italian body and a Buick aluminum V-8

- Chrysler plans to build 50 turbine-powered cars, which will be tested by motorists

▲ Chrysler's 1962 family included (*from lower left*): Plymouth Valiant and Fury, Imperial, Dodge Dart, Plymouth Fury Suburban, Chrysler 300, and (*center*) Dodge's Lancer.

▼ Valiant-like lines marked Dodge's "full-size" 1962 Darts. The 440 series included one of the line's two ragtops, which sold for $2945 with standard 318 V-8; 3166 were built.

▲ Chrysler replaced Windsors with "nonletter" 300s for '62, among them this $3883 ragtop; 1848 were sold.

▶ New for '61, Dodge's Lancer sported a new grille for '62. A hardtop with bucket seats became the $2257 GT.

▲ Sportiest of Dodge's smaller '62 "standards" were the Polara 500s: ragtop, hardtop sedan, and this hardtop coupe. Priced at $3019, the coupe found 6834 buyers.

▲ At $3268, the bucket-seat Polara 500 convertible was the costliest Dodge at the beginning of model-year '62—but not after the big Custom 880 arrived midyear.

▲ Though it looks innocent, this light base-series '62 Dodge Dart two-door sedan could be had with a 413-inch V-8, making it ideal for the dragstrip.

◀ Shown here, the "Ram Charger" V-8 converted the sleepy looking Dodge Dart into stealthy rocket. Horsepower? A formidable 410.

1962 Model-Year Production Figures								
1. Chevrolet	2,061,677		7. Mercury	341,366		13. Lincoln	31,061
2. Ford	1,476,031		8. Plymouth	339,527		14. Imperial	14,337
3. Pontiac	521,933		9. Dodge	240,484		15. Checker	1230[1]
4. Rambler	422,346		10. Cadillac	160,840		16. Metropolitan	420[2]
5. Oldsmobile	428,853		11. Chrysler	128,921			
6. Buick	399,526		12. Studebaker	89,318			

[1] Estimate, excludes taxicabs
[2] Calender-year sales

377

▲ Full-size Fords looked larger for '62, but weren't. Galaxie 500s, like this $2749 Town Sedan, were the line's big sellers.

▲ This $2674 Galaxie 500 Club Victoria found 87,562 buyers. Note the big, round taillights that became a Ford hallmark.

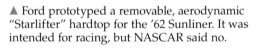

▲ Ford prototyped a removable, aerodynamic "Starlifter" hardtop for the '62 Sunliner. It was intended for racing, but NASCAR said no.

▼ Though Falcon-based, the '62 Fairlane was longer and more "grown-up," and had a V-8 option. Here, the base $2154 two-door.

▲ An "electric shaver" grille identified '62 Ford Falcons. This $2273 bucket-seat Futura sold 17,011 copies.

378

▲ Ford's Thunderbird was all-new for '61, so '62 changes were modest. This standard ragtop wears a rear tonneau borrowed from the slinky new Sports Roadster model.

▲ Thunderbird's '61 "projectile-look" front end would last through '63. This '62 convertible, which enticed 7030 buyers, stickered at $4788. It weighed a hefty 4370 pounds.

▲ Imperial looked cleaner for 1962 thanks to finless fenders and a new grille. The make's sole ragtop appeared in the midline Crown series. This is one of only 554 built.

▶ The LeBaron Southampton hardtop sedan remained the top-line standard Imperial for '62. Base price was $6422. The wide rear-quarter "formal" roof-line was exclusive to this model.

▲ Lincoln's latest Continental was little-changed for 1962. At $6720, this 5370-pound convertible sedan found just 3212 buyers.

◄ For 1962 full-size Mercurys were regrouped into low-end Monterey and uplevel Monterey Custom lines, plus Commuter and Colony Park wagons. Colony Park continued with woody-look side trim in six- and nine-passenger versions priced at $3200-$3300; 9596 were sold.

▼ Mercury issued a sporty bucket-seat big car in mid 1962. Called Monterey Custom S-55, it came either as a hardtop coupe or as this $3738 convertible with a standard 300-horse 390 V-8. Ragtop sales totaled just 1315; hardtops, 2772.

▲ Mercury Comet received a modest facelift for 1962. Here, the new $2170 Custom four-door station wagon.

▲ New for mid '62 was this woody-look Comet Villager wagon, sold only in four-door form for $2710.

▲ Oldsmobile made its big bucket-seat cars a separate line for 1962 and added this $4131 hardtop coupe with a mock-convertible roofline to the Starfire fold. The hardtop sold well: 34,839 versus just 7149 droptops.

◄ The big news for Oldsmobile's 1962 compact line was the addition of F-85 convertibles in both base and Cutlass trim. Respective output was 3660 and a healthier 9893 units. Seen here is a ragtop wearing Jetfire trim.

▲ Plymouth revived the Sport Fury name at mid 1962 for a $3082 bucket-seat convertible (1516 built) and hardtop coupe. Both had a standard 305-horse 361 V-8.

▲ Like Dodge, Plymouth shrunk its standard models to a 116-inch, intermediate-size wheelbase for '62—and watched sales plunge. This Fury hardtop coupe sold for $2585.

▲ The '61 Plymouth Valiant V200 hardtop gained bucket seats to become the 1962 Signet. Priced at $2230, it garnered 25,586 sales. The "Slant Six" again gave 101 or 145 optional horses.

▶ Plymouth's lightest '62s—the low-line Savoy sedans like this $2313 two-door—could be very speedy when equipped with one of the optional 413-cubic-inch V-8s.

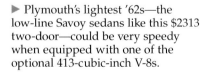

▲ Like the Buick Special and Olds F-85, Pontiac's Tempest added a convertible for '62, plus a spiffy bucket-seat Le Mans trim option (*shown*) that found immediate buyer acceptance. Total Tempest ragtop sales: 20,635.

▼ Pontiac replaced Ventura with the sportier Catalina-based Grand Prix hardtop in mid 1962. For $3490, bucket seats, console, 389-inch V-8, and unique styling touches came standard. Wheelbase measured 120 inches.

▲ Grand Prix was Detroit's most-popular sporty big car for '62, attracting a healthy 30,195 orders. Grille treatment was unique, as was the standard all-vinyl interior. The handsome aluminum wheels seen here were optional.

▲ Designer Brooks Stevens gave 1962 Studebaker Larks a Mercedes-look grille and a $185 Skytop fabric sunroof, as on this $2190 Regal four-door. Unfortunately, sales kept sliding.

383

A sample of AMC's 1963 Rambler lineup, which won *Motor Trend* "Car of the Year" honors, led by the all-new Classic sedan and Ambassador wagon.

► The Ambassador 990 wagon shown here listed at $2956, or $3018 with eight-passenger capacity. Only 8299 were produced for the model run.

1963

- Industry output soars to 7.3 million cars; car/truck sales top the 1955 record

- Chrysler adopts a 5-year/50,000-mile power-train warranty to boost sales; many others increase to 2/24,000

- The average full-time worker earns $5243; an average new car sells for $2310

- New models introduced for 1963 include the Buick Riviera; Chrysler 300-J and New Yorker Salon; Mercury Marauder and Comet Sportster semifastback hardtops; Studebaker Avanti, Super Lark, and Super Hawk

- Big-block V-8 engines grow again; four-on-the-floor gearshifts, bucket seats, and consoles continue to gain in popularity

▲ AMC's Rambler American changed little for 1963. The ragtop was in the new top-trim 440 line and sold for $2344.

▲ Buick's compact '63 Specials were in the final year of their original '61 design. Here, the $2857 Skylark hardtop.

◄ The Buick Riviera was reborn for 1963 as a stunning $4365 hardtop coupe artfully blending American and British style. Build: 40,000.

▼ Buick's sporty Wildcat returned for '63 as this $3849 hardtop coupe—and in new ragtop and hardtop sedan models costing $3961 and $3871.

• Ford offers the industry's first fully synchronized three-speed manual transmission

• Power front disc brakes are now optional on Studebakers (standard on Avanti)—a first for production U.S. cars

• Most 1963 cars have self-adjusting brakes; Studebaker was first in '47

• Half of all 1963s are ordered with power steering, three-fourths with automatic transmission, nearly two-thirds with V-8, and one-seventh with air conditioning

• Studebaker begins installation of seatbelts in March 1963; other makes follow for 1964

• Amber front turn-signal lights are adopted by the auto industry

• PCV (positive crankcase ventilation) systems are installed in all cars—but not yet trucks—to reduce pollution output

• The Dodge/Plymouth big-block expands to 426 cid, with a super-performance "Ram-charger" delivering 425 horsepower

• Pontiac offers optional transistorized ignition—an industry first

▲ A heavy 1963 restyle gave Cadillac its lowest fins in years—and they'd go lower still. Here, the Eldorado Biarritz, which was priced at $6608; 1825 were built.

▲ Chevrolet's bucket-seat Corvair Monza coupe (*shown*), which sold for $2272, and convertible remained strong sellers for '63—117,917 and 36,693 units, respectively.

◄ Again for '63, Chevrolet offered three convertibles with seating for more than two (*from top*): the $2481 Corvair Monza, $2472 Chevy II Nova 400, and $2917 full-size Impala ($3024 with the base V-8). Only the Impala sported new sheetmetal this year.

▲ Only detail and mechanical changes were made to 1963's Chevy II models. This Nova 400 Sport Coupe hardtop sold for $2267 with standard 194-cid, 120-bhp six, and 87,415 were delivered. This one has the sporty SS trim package, which added $161 to the price.

- A tilt steering wheel is now optional in most full-size General Motors cars

- Nearly nine million households have more than one car—up from 4.2 million in 1954

- The Corvette Sting Ray adopts independent rear suspension, but passes on disc brakes

- Dodge completely restyles its compact and renames it Dart, dropping the Lancer moniker

- Chrysler issues a limited-edition 300 Pace Setter hardtop and convertible to mark its official pace car status at the Indy 500 race; the 300-J comes as a hardtop only

- Ford's sporty bucket-seat Falcon Sprint hardtop and convertible are midyear arrivals

- A lightweight 289-cid V-8—with up to 271 horses—becomes available in Ford Fairlanes

- Pontiac Tempest gains a 326-cid V-8 option launches a separate Le Mans series

- A big 421-cubic-inch V-8 is newly available full-size Pontiacs

- Imperial loses its freestanding taillamps and reinstates the Crown Ghia limo (13 built)

- The rakish fiberglass Avanti coupe offers a selection of R-series 289-cid V-8s

◄ The first fully redesigned Chevrolet Corvette since the '53 original arrived for 1963 with the Sting Ray name. The convertible started at $4037.

▼ The 1963 model would be the only Sting Ray coupe with the unique "split" rear window. The coupe weighed in at lean 2859 pounds.

▲ Chrysler touted its "crisp, clean custom look" in a major 1963 restyle. The midyear $5860 Salon hardtop sedan topped the New Yorker line, but sold only 593 copies.

▲ Nonletter Chrysler 300s paced the 1963 Indy 500, and a replica "Pace Setter" convertible (*shown*) and hardtop coupe were issued. Ragtop orders totaled 1861 units.

- Experimental vehicles appearing in 1963 include the Chevrolet Monza GT and SS; Ford Allegro, Cougar II, and Mustang II; Mercury Super Cyclone and Super Marauder; Oldsmobile J-TR; Plymouth Satellite convertible; Pontiac X-400

- Full-size Fords get a 427-cid V-8 option; semifastback Galaxie 500 and 500/XL "Scat-back" hardtops bow at midyear

- Studebaker's Wagonaire wagon has a rear roof panel that slides forward to accommodate taller loads

- Goodyear introduces a premium safety tire with an inner "spare" that allows driving for 100 miles after the outer carcass blows out

- Studebaker ceases all U.S. car and truck production in South Bend on December 20, 1963, consolidating remaining output of a significantly reduced model range into its smaller Hamilton, Ontario, plant

- The consumer evaluation program for the experimental Chrysler Turbine begins as the first cars are delivered in November

◄ Chrysler launched a consumer test program of its latest automotive gas-turbine engine in 1963. The engine was packaged in this striking hardtop coupe styled by Elwood Engel, and 50 were built by Ghia in Italy.

► Styling for the 1963 Dodge Polara was toned down. Hardtops like this one found 6823 buyers. Prices started at $2965.

▼ Hastily revived mid 1962, the true big Dodge continued as the Custom 880. Here the $3109 hardtop sedan.

▼ Lancer left as Dodge's 1963 compact, replaced by the new Dart. This bucket-seat GT ragtop went for $2512.

▲ Functional hood scoops identify this as one of the rare, light-weight '63 Dodge 330 "Ramcharger" two-door sedans with the big new 426 "wedge-head" V-8.

► The sporty bucket-seat Galaxie 500/XL ragtop (*shown*) and hardtop coupe returned from 1962 as two of 1963's heavily restyled "Super Torque" Fords.

▲ Most '63 500/XLs, like this "formal" hardtop, got a 390-inch V-8, but 406 and new 427 options were also available.

▲ Ford added Galaxie "Scatback" semifastback hardtop coupes at mid 1963 for more speed in stock-car racing.

▲ Convertibles in Futura and sporty new V-8 Sprint trim expanded the '63 Falcon lineup.

▲ Fairlane's sportiest '63 was this new $2504 Sports Coupe hardtop; 28,268 were built. It was also sold with a bench front seat for $2324.

1963 Model-Year Production Figures

1. Chevrolet	2,237,201	7. Buick	457,818	13. Lincoln	31,233
2. Ford	1,525,404	8. Dodge	446,129	14. Imperial	14,121
3. Pontiac	590,071	9. Mercury	301,581	15. Checker	1080[1]
4. Plymouth	488,448	10. Cadillac	163,174		
5. Oldsmobile	476,753	11. Chrysler	128,937		
6. Rambler	464,126	12. Studebaker	69,555		

[1] *Estimate, excludes taxicabs*

▲ The '63s were the last "projectile-nose" Ford Thunderbirds, and again came in four models. This $4912 convertible attracted 5913 upmarket shoppers.

▲ Imperial lost its "gunsight" tail-lamps for '63. This is the $5243 Custom hardtop; 3264 were built.

▶ The '63 Lincoln Continental convertible sedan cost $6916 and was vastly outsold by the regular sedan: 28,095 units versus 3138. Among detail refinements made to both models that year was an extra 20 horsepower—320 total—from the 430-cubic-inch V-8.

▲ Mercury's S-55 had less success than many sporty big cars. For 1963 it came as a hardtop coupe, ragtop, and hardtop sedan. A drop-down, reverse-slant Breezeway rear window is evident on this $3650 formal hardtop.

▲ Introduced as a close copy of Ford's Fairlane, Mercury's midsize Meteor returned for '63 with more new looks and new hardtop coupes in $2448 Custom and $2628 bucket-seat S-33 trim; the latter is shown here.

◄ Like Ford's Falcon, Mercury's Comet added hardtops and convertibles for 1963. Here, the $2605 Custom hardtop; 9432 were sold.

391

▲ Crisper sheetmetal marked the big '63 Oldsmobiles, like this sporty Starfire hardtop coupe, which attracted 21,148 customers at a starting price of $4129.

▼ Oldsmobile gave its 1963 F-85 compacts more of a big-car look. This Deluxe four-door sedan was the F-85's second-best-selling '63 model, after the new Cutlass Sport Coupe hardtop, snaring 29,269 buyers with a base price of $2592. All F-85s ran with an aluminum V-8 rated at 155, 185, or 215 bhp.

◄ Plymouth styling improved greatly for '63. The midrange Belvedere series again included a hardtop coupe. Priced at $2431 with a six, or $2538 with a 318-inch V-8, it found only 9204 buyers.

► As in '62, Plymouth's 1963 Sport Fury convertible came with a standard V-8, albeit a 318 inch versus a 361.

▼ Just 9057 Plymouth ragtops were built for '63, of which 3836 were $3082 bucket-seat Sport Furys like this one.

A big-block 421 V-8 remained the top power for big '63 Pontiacs, but now delivered up to 410 horses in ultimate "High Output" tune with two four-barrel carbs. This $2859 Catalina Sport Coupe is so equipped.

◄ Pontiac's Grand Prix was even more handsome for 1963. The grille was again unique to the bucket-seat hardtop, which scored 72,959 sales at $3489 apiece.

▼ Pontiac's 1963 Tempest was squared up and slightly bulked up. The Le Mans became a separate series that year with a $2418 hardtop coupe and this $2742 ragtop, of which 15,957 were sold.

▲ Shown in '62 but not genuinely available until 1963, Studebaker's Avanti wowed everyone with its unique Raymond Loewy styling, aircraft-inspired four-seat interior, and ample V-8 power. Price: $4445. Production: 3834.

▲ Studebaker's aging Lark compacts saw tumbling 1963 sales despite cosmetic tweaks and a bucket-seat Daytona series with wagon, hardtop coupe, and a $2679 convertible.

▲ A rare optional "Euro-style" fabric sunroof graces this '63 Studebaker Lark Daytona hardtop, which carries that year's also rare 289-cid R2 V-8 option with 290 horsepower.

◄ A 1963 Studebaker novelty was the Wagonaire wagon with a sliding rear roof section, which was unfortunately prone to water leaks. This is the topline Daytona version, which sold for $2835 with the base V-8.

CHAPTER ELEVEN

1964-1971

THE MUSCLE CAR ERA

American history accelerated like some new "muscle car" in 1964-71, fueled by the power of television. Words and pictures flooded America's living rooms in a relentless electronic torrent: a man on the moon, too many men fallen in Vietnam; assassinations in Los Angeles and Memphis; riots in Watts, Detroit, and Chicago; "hippies," "hawks," and "doves"; "sit-ins," "love-ins," and "Laugh-In"; the "British invasion" and the "Motown sound"; long hair and miniskirts; thalidomide and marijuana; the rise and fall of Lyndon Johnson, the fall and rise of Richard Nixon.

If the nation seemed to be suffering the worst of times, the Big Three automakers and American Motors enjoyed some of their best. Sales shifted into overdrive, spurred by a host of flashy new models, a national economy that revved up in lockstep with America's war effort in Vietnam, and a fast-growing pool of more affluent buyers and multicar households. Thus, in 1965 the industry built over nine million cars for the first time in a single calendar year. Ironically, Studebaker ceased production the next year after closing its 112-year-old South Bend, Indiana, plant in late 1963 to make a last, short stand in Canada with "Common Sense Cars."

The keys to Detroit's success in this period were "think young" styling and unprecedented performance. Sounding the gun for another all-out "horsepower race," Pontiac stuffed a big 389 V-8 into its newly enlarged '64 Tempest to create a "muscle car." Oldsmobile unleashed its now-famous 4-4-2 package that same year. For 1965, Chevrolet listed a big-block option for its year-old intermediate Chevelle, and Buick issued racy Gran Sport Skylarks. Chrysler continued midsizers with wedge-head 426 options, then upped the ante by offering its hulking Hemi, which had been cleaning up in stock-

car racing, as a showroom option for 1966. By that time, Dearborn had jazzy Ford Fairlane GTs and Mercury Cyclones with similar big-inch powerplants.

Yet as popular and awe-inspiring as muscle cars were, Ford scored the decade's biggest coup with the Mustang, a stylish new "sporty compact" with more sheer youth appeal than anything except the Corvette. Suddenly, Detroit had yet another new breed: the "ponycar." Again, competitors rushed to lasso stampeding buyers, and by 1968 there was a menagerie of Camaros, Firebirds, Cougars, Barracudas, Javelins, and AMXs.

But "bigger" still meant "better" in these years, so bread-and-butter Detroiters all grew larger, heavier, and more complex. Even ponycars soon vied with high-power intermediates for horses and cubic inches. Symbolizing this trend was Oldsmobile's big new personal-luxury Toronado of 1966, America's first production front-drive car since the late-Thirties Cord. But radical engineering alone still didn't assure success, and dwindling sales brought on by ponycars claimed Chevy's rear-engine Corvair after 1969. More salable by far were Detroit's new lower-priced big luxury cars, the 1965 Ford LTD and Chevrolet Caprice.

Of course, the go-go good times couldn't last, and sobering new realities were evident by 1971. Demand for both ponycars and muscle cars was plummeting, and Congress was adding new requirements for safety features and exhaust emissions to the original list mandated for 1968-70. What's more, imports had made a comeback, including a new horde from Japan. The Sixties had been a weird, wild, wonderful ride, but times were changing, and Detroit, like all America, would never be quite the same.

1964

- Industry output leaps to 7.9 million cars

- New models include the Chevrolet Chevelle, Mercury Comet Caliente, Oldsmobile Jetstar 88 and Jetstar I, Studebaker Challenger

- Ford Mustang is launched on April 17, 1964, as a 1965 model; Plymouth's sporty Barracuda fastback, a '64, had already bowed on April 1

- All '64 models have front seatbelts

- More than one-fourth of the '64 cars are two-door hardtops; nearly 69 percent have a V-8 engine; 18.5 percent sport bucket seats

- Dodge marks its 50th anniversary and provides the official pace car, a Challenger convertible, for the Indy 500 race

▲ AMC's small 1964 Rambler Americans wore attractive all-new styling on a six-inch-longer wheelbase (106 inches). Here, the top-trim 440 convertible, hardtop, and wagon.

▲ The Rambler Classic Typhoon hardtop bowed in mid 1964 to introduce a modern new inline six of the same name (232 inch, 145 horse). Just 2520 were sold at $2509 apiece.

▲ A minor facelift freshened AMC's larger cars for 1964. One of four models in a slimmed-down Ambassador line, the $2985 990 wagon attracted only 4407 customers.

▲ Ambassador wagons could be dressed up with spiffy side trim and whitewall tires. A step down from the 990 shown here in the auto show spotlight was the $2651 770.

◀ Hardtop coupes graced AMC's '64 lineup for the first time since the last Nash/Hudson models of 1957. This bucket-seat Ambassador 990-H was the premium offering, priced at $2917. Just 2955 were sold.

• Studebaker arranges to buy engines from General Motors for Canadian-built 1965 and 1966 models

• Automatic-transmission selectors are standardized at "PRNDL" in some GM models; other automakers follow for 1965

• Buick's Special/Skylark models ride a new intermediate-size "A-body" platform

• An optional Cadillac heat/air conditioning system holds a preset temperature, while Twilight Sentinel controls the headlights

• For the first time, an optional V-8 (273-cubic inch) is available for the Dodge Dart and Plymouth Valiant

• Wildcat puts the Electra's 401-cubic-inch V-8 into the lighter Buick LeSabre chassis

• Dodge's "Ramcharger" is now a race-only 426-cid Hemi; everyday buyers get a tamer "Street Wedge" V-8 with 365 horsepower

• A prototype Studebaker SS roadster is shown—it will evolve into the ersatz, limited-production Excalibur

• Checker drops its Superba sedan and wagon, but keeps Marathon

◄ Buicks looked brawnier for '64. Sporty Wildcats, like this $3267 hardtop coupe, boasted a new 425-inch V-8 option with either 340 or 360 horsepower.

▲ Compacts no more, Buick's 1964 Specials rode a new longer wheelbase to become midsize cars. This $2834 Skylark ragtop saw build reach 10,225.

▲ Buick's 1964 Electra 225s wore a nice blend of soft and razor-edge lines. One of five models in that series, the $4070 hardtop coupe managed 7181 sales.

▲ There was no need to fiddle much with Riviera for 1964. But there was more standard power in the 340-horse 425-inch V-8. Output slipped to 37,658.

▲ Giving new meaning to the term "family bus" was Buick's new 1964 Skylark Sportwagon with "Greyhound Sceni-Cruiser" roofline. Body and wheelbase (120 inches) were unique to this model, which sold for around $3100.

▲ Cadillacs sported a wider look via a restyled face. Here is the lush 1964 Eldorado Biarritz convertible, which started at a breathtaking $6610. At that, only 1450 of the 4605-pound ragtops were produced for the model year.

- Chevy II adds the 283-cid V-8 and four-speed gearbox to the options list

- Corvairs adopt a camber-compensating transverse rear leaf spring spring to improve handling and save space

- A convertible returns to the letter series Chrysler 300, now called the 300-K

- The midsize Chevrolet Chevelle debuts; Malibus get a Super Sport package option

- Mercury adds a Cyclone hardtop; slant-back Marauders deliver awesome performance with a 427-cid V-8 option

- The restyled fourth-generation Ford Thunderbird features "Silent-Flo" ventilation

- Ford's Falcon and Mercury's Comet are restyled, are bigger-, bulkier-looking

- The full-size Jetstar I joins the Oldsmobile line, while the midsize Cutlass lineup adds its first muscle car, the 4-4-2, at midyear

- Pontiac offers a new Catalina "2+2" option package that includes bucket seats

◀ The full-size "Jet Smooth" Chevrolets looked a little boxier for 1964. Impala SS was again the sportiest of the lot, though this tamer hardtop coupe came with a 140-horse six for $2839.

▶ As usual, spartan Biscayne sedans anchored the bottom of Chevy's full-size 1964 fleet. This two-door stickered at $2363 with the standard 140-horse 230-inch six.

▲ Chevy Corvair standard horsepower rose to 95 or 110 for 1964. Here, the $2335 Monza four-door sedan, which attracted 21,926 buyers.

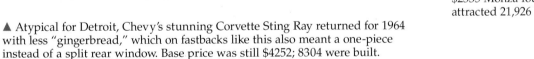

▲ Atypical for Detroit, Chevy's stunning Corvette Sting Ray returned for 1964 with less "gingerbread," which on fastbacks like this also meant a one-piece instead of a split rear window. Base price was still $4252; 8304 were built.

• Pontiac Tempest gets an inline six as the base engine; the legendary GTO, considered the first "muscle car," arrives at midyear

• Rambler debuts the specially trimmed, yellow-and-black Typhoon hardtop to showcase its new 232-inch inline six

• The last American-built Studebakers leave South Bend, Indiana, on December 20; production continues in Canada

• Experimental and show vehicles for 1964 include the Mercury Park Lane 400; GM Firebird IV, Runabout, and GM-X; Chevrolet Toronado and Super Nova; Buick Silver Arrow; and Ford Aurora station wagon

• Vetta Ventura emerges as the successor to the Apollo sports car; the targa-roofed Warrior has a rear-mounted V-4; the Griffith sports coupe wears a modified fiberglass TVR body; the scaled-down Cord 8/10

► Chrysler's "crisp, clean custom look" was tastefully warmed over for '64. Chrysler held on to hardtop wagons longer than anyone else—witness this 1964 New Yorker Town & Country. Weak model-year sales of only 2793 units made 1964 this body style's last year.

◄ The letter series Chrysler 300 convertible was reinstated for '64 after a year's absence, but the $4522 ragtop 300-K managed a production run of only 625 units.

▲ With 3022 built, the $4056 300-K hardtop coupe easily outsold the ragtop. Alas, both letter series Chryslers were even more like nonletter 300s, which cost about $600-$700 less.

▲ The nonletter 300 ragtop sold for $3803. Trim details and a 305-horse 383-inch V-8 set the 300s apart from the 300-Ks, whose standard 360-bhp 413 incher was optional on 300s.

1964 Calendar-Year Car Sales

1. Chevrolet	2,318,619	7. Oldsmobile	493,991	13. Lincoln	36,297
2. Ford	1,594,053	8. Rambler	393,859	14. Imperial	23,295
3. Pontiac	715,261	9. Mercury	298,609	15. Checker	960[1]
4. Plymouth	551,633	10. Cadillac	165,909		
5. Buick	510,490	11. Chrysler	153,319		
6. Dodge	501,781	12. Studebaker	36,697		

[1]Estimated, excludes taxicabs

▲ Obviously ready for quarter-mile action, this two-door '64 Dodge 330 is a rare "Hemi-Charger" with the factory Maximum Performance Package.

◄ To keep pace in a burgeoning new "horsepower race," Chrysler put Hemi heads on its biggest 426 wedge-head V-8 in 1964—but strictly for competition.

▲ Dodge's big 880 models wore a smoother look for '64 via tasteful restyling front and rear. Although this Custom ragtop was attractively priced at $3264, only 1058 were sold.

▲ Based on '62 tooling, midsize Dodges looked better still for '64. Vee'd C-pillars were new to hardtop coupes like this $2978 Polara 500, which found 15,163 buyers.

◄ Dodge's new compact Dart had sold well in '63, so the '64s were little-changed. A new 274-inch V-8 option with 180 horses gave sporty GTs like this hardtop coupe more satisfying go.

▲ A full lower-body reskin made Ford's compact Falcon look more "grown-up" for '64. This Futura Sprint convertible, 4278 of which were built, boasts a 260-inch V-8 option.

▲ Ford's midsize Fairlane looked a tad busier for 1964, but again offered 289-inch V-8 options with up to 271 horses. This bucket-seat 500 Sports Coupe hardtop listed at $2502.

◄▲ After years of watching Hemi-powered cars go by on the strips, Ford conjured a Fairlane drag car for 1964. Called Thunderbolt, it packed a "High-Riser" 427 V-8 (*above*) with a reported 425 horsepower (the true number was closer to 500), plus light-weight fiberglass body panels. Ford built only 100 at a cost of $5300 each, but sold them for just under $4000.

▲ Ford's personal-luxury Thunderbird picked up sales steam with all-new 1964 models featuring a "begadgeted" interior with a curved "cove" back seat. The convertible pictured here listed at $4953. It registered 9168 sales—compared to 60,552 standard hardtops and 22,715 Landau hardtops. Weight was up about 250 pounds (4586 for the ragtop).

▶ Big Fords still used a lot of 1960 tooling for '64, but it wasn't evident with that year's massive lower-body restyle. This Galaxie 500/XL hardtop coupe sold for $3233 with the standard 289 V-8; 58,306 were produced.

◀ A bona fide collectible now, the Ford Galaxie 500/XL convertible sold for $3495 in 1964. Most big XLs were ordered with a big-block 390-inch V-8 and self-shifting Cruise-O-Matic.

▶ Helping to cement Ford's advertising claim as the home of "Total Performance" for 1964 was this new big-block 427-cubic-inch V-8. Basically a bored-out version of the previous 406-inch V-8, it delivered 410 horsepower with a single four-barrel carburetor, and a mighty 425 with dual quads, as shown here.

▲ Ford opened up a big new market with the Falcon-based Mustang. Introduced on April 17, 1964, the new sporty compact sent people scurrying to Ford showrooms like nothing in years, touching off "Mustang Mania" and Detroit's greatest sales success of the Sixties. This ragtop cost $2614 with the 101-horsepower six, and scored an amazing (for a ragtop) 101,945 sales.

403

▲ This $5739 Imperial Crown took on a Lincolnesque look for '64 in a tasteful makeover by Chrysler design chief Elwood Engel (principal designer of the '61 Lincoln).

▲ Lincoln grew three inches in wheelbase for 1964 (to 126), but retained the classically simple lines of 1961-63. This convertible sedan cost $6720, but only 3328 were sold.

◀ Mercury marked its Silver Anniversary in 1964 with a facelifted full-size line led by performance-oriented Marauder semi-fastback hardtops like this Montclair.

▲ Mercury bulked up its '64 Comet compact to fill in for the midsize Meteor, which was dropped. Here, the low-line $2154 202 two-door sedan.

▲ Like Buick, Oldsmobile debuted a "split-level" wagon in mid '64. Called Vista Cruiser, this F-85 model cost around $3000, and 3394 were built.

▲ Lansing's big bucket-seat Starfire twosome received crisper styling for 1964. Demand for the $4138 hardtop dropped one-third to 13,573 units.

◀ Oldsmobile's F-85 went from compact to midsize for 1964 by adopting a handsome new "A-body" platform shared with Buick's Special/Skylark, Pontiac's Tempest/LeMans, and Chevy's new Chevelle. The sporty Cutlass became a separate series, of which this $2784 Holiday hardtop coupe was the best-seller: 36,153 units.

▲ Regarded as the first modern "muscle car," Pontiac's GTO blew in for 1964 as a Tempest-based convertible, hardtop coupe, and this $3200 pillared Sport Coupe with a standard 325-horse 389-cubic-inch V-8. Total GTO production was 32,450 units.

▲ Full-size '64 Pontiacs had a more rounded rendition of 1963 styling. The Catalina ragtop, and this $2869 Sport Coupe (74,793 built), offered a new $291 "2+2" option.

▲ Plymouth clawed its way back up the sales charts with new 1964 styling as on its still midsize "standards." This Sport Fury hardtop coupe doubled output to 23,695 units.

▲ Like Dodge's Darts, '64 Plymouth Valiants, like this $2256 Signet hardtop, could have a new 180-bhp V-8.

▲ Studebaker Larks, like this $2451 Daytona hardtop, wore a neat new look for '64—but sales still tumbled.

▲ The 1964 Studebakers, here the $2805 Daytona ragtop, would be the last to be built in South Bend, Indiana.

▶ Studebaker's Avanti returned for 1964 with a $4445 price tag and square headlamp bezels as one of the few changes from debut '63. A 240-horse 289-inch V-8 remained standard, and options ran to a 290-horse "R2" version—or a 335-horse, 305-inch "R3." Unfortunately, sales dropped from 3834 to just 809, which helped force Studebaker's exit from South Bend.

▲ American Motors tried to one-up Ford's Mustang 2+2 fastback with its mid-1965 Marlin. Priced at $3100 with the 232-cubic-inch six, it offered a wide range of options and attracted 10,327 customers.

▲ The '65 Rambler Americans showed only detail changes. AMC built 3882 of its $2418 440 ragtops that year.

▲ Ambassadors, like this $2656 990 four-door sedan, wore straight-edged lines and stacked headlamps.

◄ AMC's midsize Rambler Classic added a convertible for '65, a first for the line. Sold only in top-trim 770 guise, it stickered at $2696 with the 145-horsepower, 232-cid six. Sales were modest, as only 4953 were built.

1965

- American car production sets a record: 8.8 million for the 1965 model year

- New models include the Chrysler 300-L, Dodge Coronet and Monaco, Ford LTD, and Gran Sport (GS) editions of the Buick Skylark and Riviera

- Ralph Nader publishes *Unsafe at Any Speed,* a critique on auto safety that springboards into a potent consumer movement

- Replacing drums, front disc brakes are installed on many 1965 models

- The Automotive Products Trade Act of 1965 eliminates tariffs on new vehicles crossing U.S. or Canadian borders from either direction

- The Avanti II enters production; it's much like the original Studebaker version, but is powered by a potent Chevrolet Corvette V-8

▲ This Electra 225 Custom hardtop sedan shows off the new lines worn by all big Buicks for 1965. It stickered at $4389, and 29,932 were sold. Standard-trim Electras began at $4206.

▲ Buick's '65 Wildcat ragtop came as a $3502 Deluxe or as this $3727 Custom. All Wildcats now rode Electra's 126-inch wheelbase, rather than LeSabre's 123-inch chassis.

◄ With a standard 155-horse, 225-cid V-6, Buick's Skylark Thin Pillar Coupe was a fairly rare commodity for 1965, as just 4195 were built. The less-deluxe Special Standard Coupe, priced at $2343 (versus $2537), sold better, attracting 12,945 buyers.

► For 1965, Buick hid the headlights on the Riviera, which stickered at $4385. Build slipped to 34,586 units, but Buick wasn't too concerned because it had a new model waiting in the wings for 1966. The Gran Sport option shown here was installed on 3355 Rivieras.

- A nationwide "HELP" communications network is announced; it will use CB radios

- Chrysler products abandon the novel automatic-transmission pushbutton controls first used in 1956

- Audiophiles rejoice: FM stereo radios become available in some Chevrolets

- AMC introduces its fastback "3+3" Marlin; it's based on the Rambler Classic

- A tilt/telescope steering column is optional on some Cadillacs, as is an automatic leveling suspension

- A Gran Sport option for Buick Riviera and Skylark includes the Wildcat 401-inch V-8

- New power for Checker: Cabmaker now buys Chevrolet six and V-8 engines

- The Corvair sports all-new hardtop styling and a redesigned independent suspension; Corsa replaces the Monza Spyder

- Caprice Custom Sedan joins the Chevrolet line at as the marque's top LTD-fighter

▲ Having introduced a big new 429-inch V-8 for 1964, Cadillac completed its product renewal with trim new 1965 styling. The standard convertible, now a De Ville priced at $5639, sold 19,200 copies. Calais was the new bottom-rung series.

▲ Checker Motors of Kalamazoo began selling civilian versions of its famous taxis in 1959. This $3140 Marathon wagon was one of three '65 models. Total sales: 930 units.

▲ Chevy's midsize '65 Chevelle received only minor style tweaks that also appeared on the Chevelle-based El Camino pickup. Prices started at $2380; sales improved to 34,724.

▲ The sassy Chevelle Malibu SS got a big performance boost midyear with a big-block 396-inch V-8 option with 375 horses. Just 201 cars got one, but '66 would see many more.

▲ Early Chevelles like this '65 Malibu SS ragtop were ideally sized—much like the "classic" mid-Fifties Chevys. This model sold for $2750 with a six, $2858 with the 283-inch V-8.

- Chevrolet's Chevy II Nova gains a 327-cid V-8 option; Dodge Dart and Plymouth Barracuda offer a 273-cid "Commando" V-8

- Corvette gains optional four-wheel disc brakes, plus its first big-block V-8 engine

- Chrysler's 300-L is destined to be the last letter series model; a final 2405 hardtops and 440 ragtops are built

- Resembling the prewar Mercedes SSK, the neoclassic Excalibur SSK roadster enters limited production priced at $7250

- Dodge output starts a rapid rise; the Coronet name returns on midsize models

- Dodge's Coronet Hemi-Charger aims at the dragstrips, while the Monaco is a full-size sport/luxury hardtop

- A 2+2 fastback joins the initial Mustang coupe and soft top; 680,989 Mustangs are sold from April '64 through August '65

- Ford Falcons are now available with a 289-cubic-inch V-8 with 200 horsepower

- Thunderbirds boast "sequential" turn signals, standard front disc brakes, and a keyless locking system

▲ Chevy's big 1965 news was a totally revamped full-size line with curvy new contours. The sporty Impala SS continued as a hardtop coupe and as this ragtop, which listed for $3104 with base six; most buyers opted for a V-8.

◄ Helping to open up a new market for lower-priced, full-size luxury cars was the 1965 "Caprice Custom Sedan by Chevrolet," a $200 package option for the Impala hardtop sedan—a quick response to Ford's lush new Galaxie LTD.

◄ Chevy further cleaned up the Corvette Sting Ray's looks for '65 and added leather seats, AM/FM radio, and four-wheel power-disc brakes to the options list. Corvette sales reached another new high: 23,562 units. So did power, with the midyear addition of a 396-inch V-8 option with up to 425 horsepower.

- Ford's posh new Galaxie 500 LTD is claimed to ride as "Quiet as a Rolls-Royce"

- Mustangs can be optioned with a 271-horsepower "Hi-Po" 289 V-8

- Oldsmobile adopts a 400-cid V-8 for duty with its 4-4-2 option package

- Full-size Plymouths return; the Fury models are the biggest Plymouths ever

- Midsize Belvederes and bucket-seat Satellites join the Plymouth stable

- The Mustang-based Shelby GT-350 features a 289-inch V-8 with 306 bhp

- Studebaker drops the Lark, and offers Canadian-built sedans and wagons only

- Don Yenko offers the limited-edition Yenko Stinger—a modified Corvair Corsa

- Experimental vehicles displayed during 1965 include AMC's St. Maritz and Tahiti; Dodge Charger II; Plymouth XP-VIP; Mercury Astron; Comet Escapade and Cyclone Sportster; Lincoln Continental Coronation Coupe; Ford Bordinat Cobra, Mercer Cobra, and Black Pearl; Chevrolet Mako Shark II and Concours

◄ The Corvair Greenbrier wagon was in its final year for '65. Just 1528 were sold this year at $2609 apiece.

◄ Regular Corvairs got a new lease on life for '65 with pretty new all-hardtop styling. This $2519 Corsa coupe, of which 20,291 were built, has the 180-horse "Turbo Air" flat-six, which added $158 to the price.

▲ The last of the letter series Chryslers were the 1965 300-L hardtop and $4618 convertible, which shared a bigger, brand-new design with linemates. Build: 2405 hardtops and 440 ragtops.

▲ Crisp but not boxy describes Chrysler's 1965 styling, the work of design chief Elwood Engel. New Yorkers like this $4161 hardtop wore unique translucent taillamps.

1965 Calendar-Year Car Sales

1. Chevrolet	2,375,118	7. Dodge	489,065	13. Studebaker	19,435
2. Ford	2,170,795	8. Rambler	391,366	14. Imperial	18,409
3. Pontiac	802,000	9. Mercury	346,751	15. Checker	930[1]
4. Plymouth	728,228	10. Chrysler	206,089	16. Excalibur	56
5. Buick	600,145	11. Cadillac	182,435	17. Avanti II	21
6. Oldsmobile	591,701	12. Lincoln	40,180		

[1] *Estimated, excludes taxicabs*

▲ A 180-horse, 273-cubic-inch V-8 was standard for 1965 Coronet 500s, like this $2894 convertible, but optional big-block wedge-head engines were still available.

▲ Dodge built only a few '65 Hemi-Coronet "altereds" for drag racing. Like "Dandy" Dick Landy's mount here, they were banned by NHRA and thus ran only in AHRA.

▲ The new big 1965 Dodges wore handsome all-new styling. Models were divided into premium Custom 880s, like this $3335 ragtop, and a companion group of slightly detrimmed, lower-priced Polaras. With all this, sales of the big Dodges more than doubled: 12,705 Polaras and 44,496 Custom 880s, plus 13,096 examples of the plush $3355 Monaco hardtop coupe.

◄ The '65 Dodge Dart GT hardtop listed at $2404 with the standard Slant Six, but two small-block V-8 options boosted power to 180 or 235. A low 2715-pound curb weight helped performance.

▲ Widely advertised as being "Quiet as a Rolls-Royce," the Galaxie 500 LTD was the costliest and cushiest of the all-new 1965 full-size Fords. This hardtop sedan stickered at $3313, and notched up an impressive 68,038 sales.

▲ Ford's new '65 Galaxie 500 LTD was also offered as this $2685 hardtop coupe, but it didn't sell as well: 37,691 units.

▲ Ford's wildly popular Mustang got a revised engine slate with up to 271 horsepower for 1965. Base price: $2416.

▲ Whitewalls, wire wheel covers, and a decklid luggage rack were just three of the many options for 1965 Mustangs.

▲ This racy "2+2" fastback expanded the Mustang stable for the 1965 model year, and galloped off with 77,079 buyers.

▲ A squarer, more sculptured look marked Ford's '65 midsize Fairlanes. At $2538, this bucket-seat 500 Sports Coupe was the sportiest offering.

▲ The 1965 Falcon was the last of the 1960 design. Changes were few, save for a revised grille. Sales for the $2226 Futura hardtop coupe: 25,754.

▲ A rear-seat tonneau graces this $4953 Ford Thunderbird convertible, of which 6846 were built for '65—2352 fewer than its 1964 predecessor.

▲ Imperial's four-model lineup returned for 1965 with minor trim and equipment revisions. This Crown hardtop sedan was the top seller with 11,628 orders. Price: $5772.

▲ Lincoln Continental scored higher 1965 sales despite being largely unchanged. The "pillared-hardtop" sedan greatly outsold the ragtop sedan—this year, 36,824 to 3328.

▲ Mercury's Comet received another restyle for '65, with vertically stacked headlights. As before, Comet's lone ragtop resided in the plush Caliente series. Although affordably priced at $2664, it sold just 6035 copies.

▲ Full-size 1965 Oldsmobiles were differentiated by trim, equipment, and grille treatment. The most formal look was reserved for top-line Ninety Eight models like this $4197 hardtop coupe, of which 12,166 were built.

▲ With an extra 35 horses—345 in all—Oldsmobile's hot 4-4-2 package was hotter for 1965. As in '64, the option package was available for F-85/ Cutlass pillared coupes, hardtop coupes, and this ragtop.

◀ Like its full-size GM sisters, the big 1965 Oldsmobiles had a more flowing look. This sporty $4778 Starfire ragtop got only 2236 orders.

▲ Topping Plymouth's lineup of "Roaring '65s" was the first true full-size Fury since 1961, with a complete range of body styles. At $2863, 21,367 customers chose this top-line Fury III hardtop sedan.

▲ Plymouth's Barracuda bowed on April 1, 1964, as a Valiant-based "glassback" coupe—but not a direct reply to Mustang. Sales were good for 1965: 64,596 units.

◄ The "standard" 1962-64 Plymouth became the midsize '65 Belvedere. Sporty Satellites topped the line: a hardtop and this rare $2910 ragtop (1860 built).

▼ Big '65 Pontiacs had rakish new lines and longer wheelbases on an even wider "Wide Track" chassis. The Bonneville convertible carried a base sticker price of $3594 with standard 389-inch V-8, Turbo Hydra-Matic, and skirted rear wheels. Sales for this model: 21,050. Total '65 Bonneville production: 134,020 units.

▲ Stacked headlights continued on Pontiac's all-new big '65s, as did the performance-oriented "2+2" package option for the Catalina convertible and this semifastback Sport Coupe hardtop, which sold for $3287 so equipped.

▲ Tempests adopted a crisper look for '65, announced by newly stacked quad headlamps as on full-size Pontiacs. The droptop GTO shown here stickered at $3057 and boasted 335 standard horses, 10 up on the debut '64 "Goats."

414

▲ Rogue replaced the 440-H as the sporty hardtop in American Motors's '66 Rambler American line. Despite a reasonable $2370 price, only 8718 were sold.

▲ Ambassador also became a separate AMC "make" for 1966, and offered a swank new top-line hardtop model: DPL. It started at $2756, and 10,458 were built.

▲ Midsize '66 Buicks got a "midlife" makeover. Big-inch bucket-seat Gran Sports were now a separate line distinct from Skylarks, which included a new hardtop sedan, shown here with the $3019 GS hardtop coupe, of which 9934 were built.

▲ Buick's personal-luxury Riviera was all-new for '66, and somewhat bigger and heavier, too—but still quite elegant. Base price rose to $4408, production to 45,348 units.

▲ After record sales in 1965, Cadillac stood basically pat for '66, yet fared nearly as well. Here, the $5555 De Ville convertible, whose sales held steady at just over 19,000.

1966

- Chevrolet output trails Ford for the second time this decade; both makes top 2.2 million cars for the model year, as industry volume eases slightly to 8.6 million

- Dodge reaches fifth place in the production race, with a record 632,658 cars built

- Oldsmobile launches the personal-luxury Toronado—the first production American front-wheel-drive car since the 1937 Cord

- New models include the AMC Ambassador DPL, Rambler Rebel, and American Rogue; Chevrolet Caprice Custom Coupe; Dodge Charger fastback; Ford Fairlane GT; Mercury Comet Capri; and the Plymouth Fury VIP

- The Mars II electric car, from Electric Fuel Propulsion Inc., uses a Renault 10 body; its lead-cobalt batteries can be recharged up to 200 times for a claimed 50,000-mile life, but this sounds optimistic to most skeptics

▲ Chevrolet had a hot new number for 1966 full-size cars: "427," an even bigger big-block V-8 with 390 or 425 horses. A new grille and taillights updated the styling. Seen here is the $2947 Impala SS Sport Coupe hardtop.

◀ Chevy followed up on the success of the 1965 Caprice hardtop sedan by adding wagons and this two-door with its own greenhouse for 1966. Total Caprice output: 181,000 units.

▶ A standard big-block 396-inch V-8 and smooth new styling gave Chevy salesmen plenty to talk about in the midsize 1966 Chevelle Malibu Super Sport, or SS 396. A three-speed manual was standard, but four-on-the-floor and "Turbo-Hydro" automatic were available. Incredibly, the hardtop coupe shown here started at $2776. The wheels on this car are actually borrowed from a period Corvette.

- Pontiac's Tempest is available with an overhead-cam six—ohc motors won't arrive in force in American cars until the late '80s

- Safety first: Rear seatbelts are made standard on all 1966 models

- The average full-time American worker earns $5967 yearly; the cheapest full-size Chevrolet starts at $2379

- Ford's 428-cid V-8 powers the 7-Liter hardtop and convertible models; boasting 345 bhp, it's optional on other big Fords

- The National Traffic and Motor Vehicle Safety Act and the Highway Safety Act are enacted; the federal Department of Transportation (DOT) is established

- It's the "last hurrah" for 114-year-old Studebaker. Production ceases in March 1966; output for 1966 is just 8947 units

- New Dodge Charger is essentially a fast-back Coronet with hidden headlamps

- AMC—now a distinct make—replaces Rambler badging on Marlin, Ambassador, and will do so soon on the Rebel

◄ With GM mandating a halt to development after 1965, Chevy's Corvair changed little from that point forward. Still, it remained a desirable semisports car. The Monza Sport Coupe here cost $2350; 37,605 were built.

► Chevy dropped "fuelie" small-blocks for 1966, leaving a big new 427-inch V-8 with up to 425 horses as Corvette's ultimate 1966 power option. It came with a domed hood. The $4295 coupe sold 9958 copies this year.

◄ Dart was part of "The Dodge Rebellion" for 1966, but changes were evolutionary. A landau-style roof was a new extra for the GT hardtop, which stickered at $2417.

- The second-generation Buick Riviera is kin to the Oldsmobile Toronado, but keeps its traditional rear-wheel-drive setup

- Chevelle's Super Sport becomes the SS 396, courtesy of a 396-cid engine; big Chevrolets add a 427-cid V-8 option

- A 440-cid V-8 is now standard in the Chrysler New Yorker, and available in the big Dodge and Plymouth models

- A 425-horsepower "Street Hemi" is now available in midsize Dodges and Plymouths

- Ford Fairlanes can be had with an optional 410/425 horsepower, 427-cid V-8

- Ford station wagons feature a two-way tailgate that folds down and opens to the side

- The new Mercury Comet Cyclone GT paces the Indianapolis 500

- Ford's Falcon now ranks as a shorter version of the Fairlane; the rebodied Fairlane line is topped by the bucket-seat 500/XL

- Lincoln revives the two-door hardtop (its first since 1960) and adopts a 340-horse, 462-cid V-8—the largest on the market

- Hertz rents out 936 Shelby GT-350H fastbacks ($17 a day/17¢ a mile); many are surreptitiously raced on weekends

▲ A mid-1966 surprise was Dodge's Coronet-based Charger fastback, which had originally been slated for a mid-'65 introduction. The sleek Charger managed a healthy 37,344 sales in its abbreviated debut season. A mild 230-bhp 318-cubic-inch V-8 was included in the $3122 base sticker price, but more power was available—up to a 425-horsepower Hemi V-8.

◄ Built on a new B-body platform shared with the Plymouth Belvedere/Satellite, the '66 Dodge Coronets wore crisp, fairly conservative lines. Here, the 500 convertible (*shown*), which sold for $2600-$2900. Including the four-door sedan, 55,683 Coronet 500s were produced.

• Experimental cars seen this year include the AMC Cavalier, Vixen, and AMX; Corvair Monza SS roadster and GT twin-canopy coupe; and Pontiac Banshee

• Excalibur Series I models, now including a $7950 phaeton, are powered by Chevrolet's 327-cubic-inch Corvette V-8; production reaches 90 cars for the year

• Glassic's fiberglass-bodied Model A replica rides an International Scout chassis; this $3800 roadster will be available into 1975, when it will list for $8900

• Fritz Duesenberg displays a Virgil Exner-designed, Ghia-built prototype neoclassic sedan bearing the legendary nameplate; production never happens

▶ This '66 Dodge Coronet 440 hardtop coupe looks a tad plain, but could be a super-stormer with that year's new 440-inch wedge or Street Hemi options. Base price with V-8 was $2551.

▲ Dodge's full-size sporty car for '66 was this $3604 Monaco 500 hardtop coupe. It was a big car—121-inch wheelbase, 3895 pounds—that found modest success at 10,840 units

▲ Mid-Sixties Imperials were more tasteful than early decade models, one reason that sales improved. Here, one of just 514 Crown ragtops built for '66.

▲ What better setting for America's favorite mid-Sixties car? A '66 Ford Mustang hardtop, of which 499,751 were built, visits Washington, D.C.

▲ Ford's '66 Mustang saw only minor trim changes—no need to mess with a winner. This $2653 convertible wears styled steel wheels, a new option.

▲ Ford unleashed a new '66 Galaxie 500/XL "7-Liter" hardtop and ragtop, both boasting a big new 345-horse 428 V-8. Sales: 8705 hardtops, 2368 ragtops.

1966 Calendar-Year Car Sales

1.	Ford	2,206,639	7.	Buick	553,870	13.	Imperial	13,742
2.	Chevrolet	2,212,415	8.	Mercury	343,149	14.	Studebaker	8947
3.	Pontiac	831,331	9.	Rambler/AMC	295,897	15.	Checker	1056[1]
4.	Plymouth	687,514	10.	Chrysler	264,848	16.	Avanti II	98
5.	Dodge	632,658	11.	Cadillac	196,685	17.	Excalibur	90
6.	Oldsmobile	578,385	12.	Lincoln	54,755			

[1] *Estimated, excludes taxicabs*

◀ The midsize Ford Fairlane was all-new for 1966, wearing swoopier styling on slightly larger dimensions. Like most Fairlanes, this $2378 Fairlane 500 hardtop coupe came with a 200-inch six, with a 200-horse 289-inch V-8 optional. This model sold 75,947 copies.

▲ The Ford Thunderbird completed another three-year styling cycle for 1966 with a new pointy nose and eggcrate grille, plus wall-to-wall taillights. The soft top, shown here, stickered at $4879, but sales were down to just 5049 units. Because Thunderbird ragtop sales continued to fall, the body style would not return for '67. A 390-inch V-8, upped to 315 bhp, was still standard.

▼ This little-known limousine conversion on the 1966 Ford LTD was executed with Ford Motor Co.'s blessing by Hollowell Engineering and Dearborn Steel Tubing.

◀ First seen in 1964, the mid-engine Ford GT40 endurance racer won the gruelling Le Mans 24 Hours in 1966 in this Ferrari-eater "Mark II" guise. In addition, a few roadgoing cars were later built as "Mark III" models.

▼ Lincoln's 1966 redo added five inches of length, plus a massive 462-cubic-inch V-8. A new hardtop coupe, priced at $5485, helped boost Lincoln build to 54,755.

▲ Crisper lines marked the 1966 Lincoln Continentals. This $6383 convertible sedan captured just 3180 sales.

▶ Oldsmobile's "4-4-2" legend meant 400 cubic inches, four-barrel carburetor, and dual exhausts. Pricing began at a reasonable $2923.

▲ A design and engineering *tour de force*, Oldsmobile's new 1966 Toronado was the largest front-drive car ever attempted—119-inch wheelbase, 4366 pounds—and America's first such production car since the late-Thirties Cord. Base price: $4617.

▲ The 1966 Plymouth Barracuda showed off an unchanged "glassback" profile and squared-off nose. Priced at $2556 basic, it scored 38,029 sales—still way behind Ford's galloping Mustang. Carried over from 1965 was a "Formula S" option comprising a high-output 235-horse, 273-cid V-8—plus firm suspension, special wheels and tires, tachometer, and unique identification.

▲ Plymouth's revived full-size Fury returned for '66 with minor styling tweaks, including vertically stacked headlights, and Chrysler's new 440 big-block V-8 as an option.

▲ Accepting the challenge of the Ford LTD and Chevy Caprice was Plymouth's lush new '66 Fury VIP, a $3069 hardtop coupe (*shown here*) or $3133 hardtop sedan.

▲ As did Dodge, midsize Plymouths offered a muscular new Street Hemi option for 1966, here on a Satellite hardtop coupe. The Hemi added $907.60 to the model's $2695 price.

▲ Pontiac's hot GTO looked better than ever for '66. Standard horses numbered 333, with 360 optional. This Sport Coupe started at $2783 and saw 10,363 sales.

◄ Pontiac's personal-luxury Grand Prix ran into sales trouble starting in '66, when production dropped from 57,881 to just 36,757. This happened despite the fact that the base price was actually $5 less than in '65: $3492.

▼ As usual, Catalina was Pontiac's most-popular full-size line for '66. This sleek $2893 hardtop coupe was the series' second-best-seller, attracting an impressive 79,013 customers.

▲ Ford asked Carroll Shelby, creator of the awesome early Sixties Cobra sports cars, to turn Mustangs into race winners. His answer, the '65 GT-350, saw few changes for '66. Price: $4557.

▲ The last Studebakers were 1966 models, basically warmed-over '64-'65s with Chevy six or V-8 power. This Cruiser sedan was among the 8947 Canadian-built cars that ended the historic nameplate.

423

▲ AMC's fastback Marlin looked miles better for 1967, but the public remained unmoved, so the 3+3 coupe was dropped after a run of just 2545 units. The Marlin shared front sheetmetal with the Ambassador, so proportions were better balanced, but the fastback roof with its sweeping elliptical side-window shape was unchanged. Price was $2963 with the base 232 six.

▲ Trendy new "coke bottle" fenderlines and an updated chassis made the '67 Ambassador AMC's best big car yet. The top-line DPL hardtop coupe shown here cost $2958.

▲ AMC's '67 midsize cars were still called Rambler, but their surname changed from Classic to Rebel. Performance improved via modern new 290- and 343-inch V-8 options.

1967

- President Johnson's deficit spending for the Vietnam War is destined to lead to serious inflation—but, for now, prosperity continues and jobs remain plentiful

- Production of '67 models slips to 7.6 million; Chevrolet tops Ford, 2.2 million to 1.7 million

- The year's biggest high-performance engine is Chrysler's potent 440-inch Magnum V-8

- The Mercury Cougar and Chevrolet Camaro ponycars make their debut, followed later in the season by Pontiac's Firebird

- Other new models include the Chevrolet Chevelle Concours; Dodge Coronet R/T; Mercury Marquis and Brougham; front-drive Cadillac Eldorado; and Shelby GT-500

- A 430-cid V-8 replaces the 425 in big Buicks

▲ Though Buick built some of the most potent muscle cars of the Sixties, some models were surprisingly rare. This 1967 GS 400 convertible saw production of only 2140 units. The $3167 base price may have helped squelch demand.

◄ A sweeping new full-fastback roofline and curvy bodysides marked Buick's '67 Wildcat hardtop coupe. Offered in both base and Custom form, it attracted 22,456 buyers.

▼ Buick's 1967 Riviera had its own Gran Sport handling option and a new 360-horse 430 V-8.

- Most 1967 cars have underbodies of corrosion-resistant galvanized steel; 38 percent come equipped with the increasingly popular air conditioning

- Safety issues grow: A dual braking system is installed in all cars; collapsible steering columns emerge on some models

- Firebirds have a deflated mini spare tire; Pontiac boasts the first concealed wipers

- The Coronet R/T with a tuned 440-inch Magnum engine gives Dodge a rival to Pontiac's GTO; Plymouth's Belvedere GTX is comparable and slightly less costly

- A new 350-cid V-8 is phased in on the Chevrolet Camaro; the Impala SS 427 gets a 385-horsepower 427-inch V-8

- GM cars get buzzers that sound when the driver leaves the key in the ignition

- Dodge Dart gets a completely restyled unibody; about 38,000 sporty GT hardtops and ragtops are produced, 43 percent of them equipped with an optional V-8

- Like the Mustang, Chevy's new Camaro sports a long-hood/short-deck profile and a long, enthusiast-friendly options list

- GM, Ford, and American Motors adopt a 5-year/50,000-mile powertrain warranty

▲ The huge success of Ford's Mustang inspired Chevy's new-for-'67 Camaro. This $2466 hardtop coupe has the SS and RS packages, two of the many extra-cost items offered to entice buyers. Total Camaro sales for 1967: 220,917.

◄ Created for the recently formed Trans-Am racing series, the Camaro Z/28 option package included numerous performance goodies, including a 302-inch V-8 with 290 horses, plus disc brakes and unique badging. Only 602 were built for '67.

► The '67 Camaro ragtop listed at $2704 with the base 140-horse six, $2809 with the base 210-horse 327-inch V-8. Some 25,141 customers drove one home. Liberal use of the options list could boost the price to almost $5000.

- In just over a decade, 57 percent of the Interstate Highway System is completed

- AMC's Marlin gets longer, now based on the Ambassador chassis; only 2545 are sold

- Camaro's Z/28 competition package includes a hot 302-cubic-inch V-8; only 602 are produced

- Lincoln offers its final four-door convertible, but only 2276 are sold

- The Corvair line is trimmed to just five models—and the turbocharger is gone

- The full-size Dodge Polara and Monaco are extensively redesigned and larger, now riding a 122-inch wheelbase

- Hemi engines are still available in midsize Dodges and Plymouths

- Mercury's Cyclone GT can be had with an optional 427-cubic-inch V-8

- A four-door Landau model with rear-hinged "suicide" back doors joins the all-new Thunderbird line

426

▲ Chevrolet's Impala SS was still a separate series for 1967, but would be downgraded to option-package status in 1968. This hardtop coupe carries Chevy's big new 427 V-8 option.

▶ A mild facelift marked '67 Chevy Chevelles, like this SS 396 convertible, of which only 2286 were built. This model started at $3102, $239 more than the Malibu V-8 ragtop.

▼ An all-new Chevy Corvette was planned for '67, but development problems delayed it a year. The Sting Ray thus put in one more appearance—and looked cleaner than ever. This $4141 convertible added the $437 top-line power option, the triple-carb big-block 427-inch "L71" V-8 pumping out 435 horses. Total 'Vette sales eased to 22,940 for the year.

▲ Just 8200 Chevy II Nova Super Sports were ordered with the optional 327-inch V-8s for 1967. In place of the listed 275-bhp engine, a few got a 350-horse version, even though it was no longer officially available.

• Imperial adopts Chrysler's lighter-weight unibody construction, but on a longer 127-inch wheelbase; output increases to 17,614 (plus six long-wheelbase limos)

• Oldsmobile's lightly retouched Toronado can have front disc brakes and radial tires

• Pontiac's Firebird, a Camaro clone, accepts V-8s up to 400 cid; the base engine is an overhead-cam inline six

• Valiant is restyled, but wagon, hardtop, and convertible are gone; the similarly restyled Barracuda takes up the slack with a new convertible and notchback hardtop

• A Grand Prix convertible is marketed this year only; just 5856 are produced

• A restyled, curvier Rebel replaces the Classic as AMC's midsize series; 1686 Rebel convertibles find customers

• The Mercury Cougar hardtop, posher and slightly larger than Ford's Mustang, sports hidden headlights—but no convertible or fastback models are offered

• Ford suffers a 65-day strike in the fall; 159,000 workers are idled

• Rambler American gets a 200- or 225-bhp V-8 option and a Rogue convertible, of which only 921 are built for the model year

▲ It was hard to spot any changes in Chevy's 1967 Corvairs—like this Monza convertible—because there were none. Priced at $2540, the ragtop landed only 2109 sales.

▲ Cadillac's Eldorado was rejuvenated for 1967 as a posh close-coupled hardtop coupe based on the front-drive Olds Toronado, but on a 120-inch wheelbase. Base price: $6277.

◄ Another 1967 Cadillac Eldorado shows off its elegant, semiformal lines in a contemporary photo using the Chicago skyline as a backdrop.

▼ Big Caddys weren't neglected for '67, sporting a complete redo with more-rakish lines. Despite a $5608 price, 18,202 ragtops found buyers.

- The privately built Mohs Ostentatienne Opera starts at $19,600; a modified truck chassis accommodates International Harvester V-8s

- The fiberglass-bodied Valkyrie packs a 450-bhp Chevrolet V-8, it reaches 60 mph from a standstill in just 3.8 seconds

- An Auburn 866 Speedster replicar enters production; priced at a towering $8450

- The U.S. Department of Commerce holds a seminar on electric vehicles; Ford announces the Comuta electric, GM exhibits Electrovair II, Westinghouse displays the two-seater Markette

- GM begins a navigation study that does without maps or road signs; a driver dials in the destination and uses codes from roadside landmarks for guidance

◄ Chrysler took on a sharpened look for 1967. Wide lower-body trim identified a popular new line of Newport Customs priced above entry-level Newports. This $3407 hardtop coupe enjoyed 14,193 sales.

► Eclipsing Coronet 500 as Dodge's raciest '67 midsize model was the new R/T (for "road and track"), offered as a $3613 convertible and this $3379 hardtop.

► A 375-horsepower "Magnum" 440-cubic inch V-8 (with four-barrel carb and dual exhausts) was standard for '67 Coronet R/Ts, along with a beefed-up chassis and redline tires.

◄ Although Dodge's fastback Charger looked little different in its second year, the '67 could now be had in R/T trim as shown here. Sales plummeted to just 15,788 for the year.

▲ Full-size '67 Fords followed the industry trend to cleaner lines with a handsome restyle. This $3493 Galaxie 500/XL ragtop, which came with the 289-inch V-8, is one of 5161 built.

▲ Big-block 427-inch power was still on tap for 1967 Fairlanes, but most GTs, like this hardtop (18,670 built), ran with 270- or 320-horsepower 390s (a 289-inch V-8 was standard).

▲ Ford's Mustang took on a beefier look for 1967 via new lower-body sheetmetal, and offered a big-block 390-cubic-inch V-8 option with 320 horses for the first time.

▲ This '67 Mustang hardtop is nicely optioned with styled-steel wheels, whitewalls, vinyl roof, GT package (note rocker-panel racing stripes), and Cruise-O-Matic transmission.

◄ Paul Harvey Ford campaigned this modified 1967 Ford Fairlane 427 hardtop coupe on National Hot Rod Association dragstrips, typically spanning the quarter-mile in just under 11 seconds.

1967 Calendar-Year Car Sales					
1. Chevrolet	1,948,410	7. Dodge	465,732	13. Imperial	17,620
2. Ford	1,730,224	8. Mercury	354,923	14. Checker	950[1]
3. Pontiac	782,734	9. Rambler/AMC	235,293	15. Excalibur	71
4. Plymouth	638,075	10. Chrysler	218,742	16. Avanti II	60
5. Buick	562,507	11. Cadillac	200,000		
6. Oldsmobile	548,390	12. Lincoln	45,667	[1]*Estimated, excludes taxicabs*	

▲ Chrysler's penchant for producing rare models certainly held with the 1967 Imperial convertible—just 577 were built. Survivors like this example are rare nowadays.

▶ Lincoln's Continental kept on evolving with no great change needed, but convertible sedan output hit a new low for 1967: only 2276. That's why it wouldn't return for '68.

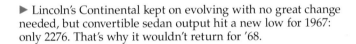

◀ Having grown from compact to midsize for 1966, Mercury's Comet carried on for '67 as a kissing cousin to Ford's Fairlane. Hottest in the line was the Cyclone GT, here in $3034 hardtop coupe form, but only 3419 were sold.

▲ The big Oldsmobiles were facelifted for 1967 to achieve a faint similarity to the singular Toronado. This $4498 Ninety Eight convertible appealed to just 3769 buyers.

▲ The '67 Olds 4-4-2 again offered 350 standard horses and a hot W-30 option with close to 375. Base price for this Holiday hardtop coupe, which saw about 16,500 sales, was $3015.

▲ Plymouth was "Out to Win You Over" in 1967. One way they did was the new Belvedere GTX, a hardtop coupe (*shown*) and convertible packing a standard 375-horsepower Super Commando 440-inch V-8, plus beefed-up chassis and racy cosmetics.

▲ Valiant was completely restyled for 1967, looking bigger and more blocky. Gone were the hardtop, convertible, and wagons, but this top-line Signet four-door sedan nonetheless looked rather dapper. Price: $2308. Production: 26,395 units.

▲ Plymouth's 1967 Barracuda added convertible and hardtop coupe models to the familiar fastback. Standard engine was a 145-bhp Slant Six. This $2779 ragtop scored just 4228 sales.

▲ The new 1967 Barracuda notchback hardtop sported an abbreviated roofline with a concave backlight. Total Barracuda sales nearly doubled from 1966, to 62,534.

▲ More, and tougher, competition hurt '67 Pontiac GTO sales, which slipped to 81,722, including 9517 ragtops.

▲ GTO's standard V-8 for 1967 was a new four-barrel 335-horse 400-incher. Here, the $2935 hardtop; 65,176 were built.

▲ To lift Grand Prix sales, Pontiac issued this $3813 ragtop as a new 1967 companion to the hardtop coupe. Both had unique hidden-headlamp front ends on a facelifted full-size "Poncho" body. Alas, with only 5856 orders, the ragtop Grand Prix ended up being a one-year-wonder model.

▶ Pontiac's Firebird bowed midyear as a Camaro cousin. The Sprint hardtop boasted a 215-bhp ohc 230 six.

▲ Carroll Shelby one-upped the restyled '67 Mustang fast-back with even more-aggressive-looking GT models with standard grille-centered driving lights. Note the hood scoop.

▲ A new big-block Shelby Mustang, the GT-500 bowed for 1967 with 355 advertised horses, but those in the know said it was surely more. Just 2050 were sold at $4195 apiece.

◄ Unveiled in 1965, the Anglo-U.S. Shelby Cobra 427 was the most brutish muscle car ever. Evolved from the early Sixties AC Ace-based small-block Cobra, the 2600-pound 427 packed 345-425 horses in various guises through 1967, when production ceased at a mere 348 numbered chassis.

► Spicing up the '67 scene was a new Jeepster on the Jeep CJ. This Sport convertible was offered along with the Commando Roadster, pickup, and wagon. With changes, including a restyling and AMC sixes and V-8 for '72, the line continued through '73. Production totaled 77,573.

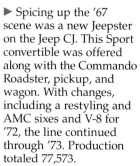

◄ AMC's Marlin was shot down for 1968 by Javelin, a hardtop coupe "ponycar" in base (*shown*) and ritzier SST trim. A six was standard, but 343- and new 390-inch V-8s with up to 315 bhp were optional.

► AMC shortened the Javelin 12 inches to create the two-seat show-car-inspired AMX coupe for '68. Price was $3245, but sales reached only 6725. Designed under AMC's Dick Teague, the 109-inch-wheelbase Javelin was one of the few ponycars that actually looked good with an optional vinyl top.

◄ Besides setting records with the AMX, land-speed-record driver Craig Breedlove ran this Javelin at the Bonneville Salt Flats in Utah in August 1968.

1968

• New federal pollution laws take effect; all makes have an exhaust-emission control system

• Despite a long strike, Ford's model-year output reaches 1.75 million cars; Chevrolet remains in first place with 2.1 million units produced

• A total of 9,403,862 new cars are registered this year, topping the 1965 record; total model-year production hits 8.4 million

• An average full-time worker earns $6657; the average new-car buyer pays $2936 (plus trade-in)

• New models include the AMC, AMX and Javelin, Ford Torino, Mercury Montego, and Lincoln Continental Mark III luxury coupe

• Nearly one million imported cars are sold, triggering a call for more American-built compacts and subcompacts

▲ Though no longer a Rambler in name, the 1968 AMC Rebel was little-changed save for a new 315-horse 390-inch V-8 option. This $2775 SST was the sportiest of the line.

▲ After one year with a convertible companion, AMC's sporty Rambler American Rogue hardtop coupe soldiered on alone for 1968 with few changes. Base price was $2244.

▲ The 1968 Buick Riviera, now weighing 4222 pounds, hid its headlamps within a restyled face. Changes were few—and mostly dictated by government clean-air mavens.

▲ The big 1968 Buicks still wore a Fifties-style bodyside "sweepspear." Wildcats, like the $3416 four-door, went like a scalded cat thanks to a standard 360-horsepower 430 V-8.

▲ The 1968 Electra 225 retained a more formal look to stand apart from lesser full-size Buicks. This hardtop coupe sold for $4221 in standard trim, $4400 in ritzier Custom dress.

▲ Government-mandated side marker lights were a subtle visual change for Cadillac's 1968 Eldorado, but a big new 375-horse 472-inch V-8 lurked beneath the hood.

- Front shoulder harnesses are required on cars sold after January 1; other mandated safety features include rear lap belts, side marker lights, and padded interiors

- The United States Postal Service issues 12-cent stamp commemorating Henry Ford

- Fords boast "controlled-crush" front ends and recessed inside door handles

- Pontiac introduces an engine-driven emergency air pump; Chrysler Corporation station wagons can be had with a washer/wiper to clean the tailgate window

- Hidden windshield wipers are seen on more General Motors cars

- An optional buzzer in AMC cars alerts drivers when the lights are left on

- The AMC badge finally appears on Ramblers; AMC introduces the Javelin ponycar and stubby, lightweight two-passenger AMX sport coupe

- Rebel offers AMC's only convertible; only 1200 are built—it becomes AMC ragtop

- Cadillac's new V-8 is designed specifically to meet tougher emissions regulations

▲ Chevy's fully restyled 1968 Corvette wasn't called Sting Ray, but it was built on the same chassis. This $4663 T-top coupe replaced the beloved fastback.

◀ As in 1966-67, a prominent hood bulge signaled big-block power in the new 1968 Corvettes. With 18,630 orders, the $4320 convertible still easily outsold the coupe. As since 1963, the 'Vette rode a 98-inch wheelbase.

▲ Full-size Chevys wore a huskier look for 1968, and the Impala Super Sport was demoted from separate model to option status. This ragtop wears the so-called "party hat" wheels included with the optional power front-disc brakes. Only 2455 SS 427s were built.

▲ A new shorter wheelbase for two-doors highlighted the 1968 Chevy Chevelles. With 325 standard horses, the SS 396 remained the line's top performer. Priced at $2899, this hardtop coupe captured 60,499 buyers.

- Pontiac GTOs flaunt "Endura," an energy-absorbing, steel-reinforced, body-color rubber bumper

- Chevy II Nova is now near midsize (111-inch wheelbase); the hardtop coupe, convertible, and wagon are gone

- Buick's restyled midsize Skylark enjoys record sales; an inline six replaces the V-6, which has been sold to Kaiser-Jeep Corp.

- The all-new Chevelle two-doors ride a shorter 112-inch wheelbase; a choice of three 396-cubic-inch V-8s are available

- The restyled Corvette stretches an extra seven inches; it sports vacuum-operated flip-up headlights

- Dodge reworks the intermediate-size Coronet and Charger, while the compact Dart adds a hot GTS hardtop and ragtop

- A no-frills Super Bee coupe with a 335-bhp 383-inch V-8 joins the Coronet lineup; it starts at $3027

- The big Oldsmobiles have a new 455-inch V-8, so Hurst/Olds stuffs a Forced-Air 455-inch V-8 into a limited-edition 4-4-2

- Road Runner is Plymouth's new budget muscle car; with prices starting at $2896, it attracts 44,599 eager buyers

▲ Chevy's Camaro got minor style changes for '68, including federally required side marker lights. Here is one of 27,844 SS-equipped cars for 1968 out of a total 235,147 Camaros.

▲ The Chevy Corvair was nearing the end of its road in '68. Base priced at $2507, this Monza coupe found 6807 buyers. Total Corvair sales skidded to an all-time low of 15,399 units.

▲ For its second year without a letter series sister, Chrysler's 300 shared a mild facelift with other 1968 models, as well as a unique hidden-headlamp front end. At $4337, the ragtop (*above*) enjoyed 2161 sales, up about 500 from '67, but the series' mainstay was still the hardtop coupe, which lured 16,953 buyers at $4010 apiece.

◄ Dodge's '68 Coronet Super Bee was a budget muscle car like Plymouth's new Road Runner. This 3395-pound member of Dodge's "Scat Pack" came only as a $3027 pillared coupe. A 335-bhp 383-inch V-8 was standard.

- Late in the season, the "personal-luxury" Continental Mark III joins the Continental sedan and hardtop; all Lincolns come with a new 460-cid, 365-bhp V-8

- A plush Torino series joins the Ford stable; the Fairlane is restyled again

- Pontiac launches the revised A-body Tempest on two wheelbases: 112 inches for two-doors, 116 for four-doors

- A new Lincoln Continental presidential limousine built by Lehmann-Peterson enters service; it wears 1969 model-year styling and bodywork

- GM and Chrysler experiment with air-activated accessories; Lincoln-Mercury and Plymouth try periscopelike devices to improve visibility; engineers experiment with inflatable gas bags to cushion occupants in the event of a collision

- The final Crown Imperial ragtops go on sale; at $6497, only 474 are produced

- Pontiac GTO has boasts freshened styling and a standard 400-cubic-inch V-8; production increases to 87,684 units

- Shelby introduces the GT-500KR "King of the Road" with a new 428-cubic-inch V-8 Cobra-Jet engine; Shelbys are now assembled by Ford

◄ The R/T convertible (*shown*) and hardtop coupe remained the sportiest and costliest of Dodge's '68 Coronets, respectively priced at $3613 and $3379. All Coronets got a new platform that year with handsome new styling.

▼ Dodge shoehorned a 383-inch V-8 into its compact Dart to create the GTS, but Hurst-Campbell Inc. went the factory one better by stuffing in 440-inch mills and even a few Hemis to create a dragstrip terror.

▲ Dodge's Charger for '68, was offered in three flavors of hardtop coupe. The most potent was this $3506 R/T, with standard 440-inch Magnum V-8.

◀ This is one of 50 special light-weight Mustangs built to showcase the new Cobra Jet 428 V-8. The cars dominated the S/S class at the '68 NHRA internationals.

▲ Midsize Fords were fully revised for 1968, and lush new Torino models were added above Fairlanes. Both lines offered racy new fastback-hardtop coupes.

▲ This Torino GT ragtop paced the 1968 Indianapolis 500. Ford also offered a notchback GT hardtop (23,939 sold), but the new slippery fastbacks were favored for stock-car racing.

▲ Ford kept pushing sporty big cars for 1968, but with diminishing success. "Peek-a-boo" headlamps were featured on the Galaxie 500/XL convertible and hardtop coupe (*shown*), with the latter using the name "SportsRoof." XL output totaled 50,048 fastbacks and 6066 convertibles.

▲ The first-ever four-door T-Bird bowed for 1967 as part of a full redo for Ford's personal-luxury flagship. Standard power came from a 315-bhp V-8. Convertibles were gone. At 21,925 units, the longer new Landau sedan wasn't as popular as the base and Landau hardtop coupes, whose sales totaled 43,006.

1968 Calendar-Year Car Sales

1.	Chevrolet	2,139,290	7.	Oldsmobile	562,459	13. Imperial	15,367
2.	Ford	1,753,334	8.	Mercury	360,467	14. Checker	992[1]
3.	Pontiac	910,977	9.	AMC/Rambler	272,726	15. Avanti II	89
4.	Plymouth	790,239	10.	Chrysler	264,853	16. Excalibur	57
5.	Buick	651,823	11.	Cadillac	230,003		
6.	Dodge	627,533	12.	Lincoln	46,904		

[1] *Estimated, excludes taxicabs*

◄ Lincoln's '68 Continentals got a new 365-horse 460-inch V-8. The ragtop sedan was gone, leaving a $5970 sedan and this $5736 coupe, which saw sales of 9415.

► The modestly restyled '68 Imperial offered two 440-inch V-8s: a standard 350-horse unit and a new dual-exhaust 360-bhp option. With 8492 orders, this $6115 Crown hardtop sedan was the most-popular model for the year. Total Imperial sales slipped from 17,620 to 15,367 units.

◄ Cougar styling was unchanged for 1968 save for side marker lights added at Washington's insistence. Here, the posh $3232 XR-7. Some 32,712 of the Mercury coupes were produced for the year.

▼ Chrysler and Mercury offered faux-wood bodyside trim as a new '68 option. Merc sold it on the Park Lane hardtop and ragtop. Only 1112 were built—how many got the "yacht planking" is unknown.

◄ The first Hurst/Olds bowed in 1968 as a limited-production coupe, pillared or hardtop, based on the 4-4-2. The 515 built featured a special 390-horse 455 V-8, Turbo Hydra-Matic, Hurst Dual Gate shifter, heavy-duty everything, H/O emblems, and a special black-and-silver paint job.

► The Sox & Martin team won drag racing fame and fortune for Plymouth throughout the Sixties. The new '68 Road Runner looked to be a natural, and the team quickly modified some for quarter-mile action at U.S. dragstrips.

◄ Plymouth got back to muscle car basics with its new '68 Road Runner, a no-frills Belvedere (except for a "Beep! Beep!" horn) with all the needed go-faster mods, including a hot 335-horse 383 V-8 and fortified chassis. This $3034 hardtop, added at midyear, sold 15,359 copies.

► This '68 Barracuda hardtop coupe wears one of that year's new options: the so-called "Mod Top," a vinyl roof covering with a "flower power" motif. Plymouth sold it as a package with seat and door-panel inserts done in the same pattern. How many of the 19,997 coupes sold got this wild option package isn't known.

442

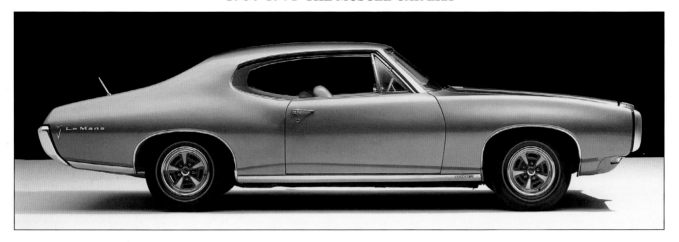

▲ A new look was featured on midsize 1968 Pontiac two-doors, which moved to a tighter 112-inch wheelbase. This $2786 Le Mans hardtop coupe, of which 110,036 were built, wears optional Rally wheels and redline tires.

▲ Pontiac's GTO lost its pillared coupe model for '68, but the new hardtop and ragtop looked great. Sales rose to 87,684; 77,704 of them roofless.

▶ Shades of Edsel—or so said some regarding Pontiac's new '68 big-car "face." Here, the $3089 Catalina hardtop coupe chosen by 92,217 buyers.

▲ Pontiac Firebird's V-8 choices were shuffled to include new, more emissions-friendly 350- and 400-inch engines. Still available was the "Sprint" ohc-six with 215 horses.

▲ Shelby Mustang GT-350 and GT-500 fastbacks and ragtops returned, with the 400-horse GT-500KR "King of the Road" arriving midyear. Shown here, an early 500 soft top.

▲ A revised nose and tail carried American Motors's big Ambassadors through 1969, when this top-of-the-line SST hardtop coupe stickered at $3622, and 8998 were sold.

▲ AMC's midsize Rebel is shown here in jazzy SST guise. This SST hardtop, which only managed to find 5405 buyers, started at $2598. Total Rebel sales reached 60,106 for the year.

◄ Shuffled trim, equipment, and color options were the main changes for AMC's 1969 Javelin, but sales dropped sharply to 40,675, with the base model suffering most of the loss. Here, the jazzy $2633 SST (23,286 were built) in early year trim with the popular vinyl top.

▶ Wild artwork adorned the cover of a catalog announcing AMC's bright new 1969 "Big Bad" color options for the Javelin and AMX.

The Big Bad Colors They're Something Else From American Motors

▲ Javelin changed its optional tape stripes in January 1969 to a "C-shape" motif, as on this SST. Dummy side pipes and a wispy roof spoiler were other new extra-cost goodies.

▲ This production 1969 AMX is done up in "Big Bad Orange" with black racing stripes. Sales of the $3297 AMX rose 1558 units to 8293. Base engine was the 290-inch V-8.

1969

- Chevrolet beats Ford again in model-year output, 2.1 million cars to 1.8 million; the industry total reaches 8.4 million units

- New models include the Mercury Marauder and the midsize Pontiac Grand Prix

- New midyear are several muscle cars: AMC's SC/Rambler Pontiac Firebird Trans Am, Dodge Charger Daytona, Mercury Cyclone Spoiler

- The last Rambler American goes on sale as simply the Rambler; this will be AMC's last use of the famous nameplate that dates back to 1902

- On the economy front, Ford introduces the midyear Maverick coupe as an early '70 model

- The federal Truth in Lending Law requires auto dealers to state costs, terms, and conditions in a clear and uniform manner

◄ The last Ramblers and Americans appeared for 1969, headed by this outrageous SC/Rambler-Hurst performance hardtop packing AMC's 315-horse 390-inch V-8. Only 1512 were sold, priced at $2998. The "Scrambler," as it was dubbed, was a joint AMC/Hurst effort and of course came with a Hurst shifter.

► Studebaker was long gone by '69, but its sporting Avanti model lived on. South Bend dealers Leo Newman and Nate Altman acquired manufacturing rights in 1965 and began building the "Avanti II" as a limited-edition luxury GT with Corvette running gear and detail styling changes. Base price was $7145 in 1969, when 103 cars were produced.

▲ Chevy's Impala SS was a $422 option for 1969, not a separate model, with a 390-horse 427-inch V-8. This ragtop has one of only 2455 SS packages installed.

▲ "Second thought" changes marked Chevy's '69 Corvettes, including a return to the "Stingray" name and 350-inch V-8s.

- An average full-time American worker earns $7095; a midsize Chevrolet Chevelle retails for as little as $2458

- All cars must now have front headrests, as per government mandate

- Warranties on '69 models are set at 1 year/12,000 miles for the entire car, 5/50,000 for the drivetrain

- GM's "telltale" odometers provide visual evidence of tampering

- Mobil discontinues its long-running annual Fuel Economy Run

- Chevrolet builds its final Corvairs; only 6000 are purchased

- Chrysler and Ford follow GM's lead and adopt concealed wipers

- The government proposes a law requiring installation of inflatable airbags to cushion occupants in the event of an impact

- A recreational vehicle (RV) boom begins; 540,000 camper-pickups are on the road

- Optional on Thunderbird and Continental is a rear-wheel skid-control braking system, which is activated by a miniature computer

▲ The Chevelle Malibu continued on for 1969 as one of America's most-popular cars—367,100 were sold.

▲ A heavy lower-body restyle marked Chevy's Camaro "ponycars" for 1969. The Z/28 hardtop saw sales of 19,014.

▲ Camaro paced the Indianapolis 500 in 1967 and again in '69, when 3675 replica hardtops and convertibles were built with white paint and "Hugger Orange" stripes and interiors.

▲ Performance whiz Don Yenko built 201 of these Yenko/SC Camaros for 1969. Chevy, meanwhile, built 69 drag-ready ZL-1 models with aluminum-block 430-horsepower engines.

◀ Bulbous "fuselage styling" came to Chrysler Corporation's full-size '69s. Sporty Chrysler 300s like this $4450 ragtop retained "peek-a-boo" headlights. This would be the next to last year for the open 300, of which just 1933 were ordered in '69. Today, big Chrysler cars of this era have sparked renewed interest among collectors.

- A grille-mounted Super-Lite gives Dodges better visibility for high-speed driving

- Pontiac Grand Prix's radio antenna is embedded in the windshield

- Corvettes come with headlight washers, a European-inspired idea

- Chrysler wagons have roof-mounted air spoilers to help keep the rear window clean

- Chevy offers Liquid Tire Chain—a device to spray sticky resins on tires to boost traction

- Chevrolet's 350-cubic-inch V-8 is now available in both Avanti II and Checker

- The Chevrolet Impala SS appears for the last time; 2455 SS 427s are built

- A Six-Pak (triple-carb) engine is new for Dodge Super Bee, Plymouth Road Runner

- New Imperials share much of Chrysler's sheetmetal; prices start at $5592

- Mercury's full-size Marauder coupe can be ordered with X-100 trim and a 429-cid V-8

- A U.S. Senate report urges the development of steam cars to cut pollution

- GM's "Progress of Power" show features five experimental vehicles

◄ Styling mods highlighted the hot midsize '69 Dodges like this Coronet R/T hardtop coupe, base priced at $3442. Powerteams were unchanged, but new "delta-theme" nose and tail treatments were notable. Just 7328 of the '69 R/Ts were built, including convertibles.

▲ Added to Super Bee's engine chart at mid '69 was the tri-carb "Six Pak" 440-inch V-8 with 390 horses. Only some 1907 cars like this hardtop got the $463 option.

▲ Dodge added a Charger 500 for 1969 with low-drag styling (note the rear window) for stock-car supertracks, but it couldn't quite keep up with its slicker Detroit rivals.

▲ Mainstream '69 Chargers saw little appearance change—not that any was needed. The R/T remained the sportiest of lot, again with standard 375-horse Super Magnum 440 V-8.

▲ Dodge's "mini muscle" Dart GTS with its 275-bhp 340-inch V-8 (or 330-bhp 383) still seemed quite incongruous in 1969, one reason sales ended after a final 6702 units.

• The Dodge Dart Swinger replaces the GTS, while the "Winged Warrior" Charger Daytona aims at winning NASCAR events

• Full-size Fords and Mercurys are restyled on longer wheelbases: 121.0 inches for Ford, 124.0 for most Mercurys

• High-performance Torino Cobras are launched by Ford; Mercury issues the similar Cyclone CJ

• Mustangs grow longer, wider, lower; the Mach 1 fastback debuts, followed by the Boss 302 and Boss 429

• As the Cougar grows bigger, so does the lineup, which adds its first convertible and a hot Eliminator hardtop

• A convertible joins the Plymouth Road Runner series (2128 are sold), and the last 700 GTX ragtops are built

• On March 8, 1969, a $724.60 Trans Am option with a Ram Air III engine debuts for the Firebird; 697 are produced

• Don Yenko issues ultrahot Corvette-engined Camaro 450s for only one year; about 50 are built

• Stutz Motor Car Company announces a Bearcat replica with an International Scout chassis; very few are actually built

▲ Ford went chasing Plymouth's Road Runner for '69 with its new Torino Cobra, a budget muscle car with a 335-horse 428 Cobra Jet V-8. This seldom-seen notchback hardtop version started at a low $3164. Most Cobras were fastbacks.

▲ For $3189, a buyer could opt for this '69 Torino Cobra SportsRoof fastback. Fat F70×14 tires on six-inch-wide rims were standard issue, as was a beefed-up suspension.

▲ The long-nose, flush-front Torino Talladega fastback was Ford's new stock-car racer in 1969. Only 754 were built. It captured 26 wins and the NASCAR Manufacturer's Cup.

▲ Mustang bulked up in a 1969 redesign. The base hardtop coupe now started at $2635, but this lush new $2866 Grandé delivered extra luxury touches, among them vinyl roof, color-keyed mirrors, wheel covers, and extra bright trim.

▲ The Mustang 2+2 became a "SportsRoof" fastback for '69. New models were Mach 1, Boss 302, and Boss 429. Here, the GT package with lower-body racing stripes, hood scoop, styled steel wheels, and heavy-duty suspension.

◀ As Chrysler adopted "fuselage" styling for 1969, so did Imperial, ending up even more Chrysler-like. But the result was pleasing—except in sales, which dropped to 22,077. Here, the $6131 LeBaron hardtop sedan, which found 14,821 buyers.

▲ Introduced mid 1968, the Continental Mark III personal-luxury coupe returned for '69 unchanged. An under-the-skin twin to Thunderbird, it listed at $6758, with many goodies standard.

▲ Lincoln's personal-luxury car Mark III was the direct successor to the 1956-57 Mark II. Ford stylist Eugene Bordinat took pains to preserve a formal look, with "classic" cues like a Rolls-Royce-style grille.

▲ Still pushing sporty big cars, Mercury revived the Marauder name for '69. This uplevel X-100 version was priced at $4091; 5635 were produced.

▲ Both '69 Marauders wore Ford's sloped "tunnelback" rooflines and a hidden-headlamp front borrowed from the uplevel Marquis.

▲ Mercury's hottest midsize street car for 1969 was this new Cyclone CJ 428 fastback coupe. A Cobra Jet 428 V-8 was included in the $3224 price.

1969 Calendar-Year Car Sales

1.	Chevrolet	2,092,947	7.	Dodge	611,645	13. Imperial	22,103
2.	Ford	1,826,777	8.	Mercury	398,262	14. Checker	760[1]
3.	Pontiac	870,081	9.	AMC/Rambler	282,809	15. Avanti II	103
4.	Plymouth	751,134	10.	Chrysler	260,773	16. Excalibur	91
5.	Buick	665,422	11.	Cadillac	223,237		
6.	Oldsmobile	635,241	12.	Lincoln	61,378		

[1] *Estimated, excludes taxicabs*

449

▲ Mercury's 1969 Cougars featured rounder styling, new convertibles, and new muscle in an Eliminator package. The last, introduced May 8, carried a standard four-barrel 351 and 12-hole wheels. The 335-bhp CJ 428 V-8 was optional.

▲ Continuing their muscle car collaboration, Hurst/Olds again offered a Cutlass-based hardtop coupe—the only body style this year—which ran with the huge 455-inch V-8 and gold-and-white paint. Horses numbered 380; cars built, 906.

▲ Oldsmobile's Toronado wore a longer tail for '69 to help visually balance its new eggcrate grille. Also back from '68 was a premium-fuel-gulping 455-inch V-8, now rated at 400 bhp. Base models started at $4835, Customs at $5030.

▲ Plymouth built only 1442 ragtop Barracudas for 1969, so this Formula S with its high-winding, 340-inch small block is a rarity. Introduced in 1968, this was the engine of choice for those seeking the best-balanced Barracuda overall.

▶ Although it wore a revised grille for '69, Plymouth's famous "Beep! Beep!" Road Runner shifted gears by emphasizing luxury options, such as bucket seats, console, and power windows.

▼ Plymouth added a ragtop Road Runner for 1969, but sold only 2128 copies. No matter, total RR volume nearly doubled to 84,420—the series' high-water mark. A new midyear "440+6" V-8 with triple two-barrel carbs boasted 390 horsepower.

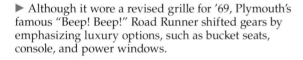

◀ Big Plymouths got Chrysler Corporation's rounded "fuselage" look for 1969. The Sport Fury came in this standard hardtop coupe, a new formal-roof model, and convertible, but total sales dropped sharply to 17,868.

▼ Grand Prix was reborn for 1969 with a smaller 118-inch-wheel-base. Power options ran up to a burly 428-cubic-inch V-8. Total sales: 112,486.

▲ Like Chevy's Camaro, Pontiac's Firebird got a lower-body restyle for '69, but demand slumped to 76,059 hardtop coupes and 11,649 ragtops.

▲ "Here come da Judge," a new $332 option package for Pontiac's '69 GTO with a 366-horse "Ram Air III" 400-inch V-8 and loud "The Judge" decals.

▲ The 1969 Shelby Mustangs were the biggest and brightest of the breed, with stripes and scoops galore, plus a prominent "loop" bumper/grille. GT-350s gained a modest 290-horse 351-inch V-8; GT-500s kept the big-block 428, but with only 375 bhp. Production: 3150 units, plus 636 reserialed "1970" leftovers.

▶ Like the GTO, lesser midsize Pontiacs wore only modest styling changes for 1969. This Le Mans convertible is equipped with the division's novel hood-mounted tachometer, as well as extra-cost wire wheel covers.

451

◄ AMC fielded an "import-fighter" in mid 1970, the Gremlin—a chopped-tail, two-door spin-off of that year's brand-new compact Hornet. Priced at a base $1879, Gremlin sold fairly well, and was a half year ahead of the new Ford and Chevy subcompacts that would bow for '71. Gremlin was identical to the bigger Hornet from the doors forward and came with the same 128-horse, 199-cid six cylinder. Trim was spartan, but options helped, including the roof rack, striping, wheel covers, and whitewalls shown here.

▲ The 1970 AMX shared its new front end with the '70 Javelin, but falling hot-car demand held sales to only 4116, meaning that the sporty coupe would not return.

▲ The 1970 AMC Javelin sported a more aggressive face and a new base 360-inch V-8. Returning options again included 390-inch engines with up to 340 horsepower.

► Racing ace Mark Donohue poses with a Javelin in Trans-Am trim outside AMC's Plymouth, Michigan, headquarters (factory still in Kenosha, of course). As chief driver for the Roger Penske team, Donohue won the 1970 T-A crown, though AMC had the only official "factory" effort in 1970.

• A recession curtails new-car sales; model-year volume slips below 7.6 million cars

• Ford is number one, turning out 2.1 million cars; Chevrolet, meanwhile, sinks to 1.46 million

• Japanese automakers offer a rising challenge as imports take a record 14.6 percent of sales

• Chrysler begins importing the Japanese Dodge Colt and British Plymouth Cricket

• Sixty percent of all new cars are now equipped with air conditioning

• Antitheft steering-column/ignition locks and front/rear side marker lights are required

• AMC introduces the compact Hornet, replacing the Rambler American

• Gremlin debuts in April as the first American subcompact; prices start at a low $1879

▲ AMC's 1970 "Rebel Machine" was a gaudy muscle car from an unexpected source. Only 2326 were built before AMC gave up on the idea. All came with a 340-horse V-8, hood scoops, fat tires, and Hurst four-speed gearbox.

▲ Styled by AMC's Dick Teague, the AMX/3 bowed at an early 1970 Rome preview as a new low-volume exotic car with a midmounted 390 V-8 and a chassis engineered by Italy's Giotto Bizzarrini. Only a half-dozen were built.

▲ No big change occurred in AMC's 1970 Ambassadors from the waist down, but sedans like this $3722 SST wore a new formal-looking roofline.

▼ A starchier face and retro-look rear fender skirts did nothing for the looks of the 1970 Riviera, or so some said. Nonetheless, it adopted Buick's new 455-cubic-inch V-8 with 370 horses. Sales slid to 37,336; base price rose $153, to $4854.

▲ An adept restyle with big new bumper/grille combinations marked full-size 1970 Buicks, like this $3700 LeSabre Custom convertible, of which just 2487 were built. Wheelbase expanded slightly to 124 inches.

• The new Monte Carlo personal-luxury coupe displays the longest hood in Chevy's history—six feet: 130,657 are sold

• All-new 1970½ Camaro and Firebird coupes arrive in February; convertibles are dropped from both lines

• Other 1970 debuts: Buick GSX muscle car, Chrysler 300-H "Hurst" hardtop, and Dodge Challenger ponycar

• Trends include plastic grilles, front seatbacks that unlatch when the door is opened, tamper-proof odometers, electrically heated rear defrosters

• Electronic skid-control braking goes into GM's Eldorado, Riviera, and Toronado

• Ford switches to a 12-month warranty with no mileage limitation

• AMC Javelin and AMX windshields have a chemically treated inner pane to reduce the possibility of facial lacerations upon impact

• The federal government awards contracts to develop a safety vehicle in which passengers could survive a 50-mph crash

• GM signs a $50 million license agreement with Curtiss-Wright Corp. for the rights to develop a Wankel rotary engine

453

▲ Chevy's 1970 Chevelle SS package included a 350-horse 396-inch V-8 in its $445 price. A new 350-bhp 402 replaced it at midyear, but badges still read "396."

▲ GM dropped its displacement limits on midsize muscle engines, so Chevy stroked its 427 to 454 cubes. SS Chevelles were rated at 360 bhp, with LS-6 versions at 450 horses.

▲ Corvette also offered Chevy's new 454 big-block option for 1970. A strike limited model-year output to 10,668 convertibles like this and 6648 T-top coupes.

▲ Chevy unwrapped a handsome new Camaro coupe for mid 1970. This is one of three concept Z/28 "Sunshine Special" prototypes proposed by Hurst.

◄ A 300-horse 350-inch engine repeated as Corvette's base 1970 V-8, with 350- and new 370-bhp options.

- AMC acquires Kaiser-Jeep Corp., suddenly becoming the country's leading four-wheel-drive vehicle producer

- AMC's "Rebel Machine" runs a potent 390-cid, 340-bhp V-8 and displays wild muscle car striping

- Chevrolet's 350-cid, 300-bhp V-8 is now standard in Avanti II, whose styling remains unchanged

- A 455-cid V-8 with 350-370 bhp is standard or available in most Buicks; the new GSX offers a hot "Stage 1" version that'll top 100 mph in the quarter-mile

- Cadillac's Eldorado V-8 displaces 500 cubic inches—it's the world's biggest production passenger-car engine (and good for up to 400 bhp)

- Chevy II changes its name to Nova, while the facelifted Chevelle more closely resembles the full-size Chevrolet

- A big-block 454 V-8 is available for big Chevys and Corvettes; the personal-luxury Monte Carlo gets an SS 454 option

- Chrysler offers an optional headlight-delay system, and releases its last big Newport/300 convertibles

▲ Chevy's new 1970 Monte Carlo coupe was a cousin to Pontiac's year-old Grand Prix. Most of the 130,657 sold had mild 350 or 400 V-8s, but 3823 got a hot SS package with the 360-horsepower 454. Still, the Monte Carlo was mostly about luxury. Prices started at a reasonable $3123.

▲ The "fuselage" Chryslers evidenced only "second thought" changes for 1970. This 300 convertible, which sold for $4580, is one of only 1077 built that model year. Engines were again 350- or optional 375-horse 440 V-8s. This unabashedly large car weighed in at a then-hefty 4175 pounds.

► Hurst converted 501 hardtops and two convertibles into white/gold 1970 Chrysler "300-H" models with a rear spoiler and power-bulge hood.

▲ With hot-car insurance premiums soaring by 1970, Dodge sold half as many Charger R/Ts as in '69—just 10,377. This example is equipped with 1970's new SE option package.

▲ Dodge entered the ponycar corral with the '70 Challenger, a close kin to that year's new Barracuda. Ragtops and hardtops were offered in base, luxury SE, and sporty R/T trim.

- The Hurst-modified Chrysler 300-H reminds fans of the old letter series models; 501 are produced

- Dodge responds to Camaro/Mustang with the new Challenger hardtop and ragtop; the redesigned Plymouth Barracuda is similar

- In this final year for the high-performance Dodge Coronet R/T series, it is rare: 2319 hardtops and 296 convertibles

- Excalibur evolves into the Series II roadster and phaeton, featuring a 111-inch wheelbase and Chevy's 350-cid V-8

- The final Ford Falcons are offered as a basically unchanged 1969 model and as a "1970½" stripped Fairlane 500/Torino

- With a $1995 base price, the import-fighting Ford Maverick sells very strongly: 578,914 are produced in a long model year

- Imperial drops its Crown series after 1587 1970 models are produced; the LeBaron series will continue alone

- Lincoln-Mercury dealers now sell the German-built Capri, a "mini-ponycar" destined to top 113,000 units in 1973

- Plymouth adds the popular Valiant-based Duster coupe and the startling winged Road Runner Superbird to its lineup

▲ This "Panther Pink" Challenger T/A was one of 2539 built to qualify the new Dodge ponycar for Trans-Am racing. Street versions boasted a "Six Pak" (triple-carb) 340 small-block V-8, as the fender logo says. It developed 290 horses, double the 145 on base Slant Six models.

◄ A "twin nostril" hood adorned the R/T version of Dodge's 1970 Challengers. Total Challenger sales were 83,032—11,000 higher than Mercury's Cougar, which Dodge had aimed to beat.

▲ Ford's big XLs were separate models for 1970, not Galaxies. This convertible styling model wears incorrect wheel covers. Only 6348 of these $3501 ragtops were built. Big Fords rode the 121-inch wheelbase introduced in '69.

▲ The '70 Ford XL "SportsRoof" retained "tunnelback" hard-top styling. Falling demand for sporty cars prompted Ford to put theirs out to pasture after 1970. The $3293 SportsRoof came with a standard 250-horse 351 V-8; 27,251 were built.

▲ Ford scored big with a smaller, 103-inch-wheelbase new compact called Maverick, arriving in spring 1969 as an early 1970 model with a low $1995 starting price. Ford built 578,914 copies, all two-door fastback sedans with standard 170- or optional 200-cubic-inch sixes.

▲ Mustang sales fell 50 percent for 1970, when minor styling changes brought a return to single headlamps. This convertible was one of only 7673 built for the model year, with a starting price of $3025. Rising insurance rates helped depress ponycar sales industrywide.

▲ Ford unleashed the potent Boss 302 Mustang to win the 1969 Trans-Am series—which it did. Just 1934 were built, followed by 6319 of the similar 1970 models like this one. Alas for Ford, AMC captured the 1970 Trans-Am crown with its Javelin.

▲ The Mach 1 fastback remained the hottest "volume" Mustang for 1970. A potent 335-horsepower 428-cubic-inch Cobra Jet V-8 was again the top power option. A 351-inch mill was standard. Mach 1 prices started at $3271.

▲ Another 1970 Ford rarity was this King Cobra, a long-nose, aerodynamic offshoot of that year's restyled Torino designed to succeed the famed Talladega on NASCAR's supertracks. But it wasn't enough to best Chrysler's winged wonders, and only a few were built.

▲ Ford's Ranchero car/pickup went through a Falcon-based design before becoming a Fairlane/Torino derivative for 1967. By 1970, it looked like this. Hidden headlamps were included on the sporty GT version and this Squire model with wood-look trim from the station wagon.

1970 Calendar-Year Car Sales

1. Ford	2,096,184	7. Dodge	543,019	13. Continental	21,432
2. Chevrolet	1,456,574	8. Mercury	324,716	14. Imperial	11,822
3. Pontiac	690,953	9. AMC	276,000	15. Checker	397[1]
4. Plymouth	684,975	10. Cadillac	238,744	16. Avanti	111
5. Buick	666,501	11. Chrysler	180,777	17. Excalibur	37
6. Oldsmobile	633,981	12. Lincoln	37,695		

[1] *Estimated, excludes taxicabs*

▲ Lincoln's 1970 Continental Mark III hadn't changed much from the '68 original, but base price was now up to $7281. Perhaps as a result, demand dropped slightly to 21,432 units. As before, a 365-horsepower, 460-inch V-8 sat beneath the mile-long hood.

◄ Mercury's Cougar Boss 302 Eliminator was something like Ford's Mustang Boss 302, with 290 horses. This one sports one of the "Competition Colors" new for 1970. The rear spoiler was more form than function.

► New outer tinware and a "gunsight" grille marked the 1970 version of Mercury's hottest midsize model, the Cyclone Spoiler. Only this notchback was offered at $3759. Mercury built a mere 1631 Cyclone Spoilers for the 1970 model year.

◀ This 1970 Oldsmobile 4-4-2 hardtop, of which 14,709 were sold, carries the max-performance W-30 option with a 370-horse 455-inch V-8. "Cooking" 4-4-2s had "only" 365 bhp.

▼ Oldsmobile switched its muscular 4-4-2s to a huskier new Cutlass Supreme platform. This convertible, which was base priced at $3567, is one of only 2933 built for the model year.

▲ Evolved from Dodge's 1969-only Charger Daytona, the 1970 Plymouth Superbird carried Chrysler's colors in NASCAR racing. Exactly 1920 were built, versus 505 Chargers. Together, they dominated the 1970 NASCAR racing season.

◀ Superbird's drooped "nose cone" (which added 17.2 inches to overall length) resembled the '69 Charger Daytona's, yet was subtly different and not interchangeable. Both models came with a four-barrel 440, with Hemi or 440 "Six Pak" optional.

▶ Plymouth's 1970 midsizers wore a nice restyle. The hot but luxurious GTX was down to this lone $3535 hardtop coupe; 7748 were built. Part of Plymouth's "Rapid Transit System," this car carries the hulking "440+6" option (triple two-barrel carbs), rated at 390 horses.

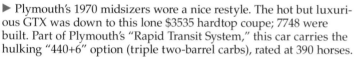

◀ A cousin to the Dodge Challenger T/A, Plymouth's 1970 'Cuda AAR was a special street version of Dan Gurney's All-American Racers' Trans-Am race car. Just 1500 were produced.

▼ Plymouth Barracuda ragtops were never high-volume sellers, and they became even rarer for 1970. Just 635 'Cuda convertibles were built.

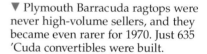

◄ Pontiac strove for a "classical" look at the front end of its 1970 full-size models like this plush Bonneville hardtop coupe, of which 23,418 were sold.

▼ Pontiac altered the GTO's styling for 1970, giving it a new Endura nose with exposed headlamps, bodyside creases, and a revised rump. Newly optional for regular GTOs, such as the ragtop pictured here, was a 360-bhp 455-cid V-8. That engine wasn't initially offered in the Judge (*left*), most of which used the 366-bhp 400-cid Ram Air III V-8. Total 1970 output came to 36,366 hardtops and 3783 ragtops.

▲ This Catalina was Pontiac's lowest-price full-size soft-top offering that year. Starting at $3604, it offered new 455-inch V-8 options with up to 370 horses; a 330-horsepower 400 came standard. Only 3686 of these open Catalinas were ordered.

▲ AMC's 1971 performance special was the Hornet SC/360, a bestriped $2663 compact two-door with a 360 V-8 giving 245 standard horses, 285 optional, and a handling suspension. Curb weight was 3057 pounds. Only 784 copies were built.

▲ American Motors chairman Roy D. Chapin, Jr., poses with the '71 Gremlin outside company headquarters. Gremlin sales totaled 53,480.

▲ AMC Javelins wore new styling for '71. The $3432 AMX, shown here, was now the high-performance Javelin. Top power choice was a new 401 V-8 with 330 horses; it cost $137 extra in the AMX.

◀ The AMC Rebel became a Matador for '71 and acquired a beefier look, front and rear, and a new hardtop roofline. Rebels listed in the $2800-$3500 range.

1971

- Once again, Ford beats Chevrolet in car production, with 2,054,351 built

- President Nixon announces a 90-day wage/price freeze and the end of the excise tax on automobiles on August 16

- Horsepower ratings continue to fall as a result of tightening emissions-control standards; hydrocarbon emissions are now 80 percent lower than in 1962 automobiles, and will fall even further

- "Closed" fuel systems on all cars control evaporation from the fuel tank and carburetor

- Plymouth grabs third place in total output, largely on the strength of its compacts; Pontiac drops to fourth place

- The "muscle car" era is nosediving into oblivion—the victim of federal safety/emissions rules, rising insurance rates, and the trend toward less-expensive cars

◄▲ Buick made big changes for '71, starting with a bigger, all-new Riviera wearing controversial "boattail" fastback styling. At 33,810 units, sales of the $5253 hardtop coupe were down nearly 10 percent from 1970. Despite a three-inch-longer 122-inch wheelbase, the 4325-pound '71 Riv was little heavier than the 1966-70 models. The standard engine was a 315-horse V-8; a 330-bhp version was optional, as was a Gran Sport handling package.

▲ A bigger new corporate C-body brought a rounder look to the '71 Cadillacs, like the popular $6498 Sedan de Ville.

▲ The 1971 full-size Chevrolets rode on a wholly new GM B-body platform with a fuller, more-rounded look.

- GM's big cars are reworked, as are the Mustang/Cougar and all of Chrysler's midsize models

- The Ford Pinto and Chevrolet Vega are introduced—the domestic-brand subcompact race is on in earnest

- Midyear additions include two compacts: Dodge Demon, a Plymouth Duster clone; Pontiac Ventura II, a Chevy Nova clone

- General Motors lowers compression ratios; other automakers wait until 1972

- GM engines run on regular or no-lead fuel, as do some from Chrysler and AMC

- The Federal Trade Commission insists that claims in auto ads be documented

- Imperial employs the first four-wheel antiskid braking system

- The Federal Highway Administration standardizes color combinations and symbols for warning signs

- Ford station wagons feature a tailgate wiper/washer; full-size GM wagons boast a "disappearing" clamshell-type tailgate

- The "Rebel Machine" and the two-seater AMX are gone from the AMC lineup; AMX is now a top-line Javelin model

◄ New low-compression engines gave '71 SS Chevelles slightly tamer performance, but cleaner exhaust pipes. Some 79,992 Super Sports were built, of which 19,292 had the big-block 454 option. An extra $485 bought 375 horses.

► Chevrolet's Monte Carlo coupe was little-changed for '71, but again offered an SS 454 package with the same 425-horse engine available in SS Chevelles. This is one of only 1919 such cars built out of 128,600 total MCs.

▲ Chevy hoped to stem a rising new tide of import sales with the innovative 1971 Vega 2300. This $2196 hatchback coupe was one of three models. Total sales: 269,905.

▲ The functional Vega "Kammback" wagon listed for $2328 and was powered by the same 140-cubic-inch four as the rest of the line. Wagons accounted for 15 percent of Vega build.

• Chrysler buys a share of Mitsubishi Motors Corp., GM purchases a portion of Isuzu—the "captive-import" business (which includes small trucks) involves Japanese as well as European companies

• Lincoln-Mercury dealers market the sleek Italian-built, Ford-powered DeTomaso Pantera; this midengined exotic lists at $9000 and 6091 will be sold from 1971 to 1974

• Automatic temperature-control air conditioning is available on some Fords

• Hornet adds an attractive Sportabout wagon and the SC/360, a hot Hornet coupe that finds only 784 buyers

• The redesigned full-size Buicks are the biggest ever: up to 228.3 inches long

• Buick introduces a radically restyled Riviera that will become known as the "boattail" Riv; it offers "Max-Trac," a computerized antiwheelspin system, a forerunner of modern traction control

• Chevrolet's 97-inch-wheelbase Vega holds much promise, but soon suffers due to a troublesome alloy-block engine that overheats and a rust-prone body

◄▲ The Dodge Charger got a new shape for '71 on a shorter wheelbase. This $3777 R/T was one of six hardtop models. They packed a 370-horse 440-inch Magnum or optional 426 Hemi.

▲ "Pocket" muscle cars seemed just the thing to combat soaring insurance rates, so Dodge added two Demons for '71, based on Plymouth's Valiant Duster coupe. For just $2721, this hot 275-horse Demon 340 pleased 10,098 buyers.

▲ Full-size '71 Dodges stayed with the "fuselage look" adopted for '69, but sales continued to slide. This $3992 Polara Custom wagon, for instance, is one of just 9682 sold (plus 5449 uplevel Monaco wagons).

▲ Ford's Maverick sold strongly for 1971, aided by a new 302-inch V-8 option, and a jazzier two-door called Grabber. The last, shown as a styling model, featured black hood and back panel, and a modest $2354 sticker price.

▲ Countering 1971's all-new big Chevys was a fully redesigned crop of full-size Fords headed by a posh new LTD Brougham sedan and hardtops ($4094-$4140). All save the cheap Custom models came with a 240-horse 351 V-8.

• Cadillac restyles the Eldorado and offers its first front-drive Eldo convertible; prices start at a hefty $7383

• Dodge releases its last convertible, a Challenger; Challenger and Charger R/T models are also in their last year

• Ford's 94-inch-wheelbase Pinto, which lists at $1919, gets off to a good start: 352,402 are built for the model run

• A sporty-looking Maverick Grabber appearance package joins Ford's compact line, as does a longer four-door sedan

• The much-changed Mustang is bigger, heavier; a new Boss 351 lasts just one year

• Automakers test 1600 units in an attempt to develop a catalytic converter that will meet projected emissions standards

• In Los Angeles, more than 5000 fleet vehicles are converted to run on clean-burning propane and natural gas

• Consumer advocate Ralph Nader publishes *What To Do With Your Bad Car: An Action Manual For Lemon Owners*

• Oldsmobile sells its last true 4-4-2 models—6285 hardtops and 1304 convertibles are built

▲ The Ford Mustang grew to Clydesdale size in a full 1971 redesign. Topping Mach 1 as the top street performer was this new Boss 351, a fastback with a hot 330-horse 351 V-8.

▲ Ford's '71 Torinos kept "shaped by the wind" 1970 styling and were still good for up to 370 bhp. The fastback Cobra hardtop was back at $3295, but only 3054 were sold.

▲ Eschewing change just for the sake of it, the 1968-vintage Lincoln Continental Mark III put in a final appearance for 1971 and scored higher sales of 27,091 units. Base price was up to $8813; the vinyl roof and body pinstriping remained standard.

◀ Oldsmobile's 4-4-2 was slightly detuned for '71, but still packed a wallop with the W-30 option, as on this $3552 hardtop; 6285 were produced.

1971 Calendar-Year Car Sales

1.	Ford	2,054,351	7.	Buick	551,188	13. Imperial	11,558
2.	Chevrolet	1,830,319	8.	Mercury	365,310	14. Checker	500[1]
3.	Plymouth	702,113	9.	AMC	244,758	15. Avanti II	107
4.	Pontiac	586,856	10.	Cadillac	188,537		
5.	Oldsmobile	567,891	11.	Chrysler	175,118		
6.	Dodge	551,386	12.	Lincoln	62,642		

[1] *Estimated, excludes taxicabs*

◄ Vacation ready, this Oldsmobile Vista Cruiser set its owner back $4008 in 1971. Total production for the year: 26,546.

▼ Mercury's Cyclone Spoiler saw few changes for '71, so high-compression 429 CJ and Super CJ V-8s still reigned. With a price of $3801, sales came to only 353.

▲ Because Mustang bulked up again for '71, Mercury's Cougar did too—and strove mightily to look like a luxury car, though hot 429-inch big-block options were still available. Here, the $3877 XR-7 hardtop coupe, which found favor with 25,416 customers.

◄ Plymouth purged midsize convertibles from its all-new '71 lineup. GTX remained the posh performer, a $3733 hardtop coupe. Only 2942 were sold, so it disappeared after '71.

▼ Plymouth's popular Valiant-based Duster fastback returned from debut 1970 with a minor facelift. The 340, shown here in "Curious Yellow," remained the top '71 performer, and attracted 12,886 buyers. A new Twister package, here in "Sassy Grass Green," offered 340 show, but not its go—and cost less to insure.

▲ Similarly, Plymouth's Road Runner was down to a single hardtop for '71, priced at $3147 with base 383-inch V-8, which dropped 30 horses to 300. The Hemi and 440s were still optional, but so was the Road Runner's first 340-inch V-8. Still, sales plunged by almost two-thirds, from 41,484 units to 14,218.

◄ Though big muscle cars were all but gone by '71, Plymouth tried one last time with its Sport Fury GT (*foreground*), a $4111 hardtop coupe with a standard 335-horse V-8. Just 375 were sold, far fewer than this lesser Sport Fury Formal Hardtop (*background*), which cost $3710.

▼ Though their faces were vaguely familiar, Pontiac's full-size '71s were all-new—and as big as American big cars would ever get. The pride of the line was a new top-line Grand Ville series that included this grandly priced $4706 convertible, which sold just 1789 units. A 325-horse 455-inch V-8 was the only engine offered.

▲ Formula remained a step down from Trans Am among performance Firebirds for 1971, but Pontiac added new 350 and 455 models to join the carryover Formula 400.

◄ A new nose marked Pontiac's 1971 GTOs, including "The Judge" hardtop coupe. This would be GTO's last year as a distinct series. Judge's 455-inch V-8 was down from 360 to 335 horses, while the base GTO's 400 V-8 dropped to 300.

▼ This base '71 GTO convertible is one of only 661 built; Judge ragtops, meanwhile, numbered a mere 17. Even base hardtop sales were little better at 9497 units.

CHAPTER TWELVE

1972-1979

THE GOVERNMENT STEPS IN

Many Americans recall the Seventies as a dour decade of defeat and disappointment, from the ignominious end of the Vietnam War to the Watergate fiasco that forced a president to resign. They were certainly years of diminished expectations—an age of disillusionment rather than the promised Age of Aquarius.

The decline was, perhaps, inevitable. After more than a decade of turmoil, the country needed to stop and take stock of what it had endured. Trouble was, we were too often disturbed by what we found. Drug abuse and urban poverty in particular loomed as growing national problems with serious long-term consequences.

So, too, the unprecedented embargo on oil shipments to the U.S., decreed in the winter of 1973-74 by a then little-known cartel called the Organization of Petroleum Exporting Countries. Suddenly, Americans who had never had to give a thought about a tank of gas were forced to wait in long lines for fuel that more than doubled in price overnight. This "energy crisis" wasn't confined to keeping cars chugging along (home heating oil was also scarce in many places that winter), but it dramatically underscored the nation's over-dependence on oil sources it could not control. Sadly, the situation would only grow worse, highlighted by a second crisis in 1979 that sparked a new economic recession to open the Eighties.

Congress had long since decided to make automakers answer for the social responsibility of their products, and the legislative hand became increasingly heavier in these years. The Clean Air Act of 1970 mandated ever-tighter limits on exhaust emissions that sapped horsepower; combined with soaring insurance premiums, they all but eliminated performance cars by 1973. That same year brought more required safety features, including bumpers able to endure five-mph impacts without damage, plus the diabolical ignition inter-lock that prevented starting up unless front-seat occupants were buckled up. The latter proved so irksome that the public got it repealed after a single year.

Of course, the first energy crisis was not forgotten. In 1978, Congress served up the Corporate Average Fuel Economy (CAFE) rule, which required smaller, thriftier engines and smaller, lighter cars to match. Actually, Detroit had already moved in that direction with "subcompacts" like the Ford Pinto and Chevy Vega, but those were meant to stem another rising import tide, including some compelling new cars from Japan. Not until GM "downsized" its biggest cars for 1977 was CAFE's full implication apparent to the car-buying public—or to GM's rivals.

Detroit convertibles went into limbo after 1976, thanks to a proposed but ultimately stillborn standard for rollover protection that would have made them illegal. To its discredit, Detroit used the threat to justify killing off ragtops, which of late had not been profitable anyway. But as we know, convertibles have a timeless appeal, and they would return.

So would performance and something like the quality workmanship we knew in the early Fifties, not to mention tasteful, rational styling. But Detroit's Seventies landscape was a mostly bleak vista of fuelish, poor-running dinosaurs with starchy stand-up grilles, "opera windows," and overstuffed velour interiors festooned with fake wood and fussy filigrees—all style passing for substance. Yet there were bright spots. The Chevrolet Corvette remained exciting, if muted from earlier days, and Pontiac's Firebird Trans Am maintained the ponycar spirit unbroken. Still, it was left to imports like the Volkswagen Rabbit and Honda Accord to point the way to Detroit's future, even as they pointed up the follies of its past.

1972

- Total industry output rises to 8.6 million cars for the model year

- Chevrolet builds 2,420,564 cars for the model run, compared to Ford's 2,246,563; Oldsmobile ranks third, Plymouth fourth, Pontiac fifth

- Congress at last revokes the price "freeze" and auto excise tax

- Ford offers 1972's only all-new lines: Torino, Montego, Thunderbird, Continental Mark IV

- Most automakers now offer a powered or manually operated sunroof; convertible sales are quickly declining

- GM cars get energy-absorbing bumpers, one year ahead of government requirements

▲ American Motors's Ambassador was little-changed for 1972. This $4018 Brougham hardtop has the optional 225-bhp, 401-cubic-inch V-8.

▲ AMC's Matador was also little-changed for '72. Hardtop coupe prices started at $2818; a 100-horsepower, 232-cubic-inch six was standard.

▲ You had to look twice to tell a '72 Hornet from a '71. This four-door sold for $2265 with the 232-inch six and $2403 with the base 150-bhp 304 V-8.

▲ AMC's sporty Javelin countered declining "go" with new "show," as on this AMX version specially ordered with the Pierre Cardin package. Overall Javelin sales eased about 1000 units to 26,184.

▲ Full-size Buicks got only detail updates for '72. This $4291 Custom convertible topped the LeSabre line. Just 2037 of these ragtops were built, each weighing 4235 pounds.

▲ Buick's 1972 Electra 225s had more-formal rooflines than LeSabres. This Custom has the even fancier Limited package and sold for $5059. A 455-cubic-inch V-8 was standard.

- Horsepower and torque ratings are now given as "net" instead of "gross"; the revised method, which is more realistic, causes published figures to drop sharply

- Nearly all cars now run on low-lead (not yet unleaded) regular gasoline

- Some 200 Mercurys with airbags go to Allstate Insurance as part of a pilot project; Eaton Corp. tests bags with live passengers

- The Pontiac Firebird, like Chevrolet's Camaro, almost expires in the early '70s as GM worries about the future of performance-oriented machines

- Chrysler and Pontiac offer solid-state (electronic) ignition systems

- The big 454 V-8 is still available in Chevelle and Monte Carlo, but the Monte Carlo SS is gone from the line

- The Detroit-based Automobile Manufacturers Association (AMA) changes its name to the Motor Vehicle Manufacturers Association (MVMA)

- Buzzers and warning lights remind occupants to fasten their seatbelts

- A 400-cid V-8 replaces the 383 in Chryslers; a plush Brougham is added to the New Yorker line

▲ The Buick GS remained pretty hot for 1972, with an unchanged 270-horse (net) Stage 1 455 V-8. But this was its swan-song season. Note the hood-mounted tach.

▲ Buick's big boattail Riviera got a new power-sunroof option for 1972. Base price eased slightly to $5149, and sales held steady at 33,728 of these controversially styled coupes.

◄ De Ville remained the best-selling Cadillac for 1972. SAE net figures pushed rated power for the 472-cid V-8 down from 375 bhp to 345, but actual performance was little-changed.

▲ Once sporty, the Impala had been reduced to just a big, heavy boulevard cruiser by 1972. Base price dropped $42, to $3979, and production jumped from 4576 to 6456.

▲ Chevy's most-popular '72 full-size model was this Impala Custom hardtop coupe. With 183,493 built, it beat out the normally top-selling four-door sedan by only 132 units.

- An electronic digital clock is standard on Imperials, optional on other Chryslers

- Buick's Skylark hardtop can be ordered with a sliding fabric sunroof; the GS 455 returns, but the GSX is reduced to an "all show, no go" appearance package

- Olds's Cutlass convertible attracts 11,571 buyers in its last year, while the 4-4-2 is now just an appearance/handling package

- An era ends as the fabled Dodge/Plymouth Street Hemi fades away—it's too costly to certify for new emissions standards

- A three-door Ford Pinto wagon debuts, including a woody-look Squire option; sales reach 197,290 units

- Ford's all-new and larger Torino gets body-on-frame construction; the short-lived Cobra muscle car is extinct

- Ford's Mustang loses its big-block V-8s and Boss 351 model

- A new larger Ford Thunderbird shares its structure with the Continental Mark IV; the sedan fades away, but production increases 60 percent to 57,814 units

- Four-wheel disc brakes are available on the Thunderbird, along with "Sure-Track," an early antilock braking system

▲ Chevelle's SS package underwent few changes for 1972, but sales dropped to just under 25,000. A 307 V-8 was the base SS engine. Only 5333 cars got big-block 454s this year.

▲ Despite few changes for its third year, Chevrolet's personal-luxury Monte Carlo was more popular than ever, scoring 180,819 sales. Base price was $3362 with the 350-cid V-8.

◄ The "shark" Corvette was five years old in 1972, but still looked tough. Making it tougher to steal was a newly standard factory alarm system. A 365-horse (270 net) 455-inch V-8 was the brawniest engine available.

▲ Changes to Chevy's compact Nova were few. For '72, power choices were down to a standard 110-horse six, and optional 130-bhp 307-inch or 165-bhp 350-inch V-8s.

▲ Chrysler added Newport Royal for 1971, and these continued little-changed for '72. All sold better than their costlier Newport Custom siblings. A 360-inch V-8 with 175 bhp was standard; Customs got a 400-inch mill with 190 horses.

• Plymouth convertibles are history, as are the GTX and big-block Barracuda; the Road Runner survives with the 240-bhp 340 V-8

• Pontiac's legendary GTO is reduced to just a Le Mans option package

• A new armor-plated Lincoln Continental with a 34-inch-wheelbase stretch is pressed into White House duty

• Prestolite introduces a maintenance-free (no need to add water) battery

• Fiberglass radial-ply tires are introduced to the public, are immediate hot sellers

• Two Corvette show cars—the GT 2-Rotor and the Aero-Vette 4-Rotor—are test beds for experimental Wankel rotary engines

• Ford signs an agreement to develop a Stirling external-combustion engine; project never advances past bench testing

• GM tests an onboard diagnostic system, an item that will become common later

• GM announces a plan to install Wankel rotary engines in the Chevrolet Vega for 1975, but they never materialize

▲ Imperial was still a separate marque in 1972 and sported revised front and rear ends. Bendix antiskid brakes returned as a worthy but seldom-ordered option.

▲ Polara remained Dodge's volume big-car line for 1972, but sales were beginning to wither. This $3898 Custom hardtop sedan attracted 22,205 customers.

▲ Dodge's low-priced Dart Swinger hardtop coupes had found success in 1971, so they continued for '72 with minor improvements—and 238,828 deliveries. Base price: $2373.

▲ Big "loop" bumper/grilles were a Chrysler hallmark in the early Seventies, as on Dodge's 1972 midsize Coronet Custom four-door sedan. It listed at a reasonable $2998.

▲ Hidden headlamps continued to set Dodge's luxury Monacos apart from the similarly sized Polaras. This hardtop coupe stickered at $4153 with the 175-bhp 360 V-8.

▲ Ford's Thunderbird was all-new for 1972, with a wheelbase stretched 5.4 inches, to 120.4. A $5293 hardtop coupe was now the sole model, shown here with the popular Landau vinyl roof option.

1972 Calendar-Year Car Sales

1. Chevrolet	2,420,564	7. Dodge	577,870	13. Imperial	15,804
2. Ford	2,246,563	8. Mercury	441,964	14. Checker	850
3. Oldsmobile	762,199	9. Cadillac	267,787	15. Avanti II	127
4. Plymouth	756,605	10. AMC	258,134	16. Excalibur	65
5. Pontiac	706,978	11. Chrysler	204,704		
6. Buick	679,921	12. Lincoln	94,560		

Some figures are estimated

▲ Full-size, formal-look 1972 Fords were much like the redesigned '71s. Here, the $3925 LTD hardtop sedan, which attracted 104,167 buyers. The fancier $4074 LTD Brougham found 23,364 homes. A 208-bhp 429 V-8 was the top engine.

▲ Ford's all-new '72 midsize Torinos were as big as recent full-size models. Sedans, hardtops, fastbacks, and wagons returned, convertibles didn't. Gran Torinos, like this $2878 "formal" hardtop coupe, stressed luxury over sportiness.

▲ Ford's Boss Mustang retired for 1972, leaving the 351-cid Mach 1 as the hottest offering. Most other models, could be ordered with a new Sprint Decor Option, as on this convertible.

▶ After being completely redesigned for 1970, Lincoln's Continental received mostly minor yearly changes. Even so, sales for 1972 rebounded to 45,969.

▲ Mercury's 1972 Cougar line again consisted of base and XR-7 hardtop coupes and convertibles. This closed $3323 XR-7 was the line's best-seller, finding 26,802 buyers.

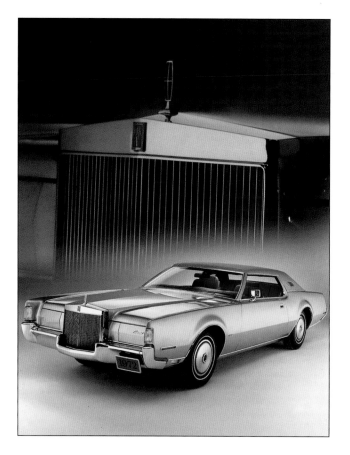

▲ Dubbed Mark IV, Lincoln's personal luxury coupe had a princely $8640 base price. Its standard 460-inch V-8 produced 212 horsepower, 12 fewer than Continental's. New oval "opera windows" were soon to be much imitated.

▲ As at Ford, Mercury reprised its full-size '72 Marquis and Monterey lines with few alterations. The Marquis editions again outsold entry-level Montereys like this $4035 Custom hardtop coupe, which found just 5910 buyers.

▲ Like most rivals, Oldsmobile's full-size '72s were mildly facelifted '71 reruns. Topping the line was this Ninety Eight Luxury hardtop sedan.

▲ After two years, the Hurst/Olds returned for 1972 with a still-potent 455-inch V-8 at 300 net bhp. Just 629 were built.

▲ The biggest engine for Plymouth's '72 Road Runner was a 280-bhp 440-inch V-8, offered with the "GTX" option.

▲ Plymouth's Barracuda fell on hard times for '72; down to base and 'Cuda hardtops, with the latter's 340 small-block option the hottest available. Optional stripes and a "scooped" hood dressed up this base model, but real muscle cars didn't wear whitewalls.

▲ Pontiac first offered its own version of Chevy's popular Nova compact as the '71 Ventura II, which continued for '72 with just a few changes. One of them was a rare sliding fabric sunroof as worn by this $2426 two-door.

▲ The 455 HO Trans Am remained Pontiac's performance Firebird for '72—with a new four-speed manual as standard. Power fell from 335 gross to 300 net, but the car was timed at just 5.4 seconds 0-60 mph. Only 1286 T/As were built this year.

▲ Like the Olds 4-4-2, Pontiac's GTO reverted to option status for '72. A 300-horse (net) 455 was the best power listed; a standard 400-inch V-8 and regular 455 both made 250 bhp. Only hardtop coupes were built, and only 5807 at that.

▲ American Motors stylists under Dick Teague designed this sporty hatchback coupe to expand the Hornet compact line for 1973. Price: $2449.

◄ By 1973, AMC had stopped making major changes to its Javelin ponycar. Now rated at 255 net horsepower, the big 401-inch V-8 was still optional. This is the top-line $3191 AMX.

▲ Pillared "Colonnade" rooflines marked an all-new fleet of 1973 GM intermediates. Among them were curvy Buicks, which got the revived Century name. This coupe has the $175 Gran Sport appearance and handling package.

▲ Buick's personal-luxury Riviera again flaunted a "boat-tail," slightly blunted for 1973—a response to the controversial '71 design. The front end was also blunted to accommodate newly required five-mph bumpers. Base price: $5221.

1973

- The October 19 OPEC (Organization of Petroleum Exporting Countries) oil embargo leads to fuel shortages, long lines, and large price hikes; it will be lifted on March 18, 1974

- Chevrolet builds 2,579,509 cars for the model year, compared to Ford's 2,349,815; Olds retains third spot, followed by Pontiac, then Plymouth

- The average new car sells for $3930, while the average worker takes home $9298 annually

- All '73 models must have five-mph front "crash" bumpers and 2½-mph rear bumpers; those built after January 1 must incorporate protective side beams in the doors

- Exhaust-gas-recirculation (EGR) valves are installed in this year's engines to cut down on emissions of nitrogen oxide

- Horsepower, torque, and compression ratios continue their sad downward trend

▲ Cadillac met 1973 crash rules with bigger bumpers and a "push-back" grille that retreated a few inches to resist damage. Here, the $7765 Fleetwood Sixty Special Brougham.

▲ Chevrolet's Monte Carlo sported GM's new Colonnade pillared coupe design—and rather florid curves. Trim levels swelled to base, S, and this $3806 vinyl-roofed Landau.

▲ A sportier roofline and blockier lower body marked the revamped 1973 Chevelles, which included this new $3179 Laguna coupe.

▲ Chevy's Corvette sported a revised profile for 1973, thanks to a restyled body-color front end that looked elegant and met the Feds' new five-mph bumper rule.

▲ Chevy's '68-vintage Nova compacts got their first major facelift for '73, most of it involving bigger bumpers dictated by new federal rules. Also new that year was this three-door hatchback version of the mainstay two-door sedan.

▲ Lincoln may have inspired the front redo on '73 Chryslers. Round headlamps in square bezels were a period design fad. The Royal was gone, so the base model was now simply Newport. This $4316 hardtop sedan found 20,175 customers.

• Subcompact and compact models enjoy record sales; big cars sink in 1973, a result of the oil crisis—but they'll be back

• Oldsmobile launches its Nova-based Omega compact, and midyear brings the related Buick Apollo; combined, they sell fewer than 100,000 units

• Hatchback versions of GM's Nova, Ventura, Omega, and Apollo appear

• GM's rebodied midsize lines feature "Colonnade" hardtops with fixed center pillars; safety concerns help kill off pillarless hardtop coupes, which will be phased out of big-car lines over the next few years

• Plymouth's "Space Duster" is similar to Dodge's "Convertriple," which blends a fold-down rear seat with a sliding steel sunroof; various Duster versions include Gold, Twister, Special Coupe, and 340

• Federal law bans odometer "roll-back," requiring dealers to formally disclose mileage before selling a used car

• The new Le Mans-based Pontiac Grand Am mixes Grand Prix luxury with Trans Am performance; Grand Prix is now on the same chassis as Chevrolet's Monte Carlo

• Extra-cost front vent windows appear, after fading away in the late Sixties

▲ Dodge's once-unique Charger had become just a two-door Coronet with 1971's "fuselage" redesign. For '73, Dodge cut in little windows to improve SE visibility (*left*). The only pillarless Charger was the $2810 standard-trim model (*right*).

▲ Because some objected to the Demon name, Dodge's fastback compact coupes were retitled Dart Sport for 1973. A "340" model (*pictured*) with that V-8 was the sportiest model.

▲ This $4001 Polara Custom hardtop sedan, which found 29,341 buyers in 1973, came with a 150-horse 318-cubic-inch V-8, with options up to a 220-bhp 440-inch engine.

▶ Except for beefier bumpers for '73, Ford's subcompact Pinto looked like it did in 1971. Here the $2021 two-door sedan. Total Pinto output for the year: 484,512 units.

- More than 72 percent of this year's cars are equipped with air conditioning

- Electronic ignition is standard on all Chrysler, Dodge, and Plymouth engines

- Swing-out bucket seats are made available in Chevelle/Monte Carlo coupes

- General Motors builds 1000 Chevrolet Impalas equipped with airbags.

- AMC's Gremlin offers a "Levi's" option wherein the interior fabric resembles that of the blue jeans, replete with red piping

- AMC's Hornet line gets a handsome fastback/hatchback coupe variant

- This year marks the final appearance of Chevelle's 454 V-8; the SS option is gone

- The SS designation and big-block engines disappear from the Camaro roster

- Buick revives the idled Century badge for its new, curvier midsize models

- Dodge's Dart Demon is renamed Sport; the devil-with-a-pitchfork logo is gone

- The '73 Cougar is the last ponycar-based Mercury, the 1974 model is much larger

▲ Midsize Fords wore a more-formal face for '73. Luxury was emphasized via new Gran Torino Broughams, here a $3071 hardtop coupe.

▲ Mustang saw few changes for '73, but rumors that ragtops would be discontinued caused convertible sales to rebound from 6121 to 11,853. Alas, the rumors were true. Top mill was a 260-horse 351-inch V-8.

▲ Ford's 1973 Thunderbird sported a front crash bumper, plus a new eggcrate grille. The new opera windows required the $137 vinyl roof. A 429-inch V-8 remained standard.

▲ Lincoln Continental's massive front end accepted 1973 crash bumpers with dignity. Shown here is the Town Car luxury package that added $467 to the $7230 price tag.

◄ The '73 Mercury Cougars would be the line's last with any pretense of sportiness until 1983. Ragtops were again rare, with just 3165 XR-7s and 1284 standard models built.

1973 Calendar-Year Car Sales

1. Chevrolet	2,579,509	7. Dodge	665,536	13. Imperial	16,729
2. Ford	2,349,815	8. Mercury	486,470	14. Checker	900[1]
3. Oldsmobile	922,771	9. AMC	392,105	15. Excalibur	122
4. Pontiac	919,870	10. Cadillac	304,839	16. Avanti II	106
5. Plymouth	882,196	11. Chrysler	234,223		
6. Buick	821,165	12. Lincoln	128,073		

[1] *Estimated, excludes taxicabs*

481

▲ Olds had done well with dressed-up Royale versions of its entry-level, full-size Delta 88s in 1972. The '73s continued the trend, but this $4442 ragtop managed only 7088 sales.

▲ Against all odds, another Hurst/Olds bowed for '73, based on the new Cutlass Supreme coupe. Some 1097 were built, all with a 455 V-8 of about 250 net horsepower.

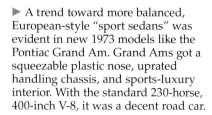

▶ A trend toward more balanced, European-style "sport sedans" was evident in new 1973 models like the Pontiac Grand Am. Grand Ams got a squeezable plastic nose, uprated handling chassis, and sports-luxury interior. With the standard 230-horse, 400-inch V-8, it was a decent road car.

▲ This Grand Ville convertible, of which 4447 were built, remained the grandest Pontiac: $4766 price tag, 4339-pound curb weight, 215-horse 455-inch V-8.

▲ A new $176 Sprint option added a dash of sportiness to Pontiac's '73 Ventura coupe. Strictly for show, it included wider wheels and tires. Ventura output reached 96,500.

▲ Pontiac's '73 Firebirds showed no sign of crash bumpers, a tribute to GM designers. This $3276 Formula listed two 455-inch V-8s: a 250-horsepower HO and 310-horse Ram Air.

◄ Plymouth tried to cash in on growing import demand in 1971 with the British-built Cricket. Though priced around $2000 with power front disc brakes, shoddy workmanship drove them from U.S. shores after '73.

▲ Still around and still pretty potent in 1973 was Plymouth's 240-bhp Duster 340 fastback, pictured here with optional tape stripes and wider Rallye wheels.

▲ Midsize Plymouths met 1973 bumper rules with a new, more-restrained front end. Road Runner still hung in, but strictly as a thin-pillar coupe with V-8s of 318, 400, or 440 inches.

483

◀ As if to answer its "What's a Matador" TV spots, AMC unwrapped this swollen coupe to replace pillarless hardtops for '74. This $3699 coupe is the sporty "X." Top engine: a 255-horse 401-inch V-8.

▲ AMC's Ambassador was down to just this $4559 Brougham and a $4960 wagon for '74, which was to be its last season.

▲ An amalgam of styling cues, the AMC Javelin was also in its last year for '74. Sales: 29,536, 4980 of them hot AMXs.

▲ You could still buy a Buick Gran Sport in 1974, but it was just a Century coupe with slightly sportier looks, bigger tires, and firmed-up suspension.

▲ Evolutionary styling changes were Cadillac's '74 news, but ultraposh "d' Elegance" and "Talisman" options arrived for the Fleetwood Sixty Special Brougham, now priced at $9537.

1974

- President Nixon requests voluntary gas station closings to curtail Sunday driving, but, as it turns out, the OPEC oil embargo will be lifted in March

- Traffic fatalities decline, with much credit going to the national 55-mph speed limit

- Industry output eases slightly to 8.1 million automobiles for the model year

- Chevrolet builds 2,333,839 cars for the model year, compared to Ford's 2,179,791; Plymouth rises to third on the strength of its compacts

- Dodge introduces rebates on the Monaco; big cars are not selling during the oil embargo

- By law, all cars now must have energy-absorbing bumpers front and rear

▲ Looking to Bicentennial 1976, Chevy offered a "Spirit of America" trim option for several '74s, including the Vega.

▲ Some 1974 Chevy Novas, like this hatchback, also wore optional "Spirit of America" dress. Package price: $140.

▲ Pending rollover standards began killing off hardtops in 1974, but this Impala Sport Coupe was still a true hardtop.

▲ Here's Chevy's new-for-'74 full-size pillared coupe in top-line Caprice Classic Custom trim. Base price: $4483.

◄ The 1974 Chevy Corvettes were the last with optional 454 big-block power—down to 270 bhp net—and the first with a restyled body-color rear end that neatly matched the previous year's new nose.

• A federally mandated interlock prevents the engine from being started until the seat-belts are fastened; this system raises a nationwide outcry and is soon abandoned

• Emissions controls are more exhaustive; fuel-mileage ratings drop as a result

• The new trim and thrifty Ford Mustang II is the first subcompact specialty car, a mechanical kin to economy-class Pinto

• The new overhead-cam 2.3-liter four found in the Mustang II is America's first mass-produced engine built to European-style metric measurements

• The Pontiac Firebird and other models adopt fiberglass-reinforced plastic noses

• While four-cylinder engines go into 13 percent of cars (up from 9 percent in '73), V-8 installations slip from 81 to 68 percent

• The final AMC Ambassadors and Javelins are built; Matador is completely reworked into a new fastback coupe, but sales are disappointing, even for the four-door

• Chevrolet's Vega plant at Lordstown, Ohio, endures a two-month strike

• Four-wheel disc brakes are standard on Chrysler Imperials, which are completely restyled; output drops to 14,426 units

▲ Topping Chrysler's '74 lineup was the New Yorker Brougham. Prices were $5931-$6063. As elsewhere in Detroit, engines were detuned to run on regular gas (unleaded).

▲ Full-size '74 Dodge Monacos—13 models strong— shared Chrysler's new big-car platform. With 10,585 sales, this $4539 Custom hardtop was a decent seller.

▲ Dodge's midsize '74 Coronets got a last-minute facelift (as hinted in this retouched factory photo), mainly to meet bumper rules. The Custom shown was the line's best-seller.

▲ A revised tail with a five-mph bumper helped add 300 pounds to the 1974 Thunderbird, now 4825 pounds. A torquier 220-horse 460-inch V-8 replaced the standard 429.

▲ Well-timed to face the energy crisis, the all-new '74 Mustang II was 14.5-inches shorter and 300 pounds lighter than the old ponycar—and scored a resounding 385,993 sales. This posh $3480 Ghia came with an 88-bhp four, or optional 105-bhp V-6.

- Buick buys back the tooling it sold AMC in 1968 so it can again build its 231-inch V-6

- Checker builds its last station wagon; Ed Cole retires from the GM presidency, to join the famous cab builder

- Chevy's sporty Laguna Type S-3 coupe, offered in 1974-76 as a replacement for the Chevelle SS, wears a "rubberized" nose

- Camaro Z28 is temporarily dropped at the end of the year, replaced by the Rally Sport

- The last big-block and LT-1 engines are installed in the Corvette, which sees production jump 23 percent to 37,502 units

- The final 16,437 Dodge Challengers are built; introduced in the waning days of the muscle era, the model never caught on

- Dodge drops the Polara, consolidating full-size models under the Monaco badge

- A Gran Torino Elite hardtop coupe joins the Ford line at midyear to battle Chevrolet's hot-selling Monte Carlo

- Mustang II comes only as a notchback coupe or fastback hatch with a four-cylinder or V-6 engine; prices start at $3134

▲ Mustang II also came as this "fasthatch" coupe in standard trim (*shown*), priced at $3328, and in sporty Mach 1 form for $3674. The latter's standard 2.8-liter V-6 was optional for other models in lieu of the 2.3-liter four.

▲ Ford began referring to four-door sedans as "pillared hardtops" for 1974, perhaps preparing buyers for the end of pillarless models. The title applied to this $4717 full-size LTD Brougham, which saw 11,371 copies built.

▲ Billed as "America's Consummate Luxury Car," the '74 Lincoln Mark IV gained a five-mph rear bumper and a new $473 Gold Luxury Group trim option.

◄ Mercury's '74 midsize Montegos lost sporty models but gained five-mph bumpers. Shown here is the $3680 MX Brougham sedan.

• Mercury's Cougar XR-7, now riding the midsize Montego platform, adopts the Thunderbird "personal-luxury" formula; output soars to 90,000 units

• The Valiant Duster enjoys another production increase, to 277,409 units; meanwhile, Barracuda output ends after only 11,734 1974s are produced

• A hulky new Plymouth Fury debuts at $1.00 per pound: minimum weight, 4125 pounds; minimum price, $4101

• The Cycolac-bodied, two-passenger CitiCar—built by a Florida firm—becomes one of the best-selling electric vehicles despite a range of only 50 miles per charge; 1801 are built in 1974 and '75

▲ Montereys still anchored the big-Mercury line for '74, but they were little-changed, and sales fell. This $4523 Custom hardtop coupe found only 4510 for the year.

▲ More-expensive full-size Mercurys were also carried over little-changed for 1974. Top of the Merc line was this $5519 Marquis Brougham "pillared hardtop."

◄ A Cutlass paced the 1974 Indianapolis 500 and led to another Hurst/Olds coupe, this time packing a 275-horse 455-inch V-8. Though just 380 were built—the lowest H/O total yet—many were used at the track for "official" duties.

► Like AMC's Javelin and the Dodge Challenger, the Plymouth Barracuda would vanish after '74, thanks to an all-but-dead ponycar market. The 'Cuda, shown here, still had a twin-scoop hood feeding a 245-horse 360-cid V-8, but found only 4989 buyers at $3252 apiece.

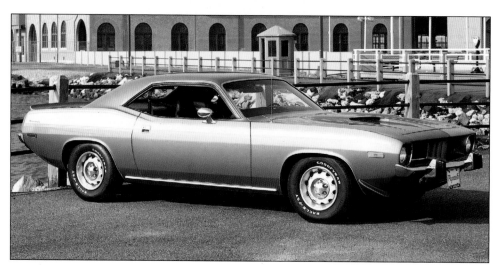

1974 Calendar-Year Car Sales

1. Chevrolet	2,333,839	7. Dodge	477,728	13. Imperial	14,426
2. Ford	2,179,791	8. AMC	431,798	14. Checker	900[1]
3. Plymouth	739,894	9. Mercury	403,977	15. Avanti II	123
4. Oldsmobile	581,195	10. Cadillac	242,330	16. Excalibur	118
5. Pontiac	580,045	11. Chrysler	117,373		
6. Buick	495,063	12. Lincoln	93,983		

[1] *Estimated, excludes taxicabs*

▲ Plymouth's '74 Duster fastback (*shown*) and its Valiant two- and four-door sedans were much like the '73s inside and out. Duster sales, 277,409; Valiant, 181,674.

▲ Road Runner remained a part of Plymouth's midsize Satellite line for '74. Though it was more "show" than "go," the 275-bhp, 440-inch V-8 was still an option. Sales fell to 11,555.

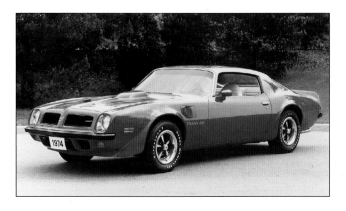

▲ Pontiac's Firebird finally showed the effects of new federal bumper rules in a handsome '74 facelift. Trans Am (*shown*) still topped the line, and more than doubled sales to 10,255.

▲ Sometimes called the "Notch Back Hardtop," Pontiac's new '74 coupe was also available as a midline Bonneville for $4572. Top engine option was the 255-horse 455-inch V-8.

▶ It says GTO, but this '74 was just Pontiac's compact Ventura with a $195 cosmetic and handling package. A 165-horse 350-inch V-8 was included along with floorshift and dummy hood scoop. After 7058 of these pretenders, the "Goat" was gone.

▲ Hornet hatchback coupes featured a big load opening and lots of carrying space. This 1975 has the sporty "X" option package. Top engine option was a 150-horse 304-inch V-8.

▲ AMC unveiled the egglike Pacer for '75. The two-door hatch cost $3299. It had been originally designed to accept a Wankel rotary engine, but one never arrived.

◄ Aimed at younger buyers was AMC's new 1975 "Levi's" package for the Gremlin. It featured faux denim upholstery, with authentic stitching.

▼ The front-engine, rear-drive Bricklin SV-1 bowed in 1974 with gullwing doors and a price around $9800. Promoter Malcolm Bricklin billed it as a "Safety Vehicle," but most considered it a sports car. Early models used an AMC 360-cubic-inch V-8.

1975

- Model-year output shrinks to 6.5 million cars

- Chevrolet volume skids to 1,755,773 cars, but tops Ford's 1,569,608 units; Oldsmobile is third, followed by Pontiac, Buick, and Plymouth

- All four major automakers install catalytic converters to reduce emissions—but the Environmental Protection Agency (EPA) charges that the devices may emit harmful sulphates

- Slow sales lead to widespread layoffs

- Automakers pay rebates to spark sales, especially subcompacts, which are selling slowly now that the gas is flowing again

- A bonanza of new (or revived) nameplates emerge: Astre, Bobcat, Charger SE, Cordoba, Elite, Granada, Monarch, Monza, Pacer, Seville, Skyhawk, and Starfire

◀ Convertibles looked to be an endangered species in 1975, when this big and brassy LeSabre Custom became Buick's last factory-built ragtop. Priced at $5133, it garnered 5300 sales.

▲ The Sedan de Ville badge still identified a four-door hard-top in the '75 Cadillac line, but rectangular headlamps and C-pillar windows were new. Base price was $8801.

▲ Cadillac's first "small" car was the 1975 Seville, a luxury special version of the GM X-body compact Chevy Nova. It had a 180-bhp, fuel-injected 350-cid V-8. Price: $12,479.

▼ Cadillac's '75 Eldorado retained its basic '71 design, but got a wider grille with rectangular headlamps. As Caddy's only ragtop, this model found 8950 buyers.

- The Chrysler Cordoba and Dodge Charger SE are built in Canada; so are the Buick Skyhawk, Chevy Monza, and Olds Starfire

- The subcompact Buick Skyhawk and Olds Starfire have standard V-6s; Chevrolet's Monza has a Vega four or small V-8

- Seville, hyped for its "international" size, is the smallest Caddy in decades; it's meant to lure Mercedes-Benz buyers

- A huge 500-cid V-8 with 190 horsepower is now standard in all Cadillacs except Seville, which employs a 350-inch V-8

- AMC's egg-shaped Pacer hatchback enters the market on March 1, and snares 72,158 buyers in the short model year

- Chevrolet's racy limited-edition Cosworth Vega arrives in April, but at $5916 attracts only 2061 customers

- The "precision-size" Granada features a mock-Mercedes look and soon becomes a top Ford seller: 302,658 in 1975

- Ford begins production of more economical "MPG" cars with catalysts: Pinto, Mustang, Bobcat

- GM's domestic market share tops 53 percent; Ford takes 28, while Chrysler captures only 14 percent

◄ The '75 would be the last Chevy Corvette convertible for 12 years. At $6537, just 4629 were built. With big-blocks killed off by emissions and economy concerns, Corvette power for '75 was handled by two 350-inch V-8s. Total sales rose to 38,465 units.

▲ Chevy offered swivel front seats as a new option for its facelifted '75 Monte Carlo. This Landau model tallied 110,380 sales, compared to the base Monte's 148,529.

▲ Full-size Chevrolets continued moving toward Cadillac style in 1975, as on this $4891 Caprice Classic hardtop sedan. Some 40,482 customers approved of the look.

◄ After years of resisting a smaller model, Chrysler tried selling a mid-size for '75. It was a cousin to Dodge's redesigned Charger, called Cordoba. "The New Small Chrysler" wasn't all that small, but at $5072 it attracted a sizable 150,105 sales. Ricardo Montalban earned a spot in TV's Hall of Fame with commercials in which he extolled Cordoba's optional "fine Corinthian leather" and other luxury features. A 318-inch V-8 was standard, with 360 and 400 engines optional.

- Borg-Warner releases its first U.S.-built five-speed gearbox, while AMC introduces an English-built overdrive transmission

- AMC's subcompact Pacer is billed as the "first wide small car," but the plan to use a Wankel rotary engine never materializes

- The Energy Policy and Conservation Act becomes law—it will set fuel-economy standards starting with the '78 models

- Experimental airbags are installed in some 1974-75 Buicks, Cadillacs, and Olds—many owners never even know they're in the steering wheel

- The "final" American convertibles are built (except for Cadillac); makers fear a federal rule on rollover protection —but slow sales are the major cause for their demise

- Chrysler's new $5072 Cordoba personal-luxury coupe is an instant hit: 150,105 are built in its first model year

- Dodge's Cordoba clone is the $4903 Charger SE, but only one-fourth as many find buyers in 1975

- Mercury pastes a stand-up grille on the Pinto hatchback and wagon, creating the $3189 Bobcat; 34,234 find buyers

◄ Dodge changed names again for 1975. What had been Chargers were once again Coronet hardtops. This is the top-trim $4154 Brougham version.

▼ The only real Dodge Charger for 1975 was this formal-looking coupe dubbed SE for "Special Edition." But special it wasn't, being nearly identical to that year's new Chrysler Cordoba. Though the Charger listed for less ($4903), it sold only a fourth as well. Was Ricardo the difference?

▲ Though conceived to replace the Maverick, Ford's new 1975 Granada emerged as a separate upscale compact with styling cribbed from Mercedes-Benz. This coupe and a four-door sedan sold in base and posh Ghia trim for $3800-$4300. It was a hit—first-year sales topped 302,000.

▲ Expanding Ford's midsize roster for 1975 was the Gran Torino Elite, a posh "baby T-Bird" and Monte Carlo-fighter, with all the expected styling cues, from "stand-up" grille to opera windows. Though not cheap at $4767, it proved very popular: 123,372 happy customers drove one home.

▲ Thunderbird's base price rose $500 for 1975, to $7701. Silver and Copper Luxury Group packages were new, as were optional "antiskid" rear brakes.

▲ Ford axed full-size hardtops for '75, but pillared two-doors appeared with gimmicky B-post opera windows. This is the $5133 LTD Brougham.

▲ Lincoln Continentals took on Cadillac-style "colonnade" rooflines for 1975. This four-door sedan jumped in price by some $1400, to $9656.

▲ Mercury put a Canadian model name on a clone of Ford's Granada to create the 1975 Monarch, a luxury compact sized and priced above Comet. Here, an uplevel Ghia four-door.

▲ Top dog among 1975 full-size Mercurys was Grand Marquis, formerly a Brougham trim option. Unique vinyl-insert lower-body moldings were featured. Price: $6469.

▲ Though muscle cars were allegedly dead, 1975 brought yet another Hurst/ Olds, a $1095 conversion of that year's $4035 Cutlass Supreme coupe.

▶ Olds quit on convertibles after 1975, but sales of the Delta 88 Royale model jumped five-fold, to 21,000—likely due to rumors that it would be the last.

1975 Calendar-Year Car Sales

1. Chevrolet	1,755,773	7. Mercury	404,650	13. Imperial	8830
2. Ford	1,569,608	8. Dodge	377,462	14. Checker	450[1]
3. Oldsmobile	631,795	9. Cadillac	264,732	15. Avanti II	125
4. Pontiac	531,922	10. Chrysler	242,330	16. Excalibur	90
5. Buick	481,768	11. AMC	241,501		
6. Plymouth	454,105	12. Lincoln	101,843		

[1] Estimated, excludes taxicabs

◀ Satellites were renamed Furys for '75, but Plymouth's restyled midsize line still offered a Road Runner. It sold only 7183 copies despite available 440-inch V-8 power.

▶ Bowing in Canada for '73 and in the U.S. for '75, Pontiac's Astre was a Chevy Vega clone, with the troublesome 78/87-bhp aluminum four.

▼ Pontiac abandoned convertibles after a final 4519 of these stately '75 Grand Villes. The only engine was a 185-bhp, 400-cubic-inch V-8.

▲ Matador became AMC's largest car for 1975. A dubious '75 facelift carried over to the '76 sedans and wagons, whose sales fell to 41,513. This four-door sedan offered six or V-8 power ($3627/$3731), with a 360-cubic-inch V-8 optional.

▲ Pacer, now in its first full year, was AMC's best-selling '76 model: 117,244. Changes were minimal, but a new two-barrel carb for the optional 258-inch six gave 120 horses to motivate this hefty 3144-pound, $3499 subcompact.

▶ The '76 AMC Hornets (the $3199 six-cylinder hatchback coupe shown) got only trim shuffles and minor mechanical enhancements. Hornet sales rose by 8000 units to 71,577.

▲ Buick's Riviera, which had lost its '71 "boattail" look in a major '74 restyle, carried on with few changes for '76. A 205-bhp 455-inch V-8 powered the $6798 luxury coupe.

▲ Along with the big LeSabre, the midsize Century line remained a Buick sales mainstay for 1976, when all models shifted to a 110-horse 231-inch V-6 as standard.

▲ Big Buicks would change dramatically after 1976, when hardtop coupes like this $5144 LeSabre Custom would vanish from the lineup. Buick built 45,669 of the posh two-doors models.

1976

• Sales leap upward after a pair of brutal years: Big Three automakers are recovering, but American Motors is showing signs of terminal weakness

• The U.S. industry produces 8,114,376 cars for the model year; domestic sales climb 22 percent

• Some 2,103,862 Chevys are built, compared to Ford's 1,861,537; Oldsmobile ranks third

• The lease/rental share of the U.S. car market is now 18 percent—up from just eight percent ten years earlier

• Inflation is still high, but no longer in budget-buster double-digit figures

• An average new car sells for $5470, while the average worker earns $11,620 annually

▲ Cadillac scored a publicity windfall with its '76 open Eldorado, the so-called last convertible. It cost $11,049 and a total of 14,000 were sold.

▲ True hardtop coupes were a thing of Cadillac's past in 1976, but this $9067 Coupe de Ville outsold every other model in the line: 114,482 units.

▲ After a major '75 redo, Chevy's compact Nova coasted for 1976, although luxury LN models became Concours. Here, a $3830 sedan.

▲ Chevy's Cosworth-Vega bowed for '75 with a 111-horse, 2.0-liter, twincam four. It was sporty—but pricey at $6066. Only 3508 were built for 1975 and 1976.

▲ Chevy's new '75 Vega-based Monza fastback got a notch-back "Towne Coupe" companion at midyear. This '76 Towne Coupe—one of 46,735—wears the new Cabriolet option.

▶ Chevy pruned Chevelle Lagunas after 1974 to a single S-3 coupe. It had a unique color-matched "shovel nose," louvered rear side windows, and appearance options like the lower-body striping and vinyl "Sport Roof." At 9100, sales disappointed, so the S-3 was canceled after '76.

- Oldsmobile's Cutlass is the top-selling model (and is during much of the '70s), beating out the full-size Chevrolet

- Several GM divisions offer an optional five-speed manual gearbox

- Front disc brakes are now standard on U.S. cars, due to federal regulation

- A Department of Transportation study finds the 10-year ownership cost of a full-size car to be $17,879—17 cents per mile

- One-third of domestic cars have an engine other than a V-8; 10 percent are fours

- No-lead gasoline averages 61 cents per gallon, "regular" sales begin to slide

- GM warns that the auto industry may have to cancel 1978 production totally, unless emissions standards are eased

- New nameplates for the year include Aspen, Chevette, Sunbird, Volaré

- General Motors reports that the average monthly payment on a car loan is now $160

▲ With the demise of the last Bel Air sedan and wagons, Impala became Chevy's entry-level full-size line for '76. This $4763 Custom coupe appealed to 43,219 buyers.

▲ A maintenance-free battery was one of the detail changes to Chevy's '76 Corvette. No ragtop was offered. Few cared—volume hit a new model-year record of 46,558 units.

▲ Rectangular quad headlamps graced Chevy's '76 Monte Carlo. The 454-cubic-inch V-8 died as a Monte option, but a 400-inch V-8 could replace the new standard 305.

◄ Looking very similar to the debut '75, the '76 Chrysler Cordoba, now $5392, again had a base 318-inch V-8, but also a new fuel-saving "lean burn" system for its optional 360- and 400-inch engines. Sales fell to 120,462.

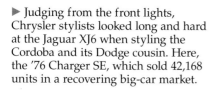

► Judging from the front lights, Chrysler stylists looked long and hard at the Jaguar XJ6 when styling the Cordoba and its Dodge cousin. Here, the '76 Charger SE, which sold 42,168 units in a recovering big-car market.

- Chrysler announces an agreement to purchase engines and transaxles from Volkswagen for installation in its upcoming front-drive subcompacts

- GM claims a fuel-economy improvement of 38 percent between 1974 and 1976, but insists that a major redesign would be needed to meet the proposed 1985 standard

- This is the last year for the "big-block" 455-cid V-8 from Buick, Oldsmobile, and Pontiac, and for Chevy's 454-inch mill

- The final Cadillac Eldorado convertibles, 14,000 of them, leave the assembly line— they'll be the last factory-built American ragtops until the 1980s open-air revival

- Chrysler's new compacts, the Dodge Aspen and Plymouth Volaré, sell well, but unfortunately will soon become the most-recalled cars to date

- Pinto introduces the Cruising Wagon, a tricked-up wagon with blanked-in rear side windows with portholes and "mod" striping; Mustang II adds a "Cobra II" trim package

◄ Dodge's new Aspen was a slightly bigger and plusher compact than the Dart it replaced for 1976. Big-car styling cues abounded, as seen on this top-line $4413 SE coupe. Aspen came as a coupe, sedan, and wagon in base, Custom, and Special Edition trim.

► Cast in the image of the great Shelby-Mustangs of the Sixties was a new $325 "Cobra II" option for 1976 Mustang II fastbacks. Included were nostalgic blue/white paint, louvered rear side windows, spoilers, snake insignia, and white-letter tires.

◄ New optional black-and-silver "Stallion" trim added visual spice to Ford's 1976 Pinto hatchback (*bottom*), Mustang II fastback (*center*), and two-door Maverick (*top*). Special snorting-horse decals and sport mirrors were part of the package. Most Stallions rolled on the styled wheels shown here, a separate extra-cost item.

• In an obvious move to boost economy, Chevy makes the new 305-cubic-inch V-8 standard in many full-size models

• The economical subcompact Chevette debuts; derived from the Opel Kadett, it's GM's first "world car"

• Stallion trim is offered for the basically unchanged Ford Pintos, Mavericks, and Mustang IIs—a stab at the youth market

• "Designer Series" packages debut on Lincolns—they include names such as Bill Blass, Cartier, Givenchy, Pucci

• A frugally tuned "Feather Duster" is Plymouth's reply to Ford's MPG models; aluminum components save some weight

• Pontiac's Sunbird is a clone of the Chevrolet Monza, but comes only as a notchback coupe for 1976

▶ Ford's Gran Torino-based Elite luxury hardtop coupe changed little for 1976, though its price rose to $4879. A standard 154-horse 351-inch V-8 was standard. Sales moved up to 146,475, yet Elite would die after this year.

▲ Lincoln's Continental Mark IV took its final bow for '76 with new "designer" trim/color options: Bill Blass, Cartier, Givenchy, and Pucci. Price was up to $11,060.

▲ Mercury entered the expanding market for small sporty coupes by importing Ford of Europe's Capri in 1970. The line was renamed Ghia II in 1975. This is the posh Ghia model.

▲ Like sister GM divisions, Oldsmobile held on to pillarless four-doors through '76, then dropped them. The '76 Delta 88s sported a new face with rectangular quad headlamps.

▲ Bowing for mid '75, the Oldsmobile Starfire was a clone of Chevy's Monza, but it ran with a Buick V-6 and offered no V-8. A $391 GT added stripes and improved handling.

1976 Calendar-Year Car Sales

1.	Chevrolet	2,103,862	6.	Plymouth	519,962	11.	Chrysler	222,153
2.	Ford	1,861,537	7.	Mercury	480,361	12.	Lincoln	124,756
3.	Oldsmobile	891,368	8.	Dodge	430,641	13.	Excalibur	184
4.	Pontiac	746,430	9.	Cadillac	309,139	14.	Avanti II	156
5.	Buick	737,466	10.	AMC	283,577			

Some figures are estimated

▲ Plymouth got a version of Dodge's new 1976 Aspen compact, which it sold with minor styling tweaks as the Volaré. The Road name moved from Plymouth's Fury line this year, becoming a Volaré option package. Here, a trio of SE models.

▲ Adopting rectangular headlamps was the '76 Pontiac Grand Prix, which inexplicably tripled sales to 228,091. Included were 4807 of these "Golden Anniversary" models.

▲ One of Detroit's few genuine performance cars in 1976, Pontiac's Firebird Trans Am was up to $4987 without extras but enjoyed a sales surge to 46,701. This one wears the "screaming chicken" hood decal, a popular T/A option.

◄ Bonneville resumed its flagship role by ousting Grand Ville as Pontiac's top 1976 full-size line. This is the base $5246 coupe, shown with vinyl roof and Rally wheels.

▲ AMC Gremlins for 1977 got an eggcrate grille and a four-cylinder base engine: an Audi-designed, 80-horse 2.0-liter built in Indiana. It was ordered in 20 percent of Gremlins.

▲ AMC's not-so-subcompact Pacer broadened its appeal for '77 with three-door wagon models. This upper-level D/L wears optional woody-look trim. Wagon base price: $3799.

◀ GM rocked the industry for 1977 with smaller, lighter full-size cars that were no less roomy inside than the gas guzzlers of 1971-76. Buick offered the "downsized" coupes and sedans under its LeSabre and Electra banners. Engines shrank to match the cars, with a standard 350-inch V-8 and a new 403 at extra cost. This Limited was one of four Electras in the $6700-$7200 range. The public responded and big-Buick sales picked up, Electras to 161,627.

▲ Doing fair business for Buick since 1975 was the hatchback Skyhawk coupe, yet another version of Chevy's Monza, but with Buick's 231-cid V-6 power. The '77 wore a new cross-hatch front in a quest for greater Buick identity.

▲ Buick brought back its Regal with a new grille for 1977. The four-door sedan, which came standard with a V-8, was again outsold ten-to-one by the coupe, which had a 231-inch V-6 standard and an available 350-inch V-8 optional.

1977

- Domestic model-year output tops 9.1 million cars; imported-car sales reach the two-million mark for the first time

- Chevrolet builds 2,543,153 cars for the model year, easily topping Ford's 1,840,427; Olds again is third, then Pontiac, Buick, and Plymouth

- American workers' real earnings start to decline after 1976, breaking a long streak of nearly constant rise

- GM's first downsizing wave hits the full-size cars, which lose up to 900 pounds and a foot in length—but are just as spacious as before

- Caught off guard, Ford and Chrysler are forced to cling to their large cars for the time being, sales suffer as a result

- Ford Thunderbird shares its platform with the hastily launched LTD II; it's lighter, cheaper, and a better seller than the full-size LTD

▲ Billed as "The Next Generation of the Luxury Car," the 1977 C-body Cadillacs shared a new downsized platform with Buick and Olds. The $10,020 de Ville sedan (*shown*) and $9810 coupe enjoyed a sales surge to 234,171 units.

▲ Still huge, Cadillac's '76 Eldorado coupe strutted a new "Custom Biarritz" option with padded vinyl half-roof, "frenched" rear-quarter windows, "coach lamps," and other geegaws. A 425-cid V-8 replaced the 500-cid unit.

◄ Full-size '77 Chevrolets looked clean and trim on their new downsized B-body platform. Models were pared to Impala and Caprice Classic coupes, sedans, and wagons. This Caprice Classic four-door cost $5237 with the 250-cid six, $5357 with the 305-cid V-8.

▲ Chevy Impalas like this one were cheaper than Caprices, but coupes of both series for 1977 gained an exclusive wrapped rear window. Coupe prices started at $4876; total build hit 130,365.

▲ After a two-and-a-half-year furlough, Chevy recalled the Camaro Z28 as a mid-1977 package. A 350-cid V-8 and colorful graphics were included in the $5170 price. Sales were strong: 14,349.

▲ Chevy's 1977 Corvette sported new black A-posts and front side lights. Price rose to $8648, but sales set a record for the second straight year: 49,213 units. Top mill was again a 210-bhp V-8.

• The Ford Elite is gone, effectively replaced by the new less-expensive Thunderbird

• President Carter names Joan Claybrook, friend of Ralph Nader, to head the National Highway Traffic Safety Administration

• Chevrolet adds the compact Concours as an upmarket Nova; prices start at $3991

• Chrysler issues the "midsize" LeBaron and Dodge Diplomat, which are based on the "compact" Aspen/Volaré

• Lincoln launches the $11,500 Versailles, but to many eyes it's a thinly disguised, well-trimmed $5000 Ford Granada sedan

• This year's new cars average 18.6 miles per gallon, 34 percent better than in 1974

• AMC adds a Pacer wagon, but total output nosedives from 117,244 in 1976 to 58,264

• The U.S. Department of Transportation orders airbag installation for new cars, to be phased in starting with the 1982 models

• A new 403-cid V-8 rated at 185 horsepower is optional in big Buicks

▲ Midsize Chevys lost their 400-cid V-8 option for '77; a 170-bhp 350 was now the top choice. This was the last of the '73 "Colonnade" generation.

▲ Chevy's Monte Carlo was in the last year of its current design in 1977. Here, the top-line $5298 Landau. Lesser S models started at $4968.

▲ T-tops were newly optional for Dodge's '77 Charger. The SE was again the only model, but the Daytona trim option returned. At $5098 base, Charger sales slid to 42,542.

◄ Chrysler's $5368 Cordoba received subtle design changes for '77, when a manual sunroof and glass T-tops appeared as options. Demand climbed by about 55,000, to 183,146 units.

▲ Dodge's midsize line dropped the Coronet name for 1977 to become the "downsized" Monaco, while the former full-size Monaco was now "Royal Monaco." This top-line Brougham four-door sold for $4217, and 17,224 were sold.

▲ Dodge tried to recapture some of the aura of the muscle-car age with a new "Super Pak" option for '77 Aspens with the R/T package. Included were a rear spoiler, louvered side windows, heavy-duty suspension, and a performance axle.

- Gremlin gets an 80-horsepower, four-cylinder Volkswagen engine option and restyled front and rear fascias

- A more efficient 425-cid V-8 (180 or 195 horsepower) arrives for most Cadillacs; sales rise again, to 358,488 units

- After peaking at 456,085 units for 1974, Chevy Vega's poor reputation catches up, cutting demand to just 78,402 for '77

- The revived midyear Camaro Z28 is welcomed, but it's less potent than early '70s predecessors; even so, 14,349 are sold

- Dodge renames its midsize models Monaco; prior Monaco full-size models newly dubbed Royal Monacos

- Lincoln debuts the Continental Mark V, which weighs 400 pounds less than the Mark IV; output jumps to 80,321 units

- Pontiac wheels out the compact Phoenix, a restyled update of the Ventura that has lingered since 1971; prices start at $4075

- Pontiac's new "Iron Duke" four-cylinder engine appears in Astre, Phoenix, Sunbird, Ventura, and soon other GM models

- Pontiac debuts Cam Am: a Cameo White Le Mans Sport Coupe with a 403-cid V-8, Rally handling package, and special trim

▲ Hidden-headlamps marked Ford's full-size '77 Landau, a luxury version of the LTD. At $5717, this coupe commanded a cool $614 premium over the base LTD.

▲ Ford "downsized" the LTD by morphing its midsize T-Bird/Torino into the 1977 LTD II. Buyers grabbed 233,324 of the "new" cars. Sedans, wagons, and coupes were offered.

▲ In another '77 "name game," Ford's Thunderbird was downsized onto the Torino platform. Prices started at $5063 (down $2727!) and ran to $7990 for this new Town Landau coupe. Sales exploded to 318,140.

▲ For 1977, Ford Mustang II's Cobra II option offered new red/white and black/gold color schemes as well as blue/white. A $607 Sports Performance Package included a 139-bhp 302 V-8, four-speed, and heavy-duty chassis.

▲ Lincoln's new 1977 Versailles was a hasty Ford Granada-derived reply to Cadillac's popular 1975-76 Seville "compact" sedan. Dressed to the nines, the four-door found only 15,434 buyers. Prices started at $11,500.

◄ Like Ford with its LTD II, Mercury switched all midsizers to a more popular name for '77: Cougar. But the ploy was less successful—though total line sales were a strong 194,823, the topline XR-7 two-door hardtop alone accounted for 124,799. This $5230 Brougham four-door saw only 16,946 copies built.

▲ Like sister GM divisions, Olds downsized its 1977 big cars on a new B-body platform, and saw sales rise. Of the Delta 88s, this $5433 Royale Town Sedan sold best: 117,571 units.

▲ The front-wheel-drive Olds Toronado scored higher 1977 sales of 34,085, with the vast majority accounted for by this $8134 Brougham coupe.

▲ An electric "Astroroof" and radical wrapped rear glass distinguished the new '77 Toronado XS. A lofty $11,132 price kept sales to just 2714 units.

▲ Oldsmobile's midsize Cutlass had become one of America's best-selling lines by 1977. By itself, this handsome $4670 Supreme coupe garnered 242,874 sales, the posher $4949 Supreme Brougham another 124,712.

▲ Ordering a 1977 Volaré coupe with the Road Runner option and new "Super Pak" option got you what Plymouth called a "Front Runner." A Dodge Aspen could be similarly equipped. The top power option was a 175-horse 360-cid V-8.

1977 Calendar-Year Car Sales

1.	Chevrolet	2,543,153	6.	Plymouth	546,132	11. Lincoln	191,355
2.	Ford	1,840,427	7.	Dodge	526,254	12. AMC	182,005
3.	Oldsmobile	1,135,803	8.	Mercury	521,909	13. Excalibur	237
4.	Pontiac	850,620	9.	Chrysler	399,297	14. Avanti II	146
5.	Buick	845,234	10.	Cadillac	358,488		

Some figures are estimated

▲ After a bevy of name changes, midsize Pontiacs by 1977 had settled into standard Le Mans and Grand Le Mans models. Grands wore rear fender skirts, as on this $4614 coupe.

▲ Faintly recalling GTO days was Pontiac's new '77 GT option for Le Mans Sport Coupes. It included special paint, "radial-tuned suspension," Rally II wheels, and full gauges.

▲ Esprit had been the "luxury" Firebird since 1970, and remained so for '77, when Pontiac's ponycars took on a handsome new "droop-snoot" nose. Both the $4551 Esprit (*shown*) and the $4270 base Firebird got a new standard engine, too: a 231-cid Buick V-6 rated at 105 bhp.

▲ Full-size '77 Pontiacs shared a platform with big Chevys, yet kept a distinct identity. They were up to 800 pounds lighter than '76 models. Here a top-line $5992 Bonneville Brougham.

▲ Pontiac's '77 Astre moved away from the Chevy Vega's troublesome engine with the new 87-bhp, 2.5-liter "Iron Duke" four. Here, the $3741 Safari wagon.

► With a formal-look facelift, AMC turned its compact Hornet into 1978's Concord line. This D/L four-door was one of 115,513 sold, up 33 percent from '77 Hornet sales.

◄ AMC offered a swank new Barcelona luxury option for '77 Matador coupes, and repeated it for '78 as Barcelona II. Though exact production is unknown, it was well under 1000 units. For Matador's last season, power steering and front-disc brakes were made standard. Base prices ranged from $4799 to $5299.

▲ A formal "Landau" roof and five-spoke road wheels dressed up this '78 Buick Skylark Custom coupe, which stickered at $4367.

▲ Now riding on GM's A- and A-Special platforms, Buick's midsize Century and Regal sported trim new profiles but stagnant sales.

▲ The sportiest Buick Century for 1978 was the hot "Aeroback" Turbo Coupe. A turbocharged, 165-horse V-6 was included in the $5051 base price.

1978

- Industry output eases slightly to just below nine million cars

- Domestic-car sales defy pessimists: 1978 ranks as the third-best year ever

- The Chevrolet Impala/Caprice is the year's top seller: 612,397 units, proof positive that Americans still want big cars

- Subcompacts account for 10.6 percent of domestic sales; compacts, nearly 28 percent

- GM's midsize cars are downsized, but new "Aeroback" models fail to induce buyers

- The compact Ford Fairmont and Mercury Zephyr debut; their "Fox" platform will serve as the basis for many future Fords

▲ After being downsized to share 1977's new Electra platform, Buick's personal-luxury Riviera saw little change for '78, but sales declined from 26,138 to 20,535. A base price increase of $1839, to $9224, didn't help matters.

▲ Buick's full-size Estate Wagons lost their eight-passenger model for '78, leaving this six-seater at $6934. Sales stayed about the same at 25,000-plus.

▲ Standard Cadillacs saw little change after 1977's overhaul. This top-line Fleetwood Brougham sedan (with the d' Elegance package) listed for $12,223.

▲ A big hit since its mid-'75 debut, Cadillac's compact '78 Seville offered a new 120-bhp, 350-cid diesel V-8 for the economy-minded luxury-car buyer.

▲ Though still wearing its familiar florid curves, Chevy's Monte Carlo was all-new for 1978. Downsized to GM's new A-body, it lost 700 pounds. Despite a wider $4785-$5828 price span, sales fell about 53,000 units, to 358,191.

▲ Chevelle was gone entirely from Chevrolet's all-new line of '78 Malibus, which, like that year's Monte Carlo, were built on GM's new A-body platform. The top-line coupe was this Classic Landau, which cost $4684 with a 3.3-liter V-6.

- Chrysler launches the first domestically built front-drive subcompacts, the Dodge Omni and Plymouth Horizon; early models come with an enlarged Volkswagen engine

- Models dropped for 1978 include AMC's Hornet, Ford Maverick, Mercury Comet, Chevrolet Vega, Pontiac Astre, Dodge Royal Monaco, Plymouth Gran Fury

- Lee Iacocca is fired from the Ford presidency by chairman Henry Ford II, then hired to head Chrysler, as that company races toward bankruptcy

- After the debut of a four-door hatchback model, Chevette becomes the best-selling U.S. subcompact: 298,973 units, more than half of them four-doors

- Chevy builds 2,375,436 cars for the model year, ahead of Ford's 1,923,655; Oldsmobile's 1,015,805 places it in third, and over one million for the second straight year

- Volkswagen begins production of the Rabbit in Westmoreland, Pennsylvania, making it the first foreign maker since the Thirties to build cars in the U.S.

▲ Having evolved from 1964 as a Chevelle offshoot, Chevy's El Camino car/pickup was downsized for '78 on that year's new Malibu design. Price: $4843.

▲ With Monza sales starting to flag, Chevy grafted a rakish nose onto the Towne Coupe to create this new 1978 Sports notchback. Price: $4100.

◄ Corvette turned 25 in 1978 and celebrated by pacing that year's Indy 500. Chevy built 6502 pace car replicas like this, priced at $13,653.

▲ Chrysler Cordoba for '78 offered a 360-cid V-8 as standard and an "economy" 318 as a credit option. Base price: $5611.

▲ Topping Chrysler's 1978 lineup was this $7702 New Yorker Brougham coupe and a companion $7831 hardtop sedan. Both still looked much like the '75 Imperials they replaced, but sales fell 41 percent from '77, to 44,559 units.

- Manufacturers voluntarily observe President Carter's price guidelines for new cars, hoping to ease inflation

- An average new car sells for $6470; the average American household earns $15,064 in annual income

- The Corporate Average Fuel Economy (CAFE) standard takes effect, starting at 18 mpg; it it will rise to 19 mpg in 1979

- Because of their propensity to catch fire in rear-end collisions, 1971-76 Ford Pintos are finally recalled for modification

- Firestone recalls 7.5 million 500-series steel-belted radials—the largest tire recall in the company's history

- Moving out: It is the final season for the AMC Gremlin and Matador, Dodge Monaco, Plymouth Fury

- Cadillac introduces "Tripmaster," a travel computer that reports elapsed time, estimated time of arrival, and fuel economy

- *Automotive News* magazine estimates that federal requirements have added $519.65 to the price of a car between 1968 and '78

- AMC's Hornet is facelifted, becoming the Concord in the process; output increases 64 percent to 117,513 units

▲ This aggressive-looking Dodge Aspen was the new-for-'78 "Super Coupe," a built-from-the-options-list street-racer package. A 360-cid V-8 was available.

► A vital new car for Chrysler Corporation was the front-drive 1978 Dodge Omni and its Plymouth Horizon twin. A small five-door hatch sedan of the Volkswagen Rabbit school, these "L-body" models even used a VW-designed 1.7-liter four-cylinder engine. Priced from $3976, Omni enjoyed fairly strong sales of 81,611. Horizon sold slightly better.

◄ An aggressive slat grille and head-lamps with flip-up glass covers marked Dodge's new 1978 Magnum XE coupe, a sportier $5509 version of that year's $5368 Charger. Bucket seats, automatic transmission, and a "lean burn" 318-cid V-8 were standard. A handling/appearance package and a T-bar roof were optional.

• Ford is still sticking to its big cars, but not for long—this is the final outing for this generation of the massive LTD

• An aggressive-looking Mustang II "King Cobra" option includes the 302-cid V-8

• A Diamond Jubilee Thunderbird marks Ford's 75th anniversary; 18,994 are built

• A fastback Pontiac Sunbird is added, along with a wagon; Le Mans is downsized to GM's new midsize A-Body platform

• A diesel V-8 and Buick's 231-cid V-6 are now available in big Oldsmobiles

• Pontiac's Ventura is gone, replaced by the very-similar Phoenix

▼ Thunderbird sales climbed 11 percent for '78, to 352,751. This $8420 Town Landau took a back seat to a $10,105 Diamond Jubilee model marking Ford Motor Company's 75th Anniversary.

▲ Replacing Maverick, the new 1978 Fairmont was the first in what would be a long line of Fords based on its sensible, compact rear-drive "Fox" platform. Sedans, a coupe, and this five-door wagon were offered. Prices started at $3624.

▲ Sending Ford's Mustang II out with a bang was 1978's overwrought new "King Cobra," a $1250 hatchback option with spoilers, wheel "spats," a big snake hood decal, a 302-inch V-8, and sport-tuned suspension.

▲ Ford's Granada got square headlamps for '78, and a sporty but subdued new ESS (European Sport Sedan) trim option, as shown on this four-door. Total Granada sales: 249,876.

▲ Newly exposed rear wheels and a freshened instrument panel spruced up 1978 Lincoln Continentals. Sales were a bit off from 1977, but still healthy at more than 88,000.

1978 Calendar-Year Car Sales

1. Chevrolet	2,375,436	6. Mercury	635,051	11. Lincoln	169,620
2. Ford	1,923,655	7. Plymouth	501,129	12. AMC	137,860
3. Oldsmobile	1,015,805	8. Dodge	467,720	13. Excalibur	263
4. Pontiac	900,380	9. Chrysler	354,029	14. Avanti II	165
5. Buick	803,187	10. Cadillac	349,684		

Some figures are estimated

▲ Lincoln's 1978 Mark V honored Ford's 75th birthday with this loaded $19,000 Diamond Jubilee special; 5159 were built.

▲ Lincoln's Versailles was little-changed for '78. Like Cadillac's Seville, its base price was higher than that of larger models: that year a princely $12,529.

▲ Mercury's big Marquis looked dated compared to trimmer new models like the Fairmont-based Zephyr. This Grand Marquis hardtop coupe listed for $7721 plus options.

▲ Zephyr breezed in to oust Comet as Mercury's 1978 compact. Though a close cousin to Ford's new Fairmont, it scored far-lower, but still healthy, sales of 152,172 units.

▲ The '78 Olds Toronado would be the last of the oversize, overweight '71 design. Change was needed desperately— sales were falling, now just a tepid 24,715 units.

▲ The '78 Plymouth Horizon offered economy-import virtues in an attractive domestic package. Sales were encouraging: 106,772 units.

▲ Like Dodge with Aspen, Plymouth issued a multitoned "Super Coupe" option on its '78 Volaré (*left*) for extroverted street racers. The Road Runner package was still around as a cousin to the Aspen R/T.

▼ Like their GM siblings, midsize Pontiacs were all-new, downsized cars for 1978. Back after a two-year hiatus was the sporty Grand Am as a $5634 sedan and this $5520 coupe.

▲ Revised taillamp bezels were the only alteration to Pontiac's full-size Catalinas and Bonnevilles for 1978. This Bonneville Brougham listed for $6784.

▲ Switching to GM's smaller new-generation A-body platform made Pontiac's 1978 Grand Prix the trimmest and lightest ever. Base, sporty SJ, and luxury LJ (*shown*) models all returned with better mileage, improved handling, and similar performance, despite smaller engines. Sales only held at their 1977 level—though that still meant a healthy 228,444 units.

▲ Again straining to look fresh, AMC's ex-Hornet Concord offered lush new Limited models for '79, including this opera-windowed two-door. Matador was dropped, and Concord saw 96,487 sales, up about 18,500 over Hornet.

▲ AMC's pudgy Pacer added Limited models for 1979. A 304-cubic-inch V-8 returned from 1978 with 125 horses as the top power option. This Limited hatchback listed for $6039. Combined Pacer sales plummeted to just 10,215.

▲ Officially discontinued for 1979, the AMC Gremlin lived on in spirit—as the Spirit, a restyled continuation offering this familiar chopped-tail two-door and a new hatch coupe.

▲ The once-proud AMX name was hauled out for this 1979 "performance" version of AMC's new Spirit hatchback coupe. Priced at $6090, it attracted just 3657 buyers.

◄ Buick's little Skyhawk hatchback was a bit more interesting with 1979's new Road Hawk option. Alas, the most power available was still a standard 115-horse 231-cubic-inch V-6 engine. Overall Skyhawk sales fell to 23,139.

1979

- The second energy crisis begins in the spring, abetted by a severe economic downturn

- Auto sales start off strong, but suffer from the oil scare and rapidly rising prices

- Calendar-year industry output drops 8.8 percent, though model-year build actually rises

- Unleaded gasoline sells for an average 90 cents per gallon—up from 67 cents in 1978

- The popularity of big-ticket power accessories begins to decline as car prices rise

- Chevrolet builds 2,284,749 cars, Ford stays in second place with 1,835,937

- Oldsmobile is third in the sales race, followed by Pontiac, Buick, Mercury, Dodge, Cadillac

- Imports sell 2,327,932 cars for a record 21.7 percent market share

▲ Full-size Buicks moved into 1979 with little change. The top-line Electra 225 returned in base, Limited, and new Park Avenue trim. This Park Avenue coupe sold for $9784.

▲ The first front-wheel-drive Buick Riviera bowed for 1979 on GM's downsized E-body platform. The base model listed at $10,684. A sporty T-type with a turbo V-6 sold for $10,960.

▲ Cadillac's Eldorado was also redesigned on 1979's new GM E-body. Engines comprised gas and diesel V-8s. Sales increased a full 44 percent, to 67,436. Base price was $14,668.

▲ Cadillac's compact Seville sedan was virtually unchanged for '79, the last year for its clean, original 1975 design. Sales remained healthy at 53,487. Base price was again $14,710.

▲ Berlinetta replaced the 1973-vintage Type LT as Chevy's "luxury" Camaro for '79. It listed for $5906 with the standard 250-cid inline six and was easily spotted via a bright-finish grille and other exclusive trimmings.

▲ Despite few changes, the base price of Chevrolet's Corvette climbed to $12,313 for '79. Styling was little-altered from that of 1978's "glassback" makeover. Still, sales were the best ever for a single Corvette year: 53,807.

- New models include the AMC Spirit, Dodge St. Regis, downsized Chrysler Newport/New Yorker, all-new Ford Mustang and related Mercury Capri

- The Buick Riviera, Cadillac Eldorado, and Oldsmobile Toronado are downsized, all with front-wheel drive; a turbocharged V-6 is standard in the sporty Riviera S-Type

- The latest cars emit 90 percent fewer emissions than at the beginning of the '70s, and deliver 35 percent better fuel mileage

- Chrysler's financial woes worsen as sales fall 17.8 percent; Lee Iacocca is elected chairman amid the turmoil

- Henry Ford II resigns as Ford chief in August 1979, but continues as chairman

- Beleaguered AMC announces an agreement with Renault: AMC dealers will sell two Renault models in the U.S., starting with the subcompact Renault 5 "Le Car"

- Renault buys 22.5 percent of AMC in October—the deal includes an agreement to build Renault-designed cars at AMC's Kenosha, Wisconsin, facility

◀ Even in standard form, the resigned 1979 New Yorker started at a steep $10,872. Though still huge, weight dropped from 4400 pounds for the previous generation to just to 3500. Power came from the buyer's choice of two 318-cubic-inch V-8s.

▲ Chrysler Corporation was fighting for survival by 1979, so most of its cars saw only evolutionary changes. That included the Chrysler Cordoba, shown here in lower-priced $5611 "S" trim. Cordoba sales dropped almost 60,000, to 124,825.

▲ A late-Seventies bright spot for Chrysler was the LeBaron, a new 1977 midsize line based on the Aspen/Volaré compacts. Town & Country "woodie" wagons joined the debut coupe and sedan for '78.

◀ For '79, Dodge dumped the Monaco line and unveiled the St. Regis. A close cousin of Chrysler's R-body Newport/New Yorker, it came with a 110-bhp, 225-cid Slant Six. A 150-bhp 360-inch V-8 was optional. St. Regis wore glass-covered headlamps and sold for only $6532. It didn't sell well, attracting only 34,972 customers.

- Turbochargers are installed on just under one percent of all domestic cars

- Only 58 percent of the '79 cars have a V-8 engine (down from 65.8 percent in 1978); fours account for 17.6 percent

- Ford finally downsizes its biggies: The LTD/Marquis weighs nearly 700 pounds less

- AMC's Gremlin gets a major facelift and a new name: Spirit

- Chevrolet's three-point automatic lap/shoulder belt marks the first such installation in a General Motors car

- The Cadillac Eldorado shrinks 20 inches, gets an independent rear suspension

- A 360-cubic-inch V-8 is now the biggest engine offered in a Chrysler-built car

- Omni/Horizon-based Dodge 024 and Plymouth TC3 fastback coupes debut; both are sporty hatchbacks

- The Dodge Charger is dropped, but the Magnum XE coupe hangs on

▲ Diplomat took over for Monaco as the mainstream midsize Dodge for 1977, and also added wagons for '78.

◀ The 1979 Omni 024 was a new hatch coupe version of Dodge's L-body front-wheel-drive subcompact. Wheelbase was 2.5 inches shorter than the boxy five-door, which helped handling.

▲ The all-new '79 Mustang was arguably the best Ford ponycar since the original '65 generation. Coupe (*shown*) and hatchback models were offered. Sales hit 369,936 units.

▲ Mustang came with four-cylinder, inline six, V-6, and V-8 engines. A Cobra model offered the best balance with its 140-horsepower, 2.3-liter turbocharged four.

▲ Production of Ford's Pinto remained strong at 199,018 units in '79 despite headlines regarding exploding gas tanks. This hatch sedan wears the new-for-1978 $370 Rallye trim group.

▲ A T-bar roof was a new extra for 1979 Ford Thunderbirds like this $8866 Town Landau. A new Heritage model, outfitted much like the '78 Diamond Jubilee, cost $10,687. Total T-Bird sales eased to 284,141.

- Excalibur moves to Chevy's 350-cid V-8, (the 454-inch V-8 is gone) and even at $28,600 per copy, 27 roadsters and 340 phaetons are sold—a company record

- The fifth-generation Ford Mustang is 200 pounds lighter; a turbocharged four is optional, and during the year an inline six replaces the German-built V-6 option

- General Motors's all-new front-drive X-body cars—Chevrolet Citation, Pontiac Phoenix, Olds Omega, and Buick Skylark—debut in April as '80 models

- The new Mustang sells well (369,936 units for '79), persevering with only one serious facelift through 1993; Mercury's similar Capri lasts only through 1986

▲ After pitching "road-hugging weight" to mileage-minded buyers, Ford finally followed GM with smaller big cars for 1979. The new LTDs comprised two- and four-door base, Landau (*shown*), and standard and Country Squire wagons (*background*). Sales improved modestly to 356,535 units.

▲ The '79 Mark V had a base price of $13,067. Designer packages like this Cartier ensemble added several hundred dollars to the sticker price. Sales perked up to 75,939 on word that 1979 would be the last year for a "big Mark."

▲ For 1979, Mercury opted for a version of Ford's redesigned Mustang to wear the Capri badge. It rejected Mustang's notchback coupe, but did offer base and luxury Ghia hatchbacks at $4872-$5237. A sporty RS package (*shown*) could be ordered with a turbo four, as on the Mustang Cobra.

1979 Calendar-Year Car Sales

1. Chevrolet	2,284,749	6. Mercury	669,138	11. Lincoln	189,546
2. Ford	1,835,937	7. Dodge	404,266	12. AMC	169,439
3. Oldsmobile	1,068,154	8. Cadillac	383,138	13. Excalibur	367
4. Pontiac	907,434	9. Plymouth	372,449	14. Avanti II	142
5. Buick	727,275	10. Chrysler	349,450		

Some figures are estimated

▲ Like Ford's '79 LTD, Mercury's full-size Marquis was fully redesigned to become smaller, lighter, thriftier, and more agile. With 32,349 produced, the line's best-seller was this $7909 Grand Marquis sedan, but total series sales dropped some 4800 units from '78, to 145,627.

▲ Mercury had the Zephyr Z-7, a compact coupe with a distinctive "basket-handle" roofline as seen on recent T-Birds. Z-7 and Zephyr as a whole always trailed Fairmont in sales by a wide margin, even though prices were quite close: for '79, $4504 for Z-7 versus Futura's $4463.

▲ The Oldsmobile Toronado shed inches and pounds to become a more balanced personal-luxury coupe. The reward for Olds was sales that almost doubled from 1978 to just over 50,000.

▼ The Olds 4-4-2 sputtered on after '72 with far more "show" than "go." Still around in 1979, it offered uprated suspension tuning and muscle-car looks. Unfortunately, the 1978-79 option was limited to the unloved "Aeroback" two-door body style.

◀ Horizon TC3 was Plymouth's version of the new-for-'79 Dodge Omni 024 coupe. Note, though, the slatted versus checked grille. Base price was identical at $4864.

▲ Midsize Pontiacs were little-changed for 1979. Here, the Grand Am coupe, which, with its sedan stablemate, accounted for just four percent of total Le Mans sales.

▲ Pontiac's Firebird got yet another "facial" for '79. This is the racy Formula model, which had a base price of $6564 and could be ordered with a 220-bhp, 400-cid V-8.

◀ Trim, color, and equipment shuffles were the only changes of note for full-size '79 Pontiacs, like this top-of-the-line $7584 Bonneville Brougham four-door sedan. As before, Bonnevilles used a 301-cid Pontiac V-8, while the lower-priced Catalinas had a 231-cid Buick V-6. Bonneville sold better than ever for '79: 179,416 units.

521

CHAPTER THIRTEEN

1980-1990
FACING THE
COMPETITION

Detroit entered the Eighties as a symbol of America's evident decline in an increasingly global economy. The industry had enjoyed three strong years, selling more than 11 million passenger cars in '77 and '78, and another 10.5 million in '79. But when a second energy crisis triggered a sharp new recession, sales dropped below nine million in 1980 for record combined losses of $4.2 billion. And sales got worse: down to 8.5 million in '81, a worrisome 7.9 million in 1982.

Was Detroit suddenly falling apart? In 1980, it sure seemed so. Everyone saw Chrysler again speeding toward ruin, but so was American Motors, and Ford's cash crisis was no less acute, though much less publicized. GM went about business as usual despite suffering its first loss since 1921. All four companies were hampered by too many plants with too much overhead and too little "quality." Worse, Japanese automakers—led by Toyota, Honda, and Datsun—had come from nowhere to claim more than 20 percent of the U.S. market, and their share was growing.

Determined to not let "Japan, Inc." overrun yet another bastion of American industry, Detroit got busy. Chrysler won needed loan guarantees from Congress, then repaid the loans early with earnings from K-car compacts and a host of derivatives, including one that proved immensely popular: the minivan. Ford, too, closed unnecessary plants, won wage concessions from workers, slashed overhead elsewhere, and streamlined management, while making the smooth "aero look" its design signature. General Motors mainly threw money at its problems, banking on costly new automated equipment to improve vehicle quality and plant efficiency. The results were sometimes laughable, but GM did have two better ideas: a new independent subsidiary called Saturn, charged with making a competitive American small car that could also make a profit, and a bold joint-production venture with Toyota.

There was plenty of precedent for "fraternizing with the enemy." The Seventies had seen Chrysler buy into Mitsubishi, Ford into Mazda, GM into Isuzu. Though the Big Three learned from their Japanese partners even as they sold some of their cars under domestic labels, the "playing field" still wasn't "level"—or so they told the Reagan Administration, which jawboned Japan into limiting car exports to the U.S. Amid a growing U.S.-Japan trade imbalance and charges that they were "dumping" vehicles at subsidized low prices, the Japanese developed a legitimate fear of protectionist legislation. But they got around the Voluntary Restraint Agreement by setting up "transplant" factories in America.

Of course, Detroit did bounce back, thanks to the kind hand of fate. By 1983, a gasoline shortage had become a gasoline glut, the economy was rebounding, people were buying again, and the Big Three were eyeing record profits. Three years later, auto sales were back above 11 million, and Detroit was back to excitement; a new-generation Camaro/Firebird, increasingly hot Mustangs, truly sporting Thunderbirds, the first new Corvette in 15 years, even specialty two-seaters called Fiero, Reatta, Allanté . . . and Chrysler's TC by Maserati. Sadly, American Motors died with the 1987 pullout of erstwhile savior Renault, but it passed to Chrysler, then on an unwise buying binge.

Ford emerged as Detroit's big Eighties winner, with strong sellers like Taurus and the most cost-effective manufacturing operation around. Significantly, Ford became America's most profitable automaker in 1986, outearning giant GM for the first time in 42 years. That remarkable achievement only underscored how GM had delayed making the kind of wrenching, fundamental changes demanded by the new world automotive order.

1980

- The recession deepens; domestic car sales suffer more than imports in an overall bad year for the industry

- Of 8,975,209 cars sold in the U.S., nearly 27 percent are imports

- Japanese automakers agree to voluntary import restraints; "Buy American" sentiment on the rise

- All four major domestic automakers finish the year in the red; GM suffers its first yearly loss since 1921: $763 million

- Chairman Lee Iacocca secures federal loan guarantees for endangered Chrysler Corporation

- The CAFE requirement rises to 20 mpg; automakers cut weights, adopt smaller engines, improve aerodynamics, push diesels

▲ General Motors's landmark X-body family of cars appeared in mid 1979 as 1980 models. The newly downsized compacts switched from rear drive to front-wheel drive. They also used transversely mounted inline four-cylinder and V-6 engines. Buick's 1980 Skylark offered two- and four-door notchbacks in base and luxury Limited trim. This Sport Coupe boasted black exterior trim and a handling suspension. Skylark base prices ranged from $5342 to $6102 with the standard four-cylinder.

▲ Big 1980 Buicks emphasized economy with an "aero" nose and minor weight losses. Electras like this $10,537 Park Avenue coupe also boasted a thriftier new 4.1-liter V-6 as standard.

▲ Cadillac's '80 Eldorado got detail styling tweaks and a new 6.0-liter V-8 with electronic fuel injection. A diesel V-8 remained optional. Base price rose to $16,141, and 52,685 were sold.

▲ Controversial "bustleback" styling marked the '80 Cadillac Seville, which moved to the front-drive Eldorado chassis, but came standard with a diesel V-8. Production was 39,344.

◀ Chevy's 1980 Corvette shed 250 pounds via greater use of lightweight materials. The standard 350 V-8 was down to 170 net horses. Sales were down too, falling 13,200 units to 40,614.

- GM's compact X-car quartet debuts to much applause, until initial models suffer a long list of factory recalls

- Fewer than 30 percent of domestic new cars have V-8 engines (half the 1979 level); four-cylinder installations nearly double

- Widely available turbochargers inject extra horsepower into shrunken engines

- Automatic transmissions lose some favor as four-speed floorshifts gain popularity in smaller "economy" cars

- Buick Century and Oldsmobile Cutlass drop "Aeroback" four-door styling, turn to traditional notchback design

- Onboard engine-management computers help to combat engine emissions

- A second-generation, front-drive Seville debuts with "bustleback" tail, standard 105-horsepower diesel V-8

- Chevrolet Caprice/Impala earn a mild "aero" reskin; V-6 power is standard in full-size models and Camaro

- New-car warranties increasingly include body-corrosion coverage

◀ Replacing Nova as Chevy's compact was Citation, the bowtie version of GM's new front-drive 1980 X-body cars. Citation came as two- and four-door hatchback sedans, plus a notchback club coupe. A sporty X-11 package (shown) was offered for two-doors.

▲ Chevy's small Monza sport coupes weren't changed much for 1980, and still had a standard 151 inline four and optional 231 V-6. This is the "2+2" fastback with the $531 Spyder package.

▲ Checker Motors of Kalamazoo, Michigan, still sold "taxi-tough" sedans in 1980, but only a few hundred of them. The "blind quarter" vinyl top is a nonfactory item.

▲ Chrysler's midsize 1980 LeBarons got new "twin waterfall" grilles and other style updates. Coupes rode a 108.7-inch wheelbase. This top-line Medallion found 10,448 buyers.

▲ The 1977-79 LeBaron coupe got a major restyling to become 1980's new "downsized" Chrysler Cordoba. Base, Crown, and sporty LS models were offered in the $6800-$7500 range with the standard Slant Six engine.

▲ Like its Chrysler LeBaron sibling, the 1980 Dodge Diplomat coupe moved to a slightly shorter wheelbase, and all models adopted a slightly crisper, creased look. Base prices ranged from $6500 to $7800.

▲ Mirada replaced Magnum as the "personal coupe" in the 1980 Dodge lineup. A close cousin of that year's Chrysler Cordoba, it listed for $6600-$6900, but sold little better than Magnum at 32,746 units.

- By 1980, only Corvette and Pontiac Firebird Turbo top 190 horsepower

- The second-generation Chrysler Cordoba debuts; a 360-cid V-8 is the biggest engine available, a six is standard

- A new overdrive automatic transmission is standard in Lincolns, available in some other Ford products as well

- The last rear-drive Buick Skyhawk and Olds Starfire fastback coupes go on sale

- AMC launches the four-wheel-drive Eagle; Pontiac's 2.5-liter four-cylinder goes into Spirit and Concord models

- On-again, off-again baroque auto builder Excalibur produces its last Series III car; a 350-cid Chevrolet engine was standard

- The Ford Thunderbird is downsized; a six-cylinder engine is available for the first time

- Mirada replaces Magnum in the Dodge lineup, close mechanical kin to the Chrysler Cordoba personal-luxury coupe

- Ford produces its last Pinto, Mercury its final Bobcat; the Crown Victoria name is revived for the top-line LTD

◀ Seeking higher sales and higher mileage, Ford again downsized the Thunderbird for 1980 by making it essentially a plush, rather overstyled two-door Fairmont. Sales fell some 18,000 units to 156,803.

▲ Ford's Granada took one last bow in original '76 form for 1980. Changes were few, but sales fell way down in a tough market from 182,000 units to just over 90,000. Here, a top-line Ghia.

▲ A new 4.2-liter (255-cid) V-8 replaced the familiar 302 option in 1980 Ford Mustangs. This is the hatch coupe with a turbocharged four and optional Cobra package.

▲ Downsizing cut the 1980 Continental's wheelbase to 117.3 inches from 127.3, and its curb weight to 3900 pounds from 4650. Luxury and formal styling cues were intact, but sales plummeted to 31,233 from 92,600.

◀ Lincoln's new 1980 Mark VI was downsized along with Continentals onto the full-size "Panther" platform. For the first time, a four-door version was offered. Opera windows were again featured on base and new Signature Series models. Coupes rode a trimmer chassis than sedans, but again offered "designer" packages such as Bill Blass.

1980 Calendar-Year Car Sales

1. Chevrolet	2,288,745	6. Mercury	347,711	11. Chrysler	164,510
2. Ford	1,162,275	7. Dodge	308,638	12. Lincoln	74,908
3. Oldsmobile	910,306	8. Plymouth	290,974	13. Avanti II	168
4. Buick	854,011	9. Cadillac	230,028	14. Excalibur	93
5. Pontiac	770,100	10. AMC	199,613		

Some figures are estimated

▲ The Mercury Cougar line was pared to one $7045 XR-7 coupe for '80. It was a near-twin to the downsized Thunderbird. The wide rear-quarter roof shown here came in a new $1987 Luxury Group. Production was down to 58,028 units.

▲ The standard 4.3-liter V-8's horsepower jumped by 15, to 120, but a subtly smoother, more aerodynamic profile yielded slightly better fuel economy on 1980 full-size Oldsmobiles, like this $7076 Delta 88 Royale coupe.

▲ Compared to the '79 models it replaced, the X-body Omega was six inches shorter in wheelbase and a full 750 pounds lighter. The SX dress-up option for standard coupes and sedans included a decklid spoiler.

▲ Pontiac's compact changed names from Ventura to Phoenix for 1977, then changed designs by adopting GM's new 1980 X-body platform with front-wheel drive. Base prices ranged from $5470 to $6100.

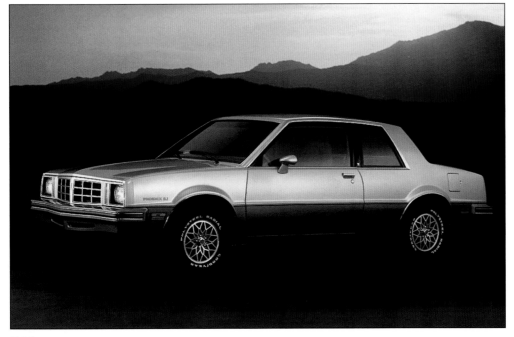

◄ For the look of performance but no extra power, the '80 Phoenix offered a sporty SJ option at $502 on notchbacks like this and $460 on hatchbacks. Pontiac's firmer Rally chassis was included. An early introduction helped push sales to 178,291 units.

◄ After a 1979 facelift, Pontiac's Firebird Trans Am paced both the Indy 500 and NASCAR races in new Turbo form, with its turbocharged 185-horsepower 301 V-8. Just 50 replicas like this one were built and later sold.

▲ Reshaped body contours and a revised engine lineup (including shelving the 350-cid gas V-8) helped improve fuel economy on 1980 full-size Pontiacs. This Bonneville Brougham sedan cost $8160; 21,249 were built.

▲ The Avanti II was still around in 1981 with its Raymond Loewy styling from Studebaker days nearly twenty years before. It switched Chevrolet engines, though, from a 190-bhp 350 V-8 to a 155-bhp 305—a sign of the times.

▲ New for 1980 and little-changed for '81, the Concord-based AMC Eagle was the country's first car with four-wheel drive. This wagon started at $8397.

▲ AMC's Spirit also offered Pontiac's 2.5-liter four as standard for 1981, and spawned four-wheel-drive Eagle Kammback and hatchback variants. Here a $5589 Spirit D/L.

1981

- Industry sales drop sharply due to continued recession and the aftermath of the energy crisis

- Production (including Volkswagen of America) totals 6,673,324 cars for the model year

- Of 8,532,672 cars sold in the U.S., 73 percent are domestically built—nearly identical to 1980

- Ford and GM offer a series of rebates to push sales; both megaliths lose market share

- Ford's board of directors ponders a merger with Chrysler, but nixes the possibility

- Ford introduces the subcompact front-drive Escort "world car"

- Chrysler adds a new Imperial to the list of cars built only in Canada

- A Buick 4.1-liter V-6 is optional in Cadillacs—its first six-cylinder engine ever

▲ Maximum power in full-size 1981 Buicks was a 150-bhp 307 gas V-8. The optional 350 diesel V-8 gave just 105. Electras, including this $11,291 Estate Wagon, also got a new standard four-speed overdrive automatic transmission.

▲ A slightly lowered nose and lifted tail cut aerodynamic drag on 1981 Buick Regals. This Sport Coupe again came with a 170-bhp, 3.8-liter turbo V-6 and automatic, though with a new lockup converter clutch. Its base price was $8528.

▲ As in 1980, the "civilian" 1981 Checker Marathon offered a choice of GM V-6, V-8, and diesel V-8 choices. Alas, Checker was failing, and total output, including taxis, was only 2950.

▲ Computerized engine control and a lockup torque-converter clutch made news for full-size 1981 Chevys like this Caprice Classic four-door sedan. Its base price was $7667 with the standard 110-horse-power V-6, or just $50 more with the 115-horse 4.4-liter V-8.

▲ Like sister General Motors models, the 1981 Chevy Monte Carlo was reshaped for less gas-wasting air drag. This uplevel Landau model stickered at $8006 with the standard 3.8-liter V-6.

◀ Chevy's sporty Citation X-11 got extra fire for '81 via a high-output 2.8-liter V-6 with 135 horses (versus 110). This publicity photo displays the unique parts in that year's model, which delivered for around $6800.

- The federally mandated CAFE requirement rises from 20 to 22 mpg

- Dodge launches its Aries K-body compact; Plymouth's Reliant differs little—both aim to help "rescue" ailing Chrysler Corporation

- Cadillac makes its new V-8-6-4 variable-displacement engine standard (optional in Seville); it lasts just one season

- Chevrolet Monte Carlo gains a handsome facelift; Chevette sales hit a new peak

- Corvette adopts a fiberglass rear leaf spring; production moves to a new Bowling Green, Kentucky, assembly plant

- Chrysler workers relinquish $622 million in salary and benefits so the company can qualify for federal loan guarantees

- Full-size GM cars gain automatic overdrive transmission

- Roger Smith becomes chairman of GM—he remains in the top spot for the duration of the Eighties

- Looking for much-needed revenue, AMC markets the French-built Renault 18i, a front-drive compact sedan and wagon

▲ Chevy's '81 Corvette offered but one 350 V-8, a new 190-bhp version (versus 230 bhp for '80) with electronic control.

▲ The second-generation Chevy Camaro would bow out after 1981 and sales of 126,139. The top-gun Z28 *(shown)* grabbed 43,272 of them at $8263 apiece. The optional 350-cid V-8 was available only with automatic transmission.

▲ Given a temporary reprieve from the chopping block, Chrysler's R-body New Yorker returned for 1981 as a $10,463 fully equipped four-door sedan. Just 6548 were sold.

▲ There was little new in Chrysler's 1981 Cordoba. A 318-cid engine replaced the 360-inch mill as top option. Sales sank by more than half to a new Cordoba low: just 20,113 units.

▲ Change was equally hard to find on 1981 Chrysler LeBarons, a situation that reflected Highland Park's low cash reserves and that year's emphasis on the all-new K-car compacts.

◀ Like 1980's Cadillac Seville, the reborn '81 Imperial wore an edgy "bustleback," allegedly inspired by Fifties British custom coachwork. The similarity with Seville was pure chance, and the Imperial's treatment was arguably better-looking—but it was still uncomfortably "me-too."

• Chrysler's biggest car is now the aging 318; New Yorker makes its last appearance in rear-drive form

• Dodge Diplomat comes only as a four-door, selling mainly to police/taxi fleets in the '80s; the last St. Regis is produced

• Ford's LTD offers its final 351-cid V-8; the new, lighter Granada is Fairmont-based

• Experimental cars include Ford's mini Shuttler, Pockar commuter car, Probe III, three-wheeled Cockpit; GM debuts Aero X

• Lincoln's traditional Town Car is selling surprisingly well—success continues through the remainder of the Eighties

• Lynx is Mercury's version of the Escort; the new Cougar is based on Ford's Granada

• John Z. DeLorean, former rising star at General Motors, markets a gullwing sports car built in North Ireland

• The Pontiac Bonneville enters its last year on General Motors's B-body large-car platform; a smaller Model G debuts in '82

• Pontiac launches the tiny Chevette-based T1000; buyers stay away

▲ The '81 Dodge Aries wagon in top Special Edition trim wore woody-look appliqué. A 2.2-liter "Trans Four" four-cylinder engine was standard.

▲ In Custom trim, the '81 Aries coupe sold for $6315. A 2.6-liter Mitsubishi four was optional for all K-cars fitted with automatic transmission.

▲ Chrysler's small 1981 L-body models, including this $6149 Dodge Omni 024, offered the K-car's Trans-4 as an option, vastly improving performance.

▲ Ford replaced Pinto for '81 with Escort, a roomier, more modern front-drive subcompact. Sales were strong, topping 320,000 for year one.

▲ Lincoln's Continental Mark VI lost its optional 351 V-8 for its sophomore '81 season. This $16,858 coupe has the Bill Blass "designer" option package.

▲ Twin to the new Ford Escort was the '81 Mercury Lynx, offered in the same body styles. Like Escort, the sole engine was a 1.6-liter four of about 70 bhp.

► Mercury's 1981 Zephyr compacts changed the name of their top trim option from Ghia to GS. This Z-7 coupe is so equipped. Base price that year was $6252. A 115-bhp, 255-cid V-8 was the top engine option.

1981 Calendar-Year Car Sales

1. Chevrolet	1,673,093	6. Plymouth	393,633	11. Lincoln	69,537
2. Ford	950,301	7. Mercury	375,756	12. Chrysler	56,726
3. Oldsmobile	873,678	8. Dodge	340,899	13. Avanti II	235[1]
4. Buick	856,996	9. Cadillac	240,189	14. Excalibur	200
5. Pontiac	489,436	10. AMC	137,125		

[1]*Estimated*

▲ The 1981 Mercury Capri offered a new Black Magic paint package with contrasting gold pinstripes. It was also available in white.

▲ The 1981 Oldsmobile Toronado switched to a 125-bhp, 4.1-liter Buick V-6 as its base power. Sales slipped nearly 1000 units from 1980 to 42,604.

▲ The 1981 was the finale for Pontiac's second-generation Firebird, as well as the Turbo Trans Am (shown). The T/A's turbo 301 V-8 was optional for the Formula. Model-year sales: 71,000.

◀ Pontiac's '81 Grand Prix slicked down a tad for better mileage, but go power had got up and gone. A 120-bhp 265 V-8 was top dog. Here, the $7803 LJ model.

▲ Chrysler was so short of cash by 1981 that its new K-cars played both Dodges and Plymouths in some publicity photos; only the badges were changed. Here a Plymouth Reliant SE.

▲ The 1981 Plymouth Reliant differed from Dodge's new Aries only in trim. Even pricing was the same—$6933 in the case of this SE four-door—though for some reason Reliant sold better.

▲ Plymouth's Gran Fury was back for 1980 as a near-duplicate of Chrysler's Newport sedan. Sold mainly for taxi and police duty, this '81 was the only Plymouth car available with a V-8.

▲ Test drivers of this '82 Avanti II found it charming but dated, with a "tack-on" approach to meeting government requirements (note the afterthought front bumperettes).

▲ Converter Griffith described its open-air Concord conversion as a "sport landau." Available through select AMC dealers, the convertible Concord found few buyers.

▲ Buick boosted midsize Century sales for '81 by replacing sloped "Aeroback" sedans with this notchback four-door. For 1982 all rear-drive midsize Buicks became Regals.

▲ And here's the reason for that '82 change: new front-wheel-drive Buick Century two- and four-door notchbacks were spawned from the X-body Skylark.

► Evoking muscle car memories was Buick's 1982 Grand National coupe, named for the Chevy-powered Regals then cleaning up on NASCAR ovals. Just 215 were built.

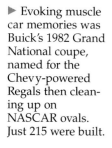

1982

- Domestic output (including Volkswagen's) sinks to 5,157,477 cars for the model year

- Of 7,978,177 cars sold in the U.S., 5,756,660 are domestically built

- Falling gasoline prices affect sales of small cars and diesel engines; high interest rates scare banks away from auto loans

- Honda builds Accord on U.S. soil, at its new Marysville, Ohio, assembly plant

- The convertible is back new droptops come from Chrysler, Dodge, and Buick

- Automakers use downsizing, powertrain shuffles, revised gearing, and wind-tunnel testing to cut weight/emissions, boost mileage

◄ Buick's Riviera was one of the few Detroit cars to gain sales in 1981, rising to 52,007. But the '82 edition dropped back to 44,071 despite technical improvements like a standard four-speed automatic.

► Cadillac's Eldorado became a touch sportier with the new 1982 Touring Coupe. It featured less chrome, a firmed-up chassis, blackwall tires on aluminum wheels, bucket seats—and no hood ornament.

▼ The shark-generation Chevrolet Corvette would bow out after 1982. Sales that year hit 25,407, including 6759 copies of this special $22,537 Collector Edition hatchback.

► A brand-new third-generation Chevrolet Camaro was one of 1982's biggest introductions. Though a bit smaller and lighter than the second-series design, it was more practical thanks to a lift-up glass hatch. Models were the familiar trio of base, luxury Berlinetta, and sport-oriented Z28 *(shown)*, with up to 165 horses available. Overall sales jumped to 182,068, including 39,744 Berlinettas and 63,563 Z28s.

• GM's J-car front-drive subcompacts debut: Buick Skyhawk, Chevrolet Cavalier, Pontiac J2000, Oldsmobile Firenza—even a Cadillac Cimarron

• Shrunken Chevrolet Camaros and Pontiac Firebirds emerge, including Z28 and Trans Am; a four-cylinder is now available

• A Collector's Edition Corvette features lift-up rear-window glass

• Wedge-shaped A-body GM compacts arrive: Chevrolet Celebrity, Buick Century, Oldsmobile Cutlass Cierra, Pontiac 6000; drivetrains are based on the X-cars

• Ford issues the Escort-based EXP sport coupe; Mercury offers the related "bubble-back" LN7—sales disappoint

• Lincoln offers nitrogen-pressurized shock absorbers—a U.S. industry "first"

• A new aluminum-block HT4100 V-8 is standard in Cadillacs (except Cimarron and limo); a European-inspired Touring Suspension is available in the Eldorado

• Renault acquires controlling interest in AMC, prepares to produce an American version of the Renault 9, the Alliance

• The new Dodge 400 is a stretched K-car; a convertible bows at midseason

▲ Chevrolet had a new Celebrity for 1982: a trimmer front-wheel-drive midsize workhorse to supplement the rear-drive Malibu. This coupe and a sedan were offered at $8313 to $8588.

▲ Supplementing the rear-drive Chevette in Chevrolet's 1982 lineup was the new front-drive Cavalier, a slightly larger subcompact offering these four body styles and four-cylinder power for as little as $6278. Cavalier was just one of the "J-cars" appearing at all five GM divisions that year.

◀ Chrysler moved its strong-selling K-car upmarket for 1982 with the Dodge 400 and Chrysler LeBaron coupe and sedan. A LeBaron ragtop bowed at midyear in base trim starting at $11,698 and as a woody-look Town & Country for $13,998. There was also a Town & Country wagon. Buyers responded well to the new LeBaron, buying over 90,000 copies.

▲ Ads proclaimed "It's time for Imperial." But this little-changed '82 got less than half the sales of the '81 model: just 2329. New this year was this Frank Sinatra Edition, complete with a set of the crooner's hits on tape.

▲ Introduced with the redesigned 1980 Chrysler Cordoba was this LS model with a "cross-hair" grille like that of legendary Letter-Series 300s of the Fifties. A "Cabriolet" roof was also included. Just 3136 of the 1982s found buyers.

- GM issues an all-new 4.3-liter diesel V-6 for midsize models; a big diesel V-8 is now available in mid- and full-size models

- GM's 2.5-liter four-cylinder engine is now fuel injected; as is the Corvette and some Camaro/Firebird engines

- Buick rises to third in production, helped by the front-drive Century and Skyhawk; midyear brings the Riviera convertible

- The last "shark" Corvettes go on sale, carrying the next-generation drivetrain; no manual transmission is available this year

- The new front-drive Chrysler LeBaron is smaller than its predecessor; the New Yorker name remains on a rear-drive model

- Midyear brings a woody-look Town & Country wagon to Chrysler, plus the first American-built convertible since 1976

- Plymouth downsizes the Gran Fury, a near cousin to the Dodge Diplomat; both sell mainly to police and taxi fleets

- DeLorean falls into receivership and is liquidated; the stainless-steel sports car failed to catch on with buyers

- Concepts include the Ford Flair and Avant Garde, plus GM's Lean Machine, TPC, and joystick-controlled Aero 2000

▲ The all-new Camaro paced the 1982 Indianapolis 500, the third such honor for Chevrolet's ponycar. Chevy built 6360 replicas, but without the checkered flags and "gumball" lights.

▲ Back for 1982 from a mid-'81 debut was Dodge's reborn Charger, a sportier Omni 024 with a standard 111-horse K-car 2.2-liter four-cylinder. Base price was $7115.

◄ Ford's subcompact Escort reshuffled models for '82 to make room for new hatchback sedans and an oddly styled coupe called EXP *(rear vehicle)*. The latter was Ford's first two-seater since the 1957 Thunderbird. Escort sales were strong—385,132 total—plus 98,256 copies of the $7387 EXP.

▲ Though little-changed for '82, the Mark VI was no longer badged Continental. The label was transferred to that year's new compact Lincoln sedan. But trim variations for the Mark continued without end. Witness this $23,594 Bill Blass coupe in new red/white livery with standard wire wheels.

▲ Ousting Versailles as a stronger challenger to Cadillac's Seville, the new '82 Lincoln Continental sedan wore its own "bustleback" on the Ford Fairmont "Fox" platform. Most every luxury amenity was included in the $21,302 sticker, but even posher Signature Series and Givenchy models were offered.

1982 Calendar-Year Car Sales

1.	Chevrolet	1,297,357	6.	Mercury	328,597	11.	Lincoln	85,313
2.	Ford	748,732	7.	Plymouth	247,936	12.	AMC	70,898
3.	Buick	739,984	8.	Dodge	241,359	13.	Excalibur	212
4.	Oldsmobile	702,340	9.	Cadillac	235,584	14.	Avanti	200[1]
5.	Pontiac	541,061	10.	Chrysler	103,310			

[1] *Estimated*

535

► Mercury hewed to tradition with its Lynx, a Ford Escort marketed with slightly better trim and higher prices. The 1982 models weren't changed much from the debut '81s, but four-door hatchback sedans like this arrived.

▼ Better equipped than the base four-door and Brougham, Grand Marquis was the costliest of Mercury's big sedans. While a police version could be had with a 351-cid V-8, the general public made do with the standard 302-inch mill.

◄ Bowing in spring 1982 to replace the Starfire, Firenza was Oldsmobile's version of GM's new J-car subcompact. It differed from Chevy's Cavalier in having a standard overhead-cam 1.8-liter four-cylinder engine.

► Oldsmobile's big cars carried over little-changed for 1982. This Regency sedan continued as one of three Ninety Eight models, all priced in the $12,000-$13,000 range. Sales held steady at a robust 90,967 units.

◀ Oldsmobile added the front-drive 1982 Cutlass Cierra to its line as its version of GM's new A-body family. Here, the $9599 Brougham four-door. It accompanied, rather than replaced, the rear-drive Cutlass, which outsold it 281,451 to 101,320.

▲ The biggest news for Plymouth's subcompact Horizon was a new top-line Custom, shown here with optional two-tone paint. The sporty TC3 two-door carried over unchanged.

▲ With aggressive looks and better handling in a trimmer package, the 1982 debut of the third-generation Pontiac Firebird Trans Am was a success. Sales rose to 52,960 units.

◀ J2000 was the "alpha-numeric" tag for Pontiac's version of the new 1982 GM J-car, offered in the same four body types as the Chevy Cavalier. The SE hatch coupe (shown) was base priced at $7654.

▲ Construction magnate Steve Blake took over Avanti in late 1982 and issued this Thirtieth Anniversary special in black, white, red, or silver.

▲ Bowing during the '82 model year, Buick's Skyhawk J-car was back for '83 with two new wagons and a sporty T-type coupe. Here a $7457 Limited.

▲ Base versions of Buick's 1983 Skylark were retitled Custom, like this two-door. As with all X-cars, recall notices were piling up.

▲ The first Buick Riviera convertible bowed in 1983 with a 125-bhp, 4.1-liter V-6 and a $25,000 base price. Painted white (*shown*) or red "Firemist," production was a scant 1750 units.

▲ A newly available four-speed automatic transmission was one of the few changes for Buick's '83 Regals. This Limited started at $9425. Regal output stayed strong at 228,239.

▲ Back for a third season, Chevy's bare-bones Chevette Scooter qualified as Detroit's least-expensive 1983 car at $5333 for this four-door hatch and just $4997 for the two-door version. Chevette sold strongly at over 169,000 units.

▲ The Chevrolet Monte Carlo SS returned in 1983 as this "droop-snoot" special with a 180-horse 305-inch V-8. Designed both for NASCAR racing and to help renew buyer interest in performance, it carried a base price of $10,474.

1983

• Excitement returns to showrooms; six different models now offer convertible versions

• Domestic model-year output totals 5,683,197 cars (including build by foreign automakers with U.S. assembly plants)

• Of the 9,181,036 cars sold in the U.S., 6,795,302 are built in North America

• Japanese automakers agree to a fourth consecutive year of import restraints

• NHTSA eases the 5-mph bumper impact standard to 2½ mph—automakers cheer, while safety advocates and insurers jeer

• Average new-car stickers reach $10,700, up from $9910 in 1982 and $6950 in '79

▲ Chrysler kept spinning out K-car variations for 1983, including this unexpected 124-inch-wheelbase Executive Sedan and a limousine with a 131-inch chassis. Styling was similar to LeBaron's, but badges simply read "Chrysler."

▲ A future "classic" ? Only 9891 Chrysler LeBaron convertibles were built for 1983, and there couldn't have been many of these woody-look Town & Countrys with the Mark Cross leather interior like this one. Base price was a stiff $15,595.

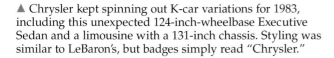

▲ A relic of "The Old Chrysler Corporation," the Cordoba was reduced to one model for its swan-song year, 1983, when changes were again minor. Sales were lower than ever at 13,471 units.

▲ Dodge's new 1983 600 was a stretched K-car sedan aimed at two markets. The base model (background) was for families, while the sportier ES sought a new breed: import intenders.

▲ Unveiled during 1983, the Shelby Charger was Dodge's small front-drive coupe heated up by legendary Carroll Shelby. Stickering at $8290, it managed a respectable 8251 sales.

▲ A five-speed manual transmission was newly available for Dodge's practical Aries line for 1983. Woodie bodyside appliqué was standard on this Special Edition wagon. Price: $8186.

▲ Chrysler showed some budget-conscious product savvy with the 1982 Dodge Rampage and Plymouth Scamp, front-drive L-body coupes stretched into compact pickups. Both versions saw little change for 1983. This Rampage 2.2 was the sportiest of the Dodges, yet reasonably affordable at $7255.

• Newly available gadgetry includes Chrysler's "talking" dashboards (which many find annoying), digital speedometers, gas-pressurized shock absorbers

• General Motors celebrates its 75th anniversary

• A General Motors and Toyota venture results in a new jointly owned California plant and a Toyota-based small car

• Pollster J.D. Power reports that domestic new-car buyers have a median age of 49.5 years and an annual income of $34,790; import buyers are younger and earn more

• Ford and GM fail to meet CAFE (Corporate Average Fuel Economy) standards

• "Domestic-content" legislation is enacted; it will play a significant role in the U.S./import battle

• Chrysler Corp. pays off its $1.2 billion in federally guaranteed loans—seven years early; the company is earning money again, mostly from its K-car platform

• Chevy's Monte Carlo SS badge is revived; the final Malibus are built

• AMC's Renault-based Alliance sedans debut; it's the last year for Spirit and Concord, but the 4WD Eagle soldiers on

▲ The 1983 Thunderbird dramatically signaled Ford Motor Company's turn to clean, low-drag styling. The standard model offered V-6 or V-8 power for $9000-$10,000

▲ After reviving a truly hot GT for 1982, Ford made Mustang even more sportier with an aero-look facelift, as displayed on this coupe, plus reborn ragtops.

▲ Ford restyled its Fairmont-based 1981-82 Granada into 1983's new "downsized" LTD, while the full-sizers were renamed LTD Crown Victoria. Here, the Brougham sedan.

▲ Heading Ford's 1983 Escort line was the GT two-door hatchback sedan with 88 horses. Improvements kept Escort at the top, but volume declined some 70,000 units to 315,370.

▶ The Lincoln Mark VI would say good-bye after this '83 edition. Few changes had occurred since its 1980 redesign, and it remained a virtual twin to the Continental Town Car.

- Convertible versions of the Chevrolet Cavalier and Pontiac 2000 Sunbird roll into showrooms

- There are no '83 Corvettes—the all-new models will be badged 1984s

- Chrysler adds a front-drive New Yorker and E Class sedan; both are stretched K-cars; the last Cordobas are built

- The Charger badge replaces 024 on Dodge's subcompact coupes; Shelby Charger is the hot rod of the lineup

- Dodge's stretched 400 sedan is called 600, it matches Chrysler's E Class for size

- Mustang gets its first convertible in a decade, plus a more-potent V-8 and a new GT Turbo hatchback

- The next Ford Thunderbird debuts with V-6, V-8, or four-cylinder turbo power, and the first manual transmission since 1957

- An upscale Fairmont-based LTD joins the Ford lineup; the final Fairmonts are built

- Mercury Capri gets a "bubbleback" rear window; the new Marquis is similar to Ford's Fairmont-based LTD

◀ The rear roofline was the biggest visual difference between the '83 Mercury Cougar and Ford Thunderbird. The cat wore an upright backlight for the more formal look thought to be favored by Mercury buyers. This LS Cougar had a base price of $10,850; the standard model started at $9521.

▲ Ford Motor Company introduced new front-drive compacts for '83: Ford Tempo and Mercury Topaz *(shown)*.

▲ Like Ford's EXP, Mercury's two-seat LN7 gained a high-output engine for '83, but sales sank from 35,000 to just 4528.

▲ Recalling the "muscle car" era, 1983's new Hurst/Olds was a Cutlass Supreme with a 180-horse V-8, firm chassis, and "Lightning Rod" shifter. Some 3000 found buyers.

▲ The Hurst/Olds package was a $1997 option on the $9848 Cutlass Supreme Calais. Buyers more interested in economy could opt for one of two diesel engines available for 1983.

1983 Calendar-Year Car Sales

1. Chevrolet	1,175,200	6. Pontiac	318,478	11. Chrysler	159,882
2. Oldsmobile	916,583	7. Dodge	304,464	12. Lincoln	101,068
3. Buick	808,416	8. Cadillac	292,814	13. Avanti	100[1]
4. Ford	783,225	9. Plymouth	273,489		
5. Mercury	359,594	10. AMC	168,726		

[1] *Estimated*

◄ Plymouth revived the Scamp name for its new 1983 twin to Dodge's Rampage pick-up. But it didn't sell nearly as well, and was dropped after one year and production of only 2129 units.

▲ A standard five-speed manual gearbox, new four-speed automatic option, and more engine choices highlighted Pontiac's 1983 Firebirds. Here, the midline $10,322 S/E. Tougher competition cut F-Bird sales more than 50 percent to 74,884.

▲ Despite few changes, Pontiac's Grand Prix registered slightly higher 1983 sales of close to 86,000. Of those, only 12 percent were the top-line Brougham model (shown); it started at $9781, $1083 more than the base coupe.

▲ By 1983, the sporty SJ was a regular Pontiac Phoenix model and delivered 135 horses from an HO 2.8-liter V-6. Sales, though, were weak: just 853 of this $8861 coupe and only 172 $8948 four-doors. Neither SJ would return for '84.

▲ Pontiac introduced a Chevrolet Chevette clone as the 1981 T1000. For '83 it was just the 1000—and a steadily declining seller: just under 26,000 sold, split between this two-door hatchback and its four-door companion model.

▲ The year-old, American Motors-built Renault Alliance returned for 1984 with few changes, but gained "bubbleback" running mates called Encore with three doors *(shown)* or five.

▲ Avanti updates continued for 1984 under the new Steve Blake regime. Most came from the previous year's Thirtieth Anniversary model. Evident here are newly available body-color bumpers, custom lacy-spoke wheels, and a handsome two-tone interior. Sticker prices now started at $31,860.

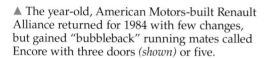

▲ Buick gave its 1984 Skyhawk a turbo four-cylinder engine, but only for the sporty T-Type. Wagon versions sold poorly: just 5285 for the year.

▲ A thin-bar grille was one of the few changes in Buick's Riviera for 1984. The $25,832 convertible returned, but only 500 were sold that year.

▲ After a year's absence, Buick's Regal Grand National returned as this "Darth Vader"-looking hot rod with 200 turbocharged horses from a 3.8 V-6.

◀ Cadillac revived a droptop Eldorado for 1984 and promptly angered those who had bought "last convertible" '76s for outrageous sums. The new Biarritz was pricey at $31,286. Just one engine was available, Cadillac's year-old 4.1-liter aluminum-block V-8. Model-year sales were predictably limited at just 3300 units.

1984

- Domestic model-year production leaps to 8,147,849 cars (including foreign automakers with U.S. assembly plants)

- Of the 10,393,230 cars sold in the U.S., more than 76 percent are domestically built; imports actually have declined slightly

- Cadillac has a convertible again, its first since '76: Eldorado is the costliest U.S. ragtop ever, and lasts only two seasons

- GM chairman Roger Smith begins a massive reorganization to restore each division to specific ranking in price and prestige; Buick-Oldsmobile-Cadillac form one group, Chevrolet-Pontiac-GM of Canada another

- GM begins importation of the small, Japanese-built Sprint and Spectrum

- The plastic-bodied, midengined Pontiac Fiero two-seater debuts

▲ The first new Chevrolet Corvette in 15 years debuted in early '83 as a 1984 model. Lighter and smaller than the old "shark," it arrived stickered at $21,800—up a cool $3510—with a 205-horsepower V-8. Sales zoomed to 51,547.

▶ Innovation in the new Corvette included an easy-access clamshell hood, practical lift-up "glassback," one-piece targa top, and a sophisticated independent suspension. Body panels were again made of fiberglass, but were hung on a strong new "bird-cage" substructure. Zero-60 mph took seven seconds.

▲ With safety and service recalls mounting, GM X-cars were little-changed for '84, though Chevy's Citation tacked on a Roman "II." This is the sporty V-6 X-11 three-door.

▲ Chevrolet's 1984 Camaro Z28 gained a more potent 305-inch V-8 with 150 horsepower, a reply to Ford's Mustang GT. Total Camaro sales boomed to more than 261,000 units.

▲ Chrysler's 1984 convertible K-cars gained rear side windows. This Town & Country ragtop again topped Chrysler's LeBaron models, with a base price of $16,495.

- The compact front-wheel-drive Ford Tempo replaces Fairmont; Mercury markets a Topaz cousin

- Lincoln introduces the Mark VII premium coupe, derived from Ford's Thunderbird; LSC is the performance-oriented edition

- Chrysler introduces groundbreaking front-drive minivans: Dodge Caravan and Plymouth Voyager

- The final Oldsmobile Omega and Pontiac Phoenix X-cars are built; Chevy Citation and Buick Skylark soldier on

- The sixth-generation Corvette has a lift-up hatch; a "Cross-Fire" V-8 and new "4+3 overdrive" manual gearbox may be ordered

- U.S. Secretary of Transportation Elizabeth Dole orders a phase-in of passive restraints, starting with 10 percent of 1987 cars

- Ford and GM again fail to meet the CAFE standard, both apply for relief; Chrysler's cars meet federal requirements

- Front-drive models account for 40 percent of Ford sales, half of General Motors's, and a whopping 87 percent for Chrysler

- The last rear-wheel-drive Buick Electras and Oldsmobile Ninety Eights roll off the assembly lines

▲ Replacing Cordoba in the '84 Chrysler line was the smaller—but sportier—front-drive Laser, the firm's latest K-car spinoff. Sold only as a hatchback, it was priced from $8648.

▲ Dodge 400s were renamed 600s for 1984, but retained the basic K-car platform with minor changes. Ragtop volume rose to 10,960. The base model started at $10,595.

◄ Chrysler's charismatic chairman Lee Iacocca gave his firm's new 1984 minivans a personal send-off at a November 1983 Detroit press preview event. Within a year of introduction, Chrysler had delivered more than 193,000 of its Dodge Caravans and Plymouth Voyagers.

▲ Having tuned the Charger, Carroll Shelby turned Dodge's sleepy Omni into a 110-horse wolf for '84. Called GLH, for "Goes Like Hell," the $7350 rocket found just 3285 buyers.

▲ The Shelby Charger itself was back for 1984 little-changed. Build eased to 7552 from the '83's 8251. Base price was up to $8541. Basic colors were still contrasting blue or silver.

- Six Chrysler models are available with a turbocharger, General Motors offers four, Ford leads all with 10

- Gadgets continue to proliferate, including video, radio, and climate controls; LCD displays; inflatable lumbar supports

- Half of '84 price hikes are attributed to federal safety and emissions requirements

- The average transaction price for a domestically branded new car now comes to $11,170

- Sticker prices range from $4997 for an economy Chevette to $31,286 for Cadillac's opulent Biarritz convertible

- The Corvette and Mustang SVO adopt directional Goodyear tires

- Mini spare tires are now the norm, but full-size spares are generally still available as extra-cost options

- J. Michael Losh becomes general manager of Pontiac; William Hoglund leaves to take over at Saturn Division

- Chevy tacks a "II" on Citation badge, an effort to distance it from plague of recalls

▲ Despite being emissions-limited to a Chevrolet 155-horse 305-cid V-8, Series IV Excaliburs were undeniably unique, especially when ordered as the rumble-seat Roadster.

▲ Appearing in late 1984 as '85 models were new Twentieth Anniversary Signature Series Excaliburs. The run consisted of 50 Phaetons (*shown*) and 50 Roadsters.

◀ Among 1984 Ford Mustangs was the new turbocharged, 175-horse four-cylinder SVO (*shown*) and a 20th Anniversary V-8 special called GT-350—the latter really just a paint-and-tape job. SVO aimed at Europhiles, but didn't make many converts, claiming just 4508 sales. One reason was the steep base price: $15,596.

▲ Ford's new 1984 LTD LX targeted enthusiasts with a "four-door Mustang GT," boasting a version of the ponycar's V-8. Just 3260 were sold before the model was axed after 1985.

▲ Released in the spring of 1983, the front-wheel-drive Tempo replaced the rear-drive Fairmont as Ford's compact with the start of the formal '84 model year.

1984 Calendar-Year Car Sales

1.	Chevrolet	1,655,151	6.	Mercury	475,381	11.	AMC	208,624
2.	Ford	1,180,708	7.	Dodge	442,527	12.	Lincoln	157,434
3.	Oldsmobile	1,144,225	8.	Chrysler	375,853	13.	Avanti	287
4.	Buick	987,980	9.	Plymouth	357,764			
5.	Pontiac	594,821	10.	Cadillac	300,300			

Some figures are estimated

▲ Reflecting Ford's newfound fondness for "aero" design was 1984's startling new Lincoln Mark VII coupe, derived from the latest Thunderbird. Prices started at $21,707.

▲ First-year Mark VII sales were 33,344, up almost 3000 over the '83 Mark VI. Surprisingly popular was this new $23,706 LSC (Luxury Sport Coupe) with "more European" features.

▲ The XR-7 tag returned to Mercury Cougar for '84 as a twin to the T-Bird Turbo Coupe. Here the $11,265 LS.

▲ Only 50 ASC/McLaren Capris were built for 1984, each with a $25,000 sticker. A 302-inch V-8 was standard.

▲ Like Tempo at Ford, the front-drive Topaz was Mercury's sole compact. Here is the LS coupe, priced at $7880.

◄ Keeping a great tradition alive, the Hurst/Olds returned from its '83 revival unchanged. A special 180-horse V-8 was again linked with the triple-stick Hurst "Lightning Rod" shifter controlling a four-speed automatic.

• The hatchback AMC Encore debuts; only a few versions of the 4WD Eagle remain as actual AMC product

• A turbo four is available for Chryslers; the rear-drive model is now called Fifth Avenue

• Dodge puts a 600 badge on the coupe and convertible formerly known as 400

• Turbocharged fours are now available in Ford EXP, Mercury Cougar XR-7, and Pontiac 2000 Sunbird

• Mustang's new SVO offering features a turbo/intercooled engine and all-disc brakes

• A 5.2-liter V-8 is the sole engine for the Dodge Diplomat/Plymouth Gran Fury

◄ Plymouth dealers sold Chrysler's new 1984 front-drive T-115 minivan under the Voyager label formerly used on full-size, rear-drive vans. Apart from trim, everything was the same as for corresponding Dodge Caravans—including the prices.

▲ The 1984 Plymouth Reliant, like its Dodge Aries twin, got a reshaped nose, plus a more modern dash. Reliant was now Chrysler's top-seller, with 152,138 built for 1984.

▲ An optional 150-horse turbo four made news for Pontiac's 1984 J-cars, which were rebadged 2000 Sunbird. This turbo SE was the official car for that year's Pikes Peak Hill Climb.

▲ Relaunched for '83 under the name Parisienne, the full-size Pontiac continued into 1984 as a near duplicate of the Chevy Caprice. This $10,281 Brougham attracted 25,212 buyers.

▲ Vying with Chevy's Corvette as 1984's most exciting new offering was the Pontiac Fiero "2M4"—a two-seat, midengine, four-cylinder coupe. Plastic outer body panels clothed a "driveable space frame." The sole engine was a 2.5-liter, 92-horse four, as this was meant to be a thrifty "commuter" runabout, not a sports car. At $8000 and up, Fiero was a hit, with sales nearing 137,000.

▲ The hatchback Renault Encore shared the 1985 Alliance's new 77-horse 1.7 engine option. This top-line LS five-door sold from $7310, a bit less than the Alliance Limited.

▲ The 1985 Electra line listed coupes and sedans, but trim levels now comprised base, the ritzy Park Avenue *(shown),* and sporty T-Type. Park Avenue came to dominate sales.

▲ Buick unveiled its next-wave compact for 1985 as the Somerset Regal, one of a trio of GM N-body models. Here a Custom, priced at $8857.

▲ Estate Wagons aside, traditional big-Buick buyers had but one choice for '85: the rear-drive B-body LeSabre. The $11,751 Limited coupe is shown.

▲ With sales falling in the wake of well-publicized recalls, Buick reduced Skylark X-cars to a pair of sedans for 1985. Here an $8283 Limited model.

◄ A carryover year for the 1985, Cadillac Seville was about to be downsized again—and more conventionally restyled. As before, engines comprised a pair of V-8s: a 4.1-liter gas and a 5.7 diesel; the former was greatly preferred for reliability. Total sales were about the same as in '84: 39,755 units.

1985

- Horsepower ratings are going up, continuing a trend that began in 1983

- Dealers are delighted by record sales—of both imported and domestic automobiles

- Inflation scales back, but sales incentives remain robust

- Domestic output totals 7,817,419 cars for the model year

- Of 11,045,784 cars sold in the U.S., 8,204,721 are domestically built

- Some Lincoln-Mercury dealers begin selling the German-built Merkur Scorpio

- The first Chevrolet Novas emerge from the GM/Toyota joint venture plant in California

- The Big Three diversify, acquiring nonautomotive subsidiaries

▲ After topping Detroit's 1984 sales chart, Chevy's Cavalier offered a zesty new Z24 option for 1985. It ran with a 125-horse V-6, as on this coupe.

▲ Moving from "Cross Fire" to "Tuned Port Injection" netted 25 horses, giving the '85 Chevy Corvettes 230, all told. Base price was now $24,873.

▲ When Camaro became the official car of the International Race of Champions, Chevy debuted the IROC-Z for 1985. Base price: $11,739.

◄ Chevy's midsize Celebrity returned for 1985 with an optional 2.8-liter V-6 switched from carburetor to port fuel injection. Also back was the Eurosport option package, offering firm suspension and blackout trim for $199. The V-6 sold separately for $250.

▲ Chrysler's aged rear-drive LeBaron was still around for '85 as a posh Fifth Avenue, with its V-8 newly bumped to 140 horses. Even at $12,865, sales were the best yet: 109,971.

▲ Another K-car spin-off bowed for '85, the H-body Chrysler LeBaron GTS. This roomy, faintly "Euro-style" four-door hatch started at $9024; 60,783 were built.

▶ Little-changed in looks, the 1985 Dodge Daytona benefited from minor changes to the electronic turbo engine. Some 8023 buyers chose this $11,620 top-dog Turbo Z.

- Ford sells 7400 special-order Tempo/Topaz models with driver-side air-bags to government and insurance fleets

- It's the last year for ill-fated GM X-cars and unpopular diesel engines

- The Saturn company is formed as a wholly owned GM subsidiary

- Chrysler launches the H-body Lancer and LeBaron GTS; GM issues the big front-drive C-body and compact N-body

- Volkswagen drops the Rabbit, produces a new Golf in the U.S.

- Ford debuts its Aerostar minivan; unlike Chrysler's vans, it is rear-wheel drive

- The CAFE standard peaks at 27.5 mpg; in September, NHTSA approves a 1.5-mpg cutback for 1986, pleasing Detroit

- AMC's Alliance adds a convertible model and a needed larger engine option

- A downsized front-drive Buick Electra debuts; ragtop Riviera departs this year

▲ Back for '85 as Dodge's top 600 model, the ES Turbo convertible offered ample power for $13,995, but sold poorly: just 5621 orders.

▲ Dodge sold a slightly different version of the new '85 Chrysler H-body and revived the Lancer name for it. This uplevel ES listed for $9690.

▲ The hot-selling Dodge Caravan moved into 1985 with newly available "convert-a-bed" rear seats and an overhead console. Here, the midline SE.

◀ Excalibur was struggling for survival by 1985. The problem was basically low performance versus high price—still around $60,000—plus a "boutique" car market besieged by fiercer competition and the cost of meeting new federal standards. Though sales were down to a trickle, Excalibur Series IVs, like this Phaeton, remained cars of impeccable high quality—and even greater rarity.

▲ Ford's 1985 Thunderbirds wore a slightly different grille, bigger "boots," and new instrumentation. Sales dipped to 151,851 units. This Turbo Coupe now stickered at $13,365.

▲ Ford boosted its 1985 Mustang SVO to 205 horses, but sales still stalled, dropping by half to 1954 units—despite a base price reduction to $14,251. Ponycar buyers wanted V-8s.

- The turbocharged Regal Grand National coupe is Buick's last gasp at high performance in the classic style

- Cadillac de Ville is sharply downsized, adopts front-wheel drive

- A Chevrolet-built V-6 is offered in the Cadillac Cimarron to squelch criticism of its poor performance

- Full-size, rear-wheel-drive Chevrolets continue to sell well, as Buick and Oldsmobile abandon that market

- An IROC-Z package with a high-output V-8 is available for the Chevrolet Camaro Z28

- Lincoln's Town Car gets an aero facelift; Mark VII LSC gets Mustang GT's V-8; antilock braking is available

- A sporty 4-4-2 option package is revived for the Oldsmobile Cutlass Salon/Supreme, it includes a 180-horsepower V-8

- The Avanti company gets yet another new owner—Michael Kelly

- The new N-body Pontiac Grand Am compact is derived from the J-car; Fiero gains a GT edition and optional V-6

▲ Like its near-identical cousin Ford LTD Crown Victoria, the big Mercury Grand Marquis was still quite popular in 1985, racking up some 161,258 sales. Here, the upper-level $12,789 LS coupe. Standard coupes started at $12,240.

▲ A new dash and minor trim changes carried Mercury's Cougar through 1985, with demand down slightly to 117,274 units. This top-line turbocharged XR-7 sold for $13,599.

▲ Despite many enhancements, Mercury's 1985 Capri languished, racking up just 18,657 total sales. This sporty RS hatchback included the 5.0L V-8 in its $10,223 base price.

◀ Oldsmobile's C-body Ninety Eight was downsized again for 1985 and, like its Buick and Cadillac sisters, switched to front-wheel drive. Most were built with a 3.8-liter V-6. Sales more than doubled, to 169,432 units.

1985 Calendar-Year Car Sales

1. Chevrolet	1,418,098	6. Dodge	500,835	11. Lincoln	166,486
2. Oldsmobile	1,165,649	7. Chrysler	420,780	12. AMC	150,189
3. Ford	1,149,427	8. Mercury	419,869		
4. Buick	1,002,906	9. Plymouth	393,711		
5. Pontiac	519,390	10. Cadillac	384,840		

Some figures are estimated

◀ The rear-drive '85 Olds Delta 88 offered more metal for the money than the new front-drive Ninety Eight. Sales neared 242,000 units. Here, an $11,062 Royale Brougham LS.

▼ Pontiac's Grand Am would prove to be the most consistently popular GM front-drive N-body compact. Like the others, it bowed for '85 in base and uplevel coupe models only.

▶ Still fighting a horde of Japanese small cars, the AMC-built 1985 Renault Alliance sported a new face and taillamps, plus a 50-month /50,000-mile powertrain warranty. Sales of L and DL ragtops totaled just 2015 units.

▲ Buick's Riviera was again downsized for 1986, and plunged 70 percent in sales. This sporty T-Type edition listed for a healthy $21,577.

▲ Coilless ignition and optional anti-lock brakes improved 1986 C-body Buick Electra. T-Type sedans like this one grabbed just 5816 sales.

▲ New for 1986 was this De Ville Touring Sedan (and Coupe). They featured a handling suspension and slightly less gingerbread.

◄ The return of Chevy's Corvette convertible symbolized a new renaissance in Detroit style and performance. This 'Vette paced the 1986 Indianapolis 500. Base price was $32,032.

◄ Chevy's Camaro kept IROC-ing along for 1986. The IROC-Z listed for $12,561, a bargain for the performance. Following a 1985 sales dip, total Camaro demand recovered to a healthy 192,128 units, 49,585 of them IROCs.

1986

- Imported-car sales rise; after a multiyear slackening, they now hold 28.3 percent share

- Domestic model-year output tops 7.8 million cars (including foreign makers with U.S. plants)

- Of the record-setting 11,463,241 new cars sold in the U.S., 8,214,662 are domestically built

- Ford earns a record $3.3 billion profit—its earnings top GM's for the first time since 1924

- The average transaction price for a new domestic car is $12,530

- The government decrees that all '86 cars must have a high, center-mounted stoplight (CHMSL)

- Ford launches the midsize Taurus (and similar Mercury Sable); most get a 3.0-liter V-6

- Buick and Olds have no more rear-drive models, except big wagons

▲ Chevy debuted a slicker Monte Carlo SS for 1986—the Aerocoupe. It was designed mainly for higher top speed on NASCAR supertracks. Because of this focus, only 200, priced at $14,191, were built for public sale.

▲ Washington's newly required third stoplamp is evident on this 1986 Chevrolet Cavalier Z24, which again featured a sport suspension and lively 2.8-liter V-6. Base price: $9068.

▲ Chrysler's 1986 LeBarons got a new engine option: a 2.5-liter version of the 2.2 "Trans-4." This Town & Country ragtop in Mark Cross trim was one of just 501 built for the year.

◀ Dodge adopted "gun-sight" grilles for most of its 1986 models. This 600 convertible sold 11,678 copies at $11,695 each; a hotter ES turbo ragtop found 4759 buyers.

• GM's all-new Riviera, Toronado, and Eldorado/Seville average 18 inches shorter; not everyone takes to the sheared-off look

• Buick LeSabre and Oldsmobile Eighty-Eight follow Electra/Ninety-Eight, downsizing to a front-drive V-6

• Making room for Taurus and Sable, the last Ford LTD and Mercury Marquis are sold

• The federal CAFE standard drops to 26 mpg, helping Detroit meet sharply rising demand for full-size cars

• A driver-side airbag is now optional in Ford Tempo/Mercury Topaz sedans sold to the public—11,000 are installed this year

• All Ford 5.0-liter V-8s are fitted with sequential-port fuel injection

• Chrysler adds a 2.5-liter, four-cylinder engine—the first domestic motor with counter-rotating balance shafts

• General Motors buys Group Lotus—not only for the British sports car, but for the company's high-tech innovations

• Donald Petersen is the newly named chairman of Ford Motor Company

▲ Chrysler's new 2.5-liter four was optional in the base '86 Dodge Daytona (*shown*), but the big news was the "C/S" sport package for the Turbo Z, named for Carroll Shelby.

▲ Back for a last stand in 1986, the Dodge Omni GLH was unchanged save sales, down from 6513 to 3629. One reason: the new and even hotter turbo-powered Shelby GLH-S.

◄▲ Widely previewed throughout 1985, the smooth, all-new '86 Ford Taurus not only replaced the dated Fairmont-based "little" LTD, but proved a much better seller. With front drive, three trim levels, sedan and wagon body styles, and a host of sensible features, Taurus became a symbol of Detroit's new "can-do" attitude. Base prices were in the $10,000-$14,000 range.

- GM ousts H. Ross Perot from its board of directors, paying him $700 million

- The last AMC Encores are offered; sales of the Renault-based subcompacts have been steadily declining

- Antilock braking is offered for bigger Buicks; the Regal T-Type and Grand National V-6 hit 235 bhp via an intercooler

- Mercury Sable features a unique "light bar" front-end grille treatment

- Cadillac Fleetwood Brougham borrows a 307-cid V-8 from Olds; it is Caddy's final rear-drive model

- Midyear adds an SS "Aerocoupe" to Chevrolet's Monte Carlo line; sporty Cavalier Z24 debuts with a V-6

- Mercury abandons the slow-selling Mustang-based Capri after this year

- Bosch antilock braking is standard in Corvettes; a convertible model arrives at midseason

- The final Chrysler Lasers are built; Dodge Daytona carries on with a C/S (Carroll Shelby) handling package now available

▲ Florida was one of many states that turned to Ford Mustangs (and Chevy Camaros) for highway patrol duty in the Eighties—enticed by special factory police packages.

▲ After a mid-1985 redo, the Ford Escort returned for '86 with this sporty GT three-door hatch at the top of the line. Boasting 108 port-injected horses, it listed at $8112.

◄ The '86 Lincoln Mark VII offered several significant improvements, including standard antilock brakes and a new high-compression V-8 that booted LSC horses to an even 200. This base model carried a "Monroney" window sticker price of $22,399.

◄ Sable replaced the smaller Marquis in Mercury's '86 line, but sold far better, attracting nearly 96,000 buyers. Developed with Ford's Taurus in a $2 billion program, the new front-drive middleweight Merc offered similarly smooth, low-drag styling for only a few dollars more. Here, the uplevel $13,068 LS station wagon.

1986 Calendar-Year Car Sales

1. Chevrolet	1,368,837	6. Dodge	450,365	11. Lincoln	156,839
2. Ford	1,253,525	7. Mercury	399,240	12. AMC	64,873
3. Oldsmobile	1,050,832	8. Chrysler	367,898		
4. Buick	850,103	9. Plymouth	350,573		
5. Pontiac	799,461	10. Cadillac	281,683		

Some figures are estimated

▲ A "light bar" grille (that didn't actually light up until 1989) made the '86 Sable unmistakable—and launched a Mercury design theme. This '86 LS sedan started at $12,574.

▲ Like Buick's LeSabre, the Olds Delta 88 was newly downsized for 1986, offering only front-drive coupes and sedans. This $13,461 Brougham coupe weighed 3170 pounds.

▲ Heading Pontiac's reshuffled 1986 Sunbird line were new GT models with a 150-horse turbo four and semi-hidden headlamps. Ragtops registered only 1268 sales.

▲ An even rarer '86 Pontiac was this NASCAR-inspired "bubble-back" Grand Prix, which revived its 2+2 name from the '60s. Just 200 were sold at $18,214 each, with a 5.0-liter V-8.

▲ Plymouth's 1986 L-body retained the Turismo name used since '83, and unchanged looks from an '84 facelift. This one wears the trim option that revived the (Valiant) Duster name for '85, and included bodyside pinstriping.

▲ A new marketing tack spelled the end of Buick's "modern muscle" GNX after 1987, when 547 were built. But these were the hottest of all, with 276 horses and blinding 4.7-second 0-60-mph ability. Base price was near $30,000.

▲ Flush "composite" headlamps and optional antilock brakes made big news for the 1987 Buick LeSabres.

▲ An extra 10 horses couldn't keep Buick's 1987 Riviera, here a $22,181 T-Type, from record-low sales of just 15,223 units.

◄ Built by Italy's Pininfarina on a shortened Eldorado chassis, the new two-seat 1987 Allanté was Cadillac's answer to the Mercedes SL convertible. A fortified 4.1-liter V-8 sent 170 horses to the front wheels through a four-speed transaxle. Rich appointments, two tops, and power everything were included for $54,700, but sales were slow—a mere 3363. Taillamps hid behind white lenses by day and glowed red by night or with the brakes applied. The trunklid emblem doubled as a high-mount center stoplamp and looked much better than the tacked-on affairs of many other 1987 cars.

1987

• The finale for AMC, both cars and company—Chrysler takes over in August, lured by Jeep, which will become Jeep-Eagle division

• A sleek hidden-headlamp Chrysler LeBaron coupe and convertible make their debut

• Shadow is Dodge's latest small-car entry; the Plymouth Sundance differs only in detail

• The Corsica sedan and Beretta coupe arrive during the year as Chevy's latest compacts; Camaro gets its first convertible in 18 years

• Cadillac's costly Allanté two-seat convertible debuts, with Italian designer bodywork

• Model-year production from U.S. plants runs 7.4 million cars (down 6.5 percent)

▲ Chevy's Cavalier got a sporty RS convertible for 1986. The ragtop sold about 5800 units each year. This 1987 model started at $13,446.

▲ Beretta bowed for 1987 as a close relative to the Corsica sedan. To test quality, almost all of the 8072 built for '87 went to rental companies.

▲ The first open-air Camaros since 1969 brightened the Chevy lineup for 1987. But at $15,000-$18,000 base, sales were small: just over 1000 cars.

▲ Built just for California in 1987 was a Camaro RS, a Z28 pretender packing (for insurance purposes) a mild V-6. The price was milder too, just $12,411.

▲ Roller valve lifters added 10 horses to give the '87 Chevrolet Corvette 240 in all. Some 10,625 ragtops and 20,007 coupes found buyers this year.

▲ Chevy took Celebrity to a new level with the 1987 Eurosport VR, a $3550 "aero" package. Of the 1623 built, all were white, red, black, or silver.

▲ The pending demise of Chevy's rear-drive Monte Carlo implied the same for sister-ship El Camino. All El Caminos sold in its last few years were built in Mexico, this to keep costs down and the model viable. Seen here is a well-optioned standard model.

▲ Though still K-cars underneath, Chrysler's new "J-body" 1987 LeBaron coupe and convertible were far more stylish, with shapely lines and neat hidden-head-lamp noses. Ragtop sales were fairly scarce at 8025, but the coupe found a more-than-respectable 75,415 buyers. Base prices ranged from $11,295-$14,000.

- Imports capture 31.1 percent of new-car sales; "transplants" (foreign companies operating in the U.S) grab 5.3 percent

- Buick drops to fifth place in production, behind Oldsmobile; Pontiac moves up to third, for the first time since 1970

- Ford earns $4.6 billion net profit—the highest ever for a U.S. automaker

- Chrysler introduces a 7-year/ 70,000-mile limited powertrain warranty

- The industry's average fuel economy is now 26.6 mpg—twice the 1974 level

- The average transaction price for a domestic car reaches $13,200

- Chrysler buys Italian maker Lamborghini

- Installation of four-cylinder engines peaks at 54 percent; only 18.5 percent of American cars now come with a V-8

- The Pontiac Bonneville is all new, joins fellow full-sizers Olds Eighty-Eight and Buick LeSabre as front-drive converts

- Mazda builds at Flat Rock, Michigan, plans with Ford to assemble Probe/MX-6

▲ Extending the appeal of Dodge's 1987 minivan was this new stretched Grand Caravan riding a longer wheelbase. Also new was a 3.0 V-6 option.

▲ Meant to replace Omni, Dodge's new 1987 Shadow arrived in two- and four-door hatch sedans. First-year sales were respectable at 76,056 units.

▲ Dodge reduced Omni in 1987 to a single model called America and gave the sedan a cut-rate $5499 base price. Options were few, but sales were good.

▲ The front-drive Dodge Daytona got its first major restyle for 1987, and expanded to base, new luxury Pacifica, and Shelby Z (shown) models. For all that, sales fell to 33,104.

▲ Despite only minor equipment changes, Ford's 1987 Taurus charged up the sales chart to nearly 375,000 units—up more than 138,000 from 1986. Here, an LX, base priced at $14,613.

▲ Following an '83 facelift, Ford's Mustang was again restyled for 1987. GTs, like this $15,724 ragtop, were more "aero" than base models, thanks to new rocker skirts and "mini-blind" taillamps. Sales dropped roughly 40 percent to 159,145.

▲ Mustang's 1987 engines were pared to an anemic 90-bhp, 2.3-liter four and the muscular 5.0-liter V-8, which gained 25 horses (for 225). The V-8 was standard in GTs (shown), and optional in LX models.

1987 Calendar-Year Car Sales

1. Chevrolet	1,384,214	6. Dodge	501,926	11. Lincoln	109,366
2. Ford	1,176,775	7. Plymouth	443,806	12. AMC	36,336
3. Pontiac	724,289	8. Chrysler	360,613	13. Avanti	300[1]
4. Oldsmobile	670,880	9. Mercury	315,147		
5. Buick	.648,689	10. Cadillac	282,582		

[1]*Estimated*

▲ A grilleless nose provided distinction to Ford's '87 Thunderbird Turbo Coupe, which gained the intercooled turbo four from the late Mustang SVO. The result was 190 horses with five-speed manual, but only 150 with optional four-speed automatic.

▲ Ford spruced up its 1987 Thunderbirds with new grilles, flush side glass, and subtly different sheetmetal. New to the line was this $15,079 Sport model packing a 150-horsepower V-8. Despite the restyle, overall T-Bird sales declined to 128,135.

◄ Like Ford with the T-Bird, Mercury restyled its Cougar for 1987, but the top XR-7 model *(shown)* again went its own way by losing its turbo four in favor of a 150-horse V-8—a sensible switch. The XR-7 listed at $15,832.

▲ The best-selling of GM's A-body quartet, Cierra enjoys new one-piece composite headlamps for 1987. A 3.8-liter V-6 was again the top power option, offering 150 horsepower.

▲ Seeking to lift Toronado from its '86 sales doldrums, Olds trotted out the Trofeo, a sportier 1987 edition with handling suspension, luxury cabin, and two-tone exterior.

- Robert C. Stempel becomes GM president

- Ford Escort/Mercury Lynx adopt motorized shoulder belts—one way to deal with the requirement for passive restraints

- GM builds a Getrag-designed five-speed manual gearbox under license, for use in high-performance models

- Pontiac Trans Am GTA gets a 5.7-liter V-8

- Chrysler pleads "no contest" to charges of disconnecting odometers from cars under test, pays a $16.4 million fine

- Dodge restyles Daytona, adds Shelby Z with Turbo II engine; Omni/Horizon drop to single low-cost "America" model

- Ford Tempo offers all-wheel drive

- Mustang's facelift includes flush headlamps; the V-6 is dropped, leaving only a four and a V-8

- Ford Thunderbird sports new sheetmetal; the Turbo Coupe adds a turbo intercooler and automatic ride control

▲ After adding four-doors like its '86 N-body sisters, Pontiac's Grand Am went sportier for '87 with a new 165-horse turbo 2.0-liter four option and an improved dash.

▲ Notchback '87 Pontiac Fieros like this SE got the nose of the mid-'86 fastback-profile GT, and all models came with a standard five-speed instead of four-speed manual.

▲ The 1987 Pontiac Firebird dropped its SE model, but still hewed to tradition with four models. Here they are (*clockwise from top left*): base coupe, Formula, Trans Am, and GTA. Newly standard for GTA and optional on Formula and T/A was the 5.7-liter V-8, rated at 210 horsepower.

▲ Plymouth shadowed Dodge's new compacts with Sundance models that differed mainly in grille and taillamp designs. Even prices were in the same $7800-$7900 range.

▲ Like its Dodge Caravan twin, the 1987 Plymouth Voyager added stretched "Grand" models. The Grand soon vied for sales honors with standard Voyagers like this midline SE.

563

◄ Conceived during Buick's sporty-car days of the early Eighties, the stylish Reatta bowed for 1988 as essentially a cut-down two-seat version of the latest front-drive Riviera with unique styling. Buick said the Reatta name was derived from a Spanish word for "lariat." Though handsome and quite roadable, the division's new image-booster did not lasso many sales at $25,000 a copy: just 4708 for the debut 1988 model year.

▲ You could still buy a sporty full-size Buick T-Type in 1988, but few people did. This $16,518 LeSabre coupe managed 6426 sales, the Electra T-Type four-door only 1869.

▲ One of three all-new front-drive GM10 coupes, the 1988 Buick Regal featured Custom and Limited models, but options allowed building a "Gran Sport" version like this.

▲ Called Fleetwood Brougham through 1985, then just Brougham, the basic rear-drive '77 Cadillac sedan was still around in 1988 with a 140-horse 5.0-liter Oldsmobile V-8.

▲ The front-drive Cadillac De Ville and Fleetwood gained a larger V-8 for 1988, upsized from 4.1 to 4.5 liters and from 130 to 155 horsepower. Base prices were around $23,000.

1988

- Domestic output totals 6,973,636 cars for the model year; 6,195,090 come from Big Three automakers, the rest come from joint ventures and foreign automakers with U.S. plants

- Market share for imports dips to 29.2 percent; costly European makes suffer biggest loss

- Chrysler profits drop for fourth straight year, but Big Three earn record profit of $11.2 billion

- The all-new Continental sedan rides a stretched Taurus platform—it's the first front-wheel-drive Lincoln, and the first with a six-cylinder engine

- Chevrolet drops to number two in production, behind Ford division

- Industry fuel-economy average rises to a new point: 28.7 miles per gallon

▶ After getting off to a very slow sales start, Chevy's compact Beretta coupe and Corsica sedan zoomed up the '88 chart. Corsica convinced over 291,000 shoppers, Beretta more than 275,000. As before, $1700-$2700 would option a Beretta into a GT model with Z51 handling suspension, bringing the price with V-6 to about $13,500.

▲ Advertising Beretta's entry into 1988 IMSA Grand Touring/Under 3-Liters racing was the new GTU, a V-6 model with skirts, spoilers, and mono coloring.

▲ Chevy's Cavalier traded its RS convertible for a sportier Z24 model, giving it a standard 125-horse 2.8-liter V-6 in the process. Just 8745 were sold at a $15,990 base price.

▲ Chrysler unwrapped a new front-drive New Yorker for 1988. This base four-door and the ritzier Landau version managed to find nearly 71,000 buyers this year.

▲ In the spirit of its old "spring specials," Chrysler added sporty GTC versions of the LeBaron coupe and convertible *(shown)* as mid-1988 sales boosters. All were white.

• GM launches midsize, front-drive W-body cars: Buick Regal, Oldsmobile Cutlass Supreme, Pontiac Grand Prix

• Dynasty is Dodge's new front-wheel-drive family sedan

• Chrysler launches another New Yorker, with a new 3.0-liter Mitsubishi V-6

• Chrysler markets departed AMC's Eagle line: Canadian-built Premier and French-made Medallion

• Buick introduces the two-seat Reatta coupe with a "3800" V-6

• The last T-Type Buick LeSabre and Riviera are produced

• Oldsmobile develops the overhead-cam "Quad-4" four-cylinder engine for use in Calais, Grand Am, Skylark

• Chrysler adds monochromatic GTC model to Lebaron, all are white

• Mitsubishi 3.0-liter V-6 sees wide use in Chrysler, Dodge, and Plymouth vehicles

▲ Dodge sharpened up the appearance of its 1988 Shadow ES *(foreground)* via a new face with integral foglamps, plus reshaped rear spoiler and revised body graphics. The ES package added $2147 to the price of a three-door Shadow.

▲ Chrysler's new 1988 C-body New Yorker was also offered as the Dodge Dynasty, though with fewer luxuries in exchange for lower list prices. This upper-rung Dynasty LE stickered at $12,226, the base model at $11,666. Sales were decent at 55,550, though many were bought by rental fleets.

▲ Still selling well, the Dodge Caravan added a 4000-pound towing package and available rear air conditioner for 1988. Here, a long-body Grand SE. LE models could reach $20,000.

▲ This '88 turbocharged Lancer Shelby was new to Dodge's H-body line—and rare, with only 279 built. Based on the '86 Lancer Pacifica, it came only in monochrome white or red.

▲ A Renault remnant from the '87 takeover of AMC, the 1988 Premier helped launch Chrysler's Eagle Division as a Canadian-built front-drive midsize sedan with a 3.0 Renault V-6. Badges read Eagle.

▲ The 1988 Ford Mustang was a rerun for 1987. Sales, however, made a gratifying leap to 211,225, led by LX 5.0 coupes *(hatch shown)*, which sold for as little as $10,611.

- This is the final year for GM's rear-drive Monte Carlo, Cutlass Supreme, and Regal coupes—plus Cadillac Cimarron, Ford EXP, AMC Eagle, Plymouth Caravelle, Dodge 600, and Pontiac Fiero bow out as well

- Cadillac adds the Seville Touring Sedan (STS), enlarges its V-8 engine to 4.5 liters, and makes antilock braking available

- The Camaro Z28 is dropped, but the IROC-Z continues as Chevrolet's high-performance V-8 machine; Cavalier gains a rounded facelift and the V-6 Z24 convertible replaces the four-cylinder RS

- The final Dodge Aries/Plymouth Reliant station wagons are built; the new Shelby Lancer boasts a 176-bhp Turbo II engine

566

▲ Unchanged, Ford's Thunderbird scored higher 1988 sales of 147,243, up almost 20,000 from '87. However, the Turbo Coupe *(shown)*, was losing ground to the cheaper but equally speedy V-8 LX and Sport.

▲ The first Lincoln with front-wheel drive and fewer than eight cylinders arrived for 1988 as the new Continental. Basically a stretched Ford Taurus, it met an enthusiastic reception, more than doubling sales of its '87 predecessor, at 41,287. Base price: $26,078.

▲ Though very long in the tooth by 1988, the '81-vintage Lincoln Town Car scored its highest production ever, at over 201,000. This Signature Series started at just under $26,000.

▲ An even-older Dearborn staple, the '79-vintage Mercury Grand Marquis wore a new face and other cosmetic updates for 1988, when coupes were dropped. Pictured is LS sedan.

◄ Olds arranged 1988 Indy pace car duties for this special Cutlass Supreme convertible, based on that year's new coupe platform. Working with C&C Inc., Olds ordered 55 replicas, all with high-tech head-up information display (HUD). A wealth of positive public response prompted Olds to offer a similar convertible for showroom sale, though it wouldn't arrive until 1990.

1988 Calendar-Year Car Sales

1. Ford	1,331,489	6. Buick	458,768	11. Cadillac	270,844
2. Chevrolet	1,236,316	7. Plymouth	336,070	12. Avanti	150[1]
3. Pontiac	680,714	8. Mercury	298,859		
4. Oldsmobile	535,015	9. Lincoln	280,659		
5. Dodge	489,645	10. Chrysler	278,287		

[1] *Estimated*

567

▲ Once a best-seller, the rear-drive midsize Olds was down to base and Brougham coupes by 1988, when it ended a 10-year run with a new name: Cutlass Supreme Classic.

▲ The new Cutlass Supreme arrived as one of 1988's front-drive GM10 coupes. Olds listed base, SL, and this sporty International Series variant. Sales reached nearly 95,000.

▲ There was no reason for much change in the hot-selling Voyager minivan for 1988, but Plymouth offered a new LX appearance package. Here, a base-trim standard model.

▲ Plymouth's 1988 Sundance again mimicked its Dodge double by adding a new sport-equipment package. The RS, for Rally Sport, included two-toning and listed for $1400.

◄ Showing its best shape in years, the Pontiac Grand Prix was all-new for 1988. As one of the front-drive GM10 models, it boasted all-independent suspension and no less room than the old rear-drive GP. GM had finally learned the folly of "cookie-cutter" styling, and it paid off: Grand Prix sales rose five-fold to 86,357. Here a sporty top-line SE. A 2.8-liter V-6 was standard.

- Ford's Tempo is reskinned to look more like big-brother Taurus; a 3.8-liter V-6 is now optional in Taurus

- Lincoln's Mark VII gets a healthy power boost—to 225 bhp

- New enthusiast editions of Oldsmobiles are called International Series; the final J-Body Firenzas are built

- Pontiac's 6000 STE features optional all-wheel drive; the top-line Bonneville SSE adds electronic variable damping

- Pontiac Sunbird adopts a rounded look, along with Chevrolet Cavalier

- The all-new GM10 Pontiac Grand Prix features all-disc brakes and four-wheel independent suspension

- Fifty Avanti Silver Anniversary coupes are built with Paxton-supercharged engines; the firm gets yet another owner, J.J. Cafaro

- Concept vehicles touring the auto-show circuit this year include Pontiac's low-snouted Banshee, Chrysler's Portofino, Cadillac Voyage, Lincoln Machete, Buick Lucerne, Plymouth Slingshot

◄ After spending $100 million to develop a new suspension for 1988, GM killed the Pontiac Fiero. This Formula was one of the final 26,402 Fieros built.

▲ The first front-drive Pontiac Bonneville returned from '87 in LE and SE trim, plus this aggressive new 1988 SSE. The SSE boasted a "3800" V-6 and antilock brakes for $21,879.

▲ Dumping the 3.3-liter V-6 as the top engine for Pontiac's 1988 Grand Am was Oldsmobile's new 2.3-liter twincam Quad-4 with 150 horses. This SE coupe listed for $12,869.

▲ When was a 1988 Firebird not a fastback? When it became a "notchback" via a new hatch, as on this prototype Trans Am GTA. It was a limited-production option, but rare because it reduced trunk space to virtually nil.

▲ Pontiac's 1988 Firebird engine roster was Sixties-confusing, but the venerable Trans Am (shown) still had fire with a choice of three V-8s and from 170 to 225 horses. Styling across the board was little-changed from a mild 1987 facelift.

▲ Recognizing the error of its downsizing ways, Buick added 11 inches to the tail of the '89 Riviera, plus more chrome. Result? Sales more than doubled, to 21,189.

▲ Buick's Somerset Regal was renamed Skylark when four-door versions bowed for '88. The '89s got a new, more potent "3300" V-6 option—and this dealer-installed vinyl top.

◄ Cadillac's 1989 Allanté received a new 200-horse 4.5-liter V-8, variable-rate shock absorbers, and standard antitheft alarm. Sales rose modestly from the previous year's 2569 to 3296.

▲ Given a crisp facelift and 4.5 V-8 for 1988, the Cadillac Eldorado returned for '89 with a Touring Suspension option that gave it surprisingly good handling. Base price: $26,738.

▲ With the bigger 4.5 V-8, Cadillac Seville sales jumped from some 18,600 to nearly 23,000 for 1988. For '89 (shown) the sporty new Seville Touring Sedan (STS) proved popular.

1989

- Domestic output totals 7.1 million cars for the model year; 6,133,530 are produced by the Big Three, the others are from joint ventures and foreign automakers with U.S. plants.

- GM's market share bottoms at 34.7 percent; it was almost 45 percent as recently as 1981

- A Japanese car, the Honda Accord, is the country's top seller, followed by Ford Taurus.

- The Geo brand is launched as a separate GM division to market imported and joint-venture models, including the Toyota Corolla-based California-built Prizm

- Chevrolet battles back to the top spot in production, ahead of Ford.

- The notchback Spirit and Acclaim arrive as Dodge/Plymouth's family sedans for the '90s.

Rolled out as an early 1990 model, Chevy's new Corvette ZR-1 (*foreground*) boasted a wider tail with square lights, ultrawide tires, and an amazing new 375-horse 5.7-liter V-8. Its new six-speed manual gearbox was shared with the "basic" 'Vette. Corvette ZR-1's "LT-5" V-8 featured an all-aluminum design with port fuel injection and twin overhead cams on each cylinder bank working a total of 32 valves. A special dual induction system with electronic control featured a "valet" key that locked out ultimate power for unauthorized—or less-experienced—users.

▲ Corvette's traditional lift-off hardtop returned as a new $1995 option for '89 ragtops, complete with heated rear window and cloth headliner.

▲ Chevy shocked many by dropping the Camaro Z28 for 1989, but the IROC (*shown*) carried on in similarly raucous style. Base IROC price: $14,145.

▲ The 1989 Chevy Cavalier Z24 gained gas-charged shock absorbers. Here, the $16,615 Z24 ragtop, of which 13,075 were built.

▲ Besides this $10,375 hatchback sedan, Chevy's '89 Corsica line added an LTZ notchback, a sort of four-door Beretta GT starting at $12,825.

▲ Once a LeBaron, then a New Yorker, Chrysler's M-body Fifth Avenue took a final bow for '89, still with a three-speed automatic and carbureted V-8.

▲ Chrysler's sporty LeBaron GTC coupe (*shown*) and convertible gained 28 horses for '89—for 174 total—via an intercooler on their 2.2-liter turbo four.

• Ford goes after family sedan performance with the new Taurus SHO, powered by a Yamaha-engineered 220-bhp V-6; no automatic transmission is available

• The Ford Probe coupe debuts; its chassis is shared with Mazda's MX-6

• The all-new Ford Thunderbird is shorter, but on a longer wheelbase; the V-8 and turbo four are gone, replaced by a V-6

• Ford Motor Co. vice chairman Harold Poling warns of excess capacity, predicting that automakers will produce 20 percent more vehicles in 1990 than customers want

• Cadillac gets a driver-side airbag and optional Pass-Key theft-deterrent system

• Thunderbird Super Coupe boasts a 210-horsepower supercharged V-6, as well as four-wheel independent suspension

• A six-speed ZF manual gearbox is available for Corvettes; it features computer-aided gear selection for forced low-speed 1st-to-4th shifts to save gas

• The average transaction price for a domestic new car climbs to $14,920

• Pontiac Grand Prix, Oldsmobile Cutlass Supreme, and Buick Regal adopt a 3.1-liter V-6 engine, dropping a weaker 2.8

◀ Lacking sufficient *chutzpah* to justify its $33,000 price tag, the new 1989 Chrysler TC by Maserati was little more than a two-seat LeBaron turbo convertible with subtly different sheetmetal and two fewer seats. The public wasn't moved, so the cars weren't either, and only some 7000 would be built through 1990.

▲ New "faces" freshened up the 1989 Dodge Daytonas, including this top-of-line Shelby model (no longer a "Z") with a 174-horse 2.2-liter "Turbo II" four engine.

▲ Dodge had a new Spirit for 1989, a rounded, roomier sedan replacing the compact 600. Sport-minded shoppers looked to this ES with its 150-horse, 2.5-liter turbo four.

▲ New to the Eagle Premier line for 1989 was this mono-chromatic Limited model with standard all-disc brakes and 3.0 V-6. Few were sold at the initial $19,200 base price.

▲ An AMC artifact new in 1988, the Eagle Medallion was the U.S. version of Renault's midsize 21—and a slow seller that departed after '89. It came in sedan and wagon form.

- The Euro-American TC Maserati is marketed by Chrysler, but never catches on; the last rear-drive Fifth Avenues are built

- Buick Riviera grows 11 inches in length; sales growth follows stretch

- Cadillac De Ville/Fleetwood are revamped; sedans now longer, sleeker

- The 20th anniversary Pontiac Trans Am boasts a 245-bhp turbo V-6; the 6000 STE comes only with all-wheel drive

- Chevrolet Caprice drops its V-6, makes the once optional V-8 standard

- A tire-pressure monitor and Selective Ride Control are optional for Corvettes

- The Quad-4 engine, available in Olds Calais and Pontiac Grand Am, comes with 150 or 185 horsepower

- Mercury launches a new Cougar, similar to T-Bird, including a supercharged XR-7

- Midyear brings Pontiac's limited-edition 200-horsepower McLaren Turbo Grand Prix

◄ Under new owners in 1987, struggling Excalibur expanded its model range in 1988-89 with this Series V Touring Sedan. Price: $73,000.

▶ One of Detroit's brightest '89 stars was the all-new Ford Thunderbird. The 210-horse supercharged SC coupe topped the line at $19,823. Though it was a bit heavier than planned, the '89 Thunderbird SC delivered grand touring performance to rival a BMW, with an easy 7.8 seconds 0-60 mph. Alas, total T-Bird sales fell slightly, to just under 115,000.

▲ Still one of America's top sellers, the Ford Taurus returned for 1989 with a hot new 220-horse SHO sedan. Workaday models like this LX wagon no longer offered four-cylinder power, but the standard 3.0 and optional 3.8 V-6s continued.

▲ Ford's Mustang turned 25 in 1989, but persistent rumors of a hot rod anniversary model proved false. Sales held steady at a still-healthy 209,769, including 42,244 ragtops. Here, the $13,272 V-8-powered GT hatchback coupe.

1989 Calendar-Year Car Sales

1.	Ford	1,502,878	6.	Mercury	474,673	11.	Chrysler	196,125
2.	Chevrolet/Geo	1,348,265	7.	Dodge	447,688	12.	Eagle	69,719
3.	Pontiac	678,968	8.	Plymouth	306,161			
4.	Oldsmobile	600,037	9.	Cadillac	266,899			
5.	Buick	542,917	10.	Lincoln	200,315			

Figures include cars made for the Big Three in plants managed by Japanese companies

▲ Mercury used the T-Bird's basic all-new design for 1989. Base LS and sporty XR-7 were offered. XR-7 returned to assisted aspiration, sharing T-Bird SC's supercharged V-6.

▲ Plymouth won Acclaim for '89: a new midsize sedan to replace its middecade Caravelle. Acclaim was a close cousin to the Dodge Spirit. Here, the top-line $13,195 LX.

▲ Olds dropped a new high-output Quad-4 engine with 185 horses into Cutlass Calais coupes and sedans to create the even-sportier 1989 International Series models.

▲ The Oldsmobile Toronado hit a new sales low for 1989 with just 9877 orders. Only 3734 were standard $21,995 Toros like this; the $24,995 Trofeo accounted for the balance.

▲ Marking Trans Am's twentieth year were 1500 copies of this $25,000 '89 model with a 245-horse turbo V-6 from Buick's late GNX. It did 0-60 mph in just 5.4 seconds. It served as that year's Indy pace car with no engine modifications. Former Indy winner Bobby Unser is pictured here.

▲ Pontiac built 1000 special Grand Prixs in 1988 as McLaren Turbos. They inspired the regular-production Grand Prix Turbo for '89, with a similar intercooled 205-horse V-6 and racy body addenda. Prices started at around $26,000.

▲ Buick unveiled a ragtop Reatta for 1990 after a year's delay. But stickered at $35,000, it proved even tougher to sell than the coupe, and only 2437 would be built through 1991.

▲ Buick tweaked its Skylarks for 1990 adding this $12,935 Gran Sport with firm suspension, alloy wheels, and upgrade interior. Most 'Larks were sold with the smooth "3300" V-6.

▲ After a major '89 restyle that added several inches to both length and wheelbase, Cadillac's 1990 De Ville/Fleetwood line got 25 more horses. Here, the $26,960 Coupe De Ville.

▲ After a sales dip for '89, the Cadillac De Ville/Fleetwood recovered to nearly 175,000 combined for 1990. The $25,435 Sedan de Ville (*shown*) was the sales leader nearing 132,000.

▲ After making do with the rear-drive Astro, Chevy added a front-drive minivan for 1990. Called Lumina APV (All-Purpose Vehicle), it sold respectably but was oddly styled. It was no threat to Chrysler, which still dominated the market.

▲ Bowing in the spring of '89 as a 1990, Chevy's midsize Lumina coupe and sedan took over for comparable Celebrity models. This base four-door, riding a 107.5-inch wheelbase, took half of the line's 295,007 debut-year sales.

1990

- The industry suffers its worst year since 1983, selling only 14.1 million cars and trucks; prospects for 1991 look bleaker yet

- Rebates in the neighborhood of $1000 lure some reluctant buyers into showrooms

- Automakers rely heavily on sales to rental agencies, but those nearly new "program" vehicles later steal new-car sales

- Antilock brakes are fitted in 7.6 percent of 1990 cars (double 1989's count); driver-side air-bags are in 30 percent of domestically built cars

- Domestic model-year output totals 6,276,459 cars (5,021,953 from Big Three automakers)

- Honda Accord beats Taurus as the sales leader for the second straight year; Cavalier and Escort are in third and fourth place

◀ Like all '90 Corvettes, this $37,264 droptop got a new dash and driver-side airbag. But big news for Chevy's sports car was that the ZR-1 finally went on sale—though in coupe form only.

▶ The ZR-1 actually was a $31,683 option package for a 'Vette coupe that listed for $59,000. But some rabid speculators shelled out double that for early examples.

▲ Though it shared a basic front-drive design with that year's revamped Fifth Avenue, higher-zoot Imperial was priced $3600 higher, at $25,000. Output was only 1370.

▲ Only a bit less posh than the reborn Imperial, Chrysler's 1990 New Yorker Fifth Avenue wore similarly square, formal lines. Calendar-year production was decent, at 41,366.

- Driver-side airbags are standard in all American-built Chrysler products (except the Eagle Talon and Plymouth Laser)

- Chevrolet releases the "King of the Hill" Corvette, the ZR-1 coupe, with a special LT1 32-valve aluminum 375-bhp engine

- Lumina replaces the high-volume Celebrity as Chevrolet's midsize offering

- The Lincoln Town Car is fully restyled; dual airbags are intended, but a shortage of bags forces Lincoln to delay installation

- GM launches a sharp-nosed minivan trio: Chevrolet Lumina APV, Oldsmobile Silhouette, and Pontiac Trans Sport

- Chevrolet drops to second place in model-year car production, behind Ford

- Congress passes a new Clean Air Act after a decade of fumbling—emissions must be halved by 1998, starting with a '94 phase-in

- The industry fuel-economy average (CAFE) slides to 28.1 mpg, down from an all-time high of 28.7 mpg in 1988

- Congress nixes a CAFE standard requiring a 40 percent decrease by 2001

▲ The 1990 Chrysler TC by Maserati exchanged its turbo four for a Mitsubishi V-6, provided you ordered automatic. But hardly anyone was ordering this $33,000 car at all.

▲ There was a new LeBaron for 1990, essentially the A-body Dodge Spirit/Plymouth Acclaim in a formal Chrysler suit. A 3.0 Mitsubishi V-6 was included in the $16,000 base price.

▲ Shelving the LeBaron convertible and wagon left the Town & Country name free for…a long-body 1990 Chrysler luxury minivan with woody trim and Chrysler's new 3.3-liter V-6.

▲ A blast from the past in name only, the 1990 Dodge Monaco was a near-copy of the ex-Renault Eagle Premier. It was introduced mainly to boost sales and keep its Canadian plant busy.

▲ The Eagle Premier was treated to all-disc brakes for 1990, plus a floor-mounted shifter for its automatic transmission. The ES Limited (shown) topped the line at $20,272 base.

◄ New in 1989 as an early '90, the Eagle Talon was a retrimmed version of Mitsubishi's new Illinois-built Eclipse sport coupe, as was Plymouth's Laser. Here, turbocharged TSi AWD (all-wheel drive).

1990 Calendar-Year Car Sales

1. Chevrolet/Geo	1,364,096	6. Mercury	390,794	11. Chrysler	185,535
2. Ford	1,321,149	7. Dodge	361,698	12. Eagle	60,646
3. Pontiac	636,390	8. Cadillac	258,168		
4. Buick	536,667	9. Plymouth	252,964		
5. Oldsmobile	511,781	10. Lincoln	231,660		

Figures include cars made for the Big Three in plants managed by Japanese companies

▲ New for '89, the front-drive Probe was intended to replace Mustang, which Ford continued after protests from loyal fans. Though based on Mazda's MX-6, Probe wore an "all-Ford" look and, for 1990, offered the 3.0-liter Taurus V-6 as an option. The sporty GT here used a turbo-four with 145 very strong horses.

▲ Having given Mustang a reprieve, Ford got to work on an all-new design. Meantime, the basic '79 package got a driver-side airbag as its main change for 1990. Here, the LX 5.0L Sport in $12,265 hatchback form. Mustang sales fell by almost half that year, to 128,189.

▲ Ford observed Thunderbird's 30th year in '90 with a $1085 package for the $20,390 Super Coupe. As shown, it added unique paint and trim. Just a few thousand were built.

▲ Fully restyled for the first time in a decade, Town Car got Lincoln's version of the "aero look" for 1990. Sales stayed strong and were in fact up by more than 19,000, to 147,160.

▲ Cross-spoke alloy wheels marked the sporty LSC version of Lincoln's 1990 Mark VII. All models gained a driver-side airbag and a reshaped dashboard. Sales slipped to 22,313.

▲ With fortunes falling, Olds dealers asked for a version of GM's 1990 front-drive minivan. Silhouette offered more luxury than Chevy or Pontiac, but the same 3.1-liter V-6.

▲ An Olds Cutlass Supreme convertible finally arrived in 1990. It had a base price of $20,995, a power roof, and a "structural top bar" not seen on the '88 Indy prototypes.

- NHTSA initiates a rule that will require cars to pass a new side-impact test, starting with 10 percent of 1994 models

- Roger Smith retires from the GM chairmanship, Donald E. Petersen retires from Ford; Robert C. Stempel and Harold A. Poling take over the respective slots

- Traction control is available in the Cadillac Allanté—a first for a front-drive car

- Corvettes get a standard driver-side airbag and advanced ABS II braking

- Dodge Daytona can have a V-6; it's the final year for Omni/Horizon

- Dodge Monaco is a rebadged Eagle Premier, sold through 1991

- Oldsmobile Toronado is restyled, adds a foot in length

- Four-door Cutlass Supremes are now available, plus the first Olds convertible in 18 years, wearing a "structural top bar"

- Diamond-Star Motors in Illinois builds the Mitsubishi Eclipse sport coupe plus American-badged cousins: Eagle Talon and Plymouth Laser

- Ford purchases legendary British carbuilder Jaguar for $2.5 billion

◄ The most enthusiastic Plymouth since Barracuda, the 1990 Laser was one of the three "Diamond-Star" 2+2 coupes built at the new Chrysler-Mitsubishi plant in Illinois. Laser was denied an all-wheel-drive version like the Eagle Talon TSi AWD, but did offer front-drive base, RS, and RS Turbo models, as shown (clockwise from left).

▲ A driver-side airbag was newly standard on 1990 Plymouth Acclaims. A Rally Sport package was optional. Shown is the top-line $13,805 LX sedan. Acclaim output was 120,440.

▲ Pontiac Firebirds got a driver-side airbag for '90. Trans Am GTA remained the hottest—and was even hotter because its 5.7-liter V-8 gained 10 horses, to 235.

▲ Pontiac's 1990 Grand Am boasted one big update: a new high-output Quad-4 engine with 180 horses standard in SE models like this one. Grand Am saw 197,020 cars built.

▲ The Pontiac Trans Sport minivan arrived for 1990 in base and SE trim. Trans Sport offered seating for five or optional 2+2+2 buckets. Base Trans Sports started at $14,995.

CHAPTER FOURTEEN

1991-1999
MARKET SHARE BATTLE

Who could have guessed that the 1990s would turn out so well for Americans—and for the American auto industry? But who could have blamed the naysayers? After all, the 8.2 million cars Americans purchased in 1991 was the weakest total since 1982—and a full quarter of those were imports. The domestic-model tally was barely six million, the lowest since 1959.

The Big Three were clearly suffering as the decade opened, though for different reasons. Ford had made great strides, yet was struggling to break even in an economy turned sour. Chrysler was flirting with financial oblivion yet again, owing to unappealing products (its minivans being the one big exception) and costly nonautomotive acquisitions in the Eighties.

Even worse off was General Motors, which couldn't stop hemorrhaging cash. The reasons were plain enough: stale, slow-selling designs; heavy capital spending with little tangible return; the industry's highest overhead; a bloated, inefficient organization. Loss piled upon loss, each reported in huge headlines, and by the fourth quarter of 1993 they made a towering $18 billion mountain. GM dropped a staggering $11.7 billion in 1992 alone.

Yet within two years, all Detroit was making money again—even GM. What happened? For one thing, the economy began a recovery that steamrolled to record growth. For another, the yen strengthened against the dollar, making Japanese cars more expensive than comparable domestic models, to the benefit of Detroit sales and profits. Prices for all cars still seemed steep, however, and many Americans discovered the advantages of leasing instead of buying. A lease counted as a sale, and that kept factories humming.

Several other factors were at work. After years of unfavorable comparisons, Detroit was by the mid Nineties perceived to have closed the "quality gap." This dovetailed neatly with the desire of many import owners to give Detroit another chance, and many did so with the 1991 launch of GM's Saturn subsidiary that featured a well-made small car, affordable "no-dicker" pricing, and exceptional customer service.

But perhaps the real key to the decade turned out to be something quite unexpected. Americans in 1990 purchased 4.6 million light trucks, barely 30 percent of total vehicle sales. By 1998, half the vehicles sold in the U.S. were light trucks—7.4 million of them. And because the imports were slow to understand America's love of big pickups and, especially, of sport-utility vehicles, the Big Three were the big benefactors.

Ford's smash-hit Explorer led the way, debuting in 1990 and going on to outsell the best-selling car in 1995, '96, and '98. Once buyers got a taste of midsize SUVs, they developed an appetite for even-larger 4×4s. Detroit responded, and soon shopping mall parking lots were crawling with 5500-pound, $45,000 behemoths like the Lincoln Navigator. By the mid Nineties, Ford and Chrysler were selling more light trucks than cars, and GM was killing off such icons as the Buick Roadmaster to devote more assembly line space to truck production. Propelled by the truck boom, 1998 ranked as the second-best year ever for U.S. car sales.

America's newfound hunger for trucks had a profound effect on automotive design. The byword as the industry raced into the new century was "hybrid." This was an altogether new category of vehicle that combined the comfort of a car with the go-anywhere attitude of an SUV. The other sea change was the consolidation of the industry itself. Small and midsize independent makes were gobbled up by giants convinced that survival in the 21st Century hinged on enormous economies of scale. Ford Motor Company acquired Jaguar, Mazda, and Volvo. GM bought out Saab. And then in 1998, Germany's Daimler-Benz AG assumed a controlling interest in Chrysler Corporation, forming a new transatlantic company, DaimlerChrysler.

The family album of the American auto had become in some ways an album of extended families. It reflected new alliances, evolving needs, unpredicted desires, and shifting tastes. It was a little like any American family album might be at the dawn of the new millennium.

1991

- Persian Gulf War tensions and a lingering recession contribute to depressed auto sales

- Model-year production in U.S. plants (including transplants) totals 5,777,211 cars

- Of 8,175,582 cars sold in the U.S., 6,072,255 are domestically built

- Sales of nearly new "program" cars (used in rental fleets) cut into the new-car market

- Ford and GM agree to require rental companies to keep cars in service fleets longer; temporarily reducing the program-car glut

- The Big Three chairmen go to Washington in March to seek Clean Air Act concessions and to oppose potentially tighter CAFE restrictions

- Chrysler chairman Lee Iacocca warns that if Japanese makers keep taking market share, Chrysler could be "gone"

▲ Buick's Regal entered 1991 with cosmetic tweaks and a 170-horse 3.8 V-6 as an upgrade to the standard 140-bhp 3.1. Base price on this Limited coupe was up to $16,455.

▲ The Buick Riviera added standard antilock brakes, five horsepower, and a vinyl-roof option for '91, but production fell again by nearly half to 13,168, a new low for the model.

▲ After 33 years, the Roadmaster name returned in 1991 on Buick's redesigned B-body Estate Wagon to replace the blocky '77-vintage design. Sales were weak at just 7466.

▲ The redesigned front-drive C-body Buicks were all Park Avenues by 1991, the Electra badge having been lost in the update. This base model was priced at $24,385.

◄ Ending a short, unhappy sales life, Buick's two-seat Reatta bowed out after 1991, when it gained an improved "3800" V-6 linked to GM's new electronic T460E automatic transaxle. Upsized wheels and tires were also included, but the Reatta had no place in Buick's future, and only 1313 of the '91s were built. Among them were just 305 convertibles, whose base price was upped nearly $1000 to $35,965. Though all Reattas stand to become collectible, the rare ragtops will surely do so before the coupes.

• Enjoying success, Toyota plans to build a second U.S. assembly plant

• Saturn is the first new American make in 30 years; dealers are "retail partners"; customer satisfaction is a primary goal

• GM offers a new 210-bhp 3.4-liter "Twin Dual Cam" (24-valve) V-6 for midsize Lumina, Grand Prix, Cutlass Supreme

• Low-cost antilock brakes (ABS VI) are offered on a number of GM models

• Smoother, more-efficient electronically controlled automatic transmissions are installed in a number of models

• Chevrolet Caprice is restyled with a softer profile, still boasts a V-8 engine and rear-wheel drive

• Oldsmobile's Ninety Eight is restyled, in time for the model's 50th Anniversary

• Buick's Reatta reaches the end of the line; a limited run of 1313 1991 models cap a disappointing stay for the two-seater

• Splitting the line, Buick offers a new front-drive Park Avenue and a rear-drive V-8 Roadmaster Estate Wagon

▲ A 4.5-liter V-8 upped to 4.9 liters gave C-body 1991 Cadillacs 200 horses versus 180. Also new were electronic automatic transmission and Computer Command Ride shocks. Here, the $34,695 Fleetwood coupe.

▲ The 1991 four-door Seville also featured Cadillac's new 4.9-liter V-8 and Computer Command Ride variable-rate shock absorbers. The sporty STS variant continued to garner buyer favor even with a base price of $37,135.

▲ The Cadillac Brougham switched to a standard Chevy 5.0 V-8 for 1991 and added 30 horses for a total of 170. A Chevy 5.7 V-8 option returned with 185 bhp. Sales dropped 6510 units in 1991, to 27,231.

▲ Chevy's redesigned Caprice line gained a wagon for '91, when output nearly doubled to 217,461. Here, a civilian sedan and 9C1 police-package partner.

▶ The big news for Chevy's '91 Lumina was spelled Z34, an enthusiast-oriented coupe packing a new twincam 3.4-liter V-6 with 210 horses, plus uprated suspension and suitably sportier appearance. It poses here with a standard four-door and APV minivan.

- Subcompact Ford Escort and Mercury Tracer receive subtle facelifts

- Cadillac Brougham now fuel injected, supplied by sister-division Chevrolet

- Chevrolet Beretta/Corsica line adds a standard driver-side airbag; Cavalier offers a convertible, replacing the promised Beretta ragtop that never materializes

- Chevy Camaro's IROC-Z badge is dropped, paving the way for the Z28's return

- Dodge sells the Mitsubishi-built Stealth, similar to Japanese maker's 3000GT

- Dodge adds a convertible to the Shadow line, while the Spirit range expands with the addition of the 224-horsepower turbocharged four-cylinder R/T

- Four-cylinder Mustangs find 17 new horsepower via a new twin-plug head

- A new 200-bhp, 5.0-liter V-8 is offered in the Ford Thunderbird and Mercury Cougar

- Lincoln's Town Car boasts Ford's first mass-produced overhead-cam V-8, a 4.6-liter "modular" engine that produces either 190 or 210 bhp

▲ A new tapered nose graced the 1991 Chevy Corvettes, and standard models got the same rear-end look as the pricey ZR-1—to the dismay of early Z buyers.

▲ Whitewall tires and wire wheel covers dressed top-line Classic Caprices. Initially only one engine was offered, a 5.0-liter V-8 rated at 170-bhp. Base price: $16,515.

▲ A larger 3.8-liter version of Chrysler's 3.3 V-6 was newly standard for the '91 Imperial. It gave only three more horses (150 total), but was torquier. Sales slipped to just 11,601.

▲ Except for optional antilock brakes, there was little '91 news for the Canadian-built Dodge Monaco, a near-identical twin to the Eagle Premier. This is the sporty ES model.

▲ Brightening the '91 Dodge Shadow line was this new ragtop, a conversion by American Sunroof Company. Offered in "Highline" trim and, as shown, a sporty uplevel ES, it came with manual-fold top, seating for four, and a choice of three I-4 engines, including a 152-horsepower 2.5 turbo.

▲ The 1991 Dodge Caravan underwent a complete redesign, the first since its 1984 introduction. Updates included all-new outer body panels (though appearance wasn't greatly altered), a more ergonomic interior, and newly optional full-time all-wheel drive. Base prices ranged from $13,215 to $21,105.

1991 Calendar-Year Car Sales

1. Chevrolet/Geo	1,161,236	6. Mercury	376,059	11. Chrysler	126,383
2. Ford	1,081,290	7. Dodge	324,595	12. Saturn	74,493
3. Buick	544,325	8. Cadillac	213,288	13. Eagle	59,347
4. Pontiac	489,812	9. Plymouth	192,193		
5. Oldsmobile	426,306	10. Lincoln	178,701		

Figures include cars made for the Big Three in plants managed by Japanese companies

▲ ES Limited, the priciest and sportiest Eagle Premier, got a new grille and standard antilock brakes for 1991. All models included air conditioning as standard. Sales for 1991: 11,300.

▲ Ford's Probe saw few changes for '91—except sales, which dropped in a tough market, as did sales of many cars that year. The tally was just under 94,000, versus 117,000 for 1990.

▲ The $20,999 supercharged SC remained Ford's top T-Bird for '91, but the big news was optional 302 V-8 power for base and midrange LX models, with 200 horses.

▲ V-8 Ford Mustangs wore handsome new five-spoke alloy wheels for 1991, when ragtops like this GT gained a slimmer "top stack." Total Mustang sales fell from 128,000 to 98,737.

▲ Like sister Ford Crown Victoria, the Mercury Grand Marquis would be revamped for '92. Here, the $19,940 Colony Park LS wagon.

▲ Mercury unveiled a very different Capri for 1991: a new front-drive convertible based on the Mazda 323 platform but styled and built by Ford Australia. A decklid spoiler identified the $15,920 XR2 with 132-horse 1.6-turbo four-cylinder.

▲ Mercury Cougar XR7 reverted to a conventional V-8 for 1991: a 200-bhp version of the venerable 302 borrowed from Mustang GT and Lincoln Mark VII. Base price was up to $20,905, versus $15,629 for the entry 3.8 V-6 LS model.

• Reworked Chrysler minivans debut, feature a standard driver-side airbag

• Cadillacs get a new 4.9-liter V-8 and electronic transmission

• All Corvettes now wear a convex tail panel, as debuted on the ZR-1

• Mercury dealers market the new Australian-built Capri roadster

• Plymouth Sundance "America" is the cheapest car built in the U.S., just $7699

• A new GTP model replaces the Pontiac Grand Prix Turbo Coupe

• Pontiac Sunbird gets its first V-6, a 3.1-liter unit; the turbo four disappears

• The Avanti Automotive Corporation files for bankruptcy

▲ Like Dodge with Shadow, Plymouth standardized a driver-side airbag for 1991 Sundance models, including new bargain-priced America versions. This is the sporty top-line RS.

▲ Plymouth's 1991 Acclaim lost its turbo option but gained available antilock brakes. This top-line LX again came with 3.0 V-6 engine and four-speed "Ultradrive" automatic.

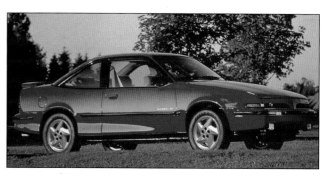

▲ The Pontiac Sunbird discarded its turbocharged four for a 3.1-liter V-6 option that was standard on this sporty $12,444 GT coupe. Larger GT wheels and tires were new.

▲ In January 1991, after the release of a Chevy Camaro ragtop, Pontiac unwrapped its first Firebird convertibles since '69, complete with a new nose inspired by the 1988 Pontiac Banshee show car. The reborn ragtop came in base or Trans Am trim, starting at $19,159. Only about 2000 were built for that model year.

▼ After eight long years and $8 billion in start-up costs, GM's much-anticipated new Saturn subcompacts debuted for 1991 with four four-cylinder models: twincam SC coupe and SL2 sedan (*foreground*), and single-cam SL and SL1 sedans (*SL1 background*). Interest was high with prices as low as $7995, but a deliberate "go-slow" policy held total production to 48,629 for the model year.

▲ A sedan joined Buick's Chevy Caprice-based Roadmaster wagon for 1992, and both models gained a 5.7 V-8 with 180 horsepower. Sedan sales reached 73,817, wagons 11,715.

▲ Ranked tops in Detroit quality by 1992, Buick's full-size LeSabre was redesigned à la Park Avenue, getting standard antilock brakes, but losing all two-door models. Pricing for top-of-the-line Limiteds like this one began at $20,775.

▲ GM's N-body compacts saw major changes for 1992, including Buick's startlingly restyled Skylark. Antilock brakes were standard on all models, including the $15,555 GS seen here.

▲ Cadillac's two-door Eldorado wore its own new design for 1992, growing 11 inches longer on an unchanged wheelbase. Its 200-horse 4.9-liter V-8 was carried over intact. Just over 31,000 Eldos found buyers in '92. Base price: $32,470.

▲ Standard antilock brakes also appeared on 1992 Buick Regal Gran Sports, but remained optional on base Customs like this $16,865 sedan. Calendar 1992 production for the line eased slightly to 97,692 units.

▶ Cadillac also restyled Seville for '92, again aiming for a more distinct look along the lines of Eldorado. Wheelbase grew three inches, while overall length was stretched more than 12.

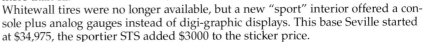

Whitewall tires were no longer available, but a new "sport" interior offered a console plus analog gauges instead of digi-graphic displays. This base Seville started at $34,975, the sportier STS added $3000 to the sticker price.

1992

- A year of relative stability: 8,210,627 cars are sold in 1992; 6,216,488 are domestically built

- Ford Taurus edges past Honda Accord to become the top seller for '92—fleet sales help

- The average transaction price for a new-car purchase is now just over $17,000

- Inspired by Saturn's success, a number of dealerships experiment with "one-price" selling

- Buick LeSabre gets a handsome redesign, similar to linemate Park Avenue; Oldsmobile Eighty Eight gets a similar treatment, as does Pontiac's sporty Bonneville

- The restyled Buick Skylark is still closely related to the Pontiac Grand Am and Oldsmobile Achieva (formerly Calais), but with unique Buick touches and available Adjustable Ride Control

◀ Chevy passed a major milestone in 1992 by building its one-millionth Corvette, a white convertible with that year's new 5.7 LT1 V-8, which replaced the old like-size L98 as base powerplant. Also new that year: standard six-speed manual gearbox, optional ASR ("Acceleration Slip Regulation") traction control, and extra-cost "Quiet Car Package." Here, the historic millionth 'Vette poses with a 1953 original at the Bowling Green, Kentucky, Corvette plant, which hosted 'Vette owners and their cars in a week-long celebration.

▲ Planned but never built for sale was this 1992 Camaro convertible with a new "Heritage Appearance" package, marking 25 years of Chevrolet ponycar history.

▲ The Z34 coupe returned for '92 as the sportiest of Chevy's midsize Lumina coupes, bolstered by newly standard antilock brakes. Base price was attractive at $18,400.

▲ Chevy added this twincam Lumina Euro 3.4 sedan for 1992 as a Z34 running mate, but limited it to four-speed automatic transmission. Base price was $15,800.

▲ The slow-selling Chrysler Fifth Avenue got a slightly rounder face for '92, but buyers resisted its $28,000 base price. Sales slipped from 44,464 to just under 38,000.

• The Roadmaster badge returns on a big rear-drive Buick sedan, joining the 1991 wagon; both get a more potent 5.7-liter V-8

• Even entry-level models get available antilock braking, including Chevrolet Cavalier and Pontiac Sunbird

• Cadillac's Seville and Eldorado are dramatically restyled, with more distinct identities; body panels are not shared

• Buick Park Avenue Ultra boasts a standard supercharged V-6 with 240 horsepower; traction control is newly available

• Corvette gets a new 300-bhp LT1 base engine, still a 5.7-liter V-8; traction control is made standard across the board

• Chevrolet Lumina gets a 3.4-liter Euro package; the option includes a 24-valve six and aero-look body addendum

• Dodge introduces the Viper roadster with a 400-bhp, 8.0-liter V-10 engine—it rivals Europe's fastest exotics in straightline performance at a bargain price: $50,000

• Ford restyles its full-size Crown Victoria, with dual airbags but a same rear-drive platform; the overhead-cam 4.6-liter V-8 is new, a Touring Sedan comes later

▲▶ Quickly evolved from a showstopping '89 concept—with help from Carroll Shelby—the new 1992 Dodge Viper *(above)* was America's hottest production sports car with its brutish 400-horse V-10. Aptly termed a "modern Cobra," it came with six-speed manual gearbox, huge wheels and tires, clip-in side curtains, and skimpy "bikini" top for $55,630. Initial output was deliberately held to 200 units, all finished in red with black interior. Standard outside exhausts gave the Dodge Viper an unmistakable sound.

▲ Dodge's aging front-drive Daytona got yet another facelift for 1992, plus this high-performance IROC R/T model, which was powered by either a 3.0-liter V-6 or optional 224-horse "Turbo III" four-cylinder. Base price: $14,098.

▲ Like the Dodge Daytona, the Mitsubishi-designed Eagle Talon got exposed headlamps and other styling tweaks for '92. This base front-driver started at $13,631 with standard 135-horse 2.0 I-4 and a five-speed manual transmission.

- Dodge's Daytona IROC R/T replaces the range-topping Shelby edition at midyear

- Mercury's Grand Marquis is restyled similar to the Crown Victoria; big Ford/Mercury wagons are history

- Ford Taurus and Mercury Sable boast a subtle restyle; twin front airbags are newly available

- Ford Tempo/Mercury Topaz get a V-6 option; the slow-selling four-wheel-drive versions are gone

- Lincoln Continental gets a passenger-side airbag; after almost ten years, the final Mark VII coupe is built

- Rumors suggest that Oldsmobile's days are numbered, but GM denies it vehemently

- A 205-bhp supercharged V-6 is an Olds Ninety Eight Touring Sedan option

- Oldsmobile's Custom Cruiser wagon gets a larger optional engine, a 5.7-liter V-8 good for 180-horsepower

- Plymouth's subcompact Sundance gets a Mitsubishi-built 141-bhp 3.0-liter V-6, but only in Duster models

▲ A new Sport option with rear spoiler, alloy wheels, and upsized tires added spice to the midline LX version of Ford's 1992 Probe, which continued with standard 3.0 V-6.

▲ Ford's Taurus became America's top-selling car for 1992, helped by a restyle that, though subtle, involved mostly all-new sheetmetal. This LX sedan carried a $17,775 base price.

▲ Ford was nearing completion of a fully redesigned Mustang by 1992, so the old '79 design was altered only in detail from '91 form. Ragtops like this $19,644 V-8 LX 5.0L continued with a no-cost power top. Sales took a beating, falling almost to 79,000.

▲ The 1992 Crown Victoria debuted in March '91 with smooth looks, reworked rear-drive chassis, and Ford's new 4.6 "modular" V-8 with 190 bhp. This police package countered Chevy Caprice's similar 9C1 group.

▼ Like fraternal twin Ford Taurus, the 1992 Mercury Sable was so subtly restyled that it almost escaped notice. A redesigned dash and optional passenger-side airbag were among other changes.

▼ With an all-new replacement just around the corner, 1992 was the end for Lincoln's Mark VII, which was down to just a Bill Blass edition and the ever-sporty LSC (shown). Both listed at around $32,000. Total model-year production was a mere 5732.

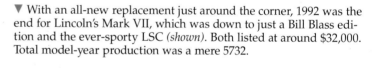

1992 Calendar-Year Car Sales

1. Ford	1,213,761	6. Oldsmobile	389,173	11. Lincoln	161,648
2. Chevrolet/Geo	1,000,891	7. Dodge	290,184	12. Chrysler	148,010
3. Buick	523,569	8. Cadillac	214,176	13. Eagle	59,216
4. Pontiac	519,925	9. Saturn	196,126		
5. Mercury	402,225	10. Plymouth	182,176		

Figures include cars made for the Big Three in plants managed by Japanese companies

▲ Oldsmobile's Eighty Eight line lost its coupes for 1992, but offered two fully redesigned sedans. Antilock brakes were among many standard features on this well-trimmed LS model, which started at $21,395.

▲ Arriving a bit behind the rest of the line, the SCX sport coupe was the quickest of Oldsmobile's new '92 Achieva compacts, with its own 190-horse Quad-4 engine and mandatory five-speed manual. Sales were slow.

▲ The Olds Toronado (shown) and Trofeo bulked up for 1990 to look more "important." Sales rose to 15,022, then dropped to 8000 of the improved 170-horse '91s and just 6436 of the similar 1992s.

▲ Rarity alone doesn't make a car collectible, but it may help the Olds Custom Cruiser, which was redone for '91 but departed after 1992, with just 12,000 sales.

▲ Pontiac's sportiest Grand Prix coupe for 1991-92 was the new GTP. Like Chevy's Lumina Z34, it packed a 3.4-liter "Twin Dual Cam" V-6 with 200/210 horses. Antilock brakes and handling suspension were included.

▲ As with Chevrolet's Camaro, the third-generation Pontiac Firebird would say goodbye after 1992, ending an 11-year run. This base coupe carried a $12,505 starting price. Firebird production hit a record one-year low: 27,566.

▲ Like its sister N-cars, 1992 Pontiac Grand Ams sported new—and rather overt—styling, plus a revived 3.3 V-6 option. Trim levels thinned to just SE and the sportier GT, here in $13,799 sedan form.

◀ Buick's '93 Riviera, on the eve of a completely new design for '95, offered just one engine, a 170-horsepower V-6. The Gran Touring package seen here had an uprated suspension.

▲ Cadillac's slow-selling, two-seat Allanté gained the world-class 4.6-liter Northstar V-8 for 1993. That bit of good news was undercut by the rumors that the Caddy convertible would not be back for 1994.

▲ Cadillac's big rear-drive Fleetwood Brougham was restyled for 1993, à la Chevy Caprice and Buick Roadmaster. Fairly popular, the big Caddy narrowly outsold Roadmaster, 31,773 to 30,958.

▲ Back for '93 from a '92 debut, Chevy's "boy racer" Beretta GTZ sported aero add-ons galore, plus a 180-horsepower version of the 2.3-liter Olds Quad-4 engine. A milder but more refined 140-bhp 3.1 V-6 was optional, and standard in the GT model, which started at $12,575, versus the GTZ's $15,590 base price.

▲ Hard to believe, but America's sports car turned a middle-aged 40 for 1993. Chevrolet celebrated with a 40th Anniversary equipment package for the standard Corvette coupe and convertible, identified by special emblems, interior trim, and Ruby Red paint treatment. Meanwhile, ZR-1 production was reduced to only 380 cars per year because of slow sales. Here, the standard $41,195 ragtop.

1993

- Safety continues to be a major industry focus: Several models offer passenger-side as well as driver-side airbags

- The trend toward sportiness and performance continues, but unemployment and the lingering economic recession hurt car sales

- Demand for used cars remains strong as people are priced out of the new-car arena

- Chevrolet Camaro and Pontiac Firebird are restyled for a midyear introduction—the first full redesign in a dozen years

- Camaro and Firebird boast standard dual front airbags, but are launched only in coupe form, convertibles will come later

- Chrysler debuts LH midsize sedans: Chrysler Concorde, Dodge Intrepid, and Eagle Vision

▲ Chevy Camaro fans cheered at 1993's new fourth-generation coupes (ragtops would be along later): a $13,399 base model with 160-horse 3.4 V-6, and a new $16,779 Z28 with a 275-bhp version of Corvette's LT1 V-8 and standard six-speed manual transmission. Also featured were modified "space frame" construction and more-ergonomic interiors.

▲ The all-new '93 Camaro paced that year's Indy 500, the fourth time the Chevy ponycar was so honored. Here, the special T-top pacer *(foreground)* and its 1967, '69, and '82 predecessors line up for a picture at the Brickyard.

◄ Chrysler wowed critics and consumers alike with its all-new 1993 Concorde, a roomy full-size sedan with front-wheel drive, V-6 power, and sleek "cab forward" styling. Prices started at $18,441. Model-year production was 56,218.

► Still built on Chrysler's compact A-body platform, the 1993 LeBaron again offered an LE model and this swankier Landau, the latter priced around $17,000. Sales were steady but slow: just 22,499 for the year.

- All three "cab-forward" LH cars have dual front airbags and offer two V-6 engines, with traction control available

- Lincoln introduces an all-new Mark VIII, again rear-drive, with a hot aluminum twin-cam 4.6-liter V-8 and dual airbags

- The redesigned Ford Probe again shares structure with Mazda MX-6; both are built in Michigan; the turbo engine is dropped

- Cadillac's final Allantés go on sale, now powered by a Northstar dual-cam V-8 rated at 295 horsepower. "Road Sensing Suspension" and traction control are new standard features this year

- Cadillac Seville and Eldorado hit 295 bhp, with the new Northstar V-8 in Touring Coupe and STS; a mildly detuned Northstar engine comes in the Eldo Sport Coupe

- Mercury launches the smallish Villager minivan, produced in Ohio on the same line as Nissan's similar Quest minivan

- Buick Century gets a new 2.2-liter base engine; ABS is standard on all LeSabres; Park Avenue gets automatic ride control

- The last E-body Buick Rivieras are produced, but the name is expected to return for the 1995 model year

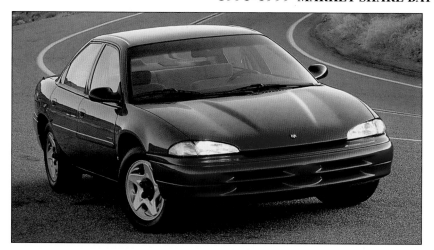

◄ Like Chrysler's Concorde, the 1993 Dodge Intrepid rode on the company's new full-size "LH" platform and boasted similarly sleek "cab forward" sedan styling. But it came with fewer standard frills and lower prices beginning near $16,000 for this base model. A sportier, uplevel ES started at $17,289.

▼ Larger tires on alloy wheels marked the 1993 Intrepid ES, which also came with all-disc brakes. Antilock brakes were optional on both base and ES models. Power was your choice of 3.3 ohv or 3.5 twincam V-6, each mated to a four-speed automatic transmission. Dodge sold a healthy 81,000 Intrepids for the year.

▲ Chrysler's new 1993 "LH" sedan was also sold (with somewhat different styling) as the Eagle Vision. It came as an ESi *(shown)* and the sportier TSi with 3.3 and 3.5 V-6, respectively. Sales totaled 30,676.

▼ The old '79-vintage Ford Mustang went out with a bang after 1993, thanks to a hot new limited-edition Cobra hatchback with tuned 235-horse 5.0-liter V-8, special upsized high-performance tires, and $20,000 base price. Meanwhile, regular V-8 models like this GT hatch were downrated from 225 to 205 horses, owing to a change in Ford's rating system. Mustang model-year sales leaped by 30,000 units to 114,228.

1993 Calendar-Year Car Sales

1. Ford	1,292,227	6. Oldsmobile	380,563	11. Chrysler	194,588
2. Chevrolet/Geo	1,049,618	7. Dodge	368,183	12. Lincoln	173,644
3. Pontiac	544,302	8. Saturn	229,356	13. Eagle	71,225
4. Buick	500,691	9. Cadillac	204,159		
5. Mercury	412,278	10. Plymouth	200,136		

Figures include cars made for the Big Three in plants managed by Japanese companies

▲ Ford's sporty Taurus SHO ("Super High Output") made do with "just" a five-speed manual and 3.0 twincam V-6 for its 1989 debut. For '93 it finally got a four-speed automatic option and a 3.2 V-6 to go with it. Still, sales remained low.

▲ Though still a cousin of Mazda's MX-6, the 1993 Ford Probe was all-new, again with unique styling and its own chassis tuning. Both the base four-cylinder hatch coupe and this sporty V-6 GT proved popular, scoring 137,422 sales.

◄ A far cry from Lincolns of old, the all-new 1993 Mark VIII boasted slick, ultraclean lines and a silky new 4.6-liter twincam V-8, whose 280 horses could run 0-60 mph in 7.0 seconds.

▲ Mercury joined the minivan melee with the 1993 Villager, sharing a front-drive design with the new Ford-built Nissan Quest. A V-6 and four-speed automatic were standard on GS and this uplevel LS at prices from $17,000. Sales were good at close to 109,000.

▲ A 1988 newcomer based on the Mazda 323, the subcompact Mercury Tracer was redesigned for '91 along with Ford's second-series Escort. The '93 lineup again included a sporty LTS four-door, with a twincam 1.8-liter Mazda four. Base price: $12,023.

▲ Mercury's big Grand Marquis sedan was fully revamped along with Ford's Crown Victoria for 1992, losing wagons but gaining a modern new drivetrain. For 1993, the LS (shown) and entry-level GS got a standard passenger air-bag and minor equipment changes.

- Saturn suffers another in a series of recalls, but turns bad publicity into a virtual party as dealers make "fixes" easy to obtain

- *Ford News* fades away after 47 continuous years of publication

- Traction control is available in the Cadillac Eldorado/Seville; passenger-side airbags become standard equipment

- Cadillac's top De Ville is now called Sixty Special; the Fleetwood badge moves to a huge, restyled rear-drive sedan

- The ZR-1 Corvette adds even more horses—now rated at 405 bhp

- Chevrolet Caprice gets rounded rear wheel openings; a bigger 5.7-liter V-8 engine becomes standard on LTZ variants

- Optional Passive Keyless Entry System available on Corvettes: Doors unlock as driver approaches vehicle

- The final Chrysler New Yorker Fifth Avenue/Salons and Imperials are built

- Dodge drops the Spirit R/T sedan, but expects to produce 800 similarly turbo-powered Daytona IROC R/T coupes

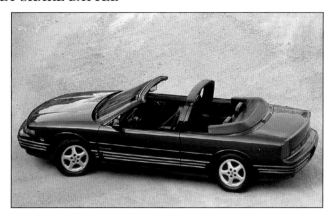

▲ Plymouth's Laser listed a new Gold Decor Package option for 1993 *(shown)*. Plymouth's sporty coupe would not return for '95, when a new U.S.-built design would appear only in Eagle Talon and Mitsubishi Eclipse versions.

▲ Having gained mini-headlamps in a 1992 facelift, the Cutlass Supreme convertible offered a "Twin Dual Cam" 3.4-liter V-6 as a new option in Oldsmobile's 95th anniversary year. Base price for the drop top: $22,699.

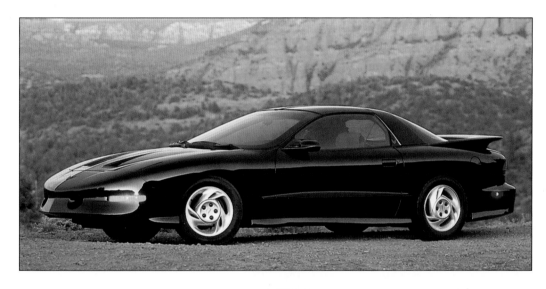

◀ A fourth-generation Firebird bowed for 1993 with the same basic design as the new Camaro, but Pontiac offered two V-8 models—Formula and Trans Am—to Chevy's one, plus a V-6 base car. Here, the Trans Am.

▲ Formula was the bargain performance buy among 1993 Pontiac Firebirds, offering the Trans Am's 275-horse LT1 V-8 and six-speed manual gearbox for about $3400 less to start: $17,995. All the new 'Birds boasted antilock brakes and styling inspired by the '88 Banshee show car.

▲ With more than 247,000 sales, the Pontiac Grand Am bowed only to the Chevrolet Cavalier as General Motors's most-popular 1993 car. That year's models were much like the fully revised '92s, but received new engine mounts and induction systems for quieter four-cylinder operation, plus a firmer "Level III" sports suspension for the top-line GT sedan and coupe *(shown)*.

▲ Buick's 1994 Park Avenues gained passenger airbags, and the uplevel Ultra *(shown)* gained 20 horses—to 225 total—via a revised supercharger. Prices started at $26,999.

▲ Cadillac's sporty Seville STS saw few changes for '94, but its base-model companion was redubbed SLS and given a high-torque, 270-horsepower version of its 295-bhp V-8.

◄ Cadillac was without a Coupe de Ville in '94 for the first time since the 1949 original. But the Sedan de Ville was redesigned on the Seville platform, with styling like that of the latest Fleetwood Brougham. Base priced at $32,990, it came with Speed Sensing Suspension and a 200-bhp 4.9 V-8.

▲ Aimed at luxury imports, the new '94 Cadillac Concours was similar to that year's redesigned Sedan de Ville, but carried the sophisticated Northstar V-8 in high-torque 270-horsepower form, plus Road Sensing Suspension. Price: $36,950.

▲ As promised, ragtop Chevy Camaros returned for 1994 in new fourth-generation guise. Like the coupes, the convertibles came in V-6 base form and high-performance V-8 Z28 *(shown)*. A power top with glass rear window was included on both. Camaro was otherwise little-changed, but traction control was a new mid-season option for Z28s with automatic.

1994

- Some 3000 Dodge Vipers are expected to go on sale, but production grinds to a halt because of poor-fitting hoods

- The Touring Sedan is dropped from Ford's Crown Victoria line, which adds a grille; a passenger-side airbag is available

- Ford Escort and Mercury Tracer go on sale early in the season, marketed under a special one-price, no-haggle program

- The Ford Taurus SHO is finally available with automatic transmission; a passenger-side airbag is made optional in the standard Taurus

- A limited-edition Ford Mustang Cobra debuts, with a modified 5.0-liter V-8 and unique body and interior trim

- A supercharged, 225-horsepower 3.8-liter V-6 is now available in the Pontiac Bonneville SSE and SSEi

▲ Renamed the Lumina Minivan, Chevy's 1994 version of the "GM200" front-drive design wore a bobbed nose that trimmed length by three inches. Options included a $295 power sliding right-rear door and $225 child-safety seats.

▲ Chevy's Corvette added traction control and a passenger airbag as new standard equipment for 1994. The hot ZR-1 returned from '93 with 405 horses versus its previous 375, but remained a tough sell. Here, the dashing $42,960 ragtop.

▶ Chevy revived the nostalgic Impala SS handle for a heated-up '94 Caprice with a 260-horse version of the Corvette LT1 V-8, plus unique styling touches and police-inspired chassis tuning. Price: $22,495.

▲ Among early '94 arrivals were two stylish new top-line Chryslers: the first "cab forward" New Yorker and bucket-seat LHS (*above*). Based on the acclaimed "LH" design, they differed in details but shared a 214-horse 3.5-liter twincam V-6.

▲ After exposing its headlamps in a '93 facelift, the J-body Chrysler LeBaron convertible returned for a final stand with a 3.0-liter V-6 as its only engine. Model choices thinned to this lone GTC, base priced at $16,999. Up for '95: an all-new replacement called Sebring, a mechanical twin of Dodge's forthcoming Avenger.

• The model year begins with sharp price hikes on most models

• Senator Richard Bryan prepares to try again for a 40-mpg CAFE standard by the beginning of the 21st Century

• The emissions focus for the later '90s shifts to carbon dioxide, rather than previously targeted pollutants

• Automakers begin using environmentally safer R-134A refrigerant for air conditioners

• Driver-side airbags are added to the Buick Skylark; Oldsmobile Achieva, Cierra, and Cutlass Supreme; Pontiac Grand Am

• Cadillac de Ville is restyled on a K-Special platform—a stretch of the Seville—with airbags that protect three front passengers

• Passenger-side airbags are newly installed in the Oldsmobile Eighty Eight and Ninety Eight, Ford Thunderbird, Mercury Cougar, Buick LeSabre and Park Avenue, Chevrolet Caprice, and Pontiac Grand Prix/Bonneville

• The new Cadillac De Ville Concours gets a 270-bhp Northstar engine, like the top versions of Seville and Eldorado

▲ After adding black to its color chart for 1993, the Dodge Viper added yellow and green, with a black/tan interior for the latter (in lieu of gray/black). Also new was a device designed to prevent the accidental selection of reverse gear.

▲ The Japanese-built Dodge Stealth continued into 1994 as close kin to Mitsubishi's 3000GT. Tops among the three available models was this racy $37,500 R/T Turbo with a turbocharged 3.0-liter V-6 sending 320 horses to all four wheels.

◄ New for 1994, the front-drive 1995 Neon brought Chrysler's "cab forward" look to the small-car arena—and made value news with prices starting as low as $8975. Sold in identical Dodge and Plymouth guises, it boasted a new 2.0-liter, Chrysler-designed over-head-cam four-cylinder engine with 132 horses. A twincam version followed about six months later. Trim levels comprised base, Highline (shown), and Sport.

▲ Though not that much sportier than other '95 Neons, the Sport version did offer antilock brakes (optional on lesser models) and a "touring" suspension with one-inch-larger wheels and tires at a modest $12,215 starting price.

▲ The '94 Eagle Visions were much like the debut '93s except for power steering with variable-instead of fixed-rate assist. This TSi was base priced at $22,773, but the entry-level ESi now looked almost the same, yet cost just $19,308.

- Chevrolet Caprice adopts dual airbags; the sporty Impala SS debuts at midseason; Beretta comes in base and new Z26 form

- Both the Chevrolet Camaro and Pontiac Firebird add a convertible body style

- No Buick Rivieras are offered this year; the 1995 models will be all-new

- Chrysler stretches Concorde to create upscale New Yorker and LHS models

- The Chrysler LeBaron is reduced to one model, a convertible, with standard V-6; the LeBaron coupe is history, along with the Imperial and Dodge Dynasty

- Chrysler's minivans meet all safety requirements through 1998

- Chrysler's LH cars offer a flex-fuel V-6 that runs on a mix of gas and methanol

- The Dodge Shadow and Plymouth Sundance return for a partial season, then are replaced by the new subcompact Neon sedans; the Shadow convertible is dropped

- Ford debuts an all-new Mustang—the first since '79; V-6 is now the base engine

▲ Aspire was Ford's chunky new 1994 replacement for its 1987-93 Festiva minicar. Offered in three-door form and this new five-door model, the Mazda-designed Aspire was built in South Korea. Prices started at $8240.

▲ The new '94 Mustang was built on a heavily modified version of the old '79-vintage "Fox" chassis, but boasted all-new styling inside and out, plus standard all-disc brakes with optional anti-lock control. Here, the bespoiled $20,160 GT coupe.

◀ Following hard on the hooves of Ford's first redesigned ponycar in 15 years was a new Mustang Cobra, launched in early 1994 with 17-inch chrome wheels, Z-rated tires, and a high-output 240-horse 5.0 V-8 among the unique features. Only some 4000 coupes like this were slated for sale.

▶ Another early 1994 entry was the modestly restyled Lincoln Continental sedan with new grille, taillamps, rocker trim, and standard leather cabin. Prices began at $33,750.

▲ The Olds Cutlass Supreme finally got a driver-side airbag for '94, plus antilock brakes. A new Special Edition sedan and coupe offered more features at a lower $16,995 "value" price.

▲ Despite its 1991 redesign, the Olds Ninety Eight still couldn't match the sales of Buick's Park Avenue. This is the top-line 1994 Regency Elite, which was just shy of $28,000.

▲ Chrysler's new 1995 Neon marked some kind of first in being sold under two different nameplates—though neither the Dodge nor Plymouth versions were actually badged as such. Here, an early example in Highline trim.

▲ After scoring just 9679 sales for '93, Firebird added convertibles for '94. Pontiac marked the Trans Am's 25th birthday with a $995 white-and-blue trim package for that year's new T/A GT coupe. Only 2000 cars were slated to have it.

▲ Like Chevy's Lumina Minivan, the '94 Pontiac Trans Sport wore a newly bobbed nose and standard driver-side airbag. An optional 170-horse V-6 gave greatly improved midrange performance.

▶ GM's Saturn brand had expanded the family by '94 to include "SW" wagons *(front)* and a lower-priced SC1 coupe.

1994 Calendar-Year Car Sales

#	Make	Sales	#	Make	Sales	#	Make	Sales
1.	Ford	1,369,268	6.	Mercury	390,407	11.	Chrysler	197,342
2.	Chevrolet/Geo	1,004,157	7.	Dodge	354,174	12.	Lincoln	179,166
3.	Pontiac	586,343	8.	Saturn	286,003	13.	Eagle	62,495
4.	Buick	546,836	9.	Cadillac	210,686			
5.	Oldsmobile	423,847	10.	Plymouth	197,813			

Figures include cars made for the Big Three in plants managed by Japanese companies

◄ Century was one of the few midsize domestic cars to still offer a station wagon body style. Engines were a 120-bhp 2.2-liter four-cylinder or a 160-bhp V-6. Prices were reasonable, ranging from $16,360 to $17,965. This is the $17,080 Special wagon. A rear-facing third seat was available.

▲ New for base versions of Buick's top-of-the-line Park Avenue was the 3800 Series II, a 3.8-liter V-6 boasting 205 bhp, 35 more than the outgoing Series I engine.

▲ Back after a one-year hiatus, Riviera returned bigger and more powerful. Buick's new coupe would find more than 41,000 buyers in 1995. Prices started at $27,632.

◄ Buick's biggest car was the 4600-pound Roadmaster Estate wagon. It listed for $27,070 in all its eight-seat, vista-roof, faux woodgrain glory.

1995

- Industry sales fall short of expectations: The 14.8 million cars and light trucks sold in calendar-year 1995 is a 2.1 percent drop from calendar-year 1994; car sales fall 4 percent, despite a rush of year-end incentives; truck sales grow to more than 6 million units

- In the last season of its original design, Ford Taurus is the best-selling car for the fourth consecutive year, despite a late sales charge by Honda's increasingly popular Accord

- Ford Motor Company sells more than 2 million trucks, topping General Motors in total truck sales for the first time since 1970

- Honda's former top U.S. sales executive, S. James Cardiges, is sentenced to jail for taking bribes in the ongoing Honda corruption scandal

- GM embarks on a $1 billion revamp of its dealer organization; reducing its number of "dualed" (multiple make) outlets is a goal

► A body-colored grille helps identify the Touring Coupe edition of Cadillac's Eldorado. For '95, its Northstar V-8 had 300 bhp, while base Eldorado's version made 275; both were 5-bhp increases over '94. The standard Road Sensing Suspension, which automatically adjusted firmness based on vehicle speed, body lean, and other factors, added steering angle to its parameters. The ETC listed for $41,535, the base model for $38,220.

◄ Fleetwood, Cadillac's only rear-wheel-drive car, had a 260-bhp 5.7-liter V-8 derived from the Corvette's LT1 engine and could tow 7000 pounds. New for '95 was an on/off switch for the traction-control system.

▲ The revamped Lumina and its Monte Carlo coupe companion were early '95 entries. Lumina was Chevy's best-selling 1995 car, at 214,595 units.

▲ The 260-bhp Impala SS bowed during 1994 as the hot version of the Caprice. For '95, green-gray and Dark Cherry joined black as SS colors.

▲ The redesigned Cavalier featured two- and four-door models, plus a convertible with power top. Priced at $17,210, it was the costliest Cavalier.

• Former Chrysler Corporation chairman Lee Iacocca joins billionaire Las Vegas businessman and Chrysler shareholder Kirk Kerkorian in a bid to take over the automaker; Chrysler's board fends off the effort, but puts a Kerkorian ally on the board of directors and pays Iacocca $21 million in deferred stock options

• Trucks account for 41.5 percent of total U.S. vehicle sales and climb to 49 percent of combined Big Three sales; for the first time ever, the top three selling vehicles are trucks as the Ford Explorer jumps from eighth place in 1994 to No. 3, behind perennial front runners, Ford F-Series and Chevrolet C/K pickups

• CarMax, AutoNation USA, and other "superstores" threaten to revolutionize used-car sales; they apply mass-retailing techniques, offering large inventories of used cars, computerized selection, warranties, and fixed prices—results are mixed, but automakers and traditional new- and used-car dealers watch closely

◄ Corvette paced the Indianapolis 500 for the third time in 1995, and celebrated with 527 near-replicas of the genuine pace car shown. With its 300-bhp LT1 V-8, the 'Vette needed no mechanical modifications to pace the big race.

◄ The 490 roadster was Chevy's entry-level 1919 model. It boasted 26 bhp and sold for $715. The '95 Camaro convertible started at $19,495 for the 160-bhp 3.4-liter V-6 model shown, while the 275-bhp V-8 Z28 ragtop listed for $23,095.

▲ The '95 Monte Carlo went on sale in the fall of '94 as this $16,770 LS model with a 160-bhp 3.1-liter V-6 or the flashier $18,970 Z34 with a 210-bhp dual-over-head-cam 3.4-liter V-6. Its NASCAR debut was in the '95 Daytona 500.

▲ Sebring followed the Dodge Avenger to market as Chrysler's version of the Mitsubishi-built front-drive sports coupe.

• Plymouth is the biggest sales loser in the U.S., declining 28.7 percent from 1994; other big losers: Geo, down 17.6 percent, Lincoln, suffering a 15.8 percent dip

• Lincoln Continental gets a major revamp, replaces its V-6 with a 32-valve V-8

• A national survey reports that the average new-car dealer spends $416 on advertising per car sold; that's up by $42 from 1994

• Ford taps its European Mondeo sedan as the base for the new Ford Contour and Mercury Mystique. They're sportier and pricier than the Tempo and Topaz they replace

• Chrysler drops the LeBaron sedan, leaving the convertible as its only LeBaron model

• At 225 inches, the rear-drive Cadillac Fleetwood is the longest production car produced in the United States

• Mainstream Caprices get the "dogleg" rear-roof pillar shape introduced last year on the high-performance Impala SS

• Optional traction control is offered for the first time for Chevrolet Camaros and Pontiac Firebirds, but only on V-8 models

• GM's midsize cars—the Chevrolet Lumina and Monte Carlo, Buick Regal, and Pontiac Grand Prix—add a passenger-side airbag

◀ Replacing the LeBaron sedan, Cirrus debuted for '95 as Chrysler's new "compact" four-door. Prices started at $17,435 for the base model and $19,365 for the plusher LXi version shown.

▲ The V-10, 400-bhp Viper continued mechanically unchanged for '95, though its cabin gained a passenger assist handle and seat-cushion storage pockets. Dodge had also begun to offer alternatives to the original red exterior/gray interior colors. Emerald Green and Bright Yellow were now offered, with a black-and-tan upholstery combination also available.

▲ Like its Cirrus cousin, the Dodge Stratus came standard with antilock brakes and dual airbags. Base prices ranged from $13,965 to $17,265. A 2.0-liter four was standard.

▲ Aggressive looks and reasonable prices were the appeal of the new-for-'95 Avenger. Dodge sold nearly 35,000 of these front-drive coupes that year. Prices started at $14,460.

- The aging but popular Chevrolet Astro minivan loses the shorter of its two bodies

- GM redesigns the Chevy Blazer and GMC Jimmy, adds a driver-side airbag to both

- Addition of a passenger airbag gives Ford Escort and Mercury Tracer dual airbags, but they both retain motorized front shoulder belts and manual lap belts

- Chrysler launches its import-fighting Neon as an early 1995 model; sold in identical form under Dodge and Plymouth brands, the front-drive subcompacts debut as sedans in January 1994, and for the start of the '95 model year, gain 2-door coupe versions—engines are single- and dual-overhead-cam 2.0-liter 4-cylinders

- Average new-car loan rate is 11.2 percent

- Chevrolet redesigns its best-selling car for the first time in more than a decade, giving the Cavalier a longer wheelbase, fresh exterior styling, and a new interior with standard dual airbags. Pontiac's version of this front-drive "J-Car" subcompact is also redesigned and changes its name from Sunbird to Sunfire

- Big Three production is 49 percent trucks

▲ Targeted at import buyers was the Eagle Vision version of Chrysler's LH cars. This is '95's top-line TSi model. It had a 214-horsepower 3.5-liter single-overhead-cam V-6.

▲ The power driver's seat was now optional, but a CD player was newly available as Mustang cantered into 1995 largely unchanged from its '94 overhaul.

▲ Replacing the Tempo for '95 was the far more competent, and more expensive, Contour. Ranging from $13,310 to $15,695, base prices were about $2400 higher.

▲ Original '55 Thunderbird: two seats, 2980-pound curb weight, $2944 base price, 16,155 sales. Forty years later: five seats, 3536 pounds, $17,400 base price, 104,254 sales.

▲ Mystique was Mercury's version of the new Contour. Both had four- and six-cylinder engines. Tight rear-seat room would be an ongoing criticism.

◄ Bowing in December '95, the new Lincoln Continental was longer and wider than before. Big change was underhood, where a 260-bhp V-8 replaced the 160-bhp V-6.

605

▲ Plain-Jane Plymouth Acclaim could be had for as little as $12,470 in '95. This was its seventh, and last, year.

▲ Supplanting Sunbird was Pontiac's Sunfire. Coupe models were this 120-bhp, $11,074 SE or the 150-bhp, $12,834 GT.

▲ Aurora bowed for '95 to signal a new direction for Olds-mobile. It targeted luxury imports and started at $31,370.

▲ Bonneville's SSEi kept its 225-bhp supercharged V-6 for '95, while base V-6s beefed up by 35 bhp, to 205.

▲ Aero trim adorned Pontiac's Grand Prix GTP. The GTP group included a 210-bhp V-6. Coupes started at $17,384.

◄ A passenger-side airbag and 15 more horsepower for the base engine were additions to the '95 Saturn line. Reasonably priced from $9995 to $13,815, these plastic-body coupes, wagons, and sedans generated strong buyer loyalty. With sales of 285,674, Saturn was GM's top-selling '95 car.

1995 Calendar-Year Car Sales

1. Ford	1,279,096		6. Oldsmobile	371,725		11. Lincoln	150,814
2. Chevrolet/Geo	1,054,071		7. Mercury	361,315		12. Plymouth	113,565
3. Pontiac	566,826		8. Saturn	285,674		13. Eagle	53,612
4. Buick	471,819		9. Chrysler	215,164			
5. Dodge	403,839		10. Cadillac	180,504			

Figures include cars made for the Big Three in plants managed by Japanese companies

◀ Buick stole a beat from its corporate cousins with the Regal GS. Its 3.8-liter V-6 was smoother, quieter, and torquier than the twincam 3.4 V-6 in the Grand Prix, Lumina, and Cutlass Supreme.

▶ Sixty years of technology separated the Buick Roadmaster from its 1936 namesake. Curb weight of the '96 sedan versus the '36, 4211 pounds to 4100; horsepower, 260 to 120; price, $25,560 to $1255.

▲ De Ville *(second from left)* replaced a 200-bhp pushrod V-8 with the 275-bhp dual-overhead-cam 4.6-liter V-8, giving Cadillac a totally Northstar-equipped front-wheel-drive lineup for '96. The others *(from left)*: Concours, Seville, and Eldorado.

1996

- Nineteen ninety-six marks the centennial of the American automobile, celebrating the anniversary of the first "motor wagons" built by brothers Frank and Charles Duryea in Springfield, Massachusetts

- For the first time, the Big Three sell more trucks than cars—5.7 million pickups, minivans, and sport-utility vehicles—versus 5.3 million cars

- Flamboyant, penny-pinching Australian Jac Nasser is appointed president of Ford Automotive Operations

- Total domestic and import truck sales increase 7.8 percent to a record 6.6 million and account for 43.7 percent of all vehicle sales. Car sales fall 1.2 percent. For the year, total vehicle sales rise by 2.5 percent, to 15.1 million units

◄ Corvette's fourth generation went out with a flourish in '96, with silver Collector Editions and this very special Grand Sport. Just 1000 of the latter were built and they used a 330-bhp LT4 V-8. Other 'Vettes had the slightly less-potent 300-bhp LT1.

▶ Borrowing Corvette's 5.7-liter LT1 V-8, albeit detuned to 285 bhp for '96, was the Chevy Camaro Z28. It was hot enough to pace NASCAR's third Brickyard 400. Base Camaros, meanwhile, traded their 160-bhp 3.4-liter V-6s for smoother 200-bhp 3.8-liter units.

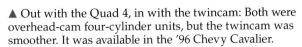

▲ Out with the Quad 4, in with the twincam: Both were overhead-cam four-cylinder units, but the twincam was smoother. It was available in the '96 Chevy Cavalier.

▲ GM shelved its big rear-drive cars after '96, including the Caprice Classic wagon. This $22,405 eight-seater came with a 5.7-liter V-8. Woodgrain was a $595 option, though.

- Ford Taurus is redesigned for the first time since its 1986 introduction

- Aided by incentives, Taurus retains title of best-selling car, but 51 percent go to fleets; next up Honda Accord, by contrast, tallies fleet sales of only 4.2 percent sales

- GM sues former VP J. Ignacio Lopez, charging that he stole company secrets when he left to join Volkswagen in 1993

- Average price of a new domestic car drops to $16,998, lowest since 1991

- GM's market share continues to shrink, to 31.1 percent during 1996. Riding the boom in truck sales, Chrysler Corporation increases its market share to 16.2 percent

- The average new-car loan rate drops to 9.8 percent, down from a decade-high 11.2 percent the previous year

- Ford Motor Company increases its holdings in Mazda Motor Corporation from 25 percent to 33.4 percent; the move costs Ford $500 million and effectively gives it full control over its long-time affiliate; Ford's best-selling 1996 car is the Taurus, at 401,049 units; Mazda's U.S. car sales are 180,975 for the year

- Dodge rolls out a coupe companion to the Viper roadster; the new GTS has 450 bhp

▲ Fully redesigned for the first time since their debut as 1984 models, Chrysler Corporation's '96 minivans were sleeker and smarter. This is the top-line Chrysler Town & Country.

▲ Replacing the LeBaron as Chrysler's ragtop was the '96 Sebring. Sebring coupes used a Mitsubishi platform, but the attractive new convertible was built off Chrysler's own JA chassis.

▲ The New Yorker nameplate, used first in 1938 and the oldest still in use in the U.S., was retired in mid '96. This sedan is the last to wear the badge. The related LHS soldiered on.

▲ Dodge's Viper RT/10 roadster was joined in 1996 by the GTS coupe. Both used a V-10, but the new coupe had 450 bhp to the RT/10's 415. No modification was required for the GTS to pace that year's Indy 500. Dodge also supplied support trucks.

► Cloned from the Mitsubishi Eclipse, Talon ranged from this 140-bhp $14,830 ESi to the 210-bhp, $20,271 all-wheel-drive TSi. Sales of 13,842 made Talon Eagle's best-selling '96 model.

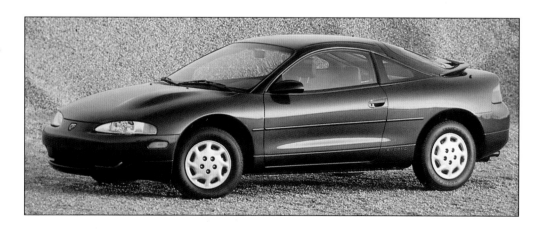

• "We have bona fide car people in sales and marketing, not Pampers people."—Chrysler Corporation's outspoken president and chief operating officer Robert Lutz, commenting on a reorganization of GM's executive ranks that brought in "brand" specialists with noncar backgrounds

• Spy photographers vie for views of the next Corvette; 1996 marks the end of the C4 generation that debuted for 1984

• Chrysler Corporation redesigns its popular minivans, giving them their first complete overhaul since their debut as 1984 models when they revolutionized the auto industry; the '96 Dodge Caravan, Chrysler Town & Country, and Plymouth Voyager feature sliding doors on both sides of the van

• Ford's Explorer gets an optional V-8, addressing what many felt was the popular sport utility's shortfall—a lack of power

• General Motors closes the book on its full-size, rear-wheel-drive cars, announcing the assembly lines that build the Buick Road-master, Cadillac Fleetwood, and Chevrolet Caprice and Impala will be converted to full-time truck production after the 1996 model year wraps up

• The only General Motors product to crack the 1996 top-10 list of best-selling vehicles is the full-size Chevrolet C/K pickup

◀ Taurus defended its title as America's best-selling car with a fully redesigned model for '96. It was larger inside and out, and more expensive. Two V-6s and, for the SHO, a V-8, were offered.

▶ Oval styling themes on the sedan and wagon drew mixed reviews. But Ford took steps—mostly in the form of rebates—to keep Taurus, which started about $1500 higher than in '95, popular. Buyers drove home 401,049 of the front-drivers, and Taurus was once again America's best-selling car.

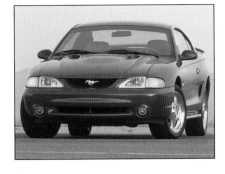

▲ Mustang's 5.0-liter had roots in the original 1965 model's V-8. For '96, a 4.6-liter overhead-cam V-8 with 215 bhp in the GT and 305 in the Cobra (*shown*) replaced the aged pushrod 5.0.

▲ Lincoln marked its 75th anniversary in '96, and the Town Car was its best-selling model. Big, pillowy, and with base prices between $36,910 and $41,960, it defined traditional rear-wheel-drive V-8 American luxury.

▲ Like its Ford Crown Victoria cousin, Mercury's '96 Grand Marquis came with a 4.6-liter overhead-cam V-8 of 190 bhp, or 210 with available dual exhausts. This rear-drive sedan started at $21,975. Sales were a healthy 99,770.

- "Why is it that people think they have to have a 55-gallon barrel of Mountain Dew to drive to work? A long time ago, there was a horsepower race. Now there's a cupholder race."—GM designer Jerry Palmer

- Average amount financed on a new vehicle in 1996: $16,987

- Tried-and-true pushrod V-8 is replaced by an overhead-cam design in the '96 Mustang

- Rick Hendrick, America's biggest auto retailer, is indicted by the United States Justice Department, charged with paying kickbacks to Honda executives in the ongoing Honda bribery scandal

- With a thoroughly redesigned Wrangler due in the spring as an early 1997 model, Jeep doesn't bother to certify a '96 model, choosing instead to build enough additional 1995s to bridge the gap

▲ Sable was also redesigned for 1996 and again shared its platform and mechanicals with the Ford Taurus. Offered in sedan and wagon form, sales increased 11 percent over '95, to 114,164. It was again Mercury's top-selling 1996 model.

▲ Sable's sedan styling was slightly more conservative than that of its Taurus cousin. Like the Ford, Sable offered a 145-bhp 3.0-liter pushrod V-6 and a new 200-bhp 3.0-liter overhead-cam V-6. But Mercury had no counterpart to the SHO.

▲ Aurora got daytime running lights and a $1295 base price increase to $34,360, for '96. Olds also fixed the rear-window distortion that had drawn complaints. Sales fell by 2827 in the car's second season, to 23,717.

▶ Achieva underachieved, selling just 40,344 units for Olds in '96. Even the homelier-still Buick Skylark sold 51,299. Pontiac's Grand Am, which shared their underskin design, buried them both, with sales of 222,477.

▲ A new logo reviving its old sailboat icon wasn't the only thing new for Plymouth in '96. It boasted a new Breeze sedan *(third from left, above)*, and the year's hottest show car, the retro hot rod Prowler. Prowler would make it to production as a '97 model.

▲ Breeze contained itself to a four-cylinder engine and limited options to keep its base price a tempting $14,310.

▲ A new factory option for Formula *(shown)* and Trans Am, Ram Air kicked the 5.7-liter V-8 from 285 bhp to 305.

▲ Revised front and rear styling and 240 bhp for the supercharged V-6 (up by 15) were Bonneville's 1996 changes.

▲ For '96, Saturns got their first styling change since their debut as 1990 models. This is the $11,395 SL1 sedan.

1996 Calendar-Year Car Sales

1. Ford	1,240,928	6. Mercury	354,848	11. Cadillac	168,703
2. Chevrolet/Geo	1,045,172	7. Oldsmobile	306,486	12. Lincoln	141,476
3. Pontiac	529,710	8. Saturn	278,574	13. Eagle	28,695
4. Buick	427,350	9. Chrysler	212,021		
5. Dodge	421,945	10. Plymouth	169,172		

Figures include cars made for the Big Three in plants managed by Japanese companies

▲ For '97, Park Avenue moved to the rigid new platform GM introduced on the Buick Riviera and Olds Aurora. Styling retained traditional Park Avenue themes, but the wheelbase grew by three inches, weight by 250 pounds.

▲ Base Parks used the 205-bhp 3.8-liter V-6 and started at $29,995. The Ultra (*shown*) included the 240-bhp supercharged 3.8, plus traction control and goodies in its $34,995 base price. Sales jumped 30 percent, to 68,777.

▲ Redesigned for '97, Buick's Century retained its conservative appeal but wrapped it in new sheetmetal. Base models started at $17,845, Limiteds (*shown*) at $19,220. Both had a V-6.

▲ Cadillac moved to attract younger, import-oriented buyers for '97 by retrimming GM's Opel Omega and calling it Catera. The compact-sized sedan started at $29,995.

▲ The huge rear-drive Fleetwood was dead, leaving the $36,995 De Ville to carry Cadillac's big sedan torch. De Ville got standard side airbags and a subtle facelift for 1997.

◄ Concours was the performance version of the De Ville. It had 300 bhp instead of 275, a more sophisticated suspension, and a starting price of $41,995.

1997

- By type, the big sales gainers were again light trucks; sales of pickups, minivans, and sport-utility vehicles gained 3.9 percent, increasing their share of the U.S. market to 45.3 percent.

- For the first time since 1991, a domestic nameplate was not the nation's best-selling car, as the Ford Taurus fell from the top spot to finish behind sales-champ Toyota Camry and runner-up Honda Accord

- Another healthy year for the U.S. auto industry, with sales of 15.1 million domestic and imported cars and trucks, a negligible increase over 1996

- Cadillac retains its crown as America's best-selling luxury brand, increasing sales 7.2 percent, to 182,624; GM executives, who had earlier shelved plans for a Cadillac SUV, could not help notice that archrival Lincoln has a hot seller in its new Navigator 4×4 wagon

▲ Chevrolet redesigned its two-seat sports car for '97, retaining a rear-wheel-drive layout, fiberglass body panels, and V-8 power, but changing most everything else. A hatchback coupe with a removable roof panel debuted first. Wheelbase grew by 8.3 inches, to 104.5, but body length increased just 1.2 inches. A new chassis eliminated the tall frame rails of the previous generation, making it easier to get into and out of the spaciously redesigned cabin. Underhood was a new all-aluminum 5.7-liter pushrod V-8 with 345 bhp. The transmission—six-speed manual or four-speed automatic—was relocated to the rear axle, for better weight distribution and more interior room. At $37,495 to start, the fifth-generation 'Vette had Ferrari-like performance: 0-60 mph in 4.7 seconds and a 172-mph top speed.

▲ Camaro marked its 30th anniversary in 1997 with an orange-stripe package that emulated the 1969 Indy 500 pace car's. The look debuted on the Camaro Z28 that paced the 1996 Brickyard 400. Here it is with its pace car ancestors.

- The Japanese automakers' share of the U.S. vehicle market in '97 climbed to 23.5 percent, while the Europeans rose to 3.9; GM (31.1 percent) and Ford (25.2 percent) held steady; Chrysler Corporation's share dropped from 16.2 percent to 15.2

- Cadillac hunts import intenders with the Catera, a luxury-trimmed version of the Opel Omega from GM of Germany

- Casting a wary eye at the trend in nontraditional superstores, Ford Motor Company attempted to, in effect, buy out its dealers in Indianapolis and Salt Lake City and form a new-age retailing venture of its own; dealers balked and refused to sell

- Most 1997 General Motors cars, minivans, and SUVs are fitted with standard daytime running lights (DRLs)

- Drivers of cars had hated them for years, but in the first hard evidence of an SUV backlash, The New York Times ran a series of articles criticizing sport-utility vehicles for fuel inefficiency and casting them as threats to smaller vehicles in collisions

- Long-awaited redesign of the Chevrolet Corvette brings new styling, a new chassis, and an all-new all-aluminum LS1 V-8

▲ The left-side sliding door that proved so popular upon its 1996 introduction became standard on all 1997 Chrysler Town & Country models. This is the top-line LXi version, which listed for $31,465 and had a 166-bhp 3.8-liter V-6.

▲ A terror on the street, Viper wasn't afraid to go racing. The GTS-R was the endurance-racing version and sported competition-ready aero addenda and suspension pieces, while boosting output of the V-10 to well over 600 bhp.

◄ Dodge's Stratus had racing in its blood, too. Its competition iteration finished first and second in the 2.0-liter class in the short-lived North American touring car series. Like production versions, the racers were front-wheel drive.

▲ Caravan sales slipped five percent coming off its '96 redesign, but Dodge still had America's best-selling minivan in 1997, with 285,736 units. This is the Grand Caravan LE: $25,825 with front-wheel drive, $28,870 with AWD.

▲ Sold by Chrysler Corporation's Jeep-Eagle division, the Mitsubishi-made Talon accounted for 10,206 of Eagle's 15,352 sales in 1997. The Vision sedan made up the balance. This is the front-drive, 140-bhp, $14,830 Talon ESi.

• Despite flat sales, Ford and GM are earning record profits, thanks mainly to more-efficient manufacturing practices plus the boom in truck sales; Ford's profits are up 58 percent and GM's 19 percent

• Changes in the ranks: Jack Telnack, 60, VP of Ford design, retires; J Mays, 43, who, as a designer at Volkswagen, was credited with the New Beetle, is appointed VP of design at Ford Automotive Operations

• Redesigns at Buick for '97: Century gets its first complete makeover since the front-wheel-drive version was introduced in 1982, and the flagship Park Avenue moves to General Motors's newest big-car platform while maintaining familiar styling and carryover powertrains

• Standard side airbags are newly standard features for Cadillac's facelifted De Ville and Concours

• Ford revamps its Escort, giving the popular subcompact and its Mercury Tracer cousin new styling inside and out

• Thunderbird flies the coupe; Ford stops production of the two-door icon, but hints that the nameplate will be back

• Eagle Vision is dropped, but Talon is on life support as Chrysler prepares to kill the Eagle brand

▲ Thunderbird's 1990-97 generation was big and heavy, and sales fell as big coupes went out of fashion. The final 1997 model weighed 3600 pounds and came with a V-6 or V-8.

▲ Topping the Taurus line for '97 was the performance-minded SHO. It had a 235-bhp Yamaha-built 3.4-liter twin-cam V-8, but lack of a manual transmission cooled its sport-sedan appeal.

▲ Escort was redesigned for 1997. Sedans and this wagon body style carried over, but with fresh styling. A 110-bhp four-cylinder was the sole engine. Prices started at just $11,015.

▲ Mark VIII was freshened at the rear, too, with a full-width neon light bar. New outside mirrors tilted down when the car was shifted into reverse.

▲ With the demise of GM's big rear-drive cars, the 1997 Mercury Grand Marquis and its Ford Crown Victoria cousin were America's only traditional full-size V-8-powered sedans.

▲ Cougar was Mercury's formal-looking version of the Thunderbird, and it, too, was suffering. Sales fell by 5499, to 30,516 for '97, while T-Bird's sank by 13,387, to 66,334.

▲ Only the second four-door sedan to pace the Indy 500, Oldsmobile's '97 Aurora could claim a kinship to the winning race car, which used a V-8 based on Aurora's production 4.0 liter.

▲ Sharing its basic structure with the new Chevy Malibu, the fresh-for-'97 Cutlass was Olds' newest midsize entry. It came with a 160-bhp 3.1-liter V-6 and started at $17,325.

◄ Chrysler Corporation design chief Tom Gale was a fan of true hot rods, and company vice chairman Robert Lutz was a "car guy." They put their money where their hearts were by championing the transformation of the Prowler from a show car to a 1997 production Plymouth. Sticker price was $38,300, but demand for the limited-edition, rear-wheel-drive two-seater pushed some early buyers to pay double that.

◄ All first-year Prowlers were purple with a black folding top. The only powertrain was Chrysler's 214-bhp 3.5-liter overhead-cam V-6 and four-speed Autostick automatic transmission with manual-shift capability. Prowler looked retro but extensive use of aluminum, including in the body, made it pretty high tech. There was only a sliver of trunk space, so Chrysler offered a matching trailer.

◄ Wide Track was back. Pontiac's redesigned 1997 Grand Prix had racy new styling and larger dimensions, including a front track wider by two inches and a rear wider by three.

◄▼ The General Motors EV1 put electric power on the street in 1997 in this aerodynamic front-drive two seater. Its plastic body's aerodynamic shape gave the EV1 a 0.19 coefficient of drag, lowest of any production car.

◄ Owners loved them, but the aged Saturns attracted fewer buyers for '97. Sales fell 10 percent, to 251,099.

1997 Calendar-Year Car Sales

1. Ford	1,009,297	6. Mercury	337,082	11. Cadillac	157,213
2. Chevrolet/Geo	980,554	7. Oldsmobile	251,663	12. Lincoln	139,540
3. Pontiac	556,662	8. Saturn	251,099	13. Eagle	15,352
4. Buick	438,064	9. Chrysler	188,929		
5. Dodge	372,832	10. Plymouth	159,417		

Figures include cars made for the Big Three in plants managed by Japanese companies

▲ Buick's Park Avenue got depowered airbags and OnStar satellite communications capability, but still saw sales slip about 16 percent, to 58,187, coming off its 1997 redesign.

▲ Sales jumped 23 percent for '98 as Buick marked Regal's 25th anniversary with a special trim package. Base price was $20,945 for the 195-bhp LS, $23,690 for the 240-bhp GS.

◄ Redesigned for '98, Seville retained front-wheel drive and Cadillac's Northstar V-8 rated at 275 bhp in the base SLS model and 300 in the STS (shown). Styling was evolutionary but the body was shorter by 3.1 inches and wheelbase longer by 1.2 inches. The STS started at $46,995, but could easily top $52,000 with such options as Cadillac's new $1202 Adaptive Seat System in which air cells in the front seats adjusted to suit body shapes.

▲ Sedans in the $29,000-$40,000 range were the fastest-growing luxury-car segment and Cadillac was there with the Catera. It started at $29,995, but sales were tepid.

▲ Eldorado spent nearly two decades as essentially a two-door Seville, but the '98 model didn't share the new platform of the redesigned Seville. Sales fell 33 percent, to just 15,765.

1998

• Propelled by the truck boom, 1998 ranks as the second-best year for U.S. car sales ever; combined sales from all makes totaled 15.6 million, behind only the 16 million recorded in 1986; trucks took 47.5 percent of the market in '98—in 1978, it was just 25.3 percent

• Times are good for car manufacturers: 1998 is the first time in history Americans purchased more than 15 million cars and light trucks for three consecutive years

• The world of business is rocked by the merger of Germany's Daimler-Benz, maker of Mercedes-Benz, and Chrysler Corporation; the new company, DaimlerChrysler, would be controlled by Daimler, but aimed to keep Mercedes and Chrysler product lines distinct

• A Ford family member is again in control of Ford, as William Clay Ford, Jr., 41, great-grandson of founder Henry Ford, is elected chairman of Ford Motor Company

◀ Chevy unveiled the sexy open-air version of its Corvette for 1998. Priced at $44,425, $6930 more than the hatchback coupe, the convertible snared about 45 percent of the 29,208 sales for the year. It shared the coupe's 345-bhp LS1 V-8.

▶ Chevrolet's big sport-utility Tahoe wasn't a hit with police, but Camaro's pursuit package, which could be had with the Z28's sport suspension and 305-bhp Corvette-derived 5.7-liter V-8, was just the ticket for highway patrol duty.

▲ Chevy also offered this Lumina police package. It had a heavy-duty suspension and seats. But with front-wheel drive, unibody construction, and a V-6, wasn't really cop-friendly.

▶ Corvette's new convertible needed no mechanical modifications to pace the '98 Indy 500. It posed with the three other 'Vettes to do the honors.

- For the 17th consecutive year, Ford's F-Series was the top-selling vehicle; second- and third-best-sellers were also trucks: the Chevrolet C/K and Ford Explorer; most-popular car was the Toyota Camry; best-selling domestic nameplate among cars was the Ford Taurus, in seventh place

- Buick Skylark and Oldsmobile Achieva, oddly styled and poorly market focused, are dropped from their respective lineups

- Oldsmobile continues its quest for a new image by introducing the 1998 Intrigue. It says the new midsize sedan is a "tightly focused" car designed to take on the world's best imports. It offers just one body style, one powertrain, one seating configuration, and one suspension setup

- General Motors loses $2.5 billion in profits and thousands of customers in a 54-day strike by the United Auto Workers

- Turning its back on the theories of its legendary brand-architect Alfred Sloan, GM in effect combines executive staffs of Chevrolet, Pontiac-GMC, Oldsmobile, Cadillac, and Buick into a single body that will serve the needs of all the divisions

- Attempting to recapture the "Standard of the World" title it admits it lost, Cadillac unveils a new Seville intended to better the quality and value of such brands as Lexus

▲ Concorde was redesigned for '98, keeping front-wheel-drive and a 113-inch wheelbase, but getting dramatic new styling and a 7.5-inch stretch in overall length. Use of aluminum in the suspension, hood, and engine cut weight by 100 pounds.

▲ Concorde offered a $21,305 base model and, for an extra $3000, a plusher LXi trim level that included leather upholstery and other amenities. Even loaded, Concorde cost less than most less-roomy, and less-zoomy-looking, rivals.

◄ America's best-selling convertible was again the Chrysler Sebring, though about half its 40,000 annual sales were to rental fleets.

▲ Just as distinct as the Concorde and even racier looking than its underskin twin was the redesigned 1998 Dodge Intrepid. The Dodge version had slightly tauter suspension tuning than the Chrysler, but both had great road manners.

▲ Intrepid and Concorde shared two new V-6s, both over-head-cam designs. The base 2.7-liter had 200 bhp and the 3.2 had 225. Intrepid offered the $19,865 base model or the $22,465 ES *(shown)*, which came with the 3.2-liter engine.

- Lincoln's Mark VIII follows its corporate relative, the Ford Thunderbird, to the grave

- Chevrolet drops the Geo badge, bringing the Toyota-based Prizm and Suzuki-based Metro and Tracker under the Chevy label. Chevy coined the Geo name in 1989 as a global-sounding sub-brand to market Japanese-sourced or designed models

- Each of the Big Three U.S. automakers register record sales years for light trucks

- Responding to new concerns regarding the dangers of airbags, the National Highway Traffic Safety Administration allows airbag-cutoff switches and permits automakers begin to phase in depowered airbags that deploy with less force

- Some auto-show concept cars don't look as advanced as the two new full-size sedans Chrysler puts into production as the Chrysler Concorde and Dodge Intrepid

- As Jeep readies a redesigned Grand Cherokee for '99, it gives the '98 a last shot of power with an available 245-bhp V-8 and creates a new category: the muscle SUV

▲ Dodge's new-for-1998 Durango offered big V-8 power and seating for eight in a compact SUV package.

▲ Both the Viper GTS coupe and RT/10 roadster now had the same 450-bhp version of the 8.0-liter (488-cid) V-10.

▶ Ford's Special Vehicle Team did its high-performance handiwork on the Contour to create the 195-bhp SVT.

▲ Dodge Avenger sales continued to slip, falling 25 percent, to just 24,084 for 1998. This is the $17,585 ES version.

◀ Escort's two-door coupe shared little with the stodgy other versions. It was called the ZX2 and had 130 bhp.

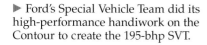

▲ Mustang's only change for '98 was 10 more horsepower, now 225, for the GT model. This is the GT convertible.

◄▲ Lincoln redesigned its Town Car for '98, giving it all-new sheetmetal and trimming it by three inches in length and 200 pounds in heft. Sales climbed five percent, to 97,547. Base prices ranged from $37,830 to $41,830, depending on trim level. All shared a rear-drive design and an overhead-cam V-8.

▲ New front and rear styling and a revamped suspension identified the 1998 Mercury Grand Marquis.

▲ Cutlass occupied the entry-level rung of Oldsmobile's midsize ladder. It outsold make mate Intrigue nearly 2-1.

▲ Gone was Oldsmobile's one-model strategy for the Intrigue. By late '98, this midsize offered three trim levels. Intrigue felt more grown-up than the brash Grand Prix and more sophisticated than the Regal. It didn't share its stablemate's available super-charged V-6, keeping the regular 3.8 for '98.

▲ Voyager didn't offer the largest V-6 available in its Dodge and Chrysler minivan siblings, and the right-side sliding door was optional. But it was Plymouth's top-selling '98 model.

▲ Breeze followed Plymouth's basic-transportation script, but it did jazz things up a little for '98 by offering an "Expresso" trim package and a 150-bhp alternative to its 132-bhp four.

▲ Dodge or Plymouth, Neon was the same two- or four-door subcompact. Plymouth didn't field a version of the Dodge edition's sporty R/T package, though it did offer the 150-bhp engine.

▲ Grand Am was in the last year of its 1992-1998 incarnation, and though sales fell 13 percent for '98, it remained Pontiac's best-selling model. This is the GT coupe. Price: $16,324

▲ Standard instead of optional on the 1998 Bonneville SSE was Pontiac's Eye-cue Head-up Display, which projected speedometer readings and other information onto the windshield.

▲ The WS6 Ram Air option added $3100 to the $22,865 Firebird Formula (shown), the $25,975 Trans Am coupe, or $29,715 convertible. It boosted the 5.7-liter V-8 from 305 bhp to 320.

▲ Saturn coupes were late to get the facelift applied to sedans and wagons. Base prices spanned $10,595 to $15,715 in this line of GM-built subcompacts.

◄ Its cars were dated, but Saturn's image was intact, nurtured by a low-pressure one-price strategy and a homey approach that included this visitor welcome center at its assembly plant in Spring Hill, Tennessee.

1998 Calendar-Year Car Sales

1.	Ford	1,064,412	6.	Mercury	324,096	11.	Lincoln	143,262
2.	Chevrolet	867,432	7.	Oldsmobile	261,986	12.	Plymouth	139,670
3.	Pontiac	477,421	8.	Chrysler	235,860	13.	Eagle	3,458
4.	Buick	398,156	9.	Saturn	231,786			
5.	Dodge	360,229	10.	Cadillac	156,818			

Figures include cars made for the Big Three in plants managed by Japanese companies

▲ A 1999 LeSabre posed with a '59 to mark its 40th birthday. The front-drive sedan was both Buick's best-selling model and America's most-popular full-size car in '99. Prices started at $22,725 for the entry-level Custom.

▲ Buick killed the Riviera early in the '99 model year. About 200 of the last 2000 built for the year were tagged Silver Arrows, after the original 1963 Riviera concept car. Riviera prices started at $33,820.

▶ Burned by the surprise success of the Lincoln Navigator SUV, Cadillac for '99 introduced the first truck in its 96-year history. Escalade moved GM's flagship division into the SUV field with a slightly restyled version of the GMC Denali, a luxury SUV based on the four-door Chevrolet Tahoe/ GMC Yukon. Escalade's base price was $45,875 with standard leather and automatic four-wheel drive.

▲ Eldorado's holdover design still didn't have side airbags, as did most rivals, but for '99, the Touring Coupe version (*shown*) did get optional massaging front seatbacks.

▲ Seville met the competition with standard side airbags, but no rival offered its optional "rolling" front-seat lumbar bolsters that massaged the lower back in 10-minute cycles.

1999

• Chrysler clips the wings of its Eagle division after clearing inventories of 1998 Talon sports coupes; the brand, launched in 1988, never caught on as an alternative to import lineups

• The Oldsmobile Eighty Eight celebrates its 50th—and last—birthday in 1999. General Motors retired the proud old nameplate as it revamped its large-car line.

• Slow sales prompt Buick to stop production of Riviera after only 2000 1999 models are built. About 200 of the last Rivs are Silver Arrow models with distinctive silver paint and special trim; Silver Arrow is the name of the 1963 concept car that spawned the original Riviera

• Cadillac examines the creation of sporty performance versions of several models

▲ Chevy's Corvette added a lightweight hardtop body style to its convertible and hatchback choices for 1999. The hardtop (*foreground*) shared the other models' 345-bhp V-8, but not luxury options new to them: a head-up instrument display and a power telescoping steering column.

◄ Camaro got a new-look nose for '98. For '99, traction control, previously exclusive to V-8 models, was made available on the base V-6 versions. Here's the base coupe.

▲ Cavalier was Chevy's best-selling car, offering coupes, sedans, and this Z24 convertible. It included a 150-bhp four-cylinder and a power folding top in its $19,571 base price.

▲ Chrysler's homegrown Sebring convertible handily outsold its Mitsubishi-sourced Sebring coupe. The JX ragtop (*shown*) listed for $23,970 and the leather-upholstered JXi for $26,285. Both came with a V-6, automatic transmission, ABS, and power top with a glass rear window and defroster.

- Despite the explosion of auto-buying information on the Internet, auto dealers and analysts say that as of 1999 it hadn't had much impact on the way cars are sold

- GM and Ford lay plans to build pickup-truck beds out of plastic instead of metal

- Pope John Paul II greets crowds in Mexico from a custom Cadillac De Ville stretched 30 inches and shorn of its top

- Ford acquires the automaking side of Volvo for $6.45 billion; with Jaguar and Lincoln, the move gives Ford a powerful array of luxury brands; Ford plans to capitalize on Volvo's reputation as an upscale, safety-minded, and environmentally conscious brand

- Nineteen ninety-nine opens with light trucks accounting for 49.7 percent of U.S. vehicle sales

- DaimlerChrysler creates a "brand bible" to ensure that Mercedes-Benz products remain distinct from Chrysler, Dodge, and Plymouth models; the document is meant to preserve Mercedes prestige by banning sharing of designs, platforms, or marketing

- Chrysler savior-turned-nemesis Lee Iacocca resurfaces as chairman of EV Global Motors Co., a maker of electric-powered bicycles

▲ New-for-'99 was this luxury version of the Chrysler Concorde. Called the LHS, its front and rear look was distinct from the Concorde, and it used a 253-bhp 3.5-liter version of Concorde's 225-bhp 3.2-liter V-6. Base price: $28,850.

▲ Companion to the LHS was the 300M, which cost the same and used the same V-6, but emphasized performance via tauter suspension settings and Chrysler's Autostick transmission, which helped the automatic mimic a manual.

◄▲ The new 300M was a spiritual descendent of Chrysler's fabled "letter-series" models of the 1950s and '60s. Unique front and rear bodywork trimmed the 300M's overall length to under 200 inches, shortest of the "LH" cars and enough to help it sell overseas.

◄ Optional on Dodge's version of the Neon coupe was the $2870 R/T package. Included were a 150-bhp twincam four, four-wheel discs, sport suspension, and body stripes. It did 0-60 mph in 8.5 seconds. Not bad for an under-$14,000 sportster.

• An analysis of the origin of cars and light trucks sold in America in 1999 shows that 85.6 percent were assembled in North America (including Canada and Mexico), 9 percent were imported from Japan, 3.8 percent came from Europe, and 1.6 percent were built in South Korea

• Worldwide, auto-production capacity is 74 million vehicles in 1999, but projections are for approximately 52 million sales

• Responding to complaints from shorter drivers, and recognizing that women make up a healthy percentage of sport-utility drivers, Ford gives the big Expedition and Lincoln Navigator an adjustable brake and accelerator-pedal cluster that moves forward about three inches

• CarMax and AutoNation USA used-car superstores blame aggressive new-car incentives for their lackluster profit picture

• General Motors markets two generations of full-size pickups as 1999 models. As production ramps up on the new-generation Chevrolet Silverado and GMC Sierra, limited offerings of the 1988-generation Chevrolet C/K and GMC Sierra Classic continue to roll into showrooms as '99 models

• Ford offers its Explorer and Windstar with a safety system that sounds a warning of objects in the way when backing up

▲► Ford's ponycar celebrated its 35th anniversary in 1999 with new styling and more power. The base model's 3.8-liter V-6 gained 40 bhp, to 190, and the GT's overhead-cam 4.6-liter V-8 gained 35 bhp, to 260. Traction control was a first-time option on these rear-drive coupes and convertibles. A wider rear track improved handling and four-wheel discs were newly standard. This is the $24,870 GT convertible.

▲ Standard seat-mounted front side airbags and an increase of 15 horsepower, to 275, for its twincam 4.6-liter V-8 were the big changes to Lincoln's front-wheel-drive Continental for '99.

▲ Town Car was America's only homegrown rear-wheel-drive luxury car and the Lincoln gained standard front side airbags for '99. Base prices ranged from $38,325 to $42,825.

- Lincoln begins training dealers to serve buyers of its coming LS luxury/sport sedan; dealers are coached to adjust to younger, more affluent shoppers who usually consider only European or Japanese cars

- DaimlerChrysler continues to consolidate Chrysler-Plymouth dealers with Jeep stores; it enters 1999 with the project about 70 percent complete, but runs into resistance from dealers who don't wish to be merged

- Longtime Corvette modifier Callaway Cars sets the price on its ultraperformance, 440-horsepower C12 version of the 1999 Corvette convertible: $211,000

- Surviving on subcompacts since its 1991 inception, Saturn prepares to introduce two midsize models, a sedan and wagon based on cars built in Europe by General Motors's Opel division; they'll be "Saturnized" with selected plastic composite body panels

- One of the worst blizzards of the century descends on the country's Midwest, snarling transportation and wrecking havoc with the North American International Auto Show in Detroit. *AutoWeek* reports a frustrated, snowbound Volkswagen executive takes a cab from Chicago to Detroit for the show and pays the $800 fare in cash

- Pontiac drops the Trans Sport moniker and renames its minivan Montana

▲ Cougar debuted for 1999 as a "new-edge" styled Mercury coupe built on the Contour/Mystique platform.

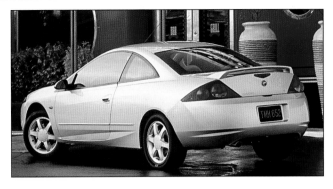

▲ Four-cylinder Cougars had 125 bhp and a base price of $16,195. V-6 models had 170 bhp and started at $16,695.

▲ Oldsmobile's Alero was a grown-up "sophisticated" GM cousin to the boy-racer Pontiac Grand Am.

▲ A 50th Anniversary Edition marked the end of the Olds Eighty Eight. Anniversary Editions started at $27,350.

◄ Oldsmobile ended production of the original Aurora at the close of the '99 model year. An evolution of its platform would return as a larger model with both V-6 and V-8 power.

• Wary of losing the domestic luxury-car sales race to Lincoln, Cadillac extends its 1998 sales reporting period to include vehicles sold through January 4, 1999; the move helps the GM division beat out Lincoln by 222 units for calendar 1998 and thereby preserve the title held since 1941

• Appalachian State University in Boone, North Carolina, offers a course entitled "A History of Southern Stock Car Racing"

• Chevrolet launches a redesigned Tracker compact SUV; it is again built from the same design as Suzuki's SUV, now called Vitara

• The IRS calculates that for the first time since 1981, the cost of owning and operating a car or truck has gone down, and announces that the standard tax deduction or employee reimbursement for use of a vehicle for business will decrease from 32.5 cents to 31 cents per mile

▲▲ Plymouth's hot rod Prowler sat out '98, then returned for 1999 with a new 3.5-liter V-6 of 253 bhp, 35 more than the engine it replaced. Prowler now did 0-60 mph in six seconds, not seven. Black, yellow, or red paint added $1000. Hot rod touches included a steering-column-mounted tachometer and central gauges in a body-colored cove.

▲ A power driver's seat was optional for the first time in the Breeze. This roomy Plymouth included standard air conditioning, tilt steering, and a folding rear seatback for $15,115.

▲ Neon sedans had an abbreviated 1999 model year, as the redone 2000 versions slid into stores early. This is the last of the '99 four-doors, which started at just $11,425.

▲ The Pontiac Grand Am, America's best-selling compact car, was redesigned for 1999. Styling was new, wheelbase increased 3.6 inches, and overall width grew by two inches.

▲ Sedan and coupe Grand Ams returned with a standard 150-bhp twincam four-cylinder engine. Uplevel models, including this $18,970 SE coupe, got a 170-bhp 3.4-liter V-6.

▲ Anticipating a redesign for 2000, the Pontiac Bonneville essentially stood pat for '99. This is the base SE model, which started at $22,800 and had a 205-bhp V-8 and standard ABS.

▲ Trans Am convertible gave Pontiac a 305-bhp rear-drive muscle car that listed for $30,245 in 1999. Its power-operated top had a glass rear window with defogger.

▲ Saturn's two-door coupes became three-door coupes during the '99 model year with introduction of a rear-opening "suicide" back door on the driver's side.

▲ Inspired by those on extended-cab pickup trucks, the new rear door on Saturn coupes eased rear-seat access, but didn't open independently of the front door. Coupe prices started at $12,445.

1999 Calendar-Year Car Sales

1. Ford	1,100,730	6. Mercury	343,404	11. Lincoln	137,243
2. Chevrolet	884,749	7. Oldsmobile	281,989	12. Plymouth	125,980
3. Pontiac	552,350	8. Chrysler	249,318		
4. Buick	445,611	9. Saturn	232,570		
5. Dodge	369,977	10. Cadillac	154,610		

Figures include cars made for the Big Three in plants managed by Japanese companies

CHAPTER FIFTEEN

2000-2005

AN INDUSTRY REDEFINES ITSELF

The most interesting thing about the turn of the century was not what had happened to the American automotive landscape, but what had failed to happen. Detroit had not crumbled under pressure from Asian competition, the SUV craze had not subsided, and private automobile ownership had not been regulated out of existence.

Most disappointing to fans of '50s and '60s *Popular Science* cover art, flying cars were still nowhere to be found. In fact, not only were cars not flying, they were still mostly the four-wheeled, gas-powered, steel-skinned, and reasonably affordable vehicles Henry Ford and Ransom Olds were building before World War I. Still, things had changed.

By the early 2000s, rare was the car that was not available with antilock brakes or keyless entry; and traction control, satellite radio, and navigation systems were becoming common.

The mood in Detroit had also changed. Japanese automakers were no longer a temporary threat whose voracious appetite for market share could be staved off by a single "home run" model or design. The Asian makers were now regular diners at the American auto-sales table, and their perpetual hunger for sales growth a permanent part of the new automotive paradigm.

By the end of 2003, Toyota had replaced Ford as the world's second-largest automobile manufacturer. General Motors was still struggling with its promise to again claim 30 percent of the U.S. market, and the DaimlerChrysler-controlled Chrysler Group had lost its once unbreakable hold on the minivan market.

Yet, despite an early decade recession and America's involvement in multiple Middle East conflicts, auto sales remained robust. More significant, far from being crushed, a reborn Detroit was showing renaissance levels of design, creativity, and market savvy.

General Motors embraced niche marketing, a practice the behemoth wouldn't consider even in the late 1990s. Examples included Cadillac's $80,000 XLR, a bold rival for Mercedes-Benz sports tourers; the half pickup, half sporty coupe Chevrolet SSR; the reborn Pontiac GTO, built from an Australian design; and the small, topless, and sporty Pontiac Solstice, a true Miata fighter.

Ford climbed aboard, too. The $140,000 retro-chic GT recalled Ford's legendary late-'60s GT40 Ferrari beater, but with even greater performance. Replacing the aged Taurus, the Five Hundred sedan with European styling and available all-wheel drive, sent Ford in a new direction, as did the hybrid-powered Escape.

Looking to recreate a bygone segment, Chrysler and Dodge made bold, unapologetic returns to their large-car roots. The rear-drive 300C and Magnum were modern interpretations of the traditional big car. Combining flagrantly American style with available "Hemi" V-8 power, Chrysler's new full-size offerings undid decades of "me-too" design. Even Jeep was preparing to challenge convention by offering the Liberty with the division's first-ever diesel.

Detroit had become more agile and opportunistic than at any point in the past 30 years, America's auto industry was again a source for forward-looking design and engineering. And while the dream of "driving the Japanese back to their shores"—as one auto executive boasted of Detroit's new batch of 1960 compacts—was all but forgotten, the prospect of reclaiming market share was very real.

Although battle-scarred by the loss of Oldsmobile and Plymouth and humbled by Asian efficiency and quality, the industry that shaped a nation had survived one of its most challenging decades intact. With renewed vigor, Detroit entered its second century, calloused and ready for its toughest battles yet.

2000

- Aided by incentives, industry light-vehicle sales reach a record 17.4 million

- Chevrolet offers the redesigned Monte Carlo and a reborn Impala on a shared midsize chassis

- The Dodge and Plymouth Neon are redesigned and offered in early 1999 as 2000-model-year cars

- Ford introduces the Focus, and Lincoln debuts the LS, both with a European flair

- Pontiac Bonneville and Buick LeSabre are redesigned on a platform shared with the existing Cadillac Seville and Buick Park Avenue

- In January, Ford announces it will launch the Th!nk brand in the U.S.; the new brand will offer environmentally friendly battery/electric vehicles

- Rick Wagoner becomes CEO of General Motors on June 1, taking over for Jack Smith who remains chairman

◀▲ Arriving a half season early, the restyled 2000 Buick LeSabre boasted gentle curves and a more-contemporary feel. Its structure was shared with Buick's Park Avenue and the Cadillac Seville, but its base price of $23,235 was a bargain by comparison.

◀▲ Sporting crisper lines, Chevy's new Impala (*left*) replaced Lumina as the make's premium midsize car. Sharing the Impala's structure was the new bustleback Monte Carlo (*above*). Both cars sported a standard 3.4-liter V-6. A 3.8-liter V-6 was optional.

▼▶ Jay Leno (*below*) paced the 1999 Indy 500 in a 2000 Monte Carlo. New for Chevy's Venture minivan (*right*) was the Warner Bros. Edition. A standard second-row videotape player was part of the deal.

- Ford buys Land Rover from BMW AG for $2.7 billion in July

- DaimlerChrysler buys a controlling 34 percent stake in Mitsubishi in July

- In August, 6.5 million Firestone tires are recalled due to tread separations that are linked to 148 traffic deaths, many in Ford Explorers; the fiasco spurs public and congressional scrutiny

- In September, Ford announces it is no longer bidding for the Korean automaker Daewoo Motor Co., leaving General Motors as the likely buyer

- DaimlerChrysler CEO Jürgen Schremp admits to the *Financial Times* that the 1998 Daimler-Benz acquisition of Chrysler Corp. was a takeover, not a "merger of equals"; major stockholder Kirk Kerkorian sues

- Chrysler group CEO Jim Holden is fired and replaced by Dieter Zetsche; company morale suffers as employees view the move as a takeover by German parent company DaimlerChrysler

- In December, GM announces it will disband its oldest division, Oldsmobile; the process will take a few years

▲ The chipper subcompact Neon was freshened for 2000. Available from Dodge or Plymouth dealers, Neon sported a standard 132-horsepower four. Prices started at $12,460.

▲▼ Europe's 1999 Car of the Year came to America as Ford's new subcompact for the 2000 model year. A two-door hatch (*above*), a wagon (*below*), and a four-door sedan comprised the all-four-cylinder lineup. Base Focus price: $11,865.

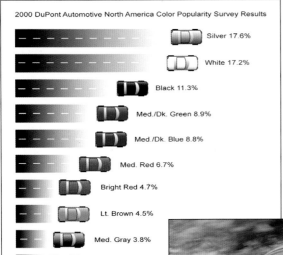

2000 DuPont Automotive North America Color Popularity Survey Results

- Silver 17.6%
- White 17.2%
- Black 11.3%
- Med./Dk. Green 8.9%
- Med./Dk. Blue 8.8%
- Med. Red 6.7%
- Bright Red 4.7%
- Lt. Brown 4.5%
- Med. Gray 3.8%
- Gold 3.5%

▲ According to industry paint-supplier DuPont, Silver was the automobile color most preferred by U.S. customers in 2000.

▶ Ford's 2000 Taurus shed its ovoid look for a more-contemporary design. A more-traditional dashboard was part of the update.

◀ When shown at Detroit's 2000 North American International Auto Show in January, Ford's retro-styled Thunderbird concept looked production ready.

◀ Big changes for GMC's big rigs brought revised sheetmetal and new engines for the 2000 model year. Twins to Chevrolet's Tahoe and Suburban, Yukon (*left*) and Yukon XL (*right*) enjoyed new "Gen III" V-8s that displaced 4.8, 5.3, and 6.0 liters.

◀▶ A sports sedan in the BMW idiom, Lincoln's new LS boasted rear-wheel drive and optional V-8 power. Meant to appeal to Euro-sedan intenders, the conservatively styled LS proved a tough sell. With a V-6, the base price was $30,915.

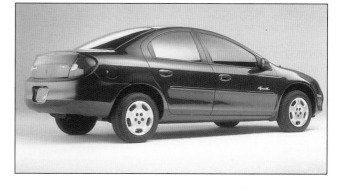

▲ Like its Ford Taurus cousin, Mercury Sable shed its bubble-look skin for a more linear design. Base price: $18,845

▲ Less cheeky than its predecessor, the restyled 2000 Plymouth Neon was positioned as an "upscale" subcompact.

◀ Clinging to its extroverted nature, the redesigned Bonneville retained most of its brash styling cues for 2000. The SSEi (*far left*) sported a 240-horsepower 3.8-liter V-6.

2000 Calendar-Year Car Sales

1.	Ford	1,089,769	6.	Chrysler	314,568	11. Lincoln	155,086
2.	Chevrolet	890,807	7.	Mercury	282,153	12. Plymouth	58,901
3.	Pontiac	542,427	8.	Saturn	271,800		
4.	Buick	404,612	9.	Oldsmobile	216,801		
5.	Dodge	367,900	10.	Cadillac	165,808		

Figures include cars made for the Big Three in plants managed by Japanese companies

◄▲ Quickening the pace for 2001, the Corvette stable added a new thoroughbred. Chevy's 385-horsepower Z06 offered supercar dash for modest cash: $46,855. Base hatchbacks and convertibles returned, but the hardtop was dropped.

▲▶ Although the rear-drive Ford Crown Victoria still dominated the police market, a growing number of law-enforcement fleets were adding Chevy's front-drive Impala (*above*) to their rolling stock. Monte Carlo (*right*) earned pace car honors at the 2000 Brickyard 400. Just 1300 replicas were built.

◄▲ The retro-chic PT Cruiser was a sales success for Chrysler. Roomy and attractive, the functional four-cylinder "mini-minivan" started at $15,935.

2001

- Helped by zero percent financing, industry light-vehicle sales reach 17 million units, down just 2.3 percent in what was expected to be a tough year

- Chevrolet offers a new high-performance Corvette, the 385-horsepower Z06

- Chrysler introduces a retro-styled compact called PT Cruiser that merges elements of 1930s cars and modern minivans

- Chrysler's Sebring line is redesigned with sedans and convertibles built by Chrysler and coupes built by Mitsubishi

- Ford introduces its first compact SUV, the Escape, in 2000 as a 2001-model-year truck

- Ford offers the Bullitt Mustang and a Harley-Davidson-edition F-150

- Pontiac introduces a crossover SUV called Aztek that is widely panned for its styling

▲ Though redesigned, Chrysler's Sebring line carried over its split heritage. Sedans and convertibles were built by Chrysler, while coupes came from Mitsubishi's Normal, Ill., factory. A 2.4-liter four was the base engine for all three Sebring models.

▲ New styling and more power marked 2001 for Chrysler's Town & Country and Voyagers. Prices started at $19,160.

▲ A fresh face and more muscle arrived for Dodge Caravan in 2001. The top engine option was a 215-horsepower 3.8-liter V-6, up 35 for the new year.

▲ This top-line Escape XLT likely came with the optional 3.0-liter V-6. Buyers on a budget could opt for the base XLS with the standard 2.0-liter four.

▲ Launched in 2000 as an early 2001, Ford's compact Escape struck a chord with buyers looking for SUV utility in a more-efficient package.

◀ A carlike interior contributed to the Escape's sales success. Buyers snapped up almost 165,000 of the "cute utes" in calendar year 2001. Base price: $17,645.

• In May, Ford recalls 13 million more Firestone tires as the death toll due to crashes caused by tire separations has risen to 271

• Firestone responds to the Ford recall by ending the companies' 100-year relationship; a federal judge grants class-action status to Ford/Firestone customers

• In September, General Motors hires 69-year-old Bob Lutz to be its product czar

• In the wake of the Sept. 11 terrorist attacks, GM announces "Keep American Rolling" zero percent financing

• With sales and quality in decline, Ford CEO Jacques Nasser is fired on Oct. 30 and replaced by Bill Ford, Jr.

• Nick Scheele, formerly of Ford of Europe, is named Ford's COO and President of Automotive Operations

• In November, Bob Lutz is named chairman of GM North America, replacing Ron Zarella; Gary Cowger is named president of GM North America

• Despite price cuts and a return to incentives, slow sales spur Chrysler to eliminate 26,000 jobs by the end of 2001

◀▲ Ford offered a snappy trio of new trucks for 2001. The F-150 Lightning (*left*) melted tires thanks to its 360-horsepower supercharged 5.4-liter V-8. Explorer Sport Trac (*top, above*) combined pickup utility with SUV interior accommodations. The F-150 Harley Davidson Edition (*bottom, above*) sported a detuned Lightning V-8 and Harley-themed decor.

◀ Big, brash, and expensive, the Harley-Davidson Edition F-150 was the ultimate biker accessory. Leather seating with sewn-in Harley emblems was included in the $33,780 price.

◀▼ Recalling Steve McQueen's legendary movie ride, the $3695 Bullitt package spruced up Ford's aging Mustang. A GT option, the Bullitt sported unique wheels, tauter suspension tuning, and five extra horsepower. Production was limited to 6500.

▲▶ The poshest Sierra yet, GMC's new C3 (*above*) took the brand's pickups up a notch. Price: $38,305. A similar Denali model spruced up the full-size Yukon and Yukon XL (*right*). A 6.0-liter V-8 powered the upscale GMCs.

▲ Celebrating its 60th anniversary in 2001, representative vehicles of the Jeep family gathered for a photo in front of the Walter P. Chrysler Museum.

◀▲ A 32-valve version of Ford's 5.4-liter V-8 distinguished Lincoln's Navigator (*left*) from Ford's similar Expedition. A new Town Car L (*above*) stretched six inches longer than the standard Town Car.

▲ Founded in 1897, and incorporated into GM in 1908, Oldsmobile entered 2001 marked for death. The announcement came as a surprise to the make's loyal customers. *Left to right:* Silhouette, Alero, Aurora, Intrigue, and Bravada. Intrigue would die first.

639

◀ A race-bred aluminum chassis and a 320-horsepower Ford V-8 combined to create the Panoz Esperante. Just 100 of these $80,000 convertibles were built in 2001.

▲ A 150-horsepower engine was added to the Plymouth Neon lineup for 2001, but only as part of the R/T or ACR packages. This car's wheels were a $410 option.

◀ The Plymouth brand was in its final season, but the popular Prowler would move to Chrysler for 2002. Here is one of the last retro roadsters to wear a Plymouth badge.

◀▼ Officially a "crossover" vehicle, Pontiac's new Aztek ventured stylistically where no make had gone before. Mechanically derived from the make's Montana minivan, Aztek's bold look polarized buyers. Base price: $21,445. Available all-wheel drive gave Aztek SUV credentials, but sales were slow. A number of "lifestyle" options were available, including a unique hatch-mounted tent.

2001 Calendar-Year Car Sales

1. Ford	978,113	6. Dodge	329,053	11. Lincoln	127,038
2. Chevrolet	830,038	7. Saturn	260,337	12. Plymouth	31,234
3. Pontiac	456,664	8. Mercury	244,167		
4. Buick	373,924	9. Oldsmobile	173,694		
5. Chrysler	342,447	10. Cadillac	130,503		

Figures include cars made for the Big Three in plants managed by Japanese companies

◄▲ Though mechanically similar to the Pontiac Aztek, Buick's new-for-2002 Rendezvous wore more restrained styling. Available six-passenger seating and copious storage space helped boost sales. Base price: $25,024.

► The last of a breed, Cadillac's Eldorado would be discontinued after 2002. Not immune to the large coupe's fall from favor, Eldorado sales slipped under 10,000 for 2001. The potent 4.6-liter V-8 carried over intact, available with 275 or 300 horsepower. The sporty top-of-the-line ETC started at $45,000.

◄▼ Based on Chevy's popular Avalanche, Cadillac's Escalade EXT became the marque's first pickup truck. A specially tuned version of GM's truck-duty 6.0-liter V-8 was the top Escalade mill.

▲ Shedding any pretense of subtlety, Cadillac's big, brash Escalade returned for 2002 with a fresh look and more power. Though mechanically related to the Chevy Tahoe, only the big Caddy could claim a 345-horsepower V-8.

2002

- Thanks to zero percent financing, industry light-vehicle sales remain strong at 16.6 million; the Big Three account for only a 61.4 percent market share, its lowest ever

- Light-truck sales outpace car sales for the first time ever

- Generals Motors introduces the Pontiac Solstice concept at January's Detroit Auto Show, showing product is king at GM

- Although it shares a minivan platform with its sister Pontiac Aztek, the new Buick Rendezvous sports less-questionable styling

- Cadillac offers its first pickup truck, the Escalade EXT, which is basically a spruced up Chevrolet Avalanche

- Chevrolet marks the final year of the Camaro with a 35th anniversary edition SS model; the Pontiac Firebird is also in its final year

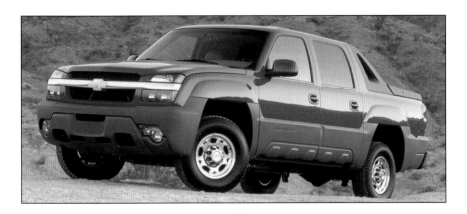

Essentially a Suburban with a pickup bed, Chevy's 2002 Avalanche created a new full-size truck category. A unique "midgate" arrangement allowed the bed to extend into the cabin for additional cargo space. An instant hit, sales neared 90,000 for '02.

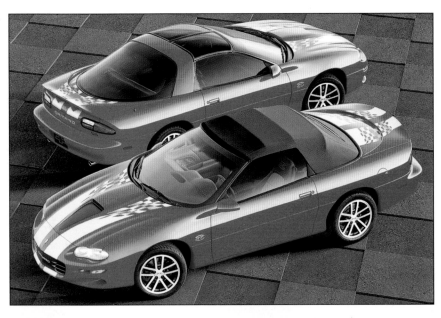

An SS 35th Anniversary Edition marked Camaro's last year in the Chevy lineup. Slow sales may have hastened the demise of the storied ponycar, but performance remained brisk. The Corvette-derived V-8 delivered 325 horsepower in SS models.

Pouring gas onto the fire, the Corvette's already hot Z06 claimed an additional 20 horses for 2000, now up to 405. For $490, buyers could take delivery of their 'Vette at the Corvette Museum in Bowling Green, Kentucky.

- Chevrolet offers a new midsize SUV called TrailBlazer that is bigger and more powerful than the Blazer, which lives on in diminished volume; Oldsmobile Bravada and GMC Envoy share TrailBlazer's design

- Chevrolet's Prizm, a cousin to the Toyota Corolla, is in its last model year

- Chevrolet and GMC offer four-wheel steering on their full-size pickup trucks

- The Plymouth brand is gone, but the Prowler remains, now with a Chrysler badge

- Dodge redesigns its Ram pickup trucks, maintaining their "big rig" image with bigger cabs and bold styling

- Ford adds the performance-oriented SVT to the Focus lineup, giving it more power and improved handling

- Ford redesigns the Explorer, making it bigger; Mercury Mountaineer shares the design

- A blast from the past returns when Ford introduces its new Thunderbird, a two-seat luxury convertible tourer

- Lincoln offers a Ford F-150-based luxury pickup called Blackwood; it is destined to become a sales disaster

◄ Upgrading your Monte Carlo SS to a Dale Earnhardt Signature Edition added $5200 the price of Chevy's midsize coupe.

▲ Wood-look trim was an $895 option on Chrysler's PT Cruiser for 2002. Budget-conscious buyers might prefer the flame-accent decals, available for only $495.

▲ GM supplemented its line of midsize SUVs with three new trucks in 2003. GMC Envoy (*left*), Oldsmobile Bravada (*middle*), and Chevy TrailBlazer (*right*) boasted spacious interiors and a 270-horsepower inline six.

◄▲ Though Ford still had a lock on the police-car market, Dodge made a credible pitch to fleet buyers with its shapely Intrepid (*left*). With the Plymouth brand now a historical footnote, the hot rod Prowler (*above*) was moved to Chrysler.

- Jeep replaces its 18-year-old Cherokee with a new compact SUV called Liberty

- Oldsmobile begins phasing out the Aurora, which will be gone by May 2003; the Intrigue is discontinued in June 2002

- Saturn introduces its third model, a crossover-type compact SUV with front- or all-wheel drive

- A bid by senator John Kerry (D-Mass.) for a 50 percent Corporate Average Fuel Economy increase by 2013 is vehemently opposed by automakers and their supporters, then denied by the U.S. Senate

- To offset profit hits caused by zero percent financing, U.S. automakers raise prices several times throughout the year: GM has three hikes, Ford and Chrysler four each

- In June, Ford closes Wingcast, the telematics arm that planned to offer concierge services and email and Internet access in Ford products; Ford invested $100 million in the failed venture

- Ford Motor Co. CEO Bill Ford, Jr., stars in the company's television commercials

▲ Redesigned for 2002, Dodge's full-size Ram pickups lost none of their "big rig" presence. Extended cabs disappeared, leaving only regular- and Quad-cab body styles.

◄ A 5.9-liter V-8 was the top dog in 1500 series Rams. An 8.0-liter was the upgrade for V-10 2500 and 3500 models.

▲ Ford's popular Explorer grew longer and wider for 2002, picking up new sheetmetal along the way. A standard 4.0-liter V-6 provided 210 horsepower. Base price: $24,585.

▲ New for Ranger was XLT FX4, a top-of-the-line off-roader with unique trim. Ford's compact pickup remained a strong seller, racking up more than 262,000 buyers in 2002.

◄ Ford scored a performance hit with the Focus SVT. Based on the two-door ZX3, SVT boasted 170-horsepower, 40 more than the standard coupe. A sport-tuned suspension, rear disc brakes, bigger wheels, and unique trim completed the package. Price: $17,480.

▲ Ford's ubiquitous midsize Taurus reached a heady milestone in 2002—its six-millionth copy.

▲▼ A melding of old and new, Ford's updated Thunderbird was a show car come to life. Sharing chassis components with Lincoln's LS sedan, T-Bird was more luxury cruiser than sports car. A 3.9-liter V-8 provided 252-horsepower, while an optional hardtop made Ford's two-seater a legitimate four-season car. Prices started at $35,390.

▲▶ GMC's C3 luxury pickup was redubbed Denali (*above*) for 2002, while adding Quadrasteer four-wheel steering to its standard equipment list. Civilian versions of the Humvee military off-roader were (*right*) now sold through GM dealerships under the Hummer brand.

▶ A High-Output 4.7-liter V-8 churned out 260 horsepower and came standard in the 2002 Grand Cherokee Overland.

▲ Moving further upscale, the line-capping Overland model was added to Jeep's Grand Cherokee family for 2002. Laredo, Sport, Special, and Limited models were also available.

◀ Replacing the 18-year-old Cherokee, Jeep Liberty had big shoes to fill. Rubicon Trail tested, the bigger, more refined Liberty proved popular with "cute ute" shoppers. More than 88,000 sales were tallied for 2002.

▲ Lincoln's Blackwood was a Ford F-150 in a tuxedo. A $51,785 price tag and lack of four-wheel drive hurt sales.

▲ Failing to capture the hearts of luxury-car shoppers, Lincoln's front-drive Continental was gone by 2003.

▲▶ Shapely but slow selling, Mercury's Cougar (*above*) was caged after 2002. Fewer than 20,000 buyers came to say good-bye. Sister ship to Ford Explorer, Mercury Mountaineer (*right*) was also enlarged and restyled for the new model year.

◀▲ Only the final 500 Oldsmobile Intrigues were adorned with commemorative seat embroidery. Intrigue was the first Olds to go, Alero would be last, surviving through 2004.

▲ Tepid sales forced an emergency freshening of Pontiac's Aztek. Cleaner flanks and monochromatic trim helped boost sales, though only slightly. Fewer than 28,000 found homes in 2002.

▲ Like its sibling, the Chevrolet Camaro, Pontiac's Firebird was dropped after 2002. Fewer than 21,000 buyers opted to buy a piece of automotive history.

2002 Calendar-Year Car Sales

1. Ford	864,903	6. Chrysler	316,493	11. Lincoln	114,522
2. Chevrolet	746,595	7. Saturn	204,771	12. Plymouth	605
3. Pontiac	441,203	8. Mercury	198,614		
4. Buick	370,549	9. Cadillac	150,104		
5. Dodge	348,218	10. Oldsmobile	118,179		

Figures include cars made for the Big Three in plants managed by Japanese companies

◄ Portholes returned from Buick's past to mark the 2003 edition of its top-line sedan. Park Avenue was little-changed otherwise. Two 3.8-liter V-6 engines were available; the standard was good for 205 horsepower and a super-charged version produced 240 hp.

◄▲ Replacing the unloved Catera, CTS was Cadillac's new entry-level model. Edgy "Art and Science" styling helped set the new-for-2003 CTS apart from the crowd, while able handling made it a hit with enthusiasts. A CTS costarred with Keanu Reeves in the movie *Matrix Reloaded* (*above*). It didn't survive.

◄▲ The new Escalade ESV (*left*) added 12 inches to Cadillac's popular SUV. Bulgari-designed instrumentation (*above*) added elegance and helped distinguish Escalade from GM's other big trucks.

2003

- U.S. light-vehicle sales total 16.7 million, down from 2002, but still the fifth best year ever; even bigger incentives than 2002 help

- For the second straight year, trucks outsell cars, accounting for 53.2 percent of sales, up from 50.6 percent

- Big Three U.S. market share dips 1.5 percent to 60.2 percent, an all-time low; Ford's market share of 19.5 percent is its lowest since 1928

- Toyota cars outsell Ford and Chevrolet cars, marking the first time since 1909 Ford or Chevy hasn't been number one

- Cadillac replaces the unpopular entry-level Catera with a new car called CTS in mid 2002 as a 2003 model

- Chevrolet celebrates Corvette's 50th year with a special-edition anniversary package

▲▶ Chevy's legendary two-seater turned 50 in 2003. All '03 Corvettes got commemorative badging to mark the occasion, but the $5000 50th Anniversary Package upped the ante with unique trim, special wheels, and magnetic ride control. The Z06 was still king of the hill, but standard 'Vettes were no slouches, boasting 350 horses.

◀▲ Big and bold, the SS was the ultimate expression of Chevrolet's full-size pickup. A 6.0-liter V-8 provided 345 horsepower and ground-pounding torque. Monochromatic trim and unique bodywork completed the package. Prices started at $39,380.

• Chevrolet adds a unique V-8-powered roadster pickup called SSR to its arsenal with a limited run late in the model year

• General Motors and AM General team up to build the new Hummer H2, a big SUV with big style and bigger thirst

• Pontiac and Toyota team up to build two new compact crossover wagons, the Pontiac Vibe and Toyota Matrix

• After 14 years, Saturn replaces its entry-level S-line with the Ion; Ion retains Saturn's trademark plastic panels

• Dodge brings back a fabled engine from the past when it offers a new Hemi engine for the Ram pickup

• Dodge redesigns its high-performance halo car, Viper, adding even more power

• Dodge jumps into the sport tuner market with a potent turbocharged version of the Neon called SRT-4

• Chrysler introduces a crossover SUV called Pacifica; initial sales are slow

• Ford Motor Company redesigns is popular Ford Expedition and Lincoln Navigator

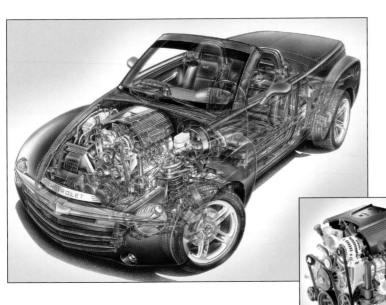

▲ Part pickup truck, part roadster, and entirely head turning, Chevy's SSR was a show car come to life. Intentionally rare, just 1664 were sold in 2003.

◄▲ A retractable hardtop and two-place seating characterized the brash SSR, as did its $42,000 price. Based on GM's midsize SUV chassis, SSR was too heavy to be truly sporty. A 300-horsepower V-8 provided the thrust.

◄ A boy racer's dream, the new Neon SRT-4 packed a turbocharged, 215-horse four and substantially upgraded brakes and suspension. *Car and Driver* magazine reported launching the sub-$20,000 subcompact to 60 mph in just 5.6 seconds. Chromed wheels added $600 to the price.

◄▲► Dodge resurrected a legend for 2003, in the form of its new Hemi truck engine. Living up to its stock-car-honed ancestry, the new 5.7-liter V-8 cranked out 345 horsepower and a stump-pulling 375 pound-feet of torque. The new Hemi added $1385 to the sticker price of a regular-cab Ram pickup.

• Ford revives an old performance name when it offers a supercharged, 390-horse-power SVT Cobra version of the venerable Mustang

• Lincoln adds the Ford Explorer-based Aviator to its lineup; Aviator has only a V-8 that is more powerful than Explorer's V-8

• Mercury offers a "hot-rodded" Marauder model to its Grand Marquis lineup

• Ford Motor Company celebrates its 100th anniversary in June with a five-day party at its Dearborn, Michigan, corporate headquarters

• GM buys the assets of Daewoo, then offers the Chevrolet Aveo, and Suzuki Verona and Forenza based on Daewoo designs

• Daewoo's U.S. auto dealers sue General Motors for ignoring the existing Daewoo distribution network

• Nissan introduces the Titan pickup truck in November, joining Toyota's Tundra as contenders in the domestic-dominated full-size-truck market

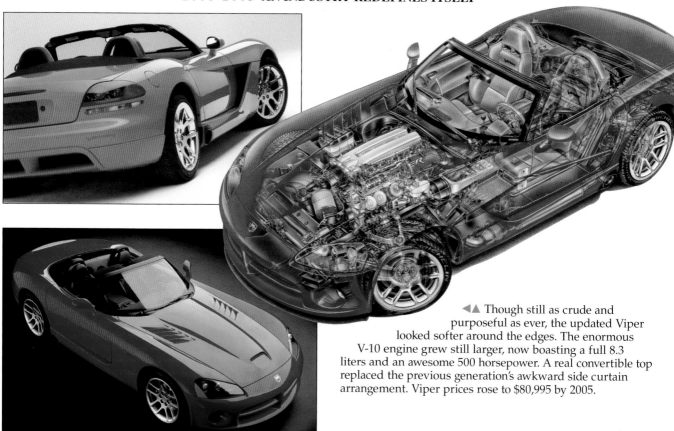

◄▲ Though still as crude and purposeful as ever, the updated Viper looked softer around the edges. The enormous V-10 engine grew still larger, now boasting a full 8.3 liters and an awesome 500 horsepower. A real convertible top replaced the previous generation's awkward side curtain arrangement. Viper prices rose to $80,995 by 2005.

▲ The Ford Motor Company celebrated its 100th year in 2003. Here, the Dearborn, Michigan, headquarters.

▲ Ford spiced up its Focus SVT models in 2003 with a new European Feature Car Package. For $3410, enthusiasts got a better stereo, high-intensity discharge headlights, revised interior trim, and thin-spoke alloy wheels.

◄ Anniversary packages spruced up a number of Ford models in 2003. The no-cost Centennial option on this F-250 Super Duty included two-tone upholstery, quad captain chairs, body-color bumpers, and special badging.

▲ A blast from the past, the Mach 1 moniker was reborn after a 23-year hiatus. Slotted between the brutal Cobra and common GT, the newest Mustang was limited to a production run of 6500 for '03. A 4.6-liter V-8 provided 300 horses.

▲ A spring-mounted "shaker" hood scoop topped the Mustang Mach 1 V-8. Mach 1 prices started at $28,705.

▲► Top horse at the Mustang ranch was the Cobra (*above*). Newly available as a convertible for 2003, the topless Cobra boasted the same supercharged 390-horsepower V-8 as its fixed-roof stablemate. Sporting a one-off coral paint job, a lucky Thunderbird (*right*) earned a cameo with Halle Berry in the James Bond thriller *Die Another Day.*

► Bringing machismo to the masses, GM's newly established Hummer division launched the Hummer H2 in '03. Based on proven Chevy full-size truck and SUV mechanical bits, the H2 became a hit with urban copyboys and the scourge of environmentalists. Prices started at $49,995.

◄▲ Capitalizing on the truck's film appearance, Jeep issued a limited edition Tomb Raider variant of its Wrangler off-roader. Based on the Wrangler's capable Rubicon model, the Tomb Raider package added Alcoa aluminum wheels, special trim, and badging. Base price: $28,815.

▲ Lincoln's big Navigator got a baby brother in 2003, the Ford Explorer-based Aviator. Prices started at $39,225.

▲► Resurrecting a name from the past, Mercury offered the Marauder as an attempt to inject some zip into the brand's sober lineup. Based on the full-size Grand Marquis, the $33,790 Marauder got a 302-horsepower V-8, bucket seats, 18-inch alloy wheels, and special gauges.

◄ Pontiac's aging Sunbird received a dramatic nosejob for 2003. The brand's smallest car was also its cheapest, at $14,870. Sedans were dropped from the Sunbird line for '03.

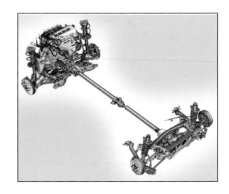

◄► Based on Toyota's Matrix, Pontiac's Vibe was a modern interpretation of the small wagon. Available all-wheel drive (*left*) made small work of winter driving.

▲ Still plastic clad, Saturn's smallest car was all new for 2003 and renamed: Ion. Rear-hinged back doors afforded easy access to coupe interiors, while a flat-folding front passenger seat created extra space. Coupe prices started at $14,030.

▲ Replacing the SL line that launched the brand in 1991, Saturn's new Ion was charged with reenergizing the make's slumping sales. Coupes and sedans featured interchangeable roof rails that were available in several contrasting colors.

◄▲ Unique four-spoke wheels adorned top-line Saturn Ions (*left*). Shown in wagon form, Saturn's midsize L-Series cars (*above*) were slow sellers. A 2003 facelift added brightwork to the grille.

2003 Calendar-Year Car Sales

1. Ford	792,313	5. Chrysler	265,834	9. Mercury	150,352
2. Chevrolet	799,479	6. Buick	259,348	10. Oldsmobile	103,073
3. Pontiac	408,673	7. Saturn	189,233	11. Lincoln	90,427
4. Dodge	298,601	8. Cadillac	151,298		

Figures include cars made for the Big Three
in plants managed by Japanese companies

◄▲ More than just a Chevy Trailblazer with a huge chrome grille, Buick's new-for-2004 Rainier boasted a quieter and more opulent interior than its midsize GM stablemates. Buick's first truck-based SUV started at $35,295.

◄► Buick's other truck moved upscale for 2004. Ultra now capped the Rendezvous line, sporting a higher-zoot interior and a new 3.6-liter V-6 power-plant. Though mechanically similar to the ungainly Aztek, Rendezvous was by far the better seller, trumping the unloved Pontiac 72,643 units to just 27,354 in 2003.

◄ Already popular with enthusiasts, Cadillac's CTS returned for 2004 with power borrowed from Chevy's Corvette. The CTS-V boasted a 400-horsepower 5.7-liter V-8, sportier suspension tuning, and unique trim all for the relatively low price of $49,995.

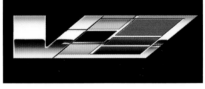

◄ Cadillac's biggest car was actually built like a tank for 2004. A new armored De Ville provided ample leg room and bulletproof body panels. Security wasn't cheap, prices started at $119,095.

▲ Appearing first on CTS-V, the "V" badge would come to adorn a number performance-enhanced Caddy models.

2004

- Buick adds Rainier, a midsize SUV based on the Chevrolet TrailBlazer, to its model lineup

- Cadillac's CTS gets a high-performance big brother called CTS-V with a 400-horsepower V-8; the regular CTS is now available with a 255-horsepower V-6

- Cadillac expands its line with two new models, the car-based SRX SUV and the XLR, a two-seat roadster with a retractable hardtop

- Chevrolet redesigns its midsize Malibu, adding a wagon called Malibu Maxx

- Chevrolet introduces Aveo, an entry-level subcompact based on the Daewoo Lanos

- 240-horsepower Supercharged SS versions of the Chevy Impala and Monte Carlo are offered

▲▶ Shaking off memories of Cadillac's ill-fated Allanté of the Eighties, GM's luxury division introduced the XLR roadster for 2004. Aimed squarely at the Mercedes-Benz SL convertible, XLR sported edgy styling and a folding steel top.

◀ Built in Korea by Daewoo, Chevrolet's new Aveo was earmarked to be the brand's value-priced subcompact for 2004. Prices started just under the magic $10,000 line.

▲ Revised for 2003, Cadillac's "Northstar" V-8, now with 320 horsepower, provided motivation for the XLR.

◀▼ Replacing the ancient S-10 line, Chevrolet's new Colorado small pickup was designed to be less truck-like and more commuter friendly. The top engine was a 220-horsepower inline five. Base price: $15,565.

- Chevrolet and GMC replace the aging S-10 and Sonoma compact pickups with the slightly larger Colorado and Canyon; they are available with GM's first five-cylinder engine

- The Chevrolet S-10 continues as only a 4WD four-door crew cab

- GMC adds a new model to the Envoy SUV line; XUV has a power sliding roof and a midgate that drops to extend the cargo floor

- Limited-edition models of the Alero, Bravada, and Silhouette mark the end of Oldsmobile's 101-year run

- Pontiac offers the first V-8 Bonneville since 1986 in the form of the 275-horsepower GXP

- Pontiac revives one of autodom's most hallowed names by bringing the Australian Holden Monaro to the U.S. under the name GTO; the U.S. car boasts 350 horsepower

- Pontiac revamps the Grand Prix, but it remains on the same basic platform

- A Honda-sourced 3.5-liter 250-horsepower V-6 replaces the Saturn Vue's 3.0 V-6

- Saturn offers a high-performance "Redline" version of the Vue

- Chrysler introduces Crossfire, a two-seater based on the Mercedes-Benz SLK

▲ The heart of the Impala SS was its 240-horse supercharged V-6. A sport-tuned suspension and alloy wheels were included in the $27,995 price.

▲ Chevy's Impala got a shot in the arm from the new line-topping SS model. Extroverted trim and an enhanced engine were part of the deal.

▲ On a platform shared with the Saab 9-3, Chevy's Malibu midsize sedan was all-new for 2004. Price in LS trim: $20,995.

▲ Don't call it a station wagon; Malibu Maxx was Chevy's new-for-'04 entry into the expanding "sportwagon" category.

▲▶ The Monte Carlo Supercharged SS shared the Impala SS's engine. A Monte Carlo paced the NASCAR's '03 Coca-Cola 600 (*above*) at Lowe's Motor Speedway.

- Chrysler adds a convertible body style for the PT Cruiser

- Dodge redesigns the Durango, making it larger and giving it more available power, including the new Hemi engine

- Ford redesigns America's best-selling full-size pickup, giving the F-150 more interior room and more power

- The existing Ford F-150 continues to be sold as the F-150 Heritage; it is only offered in regular cab and extended SuperCab form

- The Ford Windstar is revamped and renamed Freestar; the Mercury Monterey returns on the same platform

- 2004 is the 40th anniversary of America's favorite ponycar, the Ford Mustang

- DaimlerChrysler announces it will provide no more financial backing to troubled Mitsubishi, fueling speculation that the German-owned company will divest itself of its 37 percent share in the Japanese automaker

- Nick Scheele is replaced as Ford's Chief Operating Officer and head of Automotive Operations by Jim Padilla after Ford reports a $2 billion first-quarter profit; Scheele remains with Ford in a diminished role

▲ Without a large rear-drive sedan to compete with Ford's Crown Victoria for police work, Chevy pressed a few thousand rugged Tahoes into law-enforcement duty.

◄▲► Making the most of its relationship with Mercedes-Benz, Chrysler borrowed bits from the German maker's SLK to create the dramatic two-seat Crossfire. A standard 3.2-liter V-6 provided a healthy 215 horsepower. The Crossfire's interior was nearly as stylish as its bodywork. The optional automatic transmission added $1075 to the coupe's $34,495 base price.

◄► Neither van nor wagon, the Pacifica was Chrysler's entry into the loosely defined but ever-expanding "crossover" category. New for 2004, Pacifica came luxuriously outfitted with standard 10-way power seats, and dual-zone climate control. An "Autostick" shifter (*right*) permitted manual control of the standard four-speed automatic transmission. The chrome alloy wheels shown added $750 to Pacifica's base price.

◄▲ Bigger and bolder, the 2004 Durango was a huge improvement over its dated predecessor. A V-6 was new to the line, as was a 5.7-liter Hemi V-8. Durango prices started at $25,920.

▶ Though not the most practical pickup, Dodge claimed it was the fastest. Powered by the Viper's 8.3-liter V-10, the Ram SRT-10 boasted 500 horse-power and 525 pound-feet of torque. The SRT-10 package added $22,575 to the price of a Ram pickup, and reportedly topped out at more than 150 mph.

◀ Aging gracefully, Dodge's ubiquitous Stratus sedan received a needed face-lift for 2004. Still anonymous in the crowd of stiff Asian and domestic competitors, Stratus was a disappointing seller. Here, the $21,225 top-line R/T.

▲ Fighting to keep its hold on first place in the pickup sales race, Ford redesigned its perennially best-selling F-150 for 2004. Shown here: the $33,180 XLT SuperCrew shortbed.

▲ The off-road-ready member of the F-150 family, the FX4 was marked by its monochromatic grille surround. Neither a manual transmission nor a V-6 was available for 2004.

▶ A fresh face and and a new name arrived in 2004 for Ford's minivan. Previously Windstar, the Freestar boasted larger engines and a new Mercury cousin named Monterey. Base price for the full-zoot Limited shown here: $33,775.

659

▲ With an all-new model less than a year away, Ford celebrated its fabled ponycar's 40th anniversary quietly (*right*). A color-shifting Mystichrome paint treatment added $3650 to the supercharged Cobra's (*above, left*) base price.

▲ The sky was the limit for GMC's newest Envoy, literally. XUV boasted a retractable roof that opened to create a cavernous pickuplike storage area.

▲ A near twin to Chevy's Colorado, Canyon replaced the dated Sonoma compact pickup in GMC's lineup for 2004. Bigger than its predecessor in every dimension, the Canyon was marketed as a midsize truck.

▶ Carried over for a final appearance, the Sonoma pickup was available in 2004 only in four-door four-wheel-drive form. The ZR5 appearance package shown was a $1300 option.

▲ An LSE package gave Lincoln's slow-selling LS line a sorely needed shot of excitement for 2004. Chrome alloy wheels, aggressive-looking lower-body trim, and a rear spoiler were included in the package's $3395 price.

▲ Replacing the Nissan-derived Quest, Mercury's new Monterey was a mechanical clone of Ford's Freestar minivan. A beefy 4.2-liter V-6 provided 201 horsepower. This top-of-the-line Premier edition listed for $35,525.

▲ It took 30 years, but Pontiac again struck on the magic combination of elements worthy of the GTO badge. Based on Holden of Australia's rear-drive Monaro coupe, the newest "Goat" boasted subtle styling and Corvette-sourced power. A six-speed manual transmission came standard.

▲ Closely related to the Corvette's LS1 V-8, the GTO's 5.7-liter powerhouse (*above*) provided a stout 350 horse-power and 365 pound-feet of torque.

▲ Separated from the heavy cladding that had been Pontiac's signature, the 2004 Grand Prix cast a sleeker, more sophisticated shadow. Identified by its four-port exhaust and red brake calipers, the GTP was the hot rod of the GP lineup.

▶ A belt-driven supercharger (*right*) was the key to the GTP's performance. Bolted to a 3.8-liter V-6, the blower helped the torquey six crank out 260 horsepower. A 200-horse V-6 powered the less-aggressive Grand Prix GT.

◀ A lowered sport suspension was part of the Redline package for Saturn's compact Vue SUV. Top Vue power came from a Honda-sourced 3.5-liter V-6 making a heady 250 horsepower.

◄ Working double duty, the shapely new LaCrosse replaced both the Century and Regal in Buick's lineup for 2005.

▼ Failing to capture import intenders with the conservative front-drive Seville, Cadillac introduced the edgy rear-drive STS. With styling cues borrowed from the popular CTS, STS offered an optional 320-horsepower V-8.

◄ Replacing the ancient Cavalier, Chevy's new subcompact Cobalt sported cleaner styling and a platform shared with Saturn's Ion. Shown here is the the line-topping SS Supercharged, a 205-horsepower model aimed squarely at the California tuner crowd.

2005

- Buick replaces both the Century and Regal with a single model called LaCrosse

- Cadillac redesigns the Seville, giving it a new rear-wheel-drive platform and a new name: STS

- Chevrolet replaces the aged Cavalier with an all-new premium subcompact called Cobalt

- Chevrolet unveils its next-generation Corvette, the C6, with more power and exposed headlights

- Chevrolet releases a new midsize SUV called Equinox on the Saturn Vue's platform and markets it as an entry-level SUV

- Hummer adds a pickup body style to the H2 and calls it SUT (sport utility truck)

- Pontiac replaces the compact Grand Am with a new midsize sedan called G6; the G6 shares a platform with the new Chevrolet Malibu, but its wheelbase is stretched almost six inches

▲▶ The bow-tie brand's legendary sports car was redesigned for 2005. The new Corvette gained power, lost weight, and looked sleeker. The Corvette's 6.0-liter V-8 heart made 400 horsepower, and 400 pound-feet of torque. For the first time since 1963, the headlights were exposed.

◀ Based on the same General Motors Theta architecture as Saturn's Vue, Chevrolet's new Equinox finally gave the brand a contemporary model for the entry-level SUV arena. A 3.4-liter V-6 was the only available engine.

▼ Chrysler's brash new 300 marked the return of the big American sedan. Base price: $23,595. The line-topping 300C carried a 5.7-liter Hemi V-8 and started at $32,370.

- GM reworks its minivans, adding an SUV-like nose; the new models are the Buick Terraza, Chevrolet Uplander, Pontiac Montana SV6, and Saturn Relay

- The Chrysler 300 and Dodge Magnum replace the Concorde/300M and Intrepid

- The Chrysler Crossfire gets a convertible body style and a 330-horsepower high-performance model dubbed SRT-6

- The Chrysler Town & Country and Dodge Caravan are revamped and given 2nd- and 3rd-row seats that fold flat into the floor

- Ford plans to offer a gas/electric hybrid version of the Escape SUV; it is the first hybrid vehicle from a U.S. automaker

- Jeep redesigns the Grand Cherokee, giving it available seven-passenger seating, and offering new engines

- Ford replaces the Taurus with the larger Five Hundred; Mercury's Sable is similarly replaced by Montego

- After 27 years on the same platform, Ford completely redesigns the Mustang

- Ford offers a new crossover SUV called Freestyle that is based on the Five Hundred sedan's architecture; Mercury gets a similar crossover

▲ Spicing up the already sexy Crossfire, Chrysler launched the potent SRT-6 edition for 2005. A supercharger upped the output of the standard 3.2-liter V-6 from 215 to 330 horsepower. Also new for 2005 was the Crossfire convertible, available in standard and SRT-6 trim. The aggressive rear spoiler and 15-spoke wheels shown here were part of the SRT-6 equipment list.

◀ Mechanically similar to Chrysler's 300, the striking Magnum marked Dodge's return to the rear-drive big-car category. Offered only in "fastback" wagon form, the square-jawed four-door boasted up to 340 horsepower from its available 5.7-liter Hemi V-8. Price as pictured in aggressive R/T trim: $29,995.

◀▲ Chrysler's new Stow 'n Go seating for Town & Country (*shown*) and sister ship Dodge Caravan could be folded flat to create a completely level storage floor.

▶ Ford gave a nod to green enthusiasts with a hybrid version of its popular Escape compact SUV. Powered by small gasoline engine boosted by an electric motor, the Escape Hybrid traveled up to 40 miles on a single gallon of gasoline. Efficiency didn't come cheap however, with hybrids listing for roughly $3000 more than their V-6 powered counterparts.

▲► Ford launched a pair of family sized cars for 2005. Freestyle (*left*) was a car-based "crossover," with a wagonlike silhouette. A 3.0-liter V-6 was standard. Five Hundred (*right*) replaced the midsize Taurus in Ford's lineup, but was closer in size to many full-size cars. Available all-wheel drive was a boon to winter drivers in snow-belt states.

▲► Invading the world of exotic cars, Ford's 2005 GT was a masterpiece of lightweight materials and brute force. A supercharged 5.4-liter V-8 provided 500 horsepower. Base price: $139,995.

▲► The first completely new replacement since 1978, the 2005 Mustang featured a modern design with retro features. A unique three-valve design helped Mustang GT's 4.6-liter V-8 (*above, right*) churn out an impressive 300 horsepower. The standard 4.0-liter V-6 was no slouch either, providing a healthy 202 horsepower.

▲ Hummer's brash H2 line was expanded with the addition of the SUT for 2005. A collapsible "midgate" allowed for longer loads to extend into the interior. Base price: $51,995.

▲ All-new for the first time since its 1993 introduction, Jeep's Grand Cherokee was a bigger, heavier vehicle for 2005. Still "Trail Rated" by Jeep, a Hemi V-8 was newly optional.

▲ Fleshing out the Mercury lineup for 2005 was Mariner, an up-content version of Ford's Escape compact SUV. A 3.0-liter V-6 was standard.

▲ Without the division's trademark bodyside cladding, the Pontiac G6 was a clean break from the past. Replacing the ubiquitous Grand Am, G6 boasted an optional 3.9-liter V-6.

▲ Relay, Saturn's first minivan, was one of a quartet of new family haulers from General Motors. Sister ships Buick Terraza, Chevy Uplander, and Pontiac Montana SV6 all debuted for 2005.

▲ Saturn's Redlines were the top performers of their model lines. This 2005 Ion Redline boasted a supercharged engine, racy trim, and 17-inch wheels.

▶ A literal show car come to life, Solstice was Pontiac's answer to Mazda's evergreen Miata roadster. A 2.4-liter 170-horsepower "Ecotec" four was earmarked to provide motivation for the two-seater upon its debut in late 2005 as an '06 model.